Visiting the Fallen:
Arras South

Visiting the Fallen: Arras South

Peter Hughes

Pen & Sword
MILITARY

First published in Great Britain in 2015 by
PEN & SWORD MILITARY
An imprint of
Pen & Sword Books Ltd
47 Church Street
Barnsley
South Yorkshire
S70 2AS

ISBN 978-1-47382-558-1

Typeset by Concept, Huddersfield, West Yorkshire, HD4 5JL.
Printed and bound in England by CPI Group (UK) Ltd, Croydon CR0 4YY.

Pen & Sword Books Ltd incorporates the imprints of Pen & Sword Archaeology,
Atlas, Aviation, Battleground, Discovery, Family History, History, Maritime,
Military, Naval, Politics, Railways, Select, Social History, Transport, True Crime,
and Claymore Press, Frontline Books, Leo Cooper, Praetorian Press,
Remember When, Seaforth Publishing and Wharncliffe.

For a complete list of Pen & Sword titles please contact
PEN & SWORD BOOKS LIMITED
47 Church Street, Barnsley, South Yorkshire, S70 2AS, England
E-mail: enquiries@pen-and-sword.co.uk
Website: www.pen-and-sword.co.uk

Dedication

To my father, Jack, who often accompanied me to France and Belgium, and my mother, Mary, who sadly never saw the start of this project – with love and gratitude.

Contents

List of Plates

Funeral of Major Roderick Ogle Bell-Irving DSO MC, 16th Battalion, Canadian Infantry, near Cagnicourt.

The Battle of Arras near Hénin-sur-Cojeul. A small battlefield cemetery can be seen in the middle of the photograph with a shell bursting a little way beyond it near the road.

A soldier's grave near Bullecourt marked with a simple wooden cross.

Photograph taken from the high ground south of Noreuil on 14 May 1917.

After the war every effort was made to locate lost graves. Here a Grave Registration Unit is uncovering remains.

Another team begins the unpleasant, but necessary task of recovering the body of a fallen soldier after the war.

Photograph showing the bodies of soldiers arriving at a military cemetery for re-burial.

A carpenter making wooden crosses.

Windmill British Cemetery on the Arras–Cambrai Road with the remains of Monchy-le-Preux barely visible in the distance to the left of the Cross of Sacrifice.

The Faubourg d'Amiens Cemetery at Arras.

Floral tributes for a fallen soldier.

A mason's yard containing some of the many headstones required to replace each wooden cross.

Today, headstones are cut by computer-programmed machines. Here, the inscription is being done by hand.

A vehicle used by a team from the Imperial War Graves Commission.

Bodies are still being discovered on the battlefields. In 2009 a farmer found the remains of soldiers originally buried in May 1917 after the Second Battle of Bullecourt.

HAC Cemetery, Écoust-Saint-Mein, on 23 April 2013.

Acknowledgements

I would like to express my sincere thanks to the following people for their help during various stages of this work.

To Ian Small at the CWGC office in Maidenhead, who had to contend with my frequent requests for photographic material despite having to prepare for the 70th anniversaries of D-Day and Arnhem, as well as the start of the 1914–1918 centenary commemorations. With each request, Ian trawled the CWGC archives, producing whatever was available and was never less than helpful.

To Parveen Sodhi at the Imperial War Museum, London, for her courtesy and help regarding the licensing of several of the photographs used to illustrate these books.

To the team at Pen & Sword Books, but especially to Design Manager, Roni Wilkinson, for his support and guidance in the months prior to my submission of the work and for his help in procuring some of the photographs used to illustrate it. Also to Matt Jones who oversaw the production, to Jon Wilkinson who did an amazing job designing the book's cover, and to my editor, Irene Moore, for her guidance and encouragement throughout the final stages.

To Ronelda Peters, part of the team at the Canadian National Memorial, Vimy, for her help regarding matters pertaining to the memorial itself. To Nelly Poignonnec, Communication and Public Relations Officer at the Commonwealth War Graves Commission in Beaurains, France, for putting aside the time to answer all my questions regarding the work of the Commission and for introducing me to many of the staff and craftsmen at Beaurains who somehow manage to cope with the extraordinary demands placed on the organization from around the world. To Isabelle Pilarowski at the Office de Tourisme, Arras, who shares my own desire to raise the profile of Arras and its battlefields as a key destination on the Western Front – we may yet succeed.

To Barrie Duncan, Assistant Museums Officer, Leisure & Culture, South Lanarkshire Council, who was ever ready to delve into long-forgotten editions of *The Covenanter* and provide information from all corners of the regimental archive. Similarly, thanks go to Sandy Leishman at the Highland Fusiliers HQ, Sauchiehall Street, Glasgow, who was extremely helpful on matters relating to the Highland Light Infantry and the Royal Scots Fusiliers in the Great War. He and Barrie were not the only keepers of regimental archives who gave up their time to answer questions, but both were especially helpful.

To the staff at the reading rooms of the British Library, the National Archives at Kew, the Guildhall Library in the City, and the Imperial War Museum, London, for their courtesy and service during the research phase of this project. To author David Kent-Lemon, for his kind advice and support as I took my first steps towards having the work published and who was responsible for introducing me to Pen & Sword.

For many entirely different reasons, I should also like to extend recognition and thanks to the following: Hugh Harvey, friend and colleague for many years, who helped iron out some of the last remaining pieces of research required to complete this book. He has toured the Western Front with me since 1993, as have the following: Dave Beck, Jim Wilcox, Sam Oliver, Alan Oliver, Andy Cook, Douglas Mackenzie, Gareth Berry, not forgetting Dennis Harvey and Frank Wilcox, whose company we dearly miss.

To Garry Reilly, Phil Hughes, Iain Petrie, Darren Bone, and countless other ex-colleagues from Camden who have been particularly supportive since I retired in July 2010, and who, throughout the four years it took to complete this project, provided encouragement along the way. A special mention goes to Danielle Louise Mackinnon, another friend and former colleague from Camden, who always believed in my ability to write and who encouraged me to do so, as did Jane Chiarello and Simon Turner. To all those other wonderful friends, whose kind invitations to lunch, etc. I sometimes had to decline and who never once complained.

Finally, to Peter Gilhooley, who first introduced me to the Western Front Association in 1981. I made my first trip to the battlefields of France and Belgium with Peter in September that year and continued to tour with him for many years after that. His extensive knowledge and infectious enthusiasm fuelled my early interest in the Great War, an interest that has ultimately led to my writing these three books. If it were it not for that initial spark, I might never have been inspired to write them.

This work is also dedicated to the memory of Dave Pilling, who one night went out beyond the wire never to return.

Peter Hughes

Introduction

Like Ypres, Arras was briefly occupied by the Germans in the very early days of the war, but the French soon drove them out. For the remainder of 1914 and throughout 1915, French soldiers held a line just east of the town. In March 1916 the sector was handed over to the British who extended their line southwards from La Bassée. Thereafter, Arras remained in British hands. It was only in the final two months of the war, when the fighting drifted eastwards away from the town, that Arras could finally breathe a sigh of relief. It never quite suffered the destruction that Ypres did, though it was frequently subjected to heavy shelling and in many places its streets and buildings were very badly damaged. It was a town battered and bruised, but essentially still intact. Like Ypres, it had always been a front line town, and for two and a half years it served as 'home' to countless British and Commonwealth soldiers. Both towns shared, and still share, a great deal in common.

Today Arras receives far fewer visitors to its battlefields than either Ypres or the Somme. I would venture even further and say that, in comparison with the other two, it has been seriously neglected, the one notable exception being the Memorial Park at Vimy Ridge. Here, the tunnels, shell holes, craters, concrete trench reconstructions, and the crowning magnificence that is the Canadian National Memorial, provide sufficient visual stimulus to attract large visitor numbers. Sadly, for many, this is where their visit to the Arras battlefield begins and ends. I sincerely hope that the three books in this series help to change all that.

Prior to the publication of *Cheerful Sacrifice* by Jonathan Nicholls in 1990 it was difficult to find any account of the series of military operations fought between April and May 1917, known collectively as the Battle of Arras. More recently, and assisted by Jeremy Banning and the Imperial War Museum, Peter Barton produced another fine publication, one of a series of books based on panoramas, 'then' and 'now', in many ways similar in style to the ones written by John Giles in his *Then and Now* series, where original photographs were juxtaposed with their modern day equivalents. For several years, before either of these titles appeared, *Prelude to Victory* by Brigadier General Edward Louis Spears was on my bookshelf, along with the indispensable first volume of the Official History for 1917 but, sadly, that was about it; Arras was truly neglected as a subject.

As for accounts of the 1918 fighting around Arras, these were, and still are, virtually non-existent; similarly with 1916. Leaving aside Norm Christie's short history, *The Canadians at Arras, August–September 1918*, which forms part of his *For King and Empire* series, the only published sources, and not always readily to hand, were individual unit histories, the five volumes of the Official History for 1918, together with a handful of Canadian memoirs. With all this in mind, I would like to think that my three books on Arras manage to fill in some of the gaps regarding this neglected part of the Western Front, notwithstanding my slightly unusual approach to the subject. Hopefully, they will complement what little already exists, at least from a British and Commonwealth perspective, and I really hope that people find them a useful addition. Incidentally, any of the above-mentioned works are well worth reading before considering a visit to Arras and its battlefields.

However, unlike these other books, my trilogy is not an account of any particular battle that took place around Arras, nor is it a chronological narrative of any of the events that took place there; there is no conventional storyline. So, what exactly is it then?

Perhaps the best way is to describe it as a kind of *Who's Who*, though, strictly speaking, that should read: 'Who was Who', since all the 'protagonists' are dead, buried now in one of the many CWGC cemeteries that dot the landscape in and around Arras, or else commemorated nearby on one of the four memorials to the missing. The books are principally concerned with the men who fought and fell around Arras, including, in many cases, the circumstances in which they died; they are, I suppose, simply an expression of remembrance.

The 'stage' for this pageant of remembrance is the better part of the map that forms the end paper at the beginning of *Military Operations, France & Belgium, 1917, Volume One*. It stretches from Aix-Noulette and Liévin in the north to Morchies and Lagnicourt in the south; from Dury and Éterpigny in the east to Barly and Saulty in the west. Though it was conceived, researched, and originally written as a single project lasting four years, in one continuous 'flow of the pen', as it were, the work is now divided into three parts: *Arras – North*, *Arras – South*, and *Arras – The Memorials*.

The work is not really a guidebook in any conventional sense of the term. Although I have given a brief indication as to where each cemetery is located, I have deliberately steered away from the idea of anything approaching what might be referred to as an itinerary, though the cemeteries within each chapter are all grouped by reasonable proximity to each other. I would much prefer to let the visitor decide which cemeteries to visit and the order in which to visit them.

In the first two books I have tried to outline briefly the nature of each cemetery in terms of size, character, and composition, before taking the visitor through the various plots and rows of graves, halting at many of the headstones where I then talk about the individuals buried there. Similarly, the volume covering the memorials highlights many of the individuals commemorated at each of the four sites. The books only become 'guidebooks' once the visitor is inside the cemetery itself or standing in front of the memorial.

In an age of satellite navigation and the internet, reaching any of the cemeteries or memorials should be an easy enough task. The list of CWGC cemeteries and memorials can now be downloaded onto a satellite navigation system and the organization's website now includes the GPS co-ordinates for each site. For anyone not relying on modern technology, I would suggest the 1:100,000 maps produced by the *Institut Géographique National* (IGN). Unfortunately, two of these maps are required: No. 101: Lille – Bologne-sur-Mer, and No. 103: Amiens – Arras. Investing in both will also come in very handy when visiting other parts of the Western Front. Personally, I would be inclined to run with both systems whenever possible. The 'Michelin'

1:200,000 series, with the CWGC cemeteries and memorials overlaid and indexed, provide a useful pointer, but again two maps, 51 and 52, are required, and the scale is just a little too small for my liking.

With regard to maps, I know that many people will wonder why I have not included any within the body of my work. This would have been difficult to achieve with any clarity, not least because the actions described are extremely diverse, both in terms of timeline and location. I had to consult well over two hundred maps during the course of my research. To condense all the topographical information into a handful of maps would have been virtually impossible, as well as potentially confusing. My own IGN maps, the Blue 1:25,000 series, are entirely overwritten in pencil, showing redoubts, trenches, etc. Such detail and scale is essential when walking and describing the battle-fields, but perhaps less important in a work whose subject happens to be mainly people. For the really committed visitor, the 1:25,000 series are the ones to go for, though several of them will be required on account of the larger scale.

Each of my three books has been written with the curious reader in mind. At times the detail may amount to more than the average visitor requires, but I would much rather leave it to the reader to decide which bits are relevant and which are not. Every headstone and every name on a memorial represents a unique human life, and there-fore a unique story. Not all of these stories can be told, but many can, and that is really what these books are about. Although none of the three books provides a chrono-logical narrative to the fighting, I do think that, collectively, they serve to illustrate quite well many aspects of life and indeed death, on the Western Front. That, at least, was the intention when I wrote them, and partly the inspiration behind them.

When I mentioned earlier that the books were a kind of *Who's Who*, they may, at times, also bear a slight resemblance to the popular BBC television series *QI*. The reason for that is that my own curiosity often has a tendency to take me off at a tangent. Whenever something struck me as 'Quite Interesting' I found it very hard to leave it out; after all, a good story is a good story. This confession should suffice to explain away the inclusion of a mammoth, a magician, and 'Mr Ramshaw', a golden eagle, as well as one or two passing references to decent drams. (I was once fortunate enough to spend several years on the London tasting panel of the Scotch Malt Whisky Society – a tough assignment, I know, but someone had to do it.) Hopefully, and occasionally, the reader will find time to smile.

On a more personal note, I have been visiting the battlefields of the Western Front for over thirty years and have been a member of the Western Front Association since 1981. From the very first visit I have always carried a notebook with me. Anything of interest ends up in the notebook; sometimes a note regarding an individual soldier, or maybe a particular group of headstones; sometimes recurring dates, or perhaps the predominance of a particular regiment in a cemetery; in fact, just about anything unusual or interesting that might be worth pursuing once back home in England with time to research. Very often curiosity pays off, sometimes spectacularly. This has always been my way when visiting the cemeteries and memorials on the Western Front and, at least in part, this is how these three books came to be written. I hope they encourage people to delve a little deeper and to be even more curious when next visiting the battlefields.

Finally, the original title for this work was *Withered Leaves on the Plains of France*. The words are taken from four lines of a poem by Edward Richard Buxton Shanks. While he and others from the Artists' Rifles were drilling in London's Russell Square, in the heart of Bloomsbury, he noticed the autumn leaves swirling on the ground, conscious of the fact that they would soon begin to moulder before turning to mud, and eventually dust. Within that image he saw a clear reflection of his own mortality and that of his comrades, soon to leave for France and the trenches.

During my former working life I came to know Russell Square very well. Its lawns, flower beds, and the same trees that once stirred Shanks's imagination, formed a pleasant and familiar backdrop; not a place of quiet, but still a place where one could think. Over a period of time, seated outside the café there, I first conceived the idea of writing this work, though only as a single book, never imagining it would emerge as a three volume text. It was there too that I decided to use Shanks's metaphor in the title of the book. For the next four years, as the work took shape, it existed only under its original title until it was eventually changed to *Visiting the Fallen* at the suggestion of my publisher. So much for good intentions and poetic licence! However, let me say at this point that I very quickly warmed to the new title, liking it not least for its simplicity and direct appeal. I still, however, think of the 'Fallen', referred to in the title, as all those 'Withered Leaves'. A hundred years on, it remains a powerful and compelling image.

Arras South

This second volume covers Arras itself, as well as the CWGC cemeteries that lie south of the town, almost as far as Bapaume. The cemeteries that sit within the Arras battlefield of 1917 are likely to be familiar to many, but some just to the east of Monchy-le-Preux, or those behind Arras itself, receive relatively few visitors, which is exactly why they are included here. It might be argued that the cemeteries closest to Bapaume could have been left out. However, all of them can be reached easily from Arras and there seemed no reason to omit them simply because they were closer to Bapaume than Arras.

The German Offensive that swept across the old Somme battlefields, and indeed south of the River Somme during the latter part of March and the first week of April 1918, also raged briefly opposite Arras and the area south of the town. The villages here receive far less attention than those between Péronne and Saint-Quentin, and yet were no less important as the British line south of Arras came under pressure. The same villages south of Arras also featured heavily during the British advances in late August 1918, as did those east of the town that lay in the path of the Canadians during the early part of September. Scant attention has been given to these parts of the battlefield, but I hope that this volume goes some way towards correcting that imbalance.

The countryside and villages that lie south-west and south-east of Arras are a delight to visit. This part of the Western Front certainly deserves greater recognition. If this volume encourages more visitors to explore this part of northern France, then so much the better, and the time spent researching and writing it will have been worthwhile. Go there with confidence, and above all, appreciate the wealth of small cemeteries that this area has to offer.

Chapter One

Two Male Models – A Highland Tune for the Major – A Dip in the Canche

Faubourg d'Amiens Cemetery, Arras

Private Leonard Albert BYWATER, 16th Royal Warwickshire Regiment, was 19 years old when he was killed by a sniper's bullet on 3 April 1916 (Plot I.A.12). Although he was born in Stroud, Gloucestershire, the family lived in the Aston district of Birmingham. Leonard's elder brother, Private Arthur Harold BYWATER, served in the same battalion and was also killed by a sniper a few months later on 16 June (Plot I.D.52). Not only did they share a similar fate, but both are now buried here in Plot I just a short distance from each other.

Company Serjeant Major Frederick John CROSSLEY DCM, 1st Queen's Own (Royal West Kent Regiment), was killed in action on 9 April 1916, aged 41. His DCM, gazetted on 17 December 1914, was awarded for conspicuous and gallant service over a period of ten days in the trenches at Neuve Chapelle. (Plot I.A.24)

Lieutenant Colonel Henry Norrington PACKARD DSO, 46 Brigade, Royal Field Artillery, was 46 years old when he was killed in action on 12 April 1916. He was commissioned in the Royal Artillery in July 1890 and was mentioned in despatches in October 1914. In February the following year he received his DSO in connection with operations in the field. (Plot I.A.41)

Private Ernest Henry ALLEN, 1st East Surrey Regiment, died of wounds on 21 April 1916 (Plot I.A.48). His brother, Private Edward Allen, was killed in action a few months later, on 1 July 1916 near Redan Ridge on the Somme, serving with the 1st Somerset Light Infantry. He is buried at Sucrerie Military Cemetery, Colincamps.

Lieutenant Colonel Henry Thomas CANTAN CMG, 1st Duke of Cornwall's Light Infantry, was killed in action on 16 April 1916, aged 47. The *London Gazette* dated 17 May 1892 shows his promotion from colour sergeant with the King's Royal Rifle Corps to second lieutenant with the Duke of Cornwall's Light Infantry. He served with the regiment in the South African War and the *London Gazette* of 20 July 1900 refers not only to his promotion to captain, but also notes that he had been recovered as a prisoner of war. In December that year he was seconded to the South African Constabulary, but by 1908 he was again serving with his regiment. This career soldier was promoted to temporary lieutenant colonel in October 1915. His CMG was awarded soon after that, as there is a reference to it in the *London Gazette* in December. (Plot I.A.49)

Second Lieutenant Alex John REID DCM, 1st East Surrey Regiment, was killed in action on 26 April 1916. He had won his DCM a year earlier at Hill 60, near Ypres, while serving as a company serjeant major with the battalion and the award was gazetted on 3 June 1915. The citation refers to conspicuous gallantry and valuable service performed by him on 20 April 1915 when he went out of his trench across the open and brought up ammunition and reinforcements on three separate occasions. The fighting there was extremely fierce and the ground that he had to cross was constantly swept by severe machine-gun and shell fire. (Plot I.B.11)

Major Richard Archibald JONES, 15th Royal Warwickshire, the son of a clergyman from Wandsworth, London, was killed just after midnight on 21 May 1916 by a rifle grenade as he was supervising work to consolidate a mine crater that had been blown by the Germans on 19 May. JONES had been the principal of Birmingham University College and had commanded the university OTC there. He held a Master's degree and was 34 years old when he died. (Plot I.B.46)

Killed with him was Lance Corporal William HUNDY (Plot I.B.47) whose body was recovered by his brother, Hubert, a stretcher-bearer. Three other wounded men were also brought in. A glance at William's army number – 15/1 – shows that he was the first man to enlist with the 15th Battalion in Birmingham.

Private Sidney CLINCH had served with the 8th Royal Fusiliers before being posted to the 5th Entrenching Battalion. He died of wounds on 2 June 1916, aged 17. He is one of several soldiers buried here who fell aged 17. (Plot I.C.15)

Private Charles Douglas WORDINGHAM, 1st Norfolk Regiment, was killed in action on 4 June 1916, aged 21, almost certainly a casualty of the same bombardment that obliterated trenches of the 15th Royal Warwickshire Regiment that day (Plot I.C.17). His brother, Private James Reginald John Wordingham, also fell during the war whilst serving with the 9th Essex Regiment, aged 24. He died of wounds on 23 March 1918 and is buried at Merville Communal Cemetery Extension.

Lance Corporal Leslie Frank BROMWICH, 15th Royal Warwickshire Regiment, was killed in action on 4 June 1916, aged 19 (Plot I.C.62). His brother, Private Edgar John BROMWICH, served in the same battalion and was killed on the same day, aged 26 (Plot I.D.14). Their parents had two other sons who served during the war. The cemetery register states that the brothers are buried near to one another, and initially it might seem odd that they are not buried next to one another. The most likely explanation lies in the fact that Edgar was originally reported as missing in action. His body was not immediately found, although it was recovered soon after. His burial would probably have taken place a short while after his brother's interment.

On 4 June the Germans heavily shelled the trenches held by the battalion before firing three mines. Two of these were poorly aligned and were detonated adjacent to, but not directly beneath our trenches. The third one, however, exploded directly under the section held by 'C' Company and caused several casualties. The Germans then followed this up by sending across a large raiding party, which in places penetrated as far back as the British support lines before it was finally driven back.

Lieutenant John Onslow MADDOCKS, 15th Royal Warwickshire Regiment, was killed in action on 4 June 1916, aged 19. He was the son of Sir Henry Maddocks, Conservative MP for Nuneaton. (Plot I.D.29)

Captain Archibald Henry TATLOW, 15th Royal Warwickshire Regiment, was killed in action on 4 June 1916, aged 31, during the same incident in which the Bromwich brothers died. (Plot I.D.36)

Second Lieutenant Edgar George Butlin MILLSON, 4th Bedfordshire Regiment, attached 1st Battalion, was killed in action on 18 June 1916 when he was shot dead by a sniper. He was a railway engineer working in Colombia when the war broke out and returned to England in order to enlist. His father was a specialist medical psychologist and was awarded the OBE for services in that field. (Plot I.D.54)

Serjeant Frank Cyril RICHARDSON, 8th King's Royal Rifle Corps, was killed in action on 2 July 1916 (Plot I.E.26). He and Serjeant Alfred Whitfield Harrison STONE MM (Plot I.E.29) were originally reported missing in action after the Germans had detonated a mine beneath the battalion's trenches late on the night of 1 July 1916. The mine was accompanied by a heavy barrage, and although a few Germans succeeded in entering one of the battalion's trenches close to the newly-formed crater, they were repulsed by bombers under Second Lieutenant Cooke who managed to occupy the front lip of the crater, which was then quickly consolidated.
  Private John RICHARDSON, 16th Cheshire Regiment, was killed in action on 21 October 1916 (Plot I.H.3). The information in the CWGC register suggests that both he and Frank Cyril RICHARDSON were related, probably cousins. Both men came from Calverton, Nottinghamshire.

Company Serjeant Major John BEECH, 'B' Company, 15th Cheshire Regiment, was killed in action on 4 October 1916, aged 42. The 15th Cheshire Regiment was a Bantam battalion which, along with the 16th Battalion, went to France at the beginning of 1916. Both battalions served with the 35th (Bantam) Division. (Plot I.G.29)

Captain Arthur Beadon COLTHURST, 14th Gloucestershire Regiment, was killed in action on 25 October 1916 (Plot I.H.14). His third son, Flying Officer John Buller COLTHURST, served as a bomb aimer with 115 Squadron, Royal Air Force, during the Second World War and was killed in action on 24 February 1944 during a bombing raid over Schweinfurt. His Lancaster bomber was shot down, almost certainly by enemy flak, resulting in the loss of the entire crew. His body was never recovered and he is now commemorated on the Air Forces Memorial, Runnymede. The target of the raid had been the ball-bearing works producing this vital component for the German armaments industry.

Captain James Percival HODGKINSON, 15th Sherwood Foresters, was killed in action on 2 November 1916, aged 24. He is referred to in the battalion history, *The Blast of War*, published in 1986, but there is no account of his death, which strikes me as an unusual omission. (Plot I.H.31)

Captain John TILLEY, 7th Norfolk Regiment, was killed in action on 28 November 1916, aged 21. Though a relatively quiet period for the battalion, it was required to provide working parties, including wiring parties, during the latter part of November. The battalion war diary notes that Captain TILLEY was fatally wounded while inspecting the wire under the cover of mist. The sergeant with him was also wounded.

The party that went out to rescue them presumed that they had been hit by stray bullets, but the rescue party was also fired on, suggesting that a sniper could have been responsible for his death rather than random or routine fire. (Plot I.J.30)

Private John MITCHELL, Private George CUTHBERT and Private Thomas JACKSON, all of whom served with the 10th Argyll & Sutherland Highlanders, died on 6 January 1917. They were part of a platoon preparing to carry out a raid on German positions opposite them with a party from the 8th Black Watch. The raid was due to begin at 3.08pm, but at 1.00pm an accident occurred as the men of the 10th Argyll & Sutherland Highlanders were being briefed by one of their sergeants inside a cellar. A Mills bomb exploded in their midst, presumably after the pin had come loose. Two men were killed instantly and fourteen others wounded. The raiding party was quickly brought back up to strength using men from another platoon and at 2.00pm the party of two officers, nine NCOs and seventy-seven men filed up the trench known as Imperial Street and into final positions for the raid.

The raid itself lasted only twenty minutes and the unusual timing appears to have taken the Germans by surprise. Stokes bombs were used to destroy dug-outs, which in some cases lifted the roofs off. Estimates put the German dead at around a hundred, while casualties for the 10th Argyll & Sutherland Highlanders amounted to one man killed and one other man wounded. The wounded man was carried in by Second Lieutenant Robertson.

MITCHELL, CUTHBERT and JACKSON are buried together (Plot II.B.11, 12 and 13). Nearby are the graves of Lance Corporal David CRAIG and Private William KINLOCK (Plot II.B.24 and 25). It is possible that these two men either died of wounds as a result of the incident in the cellar, or that one of them was the wounded man rescued by Second Lieutenant Robertson. Both men died of wounds on 9 January 1917.

The Reverend Edward Francis DUNCAN MC, Chaplain 4th Class, was killed in action on 11 March 1917, aged 32, while going to the assistance of a man wounded by a shell. He won his MC in similar circumstances after going to help an officer who had been wounded during a raid, an act which he carried out even though he himself had been wounded. He was attached to 103 Brigade, 34th Division. His MC was gazetted on 27 November 1916. (Plot II.F.8)

Lieutenant Thomas William JONES MD Ch.B. D.Ph, Royal Army Medical Corps, was killed in action on 11 March 1917, aged 31, while attached to the 27th Northumberland Fusiliers (4th Tyneside Irish). (Plot II.F.9)

Major Royston Swire GRIFFITHS, 123rd Siege Battery, Royal Garrison Artillery, is shown in *Officers Died in the Great War* as having died on 17 March 1917, aged 31. He enlisted in 1914 with the Royal Marines, but soon switched to the Royal Marine Engineers. He was commissioned in January 1915 and then served in France with the above battery from the end of July 1916 until his death. Unfortunately he became ill and developed a blood clot that killed him. (Plot II.H.3)

Bombardier Ernest George HUMPHRIES, 260th Siege Battery, Royal Garrison Artillery, was killed in action on 22 March 1917, aged 29. The CWGC register notes that he had been headmaster of Englishcombe School, Bath, before the outbreak of war. (Plot II.J.18)

Second Lieutenant Edward Rodney Hasluck GRANTHAM, 1st Northumberland Fusiliers, died of wounds on 31 March 1917, aged 20. He was educated at Rugby School and Trinity College, Cambridge (Plot II.M.22). His elder brother, Second Lieutenant Richard Aubray Fuge Grantham, was killed in action a few weeks earlier on 4 March serving with the 2nd Lincolnshire Regiment. He is buried at Fins New British Cemetery, Sorel-le-Grand. Like his brother, Richard was educated at Rugby School, but went on to study at Corpus Christi College, Oxford. The family lived in Hampstead, London.

Private Arthur Andrew PLANK, 'C' Company, 1st South African Regiment, was wounded at Delville Wood on 18 July 1916. He was killed in action on 5 April 1917 in the run up to the opening of the Arras offensive (Plot II.O.23). Next to him is Private N.M. MAGENNIS of the same regiment. He was killed in action the previous day. (Plot II.O.22)

Company Quartermaster Serjeant Thomas S. KING, 24th Northumberland Fusiliers (1st Tyneside Irish), aged 45, was killed in action on 7 April 1917. *Soldiers Died in the Great War* shows his death occurring the following day. (Plot II.P.2)

Among the sixty soldiers of the South African Brigade buried here are three who were killed in action on Christmas Day 1916. All three are from the 2nd Battalion, South African Regiment: Private Leslie Frederick DORE (Plot III.A.9), Second Lieutenant M.F. BURLEY (Plot III.A.11), and Private John Jacob BELLARDI (Plot III.A.13).
    Buried among them are two other casualties from that day: Gunner Henry Stone ELLIOT, 123rd Battery, Royal Garrison Artillery, shown in *Soldiers Died in the Great War* as having died on active service (Plot III.A.10), and Corporal John BRODIE, 6th King's Own Scottish Borderers, shown as being killed in action (Plot III.A.12).

Second Lieutenant Harold DAWS, 10th Durham Light Infantry, was killed in action on 26 December 1916. The CWGC register informs us that he returned from Brazil in 1914 in order to enlist and that he originally served with the Artists' Rifles OTC. (Plot III.A.14)

Private Murray Stewart LE MARE, 3rd South African Regiment, was another veteran of the fighting at Delville Wood; he was wounded there on 16 July 1916. He was killed in action on 12 January the following year (Plot III.B.7). A little way along the same row is Private Arthur Douglas GRANT, 4th South African Regiment, who was also wounded at Delville Wood. He was killed in action a few days later on 18 January 1917. (Plot III.B.21)

Major John Stanley SHARP, 5th Royal Berkshire Regiment, was killed in action on 17 March 1917, aged 34. He was educated at Wellington College, then Trinity Hall, Cambridge. He was a very good sportsman and was awarded colours for rugby, cricket and hockey while at university. In 1914 he joined one of the Public Schools Battalions of the Royal Fusiliers and was then commissioned in the 5th Royal Berkshire Regiment. He went to France with his new battalion in May 1915.

On 17 March 1917 he led around 200 of his battalion in a raid on German trenches just south of Blangy. The raid was of short duration, lasting just twenty-five minutes. Most of the casualties, thirty-six in total, occurred as the party was returning to its own trenches when it was caught by retaliatory German shell fire. Eight other ranks were killed in the action and Major SHARP was one of two officer casualties. The other officer was Second Lieutenant Basil Hamilton Abdy Fellowes. He died of wounds five days later, aged 19, at a casualty clearing station at Avesnes-le-Comte and was buried there in the Communal Cemetery Extension. SHARP's body was recovered easily owing to the fact that he fell just yards from reaching the comparative safety of the British trenches. He was mentioned in despatches in May that year in recognition of his leadership. (Plot III.G.31)

Major James Robert WALKER MC, 'B' Battery, 62 Brigade, Royal Field Artillery, was killed in action on 20 March 1917, aged 40. He had previously served for twenty years with 'C' Battery, Royal Horse Artillery. His MC was gazetted on 17 January 1917, but it appears to be without a citation. (Plot III.H.30)

Private James O'NEILL, 9th Cameronians, was killed in action on 22 March 1917, aged 22 (Plot III.J.15). His younger brother, Patrick O'Neill, fell in action on 3 May that year whilst serving as a lance corporal with the Household Battalion, aged 20. He has no known grave and is commemorated on the Arras Memorial. The family came from Motherwell.

Serjeant Thomas DOYLE, 10th Argyll & Sutherland Highlanders, was 44 years old when he was killed in action on 3 April 1917. He had spent nearly half of his life as a soldier, having served in the army for twenty-one years. (Plot III.M.29)

Captain Thomas Hesketh ROSS MC, 4th Battalion, South African Regiment, was one of only four officers from that battalion to emerge from Delville Wood unhurt. His gallantry and leadership during those desperate few days in July 1916 earned him the MC. He was subsequently wounded by a bullet to the head during a raid on the night of 18/19 October 1916 near the Butte de Warlencourt. The raid, led by ROSS himself, comprised a force of 200 men, including bombers, signallers and Lewis gunners. ROSS was wounded when the Germans launched a counter-attack on Snag Trench around 5.00am using flame-throwers and bombs. They drove him and his men back to their original positions with heavy casualties, along with a party under Captain Langdale. Sadly, ROSS was killed the following year at Arras on 3 April 1917, though there is some dispute as to whether he was killed by a sniper or by shrapnel.

In 1903 he joined the Transvaal Scottish and was commissioned the following year. In 1906 he served with the Transvaal Scottish Volunteer Company during the Zulu Rebellion and later went on to command the Transvaal Scottish in South-West Africa. This unit was to become 'B' Company, 4th Battalion, South African Regiment, and he had the privilege of taking it to war in 1914. ROSS was immortalized when his face and figure were used as the model for the statue on the memorial to the 4th Battalion, South African Regiment (South African Scottish) that now stands in Joubert Park, Johannesburg. (Plot III.M.30)

Private Gavin ALLAN, 9th Cameronians, was killed in action on 6 April 1917. He came from Hamilton in Scotland, which was a key recruiting area for that regiment and is now the home of the regimental archive and museum. He joined the militia at the age of 18 and then carried on his part-time soldiering with the Territorials after their formation. The part of Lanarkshire where he lived was a coal mining area and in civilian life he had worked locally as a miner. He was wounded at Neuve Chapelle in 1915 and again on the Somme the following year. At the age of 33, when he was killed in action, he was already an experienced soldier. (Plot III.O.21)

Captain Arthur Scott BUCKTON, 100th Siege Battery, Royal Garrison Artillery, died of wounds on 9 April 1917. He was born in Plaistow, east London, where he began his education. He was a bright pupil and won an exhibition. Through that scholarship he became an engineer, working firstly for the Port of London Authority, then in Edmonton, Alberta. In 1914, just before the outbreak of war, he was working there as a land surveyor. He returned home to enlist and joined the University of London OTC before receiving his commission in the Royal Garrison Artillery in January 1915. (Plot III.P.7)

Second Lieutenant Gordon Reid MORTON MC, 7th Cameron Highlanders, was killed in action on 9 April 1917. His MC was gazetted posthumously on 11 May 1917 and was awarded for conspicuous gallantry and devotion to duty while in command of a raiding party in which he led his men in a most gallant manner, destroying an enemy machine gun, and then carrying a wounded man back to our lines. (Plot III.P.11)

Second Lieutenant Robert Woodburn Barnard SEMPLE MC, 7th Cameron Highlanders, was killed in action on 9 April 1917, aged 24. His MC was gazetted on 11 May 1917 and was awarded for conspicuous gallantry and devotion to duty. The citation states that he was the first man to enter the enemy lines and that throughout the whole operation he set a fine example to the two platoons under his charge, leading a bombing party and inflicting many casualties on the enemy. (Plot III.P.31)

Company Quartermaster Serjeant Henry James BRACEY MM, 1st Northumberland Fusiliers, was killed in action on 11 April 1917 (Plot IV.A.23). *Soldiers Died in the Great War* shows the award of the MM and the *Médaille Militaire* (France) against his name. BRACEY's MM was gazetted, along with numerous others, on 13 October 1916 and was awarded for bravery in the field. The award of the *Médaille Miltaire* was gazetted on 1 May 1917. At the time of writing this book, the record held by the CWGC contained no reference to his MM, though I have since notified the Commission so that the register entry can be amended in due course.

Captain Joseph Leslie DENT DSO MC, 2nd South Staffordshire Regiment, who was killed in action on 11 April 1917, aged 28, had served overseas since 1914. His DSO was gazetted on 1 December 1914 and was awarded for actions on 7 October when he carried out a daring scouting patrol at night, locating an enemy trench and subsequently rushing it with two sections, driving off the occupants. His MC was gazetted on 5 June 1916 in the King's Birthday Honours List. (Plot IV.A.28)

Lieutenant Colonel Herbert Edward TREVOR, Northamptonshire Regiment, attached 9th Essex Regiment, was killed in action on 11 April 1917, aged 32. He was the son of Surgeon Major Sir Francis Wollaston Trevor KCSI CB, who had served with the 60th Rifles in the Nile Campaign 1884–85 and in the South African campaign between 1901 and 1902. (Plot IV.A.29)

Captain William Grant Spruell STUART MC, 7th Cameron Highlanders, was killed in action during the fighting to capture Guémappe on 23 April 1917. His MC was gazetted on 1 January 1917 in the New Year's Honours List. (Plot IV.C.15)

Second Lieutenant George LAMBERT, 7th Cameron Highlanders, who came from Fenwick, Ayrshire, was killed in action on 23 April 1917, aged 25, serving in 'D' Company. He was the son of a clergyman and had a younger brother, Second Lieutenant William Fairlie Lambert, who served with the 9th Cameronians and who died of wounds in March 1916, aged 20. William was wounded when a German patrol carried out a trench raid near Armentières. He was taken prisoner and appears to have died soon afterwards, and so was buried behind German lines. Surprisingly, he is now buried on the Somme in London Cemetery and Extension, Longueval, which is a very long way from where he died. George, however, was killed in action near Guémappe. He was an outstanding pupil at Kilmarnock Academy and went on to Glasgow University where he gained an Honours degree in Classics. He had intended to follow his father into the Church, but when the war broke out he opted to postpone those plans and chose to enlist. (Plot IV.C.17)

The Reverend Charles Wand MITCHELL, Chaplain 4th Class, was attached to the 8th East Yorkshire Regiment when he was mortally wounded on 3 May 1917, aged 28. He had studied in Canada, where he was born, and then went on to Emmanuel College, Cambridge, passing his Theological Tripos in 1903 and his Oriental Languages Tripos the following year, reading Hebrew and Aramaic. He became Master of Hebrew at Merchant Taylors' School in London, where he taught until the outbreak of war, having already completed his Master's degree two years earlier. On 3 May 1917 he went out under heavy shell fire to attend to wounded men after his battalion had been involved supporting an attack by the 1st Royal Scots Fusiliers. The attack broke down and the survivors were forced to occupy a series of shell holes, which were later consolidated as a line of outposts. (Plot IV.E.28)

In the next row is Second Lieutenant Wilfred PRICE, 8th East Yorkshire Regiment, who also died of his wounds in the same attack, aged 21 (Plot IV.F.27).

Two more officers from his battalion who were killed in the attack, Second Lieutenant Francis McIntyre and Second Lieutenant Joseph Morton Bibby, are commemorated on the Arras Memorial, whilst another, Second Lieutenant Arthur Johnson Cox, is buried considerably further away in Cabaret Rouge British Cemetery.

A relatively rare headstone can be seen in this cemetery belonging to a member of the Army Veterinary Corps. Captain Harry Leonard ANTHONY was serving with the 1/1st Lancashire Mobile Section, Army Veterinary Corps, when he was killed in action, aged 40. Only seventeen officers of the Army Veterinary Corps were killed in action or died of wounds across all theatres of war between 1914 and 1918, although others did die in service from other causes. He was killed on 2 May 1917 and had served in the South African campaign after graduating in 1901. (Plot IV.E.30)

Major Maurice Edward COXHEAD, 9th Royal Fusiliers, was killed in action on 3 May 1917, aged 27. A keen cricketer, he had played for Oxford University and Middlesex before the war. (Plot IV.G.14)

Major John Campbell FISHER, 1st Royal Scots Fusiliers, died of wounds on 6 May 1917. He had been mentioned in despatches. (Plot IV.G.22)

Captain Walter MACFADYEN, 3rd Royal Scots, attached 2nd Battalion, was killed in action on 7 May 1917, aged 24. He was an only son. He was mentioned in despatches and had been a member of Leeds University OTC. (Plot IV.G.24)

Serjeant Alfred William HOWITT DCM, 7th Field Ambulance, Royal Army Medical Corps, died of wounds on 7 June 1917, aged 49. His DCM was gazetted on 30 June 1915 and was awarded for conspicuous gallantry and devotion to duty between December 1914 and March 1915 whilst in charge of an ambulance wagon. The citation records that on more than one occasion he volunteered for exceptionally dangerous duty and that during an action at Neuve Chapelle in October 1914 he was able to retrieve two wagons after troops had withdrawn from their positions. The award was won while he was serving as a private. (Plot IV.H.15)

Major Vernon Ommaney DOLPHIN, 17 Brigade, Royal Field Artillery, was killed in action on 8 June 1917, aged 31. He attended the Royal Military Academy, Woolwich, before receiving his commission in the Royal Field Artillery in 1906. In the years that followed he served in South Africa and in India. His death came when he was returning to his battery after assisting in the removal of a casualty. A shell burst close to him and he was killed by one of the fragments. (Plot IV.H.18)

Captain Thomas Hall WAUGH MC, 22nd Northumberland Fusiliers (Tyneside Scottish), was killed in action on 6 June 1917. His MC was gazetted on 1 January 1917 in the New Year's Honours List. (Plot IV.H.20)

On 4 July 1917 two soldiers from the 12th (Eastern) Division were executed and now lie here in adjacent graves. Around the beginning of March 1916 it was acknowledged that Private Robert Gillis PATTISON, aged 23, was suffering from shell shock while holding the line at Loos near the Hohenzollern Craters. On 6 March the enemy detonated a mine nearby, which was accompanied by a heavy bombardment. Several days later the Germans fired yet another mine and also made several trench raids in between these two incidents. Such events caused acute anxiety among even the very best soldiers. Private PATTISON was unable to stand the strain and deserted. Although it was recognized that his nerves were badly shaken, he was sentenced to a lengthy period of Field Punishment No. 1.

He was able to survive another year of trench warfare before his nerves broke down again, this time while his battalion, the 7th Royal Sussex Regiment, was at Arras and involved in the advance on the opening day of the battle. However, on 3 May he made representations to the battalion's medical officer who promptly returned him to his platoon. PATTISON's response was to go missing and he was arrested the following day in Arras. (Plot IV.J.16)

Private John Edward BARNES, 7th Royal Sussex Regiment, aged 24, went to France in late September 1915. He was already serving a suspended sentence of penal servitude for desertion when he again went missing on 10 June 1917. The subsequent court martial could see no reason for clemency and he was shot by firing squad a few weeks later. (Plot IV.J.17)

Captain Herbert Haydon WILSON DSO, Royal Horse Guards, was killed in action on 11 April 1917, aged 42. He had previously served in the South African campaign and was twice mentioned in despatches in 1901. He was the youngest son of Sir Samuel Wilson of Victoria, Australia, a successful farmer, miner and businessman who emigrated from Ireland to Australia. His DSO was gazetted on 23 April 1901 and was awarded for gallantry in defence of posts during a Boer attack at Lichtenburg. (Plot V.A.1)

His eldest brother, Lieutenant Colonel Gordon Chesney Wilson MVO, was killed in action on 6 November 1914 when commanding the Royal Horse Guards. He was mentioned in despatches and is buried in the churchyard at Zillebeke, just outside Ypres. His headstone bears the occasionally quoted epitaph: '*Life is a city of crooked streets; death is the market place where all men meet.*'

Another brother, Lieutenant Wilfred Campbell Wilson, died of wounds during the South African campaign whilst serving with the 5th Imperial Yeomanry. A third brother, Clarence, was badly wounded during the same campaign while attached to the 8th Hussars.

Lieutenant Charles Humphrey NEWTON-DEAKIN, 3rd (Prince of Wales's) Dragoon Guards, was killed in action on 11 April 1917. Between 8.30 and 9.30am on the morning of 11 April, 'B' and 'C' Squadrons, 3rd Dragoon Guards, came under heavy shell and machine-gun fire from Guémappe while occupying ground between the southern edge of Monchy-le-Preux and the windmill just west of La Bergère on the Arras–Cambrai road. It was here that the regiment suffered several casualties including NEWTON-DEAKIN. (Plot V.A.2)

Major Alexander WOOD, 3rd Royal Sussex Regiment, died of wounds on 12 April 1917, aged 37. He is also remembered on the Roll of Honour at Hampton Court Palace where his parents resided. His father was the late Major General Edward Wood CB. (Plot V.A.4)

Second Lieutenant Harry Asher HAYWORTH, 10th Argyll & Sutherland Highlanders, was killed in action on 25 April 1917, aged 21, three weeks before his brother, Second Lieutenant Frederick Hayworth. His brother's body was never found and he is commemorated on the Arras Memorial within sight of Harry's grave. Frederick served with the 7th Argyll & Sutherland Highlanders, but was attached to the 1/14th Battalion, London Regiment (London Scottish), at the time of his death on 12 May 1917. Harry had studied at Glasgow University. (Plot V.A.12)

The 8th Royal Scots was the pioneer battalion attached to the 51st (Highland) Division. Lieutenant William Ernest WALLACE, aged 38, and Second Lieutenant James Melville MONCUR, aged 24, were members of the battalion's 'D' Company. On 17 April 1917 they were with a working party as it was making its way up the Point du Jour Ridge to carry out road repair work when the group was caught by shell fire in the open. One of the shells killed both officers. They were uncle and nephew; fittingly, they now rest here, side by side. (Plots V.A.20 & 21)

Captain David ROBERTS MC, 7th Lincolnshire Regiment, died of wounds on 23 April 1917, aged 35. His MC was gazetted on 30 March 1916 and was awarded for conspicuous gallantry during operations after the commanders of his own company and those of the next company had become casualties. He then took command of both units for twenty-four hours under heavy shell fire and consolidated the newly won position, fearlessly moving about and setting a fine example. (Plot V.B.1)

Captain David ANDERSON MC, 7th Cameron Highlanders, was killed in action on 23 April 1917, aged 30. His MC was gazetted on 23 October 1917 and was awarded for conspicuous gallantry in action. When two of his gun teams had been knocked out and two further guns buried, he personally dug a gun into position and opened fire in support of an attack. The citation states that the accuracy of his fire contributed much towards the success of the operation. (Plot V.C.14)

At the start of Plot V, Row E, are six graves belonging to the 3rd Battalion, British West Indies Regiment. Private T.A. BROWN, Private H. COVER, Private Robert Samuel WILLIAMS, Private S.A. HENRY, Private Ernest POTTINGER and Private L.A. CLAYTON were all killed in action on 10 May 1917. The 3rd Battalion served on the Western Front from 1916 until 1919. (Plots V.E.3 to 8)

Second Lieutenant Iain Donald Forrest MacLENNAN, 1st Gordon Highlanders, was killed in action on 12 May 1917, aged 19 (Plot V.E.19). His father, Major John MacLennan DCM, also served with the 1st Gordon Highlanders during the war, but died at Aberdeen Girls' School, which was then in use as a military hospital, on 9 August 1916, aged 51. He is buried in Aberdeen (Springbank) Cemetery.

Major MacLennan had been invalided home after he was injured in France. He was thrown from his horse when it was frightened by shell fire. He was sent home to Aberdeen where the family lived, but unfortunately succumbed to his injuries. His DCM was won while serving as regimental serjeant major with the 1st Gordon Highlanders in the South African War. The award was gazetted on 27 September 1901. After his death, his cousin, Pipe-Major George MacLennan, wrote a piece of music in his memory entitled, 'Major John MacLennan'. At the time of writing this book the CWGC record did not show the award of his DCM, though I have since notified the Commission with a view to having the entry amended.

Second Lieutenant Benjamin STRACHAN, 12 Squadron, Royal Flying Corps, was killed in action on 18 May 1917, aged 28 (Plot V.F.4). Buried next to him is his observer, Lieutenant Arthur Gordon MACKAY, a Canadian attached to the Royal Flying Corps, who was also killed when their BE2e was shot down (Plot V.F.3). The casualty report for their squadron states that they did not appear to notice their attacker until it was too late, although MACKAY did return fire. The wings of their machine crumpled as they folded back and upwards, giving neither of them any chance of escaping as they plunged to the ground. Their death marked the fifteenth victory for German ace and holder of the *Pour le Mérite*, Leutnant Karl Allmenröder, who went on to score a further fifteen kills before his death on 27 June 1917.

Serjeant John Robert HANDYSIDE DCM, 'C' Battery, 70 Brigade, Royal Field Artillery, was killed in action on 19 May 1917. His DCM was won as a bombardier with 'D' Battery, 71 Brigade, Royal Field Artillery, and was awarded for conspicuous gallantry between 26 September and 14 October 1915, during which time his battery was constantly under very heavy shell fire and out in the open. He frequently volunteered to mend telephone lines under heavy fire, thereby successfully maintaining communications. He had also come to notice for coolness and bravery on 25 September 1915, again near Loos, where he repeatedly volunteered to repair wires under very heavy fire, even though he was suffering from the effects of gas fumes. His unit was part of the 15th Divisional Artillery. His award was gazetted on 29 November 1915. *Solders Died in the Great War* makes no reference to his DCM. (Plot V.F.13)

Captain William Maurice (Pat) ARMSTRONG MC, 10th (Prince of Wales's Own Royal) Hussars, was killed in action on 23 May 1917, aged 27, when he was shot by a sniper. He had been part of the 29th Division's Staff since the early days in Gallipoli. On 19 May 1917 his friend, Second Lieutenant Frank Stanlie Layard, 1st Border Regiment, took part in an attack east of Monchy-le-Preux, but was then reported to be among the missing. He was believed to have been hit somewhere between Cigar Copse and the Bois des Aubépines when his company came under heavy machine-gun fire. ARMSTRONG went out on subsequent nights to look for Layard, but was killed while doing so. Second Lieutenant Layard's body was found and he is buried in Dury Crucifix Cemetery. ARMSTRONG, whose family came from Tipperary, Ireland, had previously been mentioned in despatches. At the time of his death he was serving as brigade major of 86 Brigade, 29th Division. His MC was gazetted on 4 February 1916 and was won while serving as a lieutenant. I can find no citation for it. (Plot V.F.18)

Lieutenant Harold LEIGHTON MC, 88th Battalion, Machine Gun Corps, died of wounds on 26 May 1917. His MC was gazetted on 11 December 1916 and was awarded for conspicuous gallantry during an action in which he had handled his machine guns with marked courage and skill, moving them forward with the assaulting troops. By doing so, the citation concludes, he contributed greatly towards successfully holding the captured trench. (Plot V.F.21)

Major Albert Ernest BARTON, 6th Dorsetshire Regiment, was mortally wounded by a shell on 24 May 1917 while inspecting trenches and temporarily in charge of his depleted battalion owing to the heavy fighting of the previous six weeks. As a result, 'A' and 'D' companies, and 'B' and 'C', had been formed into composite units 'Y' and 'Z' respectively. By this time many of the units that had been continuously engaged at Arras were described as being tired, depleted, and not fit for purpose, according to *Military Operations, France and Belgium, 1917, Part I*. The battalion's adjutant, Lieutenant A.H. Mitchell, was wounded by the same shrapnel burst. In his absence, and pending the return of Lieutenant Colonel Moulton-Barrett in August that year, Major James, 7th Lincolnshire Regiment, took charge of the battalion. BARTON was recommended for decorations on four occasions and was mentioned in despatches. His brother served in Mesopotamia during the war. (Plot V.F.23)

Conductor Daniel MURRAY DCM, Army Ordnance Corps, formerly York & Lancaster Regiment, was killed in action on 12 June 1917, aged 36. His DCM was gazetted as part of the King's Birthday Honours List on 5 June 1916 while he was serving with the Army Ordnance Corps. It was awarded for services in the field. (Plot V.H.2)

Lieutenant Colonel Alfred John SANSOM, 7th Royal Sussex Regiment, is shown as serving with the 5th Battalion, but was commanding the 7th Battalion when he was killed in action on 5 July 1917, aged 50. (Plot V.J.1)

Buried next to him is Captain Gilbert NAGLE MC, 7th Royal Sussex Regiment, who at the time of his death was adjutant of the battalion. His MC was gazetted on 17 April 1916 and was awarded while he was serving as a second lieutenant with the 7th Battalion. The citation notes that on 3 and 4 March 1916 he showed conspicuous courage. Despite being wounded, he continued to command his men, inspiring them with confidence and carrying out a skilful defence of some newly captured craters at the Hohenzollern Redoubt and repelling two enemy attacks. (Plot V.J.2)

Both men had stepped outside their dug-out in order to observe the effect of a 'Chinese' bombardment on Devil's Trench, near Monchy-le-Preux, and to note any lights sent up by the Germans by way of response. However, both were killed by a German shell that landed next to them.

Ironically SANSOM was probably unaware that a letter from GHQ had been received that day at Corps HQ directing him to return home. The reason for his removal from active service was almost certainly that revealed in a letter to his wife in which he informed her that:

> '*I refuse to kow-tow to higher authority, or keep from expressing opinions on those who give orders which I consider cost, unnecessarily, the lives of men. But though I know my criticisms make me unpopular with higher authority, I again don't care a damn if they have the least influence in making people thoughtful for others, and I believe I have succeeded in one or two instances. What is the value of a DSO given to a gentleman sitting in an office in safety, compared to the thought that one may have saved the lives of men under one's command?*'

In August 1914 NAGLE had been a subaltern in the battalion and had since served with it continuously, initially as a platoon commander, then as a company commander, before being appointed adjutant. His career as a soldier first ran into difficulties while he was billeted with two fellow officers in Folkestone where they were at the mercy of the two elderly maiden ladies who owned the house. The men were forced to smoke clandestinely up the dining room chimney and were obliged to settle for hot milk, presumably as a substitute for something a little stronger. They left after the first day and found a more liberal-minded doctor with whom to stay. After his experience with hot milk, NAGLE's palate was again tested when billeted near Le Touquet. On this occasion he sent back a cup of 'Bovril' on the grounds that it didn't taste quite like the 'Bovril' he knew. The next day the probable cause was detected; a decomposed horse was found at the bottom of the well from which the water had been drawn to make the drink.

Captain Harold Gerard Hans HAMILTON, 7th Border Regiment, was killed in action on 27 July 1917, aged 23. The regimental history notes that he was fatally wounded at a time when the battalion was heavily depleted of officers, but it does not comment further on the manner of his death. (Plot V.J.7)

Captain Alexander Reid PRENTICE MC, 12th Cameronians, attached 10th Battalion, was killed in action on 9 November 1917, aged 22. The regimental history shows his date of death as 5 November and notes that he was previously wounded in October 1916. His MC was gazetted on 30 May 1917 and was awarded for conspicuous gallantry and devotion to duty in command of a raiding party, which he led in a most gallant manner, gaining his objective. Later he assisted in bringing in several of the wounded. (Plot VI.A.19)

Captain Arthur Yalden Graham THOMSON MC and Bar, Cameron Highlanders, was killed in action on 30 November 1917, aged 29. His MC was gazetted on 4 June 1917 in the King's Birthday Honours List; the bar, which was gazetted on 27 August 1917, was awarded for conspicuous gallantry and devotion to duty. The citation states that he was tireless in arranging the preliminaries of an attack and getting the troops into position for it. Once the objective was gained, he wasted no time in going round the new front line under heavy shell fire before bringing back a valuable report regarding the latest situation.

His grandfather, Surgeon Major Thomson, had been a physician to both Queen Victoria and King Edward VII. Arthur's father, Brigadier General Andrew Graham Thomson CB CMG, Royal Engineers, was the base commandant of Étaples at the time of the famous mutiny there in September 1917. He and several other officers were purportedly driven to a bridge over the River Canche where, according to the story, they were off-loaded into the water, much to the amusement of hundreds of onlookers. The incident was portrayed in the controversial BBC drama, *The Monocled Mutineer*, though the accuracy with which events were depicted in the series was the subject of much debate when it was screened. (Plot VI.A.28)

Captain Joseph WILSON MC, 6th Cameron Highlanders, was killed in action on 30 November 1917, aged 30. His MC, won as a second lieutenant, was awarded for conspicuous gallantry at Hill 70 on 26 September 1915 after he had collected and rallied stragglers. He had then led them through the troops of another division as they were retiring and had remained with the group throughout the night in a very advanced position in a show of great leadership. The award was gazetted on 23 November 1915. (Plot VI.A.29)

Private Frank BALL, 10th Cameronians, a Londoner who had enlisted in Glasgow, died of wounds following an accident while placing detonators in bombs at Tilloy Camp. Nine other men from 'C' Company were wounded in the explosion. A court of enquiry was later held, but found nobody culpable, concluding that the accident had probably occurred as a result of rust. (Plot VI.B.9)

Lance Corporal Frank HURST MM, 8th Seaforth Highlanders, was killed in action on 19 March 1918, aged 27 (Plot VI.B.15). His younger brother, Arthur Hurst, was killed a few months later on 21 August 1918, aged 20, while serving as a rifleman with the 1/15th Battalion, London Regiment (Prince of Wales's Own Civil Service Rifles). He is buried at Corbie Communal Cemetery Extension.

Captain John BALFOUR MC, 2nd Scots Guards, was killed in action on 21 March 1918, aged 23. His MC was gazetted on 4 June 1917 in the King's Birthday Honours List (Plot VI.B.19). His brother, Captain Robert Frederick Balfour, served with the 1st Scots Guards and was killed in action on 28 October 1914, aged 31. He is buried at Sanctuary Wood Cemetery.

Lieutenant (Quartermaster) George MASKELL, 10th Cameronians, was killed in action on 21 March 1918, aged 38. He came from Balham, south London, and had also served in the South African campaign (Plot VI.B.29). His brother, Albert Maskell, was killed in action at Loos on 30 September 1915 serving as a lance corporal with the 9th Devonshire Regiment. His body was never found and he is now commemorated on the Loos Memorial.

Serjeant John VEITCH DCM, 'A' Battery, 71 Brigade, Royal Field Artillery, was killed in action on 23 March 1918, aged 22. His DCM was won while serving as a bombardier with 'C' Battery and was awarded for conspicuous gallantry between 26 September and 14 October 1915. During that time his battery was in the open and constantly under very heavy fire. On 8 October, during an enemy attack when it was of the utmost importance that communications should be maintained, he voluntarily went out into the open on four or five occasions and repaired the telephone wires. The citation concludes that he had invariably set a fine example of devotion to duty and always showed a total disregard of danger. The award was gazetted on 29 November 1915. (Plot VI.C.15)

Serjeant Donald McARTHUR DCM, 8th Seaforth Highlanders, was killed in action on 24 March 1918. His DCM was won as a private with the 2nd Battalion and was awarded for conspicuous gallantry when the remainder of his machine-gun team had been put out of action by heavy enemy fire. He kept his gun going and, by his bravery and resource, did much to save the situation when the line began to withdraw. The award was gazetted on 11 March 1916. (Plot VI.C.23)

Major Richard Guy PURCELL MC, 31st Heavy Battery, Royal Garrison Artillery, died of wounds at No. 47 Field Ambulance on 28 March 1918. I have been unable to find any reference to his MC in any of the Gazettes, though *Officers Died in the Great War* does acknowledge the award. He is referred to in Gazettes on 18 August 1917, but there is no mention of the MC. He was gazetted as a second lieutenant on 17 January 1908. His father attained the rank of colonel in the Royal Engineers. (Plot VI.D.31)

Gunners Malcolm and William McISAAC were killed in action while serving as part of the 149th Siege Battery, Royal Garrison Artillery, on 11 April 1918. The brothers came from Falkirk in Scotland. Malcolm was 20 years old when he died and William was 26. (Plot VI.E.21 and 22)

Second Lieutenant Edward Clive GARTON, 5th Rifle Brigade, was 19 years old when he died of wounds on 2 September 1918 (Plot VI.F.17). His brother, Captain Herbert Westlake Garton, is commemorated on the Thiepval Memorial. He also served in the Rifle Brigade and was killed in action with the 9th Battalion on 15 September 1916, aged 24.

Driver Harold E. HOLLAND MM and Bar, 'D' Battery, 70 Brigade, Royal Field Artillery, was killed in action on 2 September 1918 (Plot VI.F.45). He is one of two men buried here with a bar to their MM. The other was also a member of the Royal Field Artillery and is buried in Plot VII. He is Corporal Daniel John GUILMARTIN MM and Bar, 86th Battery, 32 Brigade, Royal Field Artillery, who died of wounds on 31 August 1918. (Plot VII.E.52)

Captain Nelson Gordon JOHNSTONE MC, 9th Black Watch, was killed in action on 30 December 1917, aged 30, whilst attached to 44th Trench Mortar Battery. He originally served in France with the 1st Sherwood Foresters before obtaining a commission in the 11th Black Watch in late 1915. Whilst undergoing officer training with his new battalion, he and four fellow officers had a minor brush with the military authorities when their celebrations got out of hand fuelled by drink. Once back in France he was wounded in the hand, but the subsequent infection spread and manifested itself in the form of a rectal abscess. He was invalided back to England, but returned to France early in 1917. His death occurred in the trenches during a trench mortar demonstration. A subsequent court of inquiry concluded that a 3-inch round had been faulty and had exploded in the barrel killing JOHNSTON, who was standing next to the mortar.

His file at the National Archives makes reference to his MC, but does not show the date on which it was gazetted or why it was awarded. The award is also acknowledged in *Officers Died in the Great War*, but I can find no reference to the award in any of the Gazettes. However, the MC does appear after his name in the *London Gazette* dated 22 December 1917, although there is no prior mention of it or when it was awarded. (Plot VII.A.20)

Captain Dan Horace GEORGESON, 8th Seaforth Highlanders, was killed in action on 9 March 1918, aged 24, and was twice mentioned in despatches. The official war artist, Sir David Muirhead Bone, made a full-length portrait of GEORGESON, who at the time was serving as a lieutenant. The portrait was entitled 'A Highland Officer'. Bone made many sketches depicting life on the Western Front, including villages, battlefields, churches and other military scenes, as well as sketches of factories at home, the Royal Navy and other war-related subjects. (Plot VII.A.33)

Corporal John DONNELLY DCM, 2nd Lancashire Fusiliers, was mortally wounded on 21 March 1918. He was inside a house some miles behind the lines when a shell struck the building. He was severely wounded in the head by fragments and died a few hours later. His DCM was gazetted on 11 December 1916 and was awarded for conspicuous gallantry in action near Le Transloy. The citation records that he was buried along with his machine gun, and that after being dug out, he worked unceasingly under heavy fire to rescue his gun. Later he rescued five men who had also been buried. Two days later, on 12 October, he again risked his life by going out under heavy fire and bringing in a wounded officer. (Plot VII.B.12)

Major Francis GRAHAM DSO MC, 71 Brigade, Royal Field Artillery, was killed in action on 28 March 1918, aged 23. He was educated at Harrow, followed by the Royal Military Academy, Woolwich, and was then gazetted in the Royal Field Artillery in 1913. He was the grandson of General Sir Robert M. Stewart GCB. He went to

France with the original BEF and took part in the Retreat from Mons, the Battle of the Marne, the Battle of the Aisne, and also fought at the First Battle of Ypres with the 1st Divisional Artillery. The following year he saw action at Festubert, Richebourg and at the Battle of Loos.

His DSO was awarded for gallantry during the First Battle of Ypres while serving as a second lieutenant with the 51st Battery, Royal Field Artillery. After all the available officers from the South Lancashire Regiment were either killed or wounded, he took command of the men and succeeded in holding part of our trenches until relief arrived and the enemy was driven back. By doing so, seizing the initiative and acting very much as an infantry officer, he saved the situation in that part of the line. He was also mentioned in despatches in February 1915.

His MC was gazetted in November 1916 while he was a temporary captain and was awarded for conspicuous gallantry in action, commanding his battery with great skill. On one occasion he and another officer established an observation post in a shell hole on the edge of a village and remained there all day under very heavy fire. The citation concludes by stating that his coolness and gallantry were remarkable. In 1917 he saw action in all the main engagements. (Plot VII.C.1)

Lieutenant Aubrey Causton STRACHAN MC and Bar, 'C' Battery, 70 Brigade, Royal Field Artillery, was killed in action on 28 March 1918, aged 23. His MC was gazetted on 27 September 1917 and its citation appeared on 10 January 1918. It was awarded for conspicuous gallantry and devotion to duty when in an advanced position with his battery. He commanded his section for five hours under heavy fire and in pouring rain. During that time he personally removed those killed and wounded and, by his own example of gallantry and coolness, kept his men in action at a very critical time. The bar to his MC was gazetted on 8 July 1918 and was awarded for conspicuous gallantry and devotion to duty in bringing his section into action under heavy artillery and machine-gun fire, skilfully assisting in the capture of a village, and doing most valuable work throughout the operations. His father, Edward Aubrey Strachan, served with the Royal Inniskilling Fusiliers as a lieutenant colonel. (Plot VII.C.7)

Gunner Kenneth MacRAE, 110th Heavy Battery, Royal Garrison Artillery, was killed in action on 3 April 1918. The family lived at Beauly, near Inverness. He was one of four brothers to be killed during the war. (Plot VII.D.2)

The first to lose his life was Private Alexander Duncan MacRae, who served with the 29th Battalion, Canadian Infantry. He was killed on 7 April 1916, aged 26, and is now buried at Bedford House Cemetery, Enclosure No. 2, in Belgium. On 15 September the same year, tragedy struck again when John, a sergeant with the 27th Battalion, Canadian Infantry, was killed in action near Courcelette at the age of 28. He has no known grave and is commemorated on the Canadian Memorial at Vimy Ridge. A few weeks before the Armistice, on 25 October 1918, Private Archibald MacRae was killed in action whilst serving with the 1st Battalion, Highland Light Infantry, during an attack on Turkish positions. He is commemorated on the Basra Memorial.

Company Serjeant Major Robert DOUGLAS, 'D' Company, 9th Black Watch, died of wounds on 6 May 1918, aged 34. His death occurred during his battalion's last tour of duty in the front line before it amalgamated with the 4/5th Battalion on 16 May.

The regimental history notes that of the original members of the 9th Battalion, only one officer and eighty-three other ranks were still serving with it by May 1918. (Plot VII.D.4)

Second Lieutenant Thomas Henry MAWBY, 4th (City of London) Battalion, London Regiment (Royal Fusiliers), was killed in action on 24 June 1918, aged 28 (Plot VII.D.14). His younger brother, John Lane Mawby, served as a private with the 1/4th Leicestershire Regiment and was killed in action, aged 20, on 13 October 1915. He is commemorated on the Loos Memorial.

Captain Douglas Marsden EWART MC, 7th Battalion, Canadian Infantry, was killed in action on 26 August 1918. His MC was gazetted on 30 July 1917 and was awarded for conspicuous gallantry and devotion to duty, displaying great courage and determination in consolidating his position under heavy fire and setting a fine example to his men. (Plot VII.D.22)

Corporal Frederick HICKMAN MM, Canadian Corps Military Police, is one of just thirteen from that regiment who lost their lives during the Great War and one of only six buried on the Western Front. He was killed in action on 27 August 1918 while attached to the HQ of the 3rd Canadian Division. He was born in Elston, Nottinghamshire, but moved to Canada in 1908 where he took up farming. He enlisted in January 1916. (Plot VII.D.24)

Captain Harold Talbot VIZARD MC and 2 Bars, 'A' Battery, 121st Brigade, Royal Field Artillery, was killed in action on 1 September 1918, aged 22. His MC was gazetted on 17 April 1916 and was awarded for conspicuous courage and devotion to duty when a gun pit containing sixty shells caught fire. Despite being under heavy shell fire, he took immediate steps to have the ammunition removed and remained in the pit until the fire had been extinguished.

The bar to it was gazetted on 27 November 1916 and was awarded for conspicuous gallantry after he reorganized a party of men and then led them forward in a bombing attack, displaying great courage at a critical time. The second bar was gazetted on 26 September 1917. Its citation appeared on 9 January 1918 and was awarded for conspicuous gallantry and devotion to duty while serving as liaison officer with an infantry battalion. After hearing cries for help coming from a derelict tank, he accompanied the medical officer through a heavy barrage and machine-gun fire. Finding a badly wounded Highlander, they dressed his wounds and carried him back to a place of safety through a hail of shell and machine-gun fire. The citation concludes that there could be no praise too great for this splendid act of fearlessness and devotion. (Plot VII.E.55)

Major William Broder McTAGGART DSO, 3 Brigade, Canadian Field Artillery, was killed in action on 2 September 1918, aged 25. He was in an observation post at Dury directing the fire of his battery when he was hit by machine-gun fire, killing him instantly. His body was brought back to Arras for burial. His DSO was awarded for distinguished service in the field in the New Year's Honours List on 1 January 1918. He was wounded on four previous occasions. (Plot VII.F.1)

Lieutenant George Thomas LYE, 85th Battalion, Canadian Infantry, joined the battalion in early October 1915 and was another Canadian officer who graduated through the ranks. He was promoted to corporal while serving on the Somme in August 1916 and in June the following year was promoted to sergeant. In December 1917 he became a company sergeant major and was subsequently promoted to lieutenant on 6 June 1918. At this stage of the war he would have been one of the most experienced men in the battalion and a real asset to his unit. Sadly, he was not to see the war through; he was killed in action on 25 September, aged 23. (Plot VII.F.51)

Lieutenant Harold POTTER, 7th East Surrey Regiment, was killed in action on 9 April 1917 during his battalion's advance to its first objective, the Black Line. Three fellow officers also fell around the same time. Like POTTER, all three were from the regiment's 3rd Battalion, but were attached to the 7th Battalion. (Plot VII.G.19)

Captain Thomas Arthur NELSON, Lothians and Border Horse, attached Machine Gun Corps, was killed by a shell on the morning of 9 April 1917, aged 40. He rejoined his yeomanry regiment on the outbreak of war and eventually went with it to France at the end of 1915, attached to the 25th Division. In 1916 he spent some time as a staff officer before becoming an observation officer with the 50th (Northumbrian) Division, which at the time was near Kemmel. In November that year, he carried out the same role with V Corps during the fighting on the Somme around Beaucourt. He then returned briefly to his regiment, but soon afterwards was granted a period of leave.

During his time at home he visited a friend in London, the author John Buchan. He had been thinking of joining the Royal Flying Corps, but complained to Buchan that he was now too old to become a pilot. He was adamant that he wanted a change of circumstances, and it was Buchan who suggested that he should consider joining the Tank Corps rather than the Royal Flying Corps. Accordingly, in March 1917, NELSON took up a position as an intelligence officer at Tank Corps HQ, serving under another of Buchan's friends, Captain Frederick Elliot Hotblack. The two men were talking together on the morning of 9 April when a shell exploded close to them. Captain Hotblack was wounded, but NELSON was killed and, although he was buried nearby, his body was removed to this cemetery after the war.

NELSON and Buchan had first met at Oxford where they revived the Caledonian Club, Nelson becoming its president and Buchan its secretary, and the two men had remained firm friends ever since. NELSON had also played international rugby for Scotland. (Plot VII.G.26)

Captain Harry Cunvin HORSFORD, 5th Royal Berkshire Regiment, died of wounds on 8 April 1917, aged 29, the day before the Battle of Arras began. *Officers Died in the Great War* shows his middle name as 'Curwin'. His brother, Algernon, served with the Middlesex Regiment during the war. (Plot VII.G.42)

On 21 March 1917 Lieutenant James FLEMING MC, 11th Royal Scots, was killed in action while carrying out what the regimental history refers to as '*a reconnaissance in force*'. The German withdrawal to the Hindenburg Line south of Arras had raised the question as to whether the enemy might also be preparing to vacate their lines nearer to Arras itself. With the British offensive just three weeks away, intelligence as to the enemy's intentions was urgently needed. The reconnaissance took place at 3.30pm but unfortunately the assembled raiders were spotted by a German aeroplane. The Germans responded quickly by putting down a trench mortar barrage on our front line trenches, whilst at the same time their machine-gun positions also began to open up. Despite all this, the 11th Royal Scots dashed across no man's land and entered the German trenches as planned. A brief but desperate fight took place as the Germans defended their position using bombs. The Royal Scots replied with their rifles and, firing from the German parapets, they soon got the better of the defenders, forcing them back to their second line of trenches.

This episode not only confirmed that the Germans were there in numbers, it also gave a clear indication that they had no intention of withdrawing and were prepared to defend their positions. The engagement was broken off shortly after the enemy had been driven back and the return across no man's land was uneventful as the Germans licked their wounds.

Casualties from the raid came to five officers, one of whom was Lieutenant FLEMING, and seventy-five other ranks. FLEMING had distinguished himself the previous year on the Somme. His MC, gazetted on 27 July 1916, was awarded for conspicuous gallantry after twice patrolling through a difficult wood that was quite unfamiliar to him, but which was occupied by the enemy who knew it thoroughly (Plot II.K.1).

Of the five officer casualties, three died of wounds the following day. All three are commemorated on the Arras Memorial; they are Captain James William Brown, Second Lieutenant John George Sandilands and Second Lieutenant Herbert Charles Lunn.

The raid provoked further hostility when the Germans raided trenches held by the 11th Royal Scots at 5.00am the following morning, capturing three men who were holding a Lewis gun post. Ever determined to have the last word, the 11th Battalion retaliated the next night. Lieutenant Bertram Cash Matthews and two other men left their trenches and entered the German front line where they killed four of the enemy's garrison, one of whom was not silenced cleanly and managed to cry out.

Matthews and his two companions were attacked before they could make good their escape. Only one man returned safely and he was unable to confirm what had happened to Matthews, though he knew that his other colleague had been killed. Once it became light, sentries reported what was believed to be a body lying out in no man's land. Lieutenant Colonel Croft, the battalion's commanding officer, ordered a party to go out after dusk to investigate. However, Second Lieutenant Storey, whether unaware of the reference to 'dusk' or gallantly ignoring the fact, went out in broad daylight and reached the supposed body, only to find that it was a piece of sacking. During the advance on 9 April, Matthews's body was found and he is now buried in Bailleul West Cemetery, Saint-Laurent-Blangy.

On the far side of the Faubourg d'Amiens Cemetery, away from the entrance, is a small plot containing German graves and, a little further along, there are three separate plots containing nine native soldiers of the Indian Army. The men are buried separately according to their religion. There is one Sikh, Sowar Arjun SINGH, 'B' Squadron, King Edward's Own Cavalry, who was killed in action on 4 August 1916 (Sikh Row).

The three Hindus, who died during the early months of 1919, were attached to ammunition columns of British divisions (Hindu Row 1 to 3), as were two of the five Moslems, a driver and a gunner, who died just after the Armistice. The remaining three Moslems include a sowar from the 17th Indian Cavalry who died in August 1916; a man belonging to the Supply and Transport Corps who died in December 1917; and a man from the Central Depot, Royal Horse and Field Artillery, who died just after the Armistice. The rank of these last two men is shown as 'follower'. (Mohammadan Row 1 to 5)

The cemetery also contains eight identified casualties of the Second World War and these can be found in Plot VIII, which is situated at the far end of the cemetery where the Cross of Sacrifice stands. For all practical purposes this is more or less an extension of Plot VI. Among them are four airmen of the Royal Air Force Volunteer Reserve, three of whom are from 107 Squadron. Sergeant (wireless operator and air gunner) John Joseph BUTLER, Sergeant (navigator) Patrick John WHELTON and Flight Sergeant (pilot) Clifford Ewart TURL were all killed in action on 16 August 1943 when their Boston aircraft came down during a low-level raid on the steel works at Denain. (Plot 8, Row A. Graves 22, 23 and 24)

A fourth member of the Royal Air Force buried here is Aircraftman 2nd Class Alfred Thomas BLAGDON, who died on 16 September 1944 (Plot 8, Row A. Grave 28).

Lieutenant Francis George SIMPSON MM, 4th Regiment, Royal Horse Artillery, died on 7 September 1944, aged 34. The war diary for his unit that day contains a note stating that his body was found a week later after he had drowned. The unit had passed through Arras, Lens, and Lille, but was then halted at Menin where the Germans had blown up a bridge, thereby forcing it to alter its route. Unfortunately the diary gives no further information regarding the manner of his death. His MM, however, was gazetted on 15 October 1942 and was won while serving as a bombardier with the 2nd Regiment, Royal Horse Artillery, during the campaign in Egypt and Libya. (Plot 8, Row A, Grave 26)

Next to him are Private William TATE, who served in the Army Catering Corps, and Sergeant Donald WIGLEY-JONES, Corps of Military Police; both men died in September 1944. (Plot 8, Row A. Graves 27 and 29)

The CWGC register points out that no details are known regarding the eighth burial from the Second World War.

Finally, the special memorial referred to in the CWGC register is one of three over by the south wall. It commemorates Colonel Thomas Jonathan Jackson CHRISTIAN Junior of 361st Fighter Group, USAAF, who was killed in action on 12 August 1944. His P-51 Mustang aircraft was lost during a bombing mission on the marshalling yards at Arras and his body was never found. An explosion was seen in the centre of the railway yard and the two pilots with him that day were able to confirm that it was not caused by any of their bombs. It was therefore presumed that the explosion they witnessed was CHRISTIAN's aircraft when it came down, very likely as a result of ground fire. Colonel CHRISTIAN was a very experienced flyer. He was awarded a Silver Star for gallantry in 1942 following operations at Guadalcanal and the Distinguished Service Cross in connection with operations in Europe.

Chapter Two

Captain Murray's Pluck – A Man who knew all about Tanks – My Family and other Eagles

Arras Communal Cemetery

This civilian cemetery is situated on the east side of the town and is easily reached on foot from the railway station along the Rue de Douai. At the junction with the Rue Saint Michel turn right and then take the next left, the Rue Gustave Colin. The cemetery is at the end of the road and is approximately 800 yards from the railway station.

There are twenty-three identified graves here and one casualty whose body is known to be buried close by, but its exact location cannot now be determined. There are also three unidentified graves. All are from the Second World War.

On 20 May 1940 Hurricanes from 85 Squadron, Royal Air Force, were deployed in support of ground forces and tasked with strafing the German troop columns advancing on Arras. Three were shot down and, although one crashed some distance away between Albert and Amiens, two came down just outside Arras. There are conflicting views as to how they were shot down; some accounts point to enemy fighters as the cause, others suggest ground flak. The two pilots who fell near Arras are now buried together in a joint grave. They are: Flight Lieutenant Michael Fitzwilliam PEACOCK DFC, who was 28 years old, and Pilot Officer Richard William SHREWSBURY, aged 19, who was shot down by ground fire. The CWGC register notes that PEACOCK, a barrister at the Middle Temple in London, was also a talented rugby player who had played whilst studying at Brasenose College, Oxford, as well as for Richmond Rugby Club. He was born in South Africa, but was educated in England. His DFC was gazetted on 20 February 1940 and is listed without any citation in *The Distinguished Flying Cross and How It Was Won*. (Plot Y. Row 1, Joint Grave 64/65)

Within the same row are the graves of four more airmen: Pilot Officer Alan Charles William GRANT, Royal Australian Air Force; Sergeant Thomas BARRATT, 7 Squadron, Royal Air Force Volunteer Reserve; Sergeant William Albert Edward NEWTON; and Pilot Officer Richard Charles MARTIN, Royal Canadian Air Force. All four men were attached to 7 Squadron, Royal Air Force. They were killed in action on 16 June 1944 when their Lancaster came down near Arras during a bombing raid on the railway yards at Valenciennes. (Plot Y. Row 1, Graves 66, 67, 68 and 70)

Over half of the identified graves here are men of the 1st Welsh Guards; fourteen in all, including Warrant Officer Class II, William Islwyn MATHIAS (Plot Y. Row 1, Grave 59), and one soldier whose identity is known, but whose grave has since been lost: Guardsman John Isaac VAUGHAN (Special Memorial, Plot X, Row 1, Grave 48). The majority of them were killed in action on 22 May 1940, but two of the headstones show the earlier date of 20 May.

The remaining burials consist of a private of the 10th Durham Light Infantry, a private of the Royal Army Ordnance Corps, a sapper from 61st Chemical Warfare Company and an officer of the 4th Royal Northumberland Fusiliers, Second Lieutenant Thomas Benson BLAND, whose date of death is shown as 30 May 1940.

Ste Catherine Communal Cemetery

There are seven identified casualties from the Second World War, as well as several that are unidentified. Although the first casualty is Private Alexander FRASER, 6th Seaforth Highlanders, killed in action on 21 May 1940 (Row 2, Grave 2), the remaining six are perhaps the main focus for visitors to this cemetery. On the night of 15/16 June 1944, Lancaster bombers of 582 Squadron, Royal Air Force, a pathfinder squadron formed in April 1944 and based at Little Soughton, near St Neots, Cambridgeshire, set off on a mission to bomb rail yards at Lens. One of them was shot down over the north-west suburbs of Arras, most likely by an enemy night fighter. Six of its crew died, but one man miraculously survived. Flight Sergeant Harold HARRIS (navigator), aged 21, had made efforts to open the escape hatch to enable the crew to bail out, but he was hit and mortally wounded while doing so. Flight Sergeant (wireless) R.F. Boots not only survived, but managed to evade capture after the crash. The squadron had been involved in a similar mission the night before.

Today, Pilot Officer Norman James TUTT is buried in Row 2, Grave 4, while the remaining five are laid to rest in Collective Grave 5 in Row 2. The remaining crew members are Flight Sergeant Paul LONG-HARTLEY (air gunner), Flight Sergeant Richard Henry AMES (air bomber), Flight Sergeant Sidney PARR (flight engineer), and Flight Officer William Thomas WILLIAMS (air gunner).

Ste Catherine British Cemetery

The cemetery lies north of the ring road that runs around the town on the north side. The D.341 is the main Arras–Houdain road that passes through Anzin-Saint-Aubin. This is the road to take, but first it is necessary to come off the ring road on to the D.264. Within about 250 yards of the junction of the D.264 and the D.341 is a turning on the left. The cemetery is situated another 200 yards along this road and is set back from the road overlooking open ground. The CWGC register gives the local church as a landmark.

Although British troops took over the Arras front from the French in March 1916, very few burials were made here that year; in fact, just four privates, whose deaths occurred between early March and the end of October 1916. These graves can now be found in Rows K and M.

The first significant use of the cemetery occurred during the days that immediately followed the opening of the Battle of Arras on 9 April 1917. Around 40 per cent of the casualties buried here relate to that single day. The 9th (Scottish) Division, the 15th (Scottish) Division, the 12th (Eastern) Division and the 34th Division were all involved in the fighting on 9 April and all four divisions used this cemetery to bury some of their dead. A handful of Canadian soldiers can also be found here, along with an officer from the 2nd South African Regiment, Second Lieutenant R.E.S. HARD-WICH MM, who was also killed in action on 9 April 1917, as part of the 9th (Scottish) Division. (Plot K.7)

Royal Field Artillery and Royal Garrison Artillery units also made burials here in the weeks, and in some cases months, that followed. Among them are several gallantry awards.

Lieutenant William Thwaites WALLACE MC, 'B' Battery, 16 Brigade, Royal Field Artillery, was killed in action on 12 April 1917, aged 24. His MC was gazetted on 27 July 1916 and was awarded for conspicuous gallantry when one of the gun pits ignited causing some of the ammunition to explode. At great personal risk, he and two others remained there to extinguish the fire. (Plot A.20)

The 63rd (Royal Naval) Division was another fighting formation that made use of the cemetery towards the latter part of April 1917 after its capture of Gavrelle. There are twenty-seven burials here from this division between 23 April and 30 April 1917. Private Robert William BATTERBEE, 2nd Battalion, Royal Marine Light Infantry, who was killed in action on 26 April 1917, also lost a brother serving in the same battalion. Private Walter Henry Batterbee was killed in action on 13 November 1916 when the Royal Naval Division took part in the last significant battle that year on the Somme. The brothers came from King's Lynn and the war memorial there shows several men with this surname who may possibly be related. Walter is buried in the Ancre British Cemetery, Beaumont Hamel, and Robert is buried here. (Plot B.2)

Although this part of the Arras battlefield was never home to the Australian Imperial Force, some of its heavy artillery batteries were deployed in the Arras area in 1917 to support the Canadians at Vimy Ridge; later they were redeployed further north in preparation for the Battle of Messines. One member of 36th Australian Heavy Battery can be found here: Corporal Harry Leslie HOPE, who was killed in action on 22 April 1917. (Plot B.6)

Captain Herbert William WALLER MC, 21st Northumberland Fusiliers (2nd Tyneside Scottish), was killed in action on 10 April 1917, aged 29, while carrying out a reconnaissance in front of newly won positions. His MC was gazetted in the New Year's Honours List on 1 January 1917. (Plot B.22)

In the next row is another Northumberland Fusilier and gallantry award holder: Private John MAYBERRY MM, 26th Northumberland Fusiliers (3rd Tyneside Irish). He is listed in *Soldiers Died in the Great War* as having died of wounds, but his battalion is shown as the 24th Battalion, Northumberland Fusiliers, rather than the 26th Battalion. (Plot C.14)

Leading Seaman Charles YATES DSM, Nelson Battalion, Royal Naval Volunteer Reserve, died of wounds on 6 May 1917, aged 22. His DSM was awarded for distinguished service during the Gallipoli campaign in 1915. The DSM is quite a rare sight on a CWGC headstone; in fact, there are only nineteen named holders of this decoration buried on the entire Western Front and his is the only such headstone in the vicinity of Arras (Plot D.1). A few graves along is the holder of a more familiar gallantry medal: Leading Seaman Edward W. SILVERTON MM, Drake Battalion, Royal Naval Volunteer Reserve, who died of wounds on 7 May 1917, aged 32. (Plot D.7)

Serjeant George WILSON MM, 9th Battery, 41 Brigade, is another Royal Field Artillery gallantry award holder buried here, though his death occurred slightly later, on 8 May 1917. (Plot D.12)

Second Lieutenant Iorwerth Roland OWEN, 13 Squadron, Royal Flying Corps, was killed in action over Arras on 7 May 1917. He was commissioned from the Inns of Court OTC and was a pupil at Mill Hill School in north London. His observer that day, Air Mechanic Class II Reginald Hickling, also died when their BE2c aircraft was shot down by German ace, Karl Allmenröder, while on a photographic reconnaissance mission. Second Lieutenant OWEN is buried here (Plot D.17), but Hickling is buried in Albuera Cemetery.

Lieutenant Lyonel Hugh JACOBSON MC, 'D' Battery, 50 Brigade, Royal Field Artillery, was killed in action on 29 April 1917. His maternal grandfather was Sir Robert Pigot, 4th Baronet and MP for Bridgnorth between 1832 and 1837, and again between 1838 and 1853. His MC was gazetted on 21 December 1916 and was awarded for conspicuous gallantry in action after establishing and maintaining lamp signalling under heavy fire. The citation notes that he later returned to Battalion HQ where he reported on the situation up ahead, adding that he was also wounded and had previously done similar fine work. (Plot K.8)

There are a number of other officers and men of that Brigade buried with him, including Major Alfred James USBORNE (Plot K.9) and Lieutenant Thomas Alfred TURNER (Plot K.15), who were also killed in action on 29 April. Lieutenant Reginald John JOICE from the same unit was killed in action the following day, though he is shown serving with 60 Brigade in *Officers Died in the Great War*, which appears to be a typographical error. (Plot K.14)

Also buried among them is another gallantry award holder from the same unit. Serjeant Percy JACKSON DCM, 'C' Battery, 50 Brigade, was killed in action on 30 April 1917. His DCM was gazetted on 26 September 1916 and awarded for conspicuous gallantry in action. Although the remainder of his detachment had been ordered to leave owing to heavy shelling, he remained at his post in a signals dug-out to maintain communications. He remained there even after he was wounded and also dug out a buried comrade who had returned to the post to join him. (Plot K.12)

Among the Canadian dead are three men with gallantry awards, one of whom is an officer from the 2nd Battalion. Sergeant Hesketh COOKE MM and Bombardier Norman James CHIVAS MM, both served with 3 Brigade, Canadian Field Artillery, and were killed in action on 13 May 1917. COOKE had also served in the South African campaign. (Plots M.14 and M.17)

Lieutenant Leslie Watters TUBMAN MC, 2nd Battalion, Canadian Infantry, was killed in action on 3 May 1917. His MC was gazetted on 25 May 1917 and was awarded in recognition of his gallantry and efforts on several occasions while leading patrols, each time bringing back valuable information and carrying out fine work. He was also mentioned in despatches. (Plot M.24)

As with 1916, there are very few casualties here from 1918. Eight of the ten are in Row J, the other two in Rows F and M. There is one gallantry award among them: Serjeant Horace Edward WEBBER MM, 15th Signal Company, Royal Engineers, who was killed in action on 28 March 1918 and who formerly served with the Royal Field Artillery (Plot M.6). The one Canadian casualty among this group is Private James Ernest Wilfrid YOUNG, 5th Canadian Mounted Rifles. He held the *Croix de Guerre* (France) and fell in action on 26 August 1918, aged 20. (Plot F.28)

Private Thomas WATTS, 7th East Yorkshire Regiment, and Private Walter NEAVE, 10th West Yorkshire Regiment, were executed on the same day, 30 August 1917. NEAVE had served at Gallipoli with the regiment's 9th Battalion. He arrived in France while the Battle of the Somme was under way, and so was not present on 1 July when his new battalion was cut to pieces opposite Fricourt; he and others arrived as reinforcements to make up the losses. He was wounded in September 1916 near Hébuterne and only returned to active service the following year. However, he deserted in July 1917 while already under suspended sentence of death. There was to be no reprieve.

Private WATTS shared NEAVE's fate, perhaps because his battalion belonged to the same division as NEAVE's, the 17th (Northern) Division. Although WATTS had no previous lapses of discipline behind him, the division had already had five of its men executed and its reputation was almost certainly the overriding reason why leniency was not shown. (Plots E.32 and 33)

Private Charles KIRMAN, 7th Lincolnshire Regiment, was executed by firing squad on 23 September 1917. He was a reservist who had been called up on mobilization and who went to the front in August 1914 with the regiment's 1st Battalion. He was twice wounded, once in November 1914 and again in 1916. At his trial KIRMAN explained that soldiering had taken its toll on him, but the court was undoubtedly swayed by the fact that he had already been found guilty of absence without leave on a previous occasion for which he had been sentenced to a year's imprisonment. Again, his battalion was part of the 17th (Northern) Division and two of its men had been shot for desertion less than a month earlier. His was a case of 'for the sake of example'. (Plot F.1)

St Nicolas British Cemetery

Saint-Nicolas was a village next to Arras; now it forms part of its northern suburbs just like Sainte-Catherine further west. Take the northern part of the ring road around Arras and at the end of the Rue de la Liberté where it joins the Boulevard Robert Schuman is a large roundabout. If travelling from west to east, take the fifth exit, which is the D.63. If coming from east to west, take the first exit. Continue along the D.63 for about 600 yards and take the sixth road on the left, which should be the Rue Aristide Briand. After about 300 yards is a very small road, the Voie de la Croix. Take this road and follow it to the cemetery, which lies a short distance further along on the right. Like Sainte Catherine British Cemetery, it is set in open ground and is well tucked away and may take a little effort to find.

This cemetery is similar in character to Sainte Catherine British Cemetery. Burials here began in March 1917 and, whilst most of them relate to that year of the war, there are far fewer casualties from 9 April than at Sainte Catherine. The distinctive regimental badges of Scottish battalions belonging to the 9th (Scottish) Division, the 15th (Scottish) Division and the 51st (Highland) Division are very evident on many of the headstones found here. Although many of them date to April 1917, a number of them are from later months.

Second Lieutenant Frederick Charles LEE, 3rd Battalion, South African Regiment, was killed in action on 9 April 1917, aged 27. He was present as a lance corporal at Delville Wood in July 1916. (Plot I.B.6)

One casualty from late April 1917 is Colonel Frank Albert SYMONS CMG DSO, Royal Army Medical Corps. He studied medicine at Edinburgh University before joining the Royal Army Medical Corps and had served in the South African War where, among other operations, he took part in the Relief of Ladysmith. He was mentioned in despatches by Sir John French in October 1914, as well as on two further occasions. His DSO was gazetted on 18 February 1915 for services in connection with operations in the field and he was promoted to the rank of temporary colonel later that year. He was subsequently appointed assistant director of medical services for the 9th (Scottish) Division and was killed in action by a shell near Athies on 30 April 1917. He was 48 years old. (Plot I.B.16)

Captain James Bruce MACKAY, 21st West Yorkshire Regiment, died of wounds on 3 May 1917. His battalion was the pioneer battalion attached to the 4th Division (Plot I.B.18). A number of burials from this battalion can be found scattered throughout the cemetery, including two officers: Lieutenant Allan GREEN, who was killed in action on 19 August 1917 (Plot I.B.14); and Second Lieutenant James Philip PADGETT, who was killed in action on 5 May 1917. (Plot I.J.1)

During May 1917 the battalion had been particularly busy deepening trenches near Roeux and was frequently shelled during this period. The 4th Division spent much of its time in this area in 1917 and 1918 and many of its battalions made use of this cemetery for burials, including the 1st Somerset Light Infantry, the 1st Royal Warwickshire Regiment, the 2nd Duke of Wellington's Regiment, the 1st King's Own (Royal Lancaster Regiment), the 2nd Essex Regiment, the 2nd Lancashire Fusiliers, the 1st Rifle Brigade and the Household Battalion.

Serjeant John Stuart MacMURCHIE DCM MM and Bar, 'A' Company, 8th Black Watch, was killed in action on 3 May 1917, aged 22. His DCM was won as a drummer with the 1st Battalion at Kruiseke on 27 October 1914 when on four occasions he conveyed very important messages under very heavy shell fire. He was badly wounded a few days later on 2 November 1914. His MM was gazetted on 2 June 1916 while still serving with the 1st Battalion. The bar to his MM was gazetted on 6 July 1917. He had previously served in the Royal Army Medical Corps and the CWGC record also points out that he had been mentioned in despatches. (Plot I.B.22)

Lieutenant Colonel Harold Underhill Hatton THORNE was killed in action commanding the 12th Royal Scots on 9 April 1917, about 200 yards from his battalion's first objective, Obermayer Trench. According to regimental sources, he was probably killed by one of our own shells. He previously had served as a captain with the

4th Royal Berkshire Regiment and the 6th King's Own Scottish Borderers before transferring to the Royal Scots. He was mentioned in despatches in March 1917 just before his death. His father had also attained the rank of colonel during his military service. (Plot I.E.1)

When THORNE was killed, command of the battalion devolved to Major G.H. Hay. It was also around this time that another of the battalion's officers, Captain James Murray, displayed extraordinary pluck by shooting off his own hand after it had become badly shattered by a machine-gun bullet. He then carried on the advance until he was wounded again by a shell fragment to the groin. Murray, who was clearly in great pain, insisted that others be tended to before him and at one point had to be prevented from taking his own life with his revolver. Although not expected to live, Murray defied the odds and survived the war. Hay was wounded on 12 April for the third time in his service. The first time had been on the Marne on 8 September 1914, whilst the second occasion was on 25 September the following year at Hooge during a diversionary attack aimed at preventing the Germans from sending reinforcements to Loos. Like Murray, he also survived the war.

Second Lieutenant Cecil Wyatt MASON, 11th Royal Scots, is shown in the CWGC register as having been killed in action on 8 April 1917, the same date as in *Officers Died in the Great War*, but the regimental history records his death as 9 April. His parents ran the Golf Hotel at St Andrews, Fife. (Plot I.E.11)

Sergeant W.H. HITCHMAN, 4th Battalion, South African Regiment, was one of the many men of the South African Brigade wounded at Delville Wood in July 1916. He was wounded there on 18 July, but recovered. He was again wounded in the ill-fated attack on Greenland Hill on 12 April 1917 and died of his wounds the following day. (Plot I.E.21)

Private Malcolm LAIRD MM, 1/7th Argyll & Sutherland Highlanders, died of wounds on 19 April 1917, according to the CWGC register. However, in *Soldiers Died in the Great War* his date of death is shown as 17 April and the MM is not credited against his name. (Plot I.F.6)

Second Lieutenant John Edward HEWISON, 9th Royal Scots, died from his wounds on 19 April 1917, aged 21. He was the son of a clergyman and came from Orkney, but he was born in India and had attended schools in England, as well as his native Scotland. He was killed in action while overseeing a wiring party when he was hit by a fragment from a bursting shell and died soon afterwards. He had been recommended for the MC, but no award was ever made. (Plot I.F.17)

Lieutenant Alexander Carnegie BAXTER MC, 6th Cameronians, was killed in action on 17 April 1917. He was attached to the 154th Company, Machine Gun Corps, at the time of his death. I can find no reference to his MC in any of the Gazettes, though it is acknowledged in *Officers Died in the Great War* and on records held at the National Archives. (Plot I.F.2)

Company Serjeant Major Harry DUCKERS DCM, 2nd Lancashire Fusiliers, was killed in action on 13 May 1917. His DCM was gazetted on 11 November 1914 and was awarded for the excellent handling of his platoon during an action at Meteren on

13 October 1914, as well as for consistently good work in previous engagements. (Plot I.J.10)

Two warrant officers of the 24th Northumberland Fusiliers (1st Tyneside Irish), now buried side by side, were killed in action within a few days of each other. Regimental Quartermaster Serjeant Frederick H. WRIGHT was killed in action on 31 May 1917, aged 37 (Plot I.L.5) and Company Quartermaster Serjeant John Archer HOPWOOD died of wounds on 2 June 1917, aged 24. (Plot I.L.4)

Further along the same row is a group of fourteen Seaforth Highlanders. There is one officer among them, Second Lieutenant Alan Roper TUDOR, 9th Seaforth Highlanders, who was killed in action on 5 June 1917 (Plot I.L.9). The men buried with him are a serjeant, a lance corporal and eleven privates, all of whom were killed in action or died of wounds on 6 June. Their unit was the pioneer battalion attached to the 9th (Scottish) Division.

Captain Edward Malcolm CUNNINGHAM MC, 2nd Duke of Wellington's Regiment, attached 9th Battalion, was killed by a sniper on 5 August 1917, aged 24. Again, there is a discrepancy between the date of death given in the CWGC records and *Officers Died in the Great War*, which gives it as 4 August. He was acting adjutant at the time of his death, a role that would normally have kept him at or close to the battalion HQ. His death presumably occurred while visiting the front line. His MC was gazetted on the 30 March 1916 and was awarded for his coolness and gallantry in organizing bombing squads from another regiment after the officer in charge became a casualty. The citation also adds that during a period of heavy bombardment he kept spirits up among his own men. (Plot II.B.12)

Company Serjeant Major William Henry DICKINSON DCM, 'A' Company, 10th West Yorkshire Regiment, died of wounds on 27 August 1917, aged 26. His DCM was awarded after he had continued to advance, reorganizing and leading his men forward through a heavy barrage, despite heavy casualties and despite having already been blown off his feet. The citation notes that on other occasions he had consistently displayed great courage and resource and had set a fine example to all ranks. The award was gazetted on 18 July 1917. (Plot II.C.4)

Captain Henry Cecil PEMBER, Household Battalion, is one of two officers from that regiment buried in this cemetery. Both fell in action on 3 May 1917. PEMBER was educated at Harrow and New College, Oxford, and was a member of the Stock Exchange. He had also served in the South African War with the Queen's Own Oxfordshire Hussars. When war broke out in 1914 he rejoined his old regiment, serving with it as major before being transferred to the 2nd Life Guards. He was killed close to the German wire by machine-gun fire as he led his battalion forward in an attack near Roeux. (Plot II.C.6)

The other officer is Captain Oldric Spencer PORTAL, who had formerly served with the 1st Life Guards (Plot II.B.16). Despite sharing the same surname, he was not related to the commanding officer of the Household Battalion, Colonel Wyndham Raymond Portal, 1st Viscount, but was descended from a French Huguenot refugee, Henri de Portal, who established a paper mill at Whitchurch in Hampshire that produced the paper on which the Bank of England printed its bank notes. His brother, Sub Lieutenant Raymond Spencer PORTAL, is commemorated on the Portsmouth Naval Memorial. He died on 31 May 1916, aged 19, when HMS *Invincible* was sunk at the Battle of Jutland. Only six of her crew survived.

The cemetery contains just thirty-eight burials from 1918. Most relate either to the fighting that took place east of Arras in late March and early April when the 4th Division held the sector north of the River Scarpe, or the period between mid-September and early October that year. The majority during this latter period are from either the 49th (West Riding) Division or the 8th Division.

One of the October 1918 casualties is Second Lieutenant Gordon Eyre BAXTER, who was killed in action on 8 October. He had formerly served with King Edward's Horse, which was part of the Imperial Yeomanry, then with the Royal East Kent Yeomanry. When the war broke out he came over with a squadron of King Edward's Horse that had been formed in New Zealand where he was living at the time. The regiment then regrouped in England once the other squadrons arrived. However, when it went to France, the regiment was split up and its individual squadrons were attached to different divisions, though they were reunited in the middle of 1916 and served again as a single unit. The regiment eventually moved to Italy in December 1917 before returning once more to the Western Front in March 1918. However, by then, BAXTER had been transferred to the infantry and was killed while serving with the 2nd Devonshire Regiment. (Plot II.F.5)

Private Hector DALANDE, 8th Seaforth Highlanders, was executed at Arras on 9 March 1918. This French Canadian soldier had served on the Western Front since the latter part of 1915. However, in 1917 things began to go wrong. He committed his first offence of going absent without leave and was sentenced to a term of imprisonment. Later that year he suffered shell shock and spent some time recuperating, but he returned to the line after a couple of months. It proved too much for his nerves and he deserted for the second time, and in desperation escaped from custody. When he was eventually found he was wearing civilian clothing. At his trial, all of the above factors weighed heavily against him and there was effectively no way out for him.

Julian Putkowski and Julian Sykes include a piece of personal testimony in their work, *Shot at Dawn*. It describes DALANDE shortly before his execution and depicts him as a tragic figure who, on account of his accent and other cultural differences, felt very much an outsider among his comrades. He claimed that he would have fared better serving with the French army, but it was far too late for that. His execution followed swiftly and with the minimum of formality. (Plot II.D.1)

Private Norman TAYSUM, 9th Black Watch, and Private Thomas WARD, 8/10th Gordon Highlanders, were executed at Arras on the 16 October 1917. Both men were found guilty of desertion; their battalions were part of the 15th (Scottish) Division. TAYSUM is buried in Plot I (Plot I.D.23), and WARD is buried in Plot II. (Plot II.C.17)

Private James Stark ADAMSON, 7th Cameron Highlanders, was executed not for desertion but for cowardice, on 23 November 1917, aged 30. He was shot very close to the cemetery where he is now buried. A brief account of his execution is given in

Shot at Dawn, though the evidence and circumstances surrounding his offence are not given. His battalion was also part of the 15th (Scottish) Division. (Plot II.C.18)

Achicourt Road Cemetery, Achicourt

Nearly all the burials here are identified and are either men of the Canadian Expeditionary Force, or else casualties from the 56th (London) Division. All four divisions of the Canadian Corps that served in France are represented, though men from battalions belonging to the 2nd Division are more numerous. Almost all of the Canadian burials relate to the fighting at the end of August 1918 when the village of Wancourt was captured. Once the village fell, the Canadians were able to wheel around to the right and link up with the 52nd (Lowland) Division and the 56th (London) Division, thereby loosening the German grip on the northern end of the Hindenburg Line. None of the 56th (London) Division casualties buried here are from that phase of fighting, as all are from 1917, mainly from March and April. A glance through the CWGC register also reveals that a good number of the men from the various battalions of the London Regiment actually came from London itself.

Captain James Archer GREEN, 16th Battalion, London Regiment (Queen's Westminster Rifles), was killed in action on 27 March 1917, aged 27. He had returned from South Africa in order to rejoin his regiment (Plot A.5). Most of the March and early April casualties occurred from shell fire, including three men of the 5th Cheshire Regiment, which was the pioneer battalion attached to the 56th (London) Division, and four men from the 167th Company and the 169th Company, Machine Gun Corps, which also belonged to the 56th (London) Division.

Serjeant Edwin Cecil HOWARD, 5th Battalion, London Regiment (London Rifle Brigade) was killed in action on 21 March 1917 by shell fire. He was one of the original members of the 1/5th Battalion who had set sail for France aboard the SS *Chyebassa* on 4 November 1914. By spring 1917, as the opening of the Arras offensive approached, the self-proclaimed *Chyebassa* men were already a dwindling band of brothers. (Plot A.10)

Among the dead of the London Regiment are two casualties who held gallantry awards. Company Quartermaster Serjeant Ronald Davidson FORBES MM, 1/4th (City of London) Battalion, London Regiment (Royal Fusiliers), was killed in action on 4 April 1917, aged 22 (Plot B.4), and Company Quartermaster Serjeant Charles WATSON MM, 16th Battalion, London Regiment (Queen's Westminster Rifles), was killed in action on 8 April 1917, aged 37 (Plot E.3A). The loss of two experienced men so close to the opening of the Arras offensive would have come as a considerable administrative blow to their respective units.

A number of the 56th (London) Division men were killed in action on 9 April 1917. These include Captain Eric Fitzgerald CLARKE, 3rd Battalion, London Regiment (Royal Fusiliers), whose parents were Sir Frederick William Alfred Clark and Lady Clark of Kensington. An accountant by profession, Sir Frederick was also (Kensington) Controller of HM Customs and Excise. Their son, who was gazetted in August 1914, also served in Gallipoli where he was wounded in October 1915. In Egypt he briefly held the temporary rank of major, after which he was attached to the 13th Battalion, London Regiment (The Kensingtons). (Plot B.22)

Also buried in Row B is Rifleman Walter YEOMAN, 12th Battalion, London Regiment (The Rangers), who had only been with the battalion since January 1917. In April he went absent for a second time and was executed on 3 July 1917 by firing squad. (Plot B.16)

Another man from the 56th (London) Division who was executed is buried in the next row. Private James MAYERS, 13th Battalion, London Regiment (The Kensingtons), came from Hackney and was shot on 16 June 1917. He was already under a suspended sentence of death when he deserted for a second time. He was discovered not far away within a couple of days of going missing. (Plot C.11)

The cemetery also contains a handful of Royal Field Artillery casualties, mainly from April 1917. Among them is the holder of a gallantry award, Gunner William Augustus Terence CROOK MM, 'A' Battery, 47 Brigade, Royal Field Artillery, who was killed in action on 10 April 1917 (Plot C.15). Buried in sequence alongside him are four of his comrades from the same gun battery, all killed in action the same day or the day before.

One final holder of the MM buried here is Serjeant Timothy KEATING MM, 10th Durham Light Infantry, killed in action on 10 April 1917, although *Soldiers Died in the Great War* shows his death in action occurring the previous day. (Plot C.18)

The 52nd (Lowland) Division came to the Western Front late in the war. It arrived in Marseille between 12 and 17 April 1918 and went into the front line near Arras on 6 May. It had served in the Gallipoli campaign, then in Egypt and Palestine, where it fought with distinction. Private George Wilson LAWSON, 1/7th Highland Light Infantry, had served in all three of those theatres before dying of wounds in France on 27 August 1918. (Plot D.22)

Captain George Clark MILLER, 5th Royal Scots Fusiliers, was killed in action on 26 August 1918, aged 27 (Plot D.36). It was on this day that the 52nd (Lowland) Division took its objectives around Hénin Hill, whilst the Canadian 2nd Division, attacking the high ground around Wancourt, also went on to take the ruins of Neuville-Vitasse from the north. This success allowed both of these divisions to swing south-east, and in so doing they began the process of rolling up the Hindenburg Line. A further consequence of this movement was to facilitate progress further south by the 56th (London) Division, which had been held up around Croisilles. Incidentally, this was also the day that Monchy-le-Preux fell to the Canadians. Two other officers of the 5th Royal Scots Fusiliers were killed during these operations between 25 and 27 August 1918, but they are buried elsewhere; one at Mory Abbey Military Cemetery and the other at London Cemetery, Neuville-Vitasse.

All the Canadian casualties can be found in Row D and Row E and a number of them hold gallantry awards. The most senior in rank is Captain William Joseph ATHERTON MC, 5th Canadian Mounted Rifles, who was killed in action on 26 August 1918, aged 24. His MC was gazetted on 26 July 1917 and was awarded for conspicuous gallantry after reorganizing his men under heavy fire and leading them against the enemy, capturing twenty-five prisoners. Later he also carried out a valuable reconnaissance. The citation concludes that throughout the entire operation he set a fine example. (Plot D.34)

The other holders of gallantry awards are: Sergeant Vincent BOWEN MM and Bar, 18th Battalion, Canadian Infantry, killed in action on 26 August 1918. He died almost immediately as a result of a bullet wound to the stomach (Plot D.19); Corporal Thomas James WHITE MM, 19th Battalion, Canadian Infantry, killed in action on 26 August 1918 (Plot D.32); and Private John MACKAY MM, 29th Battalion, Canadian Infantry, who came from Stornoway on the Isle of Lewis, and who previously served for two years with the Seaforth Highlanders. He fell in action on 26 August 1918, aged 37 (Plot E.16).

Agny Military Cemetery

For one brief moment in 1916, the villages of Foncquevillers and Gommecourt became part of the Battle of the Somme. However, after 1 July 1916 these two villages fade from the battle's narrative and so disappear from public consciousness; one could even be forgiven for thinking that the line somehow ended here. Of course, there was a front beyond Gommecourt and part of it ran east of the village of Agny as the line swept northwards towards Arras. It is true that, in comparison with the main Somme battlefield, this part of the line was far quieter during the second half of 1916, but in April 1917 when attention switched to Arras, the village of Agny was just two and a half miles behind the British front line. This sector then became far more active as the 56th (London) Division took over the line between Achicourt and Agny prior to the Battle of Arras. Even in 1916 Agny had been extensively used for the billeting of troops but, in the run up to the 1917 offensive, it became even busier and was frequently shelled. The casualties in this cemetery reflect the reality of both these periods. Of the 291 identified burials, just over half are from 1916; of the remainder, all but three are from 1917.

As with most of the cemeteries that were situated behind the line throughout the war, there is a greater sense of order to the burials. There is also a greater tendency to find groups of men from the same battalion buried next to each other, or at least very close to each other, than in many of the cemeteries closer to the front line or on the battlefield. Agny was a village where battalions came and went, burying their dead in the cemetery during successive tours of duty.

The 9th King's Royal Rifle Corps has twenty burials here; men who died between 5 May and 28 December 1916, thirteen of whom died during a fairly uneventful period holding and maintaining trenches here in June 1916 and one on 1 July. In the case of the fourteen men buried here from 9th Rifle Brigade, they were killed during the space of a few weeks between the end of April and the end of May 1916, or else during a period later that year around mid-October. All are NCOs or riflemen, and both battalions belonged to the 14th (Light) Division; in fact many of the 1916 casualties are from battalions from this division or from the 12th (Eastern) Division.

There are a number of men with interesting backgrounds among the 1916 casualties. One of them, Lieutenant Charles Edward Robert HEATON-ELLIS, 6th King's Own Yorkshire Light Infantry, was killed in action on 19 March 1916, aged 22. He was the nephew of Captain Edward Henry Fitzhardinge Heaton-Ellis, Royal Navy, who had fought aboard HMS *Inflexible* at the Battle of Jutland and who went on to become Vice Admiral Heaton-Ellis KBE CB MVO.

His two sons, and therefore Charles's cousins, also served during the war. Captain David Heaton-Ellis MC, 2nd Rifle Brigade, was killed in action on 27 May 1918, aged 21, during the German offensive on the Aisne and is commemorated on the Soissons Memorial. His MC was awarded while commanding his company under repeated attacks and holding his position in spite of the company on his flank giving ground. By his coolness and skilful handling of the situation he was able to bring direct fire on parties of the enemy trying to work their way round his flanks, thereby preventing a gap from developing in the line. His brother, Sub Lieutenant Michael Heaton-Ellis, died at home on 24 January 1919, aged 20, and was laid to rest at Hendon Cemetery and Crematorium in north London. He had served on HMS *Taurus*. Lieutenant Charles HEATON-ELLIS (Plot B.9) is one of thirteen men from the 6th Battalion buried here in Rows, B, C, and E.

One of the few gallantry award holders buried here is Corporal Richard BOYLE DCM, 24th Northumberland Fusiliers (1st Tyneside Irish), who was killed in action on 28 April 1917, aged 26. His DCM was gazetted on 18 July 1917 and was awarded for conspicuous gallantry and devotion to duty in handling his machine gun with great courage and daring, taking it forward to very advanced positions and, although most of his team had become casualties, he went forward and captured an enemy machine gun by his own initiative. (Plot B.38)

Another 14th (Light) Division casualty is Second Lieutenant Harold George Harcourt DORRELL, 10th Durham Light Infantry, who was killed in action on 2 April 1916, aged 25 (Plot C.7). The case of his brother is a curious one. Second Lieutenant Evelyn Percy Dorrell, 4th Queen's (Royal West Surrey Regiment), attached 8th Battalion, was badly wounded on 13 October 1918 and died the next day, aged 22. He was part of a group of men from 'B' and 'C' companies who managed to cross the River Selle near Montrécourt using the remains of a ruined bridge and then held a bridgehead on the other side under fire throughout the day. Previously wounded at Hargicourt, he had also seen a good deal of action at Lens, Arras and Cambrai. His commanding officer is reported to have said that, had he lived, he would have recommended him for an award in connection with his work on the night of the 12/13 October, as well as for work on previous occasions when he had carried out difficult and dangerous patrols. It has always struck me as odd that his leadership and gallantry were never officially recognized. He is buried at Delsaux Farm Cemetery, near Bapaume. Their father, George Henry Dorrell, held the rank of lieutenant colonel.

Captain George Basil Stuart WALROND was serving with another battalion belonging to the 14th (Light) Division, the 6th Somerset Light Infantry, when he was killed in action on 19 March 1916, aged 40. March was described in the regimental history as being such a quiet month that the cookers were able to be brought forward as far as Agny. The month almost passed without incident, but Captain WALROND was shot through the head by a sniper while looking out over the parapet of a trench. Even during quiet periods there was no room for complacency. He was mentioned in despatches and had also served in the South African campaign. His father, the late Colonel Henry Walrond, wrote a history of the 1st Devon Militia that was published in 1897. (Plot C.4)

Perhaps the most well known and most celebrated individual buried here is the poet, Second Lieutenant Philip Edward THOMAS. He had been a pupil at St Paul's School in London before going on to study at Lincoln College, Oxford. He later became a friend of the American poet, Robert Frost, and our own Rupert Brooke. THOMAS was also a member of a group known as the Dymock poets, which included Lascelles Abercrombie, Wilfred Gibson and John Drinkwater. He enlisted in July 1915 and initially joined the Artists' Rifles, but in August the following year he was commissioned in the Royal Garrison Artillery. He went to France with his battery in February 1917 and moved up to the Arras sector within days of arrival. THOMAS was killed in action on 9 April 1917, aged 39, serving with the 244th Siege Battery, Royal Garrison Artillery. A shell exploded close to him while he was carrying out observation duties at Beaurains. Outwardly, there was no mark on his body, but he died from internal damage to his lungs. (Plot C.43)

Another gallantry award holder buried here is Corporal Matthew VANCE MM, 16th Royal Scots (2nd Edinburgh Battalion), who was killed in action on 28 April 1917, aged 23. (Plot C.46)

Second Lieutenant the Reverend Ernest John Robinson BRIGGS-GOODERHAM, Royal Irish Regiment, attached 36th Battalion, Machine Gun Corps, was killed on 13 December 1916 along with his batman, Private William DAVIS, aged 24, just after returning to their dug-out following an inspection of machine-gun positions in the front line. Their dug-out was hit by a shell and collapsed while they were still inside. Comrades dug in vain to save both men and it is fitting that they now lie side by side. (Plots F.23 and 24)

BRIGGS-GOODERHAM was orphaned when very young and had been brought up by relatives. He was a scholar and was educated at Durham School and Caius College, Cambridge, before training for the Ministry at Ripon Theological College. He enlisted in November 1914 and was gazetted on 8 March 1916.

Although there are relatively few men with gallantry awards buried in this cemetery, one of them is Private William HENDRY MM, 7th Royal Sussex Regiment, who was killed in action on 2 November 1916 (Plot F.49). He was one of several officers and men who won gallantry awards on 3 and 4 March 1916 at the Hohenzollern Craters during actions in which almost one in three men from the battalion became casualties. Fourteen NCOs and privates won the MM, all of which were gazetted in mid-September that year. The day before his death his battalion had relieved the 8th Royal Fusiliers in trenches in the Agny sector. He is buried close to three other men from his battalion who were killed in September and November 1916. (Plots F.43, F.45 and F.48)

When the Germans withdrew to the Hindenburg Line in March 1917, they not only laid waste the ground they vacated, they also left behind many different types of booby-trap. Some of these were fairly crude, but others showed a high degree of sophistication, sometimes set for delayed detonation. Second Lieutenant Robert Henry HOSE and Private Thomas PEARSON, both from the 2nd Bedfordshire Regiment, were killed by one of these booby traps on 18 March 1917. HOSE began his military service as a dispatch rider in 1915, but in October that year he transferred to the 3/5th Bedfordshire Regiment and subsequently became its adjutant. He eventually went to France and joined the 2nd Battalion on 15 March 1917, just three days before his death. (Plots G.8 and 9)

Captain John Lewis MINSHULL, 3rd Battalion, London Regiment (Royal Fusiliers), is one of a number of officers and men from battalions of the 56th (London) Division buried in Row G. He was killed in action on 2 April 1917 and had been mentioned in despatches (Plot G.34). Next to him is a fellow officer from the same battalion, Second Lieutenant Harold Torrance BURGESS, who was killed on the same day as MINSHULL, aged 23 (Plot G.33).

Just along from the start of Row G are ten men from 'A' Company, 14th Battalion, London Regiment (London Scottish), (Plots G.12 to G.21). All fourteen were killed on 28 March 1917 when a shell exploded as they were leaving billets in Agny. The battalion had arrived there the day before and had been tasked with digging assembly trenches opposite Neuville-Vitasse in preparation for the forthcoming offensive. The same shell also wounded a further thirty-nine men.

Towards the end of Row G (Plots 48 to 64) are fourteen identified casualties from the 16th Battalion, London Regiment (Queen's Westminster Rifles). All were killed on 8 April 1917, the day before the start of the Arras offensive, including Second Lieutenant Alfred Godfrey BEVILLE (Plot G.48), and Rifleman Clements David James BARNES who, according to the CWGC register, enlisted in October 1914 and had previously served at Gallipoli. (Plot G.57)

Riflemen Alfred Buckland TOLHURST and Claud Robert VALLENTINE-WARNE were killed in action on 7 April 1917. The latter is fondly referred to as 'Kimbo' by Aubrey Smith in his superb memoir, *Four Years on the Western Front*. Smith vividly describes how men and supplies were being brought up in readiness for the opening of the Battle of Arras. All the roads were extremely busy; the junction where the Doullens–Arras road meets the road to Achicourt was no exception and the German artillery was well aware of this. The cookers belonging to 'D' Company, 5th Battalion, London Regiment (London Rifle Brigade), were also located here and a direct hit killed both men, as well as several horses from the battalion's transport section. TOLHURST's father also served with the battalion's 'P' Company.

The incident is one of many described by Aubrey Smith in his outstanding memoir. Smith's convoy happened to be stationary near that location as it waited for yet another line of wagons to pass, enabling him to witness the incident. The centre of Achicourt also came under hostile artillery fire which, as its range extended, began to fall on the road where Smith's convoy waited anxiously with its wagon limbers packed closely together. Smith and VALLENTINE-WARNE had become good friends and Smith was understandably devastated when he saw yet another survivor of Ypres and Gommecourt killed in front of his eyes. TOLHURST and VALLENTINE-WARNE are buried in the same row, though not together. (Plots G.58 and G.44)

Private Ernest George HATCHETT, 6th Queen's (Royal West Surrey Regiment), is shown as having died on 1 August 1915, and yet at that time his battalion was near Le Bizet, not far from Armentières, which is a long way from Arras. The battalion war diary indicates that several men were wounded between 25 July and 1 August and the CWGC records show that three men from the battalion died between those dates. One of them was Private HATCHETT and *Soldiers Died in the Great War* notes that he was killed in action, as opposed to dying of wounds. The other two men are buried at Bailleul Communal Cemetery Extension and Cité Bonjean Military Cemetery, both of which are far closer to where the battalion actually was at the time. The reason for Private HATCHETT's burial here is therefore not at all clear. We know that 137 bodies were brought to this cemetery after the war for reburial from the battlefields east of Arras, but even allowing for battlefield clearances and cemetery closures, his burial here, so far from where he fell, is still quite puzzling. Had he been reburied in one of the larger concentration cemeteries, such as Cabaret Rouge British Cemetery, his final resting place would have made more sense. (Plot H.31)

Anzin-St-Aubin British Cemetery
Slightly fewer than 60 per cent of the identified burials here are from 1918. With the exception of three men of the Indian Cavalry, the remainder are 1917 casualties. The three Indian cavalrymen are buried in their own tiny plot in the corner and to the left of the entrance in line with the Cross of Sacrifice. Lance Daffadar Bakhtawar SINGH, 29th Lancers (Deccan Horse) and Sowar Namd SINGH, 31st Duke of Connaught's Own Lancers, attached 29th Lancers (Deccan Horse), both fell on 20 June 1916. Lance Daffadar Muhammad ALI, 23rd Indian Cavalry (Frontier Force), died five weeks later on 27 July. However, another Indian soldier, Driver Lal GHIRAJI, is not buried in the Indian plot, but in one of the four main plots (Plot IV.E.19).

A casualty from the Indian Royal Artillery is an extremely rare sight on this sector of the Western Front around Arras. CWGC records show that of the 322 identified casualties from this regiment buried in France, the only ones buried close to Arras are at Duisans, Bucquoy and Ayette. The majority of the 1917 casualties buried in this cemetery either died or were killed in the week leading up to the Arras offensive, or during the April and early May fighting; very few are from later months of that year.

Bombardier Harold Alfred LITTLEFORD, 196th Siege Battery, Royal Garrison Artillery, was one of three men from that unit killed on 5 April 1917, and another man, who was killed later on, now rests alongside them (Plot I.A.3 to 6). One of these men, Gunner William Henry CALF, had lost a brother earlier in the war (Plot I.A.6). Private Robert Noel Calf, 13th Royal Fusiliers, died of wounds on 22 November 1915, aged 20, and is now buried at Humbercamps Communal Cemetery Extension.

A little further along Row A, in Plot I, are three men of the 51st Signal Company, 154 Brigade, 51st (Highland) Division, all of whom were killed in action on 6 April 1917 (Plots I.A.18 to 20). The 1917 casualties here from Scottish infantry units come mainly from the 51st (Highland) Division, but this cemetery also contains significantly more casualties from Scottish battalions who fell in 1918, most notably men from the Gordon Highlanders and Seaforth Highlanders. In all, a total of twenty-eight Gordon Highlanders and thirty-one Seaforth Highlanders can be found here, along with seven Argyll & Sutherland Highlanders and a further eleven men from either the Royal Scots, the Cameron Highlanders or the Cameronians. The majority of these are still from battalions belonging to the 51st (Highland) Division, mainly from the summer months of 1918, though a few are from the 52nd (Lowland) Division.

Captain John Cairns RAE MC, 86 Brigade, Royal Field Artillery, was killed in action on 10 April 1917. His MC was gazetted on 4 June 1917 in the King's Birthday Honours List (Plot I.B.14). A fellow officer of the Royal Field Artillery, Second Lieutenant John McFARLANE MC, whose unit is not recorded in the CWGC register, fell on 23 April 1917. His MC was gazetted on 12 January 1917 and awarded for conspicuous gallantry during an action in which he was wounded and yet still remained with his men in order to lead them, encouraging them and inspiring them as he had done on previous occasions. He is buried in the next plot along. (Plot II.B.13)

Private James Ross COLLEY, 9th Royal Scots, was killed in action, aged 19, while attached to the 51st Division Salvage Company. His death occurred on 9 April 1917, a day on which his battalion was engaged in fighting as it advanced east of Roclincourt. The salvaging of arms and equipment, particularly during the course of a battle, might seem like rather an odd priority, and yet the official history of the 51st (Highland) Division makes it clear that this was something that the division considered to be an important task, and one that was carried out while consolidating newly won positions. Private COLLEY is also commemorated on His Majesty's Stationery Office (HMSO) roll of honour, where he worked as a boy clerk. (Plot II.A.11)

Another young casualty is Gunner Tom PARTRIDGE, 'D' Battery, 256 Brigade, Royal Field Artillery, who was killed in action on 15 April 1917, aged 17. (Plot II.B.1)

Also among the artillery's other ranks are two holders of the MM. Both were killed on the same date, 28 March 1918. They are Serjeant Frederick James HARRISON MM, 109th Battery, 281 Brigade, Royal Field Artillery (Plot III.B.12), and Gunner James Frederick HIBBERT MM, 23rd Heavy Battery, Royal Garrison Artillery (Plot III.B.5). Fourteen of the fifteen Royal Garrison Artillery casualties from 1918 are from the last week in March, during the German offensive around Arras. *Soldiers Died in the Great War* does not show HARRISON's MM.

There are several other casualties worth noting during a visit to this cemetery, including Major Joseph Stephen WALLACE MC and Bar, Royal Army Medical Corps, who was killed in action on 28 March 1918. He began his medical training at University College, London, and later worked as house surgeon at the Great Northern Central Hospital. He had also held a commission in the Territorials and was gazetted in the 2/2nd Welsh Field Ambulance on 25 December 1915, gaining his captaincy in July 1916. The following month he joined the 2/3rd London Field Ambulance.

He received his MC for actions during the Battle of Arras in 1917 while in charge of stretcher-bearer parties under shell and gas barrages. The citation states that his judgement, coolness and disregard for his own personal safety while organizing and handling those working under his directions enabled a large number of wounded to be brought in safely. The bar to his MC was gazetted on 6 February 1918 and the citation followed on 18 July 1918. It was awarded for exceptional work during the Battle of Cambrai while in charge of an advanced dressing station where he skilfully organized his bearer parties. During that time he personally guided motor ambulances to very advanced positions, thus enabling a very large number of wounded cases to be removed to safety in a short space of time. His example of coolness and courage throughout the entire operations set a splendid example to his men. He was killed while trying to locate a fellow officer who was missing. (Plot III.B.14)

Second Lieutenant Edmund John WALDEGRAVE, 'D' Battery, 286 Brigade, Royal Field Artillery, was killed in action on 10 August 1918. He had been school captain at Marlborough College and was descended from Vice Admiral William Waldegrave, 8th Earl of Waldegrave. His father and grandfather had both been members of the clergy; his grandfather had served as the Bishop of Carlisle. (Plot III.E.2)

Major John Edouard Marsden BROMLEY DSO, was killed in action on 7 June 1918, aged 36, commanding 17th Battery, 41st Brigade, Royal Field Artillery. His parents lived in Manchester Square, on the edge of London's West End, and his father was a musician. John was educated at King's School, Canterbury, where he had excelled, not at music, but at African languages; in fact, he spoke several, including Zulu. During the South African campaign he served with the Natal Mounted Police and he also saw action in the Natal Native Rebellion in 1906. His knowledge of South Africa and its people led to his appointment as Assistant Native Commissioner for Northern Rhodesia, a post he held until 1914. At the outbreak of war he returned to England where he enlisted in the cavalry, though he subsequently transferred to the artillery and went to France just a few days before Christmas in 1915. His DSO was gazetted on 1 January 1918 and was awarded for conspicuous gallantry and devotion to duty on 26 October 1917 when he assisted in rescuing wounded men from a dug-out that had been blown in and helping them to a dressing station, an action he carried out while under intense shell fire. He then put out a fire in an ammunition dump, again under heavy shell fire. Finally, after a dug-out containing fifteen men had been blown in, he worked for an hour and a half to rescue them under intense shelling, displaying splendid coolness and courage, even though he himself was wounded. On 21 May 1918 he was mentioned in despatches. (Plot IV.C.6)

Second Lieutenant Wilfrid Maurice HASTWELL, Machine Gun Corps, was killed in action on 7 April 1917, aged 21. He was educated at the City of London School, then at Queen's College, Oxford. (Plot II.A.16)

This cemetery also contains the identified remains of sixty-three men of the Canadian Corps. All of them are 1918 casualties and all are buried in Plots III and IV. Among them are officers Lieutenant Gilbert Franklin CANN, 85th Battalion, Canadian Infantry (Plot III.A.7), Lieutenant Francis Michael MURPHY, 15th Battalion, Canadian Infantry (Plot IV.E.11), as well as Private Adrien BENOIT, 87th Battalion, Canadian Infantry, who was 17 years old when he was killed in action on 26 July 1918 (Plot IV.D.14).

The period between the end of August and the first week and a half of September 1918 was one of heavy casualties for the Canadian Corps as it fought its way across the fields and woods to the east of Arras, and yet there are no Canadian casualties here from August and only two from September, one of whom is Lieutenant MURPHY. He was badly wounded in the abdomen by a machine-gun bullet during the attack on the Drocourt–Quéant Line with his battalion on the morning of 2 September 1918. Despite receiving medical attention, he died later that day. Of the sixty-three Canadian dead here, thirty-four of them, from a dozen different infantry battalions, fell in July 1918 along with some sappers and some gunners.

Finally, a further four men are buried here who held the MM, one a Royal Engineer (Plot III.D.4), and three British infantrymen, two of whom belonged to the 1st King's Royal Rifle Corps. Both men are buried in Plot I, Row C and both are 1917 casualties. The other man is Private Arthur Ewart AUSTIN, a Seaforth Highlander serving with the 5th Battalion, who was killed in action on 20 August 1918. (Plot III.E.11)

Anzin-St-Aubin Churchyard

There are five burials in total, two of whom are unidentified. All are casualties from the fighting around Arras in May 1940. Gunner Moses BROOKS, who was a member of 208th Battery, 52nd Anti-Tank Regiment, Royal Artillery, died on 23 May. One of the two identified infantrymen, Sergeant Archie MURDOCH, 2nd Royal Scots Fusiliers, also died on 23 May, while Private Thomas BREMNER, 2nd Seaforth Highlanders, fell in action two days earlier.

Beaurains Road Cemetery, Beaurains

The overwhelming majority of burials here are from 1917. Of the 308 identified casualties, just over 90 per cent are from that one year. Perhaps more significant is the fact that almost 40 per cent of the headstones bear the date on which the Battle of Arras began, 9 April 1917. Beaurains had been in German hands until it was captured on 18 March 1917. Units belonging to the 3rd Division and the 14th (Light) Division are well represented here, including a number of men from the 89th Field Company, Royal Engineers, which formed part of the latter division. Six of its sappers were killed in action on 22 March 1917 and are buried consecutively. (Plots C.18 to C.23)

Lieutenant Aubrey Fletcher CHAPLIN, Northamptonshire Yeomanry, was killed in action on 10 April 1917, aged 35 (Plot A.1). He was the first of four officers from that regiment to be killed in action that month. The other three were killed or died of wounds the following day, one of whom is buried at Duisans British Cemetery whilst the other two are commemorated on the Arras Memorial. The Northamptonshire Yeomanry was in action on the opening day of the Battle of Arras and passed through the infantry at around 5.00pm. On reaching the crossroads at Fampoux it encountered some opposition, but acquitted itself well by driving off several snipers and capturing six field guns. More importantly though, it secured the road and railway bridges across the Scarpe. This was crucial as it provided a link between the 15th (Scottish) Division south of the river and the 4th Division north of it.

There is just one other cavalryman buried in this cemetery: Private Thomas McFADDEN, 3rd (Prince of Wales's) Dragoon Guards, who died of wounds on 12 April 1917. (Plot G.48)

Lieutenant Colonel Meredith MAGNIAC DSO, 1st Lancashire Fusiliers, had been with the regiment since 1898 and was a veteran of the Boer War (Plot B.4). He opted to leave a staff appointment in 1915 in order to return to his regiment and his DSO was gazetted the following year on 3 June 1916 in the King's Birthday Honours List. He commanded the 1st Battalion, Lancashire Fusiliers, on 1 July 1916 at the Somme when it tried to take Beaumont Hamel. He was killed by a shell on 25 April 1917 as he and the battalion's adjutant, Lieutenant Bloodworth, were sitting with bombing officer, Lieutenant William Robert Brown Caseby, under a waterproof sheet in a recess of a communication trench on the east side of Monchy-le-Preux. When the shell struck the edge of the trench, Lieutenant Bloodworth was wounded, and the other two men were killed.

The battalion also had twenty-five other ranks killed between 23 and 26 April, most of whom died as a result of shelling. The ground here was very open and the trenches, which were not very substantial, were frequently subjected to heavy shell fire. No fewer than thirteen runners from the battalion were either killed or wounded during that four-day period. A further four officers were wounded, as were 137 other ranks, and another five men were recorded as missing. Such casualty figures are indicative of the lack of cover for troops holding this part of the line during this uncertain period of the battle. Lieutenant Caseby is commemorated on the Arras Memorial.

Lieutenant James Westhall BROWN, who was 32 years old, and his observer, Lieutenant Edward John McCormick, aged 28, were killed in action together on 14 May 1917 while serving with 8 Squadron, Royal Flying Corps. BROWN, who had previously served with the Royal Field Artillery, is buried here (Plot E.31), but McCormick, who formerly served with the 7th Royal Inniskilling Fusiliers, is buried in Bucquoy Road Cemetery, Ficheux.

Major Hero Wilhelm Oswald HILLERNS, 'B' Battery, 251 Brigade, Royal Field Artillery, was killed in action on 14 April 1917, aged 35 (E.38). He is one of thirty-two men of the Royal Field Artillery buried here. All of them were killed or died of wounds during the Battle of Arras between 9 April and the middle of May 1917 or in the run up to it. Half of them fell on the opening day and thirteen are from 'C' Battery, 71 Brigade, Royal Field Artillery. Although the majority of these artillerymen were gunners, bombardiers or drivers, there are two farrier serjeants among them and one saddler, James Edward WAITES, whose brigade was the 71st, not 714 Brigade, as shown in the CWGC register.

Beaurains was very close to the British front line on the opening day of the Battle of Arras, and even by the middle of May 1917 the new line only just ran to the east of Monchy-le-Preux and Wancourt. Much of the British heavy artillery had not moved very far forwards, so consequently there are few casualties here from the Royal Garrison Artillery; just four from that year, all of whom are April casualties, and one other killed in the early autumn of 1918. The Royal Horse Artillery, however, has a number of burials here. Nine of the fourteen are from the 15th (Warwick) Brigade, eight of whom fell on 9 April 1917. The brigade was a Territorial Force unit.

With regard to the 1918 burials, of which there are only twenty-six, thirteen are Canadian infantrymen from several different infantry battalions and one is from the

Canadian Machine Gun Corps. Though most are casualties from the fighting around the Drocourt–Quéant Line in early September, two are from April 1918.

There are three holders of the MM in this cemetery and one holder of the MC. Second Lieutenant William Bell McARTHUR MC, 1st Royal Scots Fusiliers, was killed in action on 9 April 1917. His MC was gazetted on 18 May 1916 and was awarded for conspicuous determination while in charge of a working party when he and twelve men captured forty of the enemy who were armed. (Plot G.30)

Private Ernest Ward POOLE MM, 6th King's Own Yorkshire Light Infantry (Plot C.24), Acting Bombardier Maurice Buller GROVE MM (A.12), and Private Joseph FERGUSON MM, 5th Border Regiment (Ronville Military Cemetery, Memorial 7), all fell in March or April 1917. *Soldiers Died in the Great War* makes no reference to FERGUSON's MM.

Beaurains Communal Cemetery

There are just seventeen graves here and all are Second World War casualties. The most notable is that of Major Gerald HEDDERWICK MC, 7th Battalion, Royal Tank Regiment, who was killed in action on 21 May 1940 while leading a tank attack against superior numbers of German armoured units in an effort to disrupt their advance. Among the German formations that day was Rommel's 7th Panzer Division; in fact Rommel's ADC, Leutnant Most, was killed during the battle.

The British counter-attack was led by the 4th and 7th Battalions, Royal Tank Regiment, which went into battle on the south-east side of Arras, between Beaurains and Telegraph Hill. The plan envisaged the 6th Durham Light Infantry working on the left with 4th Battalion, Royal Tank Regiment, and 8th Durham Light Infantry supporting the 7th Battalion, Royal Tank Regiment on the right, but both infantry units were delayed. When they did arrive the men were tired and had lost much of their transport owing to aerial attacks. HEDDERWICK, with six tanks, had been detailed to operate with 4th Battalion that day rather than 7th Battalion, but he was soon killed in battle near Telegraph Hill. The British tanks really fought what amounted to independent actions that day without the benefit of wireless communication and, although the blow inflicted by him and the two tank battalions was not a fatal one, it did deliver a bloody nose and was sufficient to delay the German progress for twenty-four hours.

Major HEDDERWICK and his brother, Second Lieutenant Charles Stuart Hedderwick, 'B' Company, 2nd Royal Scots, both fought in the First World War. Charles was killed on 28 February 1915, aged 25, and is buried in Godezonne Farm Cemetery in Belgium. Gerald, who attended Loretto School in Musselburgh, served as a sergeant in the OTC before going on to Clare College, Cambridge, where he graduated with an Honours degree in History. He went to war in October 1914 as a corporal with a signalling unit and obtained a commission in the Royal Scots the following month. His promotion to captain came in September 1916, but he transferred to the Machine Gun Corps, Heavy Branch, i.e. tanks, in November that year.

His MC was won while serving as a temporary captain and was awarded for conspicuous gallantry as the second in command of his company, displaying great zeal in bringing his tanks into action. During the action he found himself continually exposed in his efforts to help his company and bring back valuable information regarding the operation, which on several occasions involved having to pass through a heavy enemy barrage. The citation concludes that the success of his company was due to his fearlessness and devotion to duty. The award was gazetted on 10 January 1918.

He served throughout the latter part of the 1914–1918 conflict with this developing arm of warfare, and indeed beyond it until 1922, when he was on a committee set up by the War Office to examine matters relating to the tank and its future. He was also a keen rugby player and between 1919 and 1922 he played for the Army, as well as for London Scottish. In 1923 he returned to his old school in order to teach, but with another war looming, he rejoined the Royal Tank Regiment at the end of 1939 and went to France on 5 May 1940, shortly before his death. Having served at Arras in 1917, he would have been very familiar with the area around Telegraph Hill when he returned there for that second and final encounter. (Special Memorial, Row C, Grave 3)

Three other members of the Royal Tank Regiment are buried here with Major HEDDERWICK. They are Second Lieutenant Richard Trevor RIDINGS, who served with HQ 2nd Armoured Reconnaissance Brigade, and who was killed in action on 20 May 1940, aged 21. He is buried in Row C, Grave 2. The other two men, Sergeant Sydney James TEMPLE and Trooper George William MILLS, are buried in Row A. Graves 1 and 3 and both were killed on 21 May 1940.

There are also nine men from the 6th Durham Light Infantry who died between 10 and 31 May 1940, as well as three men from the 4th Royal Northumberland Fusiliers who were killed between the 20 and 21 May.

Last, but not least, there is one Royal Air Force casualty from the Second World War. Pilot James CATERER, 635 Squadron (Pathfinders), Royal Air Force, was killed in action on 16 June 1944 while taking part in a raid on Lens. His grave lies in the north-east corner. The squadron, which was based at Downham Market in Norfolk, was formed in March 1944 and was equipped with Lancaster bombers. It took part in many bombing raids over Germany between its formation and the end of the war.

Dainville British Cemetery

Dainville is now part of the western suburbs of Arras. The cemetery lies on the western edge of Dainville, just east of the N.25. From Arras the easiest approach is to head from the Arras Memorial and the Faubourg d'Amiens Cemetery to the main crossroads just north of that location. The turning on the left is the D.265 and leads away from the town towards Dainville. Just under half a mile further on, there is a large roundabout. The D.59, which is the Arras–Warlus road, runs off the round-about. Follow this road, L'Avenue Lavoisier, for about a mile and a quarter and the cemetery is set back on the right hand side of the road.

At the moment the cemetery is pleasantly set against a backdrop of open fields and small plots of woodland. It is not large and has just 131 identified graves, as well as a few German graves at the far end of the cemetery.

The cemetery was started in April 1918 by the 56th (London) Division and was used by the Canadian Corps when it took over this part of the line in July that year.

This is very evident when walking around the cemetery today; there are now seventy-eight men of the London Regiment, seven men of the 8th Middlesex Regiment and three men from Royal Engineer units attached to the 56th (London) Regiment. Canadian casualties amount to fifteen.

Second Lieutenant Alec Scott BARTHORPE, 1/14th Battalion, London Regiment (London Scottish), was killed in action on 25 April 1918, aged 21. His brother, Edwin John Barthorpe, also enlisted, but was invalided out of the army owing to ill health. He is one of fourteen men from the London Scottish buried here. (Plot I.A.14)

Private Charles Henry CABLE, 1/2nd (City of London) Battalion, London Regiment (Royal Fusiliers), was killed in action on 27 April 1918, aged 35. He came from Halstead in Essex (Plot I.A.16). Another man from Halstead is buried in Row D: Private Morton Horace SARGENT, 'A' Company, 1/1st (City of London) Battalion, London Regiment (Royal Fusiliers), was killed in action on 28 May 1918, aged 24 (Plot I.D.5). His brother, Private Cecil Herbert Sargent, also fell, while serving with the 23rd Middlesex Regiment, on 31 March 1917 near Ypres. He is buried at Dickebusch New Military Cemetery.

Serjeant Alexander Nimmo NEISH MM, 1/13th Battalion, London Regiment (Kensingtons), is one of two men buried here with that particular gallantry medal. He was killed in action on 3 May 1918, aged 22. His family came from Glasgow. Sadly, the MM is not shown next to his name in *Soldiers Died in the Great War*. (Plot I.B.6)

Second Lieutenant William Pryor HUMPHREY, 1/4th (City of London) Battalion, London Regiment (Royal Fusiliers), was killed in action on 27 May 1918, aged 29. He had previously served as a private with the Cambridgeshire Regiment before being gazetted to the London Regiment. He had only been married a few months before he was killed; his wife died three years later in 1921. (Plot I.C.12)

Private Shaer GILBERT, 1/4th (City of London) Battalion, London Regiment (Royal Fusiliers), was also killed the same day as Second Lieutenant HUMPHREY. He came from the Jewish community that lived around Whitechapel in London. His parents are shown as still residing in Warsaw, Poland. Ironically, from a historical perspective, many of Russia's 4 million Jews welcomed German occupation of former Russian territories after years of persecution and oppression under the Tsarist regimes. Private GILBERT is shown in *Soldiers Died in the Great War* as 'Sidney' GILBERT. (Plot I.C.13)

The Reverend Richard Arthur Pell COLBORNE, Chaplain 4th Class, Army Chaplains' Department, was killed in action on 28 May 1918, aged 31, and was attached to the 1/1st (City of London) Battalion, London Regiment (Royal Fusiliers) when he died. (Plot I.D.1)

Sergeant Frank James WHERRETT, 1/16th Battalion, London Regiment (Queen's Westminster Rifles), was killed in action on 15 June 1918 whilst serving with 'B' Company. His parents lived in Chester Terrace, Belgravia, with their six children. The CWGC register also notes that Frank attended Westminster School. He is one of twelve men buried here from the Queen's Westminster Rifles, of whom all were killed or died of wounds between April and July 1918. (Plot I.D.13)

The highest-ranking officer here is Lieutenant Colonel Philip Mannock GLASIER DSO, 16th Battalion, London Regiment (Queen's Westminster Rifles), who was killed in action on 2 June 1918, aged 28. His DSO was gazetted on 4 February 1918, but the citation only appeared on 5 July that year, a little over a month after his death. It was awarded for conspicuous gallantry and devotion to duty. The citation states that, by his personal energy and leadership, he succeeded in assembling his battalion in a shallow trench very close to the enemy. It goes on to say that the subsequent attack was carried out successfully and resulted in the capture of seventy prisoners, three machine guns and a trench mortar. Prior to the attack he had, with persistence and resource, organized a series of very successful offensive patrols in which prisoners were taken and serious losses inflicted on the enemy.

GLASIER had commanded the battalion at Cambrai in November 1917, and also with great skill and gallantry near Gavrelle on 28 March 1918. In spite of a number of heavy attacks by the enemy and problems on his right flank, after the 1st Lancashire Fusiliers had been forced to withdraw, he showed great ability in organizing a series of defensive positions from which his men were able to halt any advances over open ground, forcing the Germans to take the slower route through Humid Trench and Naval Trench to make progress. Even when the British artillery, with the best of intentions, destroyed a vital block that GLASIER and his men had set up at the junction of Towy Trench and Naval Trench, he again reorganized his line using parts of a nearby communication trench and a series of posts and shell holes to seriously delay the enemy's advance and cause further heavy losses. Eventually the enemy's efforts began to run out of momentum in front of the Bailleul–Willerval Line. GLASIER's battalion shrank from twenty-three officers and 564 other ranks to eight officers and sixty men. It seems remarkable that his leadership and courage were not recognized on this occasion too.

His nephew, Phillip Edward Brougham Glasier, became a leading expert on falconry, a passion he inherited from another uncle, Charles Knight. Knight would often lecture with his golden eagle, 'Mr Ramshaw' on his arm. Some of his uncle's eccentricity clearly rubbed off on the young Phillip, who looked after some of his uncle's birds when he was away on his travels. One bird in particular, an African hawk eagle, would sometimes accompany the boy to school, settling down on the luggage rack for the duration of the train journey. (Plot I.E.1)

Second Lieutenant Isidore Herbert GREENWOOD, 10th Middlesex Regiment, attached 8th Battalion, died of wounds on 6 July 1918, aged 27. There is an interesting entry in the *London Gazette* dated 21 May 1915 relating to him and his family. It reveals that he, along with his father and mother, three brothers and two sisters, gave public notice of their desire to change the *'foreign name of Grunebaum'* to Greenwood. The notice shows Isidore serving as a second lieutenant. All the addresses given in the notice are located in highly respectable areas of London and it is clear that the family lived very comfortably. The family ran a cigar importation business. (Plot II.A.7)

Gunner Samuel SHEARE, 1/1st (Lowland) Battery, Royal Garrison Artillery, was killed on 27 April 1918. He is another soldier of Jewish ethnicity. His parents are shown as living in Russia, although his wife resided in Newcastle-on-Tyne. There is no trace of him in *Soldiers Died in the Great War*. (Plot II.A.12)

Corporal Richard Charles HAWKEN MM, 1/13th Battalion, London Regiment (Kensingtons), was killed in action on 14 August 1918, aged 27. The award of the MM is not shown next to his name in *Soldiers Died in the Great War*, but it was gazetted on 7 October 1918. Two other men with the same surname who came from the same Cornish village as Corporal HAWKEN also served during the war but survived, raising the possibility that Albert and Frederick Hawken were his brothers. The CWGC records show a number of men with this surname whose families came from Cornwall. (Plot II.A.16)

Lieutenant Colonel Lord Alfred Eden BROWNE DSO, 186 Brigade, Royal Field Artillery, was killed in action on 27 August 1918, aged 39. He was the son of the 5th Marquess of Sligo, Henry Ulick. His DSO was gazetted on 16 September 1918 and was awarded for conspicuous gallantry and devotion to duty during the March Retreat. The citation states that he displayed great skill in artillery rearguard actions, remaining in action until the last moment, running it very fine on three occasions before withdrawing by batteries or by sections, as appropriate. It goes on to say that he was always cool and showed great power in his ability to keep in touch with both the infantry and the officer commanding the divisional artillery. Sadly, his wife, Cicely, died on 10 August 1918 a couple of weeks before his death. They lived at Sheepwell House, near Potters Bar, a 113-acre estate that was subsequently sold and which in 1925 became Queenswood School for Girls. The prestigious school still exists today. (Plot II.C.1)

Captain Percy Vere BINNS MC, 1st Brigade, HQ Canadian Engineers, died of wounds on 28 August 1918, aged 25. The CWGC register notes that he was born in Port Antonio, Jamaica. Both his parents were also born in Jamaica and the family was sufficiently comfortable to be able to send their children to school in Canada. Percy went on to attend Toronto University where he graduated in 1914 with a Bachelor of Science degree in Engineering. He went on to apply his knowledge working for the Hydro-Electric Power Commission in Kenora, Ontario. His career in civil engineering was, however, short lived and he enlisted in the 1st Field Company, Canadian Engineers, in November 1915. By summer 1916 he was serving on the Western Front with the 1st Field Company.

He was wounded the following year on the Somme where he won the MC. It was gazetted on 1 January 1917 and was awarded for providing valuable service in the construction of jumping off trenches in front of the village of Courcelette. His skill and experience led to his posting in September 1917 as assistant adjutant, 1st Division, Canadian Engineers, during the Third Battle of Ypres. The following year he took part in the Battle of Amiens, but later that month, while travelling by motorcycle to Canadian forward positions in order to set up an advance engineer dump, he was badly wounded by a shell. The incident happened in the Rue Saint Quentin, just east of the railway station in Arras. As well as being wounded by shell fragments, the motorcycle ended up on top of him and its engine caught fire, which caused him severe burns. He died soon afterwards.

His three brothers served during the war and they all survived. Corporal Edward Ellis Binns served with the Canadian Army Medical Corps, Private Ray Ellerton Binns served with Borden's Motor Machine Gun Battery and Ralph Spencer Binns served as a lieutenant in the American Expeditionary Force. Binns's parents later moved to England via Philadelphia and settled in Lee in the London Borough of Lewisham. (Plot II.C.2)

Dainville Communal Cemetery

The cemetery is closer to Arras than Dainville British Cemetery, although the cemetery lies on the same route. From the roundabout where the D.59 meets the D.265, take the D.59, L'Avenue Lavoisier, for just over half a mile. The cemetery is at the far end of the avenue just before the next roundabout and it lies on the north side of the road. The CWGC graves are easily located near the Cross of Sacrifice. There are thirty-nine relating to the Great War and just one from the Second World War.

Dainville was used for billeting and other purposes from March 1916 when the British first came to Arras and the cemetery was used sporadically between then and April 1918.

There is just one officer buried among the group, Lieutenant Reginald Pole HAYES, 6th Somerset Light Infantry, who was killed in action on 12 March 1916, aged 29. The CWGC register notes that he and his wife lived in Natal, South Africa, though he was not a native of that country; he was born in Devon where he is listed on the war memorial at Instow. (Plot A.1)

The three men next to Lieutenant HAYES died on the same day. One is a gunner from the Royal Field Artillery and the next two are a serjeant and sapper from the 89th Field Company, Royal Engineers. Sapper Thomas DUNN and Serjeant Howard Charles LONG were accidentally killed during the construction of a gun emplacement when the roof of an excavation collapsed, burying several men. The 89th Field Company, Royal Engineers, was part of the 14th (Light) Division, as was the 6th Somerset Light Infantry. (Plots A.2 and A.3)

There are nine casualties here from the Canadian Expeditionary Force, all killed in the early part of April 1918. Two of the nine had been awarded the MM: Private John James SEAGRAM MM, 13th Battalion, Canadian Infantry (Plot A.23), and Private Charles Bruce DUXBURY MM, 2nd Battalion, Canadian Machine Gun Corps (Plot B.7). The CWGC register notes that DUXBURY had studied at Manitoba University, where he had been a member of the OTC, and that he was born in Lancashire. The surname is fairly common in the north-east of the county and CWGC records include a number of men from that area.

One of the Canadians, Lance Sergeant Frederick Patrick BUTLER, 14th Battalion, Canadian Infantry, had previously served in the South African War. He was killed in action on 7 April 1918, aged 36. (Plot A.24)

The 13th Battalion, London Regiment (Kensingtons), has seven of its men buried here, all killed in April 1918, six of whom died on 8 April. All six men are buried consecutively, four in Row A, and the other two at the start of Row B. One of the men, Private George Atkinson CHICKEN, who was a member of the Worshipful Company of Stationers, was also a Freeman of the City of London (Plot A.30). Two of the six men are shown in the CWGC register under the rank of drummer.

Lance Corporal Denis Byrne O'REILLY, CC Cable Section, Royal Engineers, who is referred to in the CWGC register as '*soldier, scholar and athlete*', was killed in action on 11 December 1916, aged 25. He came from Londonderry. (Plot A.12)

Private Phillip William DALY, 2/1st (London) Field Ambulance, Royal Army Medical Corps, was killed in action on 9 April 1918, aged 24. The CWGC register notes that he was a stockbroker's clerk, and also that he was a fine runner and athlete, though, as in the case of O'REILLY, the notes do not elaborate further. (Plot A.28)

Many visitors to Arras will visit the Wellington Quarries on the road out to Beaurains. The experience is well worth it. The excavation is just a small part of the Ronville Tunnel complex and was developed from medieval subterranean quarry workings by men of the New Zealand Tunnelling Company. In the same way that many trenches were named after locations back home by the troops above ground, so the New Zealand Tunnelling Company named their tunnels after locations in New Zealand, for example, New Plymouth, Auckland, Wellington, Nelson, Blenheim, Christchurch and Dunedin. The unit had its share of casualties between 1916 and 1918 and operated in Belgium as well as France. The majority of the casualties who fell at Arras are buried in the Faubourg d'Amiens Cemetery, though a few who died of wounds are buried at Duisans British Cemetery, Aubigny Communal Cemetery Extension and Habarcq Communal Cemetery Extension. One of those New Zealand tunnellers can be found here: Sapper George William ROLLS, who died on 12 April 1918. (Plot B.6)

Chapter Three

Goings on at Monchy – A Chapel and a Windmill – Port for the Duke's Table

Monchy British Cemetery, Monchy-Le-Preux

Monchy British Cemetery lies between the A.1 Autoroute and Monchy-le-Preux itself, about half a mile north of the D.939 Arras–Cambrai road. Either of the two tracks that run west from the village will lead to the cemetery, which is situated at the point where the two tracks meet. It is not large and has 581 graves, of which 523 are identified. Once Monchy had been captured, the cemetery was used to bury front line casualties until the British withdrew from there at the end of March 1918 during the German Offensive. Some graves were lost between then and the recapture of Monchy by the Canadians on 26 August, and so a number of casualties are commemorated by special memorials.

The capture of Monchy-le-Preux on 11 April 1917 is often ascribed to the 37th Division, but there is evidence that men of 15th (Scottish) Division also captured part of it. This division had the task of breaking through the narrow gap between Monchy and the River Scarpe; its leading unit was the 10/11th Highland Light Infantry. Heavy fire, some of it from the opposite bank of the Scarpe near Roeux, caused its men to veer right. As they approached the north side of Monchy-le-Preux they also came under direct fire from German positions within the village. This threatened to enfilade the 15th Division's advance and had to be dealt with if its objectives were to be taken. Two companies peeled off to deal with it, which they did very successfully. Their account is supported by German narratives that tell of their positions defending the west side of the village being taken from the rear.

The 37th Division's initial attack on the village suffered several checks from heavily defended positions among the buildings on the west side before its men were able to force their way in. What seems likely is that the defenders' grip may have been loosened when the Highland Light Infantry infiltrated behind them.

Based on the same information and believing that it signalled the capture of the village, the 3rd Cavalry Division also began moving towards its objectives on Infantry Hill, but the move was premature. German machine-gun fire to the north and east of Monchy made progress impossible for the Essex Yeomanry and the 10th Hussars, and the 3rd Dragoon Guards only managed to reach the Monchy–Wancourt road where it was forced to dismount, partly owing to machine-gun fire from Guémappe. German shelling increased later that day, causing heavy casualties, especially in Monchy itself.

The earliest burials here are from 9 to 11 April, but only fifty-three graves relate to these dates. This will probably come as a surprise given that the cemetery lies in the path of the advance on the village. Overall, the 12th (Eastern) Division has the lion's share. Its burials begin to appear in June 1917. All July casualties here are from this division, a total of 117, including men from all thirteen of its battalions. The second highest tally of dead for that month comes from the division's pioneer battalion, the 5th Northamptonshire Regiment, just two behind the 9th Essex Regiment's total of twenty. The following two months show a similar picture with casualties from twelve of the division's battalions reflecting the rotational tours of trench duty. A glance at the CWGC register also shows that the vast majority of these men were local to the county regiments in which they served: the counties of east and south-east England.

Much has been written about the capture of Monchy-le-Preux, but little about the months that followed through to the end of March 1918. This cemetery tells that story very well. The fighting, particularly in July, involved beating off counter-attacks, raiding enemy trenches and consolidating the line that ran to the north and east of the village, almost always under shell fire. Having been forced out of Monchy, the Germans were determined to make it uncomfortable for the new occupants. The fighting was on a relatively small scale, but it had all the familiar characteristics of attrition common to localities that were prized by both sides. Monchy gave the British decent observation over the enemy's positions west of the Drocourt–Quéant Line, which the Germans were now busy improving and strengthening, and it was for this reason that Monchy suffered frequent heavy shelling.

Another unit familiar with this sector was the 3rd Division. At 7.20am on 14 June the division was tasked with taking two trenches that protected enemy positions in Bois du Vert, on the south-west slopes of Infantry Hill. This was intended as a pre-liminary to capturing the hill itself. The 1st Gordon Highlanders and the 2nd Suffolk Regiment attacked Hook and Long Trenches with initial success, but later that after-noon the Germans launched a heavy counter-attack that continued for the next four days. The British held their initial gains, but thoughts of advancing to Infantry Hill were postponed. The initial capture of both trenches cost the 3rd Division fewer than fifty casualties, but by 18 June casualties had escalated to twenty-eight officers and 870 other ranks, illustrating that the defence of key positions was often far more expensive than the cost of taking them.

Although the British trenches ran in a semi-circle of about 1,000 yards radius around Monchy, the forward trenches were neither continuous, nor particularly well wired. Listed in order from west to east, the northern end of Shrapnel, Dale, Hill and Hook Trenches hung in the air. The furthest British position, Spoon Trench, just opposite the Bois du Vert, was really just an outpost in a line of shell holes rather than part of a conventional trench system. Deep trenches and dug-outs were difficult to construct and maintain in these forward positions, due partly to enemy activity, but also because a number of springs emerge here making the ground very wet. The prob-lem was so bad that the 12th (Eastern) Division's engineer companies had to construct another trench, East Reserve Trench, behind the above four, consisting of footboards supported on wooden piles and with pumps to manage water levels.

In the last ten days of June, the 12th (Eastern) Division had eight officers killed, along with fifty-four other ranks, and a further fifteen officers and 257 other ranks were wounded. There was no battle going on; this was simply attrition, the British trying to hold on to their hard won positions, whilst the German intention was to make this as costly as possible. This was not part of the Battle of Arras, but it was a consequence of it. This has to be understood if the visitor is to make any sense of Monchy British Cemetery.

The pattern was now set for the remainder of the year and some of the fighting was utterly savage. On 11 July the Germans pre-empted a raid on their trenches by the 6th East Kent Regiment (The Buffs). After a heavy bombardment the Germans used flame-throwers, overcoming the posts in Hook and Long Trenches. The 9th Essex Regiment defended parts of Hook Trench and after a desperate struggle managed to prevent further progress by the enemy.

An operation to recover these lost posts on 15 July was postponed until the 17th owing to torrential rain. The attack by the 6th Queen's (Royal West Surrey Regiment), the 6th Queen's Own (Royal West Kent Regiment) and the 9th Essex Regiment went in at 4.45am and was successful, but it proved a long day and pockets of resistance were only cleared at 1.00am the following morning. However, it was decided that Long Trench was not worth retaining and, rather than occupy it, it was filled with wire and abandoned.

On 19 July the 5th Royal Berkshire Regiment carried out an attack to redraw slightly the line north of Infantry Lane and east of Hook Trench. After briefly occupying both positions they were driven out. This was the exact location where the 7th Royal Sussex Regiment had failed on 4 July. On 25 July the Germans retaliated, again using flame-throwers against the 7th Royal Sussex Regiment. All these dates can be seen on many of the headstones in this cemetery.

Several future operations were on a much larger scale. Emphasis now changed from trying to capture enemy positions to raiding them. At 2.45am on 9 August 1917 the 7th Suffolk Regiment raided Bois du Vert and the 'Mound'. During the operation 350 of its own men, eighty from the 7th East Surrey Regiment, and eighty from the 6th East Kent Regiment (The Buffs) spent forty-five minutes in the German trenches. Royal Engineer parties accompanied the raid and used demolition charges to wreck dug-outs and other trench infrastructure during the operation. At Beaurains, preparations for the raid had included a 1:100 model of the ground as a briefing aid for those taking part. The 9th Royal Fusiliers carried out another raid on 2 September with few losses, and on the 24th, as the Germans were forming up for a raid of their own, British artillery fire smashed the attempt before it began.

On 14 October an even bigger raid took place. Just over 750 men from the 6th Queen's (Royal West Surrey Regiment), the 6th Queen's Own (Royal West Kent Regiment) and the 7th Norfolk Regiment, supported by Royal Engineer demolition parties, spent another forty-five minutes causing considerable damage. Six officers and seventeen men were killed, three officers and 144 other ranks were either wounded or unaccounted for. The raid was backed by 144 artillery pieces of various calibres.

All these accounts serve to illustrate the hard reality of holding the line, but hopefully they also enable the visitor to this cemetery to make sense of the various dates on the headstones. The 138 headstones bearing dates from September through to November 1917 will mean very little to most visitors without any accompanying explanation. This cemetery really has very little to do with the Battle of Arras itself.

Second Lieutenant William Edward HOBDAY DCM and Bar, 13th Rifle Brigade, fell during the attack on 11 April 1917, aged 22. His DCM was gazetted on 14 January

1916 and the accompanying citation appeared on 11 March that year. He won it for conspicuous gallantry as a private with the 8th Rifle Brigade, firstly acting as a stretcher-bearer, then assisting a machine-gun detachment, and finally working with the bombers. He showed great bravery and coolness, continuing with his duties until wounded. The bar to his DCM was awarded for conspicuous gallantry when he took out a small party in bright moonlight under heavy rifle and machine-gun fire and brought in a wounded officer who was lying in front of the enemy lines, even though several previous attempts had failed. The award was gazetted on 16 March 1916 and won while serving as a temporary corporal with the 8th Battalion. (Plot I.A.19)

Private Albert MERCER, Monmouthshire Regiment, is shown as 1/5th Battalion, which never actually existed. He was, in fact, from the 1/2nd Battalion and had formerly served with the South Lancashire Regiment. His unit was the pioneer battalion of the 29th Division. He was killed in action on 1 June 1917. (Plot I.E.12)

There are just a handful of cavalrymen buried here: Private Walter ARCHER, 3rd Dragoon Guards, who was born in New York, was killed in action on 11 April 1917 during the advance on Monchy by the 3rd Cavalry Division (Plot I.E.26). Nearby is Serjeant William FIELD, 3rd (King's Own) Hussars, who was killed in action on 21 May 1917. (Plot I.E.29)

Captain John William BOWYER, 13th Rifle Brigade, was killed in action on 10 April 1917 when his battalion's attack was held up by heavy fire. It was forced to dig in near Feuchy Chapel until the attack was renewed the following day. (Plot I.E.28)

Serjeant Frederick William GREENING DCM, 9th Royal Fusiliers, died of wounds on 30 June 1917, aged 29. His DCM was gazetted on 18 July 1917 and was awarded for conspicuous gallantry and devotion to duty, leading his men with the utmost skill and coolness under heavy fire. His pluck and determination while under fire set a fine example to his men. (Plot I.F.11)

Captain Frederick William LING, Royal Fusiliers, was adjutant of the 8th Battalion at the time of his death on 27 June 1917. He had begun his soldiering with the Territorials when he joined the 5th Cameronians in 1912. However, at some point he joined the London Regiment, serving with the 15th Battalion (Prince of Wales's Own Civil Service Rifles) and was one of the '17th March' men; in other words, one of the original contingent that embarked for France in 1915. He was badly wounded near Festubert after barely two months in the trenches. The gunshot wound to his thigh required hospitalization and four months away from the front line. He was then commissioned in November 1915. On 17 September the following year he received another gunshot wound, the bullet entering the right thigh and exiting via the right buttock, causing significant tissue damage. *The History of the 12th (Eastern) Division in the Great War* shows the MC against his name, but there is no reference to it in *Officers Died in the Great War*, nor is there any note of it on his file at the National Archives. Also, I can find no trace of the award in any of the Gazettes. (Plot I.F.17)

Captain Charles Frederick William MORBEY, 7th Suffolk Regiment, was killed in action on 9 August 1917, aged 28. He resided in Soham, Cambridgeshire, where his family lived in some style, building a large home, Beechurst House. The family also owned land in the area, as well as Brandon Hall, a large Queen Anne house in Suffolk. His father, also named Charles, had made his money in the world of horse racing and had begun life as head groom to Lord Manvers. After working as a jockey, he progressed to training race horses by which he made substantial sums of money. He was well connected in East Anglia and used to shoot at Sandringham with the Royal Family. (Plot I.K.8)

Corporal Arthur Leonard GUISE DCM MM, 9th Royal Fusiliers, was killed in action on 21 October 1917. His DCM was gazetted on 22 October 1917 and the citation followed on 26 January 1918. It was awarded for conspicuous gallantry and devotion to duty during a raid on enemy trenches. He was the first of his party to enter the enemy sap, immediately bayoneting two sentries before they could react. He then began to work his way along the trench to where a block had to be established, and in doing so he killed several more of the enemy using their own bombs which he had found in the trench. He reached his objective with his own party and successfully held it, eventually covering the withdrawal. The manner in which he and his men carried out their task greatly contributed to the raid's success. His MM was gazetted on 18 July 1917. (Plot I.0.20)

Second Lieutenant Frederick Haughton HADEN, 1st Rifle Brigade, was killed in action on 4 November 1917. (Plot II.A.4)

Second Lieutenant Rand Edwin John WALDEN, 2nd Lancashire Fusiliers, was killed in action on 16 November 1917, aged 35. He was the only casualty of a raid that took place at 2.00am that day. He not only led the raid, which consisted of twenty men, but personally carried out the reconnaissance on the three successive nights leading up to it. Some of the trench mortars supporting the raid fell short and close to the raiding party, delaying it and causing some disorganization. The party set off, but the recall signal was given just as it was approaching the German trenches. The party managed to silence a machine-gun post before withdrawing, although it returned without any prisoners or identifications. (Plot II.A.11)

Second Lieutenant Robert Cuthbert STOWELL, 1st King's Own (Royal Lancaster Regiment), was killed in action near Monchy on 20 November 1917, aged 29. He was in support trenches in charge of a smoke party covering a raid that was carried out in order to obtain identifications (Plot II.A.12). His brother, Second Lieutenant Wilfred Stowell, 2nd Leinster Regiment, was killed in action on 22 March 1918, aged 27. He has no known grave and is commemorated on the Pozières Memorial.

Second Lieutenant Guy Henry Goud CROSFIELD, 5th Rifle Brigade, attached 1st Battalion, was killed by trench mortar fire on 26 January 1918, aged 20, while patrolling east of Monchy (Plot II.B.21). Two attempts were made to recover his body which was recovered on the third occasion. One of the men who brought him back, Serjeant Cooke, won a bar to his MM for this action, whilst the other man with him won the MM. Cooke went on to win a DCM in June 1918 at La Pannière when he and others carried out a raid in daylight, killing twenty of the enemy and capturing a further twenty. The raid was brought to a conclusion by heavy machine-gun fire, but not before Cooke had again shown exceptional coolness by bringing in a wounded man under fire. His MM had been won near Arras on 11 May 1917 when in charge of a mopping up party that captured prisoners and other valuable material.

Second Lieutenant Arthur Charlewood TURNER, 6th Rifle Brigade, was killed in action on 16 January 1918, aged 37. His father, the Right Reverend Charles Henry Turner DD, was the Anglican Bishop of Islington between 1898 and 1923 and also chaplain to the Bishop of London. Both father and son attended Trinity College, Cambridge, where Arthur was a Fellow. (Plot II.C.1)

In December 1996, west of the cemetery, an archaeological dig unearthed four locations containing the bodies of British and Commonwealth soldiers. The work was being carried out prior to the construction of a new industrial area close to the TGV line and the A.1 Autoroute. Twenty-seven bodies were found and the usual efforts were made to identify them. Two of the men, Private Frank Harold KING (Plot II.C.28) and Private George Hamilton ANDERSON (Plot II.C.29), 13th Royal Fusiliers, were identified by alloy identity discs in their possession. These were not standard issue, but almost eighty years on they provided vital clues regarding the identity of the two men.

KING and ANDERSON were killed in action on 11 April 1917 in the 37th Division's attack on Monchy. The four original graves had been carefully and deliberately made with each body reverently laid out. It is quite likely that many, if not all, of the men found belonged to the 37th Division, though this cannot be stated for certain. All twenty-seven men were reburied here with full military honours in April 1998.

There are relatively few Canadian burials here, in fact just twenty-three. They are buried in three small groups in Plot II, Rows C and D.

Lieutenant Daniel Lionel TEED MC, 9 Brigade, Canadian Field Artillery, was killed in action on 1 September 1918, aged 24. His MC was gazetted on 3 June 1918 in the King's Birthday Honours List (Plot II.D.20). His brother, Lieutenant Hugh Mariner Teed, died serving with the 2nd Battalion, Canadian Infantry, on 7 January 1917. Canadian records show that he died from accidental injuries. The war diary only notes that the battalion was out of the line and engaged in training, including bombing practice, which is probably how the accident occurred. He is buried at Bruay Communal Cemetery Extension.

Major John SUTHERLAND DSO, 116th Battalion, Canadian Infantry, won his DSO for gallantry and ability during an attack in which he took charge of three companies and completely outflanked the enemy occupying high ground. He succeeded in getting behind their position, capturing a wood and twelve enemy guns, which included a battery of 5.9 howitzers. Throughout the operation he set a fine example of coolness and skill. He then quickly consolidated the newly won position and prevented the enemy from putting in a counter-attack on it. He was also mentioned previously in despatches. The DSO was gazetted on 11 January 1919. He was killed in action on 27 August 1918. (Plot II.D.30)

Captain Thomas Harold BROAD, 116th Battalion, Canadian Infantry, was killed in action on 17 September 1918, aged 23 (Plot II.D.33). His elder brother, Lieutenant

William Edward Lee Broad, was killed in action with the 5th Battalion, Canadian Infantry, on 9 April 1917, aged 24. His death occurred when a shell exploded close to him after he had left an assembly trench on Vimy Ridge. He is buried at Écoivres Military Cemetery.

Captain Franklin Walter OTT MC, 116th Battalion, Canadian Infantry, was killed in action on 17 September 1918, aged 25. His MC was gazetted on 11 January 1919 and was awarded when he was in charge of a company during an advance in which he showed the greatest courage and skill in handling his men. He organized bombing parties and led them against enemy posts, capturing several prisoners and two machine guns. During the enemy's counter-attack he collected eight men and repulsed several attacks, setting a great example to his men. He was the last to leave the post, and only did so when forced to retire against very heavy odds. He then organized a party and retook the position. He showed great initiative in consolidating and holding the position against all further counter-attacks. (Plot II.D.34)

There are twelve holders of the MM buried in this cemetery, seven of whom fought with battalions of the 12th (Eastern) Division. All apart from two fell in 1917. Many of these men are buried in Plot I, rows N and O, including Private Douglas D'Arcy SULLIVAN MM, 'D' Company, 9th Royal Fusiliers, who was just 20 years old when he was killed in action on 26 September 1917. He had previously served with the Royal Army Medical Corps. The CWGC register tells us that he enlisted on 8 August 1914. There is, however, no reference to his MM in *Soldiers Died in the Great War*. (Plot I.N.1)

Happy Valley British Cemetery, Fampoux

Just north of the D.33 in the village of Monchy-le-Preux is the Rue de la Chaussy where the memorials to the Newfoundland Regiment and the 37th Division are situated. Moving between these two in an anti-clockwise direction, follow the road round, which becomes the Rue de Tilleul. Follow this road out of the village to a point roughly 200 yards before the road passes beneath the A.1 Autoroute. The cemetery lies down a small track in fields off to the left.

Happy Valley was the name given to the valley that runs from the east side of Orange Hill down towards the river. It witnessed fighting on 10 April and again the following day during the attack on Monchy-le-Preux, although the burials here hardly reflect this; only two relate to that month.

The cemetery was begun by the 12th (Eastern) Division soon after Monchy was captured by the 37th Division. Its casualties are mainly from May and June 1917. It was re-used in December that year by the 4th Division, particularly the 1st East Lancashire Regiment, the 1st Rifle Brigade, the 1st Hampshire Regiment and the 1st Somerset Light Infantry, which made up 11 Brigade. That division had begun burials here as early as July and continued to use it until the end of the year. There are two 37th Division casualties from 11 April 1917, both of them from the 8th Somerset Light Infantry.

This is a very small cemetery with only seventy-six burials, seventy of which are identified. Today, it is very isolated in its location; even the small wood to the north-east of it was named Lone Copse. In April and May 1917 the ground here, which is very open, was extremely vulnerable to machine-gun fire from Roeux, just across the river. Although Monchy was captured on 11 April, Roeux held out for another month. The devastating field of fire from that direction can be readily appreciated from here by glancing across the river towards Roeux.

There are four gallantry award holders here and just one officer. In that sense it is very much a soldiers' cemetery and a very good example of the type of small battlefield cemetery that was often allowed to remain after the Armistice.

Private Sidney George BEADLE MM, 11th Middlesex Regiment, was killed in action, aged 23, on 12 May 1917. (Plot A.7)

Second Lieutenant Ernest William RUSH, 7th Suffolk Regiment, had previously served as a company serjeant major with the 2nd Battalion and had only just been commissioned when he was killed in action on 28 April 1917. He was killed by machine-gun fire from the direction of Roeux during an attack by his battalion across the fields east of the cemetery between the river and Monchy. (Plot A.12)

Private Robert WALL, 1st Hampshire Regiment, was killed in action on 23 July 1917. He was a married man and his wife was from Lamorlaye in the Département of the Oise. He was born at Chantilly, in the same Département where he and his wife resided before the war, although he returned to England and enlisted in Winchester. (Plot A.26)

Private Charles Thomas QUELCH MM, 1st Hampshire Regiment, died of wounds on 28 July 1917, aged 26, though *Soldiers Died in the Great War* records his date of death as the previous day. (Plot B.23)

Private John PAGE MM, 'A' Company 1st Royal Warwickshire Regiment, was killed on 16 December 1917, aged 34. He served under the name of 'RADFORD' and came from Birmingham. (Plot C.8)

Company Serjeant Major Albert E. BROWN MM and Bar, 1st East Lancashire Regiment, was killed on 25 August 1917, aged 22. His MM was gazetted on 11 November 1916, and the bar to it on 12 March 1917. *Soldiers Died in the Great War* does not show this second award. Both were won while serving as a serjeant with the battalion. His actual grave was lost, but he is known to be buried in this cemetery and is now commemorated by way of a special memorial.

Houdain Lane Cemetery, Tilloy-lès-Mofflaines

The cemetery lies out in open fields about three quarters of a mile north of the D.939 Arras–Cambrai road. From the eastern suburbs of Arras, take the D.939 as far as the junction with the D.37. Come off left onto the D.37 and just where it looks to be leading into an industrial estate, turn left, which is still the D.37 as it heads north to Feuchy. Follow the road, but take the first track off to the left, then the second track on the right. This is a farm track that leads directly to the cemetery.

This is a small battlefield cemetery that is visually dominated by headstones belonging to the Royal Fusiliers. There are twenty-six identified casualties from that regiment among the seventy-six burials here, nine of which remain unidentified. For me, it is splendidly isolated and seems much further than it actually is from the relentless industrial development that has spread out from Arras and which has already swallowed up a lot of the battlefield immediately east of the town.

Around two thirds of the identified burials are from the opening day of the Battle of Arras, 9 April 1917, including thirteen NCOs and privates from the 13th Royal Fusiliers. Another two men from this battalion who died on 10 and 11 April are also buried here. Despite belonging to the same unit and dying within days of each other, the whole group is scattered throughout seven of the eight rows of graves within the cemetery. These men, like the four privates from the 10th Royal Fusiliers killed on 10 and 11 April, were part of the 37th Division. One of the 13th Royal Fusiliers is 17 years old Lance Serjeant William Henry WOLSTENHOLME. (Plot H.2)

Other battalions of the 37th Division with casualties here are the 13th King's Royal Rifle Corps, the 13th Rifle Brigade and the 8th East Lancashire Regiment. All were killed during the first three days of fighting that culminated in the capture of Monchy-le-Preux.

The 12th (Eastern) Division is also represented here by men of the 8th Royal Fusiliers, the 9th Essex Regiment, the 5th Royal Berkshire Regiment, the 7th Norfolk Regiment and the 6th Queen's (Royal West Surrey Regiment) Regiment. Most of them are from 9 April 1917.

The 15th (Scottish) Division has a number of burials, mainly from the 12th Highland Light Infantry, but also some from the 7th Cameron Highlanders and the 10th Cameronians. Again, all of them were killed between 9 and 11 April 1917.

There are also two 1918 casualties, both Canadians who fell on 31 August 1918. One of them, Lieutenant Charles Victor ALLAN, is the only officer buried here. He and Driver Alexander HENRY were both serving with 8th (Army) Brigade, Canadian Field Artillery, when they were killed in action. (Plots E.1 and F.1 respectively)

Bunyan's Cemetery, Tilloy-lès-Mofflaines

This is another small battlefield cemetery that lies just over half a mile north-east of Tilloy-lès-Mofflaines. It is signposted from the D.939 Arras-Cambrai road and lies about 500 yards north of the main road down a small track. It is easily visible from the track. Houdain Lane Cemetery lies a little further north out in the fields and can also be reached via this route rather than the D.37.

There are no unidentified casualties in this cemetery and all are from the 12th (Eastern) Division, with just one exception. The infantry casualties are all from the opening day of the Battle of Arras as successive waves of men moved forward across the battlefeld. Thus, the 11th Middlesex Regiment was part of the initial advance at 5.30am and captured the Black Line. The 9th Royal Fusiliers and the 6th Queen's Own (Royal West Kent Regiment) advanced at 7.30am and faced various degrees of opposition before capturing the Blue Line. The 7th Norfolk Regiment, the 9th Essex Regiment and the 5th Royal Berkshire Regiment then moved off towards the Brown Line, advancing at 12.30pm. All of these battalions have at least one casualty buried here. The one infantryman not from the 12th (Eastern) Division is a private belonging to the 1st Royal Scots Fusiliers who was also killed on 9 April 1917. All the infantry burials are in Row A.

The remainder of the cemetery is made up entirely of men from 62 and 63 Brigades, Royal Field Artillery, each of whose three 18-pounder batteries and one

4.5-inch howitzer battery made up the 12th (Eastern) Division's Artillery, along with its supporting Ammunition Column. There are no casualties from its Medium Trench Mortar batteries buried here.

On 9 April 1917, 62 Brigade, Royal Field Artillery, began its move forward at 11.30am in support of the infantry, which had experienced some delays around the Blue Line. Despite being behind schedule, 62 Brigade did remarkably well and was in place forty minutes later to lend support to the attack on the Brown Line; 63 Brigade performed similarly well. It was able to bring down a barrage to support the advance to the Brown Line, though this objective was not secured until the following day when again both brigades gave excellent service.

Second Lieutenant Robert Herbert de Mussenden LEATHES, 'B' Battery, 62 Brigade, Royal Field Artillery, was killed on 18 April 1917. The Leathes family came from the Suffolk area where it had played a prominent part in local life since the eighteenth century. One of the family, Reginald Carteret de Mussenden Leathes CB LVO OBE, served with distinction during the Second World War with the 1st Battalion, Royal Marines and Royal Marine Commando, retiring in 1962 as a major general, Royal Marines. (Plot B.1)

The officer next to him also served with the same battery and, according to the CWGC records, was killed in action on 19 April 1917, though *Officers Died in the Great War* shows his death occurring the previous day. Lieutenant Harold Francis HUGHES-GIBB was educated at Trinity College, Cambridge, and the family home was a 75-acre estate attached to the manor house in the Dorset village of Tarrant Gunville. His sister, Gwendolen, was the wife of Sir Philip Woolcott Game GCB GCVO GBE KCMG DSO, who served in the South African campaign and also during the Great War with the Royal Flying Corps, becoming staff officer to Lord Trenchard. He went on to become an Air Vice Marshal in the Royal Air Force, eventually retiring in 1929, and, like Lord Trenchard, also served as Commissioner of the Metropolitan Police, a position he held between 1935 and 1945. (Plot B.2)

Gourock Trench Cemetery, Tilloy-lès-Mofflaines

This small cemetery is tucked away on an industrial estate on the east side of Arras, just off the D.60 road between Tilloy-lès-Mofflaines and Saint-Laurent-Blangy and about 250 yards south of the Arras–Douai railway line. The cemetery now lies on what would have been part of the German front line trench system on the opening day of the Battle of Arras, which is reflected in the date on 75 per cent of the headstones. There are just forty-four burials, four of which are unidentified.

Burials are predominantly from the 8th Royal Fusiliers, along with three men from the regiment's 9th Battalion, all killed in action on the opening day of the Battle of Arras, 9 April 1917. Other burials from that day are from the 7th Royal Sussex Regiment and the 9th Essex Regiment which, like the two battalions of Royal Fusiliers, were part of the 12th (Eastern) Division. There are also a handful of men from the 15th (Scottish) Division killed that day and a few from 12 April. There is one private from the 8th Lincolnshire Regiment, part of the 37th Division, whose date of death was 16 April, after which there are no more 1917 burials.

There is a lone gunner killed in action on 28 March 1918 whilst serving in the Royal Garrison Artillery, as well as four Canadian soldiers, including one officer, Second Lieutenant Francis Nicholas CLUFF (Plot B.9). He was killed in action on 28 August 1918 along with another man, whilst the other pair died two days earlier. The war diary for the 49th Battalion, Canadian Infantry, gives little information on CLUFF's death, except that he was one of two officers from his battalion killed that day, but infers that he was killed early during operations to capture the village of Pelves.

Orange Hill Cemetery, Feuchy

Orange Hill, little more than a small rise, lies to the north-west of Monchy-le-Preux between Feuchy Chapel and the village of Feuchy in the Scarpe Valley. The Wancourt–Feuchy Line, or the Brown Line as it was also known, lay roughly 500 yards to the west of the crest of the hill. By nightfall on 9 April 1917 the British had established a foothold on the northern part of the hill, extending north as far as the railway line just beyond Feuchy itself. The cemetery, therefore, lies in the heart of the 1917 battlefield, and yet it contains not a single casualty from that year. All the casualties here are from August and September 1918, and all, apart from one, are from Canadian units.

Corporal Arthur ALDWORTH, 11th Divisional Signal Company, Royal Engineers, is the only British casualty here and he was killed in September 1918 (Plot C.1).

There are forty-three identified burials in all. The cemetery is located in fields at the end of a track that runs off the D.37 between Feuchy Chapel and Feuchy. Most of the casualties are from the 1st and 4th Battalions, Canadian Mounted Rifles, and were killed in action on 26 August 1918, though there are also two men from the regiment's 5th Battalion buried with them who were killed the same day.

The attack on Monchy-le-Preux was scheduled for the previous day, but was postponed until 3.00am on the 26th. The Canadians deployed two of their divisions for the attack; the sector between the Arras–Cambrai Road and the River Scarpe was allotted to the 3rd Division, whilst the 2nd Division attacked south of the road. The 2nd and 4th Battalions, Canadian Mounted Rifles, advanced from the valley near Feuchy towards the German positions in front of and astride Orange Hill, whilst the 1st and 5th Battalions, Canadian Mounted Rifles, attacked the village of Monchy-le-Preux, which was captured just before 8.00am. German defences around Orange Hill fell quickly to the assault and the attack was continued by other units, including the Royal Canadian Regiment.

The 4th Battalion, Canadian Mounted Rifles, has eleven of its dead buried in this cemetery, including two officers. Lieutenant Alastair Norman BROWN was tragically killed by British machine-gun fire, which had swept too far to the right from across the river on the battalion's left flank (Plot A.1). Captain Herbert Charles ROUNDS is buried further along in Row A. He transferred to the 4th Canadian Mounted Rifles in November 1916 and was wounded at Méricourt on 10 May 1917 while his battalion was carrying out a relief. He was mortally wounded on 26 August 1918 by two machine-gun bullets to the abdomen while leading his company against Italian Trench near Monchy-le-Preux and died the same day. (Plot A.13)

Another headstone of note is that of Lance Corporal James Harold HANNAH DCM, 4th Battalion, Canadian Mounted Rifles. He won his DCM as a private while acting as a runner during an attack in which his company commander and two other men were badly wounded by sniper fire as they advanced. He crept forward, shot the foremost sniper and then captured the remaining four. He then compelled them to carry his wounded officer back to our line. After that, he returned to his company and assisted it to consolidate the captured position. He set a splendid example of courage and initiative throughout the day. His award was gazetted on 28 March 1918. (Plot A.2)

Among the dead of the 1st Battalion, Canadian Mounted Rifles, is Lieutenant Alexander Pearson MacMILLAN MC. He was the son of a clergyman and had enlisted in early June 1915, initially joining the 45th Battalion, but transferring to the Canadian Mounted Rifles the following year. He took part in the Somme fighting in 1916 where, in October, he was wounded in the right lung. His MC, gazetted on 13 January 1919, was won during the initial part of an attack when his platoon was held up by strong resistance that threatened to delay the entire advance. Without hesitation, he led his platoon around the obstacle in a flanking movement before attacking it, killing and capturing a number of the enemy, after which the advance was able to continue. He then led his platoon to its final objective. He was killed in action on 26 August 1918, aged 28. He had also taken part in previous operations at Arras and Amiens. (Plot A.23)

Another holder of the MC from the 1st Battalion, Canadian Mounted Rifles, killed in action on 26 August, was Lieutenant John Henry (Jack) SYDIE MC. He had enlisted on New Year's Eve 1914 and fell in action, aged 33. His MC was gazetted on 30 July 1917 and was awarded for gallantry as a company sergeant major after he rallied his men and assisted in the consolidation of a position. Later he led reinforcements up to the front line under heavy fire (Plot A.18). Another two officers from this battalion, Lieutenant Robert SHANNON, who had previously served with the 1st Life Guards, (Plot A.4) and Lieutenant Leonard Whitman SMITH (Plot A.5), lie buried here along with nine of their men.

Captain Thorburn Stephens ALLAN MC, Royal Canadian Regiment, was killed in action near Monchy-le-Preux on 26 August 1918, aged 22. He had won his MC for his leadership and gallantry during the capture and consolidation of an objective, setting a fine example to the men of his platoon. The award was gazetted on 30 July 1917. He enlisted in November 1916 and had also been mentioned in despatches in May 1918. He died at a nearby dressing station from a bullet wound to the right lung (Plot B.17). Next to him is Lieutenant Arthur Milton FRASER, who was also killed in action with the Royal Canadian Regiment on 26 August, aged 22. (Plot B.16)

The cemetery contains six privates from the 3rd Battalion, Canadian Machine Gun Corps, killed in action on 26 August, or the following day, when the advance continued east of Monchy and where the fighting was particularly heavy. There was some initial success during which the Bois du Vert and the neighbouring wood, the Bois du Sart, were captured, lost, and then recaptured, but the German defences in the Scarpe Valley offered stubborn resistance throughout the day, especially around the village of Pelves, on the left flank of the 3rd Division's attack.

On 28 August the 3rd Canadian Division fared better in its attacks. The 58th Battalion was able to push beyond the 52nd Battalion and the 4th Canadian Mounted Rifles and capture Boiry-Notre-Dame. The 58th Battalion was relieved after the attack and three days of fighting. The following day the battalion was resting and refitting near Feuchy when the location was shelled and eight men from the battalion, now buried here, were killed by one of the shells. They are buried together in Row B, Graves 8 to 15. A further sixteen men were wounded by the explosion, according to the battalion's war diary.

Orange Trench Cemetery, Monchy-le-Preux

This cemetery lies to the north-west of Monchy-le-Preux on the road to Fampoux and is set slightly off the road in fields. Happy Valley British Cemetery lies a little further on and Monchy British Cemetery is about 500 yards away to the south-west. The part of the road between Monchy and the A.1 Autoroute was known in 1917 as Lancer Lane. This cemetery, as its name suggests, is very much a battlefield cemetery and was constructed on the site of a captured German trench. All the burials are from April and May 1917, but only half the graves are identified. Six special memorials now commemorate a number of men known or believed to be buried here.

Two thirds of the identified casualties relate to the fighting in April 1917, mainly 11 April, and mainly privates. The majority are men of the 6th Cameron Highlanders, the 6/7th Royal Scots Fusiliers and the 10/11th Highland Light Infantry, all battalions belonging to the 15th (Scottish) Division. Of the nine officers buried here, three are April casualties. With one exception, the May casualties are from the 29th Division, mainly the 1st Essex Regiment. Although the CWGC register informs us that Private Percy William CANT served with the 4th Essex Regiment, he was killed in action with the 1st Battalion and had formerly served with the Hertfordshire Regiment. (Plot D.19)

Lieutenant Mountenay Coesvelt William KORTRIGHT, 1st Essex Regiment, was killed in action on 21 May 1917. He was an only son who, after Harrow, attended the Royal Military College, Sandhurst, before going to Gallipoli in August 1915 where he served until the 29th Division left the peninsula. KORTRIGHT's father had served as a lieutenant with the 3rd (King's Own) Hussars. (Plot A.1)

Captain Meredith André CHAWNER, 2nd Essex Regiment, was killed in action on 21 May 1917 (Plot A.2). His father, Major William John Hampden Chawner, served in Malta and in India where Meredith and his elder brother, Lieutenant Alain Percy Mark Chawner, were born. Both brothers served with the Essex Regiment. Alain, who had been mentioned in despatches, was killed in action on 21 October 1916 while attached to the 1st Battalion from the 3rd Battalion. He had initially served with the East Surrey Regiment and is buried on the Somme at Bernafay Wood British Cemetery, Montauban.

Captain Keith Morris WEARNE and Lieutenant Bernard Oldershaw WARNER, 3rd Essex Regiment, are commemorated on the same special memorial. At the time of their deaths, both were attached to the 1st Battalion, although they were killed two days apart (Special Memorial 3). Although the CWGC register contains no biographical or family detail in relation to WEARNE, he was a regular army officer who was commissioned in the 1st Essex Regiment from Sandhurst prior to the outbreak of war.

He was the eldest of three brothers who served during the war. The youngest brother, Geoffrey, was a private with the 19th Battalion, Canadian Infantry, and survived the war. The other brother, Second Lieutenant Frank Bernard Wearne, won the VC and was killed in action on 28 June 1917, barely a month after Keith's death, while serving with the 11th Essex Regiment. He is commemorated on the Loos Memorial.

Frank was severely wounded in July 1916 and only returned to active service in May 1917 following convalescence. He was killed during a raid on enemy defensive positions around Nash Alley that included a team of Australian tunnellers to blow up and destroy enemy dug-outs. Frank's party was heavily counter-attacked and, realizing the implications for the other two parties if he and his unit failed to hold their position, he climbed onto the trench parapet and, under a hail of rifle and machine-gun fire, fired his revolver and hurled bombs at the enemy. He encouraged his remaining men to follow him and drive the enemy back along the trench away from the other parties still carrying out the raid. He was twice wounded while the raid was in progress, and was wounded once again as the parties withdrew, this time fatally. CWGC records and *Officers Died in the Great War* show Frank serving with the 10th Battalion at the time of his death, which is incorrect. He would have been aware of Keith's death, which occurred on 21 May 1917. Lieutenant WARNER was killed two days earlier.

Second Lieutenant Andrew Gemmell CARMICHAEL, 6th Cameron Highlanders, was killed in action on 11 April 1917, aged 24. He had studied Medicine at Edinburgh University between 1910 and 1914 and was a member of its OTC for three years. (Plot C.9)

There are four 13th Royal Fusiliers who fell on 10 April, one of whom is Captain Donald Stanley HARDING MC, aged 32. HARDING and his men had taken part in an advance beyond Orange Hill on 10 April with the 10th Royal Fusiliers on their right. By nightfall both battalions were still short of their objective, Monchy-le-Preux, which was captured the following day. His MC was gazetted on 3 March 1917 and was awarded for conspicuous gallantry in action, leading his company on a dangerous reconnaissance, despite having been wounded, but remaining on duty, setting a splendid example to his men. The CWGC register notes that he had previously served in German South-West Africa with the Natal Carabineers. (Plot D.21)

The 88th Company, Machine Gun Corps, has three men buried here who were killed in action by shelling on 25 May 1917. Since its capture by the British, German aircraft had regularly flown over this part of the battlefield. The purpose of these flights was to carry out spotting and target registration, an activity in which both sides were constantly engaged. Second Lieutenant William John HUTCHINSON, Corporal Godfrey Henry HALLS and Private Robert Gilchrist GRIEVE were killed when they were in an area being shelled deliberately rather than by random firing. (Plots E.6, 7 and 8). Second Lieutenant Noel GRANT was also killed with them (Plot E.5).

However, another more disturbing explanation is that the targeting may have been a response to information passed to the Germans by a deserter. A man had gone unaccountably missing on the night of 18 May, hours before a local raid was carried out. The raid was instantly met by machine-gun fire and shrapnel. Another man from the division also went missing in similar circumstances before a raid a week later with similar results. It is therefore perfectly possible that targeted shelling around this time was carried out on the basis of information passed to the enemy.

Feuchy British Cemetery

The cemetery can be found on the south side of the village, close to the church. It sits just off the roundabout where the Rue de la Chapelle meets the Rue d'Athies, which is the D.37. To the rear of the cemetery is the Arras–Douai railway line. Though the village was captured on 9 April 1917 by the 15th (Scottish) Division, the cemetery was actually begun by the 12th (Eastern) Division soon after the opening day's events. The cemetery has 209 burials, although two are special memorials where the graves were later destroyed by shelling.

In the days following the initial British attack at Arras on 9 April, the area around Feuchy was cleared to make way for artillery and other supporting arms, services and supplies. Almost half the burials in this cemetery belong to either the Royal Field Artillery or Royal Garrison Artillery and, with very few exceptions, they date to April and May 1917 when the Battle of Arras was in progress, though Rows D and E do contain burials from June, July and August, mainly from the Royal Garrison Artillery. Very few casualties from these artillery units are officers; the majority are other ranks, mainly gunners, among whom there are three holders of gallantry awards, two with the MM, the other with the DCM.

Infantry burials are mainly from the 12th (Eastern) Division and 17th (Northern) Division. There are also some from the 4th Division, the 15th (Scottish) Division, the 29th Division, and the 37th Division, but far fewer in terms of numbers. Most date to April and May 1917, but because the 12th (Eastern) Division spent the entire summer and early autumn that year between here and Monchy-le-Preux, some casualties from this later period can also be found. The Essex Regiment has twenty-two casualties here. The later burials are from the regiment's 2nd Battalion, which was part of the 4th Division, whilst the earlier ones tend to be from the 9th Battalion, which was part of the 12th Division.

Two of the three artillerymen with gallantry awards are buried in Plot I. Serjeant Albert KENNARD MM, 'D' Battery, 70 Brigade, Royal Field Artillery, died of wounds on 24 April 1917 (Plot I.B.6). Acting Bombardier William Henry REY-NOLDS MM, 'D' Battery, 51 Brigade, Royal Field Artillery, was killed in action on 23 April 1917 (Plot I.D.1). Both brigades were attached to Scottish divisions; 70 Brigade was part of the 15th (Scottish) Division, 51 Brigade part of the 9th (Scottish) Division. There are several men from these two brigades buried here, as well as members of 156 Brigade, Royal Field Artillery, which was also part of the 15th (Scottish) Division.

A couple of yards along from REYNOLDS is Private Fred BETTLES MM, 2nd Essex Regiment, who was killed in action on 4 July 1917, aged 37. He came from Oundle, Northamptonshire. (Plot I.D.7)

Second Lieutenant Augustine BONNER, 13 Squadron, Royal Flying Corps, was killed in action on 30 April 1917, aged 20. He enlisted in 1914 in one of the Birmingham City battalions and was later commissioned in the South Staffordshire Regiment before joining the Royal Flying Corps. He was wounded in spring 1916, but in September that year he returned to the front. He transferred to the Royal Flying Corps in December 1916 as an observer (Plot II.A.1). His pilot that day, Second Lieutenant William Kennedy Trollope, died of wounds a few days later at Aubigny on 3 May where he is now buried in the communal cemetery extension.

Another gunner buried here is Gunner William James Woodger GAMESTER, 'D' Battery, 48 Brigade, Royal Field Artillery, who, although just 19 years of age when he was killed in action on 7 May 1917, had gone to France with the 1st Division as part of the original British Expeditionary Force in August 1914. (Plot II.B.13)

As well as the artillery, a number of Royal Engineer and Royal Army Medical Corps units also had dug-outs and supply dumps in and around Feuchy. Today, there are nineteen burials from these two branches of the army, two of whom hold gallantry awards. Serjeant William HOLDEN MM, 87th Field Company, Royal Engineers, was killed in action on 8 May 1917 (Plot II.B.8). A few graves along from him is Serjeant Charles SMITH MM, 69th Field Company, Royal Engineers, who was killed in action the day before and who held the Bronze Medal for Valour (Italy). (Plot II.B.14)

There is just one Canadian burial here. Sergeant William L'HIRONDELLE MM, 10th Battalion, Canadian Infantry, was killed in action on 30 August 1918, aged 22. His MM was gazetted on 19 November 1917 and was awarded for carrying out several very dangerous and very difficult reconnaissance patrols at Hill 70 on 15 August 1917. He returned each time, giving clear and concise reports regarding his findings. On each occasion he displayed the utmost courage and disregard for his personal safety (Plot II.C.1). He is one of just seven casualties from 1918 buried in this cemetery. All of them are to be found in Plot II.

Second Lieutenant William SHAND-KYDD, 'A' Battery, 51 Brigade, Royal Field Artillery, was killed in action on 19 May 1917. He was a former member of the University of London OTC, but its Roll of War Service shows his date of death as 16 May 1917. He came from Highgate in north London where his family owned and ran a sizeable wallpaper factory just down the hill from Highgate village, near Kentish Town. The business was built up by Norman Shand-Kydd whose son, Peter, married the Honourable Frances Shand-Kydd, née Roche, daughter of the 4th Baron Fermoy. She was the mother of the late Diana Spencer, Princess of Wales, by virtue of her previous marriage to Viscount Althorp, later the 8th Earl Spencer and, of course, Diana's father. (Plot II.E.9)

Gunner Robert Henry OXTOBY DCM, 'B' Battery, 162 Brigade, Royal Field Artillery, was killed in action on 16 May 1917, aged 20. The citation for his DCM is a short one, stating only that he had shown great courage and determination as a cyclist orderly, maintaining contact between his battery's position and the wagon lines. His award was gazetted on 13 February 1917. (Plot II.E.11)

Feuchy Chapel British Cemetery, Wancourt

In terms of its location, this cemetery is very easy to find. It lies on the south side of the D.939, the main Arras–Cambrai road, about three miles east of Arras. Nearby is the 12th (Eastern) Division Memorial.

The vast majority of casualties in this cemetery, approximately 80 per cent, are from 1917; the remainder are from the following year. Seventy-two of the 525 identified burials here are from 9 April, most notably from battalions belonging to the 12th (Eastern) Division, such as the 9th Essex Regiment, the 6th Queen's Own (Royal West Kent Regiment) and the 8th and 9th Royal Fusiliers. These can be found in Plots II and III.

Private Herbert SWAN, 9th Essex Regiment, was killed in action on 9 April 1917, the same day as his elder brother, Private William Swan. William was five years older than Herbert and died serving with the 2nd Essex Regiment, aged 24. The two units were in action that day on either side of the River Scarpe, little more than three miles from each other. Herbert is buried in this cemetery along with thirteen others of his battalion, all of whom were killed in action on the opening day of the Battle of Arras (Plot I.A.22). His brother William is buried in Fampoux British Cemetery on the other side of the river.

Plot I, Row, C contains eleven riflemen from the 20th King's Royal Rifle Corps (British Empire League Pioneers). All of them are buried in sequence in Graves 27 to 37. The 20th Battalion was raised in September 1915 and went to France in March 1916 in time to play its part in the Battle of the Somme as pioneers to the 3rd Division. On 4 July 1916 it moved from Poperinghe to Carnoy where it was employed on road construction and bridging.

Another officer with interesting family connections is Second Lieutenant Cecil Alberic Hardy WARRE, 88th Battalion, Machine Gun Company, who was killed in action on 24 April 1917. His mother lived in Brazil and was a member of the Warre family, the oldest British-owned shippers of port. The company was established in 1729 when William Warre became a senior partner in the business. The family held sole ownership of the company until 1912. Lieutenant General William Warre served with Wellington during the Peninsular War and is reputed to have supplied him with port for his table. (Plot I.C.39)

As the battle developed throughout April and into May 1917, the area either side of the main road near Feuchy Chapel became one of the main routes leading up to Monchy-le-Preux and the new sections of recently captured front line. As such it was subjected to frequent and heavy shell fire, which often resulted in casualties. The 2nd Suffolk Regiment took over defences around Monchy-le-Preux on 4 May and was relieved on 14 May 1917. Twenty-two of its casualties from that tour of duty can be found here in Plot I, Rows D to F, a good example of the routine attrition very often associated holding trenches on any given day.

Plot I contains the graves of two airmen killed in action on 23 April 1917. Second Lieutenant Arthur RALPHS, 12 Squadron, Royal Flying Corps, who previously served with the 12th King's (Liverpool Regiment) and the Royal Field Artillery, was an engineer in civilian life. He was 23 years old when he died (Plot I.D.31). Nearby is his observer, Second Lieutenant Lewes Woodham MOTT, who formerly served with the 9th Essex Regiment (Plot I.D.35). Both men were killed when their BE2e aircraft came down during a spotting mission on behalf of the artillery. They were not shot down by any enemy machine, but may have been hit by ground fire, although some malfunction may have been responsible, such as engine failure.

Captain Mortimer Frederick HAYES, 8th East Yorkshire Regiment, had enlisted at the outbreak of war, originally serving with the 28th (County of London) Battalion, London Regiment (Artists' Rifles), before receiving his commission. He was killed by a shell on 29 April 1917, aged 26, while his battalion was holding the area around Fosse Farm, on the Arras–Cambrai Road, which had formed part of the Feuchy Line prior to capture. His date of death in *Officers Died in the Great War* is recorded as 10 July 1916, but this is clearly an error, as his battalion was on the Somme near Caterpillar Valley around that time and was preparing to move up for the attack that would take place on 14 July between Bazentin-le-Grand and Longueval. (Plot I.D.40)

Captain Alexander BOTHWELL MC, 1st Gordon Highlanders, was mortally wounded on 26 April 1917 when a shell burst next to him, killing Second Lieutenant Louis Francis Huntly, whose body took the full blast and whose remains have never been identified. BOTHWELL's body, however, remained intact. He was born in West Ham and had previously served with the 1/14th Battalion, London Regiment (London Scottish). He had also been wounded twice previously. One of those occasions was connected to the award of his MC, which was gazetted on 18 May 1916. When his company commander was killed during a very heavy bombardment, he took command and greatly distinguished himself by his coolness and bravery, thereby saving the situation at a critical time. Despite being wounded the next morning, he remained in command of the company. The battalion war diary comments on the shelling, pointing out that the Battalion HQ had to be moved to one occupied by three other battalions of the 3rd Division. Sniping was also a huge hazard around this time; on 29 April it accounted for five of BOTHWELL's men. (Plot I.E.23)

Next to BOTHWELL is the grave of Second Lieutenant David Lyon SCOTT, 4th Gordon Highlanders, attached 8/10th Battalion, who was killed in action on 9 April 1917, aged 23. He had enlisted in September 1914 and eventually in February the following year he went to the front. In June 1915 he suffered shell shock, but was back in action in September that year at Hooge, where he was again wounded. (Plot I.E.22)

Second Lieutenant George Harry PRIDMORE, 21st West Yorkshire Regiment, was killed in action on 31 August 1918, though at the time of his death he was attached to the 1st Essex Regiment (Plot I.F.10). Three of his brothers died during the war. Private John Thomas Pridmore, 2nd King's Own Yorkshire Light Infantry, was killed on 14 October 1914 and Serjeant Arthur Edward Pridmore, who served in the same battalion, was killed four days later on 18 October. Both men are now commemorated on the Le Touret Memorial. Private Albert Pridmore, 1/4th York & Lancaster Regiment, died on 22 June 1917 and is buried in Sheffield where the family lived.

The CWGC records show one 1916 casualty buried here, Private Alven Edward DENNING, 28th Battalion, Canadian Infantry, who died on 26 August 1916

(Plot I.G.3). I have considerable doubts as to whether this date of death is accurate. At the time of his supposed death his battalion was in Belgium. However, on 26 August 1918 the battalion was in the Arras area. It had sustained a few casualties on the 23rd while occupying trenches on Telegraph Hill. Shortly afterwards it moved to Blairville, south of Arras, and behind our front line. I believe that the correct year of death should therefore be taken as 1918.

Lieutenant Leonard Patrick VERNON MC, 10th Royal Welsh Fusiliers, was killed in action on 18 June 1917. He was gazetted on 1 July 1916 as a temporary second lieutenant with the Royal Welsh Fusiliers when he was transferred from a reserve battalion to the front. There is no reference here to his MC. However, he is referred to again in Gazettes on 9 January 1917 with regard to his appointment as a temporary lieutenant and this entry shows the award of the MC against his name. I believe his MC may have gazetted in the New Year's Honours List in 1917. The regimental history and *Officers Died in the Great War* both acknowledge the award of the MC. (Plot I.G.15)

Captain Richard Alfred COPPIN, 'B' Company, 6th Queen's (Royal West Surrey Regiment), was killed in action on 12 April 1917, aged 19, together with six other ranks from his battalion, though none are buried in this cemetery with him. (Plot I.G.36)

There are a handful of cavalrymen buried here, not surprisingly from 11 April 1917. There is Trumpeter Arthur Henry William STOWELL, 'B' Squadron, Essex Yeomanry (Plot II.A.1), two privates from the 1st (Royal) Dragoons in Plot II, Row E and B, as well as four men of the 1st North Somerset Yeomanry in Plot III, Row D, two of whom are commemorated by way of special memorials. Both men are known to be buried nearby, but their bodies could not be located after the war when the current cemetery was being constructed.

Captain Arthur Clive KEEN, 1/7th Middlesex Regiment, remained behind at the start of the war to take up the post of adjutant to the 2/7th Middlesex Regiment and to assist with its training at their depot in Hornsey, north London. He then transferred to the 16th Middlesex Regiment and served with it in France. A couple of days before his death he visited his old battalion in the trenches at Tilloy-lès-Mofflaines and was intending to seek a transfer back to it. While he was there he took out a working party and was killed as he was supervising it on 10 May 1917. Plot II.D.11)

Regimental Serjeant Major John Alexander MUNRO MC, 7/8th King's Own Scottish Borderers, was killed in action on 12 April 1917, aged 24. His MC was awarded posthumously for actions on 9 April, three days before his death, which included the rescue of Private James Byers Morrison, who unfortunately died that day. Morrison is commemorated on the Arras Memorial. After carrying out this act of gallantry, MUNRO was mortally wounded as he was returning to Battalion HQ. The citation makes no mention of the rescue, but refers to his supervision of carrying parties, his reorganization of the line after the advance had been held up, and his setting up ammunition dumps while under shell and machine-gun fire. The award was gazetted on 20 July 1917. He was promoted on the Somme during the winter of 1916 where he served as a company serjeant major. When his battalion returned to this part of the Arras battlefield in 1918 his comrades noticed that his grave was still there, clearly identifiable, intact and undamaged. (Plot II.G.18)

Second Lieutenant George Allsop ADAMS, 7th East Surrey Regiment, was killed during his battalion's advance to the Black Line on 9 April 1917, aged 19. He was originally posted missing in action, according to the battalion war diary, but his body was subsequently recovered. It goes on to record that all local objectives had been taken that day with the exception of the redoubt at Feuchy Chapel, which fell the next morning. (Plot II.H.13)

Private James MacMILLAN, 'C' Company, 13th Royal Scots, was killed in action on 28 March 1918, aged 32 (Plot III.A.20). He was the eldest of three sons who were killed during the war. Private Gavin MacMillan, now commemorated on the Menin Gate, was killed in action at Ypres on 10 May 1915, aged 24, serving with the 1/9th Argyll & Sutherland Highlanders. The other brother, Private John Murchie MacMillan, was killed in action on 11 April 1918 with the 1st King's Own Scottish Borderers and is commemorated on the Ploegsteert Memorial.

Second Lieutenant Cyril John PILE, 12 Squadron, Royal Flying Corps, died of wounds when his machine broke up in aerial combat on 29 April 1917 (Plot III.C.19). He was the son of Sir Thomas Devereux Pile, 1st Baronet, of Kenilworth House, Willesden, London, who had served as High Sheriff of Dublin in 1898 and as Mayor of Dublin in 1900. Another son, Frederick Alfred Pile, also served during the war and was present during the Retreat from Mons. He later became a staff captain with the 1st Division, a brigade major with the 40th Division in 1916, and towards the end of the war, a general staff officer with XXII Corps in France. He was awarded both the DSO and the MC and inherited his father's baronetcy. He held various posts after the war, firstly with the Royal Tank Corps, then as Assistant Director of Mechanisation at the War Office in 1928. During the Second World War he was in charge of Anti-Aircraft Command and was responsible for air defences over the United Kingdom. He was also awarded a GCB in recognition of a lifetime of service to his country.

Second Lieutenant Duncan Hinshelwood STEWART, 'C' Company, 9th Argyll & Sutherland Highlanders, attached 11th Battalion, was killed in action on 20 April 1918. His battalion carried out a raid that morning to recover ground that the 15th (Scottish) Division had been forced to abandon during the final few days of March three weeks earlier. Some ground was retaken, including a German position known as 'Q' Gun Pit. Around mid-morning the enemy counter-attacked from the direction of Pelves Lane and advanced on several of these newly captured positions. STEWART, whose platoon had been responsible for 'Q' Pit, reported that the position had been lost and was later tasked with its recovery. The gap in the wire leading to the position was under heavy artillery fire and STEWART was killed during the renewed attack. (Plot III.G.7)

Second Lieutenant Thomas William RICHARDSON MC DCM, 32 Brigade, Royal Field Artillery, was killed in action on 28 March 1918, aged 28. He won his DCM, gazetted on 17 December 1914, while serving as a corporal with 16th Battery, Royal

Field Artillery. The citation states that he was continually employed on the hazardous work of laying and repairing telephone wires in exposed places and goes on to state that his gallant work materially assisted his battery. At the time of his death his unit was part of the 4th Division's artillery. His MC was gazetted on 18 January 1918 and the citation appeared on 25 April after his death. It was awarded for conspicuous gallantry and devotion to duty while in command of his section under heavy fire during an attack. When two ammunition dumps were set on fire, he personally extinguished them, thereby saving much ammunition and potentially lives as well. (Plot III.G.19)

Captain Roy Granville Kyrle MONEY, 3rd East Kent Regiment (The Buffs), attached 6th Battalion, was killed in action on the opening day of the Battle of Arras (Plot III.I.6). He was one of three brothers who fell during the war. Serjeant Sydney Aubrey Kyrle Money, 1st Honourable Artillery Company, was killed in action at Hooge on 16 June 1915 and is commemorated on the Menin Gate. The other brother, Second Lieutenant Gerald Hugh Kyrle Money, 18th Durham Light Infantry, was just 19 years old when he was killed in action on 27 July 1916. He is buried at St. Vaast Post Military Cemetery, Richebourg l'Avoué. The boys came from Walthamstow, east London.

Captain Frederick Williamson SPRANG, 'D' Company, 6th Dorsetshire Regiment, was killed in action on 12 April 1917, aged 25 (Plot IV.C.14). The battalion had only recently taken over trenches from units of 44 Brigade on the night of 11/12 April and had spent the previous afternoon watching the bombardment on the other side of the Scarpe in preparation for the 9th (Scottish) Division's attack on Greenland Hill and Roeux. A quarter of an hour before that attack, SPRANG and fellow company commanders were informed that the 6th Dorsetshire Regiment had been ordered to attack Rifle and Bayonet trenches, their objective being the Pelves–Monchy road. When the battalion made its attack it came under heavy fire.

Two fellow officers, Second Lieutenants Leslie Harrie SHAVE, aged 19, and Lionel Theodore LEMON, were killed with SPRANG during that attack and are commemorated here by special memorials A.5 and A.6. A fourth, Second Lieutenant Eric George Goodman, is commemorated on the Arras Memorial. Goodman was last seen on the skyline waving his men on with his walking stick as he advanced with Serjeant John Briers, who is also commemorated with him on the memorial. Four other officers from this battalion were wounded that day. Total casualties for other ranks came to eighty-four.

The 6th Dorsetshire Regiment was in action again on 23 April. Several casualties from that attack are to be found in this cemetery, including Second Lieutenant Francis Reginald PALMER, aged 23, who is commemorated by special memorial B.7, and Second Lieutenant John Lancelot TILLOTSON, aged 19, who had also been mentioned in despatches (Plot V.A.15). Four other officers from the battalion were wounded in the operations that day and total casualties among the other ranks came to 104, though only four of the dead are buried or commemorated here.

Private Alexander F. CRUICKSHANKS MM, 7th King's Own Scottish Borderers, attached 46th Trench Mortar Battery, also held the *Croix de Guerre* (France) and was killed in action on 6 March 1918 (Plot V.H.3). Around half of the casualties here from February, March and April that year belong to the 15th (Scottish) Division, including Lieutenant John MORRISON, Highland Cyclist Battalion, who was killed in action on 28 March 1918. (Plot II.I.20)

In total there are nine holders of the MM buried here, one of whom has already been referred to above. The remaining eight are listed below.

Serjeant Wilfred HOWARD MM, 'C' Battery, 63 Brigade, Royal Field Artillery, killed in action on 6 May 1917. (Plot I.A.20)

Company Serjeant Major Robert CRONE MM, 1st Border Regiment, killed in action on 14 April 1917, aged 28. (Plot I.B.35)

Gunner H. JAMES MM, 232 Brigade, Royal Field Artillery, killed in action on 27 April 1917 (Plot I.D.36). There appears to be no trace of this man in *Soldiers Died in the Great War*.

Driver Arthur POWELL MM, 71 Brigade Headquarters, Royal Field Artillery, killed in action on 28 March 1918. He shares a grave with another artilleryman, Gunner Thomas Henry CURTIS, 'C' Battery, 71 Brigade, Royal Field Artillery, almost certainly killed with him in the same incident, presumably as a result of shell fire. (Plot II.H.14)

Corporal Albert MILLHAM MM, 'D' Battery, 71 Brigade, Royal Field Artillery, killed in action on 24 April 1917. (Plot III.A.19)

Corporal Charles Walter KETLEY MM, 15th Division, Signal Company, Royal Engineers, killed in action on 11 April 1917. (Plot III.C.6)

Lance Corporal Alexander SIMPSON MM, 11th Argyll & Sutherland Highlanders, killed in action on 20 April 1917. (Plot III.G.10)

Private Charles REED MM, 9th Royal Fusiliers, killed in action on 3 May 1917. (Plot IV.B.14)

Windmill British Cemetery, Monchy-Le-Preux

Windmill British Cemetery sits on the north side of the main Arras–Cambrai road, the D.939, about 100 yards west of the junction with the D.33, the road that links Monchy-le-Preux with Wancourt to the south. It is about 4 miles east of Arras. The D.939 is extremely busy and carries fast moving traffic and heavy goods vehicles, so do be careful if parked up on the hard standing area between the cemetery and the main road, especially getting in or out of a vehicle.

This cemetery, begun by the 29th Division in May 1917, is almost evenly divided between 1917 and 1918 casualties. After the capture of Monchy-le-Preux on 11 April the British front line ran very close to the cemetery at right angles to the Arras–Cambrai road, the D.939. A hundred yards east of the cemetery is the D.33, which leads to Monchy. This road was known to the troops as Hussar Lane and a little further east is Dragoon Lane, now a track that arches back to meet up with Hussar Lane. On the other side of the road, the D.33 runs in the direction of Wancourt. Here it was known as Spears Lane. The location was vulnerable to shelling and machine-gun fire, particularly until Guémappe was captured on 23 April 1917.

Today the earliest casualties are from the 37th Division, killed on days of contrasting fortune. Whilst 10 April 1917 was a day of disappointment and little progress,

11 April, which culminated in the capture of Monchy-le-Preux, offered hope and heart to all involved, from those on the battlefield to everyone at General Allenby's HQ.

Of the seventeen casualties here from these two days, eleven are from the 10th Loyal North Lancashire Regiment. Though killed on the same day, 11 April, they are scattered throughout Plot I in Rows A, C and D. Among this group is Private James Frederick BARRETT, who was 21 years old when he died. He enlisted in Bristol in the Army Cyclist Corps (Plot I.C.23). His brother, Company Quartermaster Serjeant Walter Frank Barrett, was killed in action on 29 May 1918 while serving with the 41st Divisional Train, Army Service Corps. He is buried in Belgium at Dozinghem Military Cemetery.

Second Lieutenant William Kenneth Mackay SPENCE, 13th Royal Scots, was killed in action on 23 April 1917, aged 20. Originally from Aberdeen, his parents lived in Kensington, London (Plot I.C.20). He and men from his battalion began their attack from assembly trenches near to where Hussar Lane and Spears Lane meet the main Arras–Cambrai road, a point known as La Bergère. They immediately came under heavy rifle and machine-gun fire, especially from the south, causing 'B' and 'D' Companies to veer northwards and forcing the other two companies to fill the developing gap on the right. Germans in Dragoon Lane poured heavy fire onto the attackers and soon every officer involved in the attack was either killed or wounded leaving fewer than a hundred men unscathed. As the survivors retired they had to endure the same heavy fire.

SPENCE is one of fifteen officer casualties from his battalion that day, eleven of whom were killed or unaccounted for. Twenty-one other ranks were killed, with a further 169 wounded and seventy-one missing. Regimental sources describe the British barrage that preceded the attack as being 'more noisy than effective'. Dragoon Lane was captured by the supporting battalion, the 6/7th Royal Scots Fusiliers, whose men were able to creep unseen down a ditch that ran parallel to the main road and capture the position and its support trench. This, however, was only possible once it became obvious that its garrison had begun to run low on ammunition.

Private William ENTWISTLE DCM, 8th East Lancashire Regiment, won his DCM for gallantry with the 2nd Battalion on 12 March 1915 at Neuve Chapelle. The original recommendation was for the VC. Throughout the entire day he showed conspicuous gallantry and untiring zeal rescuing the wounded under heavy rifle and shell fire. On one occasion, as a stretcher-bearer, he saw a sapper lying badly injured under very heavy shell fire. He immediately left the cover of his trench to get to the man whom he found with one leg blown off. Still under heavy shelling, he managed to stop the haemorrhage long enough for the medical officer, Captain Craig, to arrive and apply a tourniquet. Between them they succeeded in carrying the wounded man back to the safety of a trench whereupon they amputated the man's leg and saved his life. The award was gazetted on 3 June 1915. ENTWISTLE was one of several men from his battalion who received gallantry awards in connection with their work and courage that day. He was killed in action on 11 April 1917, aged 23. (Plot I.D.20)

Private Percival Hugh LIONETT, 1st Royal Warwickshire Regiment, was killed in action on 1 November 1917 (Plot I.F.5). The CWGC register tells us that his brother also fell, but gives no further details. His brother was Lance Corporal Stanley Newton Lionett who, in fact, served in the same battalion as his brother. Stanley died of wounds earlier in the war on 28 April 1915 as a result of fighting at the Second Battle of Ypres and is now buried at Hazebrouck Communal Cemetery.

Second Lieutenant Frederick Holland VICAT, 3rd Duke of Wellington's Regiment, attached 2nd Battalion, was killed in action on 8 December 1917, aged 25 (Plot I.G.24). His brother, Lieutenant Horatio John Vicat, 1st Queen's Own (Royal West Kent Regiment), was killed in action on 13 September 1914 near the river crossing at Missy on the Aisne. *Officers Died in the Great War* shows his date of death as 18 September. He has no known grave and is commemorated on the La Ferté-sous-Jouarre Memorial.

Captain Dennis Arthur BALLARD, 1st King's Own (Royal Lancaster Regiment), was killed by sniper fire on 12 December 1917, aged 20, during a relatively quiet tour of duty in trenches near Monchy. He had also been wounded in the trenches with the 2nd Battalion at Loos, near 'Big Willie', between 2 and 6 October 1915 (Plot I.H.2). A week before his death, twelve other ranks were killed when gas entered their dug-out on 5 December and eleven of them are now buried here consecutively (Plots I.G.5 to 14). The CWGC records show nine of them dying on 4 December rather than the following day, suggesting that their deaths may have occurred late on the 4th and that the other two men died sometime after midnight and before they could be evacuated. Another discrepancy is the fact that the CWGC register shows one of the men, Private George EVANS (I.G.7), having the MM; the regimental history does not show him among those awarded gallantry medals during the war, nor does *Soldiers Died in the Great War*. However, his MM was gazetted on 18 June 1917 while serving with the King's Own (Royal Lancaster Regiment). He had also served as a private with the Lincolnshire Regiment.

Rifleman George Albert BURTENSHAW MM, 1st Rifle Brigade, was killed in action on 31 January 1918, aged 28, whilst holding trenches east of Monchy-le-Preux. The regimental history describes him as one of 'C' Company's *'famous pair of stretcher-bearers'*. His MM was gazetted on 17 December 1917. (Plot I.J.15)

Captain Archibald Edward VANDERPUMP MC, 52nd Battalion, Canadian Infantry, was killed in action on 27 August 1918. His MC was gazetted posthumously on 11 January 1919 and was awarded for conspicuous gallantry and initiative when his battalion was heavily counter-attacked. Under severe machine-gun and artillery fire, he steadied his men and then led them forward in support of the right flank. His men withstood and overcame the counter-attack, which was largely attributed to his coolness and initiative at that critical time. (Plot II.C.4)

Captain Geoffrey Grenside BOWEN MC, 'B' Company 2nd Lancashire Fusiliers, had been with his battalion from the start. On 21 October 1914 he was wounded while rescuing a wounded man during heavy fighting near Le Touquet. He led his company on 9 April 1917, and again on the 11th when they were in support of the 1st King's Own (Royal Lancaster Regiment) as the 4th Division attempted to advance the line towards Roeux and Greenland Hill. It was for his conspicuous leadership during these few days that he was awarded his MC, gazetted on 18 July 1917.

In July 1918 he trained a platoon from his company for a small, but daring daylight raid on some German posts located in shell holes among standing corn near Pécaut Farm, north of Hinges. In order to make the training as realistic as possible, he made his men practise creeping through cornfields, believing that attention to fine detail was the key to success. At 9.30am on 6 July twenty-six men carried out the raid successfully and returned with only one man slightly wounded. BOWEN's death occurred on 2 September 1918 during the attack on the Drocourt–Quéant Line; he was killed shortly after the attack had begun, leading his men forward. His loss was deeply mourned by his company, both officers and men, many of whom attended his funeral two days later. This fine officer was only 23 years old when he died. (Plot II.D.18)

Returning to the 1st King's Own (Royal Lancaster Regiment), there are nineteen of its men buried in Plot II, Rows D and E. All were killed on 2 September 1918 and what is striking is their age; many were 19 years old when they died, one was just 18, and very few were older than 25. This was typical of the composition of most British battalions in the summer and autumn of 1918 when many of the soldiers were young and fairly inexperienced. Success or failure often depended on a dwindling band of experienced officers and NCOs, survivors of previous operations.

In early September 1918 the British 4th Division was attached to the Canadian Corps, which on 2 September attacked the Drocourt-Quéant Line. Owing to casualties on previous days, the 4th Division was only able to contribute one brigade, 12 Brigade. The advance was uphill towards Étaing and Prospect Farm where the German defences consisted of a front and support line, each with two trenches. Whilst not as strong as the Hindenburg Line, the defences incorporated villages, farms and woods and were very reminiscent of those on the Somme in 1916.

For the 1st King's Own (Royal Lancaster Regiment) on the left, things did not go entirely to plan. Machine-gun fire took a heavy toll of officers and resistance from the support trenches was stronger than anticipated. Although tanks were allocated to the attack that day, none could be used on the front covered by the 1st King's Own owing to the marshy nature of the ground. Unable to advance further, the battalion made blocks in the enemy's trenches and waited while other units and tanks further north were able to work in behind the German defences. Initially, the tanks there had mistakenly advanced on Étaing Wood rather than the village, delaying support to the King's Own.

Overall, the operation that day proved successful and by the next day the German defences had been sufficiently compromised to force them to evacuate part of their line. On the afternoon of the 3rd, one company of the 1st King's Own attacked and captured Prospect Farm. The village of Étaing, however, with its well-placed machine guns, was able to hold out longer.

Rifleman Charles JEFFREY, 1/16th Battalion, London Regiment (Queen's Westminster Rifles), was killed in action on 17 September 1918, aged 24 (Plot II.E.22). His entry in the CWGC register refers to the fact that his father, Ernest Jeffrey, fell during the war, but further examination of the Commission's records fails to show any corresponding entry. Variations on spelling produce no match either.

Lieutenant Hubert Weeks DRIVER, 5 Squadron, Royal Air Force, was killed in action on 19 September 1918, aged 20, flying an RE8. His observer, Second Lieutenant H. Greenyer, was wounded when their aircraft came down. (Plot II.F.17)

Second Lieutenant Stuart White NEVILLE (Plot II.F.19) and Second Lieutenant Robert Deudney SIMMONS, 7th Battalion, London Regiment (Plot II.G.2), were killed within a couple of days of each other; NEVILLE on 21 September 1918 and SIMMONS on 23 September, aged 18. Both men had resided in South Africa before the war.

Major James Christian Lawrence YOUNG is shown somewhat confusingly in the CWGC register as serving with the Regimental Depot (Alberta) when he was killed in action on 13 October 1918. At the time of his death he was actually serving with the Canadian 1st Division Headquarters, to which he had been seconded. The register also notes that he was the son of a Lieutenant Colonel James Young, but gives no further details. (Plot II.H.17)

Lieutenant Robert Drummond McMILLAN MC, 2 Brigade, Canadian Field Artillery, was killed in action on 13 October 1918, aged 26. Canadian army records confirm the award of the MC, but I can find no trace of it in any of the Gazettes. (Plot II.J.1)

The remaining holders of the MM, not already referred to, are listed below:
    Corporal Frederick HALL MM, 'Y' 12th Trench Mortar Battery, Royal Garrison Artillery, killed in action on 16 September 1917, aged 23. (Plot I.E.9)
    Corporal Nelson SOANE MM, 6th Queen's Own (Royal West Kent Regiment), killed in action on 17 September 1917, aged 36. *Soldiers Died in the Great War* makes no reference to his MM. (Plot I.E.10)
    Lieutenant Harold SHACKLETON MM, 9th Battalion, Tank Corps, killed in action on 26 August 1918, aged 21. He was also mentioned in despatches. He is one of eight men from the 9th and 11th Battalions, Tank Corps, buried here who were killed in action on 26 or 27 August 1918. All are buried in Plot II, Rows B and C. (Plot II.B.11)
    Corporal Clifford Raymond KIRKLAND MM, 21st Battalion, Canadian Infantry, killed in action on 26 August 1918, aged 22. (Plot II.B.18)
    Sergeant Louis William CORRIS MM, 19th Battalion, Canadian Infantry, killed in action on 27 August 1918, aged 21. (Plot II.C.11)
    Gunner Samuel PROCTOR MM, 86th Battery, 32 Brigade, Royal Field Artillery, killed in action on 31 August 1918, aged 25. (Plot II.C.23)
    Serjeant Arthur Wesley CHAMBERS MM and Bar MSM, 11th Division Signal Company, Royal Engineers, killed in action on 2 September 1918. There is no reference to the bar in *Soldiers Died in the Great War*. (Plot II.C.30)
    Gunner Percy Clement HOPKINSON MM, 321st Siege Battery, Royal Garrison Artillery, killed in action on 3 September 1918, aged 35. (Plot II.D.8)
    Company Serjeant Major Charles Samuel TAYLOR MM, 1/2nd Battalion, London Regiment,(Royal Fusiliers), died of wounds on 17 September 1918. *Soldiers Died in the Great War* makes no mention of his MM. (Plot II.E.20)

Sapper Harry THURGOOD MM, 68th Field Company, Royal Engineers, died of wounds on 17 September 1918, aged 31. There is no reference to the MM in *Soldiers Died in the Great War*. (Plot II.F.10)

Bombardier Richard Ernest SNEAD MM, 195th Siege Battery, Royal Garrison Artillery, killed in action on 24 September 1918, aged 22. (Plot II.G.9)

Pelves Communal Cemetery

The village of Pelves is situated on the south bank of the River Scarpe about 6 miles east of Arras. The cemetery is on the south side of the village adjacent to the D.33E1, which leads out towards Monchy-le-Preux. The CWGC plot can be found in the north corner.

There are just three burials here, all of them privates of the 2nd Wiltshire Regiment who were killed in action during May 1940 close to the village, though one of the three, Private Ernest Douglas MUNDY, is shown as having died sometime between 22 May that year and 11 February 1941. This is not uncommon. The likelihood is that he was killed or died of wounds in May 1940, but his body may not have been found immediately. The latter of the two dates probably reflects this. (Grave 2)

Chapter Four

A Father and Son meet for the Last Time – 'Awly Magawly' and some Cavalrymen – We also fell on 1 July 1916

Wancourt British Cemetery

The cemetery sits on high ground to the east of the village of Wancourt. If approaching along the D.33 from the south, the cemetery can be seen easily on the sloping ground over to the right. This road runs along the eastern edge of the village. Where it intersects with the D.34 is where to turn off and head east along a small road, the Rue d'Alsace, away from the village. The cemetery lies at the end of this road.

The cemetery was begun by the 50th (Northumbrian) Division in April 1917 and a number of its units erected wooden crosses there as battalion memorials. This was not uncommon at the time, but they are now long gone. The position where the cemetery now stands was captured on 12 April 1917, but it fell back into German hands in late March 1918 before being retaken on 26 August that year by Canadian troops.

Not surprisingly, many graves were lost as a result of shelling, and today there are seventy-six special memorials commemorating men known or believed to be buried here. After the war the cemetery was enlarged by bringing in the dead from a number of other sites around the villages of Héninel, Hénin, Chérisy and Saint-Martin. Although there are 1,111 identified casualties, 43 per cent of the headstones in this cemetery are those of unidentified soldiers. The CWGC register notes that twenty men are now commemorated on a memorial next to the War Stone. These men were originally buried in Signal Trench Cemetery, but their graves were subsequently lost.

The initial phase of fighting between the opening of the Battle of Arras on 9 April and the capture of the position where the cemetery now stands, on 12 April, accounts for 167 of the identified burials. The period between 24 and 28 August 1918 accounts for 225 burials, substantially more than the 155 from a similar period of heavy fighting that took place in this locality between 23 and 28 April 1917.

Overall, there are just over 700 identified burials here from 1917 compared with a little over 400 from 1918. The CWGC register does show one casualty from 1915, but Private Alfred SYDENHAM, 7th East Kent Regiment (The Buffs), was killed in action on 3 May 1917, not 3 May 1915 as shown. (Plot V.A.24)

An observant visitor will notice that a number of the Northumberland Fusiliers' headstones carry the Tyneside Scottish and Tyneside Irish badges rather than that of the Northumberland Fusiliers. By contrast, the headstone of Second Lieutenant Andrew TATE, 24th/27th Northumberland Fusiliers (1/4th Tyneside Irish), who was killed in action on 20 January 1918, carries the badge of the Northumberland

Fusiliers rather than that of the Tyneside Irish, possibly because he was merely attached to the latter unit at the time of his death. (Plot I.D.30)

Similarly, there are a number of headstones elsewhere in this cemetery that bear the cap badge of the Queen's Edinburgh Rifles rather than that of the Royal Scots. This battalion was the 4th Royal Scots, the 1/4th Battalion being known as the 1st Queen's Edinburgh Rifles, the 2/4th Battalion as the 2nd Queen's Edinburgh Rifles.

Second Lieutenant Frederic Alan RANKIN is recorded as serving with the 1/5th Border Regiment, but he was killed in action on 23 April 1917 serving with 'D' Battalion, Machine Gun Corps (Heavy Branch), as was the man buried with him, Gunner James MILLER. Second Lieutenant RANKIN had previously served with the 10th (Scottish) Battalion The King's (Liverpool Regiment) and both men were killed when their tank received a direct hit. (Plot I.D.23)

Lieutenant Albert GITTINS MC, 5th King's Shropshire Light Infantry, is one of five holders of the MC buried here. He was commissioned in November 1915 and his award was gazetted the following year on 3 June in the King's Birthday Honours List. He was killed in action on 25 May 1917. (Plot I.E.4)

The cemetery also contains 217 Canadian troops who were killed in action or died of wounds between 26 August and 3 September 1918, a period that covers the combined operations against Monchy-le-Preux and Wancourt, as well as the subsequent attacks on the Drocourt–Quéant Line on 2 September. The majority of these burials are from the 2nd Canadian Division, the predominant dates being 27 and 28 August 1918. A further five Canadians are buried here who fell outside the above dates.

Private George Gibson FRENCH DCM, 27th Battalion, Canadian Infantry, was killed in action on 27 August 1918, aged 23. His DCM was gazetted on 28 March 1918 and was awarded for conspicuous gallantry and devotion to duty. When two hostile machine guns in a strongpoint opened fire, holding up the flank of his company, he immediately organized a party that successfully worked its way round to a flank and rushed the strongpoint from the rear capturing the two guns and a large amount of ammunition. The citation concludes by stating that his devotion to duty won the admiration of his comrades and that his resourcefulness and courage prevented what might otherwise have turned out to be a dangerous delay in the attack. (Plot III.A.6)

Captain Gordon Henry APPLEGATH MC, 19th Battalion, Canadian Infantry, was killed in action on 27 August 1918. His MC was gazetted on 4 February that year, the citation appearing some months later in early July. It was awarded for conspicuous gallantry while holding a front line that consisted of a number of detached posts. When the enemy counter-attacked in heavy numbers, his fearless example inspired his men to hold fast and repel the attack. He also took an active part in this action by bombing back the enemy. (Plot II.B.7)

Lieutenant Colonel Archibald Ernest Graham McKENZIE DSO and Bar, 26th Battalion, Canadian Infantry, was killed in action on 28 August 1918, aged 39. He studied Law at the University of New Brunswick, where in 1904 he gained a Master's degree, before moving on to London where he became a Bachelor in Civil Law at King's

College in 1907. He was adjutant of a militia unit in Canada when the war broke out and went on to command the 26th Battalion from 1916. His DSO was gazetted on 1 January 1917 and the bar posthumously on 11 January 1919. The bar was awarded for conspicuous skill in handling his battalion during the capture and consolidation of his objective, inspiring all ranks by his coolness and fine example. The citation goes on to state that the battalion's success in achieving its objective was due in large measure to his leadership and courage. He was also mentioned in despatches for his capable leadership (Plot II.C.9)

The 72nd Battalion, Canadian Infantry (Seaforth Highlanders), has sixty of its men buried here, including Major Arthur Vincent WOOD MC who was killed in action on 2 September 1918, aged 31. His MC was gazetted on 11 May 1917 and was awarded for conspicuous gallantry while in command of five offensive patrols, which he controlled with marked ability, setting a fine example to his men. Later in the operations he carried out a skilful withdrawal under the most difficult conditions. (Plot II.D.12)

When the 72nd Battalion was eventually relieved on 5 September it moved back to some trenches west of Triangle Wood. Rather than leave their dead on the battlefield to be collected by the divisional burial parties, the survivors, even though tired from their recent exertions, went out and gathered up all their fallen comrades and buried them here. Regimental records note that a funeral service was then held for the sixty men who had been laid to rest. To find virtually all the dead from a particular operation in one cemetery is a rare occurrence. After the Armistice, a small number of the battalion's missing were found and buried elsewhere.

Another gallantry award holder is Regimental Sergeant Major James HENNESSY MM, 24th Battalion, Canadian Infantry. He was mortally wounded near Chérisy on 27 August 1918, just before his battalion was about to carry out its attack. He was hit in the chest by shrapnel and died before he reached the dressing station. His MM, gazetted on 10 August 1916, was won on 22 May that year. Heavy shelling had destroyed the parapet of his trench in three places and had already caused eighteen casualties. Despite the shelling, he went to the assistance of the wounded and helped to dig out several men who had been buried. When a bomb store was also hit, many of the bombs began to explode, but with total disregard for his own safety, he passed by it in order to carry on dealing with the situation. (Plot III.B.1)

He is one of seventeen holders of the MM from Canadian units buried in this cemetery. One of those men was also awarded a bar to the medal: Sergeant David Brown BELL MM and Bar, 21st Battalion, Canadian Infantry, was killed in action the same day as HENNESSY. BELL, who enlisted in November 1914, worked in Canada as a crane operator before the war, though he originally came from Galashiels in Scotland. (Plot II.B.13)

A small number of cavalry casualties who fell during the first three days of the Battle of Arras are buried here, though not as many as at Tilloy British Cemetery. They are Private Harold BEADLE (Plot IV.B.3), Private Thomas Harry PIPKIN (Plot IV.D.2), Captain Montagu Locke YEATHERD (Plot IV.D.3) and Private William WALKER (Plot IV.D.6), all killed in action between 10 and 12 April 1917 whilst serving with the 12th (Prince of Wales's Royal) Lancers. Buried with them are Trumpeter Lancelot

George REED (Plot IV.D.5) and Private John Dennis ANDERSON (Plot IV.D.7), both of whom fell in action on 10 April with 2nd Dragoons (Royal Scots Greys).

Captain Wilfred Joseph BUNBURY, 4th Northumberland Fusiliers, is one of the many casualties here from the 50th (Northumbrian) Division and one of fifty-two Northumberland Fusiliers buried in this cemetery. Although shown as 4th Battalion, he was killed in action attached to the 6th Battalion. Before the war he had worked for a firm of stockbrokers, but on 4 August 1914, as war was declared, he joined the 4th Northumberland Fusiliers and immediately volunteered for service abroad. At the end of December that year he received his commission and went to France with his battalion on 20 April 1915, two days before the start of what became known as the Second Battle of Ypres. He was wounded there on 24 May 1915 and after recovering he was posted to Ireland, where he was retained as a physical training and bayonet instructor. He returned to the front in March 1917 and was killed leading his men in an attack on an enemy position on 15 April 1917, shot through the head as he reached his objective. His grave was subsequently lost and he is one of the seventy-six men commemorated here by way of special memorial. (Special Memorial 72)

The Durham Light Infantry is another regiment strongly represented within the cemetery with fifty-four burials. The 5th, 6th, 7th, 8th and 9th Battalions were part of the 50th (Northumbrian) Division and all of the regiment's casualties here, with the exception of four NCOs, are from one or other of these five battalions. The majority fell not during the Battle of Arras, but during the summer months of July and August 1917 while holding the line. The four exceptions, killed in action on 14 May 1917, are from the 10th Battalion which was part of the 14th (Light) Division.

Other regiments that also have a strong presence here are the Wiltshire Regiment, the East Yorkshire Regiment, the Yorkshire Regiment and the Manchester Regiment. The 2nd Wiltshire Regiment has thirty-seven identified casualties buried here, the majority of whom are to be found in either Plot V or Plot VI, all from 9 April 1917.

The Manchester Regiment has thirty-three officers and men buried here, all casualties from 2 April 1917 during the renewed attacks on the villages and outposts in front of the Hindenburg Line, or from the Battle of Arras itself, between 10 and 23 April.

The East Yorkshire Regiment has thirty-one men from the regiment's 1st and 4th Battalions, nine of whom are officers, including Captain Cyril EASTON MC, 4th East Yorkshire Regiment. One of the many outstanding memoirs to emerge from the Great War is *Grandfather's Adventures in the Great War 1914–1918* by Cecil Moorhouse Slack MC and Bar. He was a captain in the 1/4th East Yorkshire Regiment who, during the fighting at Arras in 1917, served as the battalion's adjutant. In a letter to his parents, written on 29 April 1917, he described his battalion's attack on the German positions east of the Wancourt Tower. Initially, the news had been positive, but by late morning it was becoming increasingly clear that the new position, unsupported on either flank, was very exposed and therefore vulnerable. The Germans took advantage of this and counter-attacked. During the fighting that day Slack lost several of his fellow officers of whom he speaks fondly in his narrative.

Second Lieutenant Harold OUGHTRED, 4th East Yorkshire Regiment, who had gained a Master's degree at Oxford before the war, was 39 years old when he was killed in action on 23 April 1917, along with Captain Cyril EASTON MC, aged 32, and Second Lieutenant Charles Cape BOYLE, aged 21. BOYLE was the only son of a widow. All three men were originally buried together on the battlefield near Wancourt in makeshift graves marked only by a rifle set into the ground. Later, when the battalion found itself back in the same sector, the commanding officer wanted crosses to be erected where their bodies lay and Slack was given the job.

Though the spot where the three men were buried was not within rifle range, it was in full view of the enemy's guns during daylight. Slack therefore went out at night with a small party and located the graves. He describes the terrible stench as the bodies were uncovered, and how he and the rest of the party had to wear gas masks. By uncovering the graves, Slack was able to recover some personal effects that were later cleaned up and sent back to the mens' relatives. As daylight began to break a shell fell near their location, indicating that the party had probably been spotted, and so, having completed their gruesome task, they made their way back.

EASTON had only been back with the battalion a month before he and the others were killed on 23 April 1917. BOYLE had also been one of nine officers invited to a dinner given by Slack to celebrate his engagement to his fiancée, an event that he covered in a letter dated 13 January 1917.

Today, all three men are commemorated within this cemetery, though sadly, they are now separated from each other. EASTON, whose MC was gazetted on 14 January 1917, is commemorated by special memorial 61, whilst BOYLE and OUGHTRED are buried in separate plots (Plot I.B.4) and (Plot V.C.39).

Before the outbreak of war the 2nd Lincolnshire Regiment was stationed in Bermuda. When war finally came, the island itself raised a force of eighty men, known as the Bermuda Volunteer Rifle Corps, hoping that it could serve as part of the 2nd Lincolnshire Regiment, thereby preserving the ties between the island and the battalion. Unfortunately, the best that the War Office could offer was to send the men to the regiment's 1st Battalion in order to make up a shortfall. They therefore went to the Western Front where they served with the 1st Lincolnshire Regiment. There are thirty-six men from the 1st Lincolnshire Regiment buried here, two of whom belonged to the Bermuda Volunteer Rifle Corps. Both were killed in action on 11 April and their regimental numbers are very close. The two are Serjeant Patrick Joseph FARRELL, aged 39 (Plot VI.G.3) and Private William Henry ARNOLD, aged 27 (Plot VII.B.32).

Much to its credit, Bermuda maintained its initial commitment to the imperial effort by keeping its contingent of eighty men up to strength throughout the war. According to the historian and author, Martin Middlebrook, 75 per cent of all those who served with the Bermuda Rifles became casualties. Forty of its members were killed or died of wounds during the war, fifteen of whom are buried or commemorated in France, with a further nine in Belgium. Of those fifteen in France, the only other man to be found in the Arras area is Lance Corporal Basil Louis Turini, who is commemorated by special memorial in Cojeul British Cemetery, Saint-Martin-sur-Cojeul. He was also killed in action on 11 April 1917.

The Highland Light Infantry has fifty-three officers and men buried here, all of whom were part of the 52nd (Lowland) Division, all killed in action between 24 and 28 August 1918. They are now buried in Plot VII, Rows C to H, though predominantly in Rows F and H.

Second Lieutenant Kenneth Alexander MACKINTOSH, 6th Highland Light Infantry, was killed in action on 24 August during the fighting for Hénin Hill (Plot VII.F.25), as was Second Lieutenant Elliott Douglas TURNER, 5th Battalion, who had enlisted in 1914 and who had also been wounded on the Somme. (Plot VII.F.18)

Two other Highland Light Infantry officers are buried in Row E: Lieutenant Robert John Alfred CUMMING, 7th Battalion, attached 6th Battalion (Plot VII.E.34) and Second Lieutenant Frederick George SMITH, 9th Battalion (Glasgow Highlanders), attached to 6th Battalion (Plot VII.E.37). Both were killed in action on 27 August, the latter while manning an observation post located at Summit Trench.

The 52nd (Lowland) Division was a relative newcomer to the Western Front, arriving in France between 12 and 17 April 1918. It had, however, fought at Gallipoli in 1915 before moving to Egypt in 1916. In 1917 and early 1918 it played a significant and distinguished part in operations in Palestine.

Major Henry Archer JOHNSTONE, 152 Brigade, Royal Field Artillery, was killed in action on 21 March 1918, aged 28 (Plot VIII.A.5). His younger brother, Second Lieutenant William McCall Johnstone, also served with the same unit, but was killed in action on 13 February 1916, aged 24. He is buried at Erquinghem-Lys Churchyard Extension. Another brother, Serjeant John Gordon Johnstone, also served, survived the war, but unfortunately died in 1922.

Plot VIII, Row A, contains the graves of five officers, all of them second lieutenants of the 1st East Yorkshire Regiment. Second Lieutenant Bernard COOKSON is shown as having died on 10 April 1917 (Plot VIII.A.6), whilst the other four were killed the previous day and are buried next to him (Plots VIII.A.7 to 10). The others are Second Lieutenant George HOLMES, who was 21 years old and was educated at King Edward VII School, Sheffield, followed by Magdalene College, Oxford; Second Lieutenant William Wesley GREEN, aged 25; Second Lieutenant Boswell Victor JALLAND; and finally, Second Lieutenant Ronald MacDonald MORRISON, aged just 19. The CWGC register shows JALLAND serving with the 3rd Battalion, but he was attached to the 1st Battalion.

The battalion did not advance until mid-afternoon on the opening day of the Battle of Arras and did not sustain any casualties while it was forming up. However, soon after its advance had started, it ran up against uncut German wire and Stokes mortars had to be brought up to create more gaps. Captain Daniel Pisa, the man who directed the fire of those Stokes mortars, was killed, aged 44, during this phase of the fighting. He has no known grave and is commemorated on the Arras Memorial where the CWGC register shows his surname as 'Piza'. The regimental history also claims that the 1st East Yorkshire Regiment was the only battalion to breach the Hindenburg Line on 9 April 1917.

The Yorkshire Regiment has thirty-one of its dead buried here, the majority of them killed in action on 23 April 1917 with either the 4th or the 5th Battalion. Captain

Wilfrid VAUSE MC, 5th Yorkshire Regiment, was one of the men who fell on 23 April. His MC, gazetted on 25 November 1916, was won whilst serving as a lieutenant and was awarded for conspicuous gallantry in action leading his company courageously and with initiative as it entered the enemy trenches. Under his leadership it then held its position against counter-attacks, and later on he organized a bombing attack that contributed to the final success of the operations. (Plot VIII.E.4)

There are also five men from the Household Battalion buried here, three of whom are shown as privates in the CWGC records, but two still show their appropriate cavalry ranks: Trooper Robert WATSON, formerly Ayrshire Yeomanry, was killed in action on 9 May 1917 (Plot VIII.F.9). Squadron Corporal Major William S.G. MARRIAGE, formerly 1st Life Guards, died of wounds on 22 August 1917 (Plot VIII.F.11). All five men are buried next to or near to each other in Plot VIII, Row F.

Of the thirty-seven holders of the MM buried here, a couple have already been referred to. Among this group is another man with a bar to his medal: Corporal James RICHARDSON MM and Bar, 6th Seaforth Highlanders. He was killed in action on 19 October 1917, aged 24. (Plot I.B.56)

Two others may be of interest; one an older man, the other an officer. Company Quartermaster Serjeant Arthur Newton DICKINSON, MM, 6th King's Own Yorkshire Light Infantry, was killed in action on 8 May 1917, aged 46 (Plot I.C.3). Second Lieutenant Robert Dickson WILLS MM, 5th Border Regiment, was killed in action on 23 April 1917. In civilian life he had worked in the Architects' Department of the London County Council. He had clearly been commissioned from the ranks (Plot V.C.30).

Wancourt Communal Cemetery
The cemetery can be found on the D.34, about 1,000 yards west of the church on the road leading out of the village towards Neuville-Vitasse. There are three identified burials in this cemetery, all from 1940, out of a total of six. The first of these is Flying Officer (Pilot) John William GRAAFSTRA, 242 Squadron, Royal Air Force, who was killed on 23 May 1940 when his Hawker Hurricane Mark I was shot down by enemy aircraft. He came from Canada and was 27 years old when he died (Grave 2). Graves 6 and 7 are those of Private Alfred McCONOCHIE, 10th Durham Light Infantry, and Private James William RIGBY, 11th Durham Light Infantry, who, at the age of 21, was two years younger than his comrade. Both died on 20 May 1940 when they were machine gunned coming out of a café in Wancourt by a German combination motor cycle.

Tilloy British Cemetery, Tilloy-lès-Mofflaines
The cemetery is located on the south-east side of the village of Tilloy-lès-Mofflaines on the north side of the D.37E next to a wooded area. The larger wood about 250 yards north-east of the cemetery is the Bois des Boeufs, which is often referred to in narratives covering this part of the front on the opening day of the Battle of Arras.

This cemetery, with its total of 1,031 identified burials, is mainly composed of officers and men from British fighting units. There are, however, some soldiers from several parts of the Commonwealth. This is not an obvious location to find Australian soldiers, but there are twenty-two, most of whom are in Plot V. All twenty-two casualties are from the first six weeks of the Battle of Arras in 1917. The prominent date on their headstones is 11 April and all those who were killed or died of wounds that day are from the 4th Australian Division and the First Battle of Bullecourt, which took place south of this location. The few Australian casualties from the early part of May are from a more mixed group belonging to the 1st, 2nd and 5th Australian Divisions.

There are also some men of the South African Brigade buried here, though not many. They are all men of the South African Heavy Artillery, and all died during the latter part of April 1917, with the exception of one man, Gunner Charles FURNESS, 72nd Battery, South African Heavy Artillery, who was killed on 31 August 1918. (Plot II.C.1)

There is just one New Zealander: Private John Brown SMITH, 1st Battalion, Auckland Regiment, whose date of death is shown as 23 April 1917 (Plot IV.C.4). The cemetery register points out that he was one of a number of men whose bodies were brought here when Maison Rouge British Cemetery was closed. That cemetery was situated not very far from here in the village of Tilloy-lès-Mofflaines. Even so, his presence here seems very out of place, as the New Zealand Division was near Messines, not at Arras, when he died.

The largest group of Commonwealth troops buried here, as one might expect, are men of the Canadian Expeditionary Force, though they make up only a small proportion of the cemetery; there are just fifty-one. Only two of them are 1917 casualties, the remainder are from the following year and can be found predominantly in Plot II, Rows A and B.

Captain Daniel Edward BRADBY, 'B' Company, 9th Rifle Brigade, was killed on 9 April 1917, aged 20 (Plot I.BB.12). He was the man responsible for raising the battalion's fine Rugby XV, which had won all of its matches to date with the exception of one which had ended in a draw. Many of the team were from public schools, such as Uppingham, Marlborough, Christ's Hospital, Haileybury and Cheltenham, and a number had also attended Oxford or Cambridge. BRADBY himself was educated at Rugby School. The remainder of the team was made up of other ranks, mostly Northern Union players.

BRADBY was shot through the heart as he and his men tried to rush some machine guns within a triangular-shaped redoubt that lay at the junction of 8 and 43 Brigades. The machine guns were subsequently dealt with by Captain Joseph Michael Buckley and eight men from 'D' Company, though they were also assisted by the timely arrival of some men of 8 Brigade who had managed to approach the redoubt from the north. Sixty prisoners and two machine guns were captured from the position. Buckley was awarded the MC for this exploit, but was killed later that year on 22 December 1917 near the dressing station at Waterloo Farm, north-east of Gravenstafel, in the Ypres Salient. He is buried in White House Cemetery.

Second Lieutenant Arnold WYNNE, 'B' Company, 13th King's (Liverpool Regiment), was killed in action by a shell while in the assembly trenches waiting to advance on 9 April 1917, aged 37. The CWGC register notes that he was a lecturer at the University of Cape Town. *Officers Died in the Great War* records his death as occurring on

8 April. This minor discrepancy can easily be accounted for. From the initial safety of the Crinchon Sewer and Auckland Cave the battalion had made its way to the assembly trenches late on the evening of the 8th, completing the move by 3.40am on the 9th. (Plot I.C.3)

Lance Corporal Frederick SOUCH, 7th Royal Sussex Regiment, died of wounds on 10 August 1917, aged 35, and is one of several men buried here who had served in the South African campaign (Plot I.J.12). Corporal Henry Wellesley GRATTAN, 'C' Company, 1st Royal Scots Fusiliers, killed in action on 10 April 1917, aged 36, was another veteran of that campaign (Plot IV.E.21); Gunner James Campbell BALLAN-TYNE, 31st Siege Battery, Royal Garrison Artillery, also saw action there. He had previously served with the Argyll & Sutherland Highlanders and had twenty years army service. He was killed in action on 21 May 1917, aged 36. (Plot I.C.5)

Captain John Cook BANKS MC, 20th King's Royal Rifle Corps, was killed in action on 2 May 1917, though *Officers Died in the Great War* shows his date of death as 1 May. His MC was gazetted on 1 January 1917 in the New Year's Honours List. The *King's Royal Rifle Corps Chronicle* for 1917 makes no reference to him in the obituary section and the section covering the 20th Battalion merely states that after 23 April it was in trenches south of Tilloy, where the companies were divided between 76 Brigade and 8 Brigade. The 20th Battalion was the pioneer battalion attached to the 3rd Division. BANKS is referred to in the *Chronicle* for 1916 where it notes that he and another officer had done particularly fine work when the battalion was in the Loos area in September that year. Regimental records show his death occurring on 1 May rather than 2 May 1917. (Plot I.C.10)

Major James Donaldson Dulnay BRANCKER DSO, 116th Siege Battery, Royal Garrison Artillery, was killed in action on 1 May 1917, aged 39. His DSO was gazetted on 4 June 1917 in the King's Birthday Honours List in connection with services in the field. (Plot I.D.23)

Major Wilfrid Frank ROGERS DSO, 45th Battery, Royal Field Artillery, part of the 3rd Divisional Artillery, was killed in action on 19 May 1917, aged 26. He was commissioned in the Royal Artillery in July 1912. His award was gazetted on 4 June 1917 and was awarded for distinguished service in the field. (Plot I.F.2)

Second Lieutenant James Eric PARKES, 69th Field Company, Royal Engineers, was killed in action on 20 July 1917, aged 21. The CWGC register notes that he was a prize cadet at the Royal Military Academy, Woolwich. (Plot I.J.6)

Private Harry EDGINGTON DCM, 7th East Surrey Regiment, was killed in action on 21 September 1917, just four days after his award had been gazetted (Plot I.J.24). Along with two other men, he had held a block in one of our trenches against a strong party of the enemy at a most critical moment after the advanced posts had been captured. He subsequently positioned himself and his comrades in shell holes from where they caused heavy casualties when the enemy renewed their attack on the position, forcing them back into cover. By their exceptional gallantry and initiative, EDGINGTON and the other two men were able to retrieve an awkward situation and prevent further progress by the enemy. The action took place on the night of

11 July 1917 near Long Trench, just east of Monchy-le-Preux; EDGINGTON's citation appeared in the *London Gazette* on 17 September 1917.

Private West was the man who assisted EDGINGTON to erect the block while Private Mapston covered them. Mapston received the MM for his part in the action, which was also gazetted at the same time as EDGINGTON's award, though there is no mention of any recognition for Private West. Mapston went on to win a DCM in 1918 in connection with operations around Bousies on 23/24 October. It was gazetted on 12 March 1919 and the citation for it, which is quite lengthy, appeared on 2 December 1919. During that action he was wounded three times in the leg.

Second Lieutenant Cecil Fred ROWLAND, 231st Siege Battery, Royal Garrison Artillery, was killed in action on 21 March 1918, aged 35. The CWGC register informs us that he was organist at St Mary's Church, Stafford, and also deputy organist at Gloucester Cathedral. (Plot II.A.18)

Private Albert Roy FENWICK DCM, 21st Battalion, Canadian Infantry, was killed in action on 26 August 1918. When all but one of his Lewis gun crew had become casualties, he pressed forward and put three successive enemy machine guns out of action. He then followed this up by capturing four more machine guns, one officer and twelve men. The destruction of these posts enabled his platoon to go forward without delay. The award was gazetted on 15 November 1918. (Plot II.B.5)

Lieutenant Arthur Egbert BELL, 2nd Battalion, Canadian Machine Gun Corps, is shown as having died on 26 August 1918. He died of wounds on the battlefield just a few miles from here, somewhere between Sun Quarry and Upton Wood, where he and his battalion had been in action that day. His battery, 'L' Battery, had been held up by enemy machine guns and strong resistance, but these enemy positions were eventually dealt with. BELL had been responsible for rushing one of the machine-gun posts and capturing its crew. Despite being severely wounded prior to this act of bravery, he had insisted on remaining with his men, a decision which may have cost him his life. Prior to the war BELL had been a school teacher. (Plot II.B.19)

In the two days of fighting that followed, his unit lost several more officers and men, a number of whom are now buried in Quebec Cemetery. The Canadian Machine Gun Corps had fifty-six officers and men killed between 26 and 28 August 1918 as it provided vital support to the infantry attacks.

Captain Stanley Lavell CUNNINGHAM MC, 21st Battalion, Canadian Infantry, was killed in action on 27 August 1918, aged 35. He died in a motor car while travelling up the Arras–Cambrai road. He had just left 3rd Canadian Divisional HQ and was trying to ascertain the position of troops when a shell burst next to the car. He had initially enlisted as a private in 1914 and was a civil engineer by profession. In Canada, he and his brother, J.E. Cunningham, had their own company, 'The Cunningham Land Company'. The local newspaper in Red Deer where he lived reported on 11 September 1918 that he had won the DSO, but although he had been recommended for the DSO, he was actually awarded the MC instead, which was gazetted on 2 January 1918 in the New Year's Honours List (Plot II.B.32). His other brother, A.B. Cunningham, served during the war as a colonel.

Gunner George SHOEBRIDGE, 239th Siege Battery, Royal Garrison Artillery, was killed in action on 29 August 1918, aged 23 (Plot II.B.38). His brother, Private Lionel Shoebridge, who is buried at Guillemont Road Cemetery on the Somme, was killed in action two days earlier on 27 August 1918, aged 18, serving with the 2/2nd Battalion, London Regiment (Royal Fusiliers).

Rifleman Michael John PRICE MC, 9th King's Royal Rifle Corps, was killed in action on 9 April 1917. *Soldiers Died in the Great War* makes no reference to the award of the MC, which in any case would not have been awarded to an ordinary ranking soldier. Occasionally, an officer or warrant officer, to whom the MC could be awarded, did choose to relinquish his commission in order to serve in the ranks. In such cases, the award would still be shown on record. There is also no reference to the award in any of the *Chronicles* of the King's Royal Rifle Corps. (Plot II.H.9)

There is an interesting note in the CWGC register relating to the determination of a young Londoner, Private James STEDMAN, 'C' Company, 6th Duke of Cornwall's Light Infantry, who was killed in action on 10 April 1917, aged just 17. He had originally served for six months with the 7th Norfolk Regiment, but was then discharged when it was discovered that he had enlisted under age. He was clearly set on serving his country as a soldier, re-enlisting at Holborn in central London, and he was still under age when he was killed. He was born in Canning Town, on the edge of London's East End, but resided in Clerkenwell, a short distance from Holborn (Plot III.E.19). STEDMAN and another soldier, Private Ernest William BALDRY, 7th Suffolk Regiment, who was also aged 17, are the youngest burials in this cemetery. BALDRY fell sometime between 9 and 10 April 1917 (Plot II.H.15).

Somewhat scattered amongst the rows are several officers of the 8th East Yorkshire Regiment who were killed in action on 9 April 1917. The youngest, Second Lieutenant John McIntyre TYRRELL, was killed by a sniper not far from the German defences known as 'The Harp'. He was 19 years of age when he died. (Plot II.H.28)

As the afternoon drew to a close, the battalion had still not reached its objective, the Brown Line. It made a further attempt, but heavy machine-gun fire from the direction of Feuchy only caused further casualties. Second Lieutenant Frederick Harold PRINCE, aged 20 (Plot I.A.26), and Second Lieutenant William HOYLE, aged 25 (Plot I.B.23), were both killed that afternoon. Company Serjeant Major Samuel APPLEBY, who was killed as his company was making its way through the Bois des Boeufs, is buried a few yards from Second Lieutenant PRINCE (Plot I.A.30). TYRELL's middle name is shown as 'McIntosh' rather than 'McIntyre' in *Officers Died in the Great War*. Another discrepancy is the date of APPLEBY's death, which is shown in *Soldiers Died in the Great War* as 13 April, though the regimental sources are more likely to be correct.

Lieutenant Philip Howson Guy PYE-SMITH, 11th King's (Liverpool Regiment), was killed in action on 15 May 1917, aged 21. His father, Philip Henry Pye-Smith MD FRCS, had served as Vice-Chancellor of the University of London between 1903 and 1905 and was a distinguished physician who practised at Guy's Hospital in London where he specialized in skin diseases. Philip was his only son. (III.E.1)

He was related to Lieutenant Colonel Charles Derwent Pye-Smith DSO and Bar MC, Royal Army Medical Corps, who was also a Fellow of the Royal College of Surgeons and whose father was John William Pye-Smith, a former Mayor of Sheffield. Both DSO awards were for acts of gallantry, the first of which involved rescuing wounded men under heavy fire over a continuous period of sixty hours.

Captain Frederick WORTHINGTON, 10th Lincolnshire Regiment (Grimsby Chums), was killed in action on 28 April 1917 during the attack on Roeux when he and around twenty men from 'B' Company were cut off by a German patrol near the railway embankment. Most of his party were killed in the fight, but some were captured. WORTHINGTON had had a narrow escape earlier that month when the company HQ was blown in on 6 April. Fortunately, he and a fellow officer managed to crawl out via a small hole. He originally hailed from Salford in Lancashire, but had been working in the Town Clerk's office in Grimsby, hence his serving with the 10th Battalion. Survivors from the original Grimsby Chums often commented that the character of the battalion changed forever after the fighting in April 1917, by which time so many of the original Chums had already fallen. (Plot III.F.3)

Captain Harry PRIDE MC, 10th Middlesex Regiment, was killed in action on 23 April 1917, aged 23. His MC was gazetted posthumously in the King's Birthday Honours List on 4 June 1917. (Plot III.F.19)

Lieutenant Sidney Grant MARTIN, 13th Battery, 17 Brigade, Royal Field Artillery, was killed in action on 18 April 1917. The CWGC register notes that he had gained a Bachelor of Arts Degree in Classics from London University. (Plot IV.D.18)

Another man from the same unit, acting Bombardier Sidney John MAYO, who was killed in action a few days later on 22 April 1917, held the Serbian Gold Medal, but he is buried in a different plot. (Plot III.G.14)

Among the twenty-two holders of the MM buried here is an older man, Private Jesse HOLLOWAY MM, 5th Oxfordshire & Buckinghamshire Light Infantry. He was killed in action on 9 April 1917, aged 48. (Plot III.J.9)

Captain Albert Edward SIDWELL MC, 9th Royal Fusiliers, was killed in action on 7 July 1917, aged 28. His MC was gazetted on 20 July 1917, just after his death. It was awarded for conspicuous gallantry and devotion to duty whilst leading an attack against a highly organized strongpoint where he succeeded in overcoming the enemy and captured a large number of prisoners. He went on to clear another two lines of trenches, taking in total over a hundred prisoners, a trench mortar and a machine gun. (Plot III.J.14)

Private Andrew TURNER, 2nd Royal Scots, was killed in action on 10 April 1917, aged 26. The CWGC register notes that his widow lived at Boulogne-sur-Mer which, according to *Soldiers Died in the Great War*, is where he resided before he enlisted in Edinburgh. (Plot IV.C.17)

Second Lieutenant Charles Sidney HALL, 60 Squadron, Royal Flying Corps, was killed in action on 7 April 1917, aged 18, flying a Nieuport 23 single-seat fighter. He and others from his squadron were on patrol when they were attacked by four enemy Albatros aircraft, one of which was piloted by Manfred von Richthofen. HALL's machine was one of three from 60 Squadron shot down during the encounter, though one of the pilots survived and was taken prisoner. Manfred von Richthofen accounted for one of the victims, but records appear to show that HALL was credited as a shared victory between two other pilots, one of whom was Kurt Wolff. HALL, who before the war had been studying to become a mining engineer, had cut short his studies at Durham University, where he was also a member of the OTC, in order to enlist. He also held a Royal Life Saving Society medal and an honorary instructors' certificate, though the medal may only have been a proficiency award. Two of his brothers also served: Captain L.W. Hall with the Royal Flying Corps, the other with the Royal Engineers. (Plot IV.C.28)

Second Lieutenant John Hastings Folliott SCOTT, 3rd Oxfordshire & Buckinghamshire Light Infantry, attached 5th Battalion, was killed in action on 9 April 1917, aged 22 (Plot IV.D.24). Two of his brothers also served. The eldest, Lieutenant Richard Thomas Folliott Scott, fell in action when he was hit by an enemy bullet on 16 March 1915 whilst with the 1st East Yorkshire Regiment near Armentières. According to his commanding officer, he was sitting in a trench when a random bullet passed through a weak point in the sandbagged parapet killing him instantly. He is buried at Houplines Communal Cemetery Extension. He, like his brother John, was educated at the Knoll School and Lancing College. The other brother, Second Lieutenant C.W.F. Scott, who served with the Gurkha Rifles and survived the war, was John's twin. Their father, a clergyman, was chaplain to the Bedfordshire Yeomanry. John had been in Ceylon as a tea planter at the outbreak of war, but returned to England in order to serve his country. The family came from Bletchley.

This cemetery also has the distinction of holding more identified casualties from British cavalry regiments than any other on the Arras battlefield. Wancourt British Cemetery has the next highest number and a few other cavalrymen can be found nearby at Hibers Trench Cemetery, Beaurains Road Cemetery, London Cemetery Neuville-Vitasse and Monchy British Cemetery. Cavalrymen can also be found in cemeteries behind the Arras battlefield. Those buried here are:

Private William John WARREN, 5th (Royal Irish) Lancers, killed in action on 9 April 1917, aged 41. (Plot I.A.19)

Lance Corporal Sam Lance DAVIS, 16th (The Queen's) Lancers, aged 19, killed in action on 10 April 1917. *Soldiers Died in the Great War* gives his date of death as 11 April 1917. (Plot II.D.21)

Private George Abraham BUTLER, 16th (The Queen's) Lancers, killed in action on 11 April 1917. (Plot I.B.22)

Private Jenkin D. JONES, 16th (The Queen's) Lancers, killed in action on 10 April 1917. (Plot II.G.26)

Private Frank RAVEN, 'A' Squadron, 12th (Prince of Wales's Royal) Lancers, killed in action on 11 April 1917, aged 41. (Plot IV.D.2)

Private Arthur BRADING, 12th (Prince of Wales's Royal) Lancers, killed in action on 11 April 1917. (Plot I.C.21)

Private Charles GENT, 10th (Prince of Wales's Own Royal) Hussars, died of wounds on 11 April 1917. (Plot II.D.19)

Private Jewitt Melville RANSOME, 10th (Prince of Wales's Own Royal) Hussars, killed in action on 11 April 1917. (Plot VI.C.3)

Shoeing Smith Corporal Ralph NORMAN, 10th (Prince of Wales's Own Royal) Hussars, killed in action on 11 April 1917, aged 34. (Plot XI.C.18)

Serjeant Ernest Harold PRICE, 'A' Squadron, Queen's Own Oxfordshire Hussars, killed in action on 10 April 1917, aged 23. (Plot II.G.30)

Private John HANDS, 2nd Dragoons (Royal Scots Greys), died of wounds on 10th April 1917. (Plot IV.D.10)

Private John HENDERSON, 2nd Dragoons (Royal Scots Greys), killed in action on 11 April 1917. *Soldiers Died in the Great War* shows his date of death as 10 April. (Plot I.B.37)

Lance Serjeant Leonard ASH, 3rd (Prince of Wales's) Dragoon Guards, died of wounds on 11 April 1917. (Plot II.H.16)

Trooper Albert Ernest HERON, Royal Horse Guards, died of wounds on 12 April 1917, aged 29. (Plot II.F.21)

Privates Albert George WRIGHT and William Henry METCALFE, 8th Squadron, Machine Gun Corps (Cavalry), both killed on 11 April 1917. WRIGHT originally served in the Royal Buckinghamshire Hussars and METCALFE with the 2/1st Essex Yeomanry. (Plot VI.C.20 and 21)

There are also a number of burials between April and June 1917 of men from the Royal Horse Artillery, including members of 'L' Battery, which won lasting fame at Néry on 1 September 1914. Judging by his army number, Fitter Staff Serjeant Alfred TAYLOR, MM, 'L' Battery, may well have taken part in the action at Néry. His MM was gazetted on the 26th March 1917 (Plot III.J.12)

Private William MAY, 13th Essex Regiment, was killed in action on 1 July 1916, aged 19. The battalion had not been in France very long and on the night of 1 July it took part in a raid on enemy trenches near Vincent Street where it joined the German front line and where an enemy strongpoint was located. Once in the German trenches the raiders were successful, killing around forty of the garrison during the fifteen minutes that the raid lasted. There was only one casualty during the raid itself, but further casualties occurred as the men were scrambling back over their own parapet. Of the four other ranks killed, William MAY is the only one buried here. (Plot V.C.27)

Second Lieutenant Cecil Victor de Burgh ROGERS, 29 Squadron, Royal Flying Corps, was killed in action on 21 April 1917 while flying a single-seater Nieuport aircraft. I am unaware of any account of his death, other than the fact that he and his aircraft failed to return. (Plot VI.A.8)

Privates Roland Herbert CLARKE and Walter Richard RAE, 8th King's Royal Rifle Corps, died on 1 July 1916; CLARKE died of wounds, RAE was killed in action (Plots VIII.A.8 and 10).

The day had passed quietly until 10.45pm when the enemy fired a mine. It was bigger than the Royal Engineers had predicted and it was blown earlier than antici-pated, though our line had already been cleared as a precaution for some thirty yards either side of its location. Nevertheless, it completely destroyed one of the posts, bury-ing the occupants, and when the Germans advanced to take the crater they also killed a sentry in one of our sap heads. However, the 8th King's Royal Rifle Corps responded quickly and seized both lips of the crater, beating back the attackers as they approached.

Once assistance from the 8th Rifle Brigade and the 7th King's Royal Rifle Corps had arrived, the new position was consolidated by wiring it and linking it up with the existing British line. By daybreak, consolidation of the crater was complete. The crater itself measured 160 feet in diameter and its lips were around 35 feet high, easily high enough to overlook the German trenches, though the Germans responded by deepening them. Between CLARKE and RAE is Private Henry Edward ALLEN, who may have been one of the twenty-five wounded on 1 July, or one of three fatalities that occurred the following night, during which the enemy continued to harass the British garrison by means of trench mortar fire. (Plot VIII.A.9)

Other 1 July 1916 casualties buried in this cemetery are listed below.

Private Arthur DENT, 11th East Lancashire Regiment, aged 19, killed in action. (Plot VII.B.10)

Private Walter SWIFT, 13th York & Lancaster Regiment (1st Barnsley Pals), and Private William HAGUE, 14th York & Lancaster Regiment (2nd Barnsley Pals), both killed in action. (Plot VII.A.4) and (Plot VIII.B.15).

Private Robert WILSON, 1/7th Sherwood Foresters, also died on 1 July 1916 when his battalion attacked at Gommecourt on the opening day of the Battle of the Somme. He may have died of wounds in German hands. (Plot XI.A.4)

DENT, SWIFT and HAGUE belonged to battalions that were in action opposite Serre on the opening day of the Battle of the Somme. Like WILSON, they could have died as prisoners of war. Their bodies would have been brought here for burial after the Armistice.

Lance Corporal William Henry JEFFERY, 2nd Yorkshire Regiment, was killed in action on 2 April 1917 (Plot XII.A.11). The CWGC register notes that his two brothers were killed in action during the war. They are to be found in the CWGC records under a different spelling and neither has any known grave. Private George David Jeffrey, 2nd Lincolnshire Regiment, was killed in action on 21 March 1918, the opening of the German March Offensive; he is commemorated on the Pozières Memorial. Private Lawrence Frederick Jeffrey, 10th East Yorkshire Regiment, was killed in action on 29 October 1916 and is commemorated on the Thiepval Memorial. William had previously served with the East Yorkshire Regiment. All three brothers came from Hull.

Neuville-Vitasse Road Cemetery, Neuville-Vitasse

This is not a large cemetery and has just seventy-five identified burials, but it is rich in interest. It sits in fields by the side of a minor road that links Saint-Martin-sur-Cojeul with Neuville-Vitasse, about half way between the two villages. Though Neuville-Vitasse was captured by the 56th (London) Division on 9 April 1917, the cemetery was actually begun by the 33rd Division. Apart from four burials, all the casualties here are from the opening day of the Battle of Arras, though all the burials are from 1917. Those killed on 9 April 1917 are from 21 Brigade, which was part of the 30th Division, and mainly belong to three battalions: the 18th King's (Liverpool Regiment), the 2nd Wiltshire Regiment, and the 2nd Yorkshire Regiment.

21 Brigade began its advance just after 11.30am on 9 April. The 2nd Wiltshire Regiment and the 18th King's (Liverpool Regiment) encountered their first opposition when they came level with the Hénin–Neuville Road, about 300 yards west of the cemetery. As they were crossing it they came under artillery fire, followed shortly by heavy machine-gun fire. On reaching the enemy's wire, there were too few men remaining to make any real progress through the gaps and, realizing that their position was hopeless, they withdrew to the Saint-Martin-Neuville road, level with today's cemetery, where they were joined by men of the 19th Manchester Regiment. Here they dug in. Casualties were heavy, especially among the 2nd Wiltshire Regiment, which sustained a total of 342 among all its ranks. This was additional to the thirty-seven that had resulted from an attack in the early hours that morning on the mill near the Hénin–Neuville road, the ruins of which housed a strong garrison and two machine guns.

As this is such a small cemetery it is easy enough to cover the various entries by battalion rather than working through each row in turn. Today, one officer and thirty-five men of the 2nd Wiltshire Regiment are buried here, but they are fairly scattered throughout the cemetery. The officer is Second Lieutenant Stanley Tom HORTON, who was killed in action, aged 20, and had originally enlisted in August 1914 in one of the Public Schools Battalions of the Royal Fusiliers. (Plot B.2)

Two of the men buried with HORTON are holders of gallantry awards. Corporal Sidney Albert MERRITT DCM, 2nd Wiltshire Regiment, had won his medal repairing telephone wires on no fewer than seven occasions after they had been severed by shell fire. All the other wires running through the wood had been cut and it was his line alone that enabled information to be sent back. His award was gazetted on 26 September 1916. (Plot D.13)

The other man, Private Reginald SKULL DCM MM, 2nd Wiltshire Regiment, was awarded his DCM posthumously. His award was gazetted on 9 July 1917 in recognition of his invaluable work as a runner and for his coolness on many occasions when under fire. The award of his MM was also announced posthumously and gazetted on 4 June 1917. He was just 20 years old when he was killed. (Plot B.10)

Like HORTON, Corporal William Granthan MILLEN, 2nd Wiltshire Regiment, had enlisted in 1914 and had served in Gallipoli. In civilian life he was a journalist. Like HORTON, he was killed in action on 9 April 1917. (Plot B.5)

Serjeant John COLLETT's military career had begun much earlier as he joined the Wiltshire Regiment in March 1908. The CWGC register shows that he had previously served in South Africa and Gibraltar. He was 26 years old when he was killed in action. (Plot B.13) His brother, Private Ernest George Collett, was killed in action on

12 March 1915 whilst serving with the 1st Wiltshire Regiment; he is commemorated on the Menin Gate, Ypres.

Among the dead of the 18th King's (Liverpool Regiment) is Second Lieutenant Frederic ASHCROFT (Plot B.1). He was an accomplished cricketer as a schoolboy in Birkenhead and was considered to be a good all-rounder at sport. Academically, he also did well, gaining a Classical Exhibition at Emmanuel College, Cambridge, and he later went on to become a schoolmaster. In August 1914 he enlisted in the 17th King's (Liverpool Regiment), but while undergoing training in England he applied for a commission, which led to his transfer as a temporary second lieutenant to the regiment's 18th Battalion. However, he did not accompany the battalion when it went to the front and it was only in January 1917 that he joined it in France. Like all the men from the King's (Liverpool Regiment) buried in this cemetery, he was killed in action on 9 April 1917 south of Neuville-Vitasse.

ASHCROFT's two brothers fell in 1918. Lieutenant William Ashcroft, 19th King's (Liverpool Regiment), was killed in action near Roupy on 22 March 1918 and is commemorated in Savy British Cemetery by way of a special memorial. Lieutenant Edward Stanley Ashcroft, 17th King's (Liverpool Regiment), died of wounds in German captivity on 12 May 1918 and is buried at Harlebeke New British Cemetery, Belgium. The CWGC register shows Edward serving with the 11th Battalion which, according to regimental sources, would appear to be an error.

Another officer casualty from the same regiment is Second Lieutenant John Nelson STEWART. He is shown as serving with the 5th King's (Liverpool Regiment), but that battalion, which was part of the 55th (West Lancashire) Division, was not involved in the Battle of Arras on 9 April 1917. He would very likely have been attached to one of the four 'Liverpool Pals' battalions that formed part of the 30th Division.

Another man, Lance Corporal Frederick James ELTON, is shown as serving in the 4th King's (Liverpool Regiment), which was part of the 33rd Division, but that division did not play any part in the fighting on 9 April when it was held in reserve. In fact it only moved into the battlefield area on 12 April. CWGC records show ELTON as having been killed in action on 9 April 1917, but if that were the case, his burial here makes little sense. He was actually killed serving with the regiment's 18th Battalion. *Soldiers Died in the Great War* shows his date of death as 4 September 1917, but this is a misprint and should be 9 April 1917; at some stage it was obviously written down as 4.9.17 rather than 9.4.17. (Plot D.14)

The eleven casualties from the 2nd Yorkshire Regiment are dotted throughout the cemetery. All are casualties from 9 April 1917 and all are either privates or NCOs. None are particularly young by the standards of the day, and all those with personal details shown in the register came from the north of England, if not Yorkshire itself. On 9 April the battalion's objective was the capture of Hénin-sur-Cojeul and it was supported in this task by two companies of the 19th Manchester Regiment whose job it was to 'mop-up'. After a fight lasting nine hours, the remaining strongpoint in the ruins of the *Mairie* was overcome after being bombarded by a Stokes mortar brought up to finish the task.

Only four burials here are not from the 30th Division: two from the 8th Durham Light Infantry and two from the 56th (London) Division. Company Serjeant Major Thomas CHRISP MM, 1/8th Durham Light Infantry, was killed in action on 22 June 1917. His MM was gazetted on 9 December 1916 and was won while serving as a serjeant with the battalion. Before the war he was a schoolmaster at St Bede's Catholic College, County Durham. His battalion was part of the 50th (Northumbrian) Division. (Plot C.2)

Rifleman Arthur Thomas GILRUTH, 5th Battalion, London Regiment (London Rifle Brigade) is one of the two 56th (London) Division men buried here (Plot D.8). GILRUTH and another man from his battalion, Rifleman Sydney Edwin Herink, died from exposure on 11 April 1917. His company had been occupying some badly damaged trenches that offered little shelter from the biting sleet, snow and freezing winds, which unfortunately proved too much for both men. Herink is not buried with GILRUTH, but is commemorated on the Wancourt Road Cemetery No. 2, Memorial Panel 3, in the London Cemetery, Neuville-Vitasse. Both men would almost certainly have been buried at the same location, but Herink's original grave was lost or destroyed later on in the war.

The battalion had been ordered to dump greatcoats before moving forward, perhaps because it was thought that the extra weight would hinder movement, even though they would have given the men greater protection from the weather. *Soldiers Died in the Great War* records both men as being killed in action, which they clearly were, but the regimental history is also honest enough to acknowledge the true manner in which they died. GILRUTH's brother, Private Reginald William Gilruth, was killed in action on 21 September 1916, aged 20, serving with the 43rd Battalion, Canadian Infantry. He is commemorated on the Canadian Memorial at Vimy Ridge.

London Cemetery, Neuville-Vitasse

A very good way to spend a day on the Arras battlefields is to travel the length of the D.5 as far as the village of Lagnicourt where the Germans carried out a large scale raid on the Australian gun batteries on 15 April 1917. Pick up the D.5 at Beaurains and take in the various cemeteries situated around Hénin-sur-Cojeul, Saint-Martin-sur-Cojeul, Croisilles, Noreuil and Lagnicourt. Though not strictly part of the Battle of Arras in 1917, operations were carried out between Lagnicourt and Hermies at around the same time. On 9 April when the Battle of Arras was set in motion, I Anzac Corps, under Lieutenant General Birdwood, captured the villages of Boursies, Demicourt and Hermies. These villages are situated a few miles south-east of Lagnicourt near the main Bapaume–Cambrai road.

Leaving Beaurains on the D.5, continue south-east for just over half a mile and London Cemetery is on the west side of the road, exactly half way between the D.60 and Neuville-Vitasse itself.

The cemetery register tells us that of the 747 burials and commemorations here, 318 have no headstone, but are commemorated on a wall inside the cemetery. These burials, originally in four former cemeteries, were destroyed by shell fire during and after the Battle of Arras. Here, 147 of the 747 casualties are from the opening day of the battle.

The 56th (London) Division, which attacked Neuville-Vitasse on the opening day, had actually attempted to capture it two days earlier on 7 April. The 1st (City of London) Battalion, London Regiment (Royal Fusiliers), had tried to eliminate a strongpoint around Neuville Mill, the position of which would catch any future advance in enfilade. The position proved too strong and it was decided that tanks could better deal with it on the opening day. Nine men killed in the attack on 7 April 1917 can be found in this cemetery, seven of whom are commemorated on the wall panels. The mill was situated half way along the road leading out of Neuville-Vitasse to Mercatel, the D.34, just by the farm track that runs roughly north-east between the two villages.

Another aspect of this cemetery is that no fewer than forty-eight British regiments have casualties buried or commemorated here, though some are represented by no more than a couple of men. There are just two Australian infantrymen, as well as twelve Canadians, most of whom belonged to the 24th Battalion and were killed in action on 11 April 1918. Though largely forgotten these days, this was a day of pro-longed and heavy fighting for the 24th Battalion. It came under bombardment for three and a half hours before two detachments of German 'storm-troopers', each numbering around eighty men, assaulted trenches held by 'A' and 'B' Companies near Neuville-Vitasse. The attack was initially beaten back, but the trenches were again subjected to a renewed bombardment for several more hours before the enemy launched another determined assault on them. This time some Germans managed to get into the Canadian trenches, but they were soon bombed out in a short, but fierce fight. The Germans, who had initially gained about 60 yards of trench, were even-tually driven back to their original line. Several men were recommended for decora-tions, but the fight left seventeen of the battalion's men dead and another forty were wounded. Nine of the dead are buried here, though they are spread throughout Rows, B, D and E in Plot II.

Not surprisingly, the 56th (London) Division's dead from the opening day of the Battle of Arras feature prominently here. The 1st (City of London) Battalion, London Regiment (Royal Fusiliers), was in support behind the leading two battalions of 167 Brigade: the 3rd (City of London) Battalion, London Regiment (Royal Fusiliers) and the 8th Middlesex Regiment. The 3rd Battalion, London Regiment, assisted by two tanks, dealt with Neuville Mill, whilst the 8th Middlesex Regiment took Neuville-Vitasse itself, where it had to overcome strong resistance near the church by outflanking it. A number of men from the 8th Middlesex Regiment are buried or commemorated here, as are men from the 3rd Battalion, London Regiment, though some were killed during the two days that followed.

One of the men from the 8th Middlesex Regiment, Serjeant Francis William George LYNE, had been awarded the MM. (Neuville-Vitasse Military Cemetery Memorial, Panel 4)

Between them the 7th and the 8th Battalions of the Middlesex Regiment have a significant number of dead buried within the cemetery or commemorated on its walls: thirty-seven men who were killed or who died of wounds on 9 and 10 April 1917. A couple of them are shown in the CWGC register as belonging to battalions of the Middlesex Regiment that never served in France or Belgium, but they had obviously been transferred or posted to the 7th and 8th Battalions at some stage. The same is true with regard to the single casualty from the 11th Battalion, London Regiment, as well as the two from the 10th Battalion, since both battalions served in Gallipoli and Egypt with the 54th (East Anglian) Division, and were never on the Western Front.

Second Lieutenant Bernard Theobald SARGEANT, 8th Battalion, London Regiment (Post Office Rifles) (Plot I.B.31) and Second Lieutenant Richard Ivor RICHENS, 18th Battalion, London Regiment (London Irish) (Wancourt Road Cemetery, No. 2 Memorial) are shown belonging to battalions that were part of the 47th (London) Division, but they too had obviously been transferred to battalions of the 56th (London) Division, presumably after receiving their commissions.

The 12th Battalion, London Regiment (The Rangers), has sixty casualties buried or commemorated in this cemetery, fifty-nine of whom fell on the opening day of the Battle of Arras. All fifty-nine are identified and are buried in Plot I, Row A. The 13th Battalion, London Regiment (The Kensingtons), attacked with the London Rangers, but have just sixteen casualties from 9 April, five of whom are commemorated on the Beaurains Road Cemetery No. 2 Memorial. The 13th Battalion made its attack across the fields between the cemetery and the northern edge of Neuville-Vitasse, whilst the 12th Battalion attacked to the left of them. Thirteen of the seventeen men buried or commemorated here from the 14th Battalion, London Regiment (London Scottish) can also be found in Plot I. All thirteen were killed on 9 April. (Plots I.A.5 to 17)

Second Lieutenant Edwin Robert Richmond PECK MC, 8th Suffolk Regiment, was killed in action by shell fire on 3 May 1917 during an attack on enemy positions near Chérisy. He won his MC on the Somme near Thiepval and the Schwaben Redoubt the year before. It was gazetted on 25 November 1916. His family, who held a memorial service for him at Holy Trinity Church, Ipswich, received several letters of condolence from his peers, as well as from his commanding officer. (Plot I.A.19)

Lieutenant Colonel Valerio Awly Magawly De CALRY DSO, 6th (Inniskilling) Dragoons, was killed in action on 10 May 1917, aged 34. He was the son of the 6th Count Magawly Cerati De CALRY and had also been awarded the *Légion d'Honneur*. His DSO was awarded for distinguished service in the field and was gazetted in the New Year Honours List 1917. The De Calry family claims to be able to trace its ancestry back to the Norman Conquest, but its control and power waned after Cromwell's campaign in Ireland. Some of the family moved abroad to seek service in foreign armies. One of them became a Field Marshal in the army of Charles IV and served as Governor of Prague; another served under Pope Pius VII as Papal Nuncio to Napoleon Bonaparte in 1814. (Plot I.B.7)

Regimental Sergeant Major Henry James BARTHOLOMEW DCM, 6th Royal Berkshire Regiment, was killed in action on 8 May 1917 by a shell, aged 37 (Plot I.B.49). He was standing outside a dug-out and overseeing the distribution of rations when a random shell exploded, killing him instantly. He had served as a police officer in Southampton, but had also had a varied career in the army and, although it was occasionally tarnished during the early years by drink, he remained a well-respected figure within the regiment.

In 1904 he served overseas with the Gold Coast Regiment in West Africa, after which he became a reservist, rejoining in 1910. He was discharged in May 1914, but re-enlisted when war broke out and went to France with the battalion in July 1915. His DCM, gazetted on 20 October 1916, was awarded for conspicuous gallantry during operations in which he organized and maintained a constant supply of ammunition and bombs and went fearlessly on many occasions through the enemy's heavy barrage, utterly indifferent to personal danger. The 'operations' referred to in the citation took place near Montauban on 1 July 1916 during the advance by the 18th (Eastern) Division on the opening day of the Battle of the Somme. He was serving as a company serjeant major at the time he won his award, but was acting as regimental serjeant major at the time of his death. He had also been mentioned in despatches.

The same shell that killed him also killed two other men, Private Arthur William ALLEN and Private John RAZEY, who are buried either side of him. ALLEN is listed as serving with the 8th Battalion in *Soldiers Died in the Great War*, but was clearly with the 6th Battalion at the time of his death. An officer from their battalion killed in action a few days earlier, Second Lieutenant Alfred PEEL, is buried in Row A, Grave 20, in Plot I.

Although the CWGC register shows four casualties from the Royal Flying Corps, there are actually five. Lieutenant Alfred Henry Templeman Loraine SPEER, 11 Squadron, Royal Flying Corps, is shown in the register as serving in the Royal Field Artillery. He was commissioned in the artillery, but then obtained his aviator's certificate in January 1916 and became a pilot. He flew operatons continuously between March and 9 July 1916, the date on which he is known to have been killed in combat over enemy lines. His observer that day, Second Lieutenant William Armstrong WEDGWOOD, also died when their machine came down and both men are now buried here together in the same grave (Plot I.C.1). SPEER was educated at Malvern College where he was a member of the OTC. He was an undergraduate at Trinity College, Cambridge, and was 22 years old when he died.

Private Samuel CUNNINGTON, 2nd Royal Warwickshire Regiment, was eventually shot for desertion on 19 May 1917, aged 20. He had previously been tried for desertion in January 1916 for which he received twenty-eight days imprisonment. He then went missing later that year, just before his battalion took part in the Battle of the Somme. He remained at large for several months before he was arrested. His trial only took place at the end of April 1917 after a significant period of time had elapsed, something which was fairly unusual. The authors, Julian Putkowski and Julian Sykes, suggest that he may well have escaped while awaiting trial, since his subsequent trial was for two offences of desertion. If so, and given his other antecedent history, there was no realistic chance of clemency or leniency. (Plot I.C.1)

This brings us to the curious case of Plot I.C.1. The CWGC register uses this grave reference for seven men, some of whom have already been referred to. The dates of death vary between July 1916 and May the following year. The CWGC register makes no comment on this feature of the cemetery and I can only assume that this is a communal grave made once the bodies were found after the war. Although there seems to be some degree of certainty over who they are, it suggests that the individual remains could not be positively distinguished.

Captain Paul Raymond MEAUTYS MC, 2nd North Staffordshire Regiment, was killed in action on 16 June 1917, aged 26. He was serving as a brigade major when he was killed and his MC was awarded in the New Year's Honours List on 1 January 1917 (Plot II.B.20). A few days before his death Paul had met his father, Major Thomas A. Meautys, who worked at the War Office and who happened to be in France at the time.

The CWGC register makes no reference to either of his two brothers who also fell during the war. The first to die was the eldest brother, Thomas Gilliat Meautys, a lieutenant in the 1st West Yorkshire Regiment. He was killed in action on the Aisne on 22 September 1914, aged 25. Like both his brothers, he was a very keen sportsman. He was educated at Marlborough School where he played rugby and also boxed, after which he went on to the Royal Military College, Sandhurst, and served in India between 1910 and 1911. He was killed while making a reconnaissance for gun positions and is buried at Vendresse British Cemetery. He left behind a widow, and a son whom he never saw. The son, also christened Thomas Gilliat Meautys, went on to serve as a captain in the 14/20th King's Hussars, Royal Armoured Corps, during the Second World War, but died in 1947 while still serving in the army.

Lieutenant Denzil Hatfield Meautys, the youngest brother, was the next to fall. He also served with the 1st West Yorkshire Regiment, but was attached to the 12th Battalion when he died of wounds on 7 May 1917, aged 19. He is buried at Étaples Military Cemetery. He also attended Marlborough School and excelled at boxing and gymnastics.

Air Mechanic F. SMITH, 55 Squadron, Royal Flying Corps, was killed in action on 23 August 1917 (Plot II.G.13). Another Royal Flying Corps casualty buried near him is Second Lieutenant Sidney Edgar STANLEY, 11 Squadron, who died of wounds on 19 October 1917, aged 19 (Plot II.G.15). His observer that day, Second Lieutenant E.L. Fosee, was taken prisoner when their Bristol F2B came down.

Second Lieutenant Stephen DENDRINO, 27 Squadron, Royal Flying Corps, was killed in aerial combat by the German ace, Oswald Boelcke, on 27 September 1916. Although he had been hit and was either dead or seriously wounded, his aircraft was observed to fly around in circles before it fell to earth, apparently because the controls of his machine had been secured by means of rubber bands. Before joining the Royal Flying Corps he was an officer with P&O and served in the Mercantile Marine. He had also taken part in the landing and re-embarkation of the Indian Expeditionary Force at Tanga in East Africa in December 1914. Having joined the Royal Flying Corps, he gained his 'wings' in just six weeks and was soon on active service. (Beaurains German Cemetery Memorial, Panel 5)

Lieutenant Colonel Maurice Edwin McCONAGHEY DSO, 1st Royal Scots Fusiliers, was killed in action on 23 April 1917 near Chérisy. He had joined the Royal Scots Fusiliers back in December 1897, aged 20, and at one point during the South African War he served as a temporary lieutenant colonel, still with the Royal Scots Fusiliers. His DSO was gazetted for distinguished service in the field on 3 June 1916, the day after his 39th birthday. He had also been mentioned in despatches and was a keen cricketer (Plot III.C.13). He is one of six lieutenant colonels killed in action on 23 April 1917, five of whom fell on the Arras battlefield.

Company Serjeant Major Joseph CUNNINGHAM DCM, 24th Northumberland Fusiliers (1st Tyneside Irish), was killed in action on 12 December 1917, aged 21, and had been wounded twice the previous year. His DCM was gazetted on 4 March 1918. The citation notes that he had continually visited the men of his company under very heavy shell fire, cheering and encouraging them. Later on that day, when enemy snipers were active, he organized a party of men and took them up to positions in front of the line from where they carried out successful sniping operations against the enemy, thus preventing many more of his men becoming casualties. It concludes that his personal example and disregard of danger were an inspiration to all his men. (Plot III.D.7)

Captain Dudley Charles ISAAC, North Staffordshire Regiment, was killed in action on 10 April 1917, aged 24. He had been mentioned twice in despatches. (Plot III.D.14)

Second Lieutenant Sydney Bailey HURST, 5th Royal Scots Fusiliers, was aged 20 when he died on 26 August 1918. He was killed in action near Hénin Hill, a short distance away to the south of this location. (Plot III.F.15)

Private Cecil WOODS DCM, 1st (City of London) Battalion, London Regiment (Royal Fusiliers), was killed in action on 30 August 1918. His DCM was gazetted on 13 December 1916 and was awarded for conspicuous gallantry in action. He was unceasing in carrying in the wounded across open ground swept by fire. Later, he brought in three more wounded men under intense fire by carrying them on his back. (Plot III.K.10)

Another grave of interest is that of Corporal Chesney James MIFFLIN, 1st Battalion, Newfoundland Regiment, who was killed on 14 April 1914, the day on which his commanding officer, Lieutenant Colonel Forbes-Robertson VC DSO & Bar MC, with just a handful of men, made a famous stand just to the east of Monchy-le-Preux, where they broke up a German counter-attack on the village. (Plot IV.A.6)

The Royal Field Artillery has thirty of its ranks buried or commemorated within the cemetery, most of whom are from units attached to either the 14th (Light) Division or the 50th (Northumbrian) Division. They fell on various dates between the latter half of April and the end of June 1917, though there are a few from March and April 1918.

Finally, there are a number of gallantry award holders buried or commemorated here who have not already mentioned. They are as listed below.

Bombardier John Joseph CLARKE MM, 'A' Battery, 47th Brigade, Royal Field Artillery, killed in action on 3 May 1917. (Wancourt Road Cemetery No. 2 Memorial, Panel 1)

Corporal Joseph NEARY MM, 'X' 14th Trench Mortar Battery, Royal Garrison Artillery, killed in action on 21 April 1917. There is no reference to his MM in *Soldiers Died in the Great War*. (Wancourt Road Cemetery No. 2 Memorial, Panel 1)

Second Lieutenant Charles William Stephen LITTLEWOOD MC, 7th Field Company, Royal Engineers, killed in action on 10 July 1917, aged 19 (Wancourt Road Cemetery No. 2 Memorial, Panel 1). *Officers Died in the Great War* shows the award of the MC against his name, as does the war memorial in the village of Ingham in Norfolk, however, I can find no trace of his MC in any of the Gazettes. His file at the National Archives refers to the MC, but does not contain any reference to the date on which it was gazetted or the circumstances in which it was awarded. His father, Lieutenant Colonel William Littlewood, is shown in the file as serving with the Royal Army Medical Corps at the 2nd Northern Base Hospital, Beckett's Park in Leeds. Letters of Administration show his as father living in Egypt in 1919.

Serjeant William James BENNETT MM, 18th King's (Liverpool Regiment), killed in action on 9 April 1917. (Wancourt Road Cemetery No. 2 Memorial, Panel 2)

Serjeant William Thomas HARPER MM, 1/3rd (City of London) Battalion, London Regiment (Royal Fusiliers), killed in action on 11 April 1917. (Neuville-Vitasse Mill Cemetery Memorial, Panel 5)

Serjeant Charles SHUFFEBOTTOM MM, 21st Manchester Regiment, died of wounds on 27th March 1917. His date of death in *Soldiers Died in the Great War* is shown as 26 March. His MM was gazetted a couple of weeks before his death. (Plot I.C.1)

Private Frank Arthur BREARLEY MM, 10th Royal Fusiliers, killed in action on 8 October 1918. (Plot II.J.18)

Pioneer David HUGHES, MM, 3rd Divisional Signal Company, Royal Engineers, killed in action on 28 March 1918. (Plot III.C.1)

Guémappe British Cemetery, Wancourt

Although the cemetery takes its name from the village of Guémappe, it really lies well outside the village to the west, roughly half way between Guémappe and Wancourt. It can be found south of the D.34 close to where it joins the D.33 about 800 yards northeast of Wancourt. It is reached via a small track.

The village of Guémappe was captured by the 8th Seaforth Highlanders on 23 April 1917. After initial resistance, the Germans relinquished their hold on it and withdrew to the ruins of Cavalry Farm and its supporting trench system. Guémappe was vulnerable to heavy fire from the high ground south of the River Cojeul and its capture depended on the 50th (Northumbrian) Division being able to clear the area around Wancourt Tower. The sacrifice of the 8th Seaforth Highlanders is immediately evident on entering the cemetery, particularly in Plot I, but also in Plot II. There are now eighty-seven officers and men from that battalion buried here.

One of the officers, Second Lieutenant Richard Forsyth McGIBBON, is shown serving with the 10th Seaforth Highlanders, but like the other eighty-six men buried with him he fell on the same fateful day, 23 April 1917 (Plot I.E.5). The 10th Battalion never served abroad and at some stage he had evidently been posted to the 8th Battalion. He had been a student at Glasgow University. His cousin, also named Richard Forsyth McGibbon, served as a second lieutenant with the 15th Highland Light Infantry and died on 16 November 1916 from wounds received just north of Beaumont Hamel. He is buried at Puchevillers British Cemetery. I have been unable to establish whether they were related to the Scottish architect, William Forsyth McGibbon, who carried out much of his work in Glasgow where their families lived.

Buried here with Second Lieutenant McGIBBON in Row E are fellow officers from the battalion starting with Second Lieutenant William BLAIR (Plot I.E.2); Second Lieutenant Albert Abercrombie GARDNER (Plot I.E.3); Second Lieutenant James Hector ROSS (Plot I.E.4); and Captain Ian Herbert Sydney JAMESON (Plot I.E.6). At the start of the row is Serjeant Gilbert TAYLOR from the same battalion (Plot I.E.1).

The Scottish character of this cemetery is reinforced by the presence of twenty-three identified officers and men of the 9th Black Watch, five men from the 11th Argyll & Sutherland Highlanders, four from the 7th Cameron Highlanders and a solitary NCO from the 8/10th Gordon Highlanders, all of them killed between 23 and 28 April 1917 near Guémappe and Cavalry Farm.

Among the Black Watch casualties are Second Lieutenant John WILSON (Plot I.E.7) and Second Lieutenant Alastair Fisher WATSON (Plot I.E.8), both killed in action on 23 April. WATSON had been wounded previously in August 1916 on the Somme.

Next to him is Captain Leonard Graeme MORRISON (Plot I.E.9), who had arrived in France during the first part of October 1915 to replace losses after the fighting at Loos. He was killed in action during the latter part of 23 April. Earlier that day, he and around seventy of his men had held an exposed position for four hours just north of Guémappe, in Hammer Trench and Dragoon Lane, after the 8th Seaforth Highlanders had been temporarily forced to withdraw. MORRISON and his party were later ordered to withdraw in order to straighten out the line and also to avoid further casualties, since throughout the day the British artillery had been unaware of their presence forward of the positions held by the rest of 44 Brigade. Around 6.00pm MORRISON organized another assault on Hammer Trench and Dragoon Lane and, although he was killed leading this attack, his mixed party of Black Watch, Cameron Highlanders and Seaforth Highlanders managed to retake both positions and even push beyond them.

Losses for the 9th Black Watch during its fifteen days of fighting during the Battle of Arras in 1917 amounted to twenty-nine officers and 466 other ranks. By contrast, the battalion lost a total of 488 casualties during forty-four days of fighting on the Somme. These figures illustrate very well the severity and intensity of fighting during the Battle of Arras.

The only gallantry award in this cemetery is also from the 9th Black Watch. Lance Corporal William REID MM, from Perth, was killed in action on 26 April, aged 22, during a night attack near Cavalry Farm towards the Saint-Rohart Factory. (Plot I.B.3)

Subsequent burials were made during the summer and autumn of 1917, first by the 56th (London) Division in June, and then by the 50th (Northumbrian) Division between July and October. There are also three Seaforth Highlanders not from the 8th Battalion, but from the 4th Battalion, who fell on 7 October 1917. Despite dying on the same day, they are buried apart from each other. They are Second Lieutenant

Cecil Barclay SIMPSON (Plot II.C.10), Lance Corporal John G. HOUSTON (Plot I.A.19) and Private Alexander D. SIMPSON (Plot II.B.9).

The 50th (Northumbrian) Division casualties buried here are from the 5th Border Regiment, the 7th Northumberland Fusiliers, the 8th Durham Light Infantry, the 4th Yorkshire Regiment and the 5th Yorkshire Regiment. They represent routine attrition during the summer months while holding the line. Although there was no heavy fighting here during these months, both sides exerted pressure to ensure that neither was able to thin its line and send troops north to the Ypres Salient where the main contest was then being fought. There was constant patrolling and wiring; trenches had to be maintained, and new trenches had to be dug, often under artillery fire. Both sides also carried out raids throughout July, August and September, though only one identified casualty here matches the date of one of those raids, and even this casualty is not from the unit directly involved. It is likely that most of the 50th (Northumbrian) Division's casualties died from shell fire, especially as the German front line lay on a reverse slope, so that at no point was the 50th Divisional front directly visible from it.

There is only one 1918 burial in this cemetery: a serjeant from the 103rd Battalion, Machine Gun Corps, which was part of the 34th Division. He was killed in early January. The division also has a handful of burials here dating from November and December 1917.

Tank Cemetery, Guémappe

All the burials in this cemetery are from 1917, mainly from April and May. The most notable aspect of this cemetery is also its most poignant; the burial of sixty-four NCOs and men of the 7th Cameron Highlanders in what was a single battlefield trench that was used to bury them. Their resting place has never been disturbed and it now forms one continuous row (Plot F.1). The men were buried side by side, close to each other and on their sides, each man's arm placed over the man in front, uniting all of them in death. The men fell on two dates, 23 April and 28 April 1917.

The village of Guémappe was captured on 23 April after the Germans withdrew to some ruined buildings known as Cavalry Farm, but the 7th Cameron Highlanders were held up at Bullet Trench by intense rifle and machine-gun fire and were unable to make any further progress towards capturing the farm. On the night of 26 April, after an artillery bombardment, the 7th Cameron Highlanders and the 9th Black Watch renewed their efforts to take Cavalry Farm. They managed to rush it and briefly occupied parts of it, but the intensity of fire from the surrounding area made it untenable, though a post was established just east of it. However, the attack did succeed in driving the enemy out of the farm's ruins, denying them access to it as a defensive position. On 28 April the farm was eventually secured.

The history of the 9th Battalion, London Regiment (Queen Victoria's Rifles), suggests that at some point the Germans did briefly manage to re-enter the ruins of the farm and that its own men rushed and cleared it on 29 April after a short trench mortar bombardment. The narrative goes on to state that as late as 4 May two officers and fifteen other ranks from the 41st German Infantry Regiment surrendered in the farm and that a sergeant from the 2nd Battalion, London Regiment, who had been held by them as a prisoner was released.

There are three gallantry awards in Row F: Serjeant John DRYSDALE DCM, Lance Corporal John KELLY MM and Lance Corporal Ernest Blair THOMSON MM. All three were killed in action, DRYSDALE on 23 April 1917, and the other two five days later on 28 April. DRYSDALE had won his DCM as a lance corporal and it was gazetted on 16 November 1916. It was awarded for conspicuous gallantry during the capture of part of an enemy trench when he and another NCO took charge of bombing operations and then, with great courage and skill, held the enemy in check until their bombs ran out. Later he rendered valuable service by making a block and organizing a counter-bombing attack, during which he was wounded. (Plot F.1)

There are also twenty-nine NCOs and men from the 11th Argyll & Sutherland Highlanders, though one is shown as serving with the 9th Battalion in the cemetery register. All of them were killed on 23 April, along with a further twenty-three from other Scottish battalions belonging to the 15th (Scottish) Division. The only officer among them is Lieutenant William Alexander MACKENZIE, 9th King's Own Scottish Borderers, who was attached to the 197th Company, Machine Gun Corps. He was killed on 17 May 1917 (Plot B.1). The regiment's 9th battalion never served abroad and was a reserve battalion that provided reinforcements for other battalions of the regiment. His death would have occurred while serving with or attached to the 7/8th Battalion of the regiment.

The 56th (London) Division also fought in this locality in May 1917 and some of its men can be found within the cemetery. Fighting still ebbed and flowed around the ruins of Cavalry Farm, which was situated on the main Arras–Cambrai road. The division recaptured it on 3 May, but the position could not be held or consolidated.

A further attempt was made on 11 May by the 14th Battalion, London Regiment (London Scottish) and the 4th (City of London) Battalion, London Regiment (Royal Fusiliers). The attack, which took place at 8.30pm, seems to have caught the Germans off guard; few of them were armed and the mail and rations had recently been brought up, which obviously proved a distraction. The 4th Battalion swept through Cavalry Farm with little opposition, but the London Scottish sustained some casualties in their attack on Tool Trench, mainly among 'D' Company, which lost two officers, Captain William MACKINNON (Plot C.23) and Second Lieutenant Herbert Edward HAWKINS (Plot C.24). At the close of this action, the northern section of Tool Trench and beyond it, Hook Trench, were still in German hands, so a block was created by filling in about 40 yards of trench. The captured positions were then consolidated.

Between 20 May and 9 June, the 56th (London) Division was out of the line, but it then returned to the same trenches, though its frontage now extended south towards Wancourt Tower. On 14 June the 3rd Division carried out a successful attack on Hook Trench, and when the Germans gathered to make a counter attack, sentries from the 56th (London) Division near Wancourt Tower spotted the enemy in numbers and sent a message back to the British artillery. When the counter-attack was launched at 5.30pm it was entirely smashed. A further enemy attack at 2.30am on

16 June was also spotted and broken up by the combined efforts of the 3rd and 56th Divisions' troops in the front line. All these dates are reflected here among the 56th (London) Division's casualties.

Captain John Bond SYMES, 2nd (City of London) Battalion, London Regiment (Royal Fusiliers), was killed in action on 3 May 1917 (D.10). Another officer from the battalion, Second Lieutenant Alfred NOEL, also killed in action that day, is buried elsewhere in this cemetery (Plot B.5). Just a little further along the row from Captain SYMES is Second Lieutenant Douglas Muir SCOUGALL, 4th (City of London) Battalion, London Regiment (Royal Fusiliers), who was killed in action on 4 May 1917, aged 19. (Plot D.16)

Corporal Stephen MORRIS MM, 49th Battery, 40 Brigade, Royal Field Artillery, is another of the gallantry award holders buried here. He was killed in action on 4 May 1917. He is one of only three men buried here not serving with an infantry unit. (Plot D.15)

Second Lieutenant Percy Cargill REID, 16th Battalion, London Regiment (Queen's Westminster Rifles), was killed on 6 May. The CWGC register makes the point that he had originally served in one of the Canadian regiments as a private soldier and had gained his commission as an officer in 1916. The Canadian unit was, in fact, the 62nd Battalion. His family lived in Notting Hill, London, but it also states that he was educated in New Zealand. Canadian army records show that he was born in India. (Plot D.22)

The 10th Loyal North Lancashire Regiment has ten of its men buried in Row A; all are identified and were killed in action on 11 April 1917. The 6th Bedfordshire Regiment, also part of the 37th Division, has nine identified burials here, though seven are represented by special memorials and carry the inscription: 'buried near this spot'. They were killed between 21 and 23 May 1917. One of the men from the 10th Loyal North Lancashire Regiment, Private Joseph William BRIGGS, had been awarded the MM and had formerly served with the Manchester Regiment. (Plot A.17)

There is a solitary member of the Newfoundland Regiment, Private Joseph OLSEN, who was killed in action on 14 April 1914 (Plot A.16). The tragedy that befell the regiment on the Somme on 1 July 1916, when it suffered 684 casualties, is well known. However, the regiment also lost heavily on 14 April 1917; the CWGC records show 151 men killed that day, the majority of whom are commemorated not on the Arras battlefield, but on the Newfoundland Memorial at Beaumont Hamel on the Somme. Those buried around Arras are widely scattered, as far forward as Dury Crucifix Cemetery and Cagnicourt British Cemetery, and as far back as Duisans British Cemetery, Étrun. A significant number were also captured.

Rifleman Godfrey Stewart MIDDLEMISS, 5th Battalion, London Regiment (London Rifle Brigade), was killed in action on 18 May 1917, aged 23. His brother, Rifleman Guy Middlemiss, also aged 23, was killed in action on 6 May 1915 serving with the Ceylon Planters' Rifle Corps. He is buried at Beach Cemetery, Anzac, on the Gallipoli Peninsula. Guy and Godfrey were born in Rawalpindi, modern Pakistan, while their father, Charles Stewart Middlemiss CIE FRS, was carrying out work on behalf of the Geological Survey of India. (Plot A.35)

Tigris Lane Cemetery, Wancourt

The cemetery takes its name from a nearby trench and was begun by the 14th (Light) Division after the capture of Wancourt on 12 April 1917. The position was retaken by the Germans at the end of March 1918, but was recaptured by the Canadian 2nd Division on 26 August that year.

The earliest burials, dated 9 April 1917, are from the 14th (Light) Division's 43rd Brigade, notably the 6th Somerset Light Infantry, and the 3rd Division's 8 Brigade, particularly the 2nd Royal Scots and the 7th King's Shropshire Light Infantry. The 14th (Light) Division's 41 Brigade was in reserve for the opening day of the Battle of Arras, but its troops came into action over the next few days, accounting for the casualties that are now buried here from 7th King's Royal Rifle Corps, the 7th Rifle Brigade and the 8th Rifle Brigade. A few men of the 6th Duke of Cornwall's Light Infantry killed on 10 April 1917, and from 43 Brigade, are also buried in the cemetery, though not together.

Among the nineteen men of the 6th Somerset Light Infantry is Regimental Serjeant Major Charles Henry BUSS DCM. Unlike the majority of them, he and one other man were killed in action, not on 9 April, but on 3 May 1917. His DCM was awarded, not for any single or specific action, but for consistent good work and gallant service and always setting a fine example to those under him. (Plot I.C.6)

Buried here with them are three of the battalion's officers killed on 9 April: Major John Neill BLACK, aged 22, previously mentioned in despatches (Plot I.E.12), Second Lieutenant Arthur Philip ABECASIS (Plot I.E.7) and Second Lieutenant Arthur Lincoln SPRINGFIELD (Plot I.B.7). The last two were attached to the 6th Battalion from other battalions of the regiment.

The Rifle Brigade's 7th and 8th Battalions have between them ten casualties from 10 and 11 April 1917, including Second Lieutenant Henry ANSTEY (Plot I.C.23). The 7th King's Royal Rifle Corps has fourteen identified casualties from those two dates, including Second Lieutenant Percy Frederic WALFORD. The *King's Royal Rifle Corps Chronicle* for 1917 makes no reference to Second Lieutenant ANSTEY's death, which is highly unusual. Second Lieutenant WALFORD is mentioned only as one of four officers killed between 9 and 12 April 1917. (Plot I.B.17)

Just under a third of the identified burials here are from Canadian units, all of whom fell between 26 August and 3 September 1918. All of them are buried in Plot II. The infantry are either from the 2nd Division's 18th, 19th and 20th Battalions, or from the 4th Division, particularly the 72nd Battalion, but also the 38th Battalion.

After the capture of Monchy-le-Preux by the Canadian 3rd Division on 26 August 1918, the Canadian 2nd Division continued to apply pressure the following day by attacking the German defences that ran north to south in front of Chérisy. Its 18th and 19th battalions, supported by the 20th and 21st battalions, attacked just south of the Arras–Cambrai road, towards Vis-en-Artois, and although successful, the attack took its toll, weakening many of the battalions involved.

A few days later on 2 September, the Canadian 4th Division attacked the Drocourt–Quéant Line near Mont Dury, but the Germans also made a pre-emptive strike the night before, attacking the jumping off positions occupied by the 38th Battalion. Private Thomas TOWNSEND, 38th Battalion, Canadian Infantry, is a casualty of this assault. (Plot II. B.2)

The attack by the Canadian 4th Division came under very heavy machine-gun fire from strong defensive positions. The 72nd Battalion, Canadian Infantry, attacking immediately south of the Arras–Cambrai road, crossed the crest of Mont Dury but was then caught in a cross fire from the villages of Dury and Villers-lès-Cagnicourt, as well as from the sunken lane linking the two.

There are a number of gallantry awards among the Canadian dead. Private Frederick STEVENS DCM MM, 18th Battalion, Canadian Infantry, was killed in action on 27 August 1918, aged 26. He won his DCM for conspicuous gallantry and devotion to duty after the NCO in charge of his section had become a casualty. He assumed command and maintained his Lewis gun in its position in good working order while under continuous and heavy shell fire. The citation concludes that his coolness set a fine example to the men of his platoon. The award was gazetted on 21 October 1918. His MM was gazetted on 13 March 1918. (Plot II.A.13).

Company Sergeant Major Thomas GALBRAITH MM, 21st Battalion, Canadian Infantry, who was also killed on 27 August 1918, was invalided back to England after breaking his ankle badly in an accident on 16 May 1917, not in trenches but in a rest camp. After an operation on it he spent some time convalescing in Dundee. His MM was gazetted on 12 March 1917. (Plot II.A.18)

Lieutenant James McDONALD MC, 72nd Battalion, Canadian Infantry, was killed in action on 2 September 1918, aged 41. His MC was gazetted on 11 November 1918 and was awarded for conspicuous gallantry during a daylight raid in which he led his party through two strong belts of wire, up a steep embankment, and into the enemy's trenches, where he secured valuable identifications. He then conducted the withdrawal of his men without incurring a single casualty, demonstrating splendid leadership and rendering valuable service. (Plot II.B.11)

Among the Canadian dead are several from the supporting arms, such as the three men of the Canadian Corps Cyclist Battalion (Plots II.B.6 to 8); one from the Canadian Army Medical Corps (Plot II.B.9); and four from the Canadian Machine Gun Corps, one of whom, Private William SCOTT, died on 27 August 1918, aged 17 (Plot II.A.15). There are also three men of the Canadian Field Artillery, one of whom was a battery sergeant major, as well as a corporal from the Canadian Corps Military Police. (Plot II.A.2)

One of the three men from the 1st Battalion, Canadian Machine Gun Corps, Lieutenant Le Roy Eaton AWREY (Plot II.A.3), is shown in the CWGC register as having been killed on 30 August 1916. However, the two men next to him, also from the same unit, are shown killed in action on 29 August 1918 (Plots II.A.4 and 5). I would suggest that the '1916' in relation to AWREY's death should read '1918', an assumption supported by Canadian military records. The register tells us that AWREY was a barrister by profession.

Finally, Corporal Harold Russell ENGLAND, Canadian Corps Military Police, who has already been referred to, was killed in action on 31 August 1918. He is one of only six men from the Canadian Corps Military Police buried in France and Belgium between 1914 and 1918, and one of only thirteen from that regiment to die in service during that period. (Plot II.A.2)

Hibers Trench Cemetery, Wancourt

The cemetery lies just west of the A.1 Autoroute on the Rue d'Artois, the D.34. Burials began almost as soon as the German positions around Wancourt Tower had been cleared. The Tower was captured on 13 April by the 50th (Northumbrian) Division. The position remained in British hands until the Germans overran it in late March 1918, though it was recaptured by the 2nd Canadian Division on 26 August. The five rows of graves follow the curvature of the slight swell in the ground, so that it is visually very pleasing, though these days a little noisy thanks to motorway traffic.

Leaving aside for the moment the significant number of artillery casualties, the cemetery contains mainly casualties from two divisions, the 14th (Light) Division and the 50th (Northumbrian) Division. The first of these was made up entirely of Rifle or Light Infantry units, the second comprised battalions taken from regiments in the north of England. There are also two men from the 2nd Dragoons (Royal Scots Greys) buried here from 11 April 1917, a day that saw cavalry units in action around Monchy-le-Preux. Serjeant William PATTERSON (Plot B.25) and Private Ernest BRUCE (Plot B.26) were both killed in action that day. (Plot II.A.4 and 5)

There are seventeen identified casualties from the three battalions of the King's Royal Rifle Corps that made up a quarter of the 14th (Light) Division. Among them are three officers from the regiment's 7th Battalion. This battalion took no active part in fighting on the opening day of the Battle of Arras, but was in reserve along with the rest of 41 Brigade. The other two brigades did attack that day south of Tilloy-lès-Mofflaines towards Telegraph Hill and 'The Harp'. The following day the 7th King's Royal Rifle Corps moved up with the 7th Rifle Brigade on its right. The intention was to relieve 43 Brigade about half a mile west of Wancourt. However, the 7th King's Royal Rifle Corps found itself in a snow storm opposite a gap that 43 Brigade had failed to cover. The enemy had already taken full advantage of this; not only did they still hold the gap, they had also reinforced it overnight. Once they became aware of this, the men of the King's Royal Rifle Corps rushed the main defensive position in a sunken road and captured it, but sustained heavy casualties from machine-gun fire that came from the hill just south of Wancourt. The 8th Rifle Brigade tried to deal with this, but came up against uncut wire and was unable to take the position, sustaining heavy losses in its attempts.

Second Lieutenant Felix Roland WILLIAMS, commanding 'D' Company, 7th King's Royal Rifle Corps (Plot B.30) and Second Lieutenant Francis Joseph St AUBYN (Plot B.31) were both killed in the operations on 10 April. The regimental history also notes that Second Lieutenant Percy Frederic Walford was the 7th Battalion's third officer fatality on 10 April, though the CWGC register records that he died a day later, as does *Officers Died in the Great War*. He presumably died from wounds, which may well account for why he is buried elsewhere, though not far away in Tigris Lane Cemetery. His body may also not have been discovered until the following day, which could account for the ambiguity over his date of death. Another officer, Second Lieutenant Kenneth Harper Williamson, who was also wounded on 10 April, was evacuated that same day to Étaples, where he died on 19 April.

On 11 April, an hour before 41 Brigade renewed its efforts to advance, the 56th (London) Division made a gallant, but unsuccessful attempt to take the machine-gun position on the hill south of Wancourt. This made a repeat of the previous day almost inevitable for the 7th King's Royal Rifle Corps, and again, its casualties were heavy. Captain Charles WHITELEY MC, 7th King's Royal Rifle Corps, was killed in the attack (Plot C.15) and another officer, Captain George Hamilton Williamson MC, who is buried at Warlincourt Halte British Cemetery, died the following day from his wounds. Both WHITELEY and Williamson had won their MCs the previous year on the Somme. WHITLEY's MC was awarded after he had remained in command of his company in spite of a wound to the arm and had even advanced with it in that condition, capturing and consolidating the enemy's trench. After that he remained on duty for twelve hours until relieved. The award was gazetted on 20 October 1916. George Hamilton Williamson was the brother of Kenneth Harper Williamson referred to above, though neither CWGC register alludes to this fact.

The St Aubyn family was a distinguished one that had traditionally served with the King's Royal Rifle Corps. Nine of the family served during the Great War, four of whom lost their lives. Eight were Old Etonians, two attained the rank of brigadier general, one became a lieutenant colonel of the 15th King's Royal Rifle Corps, and two more, who survived the war, served with the Grenadier Guards and King's Royal Rifle Corps respectively. St Michael's Mount is the family home.

One of the four to die in conflict, Major the Honourable Edward Stuart St Aubyn, was drowned in the Mediterranean on 30 December 1915, aged 57, when the SS *Persia* sank. He is commemorated on the Chatby Memorial, Alexandria, Egypt. He was the second son of the 1st Baron St Levan and had served in the Egyptian campaign in 1882 and also on the staff during the South African campaign. Second Lieutenant the Honourable Piers St Aubyn, 2nd King's Royal Rifle Corps, was killed in action on 31 October 1914. He also served in the South African campaign as a second lieutenant in Thorneycroft's Mounted Infantry. He was Lord St Levan's fifth son and is commemorated on the Menin Gate, Ypres. Major Morice Julian St Aubyn MC, 7th King's Royal Rifle Corps, who was wounded on the Somme in September 1916, was killed in action on 22 March 1918. He also has no known grave and is commemorated on the Pozières Memorial.

The cemetery also contains one officer and seventeen identified other ranks of the 7th and 8th Rifle Brigade. Both battalions were part of 41 Brigade. Thirteen were killed in operations between 9 and 12 April 1917, and the remainder between the end of April and mid-May, including the officer casualty, Second Lieutenant Norman Thomson COSSAR, who was killed in action on 15 May. (Plot D.19)

Row B, 1–10 contains one officer, Second Lieutenant Ernest Cecil WELBOURNE, 5th Yorkshire Regiment, and nine NCOs and men of the 4th Yorkshire Regiment, all killed on 21 April 1917 by shell fire. The 4th Yorkshire Regiment was not in action that day, but the trenches that it had taken over offered little protection. Between 6.00pm and 8.00pm that evening, while the 4th Yorkshire Regiment was busy consolidating its position, the Germans put down a heavy bombardment killing all the above and wounding others. Six of the nine men were from North Yorkshire, as was Second Lieutenant WELBOURNE. He had served with the Army Service Corps earlier in the war before gaining his commission in the 5th Yorkshire Regiment. He transferred to the 4th Battalion in early 1917 (Plot B.3). Buried next to him is a gallantry award holder, Serjeant Fred SHORE MM (Plot B.4). The pioneer battalion of the 50th (Northumbrian) Division, the 7th Durham Light Infantry, also suffered casualties in the same bombardment, three of whom are buried next to each other in Row D, 24–26.

The sixteen identified officers and men of the 56th (London) Division are all 1917 casualties and are from several battalions of the London Regiment, as well as the 7th and 8th Middlesex Regiment. Two of them were killed in action on 11 April 1917 in the attack referred to above, whilst the rest of them fell during the months of May and June. Among them is one officer, Second Lieutenant George Rodolph De SALIS, 8th Middlesex Regiment, who was killed on 21 June 1917, aged 19 (Plot E.16). His brother, Second Lieutenant Jerome Joseph Fane De Salis, 3rd Middlesex Regiment, died of wounds at home in England on 3 October 1915, aged 19. He is buried in St Peter and St Paul churchyard, Harlington Cemetery.

The cemetery also contains a fair number of artillerymen: twenty-three from the Royal Field Artillery and eight from the Royal Garrison Artillery. Most of the former were killed between mid-April 1917 and the end of the month, the others the following month. The Royal Garrison Artillery casualties are all 1917, but cover a wider span of dates, extending into the autumn. Among them are two winners of the MM: Acting Bombardier Thomas MARTIN MM, 'D' Battery, 250 Brigade, Royal Field Artillery (Plot E.7) and Corporal Frederick ROGERS MM, 113th Heavy Battery, Royal Garrison Artillery (Plot E.24).

Whilst this cemetery is primarily concerned with 1917, there are four identified burials dating to 1918; two privates of the 1st Gordon Highlanders, killed in action on 26 March 1918, two days before the main German push on this part of the battlefield, and two men involved in fighting during late August and early September, both of whom served with the Canadian Corps.

Two men who died after the Armistice can also to be found here. Private Harold John WILKINSON (Plot A.15) and Private Albert Percy SWIFT (Plot A.16) are both shown serving with the York and Lancaster Regiment and died about six weeks apart on different dates in 1919. Their battalion is not shown in the CWGC register, nor is there any trace of either in *Soldiers Died in the Great War*.

Chapter Five

Rooks, Cuckoos and Calvaires – Fighting a Lost Cause – A Childbirth ends in Tragedy

Bootham Cemetery, Héninel

The cemetery is a small triangular plot situated about a mile east of the village of Héninel and about six miles south-east of Arras. From the centre of Héninel, take the road leading to Chérisy, the Rue Saint-Germain, and the cemetery is on the south side of the road. Héninel was captured on 12 April 1917 by the 56th (London) Division and the 21st Division.

The cemetery derives its name from a nearby trench that was named after Bootham School in York. Despite that, there are no burials from any of the Yorkshire regiments among the 115 identified casualties. The 56th (London) Division was responsible for the first burials here in April 1917. The cemetery, situated on the road between Héninel and Chérisy, has an unusual layout; all five rows are arranged in one long line to reflect the original trench. All the casualties here fell within a very short distance of where they are now buried. It is one of those very intimate battlefield cemeteries, similar to many of those on the Somme, where the sense of comradeship and loss is still very tangible.

Although just over 60 per cent of the 186 burials here are identified, only two battalions are represented. The 16th Battalion, London Regiment (Queen's Westminster Rifles) accounts for forty-three, all killed in action on 14 April 1917 near Héninel, the village immediately west of the cemetery. The battalion had gone forward, but was met with heavy enfilade fire from the direction of Guémappe, which was still in enemy hands. The battalion's left flank was left completely uncovered by units of the 50th (Northumbrian) Division, which had also been held up by heavy fire from Guémappe. Twelve of the battalion's officers became casualties, five of whom were killed in action; total casualties among the other ranks came to 300.

The remainder of the known casualties in this cemetery are from the 2nd Royal Scots Fusiliers, or men attached to it from other battalions of the regiment. There are now seventy-one 2nd Battalion men buried here who fell in action on 23 April 1917, the opening day of the Second Battle of the Scarpe, including two officers. The battalion was part of the 30th Division, one of nine British divisions that took part that day. The only tactical successes were the capture of Gavrelle by the 63rd (Royal Naval) Division and the capture of Guémappe by the 15th (Scottish) Division. The high ground overlooking Chérisy had been the objective for the 30th Division, but its two leading battalions, one of which was the 2nd Royal Scots Fusiliers, were cut down near the German front line. Among them is Private William DOHERTY, aged 37

(Plot C.10). He had previously served in the South African War, though he is not the oldest casualty here; Private Colin FYFE, also 2nd Royal Scots Fusiliers, was killed in action the same day, aged 44 (Plot C.40).

Chérisy Road East Cemetery, Héninel

The cemetery was originally made by the 30th and the 33rd Divisions in April 1917. It lies about 600 yards east of Héninel where the road forks. The right hand fork is the road leading to Fontaine-les-Croisilles and in 1917 was known as Rotten Row. The cemetery is located along this road just after the fork. The other fork leads to Chérisy and Bootham Cemetery.

All sixty-three identified burials are from April 1917. The earliest group dating from the 14th consists of seven men of the 1/6th and 1/8th Durham Light Infantry, plus one from the 151st Company, Machine Gun Corps, all of whom are 50th (Northumbrian) Division casualties. A second group, consisting of eight men, is split between the 5th Battalion, London Regiment (London Rifle Brigade), the 9th Battalion, London Regiment (Queen Victoria's Rifles) and the 16th Battalion, London Regiment (Queen's Westminster Rifles), all of whom were part of 169 Brigade, 56th (London) Division.

The 30th Division also has casualties buried here. These men belong to the Liverpool and Manchester Pals Battalions, as well as the 2nd Royal Scots Fusiliers, and there are also two men of the 1/5th Yorkshire Regiment.

All the Manchester Regiment casualties date to 23 April, as do all ten of the Royal Scots Fusiliers and both of the men from the Yorkshire Regiment. Casualties from the King's (Liverpool Regiment) died between 23 and 28 April 1917 and all but one are from either the 17th or the 18th Battalions.

The only officer buried in this cemetery is Second Lieutenant Lawrence BAND of the 17th King's (Liverpool Regiment), who was killed in action on 28 April, aged 31. He enlisted in the 17th Battalion (1st Liverpool Pals) in September 1914, but later transferred to the Inns of Court OTC, where he trained as an officer before going to France in February 1917.

Cojeul British Cemetery, Saint-Martin-sur-Cojeul

The cemetery lies south-east of the village of Saint-Martin-sur-Cojeul close to the A.1 Autoroute. The D.33 runs though the village and the Rue de Fontaine, which runs off it to the south-east, leads directly to the cemetery. There are 394 casualties buried here, thirty-one of them commemorated by special memorials. There are also thirty-five unidentified casualties. It was begun in April 1917 and continued to be used until October that year. The village of Saint-Martin-sur-Cojeul was captured by the 30th Division on 9 April 1917.

The 21st Division accounts for most of the burials, particular its 64 Brigade. The 1st East Yorkshire Regiment has fifty-one of its dead buried here from 9 April 1917 and a further nine from subsequent months. The 15th Durham Light Infantry has seventy burials, almost all of whom fell on 9 or 10 April 1917, and the 9th and 10th Battalions of the King's Own Yorkshire Light Infantry have fifty-three burials from the first two days of fighting at Arras and a further seventeen from subsequent days through until late July.

All the 1st East Yorkshire Regiment's casualties are privates or NCOs, apart from one officer casualty, Captain Arthur Frank CEMERY, who was killed on 19 July 1917 (Plot E.20). With just two exceptions, the battalion's 9 April casualties are to be found in Rows B and C. There is one gallantry award holder buried among them, Corporal William MATES MM. (Plot C.18)

The 15th Durham Light Infantry's casualties also consist of privates and NCOs, apart from one officer, Second Lieutenant Robert WEIR (Plot D.5). All of them are spread across the first four rows, including some commemorated by special memorials. There are three gallantry award holders among them: Serjeant Joseph BLAKE MM (Plot A.24) and Serjeant Alfred PHARAOH MM (Plot C.56) were killed in action on 10 April 1917; Private George William CROFT MM was killed in action on 3 May 1917 (Plot C.66).

Among the men of the King's Own Yorkshire Light Infantry is Private Horace WALLER VC, who was killed in action on 10 April 1917, aged 20. He had only been at the front for a few months, having had difficulty meeting the medical requirements for enlistment. He won his VC on 10 April 1917 with the 10th King's Own Yorkshire Light Infantry. He was part of a bombing section that had formed a block in an enemy trench just south of Héninel. At 8.00am the first of two counter-attacks was launched against the position. Five of the garrison were killed as WALLER continued to throw bombs for over an hour, eventually repelling the attackers. The Germans counter-attacked again in the evening, during which all the garrison were killed except for WALLER. Despite being wounded himself, he continued to throw bombs for another half an hour until he was killed at his post. (Plot C.55)

There are now seventy men from the King's Own Yorkshire Light Infantry buried here, all from either the 9th or 10th Battalions, including two officers: Captain Archibald Graham SPARK MC, 9th Battalion (Plot D.3) and Second Lieutenant Robert Rowland AKRILL-JONES, shown as 4th Battalion, but attached to the 9th Battalion (Plot D.4). His brother, Lieutenant Edward Trevor Akrill-Jones, 4th Sherwood Foresters, attached Royal Flying Corps, was killed on 18 March 1918, aged 19. He is buried at St Mary's Old Churchyard, Bolsover, in Derbyshire. Captain SPARK's MC was gazetted on 4 June 1917 as part of the King's Birthday Honours List. He had arrived in France with his battalion in September 1915 and was one of its original members. Among them are two holders of gallantry awards. Private Albert SILVESTER MM, 9th Battalion, was killed in action on 9 April 1917, aged 32 (Plot A.14), while Serjeant Percy HEATH MM, 9th Battalion, was killed in action on 25 April 1917. (Plot B.13)

The 21st Division's 62 Brigade is also represented. Of the eighteen burials from the Yorkshire Regiment, seventeen are from its 10th Battalion, largely in Row A. There are also burials from the 1st Lincolnshire Regiment, which also formed part of 62 Brigade.

One particular soldier within this group deserves a mention. Lance Serjeant Arthur WALKER, 1st Lincolnshire Regiment, was killed in action on 11 April 1917. As he and his comrades advanced on the German wire they found three gaps. The 10th Yorkshire Regiment next to them was less fortunate and found only a single gap.

The Germans, aware of these openings, had machine-gun and rifle fire trained on them. WALKER, who was in charge of a Lewis gun section, managed to get into a shell hole just beyond the wire from where he made determined efforts to subdue the enemy's machine-gun fire. He kept the gun in action for six hours, crossing open ground in full view of the enemy on seven occasions to bring back ammunition to keep the gun in action. He was finally killed around 12.30pm.

Though his gallantry was witnessed, his incredible tenacity and heroism were never recognized by the VC, the only award which could be given posthumously. However, his commanding officer did have this to say: '*To keep fighting a lost cause for six hours from an exposed position needs a determination that is given to few. I know of nothing finer in the war.*' Ironically, the Germans abandoned that part of the line the following morning and the 1st Lincolnshire Regiment was able to occupy it unopposed, recovering WALKER's body in the process. (Plot A.73)

The 33rd Division also has a claim to this cemetery. Its burials are from the 4th King's (Liverpool Regiment), the 1st Battalion and the 5/6th Battalion, Cameronians, the 1/4th Suffolk Regiment, the 1st Middlesex Regiment and the 20th Royal Fusiliers. All date between mid-April and 23 April, which was the opening day of the Second Battle of the Scarpe. Second Lieutenant Louis William Alexander BACK, 4th King's (Liverpool Regiment), was just 19 years old when he was killed in action that day (Plot A.58). The battalion had been in brigade reserve, but 'A' Company had been given the role of carrying bombs forward in support of the main attack on the Hindenburg Line by the 1/4th Suffolk Regiment. The 2nd Argyll & Sutherland Highlanders and the 1st Middlesex Regiment managed to reach their objectives, but the 1/4th Suffolk Regiment and the detachment of men from the King's (Liverpool Regiment) met strong opposition once in the enemy's trenches and were forced back to their original line by German counter-attacks. Next to Second Lieutenant BACK is Second Lieutenant Hector Shields ASLACHSEN, whose date of death is shown in the CWGC register as 25 April, but which should read 23 April. (Plot A.59)

Captain Arthur HENDERSON VC MC, 4th Argyll & Sutherland Highlanders, attached 2nd Battalion, was killed in action on 23 April 1917, aged 23 (Plot B.61). He was born in Paisley and had begun working as an accountant and stockbroker in Glasgow. When the war broke out he enlisted as a private and was commissioned within the regiment. His MC was gazetted on 10 January 1917 and was awarded for conspicuous gallantry in action on the Somme in July 1916 after leading his company in an attack with great courage and determination, advancing the line and consolidating the position with great skill. The citation concludes that he had previously done fine work. His VC was won in an action when his party faced growing casualties from heavy fire and was also being attacked from the rear. Though wounded in the left arm, he led a bayonet charge with three other men against a large body of the enemy.

His brother, Private George Henderson, was killed in action a couple of weeks earlier on 9 April whilst serving with the 2nd Canadian Mounted Rifles and is commemorated on the Vimy Memorial. The brothers had met briefly at home in November 1916.

There are also four graves of men belonging to the 16th (Irish) Division, which arrived in the area after the Battle of Arras. The 7th Royal Irish Rifles arrived in France in August 1917 where it became part of the division's 49 Brigade. However, by the middle of October it was transferred to the 36th (Ulster) Division's 108 Brigade. Its three riflemen fell shortly before the move and are now buried in Row F.5 to 7. The 8th Royal Dublin Fusiliers had landed with the 16th (Irish) Division in December 1915, but the battalion was amalgamated with the regiment's 9th Battalion in October 1917. Private Patrick COSGROVE, 8th Battalion, is buried in Row F.3.

A further two holders of gallantry awards can be found in this cemetery: Driver Frank MILLER MM, 83 Brigade HQ, Royal Field Artillery, killed in action on 23 May 1917, aged 32 (Plot A.75); and Lance Corporal Fred BLAKELEY MM, 17th Manchester Regiment; killed in action on 23 April 1917, aged 22 (Plot D.62).

Cuckoo Passage Cemetery, Héninel

This cemetery is dominated by the fortunes of two battalions of the 30th Division, the 17th and 18th Manchester Regiment, and is named after a trench that ran alongside it. Forty-one NCOs and privates from these two battalions now rest here, all killed in action on 23 April 1917 in what is officially known as the Second Battle of the Scarpe. The division's objective that day was the high ground overlooking Chérisy. The 17th Manchester Regiment (2nd Manchester Pals) and the 2nd Royal Scots Fusiliers had taken part in the initial attack, but this was soon broken up and lost its momentum. The 18th and 19th Battalions, Manchester Regiment (3rd and 4th Manchester Pals), then renewed the attack with limited success. It is interesting to note that on this occasion it was the intensity and speed with which the enemy's barrage came down that brought the initial attack to a halt, rather than machine-gun fire as was more often the case. The renewed attack by the 18th Manchester Regiment made some ground, but was then driven back with heavy losses, including all the officers who took part. The 19th Manchester Regiment, however, was able to gain a foothold in the enemy's trenches and managed to hold the position.

Set in quiet isolation about half way between Héninel and Fontaine-les-Croisilles, this small battlefield cemetery is another that feels very intimate, even very private. It contains just fifty-four graves, all of which are identified with one exception. There are no officers and no gallantry awards here; in it lie very ordinary, unremarkable men, so typical of the majority who died doing their duty and their best. Many of these Manchester men would have known each other, probably quite well, and walking among them it is not hard to imagine something of the deep sense of comradeship they would have shared during their time together. The cemetery has very much a 'Pals' character and feel to it.

Within this small cemetery it will not go unnoticed that there are a few headstones belonging to men of the 9th Battalion, London Regiment (Queen Victoria's Rifles), all of whom were killed in action on 14 April 1917. These eight men are not isolated casualties, but part of the 121 from that battalion who were killed or died of wounds that day. Others can be found scattered among four neighbouring cemeteries, but the vast majority have no known grave and are commemorated on the Arras Memorial. Many were killed by machine-gun fire in the initial attack by the 56th (London)

Division south of the ruined Wancourt Tower, but others were killed when the Germans counter-attacked.

The remaining four identified casualties are from battalions of the 18th (Eastern) Division and the 21st Division, all of them killed in action on 3 May 1917, the opening day of the Third Battle of the Scarpe.

Hénin-sur-Cojeul Communal Cemetery

There is just one identified casualty buried here. Fusilier Nicholas Frederick HILL, 8th Royal Northumberland Fusiliers, was killed sometime between 19 and 22 May 1940 and was 20 years old when he died. The cemetery lies about 800 yards south of the village of Hénin-sur-Cojeul on the D.12E. The communal cemetery extension lies adjacent to it.

Hénin Communal Cemetery Extension, Hénin-sur-Cojeul

The communal cemetery and its extension are situated on the south side of Hénin about half a mile from the centre of the village on the D.12E. The extension contains 175 identified casualties, including several from August 1918 when the village was recaptured by the 52nd (Lowland) Division. It was enlarged after the war by the addition of sixty-eight graves brought in from Hénin British Cemetery. It was originally used between April and November 1917 and the infantry burials within it come mainly from the 21st, 30th and 33rd Divisions, and from two Yorkshire Regiments in particular: the King's Own Yorkshire Light Infantry and the Yorkshire Regiment.

All twenty-eight men of the King's Own Yorkshire Light Infantry are from either its 9th or its 10th Battalions. Both of these were part of the 21st Division, and some of the officers were attached from other battalions of the regiment. Second Lieutenant Arnold William HOBBS MM (Plot I.A.5), for example, was attached to the 10th Battalion from the 3rd, and prior to that, like Second Lieutenant Frank WHALEY, 2nd Yorkshire Regiment, he had originally enlisted in the 18th Royal Fusiliers (1st University and Public Schools Battalion) and had served since 1914. He was killed in action on the opening day of the Arras offensive on 9 April 1917. His MM, which was gazetted on 11 November 1916, was awarded for bravery in the field while serving as a corporal in the Royal Fusiliers. (Plot I.A.5)

Second Lieutenant Vincent Harvey WISEMAN, 4th King's Own Yorkshire Light Infantry, was killed in action on 9 April 1917, aged 20 (Plot I.A.7). His brother, Private Charles Wiseman, 12th York & Lancaster Regiment, was killed in action on 26 May 1918, aged 24. He is buried at Bienvillers Military Cemetery and, although CWGC records show him as serving with the 12th Battalion (Sheffield Pals), he was actually killed with the 2/4th (Hallamshire) Battalion of the regiment, as the 12th Battalion was disbanded in February 1918. His regimental number indicates that he was one of the original Sheffield Pals, so many of whom were killed on the opening day of the Battle of the Somme.

Captain Ralph Hugh HINE-HAYCOCK, 10th King's Own Yorkshire Light Infantry, attached from the 1st Battalion, was killed in action on 3 May 1917. He was a member of the MCC (Plot I.B.4). The majority of men buried here from that regiment fell in early May during the Third Battle of the Scarpe, or during the following two months once the main fighting on this part of the front had ceased. Captain Harold BURKETT, 10th King's Own Yorkshire Light Infantry, the battalion's adjutant, was one of nine killed in the first week of June 1917. (Plot I.D.9)

Second Lieutenant John Ernest CUNDALL, 5th King's Own Yorkshire Light Infantry, was killed in action on 3 May 1917, aged 36 (Plot II.B.2). CWGC records suggest that other members of his family may also have died or been killed during the war, though I have not been able to confirm this. Second Lieutenant Stanley Cundall, 10th King's Own Yorkshire Light Infantry, who was killed in action on 21 April 1918, may also be related. He is buried at Klein Vierstraat British Cemetery, Belgium, and is also commemorated on the Chingford War Memorial. CWGC records show a possible link between families of that name in both Yorkshire and the north London area.

The first burials here are from the 2nd Yorkshire Regiment. Second Lieutenant Frank WHALEY (Plot II.D.23) and three other ranks were killed on 31 March 1917 as units of the 30th Division edged towards the village of Henin-sur-Cojeul as part of a general advance to the Hindenburg Line. One of the men, Serjeant Albert BROWN, held the MM. He was badly wounded and died later that day (Plot II.D.27). WHALEY originally served with the 18th Royal Fusiliers (1st Public Schools Battalion).

A few days later, on 2 April, their battalion led the assault on the village under an artillery barrage, supported by two companies of the 19th Manchester Regiment. Fierce fighting took place when two of the companies from the 2nd Yorkshire Regiment entered the village from the south-west, followed by the 19th Manchester Regiment whose job it was to mop up. A German strongpoint was situated in the *Mairie* and the position was only overcome after it was bombarded by one of two trench mortars used in the attack. By early afternoon the village was in British hands, but only after a fight that had lasted nine hours.

Of the sixty-four men of the 2nd Yorkshire Regiment killed during the capture of the village, twenty-six are buried here in Plot II, mainly in Row D. Among them are Captain Robert Alister FIELD MC, aged 22 (Plot II.D.22) and Second Lieutenant Herbert Melville WRIGHT, aged 19 (Plot II.D.14). FIELD's MC was gazetted on 10 January 1917 and was awarded for conspicuous gallantry in action after displaying great courage and initiative during a bombing attack. Meeting an obstacle in the trench, he went along the parapet under heavy fire before jumping back into the trench and killing one of the enemy.

Another of those killed that day was Private James William HOWARD DCM, 2nd Yorkshire Regiment, aged 25. His DCM, gazetted on 15 March 1916, was awarded after volunteering to carry out rescue work at great personal risk. Whilst doing so, he himself was wounded, though he continued working until compelled to stop through loss of blood. (Plot II.D.21)

The 19th Manchester Regiment also has thirteen of its dead here in Plot II, Rows D and E, all killed 'mopping up' on 2 April, including one officer, Second Lieutenant Edward MURPHY. (Plot II.D.11)

The remaining infantry burials from 1917 are either from the 21st Division, or else mainly from battalions of the 33rd Division and the 50th (Northumbrian) Division.

There is also a solitary Canadian casualty from 1917 in Plot II: Sapper Alexander Stanley Walter STARK, 6th Battalion, Canadian Railway Troops, killed in action on 25 August 1917. (Plot II.B.16)

The largest number of men represented here from any one regiment belongs to the Royal Garrison Artillery; its forty-three officers and men account for 25 per cent of the identified burials in this cemetery. The majority are from May and June 1917, once the Battle of Arras was officially closed. Though small in scale, this bears testimony to the continuing attrition that was a constant feature of holding any important part of the line, during which artillery action and counter-battery fire was almost a daily routine. Three heavy artillery units, the 36th Siege Battery, 213th Siege Battery and the 156th Siege Battery, Royal Garrison Artillery, lost five officers between 28 April and 31 May 1917, including Second Lieutenant Frederick William CHALLINOR, 156th Siege Battery. His father, Frederick Arthur Challinor, was a very successful composer and an Associate of the Royal College of Music. (Plot I.C.16)

In addition to the casualties of the Royal Garrison Artillery, there are eighteen identified burials from the Royal Field Artillery. In the main, their dates of death are slightly earlier, encompassing the Second Battle of the Scarpe. Among the dead is Gunner Herbert BROWNE, 'A' Battery, 14 Brigade, Royal Field Artillery. He was killed in action on 20 April 1917, though *Soldiers Died in the Great War* shows him as dying on 24 April (Plot II.C.21). His brother, Serjeant George W. Browne, also served as a gunner with the 82nd Battery, Royal Field Artillery.

The small number of 1918 casualties, mainly from the fighting in August around Hénin and Hénin Hill, are from the 52nd (Lowland) Division or men of the 56th (London) Division. Privates James FINLAY and Edward O. BOOTH MM (Plots II.C.9 and 10), are both shown as 2/5th Highland Light Infantry. This battalion had been stationed in Dublin and the Curragh as part of the 65th Division, but was broken up in March 1918 and disbanded in May two months later. They, like the other Highland Light Infantry men here, are from the 1/6th and 1/7th Battalions and, along with one man from the 1/4th Royal Scots, were all part of the 52nd (Lowland) Division, which arrived in France from Palestine in April 1918. All of them were killed during the last week of August and are buried in Plot II, Row C, with two artillerymen from the 28th Battery, 9 Brigade, Royal Field Artillery (Graves 9 to 18). Three of the four men from the 56th (London) Division are also buried in Plot II. Row C.

Lieutenant Archibald Houlder MALCOLM, 9th Highland Light Infantry, attached 5th Battalion, was killed in action near Hénin Hill on 24 August 1918. He had been wounded previously in the shoulder and had also suffered shell shock on 20 August 1916 during an attack at High Wood in which part of Wood Lane was captured by two companies of the 9th (Glasgow Highlanders) Highland Light Infantry. (Plot II.C.8)

Hénin Crucifix Cemetery

This is a very small cemetery that derives its name from its proximity to one of the many *calvaires* frequently found throughout the French countryside. It lies just north of Hénin on the D.5. The CWGC register notes that the village fell at the end of March 1918 after a stubborn defence by the 40th Division and that it was recaptured on 24 August by the 52nd (Lowland) Division. Despite this there are no casualties here from 1918.

Two dates reveal the story behind this cemetery. On 2 April 1917 the 2nd Yorkshire Regiment and two companies from the 19th Manchester Regiment, both part of the 30th Division, carried out an operation to capture the village of Hénin-sur-Cojeul. The village was one of several included in the day's operations to clear a line of temporary outposts in front of the Hindenburg Line. The plan was to work around the village on either flank and then to establish strongpoints covering all the exits. Two companies would then enter the village from the south-west, followed by the two Manchester companies to mop-up. The encounter, which lasted all morning and continued into the afternoon, was described as typical street fighting as ruined building after ruined building was cleared. The last building to fall was the *Mairie*, where the Germans had formed a strongpoint, and by 3.00pm, after nine hours of fighting, the village was eventually captured.

There are eleven identified casualties from the 19th Manchester Regiment and thirteen men from the 2nd Yorkshire Regiment buried here who fell during that attack, including one officer, Second Lieutenant Allan COPLEY, 19th Manchester Regiment, who originally served as a private in the Honourable Artillery Company before transferring to the Artists' Rifles. (Plot A.4)

The other key date is the opening day of the Arras offensive a week later. One officer and thirty-two identified casualties from the King's (Liverpool Regiment) lie buried here from the first three days' fighting. The majority are from 9 April and from the regiment's 20th Battalion. Its left flank had to be withdrawn during the evening to a position north-west of Saint-Martin after the 2nd Wiltshire Regiment had failed to make progress. This allowed a further bombardment to take place overnight before the attack was resumed the following day. Second Lieutenant Alfred Rothwell CARR, despite being shown as 9th Battalion, was one of two officers from the 17th Battalion killed in the initial advance on 9 April. The 17th Battalion had been designated to mop-up, but in reality had little to do that day owing to the day's events during which the 19th and 20th Battalions made little progress.

The one gallantry award is Serjeant Austin BUTT MM, 89th Company, Machine Gun Corps, who was killed in the same action as the main group of King's (Liverpool Regiment) men on 9 April, and was part of a machine gun detachment supporting their attack (Plot A.42). The last recorded casualty here also came from the same brigade, the 89th, and is a private from the 2nd Bedfordshire Regiment who was killed in action on 11 April 1917.

Héninel Communal Cemetery Extension

The cemetery lies outside the village on its north-east side and along the road leading to Chérisy. It is reached by a small track and is quite isolated. The village fell on 12 April 1917 and the cemetery was begun soon after that.

The counties of northern England, Durham, Northumberland, and the Ridings of Yorkshire, are well represented in this cemetery. Regiments from these counties were the mainstay of the 50th (Northumbrian) Division and the cemetery was originally made by its burial officer. It now contains 140 burials, of which 133 are identified. Twelve of the thirteen infantry battalions that made up the 50th (Northumbrian) Division have men buried here, the 4th Yorkshire Regiment being the only exception.

The 5th Yorkshire Regiment has twenty-eight burials and there are also thirty-one burials from the five battalions of the Durham Light Infantry that formed part of the division. The division was present in this sector for the better part of six months, from the beginning of April to the beginning of October 1917. However, at the end of April, the division was taken out of the line with a view to using it to exploit any success following the attacks planned for the beginning of May. When those attacks failed to deliver the anticipated results, the division was placed in Army Reserve where it was allowed to rest and refit until the middle of June. This came as a much needed respite, as it had sustained almost 2,750 casualties during April, including sixty-six officers and 1,400 other ranks on 23 April alone.

The 50th (Northumbrian) Division took over the area east of Wancourt and Héninel on 12 April 1917 after relieving the 14th (Light) Division. On 14 April it took part in an attack with the 56th (London) Division on its right. In the original plan the 3rd Division was to have attacked Guémappe, but it was then relieved by the 29th Division, and so neither was in a position to contribute to the attack that day. Supported by the 5th Border Regiment, the 6th and 8th Durham Light Infantry went forward, but their advance, like that of the 56th (London) Division, was brought to a halt by a combination of shelling and machine-gun fire from Guémappe. Where the two divisions met, troops became mingled, which only added to the confusion. A number of casualties from this attack are buried together in Row A (Plots A.2 to A.8) whilst several others are buried in Row F.

The 50th (Northumbrian) Division was again in action here on 23 April 1917, the opening day of the Second Battle of the Scarpe, and also for the Third Battle of the Scarpe, on 3 May 1917, when it was in reserve, but took no part in the day's action. It later returned to the front line opposite Fontaine-les-Croisilles and Chérisy where the German trenches ran on the reverse slope about 500 yards west of both villages.

The summer months and early autumn in this sector were characterised by strenuous and very active trench warfare, in which the guns of both sides were more or less continuously engaged. There was also much active patrolling of no man's land, including several raids, whilst pioneers and Royal Engineer field companies were constantly engaged, improving defences and maintaining trenches and other infrastructure, including approaches to the front line.

A raid by the 9th Durham Light Infantry on 13 July was followed six days later by a large German raid on the 19th. The enemy's raid took place at six locations along the divisional front, but good wiring and determined fire from our Lewis guns prevented them from penetrating our line. However, the raid resulted in eighty casualties among the various battalions that were holding and supporting the line that day, eighteen of whom are now buried within this cemetery. These now lie in an unbroken line, all killed on 19 July 1917 by shelling (Plots C.11 to C.28).

Twelve of them were the victims of a single shell that blew in the section of their trench. Corporal John Henry DEVLIN, aged 20 (Plot C.16), was dug out by comrades, but attempts to revive him failed. The row consists of three men from the 4th East Yorkshire Regiment (Plots C.11 to C.13), followed by fifteen from the 5th Yorkshire Regiment. There is one gallantry award holder among them: Lance Corporal W. COCKERILL MM, 5th Yorkshire Regiment. (Plot C.23)

The cemetery contains three other gallantry awards, two of them officers. Lieutenant Hugh HALL MC, 9th Durham Light Infantry, was killed in action on 15 September 1917, aged 25 (Plot E.6). HALL and seven other men from his battalion were killed in a successful raid that was part of a series of connected operations by 151 Brigade of the 50th (Northumbrian) Division. HALL and his men formed one of two detachments whose role it was to protect the flanks of the raid. The raiders from 'A', 'B' and 'C' Companies attacked at 4.00pm on 15 September and spent half an hour in the German front and support trenches west of Chérisy, where they killed an estimated seventy Germans and captured twenty-five, all of whom were taken by surprise. While in the German trenches, eleven dug-outs were damaged or destroyed by demolition teams from the division's Royal Engineer units.

A further raid was carried out later that evening by the 8th Durham Light Infantry and, at 4.00am the following morning, 552 gas canisters were discharged into the German lines. Four of the seven men killed with HALL on 15 September are buried next to him or nearby: Private Walter MILLER (Plot E.5), Private Henry WEST-WOOD (Plot E.4), Private William BROWNLESS (Plot E.3) and Private William WINCHESTER (Plot E.19). Of the remaining three, Private Richard Hibbs, Private Abel Williams, and Lance Corporal John Colgan MM, are commemorated on the Arras Memorial. Another of their comrades, Private James Dennis, died of wounds later that day and is buried in St Martin Calvaire British Cemetery, Saint-Martin-sur-Cojeul.

The other officer with a gallantry award is Captain Hugh Richard LONGBOURNE DSO, 'C' Company, 7th Queen's (Royal West Surrey Regiment). He was 32 years old when he was killed by a sniper's bullet on 3 May 1917 at around 1.15pm (Plot B.17). He joined the Queen's Regiment in 1916, but six months before the outbreak of war he was responsible for raising a company of the Huntingdon Cyclist Battalion. His death occurred as he was taking his company up to support the 8th East Surrey Regiment, which had been counter-attacked on the right flank of the brigade's attack on Chérisy.

His DSO, gazetted on 25 November 1916, was awarded for conspicuous gallantry in action at the Schwaben Redoubt on 28 September 1916, during which he had crawled to within 25 yards of an enemy strongpoint before bombing it. Later, with two other men, he rushed the strongpoint, capturing a machine gun and forty-six unwounded prisoners. After most of his battalion had been relieved in the early hours of the following morning, LONGBOURNE and a number of his men remained in their position on the southern part of the redoubt until they could be relieved, only rejoining the rest of their comrades at around 11.00am that day. Soon after, on 13 October 1916, he returned to England to attend a commanding officers' course at Aldershot, and had clearly been marked as a natural leader with greater potential. On 8 April 1917 he was presented with the Silver Medal for Bravery (Montenegro).

His brother, Francis Cecil Longbourne, who had previously seen action with mounted infantry in the South African War, also served in the Queen's (Royal West Surrey Regiment). He also won the DSO for services in the field, gazetted on 15 February 1915, and went on to command 171 Brigade as a temporary brigadier general between 23 September 1917 and 30 October 1918. During his distinguished military career he was mentioned in despatches on eight occasions. He also held the French *Légion d'Honneur*, and was made a CMG in 1919.

In the next grave to LONGBOURNE is another officer from the 7th Queen's (Royal West Surrey Regiment). Captain Valentine HOOK was killed in action on the same day as LONGBOURNE, aged 21. He had been a pupil at Westminster School, London. (Plot B.18)

Other units attached to the 50th (Northumbrian) Division can also be found here, such as the five men with headstones carrying the regimental badge of the Machine Gun Corps. They are from the 149th Company, which was attached to 149 Brigade. The 446th and 447th Field Companies, Royal Engineers, which were also attached to the division, have a few men buried throughout the cemetery.

The Royal Field Artillery also has several burials. Five of the men, all members of the 62nd Trench Mortar Battery, were killed in action on 15 September 1917 and, although their graves are not consecutive, they are buried close to each other. With them, and killed the same day, is a gunner attached to the 50th Division Ammunition Column (Plot D.23). They were all killed during shelling, no doubt in response to the raid carried out that day by the 8th and 9th Durham Light Infantry.

Finally, men from various battalions of the London Regiment can be found scattered throughout Rows A, B and C. All of them are from the 56th (London) Division, and most were killed during the middle of April 1917 before the start of the Second Battle of the Scarpe.

Héninel-Croisilles Road Cemetery

The cemetery is located about 1,500 yards south of the village of Héninel along the Rue de Croisilles in open farm land on the road out to Croisilles. The CWGC register notes that it was the 21st Division that captured Héninel on 12 April 1917. The 33rd Division then took over this sector as the battle continued.

Around one third of the burials here are unidentified and, although the earliest burials are men of the 1st East Yorkshire Regiment who were killed in action on the opening day of the Battle of Arras (Plots I.B.21 to 31), the majority of burials are from units of the 33rd Division. Three of its battalions, the 2nd Argyll & Sutherland Highlanders, the 1st Middlesex Regiment and the 20th Royal Fusiliers, take up a large proportion of the cemetery. Of the fifty-one men of the 2nd Argyll & Sutherland Highlanders and forty-seven of the 1st Middlesex Regiment, almost all died on 23 or 24 April 1917. The fifty men of the 20th Royal Fusiliers were all killed in action a week earlier during a phase of minor operations that took place between the opening day of the Battle of Arras and the Second Battle of the Scarpe; all except one were killed on 16 April.

Serjeant Frederick PALMER DCM, 20th Royal Fusiliers, was killed in action on 16 April 1916. He had previously served with the 2nd Battalion, Royal Fusiliers, at

Gallipoli. It was there, during operations at Cape Helles, that he won his DCM serving as a private. It was gazetted on 3 July 1915 and was awarded for gallantry and marked ability after he had collected up men whose section leaders had been killed and whom he then went on to lead during the attack. Unfortunately, the DCM is not referred to in *Soldiers Died in the Great War*. (Plot I.A.18)

During the attack on 2 April 1917 the 1st Middlesex Regiment and the 2nd Argyll & Sutherland Highlanders became pinned down in front of their first objective, which was a small copse. However, 'C' and 'D' companies of the Middlesex Regiment, and some of the Highlanders from 'A' Company, managed to work their way around it. In doing so, they found themselves cut off and were forced to dig in and defend their position against counter-attack. By noon the remainder of the two battalions were back in their original positions, but the three companies were left isolated. Attempts to renew the attack later in the day achieved little and failed to come to the assistance of those cut off. The following day the Germans withdrew, but it was evening before the remnants of the three companies could be relieved.

Second Lieutenant George Lionel John BAKER, 1st Middlesex Regiment, was killed in action on 23 April, as were the two officers from his battalion buried next to him. He was educated at Sherborne School, where he had captained the Rugby XV, and then went on to Oriel College, Oxford, to study medicine. (Plot I.B.2)

Among the dead of the Argyll & Sutherland Highlanders is Second Lieutenant Hugh Drummond ALLAN. He went to Canada to work as a land surveyor before the war, but returned to Scotland to enlist when war broke out. He went to France in April 1915 and was wounded in 1916. Just before his death on 24 April 1917, his wife tragically died in childbirth (Plot II.C.37).

With him in the cemetery are several officers from his battalion: Captain Alexander Baird TYSON (Plot II.B.1), Second Lieutenant Arthur Alexander WILSON (Plot II.B.2), Second Lieutenant Andrew FULTON (Plot II.B.3), Second Lieutenant Joseph Moule Hamilton MAITLAND (Plot II.C.35) and Second Lieutenant William CLARK (Plot II.C.36). MAITLAND died of wounds, but all the others were killed in action on 23 April. MAITLAND's grandfather, Charles, had been the senior partner and managing director of the Bass Crest Brewery and learned his trade as a Master Brewer in Alloa.

The 1st Battalion and the 5/6th Battalion, Cameronians, were also part of the 33rd Division and have nineteen identified casualties buried here between them, including two officers from the latter battalion. Captain Kenneth ASHBY-BROWN, aged 29, from Glasgow, and a former student at the university there, was killed in action on 14 April 1917 (Plot I.B.11). Captain Douglas Cameron FOSTER, aged 26, from Salcombe in Devon, was also killed in action on the same day (Plot II.A.17). His father was Brigadier General Turville Douglas Foster MVO, who died in February 1915, aged 50. He had served as assistant quartermaster general at the Staff College and as inspector general, Army Service Corps.

Listed below are a number of men with gallantry awards who are buried here.

Captain Robert Thomas PATEY MC, 1st King's (Liverpool Regiment), attached 4th Battalion, was killed in action on 20 May 1917 leading a bombing attack along trenches between the Hindenburg Line and its supporting lines. He had served in the South African War with the Worcestershire Regiment and had been serving as regimental serjeant major before he was commissioned in the King's (Liverpool Regiment) in November 1914. He went to France in the autumn of 1916 where he soon won the MC for his courage and leadership as a lieutenant in charge of 'A' Company on 28 October 1916 in a bombing attack on Dewdrop Trench. The position was captured along with a significant number of prisoners. (Plot II.B.7)

Second Lieutenant Arthur CORBRIDGE MC, 4th King's (Liverpool Regiment), was killed in action the same day as PATEY. He had also taken part in the attack on Dewdrop Trench with PATEY on 28 October where he had been responsible for bombing dug-outs located in a sunken lane nearby, and for which he was also awarded the MC. Both awards were gazetted on 11 December 1916. (Plot II.B.5)

Serjeant Arthur HOUGH MM, who originally served with the Cheshire Regiment before the war, was killed in action on 23 April 1917 whilst serving with the 11th Field Company, Royal Engineers. (Plot II.D.1)

Although the story of this cemetery is essentially confined to 1917, there appear to be two burials from the years either side. According to *Soldiers Died in the Great War*, Private Shadrack WHITE, 7th Northumberland Fusiliers, died on 14 November 1916, aged 26, from causes other than wounds. However, this has to be in doubt, since the 7th Northumberland Fusiliers were still fighting on the Somme on that date, just east of Le Sars. A section of trench known as Hook Sap was recaptured by the Germans in a counter-attack and it seems far more likely that SHADRACK was captured and died of wounds later that day in German captivity. His body was very likely moved here after the Armistice. (Plot II.F.4)

Captain William BROWNLIE MC, Royal Army Medical Corps, attached 13th Yorkshire Regiment, was killed in action west of Croisilles on 25 March 1918, aged 36. (Plot II.A.7)

Finally, there is the grave of Private Horace PLACKETT, 2nd Royal Irish Regiment, who was killed in action on 22 November 1917 during a successful operation that resulted in the capture of Tunnel Trench (Plot II.D.32). It is the only grave in this cemetery connected with this particular operation. Parts of this formidable defensive structure, which formed part of the Hindenburg Line, had been captured in April earlier that year by the 33rd Division, but the section south of Fontaine-les-Croisilles remained in German hands until the attack on 20 November 1917. This subsidiary operation was carried out by the 16th (Irish) Division and the 3rd Division and was specifically scheduled to coincide with the opening day of the Battle of Cambrai. As Private PLACKETT is now separated from the rest of his comrades who fell in this operation, it seems a satisfactory note on which to conclude a visit to this cemetery.

Rookery British Cemetery, Héninel

There is a somewhat unusual configuration to this cemetery. Row A has two separate graves that are offset from the main row. Row B consists of two small blocks, and again ends with two separate graves. In common with many of the smaller cemeteries on the Western Front, there is no War Stone, but, unusually, there is no Cross of Sacrifice either. The cemetery itself lies about 1,500 yards south of the village of Héninel, very close to Cuckoo Passage Cemetery, and derives its name from a group of trenches that were originally located here. It was started by the 50th (Northumbrian) and 18th (Eastern) Divisions in spring 1917 and was in use until November that year. There are just two burials from 1918.

There are just fifty-five burials here, of which fifty-four are identified. Although the cemetery lies in ground that was fought over in April and May 1917, the casualties buried here are from the period that followed, mainly June and July 1917. Exactly half of the identified casualties are from the 18th (Eastern) Division. This division had spent April 1917 in GHQ Reserve, but did take part in fighting on 3 May. The division's casualty figures reflect this: fifty-three for April compared with 2,351 for May. The division continued to hold the line throughout the early summer before moving up to Ypres.

The two earliest casualties are from the 18th King's (Liverpool Regiment), although Lieutenant Charles David CALCOTT is shown in the CWGC register as serving with the 15th Battalion (Plot C.23). The other man is Company Serjeant Major John Daniel JONES (Plot C.19). Their battalion formed part of the 30th Division, together with the other three of the regiment's 'Pals' Battalions: the 17th, 19th, and 20th Battalions. All of these units are well represented in nearby cemeteries. Both men fell on 23 April 1917.

The first casualty from the 18th (Eastern) Division is a soldier from the 6th Northamptonshire Regiment, whose death occurred on 30 April 1917 (Plot C.21). There are also a handful of casualties from late May belonging to the 7th Queen's Own (Royal West Kent Regiment), (Plots C.24 to C.27) and 10th Essex Regiment (Plot C.20). Both battalions were part of the 18th (Eastern) Division.

The cemetery starts to take on part of its character thereafter with the consecutive burial of six privates from the 8th Suffolk Regiment following their death on 1 June 1917 (Plots C.13 to C.18). There are also eleven men of the 6th Northamptonshire Regiment buried a little further back in the same row, all killed in action between 3 and 9 June 1917 (Plots C.1 to C.11).

In between these two groups is Second Lieutenant Ferdinand Nigel SHERWELL, 7th Bedfordshire Regiment, who was killed in action on 13 June. He was commissioned in the Bedfordshire Regiment in September 1914 and went to France the following July with the regiment's 7th Battalion as part of the 18th (Eastern) Division. He fought with it on the Somme, where the division established its reputation as a very good fighting unit. He came from a large family and had eight brothers. (Plot C.12)

The other significant group of men now resting here are the thirteen identified casualties from the 1/4th Yorkshire Regiment, part of the 50th (Northumbrian) Division. They are buried in Rows A and B and fell in action between late June and mid July 1917. In one of the separate graves at the end of Row A is Company Serjeant Major Frederick James HOPPER, who was killed in action on 27 June 1917, aged 32. He was also mentioned in despatches. (Plot A.14)

Also from the 50th (Northumbrian) Division are four graves belonging to men from the 1/5th Durham Light Infantry who were killed or died of wounds at the end of June 1917. One of them, Serjeant Fred Hardwick MERRYWEATHER MM, is the only gallantry award holder to be found in this cemetery. He and his battalion had taken part in a raid with men from the 5th Yorkshire Regiment on 26 June. Although the raid succeeded in capturing York and Fontaine Trenches with very few casualties, the German retaliation had severe consequences for the 4th East Yorkshire Regiment, which had come up to relieve them on the evening of the raid. The Germans never even counter-attacked and allowed their former trenches to be captured, but then put down a devastating bombardment the following day, resulting in just over a hundred casualties to the East Yorkshiremen. MERRYWEATHER may have been wounded during the raid, or possibly during the relief, but he died of wounds nearby on 27 June (Plot C.29). The other three men from his battalion are buried in Row A.

There are just two 1918 casualties here. Both men were killed in action at the end of August 1918.

Captain Kenneth MacKENZIE, 9th Royal Scots, attached 7th Battalion, was killed in action on 27 August 1918. *Officers Died in the Great War* causes some confusion and shows his date of death as 9 September 1918. However, not only is the earlier date supported by the regimental history, there is also a very impressive monument to him back in Scotland, erected on the family estate at Kippet Hill, near Dolphinton in the Borders, which confirms the date of death as 27 August. He was a Justice of the Peace for Lanarkshire and a Writer to the Signet in Edinburgh, as was his father. His maternal grandfather was Sir Thomas Kirkpatrick of Closeburn, 5th Baronet. MacKENZIE's wife remarried after his death and was later awarded the OBE and a CBE. He is the most senior casualty buried here. (Plot C.31)

The other 1918 casualty is Gunner William Henry DEANS, 8th Heavy Artillery Group HQ, who was killed in action on 29 August 1918, aged 40. (Plot C.30)

St Martin Calvaire British Cemetery, Saint-Martin-sur-Cojeul

The cemetery was named after a *calvaire* situated alongside it which was destroyed during the war. The village of Saint-Martin-sur-Cojeul was captured on the opening day of the Battle of Arras by the 30th Division. The cemetery, which lies to the southeast of the village and west of the A.1 Autoroute, is situated roughly 350 yards along the Rue de Fontaine. Only five of the 228 graves are unidentified.

The King's (Liverpool Regiment) and the Northumberland Fusiliers are here in significant numbers; the former has forty-two identified burials, whilst the latter has thirty. Their casualties are from 1917 and 1918, and so cover a number of different battalions of both regiments. There are twenty-four men from the 17th and 19th Battalions, King's (Liverpool Regiment), all of whom were killed in action on 9 April 1917, including one officer. Among them is Private Reginald Vaughan DAVIES, aged 21, 19th King's (Liverpool Regiment), who had previously served with the Royal Marines at Dunkirk and Antwerp in 1914. He had also served with the Manchester Regiment (Plot I.A.26). All twenty-four men can be found in Plot I, Row A.

Among the casualties of the King's (Liverpool Regiment) who fell in 1918 are three from the 13th Battalion who were killed on 12 March, shortly before the German Offensive (Plots I.F.8, 9 and 10). The remainder are from the fighting during the final days of August and the first days of September 1918 and are men belonging to the

2/7th and 2/9th Battalions. One of the 9th Battalion casualties who fell on 28 August 1918 is Major Frank Harvey BOWRING (Plot II.B.1). The CWGC register tells us that BOWRING was born in Newfoundland. The family, whose business was originally watchmaking, emigrated from England to Newfoundland. From there it branched out into shipping and the insurance business. Frank's father, the Honourable Charles Bowring, ran the family firm. Frank was educated in England at Shrewsbury School, then at Christ Church College, Oxford, after which he became a solicitor and a member of the Liverpool Stock Exchange. Three of his brothers served during the war. Harold served as a medical officer with the cavalry, William as a lieutenant with the 9th Cameronians, and Cyril as a captain with the Royal Welsh Fusiliers; all three survived. The Bowring family purchased land for a park in St John's, Newfoundland. There is a Royal Newfoundland Regiment memorial caribou there.

Close together in Plot I, Row B, starting at grave 12, there are seven men from the 8th Royal Sussex Regiment, including Captain Alfred David FOSTER MC, killed in action on 5 May 1917 (Plot I.B.18). Three of the men were killed the same day as FOSTER, the other three on 13 May 1917. His MC was gazetted on 23 October 1916 and was awarded for conspicuous gallantry in directing the work of his platoon and opening up communications across no man's land whilst under heavy fire. Though wounded earlier in the day, he refused to leave his post until he was ordered to go back. The 8th Royal Sussex Regiment was the pioneer battalion of the 18th (Eastern) Division. Pioneer battalions were nearly always called upon to consolidate and improve recently captured trenches, a task which frequently had to be carried out under shell fire.

Captain Charles SPROXTON MC, 4th Yorkshire Regiment, was killed in action on 19 July 1917, aged 26, and at the time of his death he was serving as the battalion's adjutant (Plot I.B.22). Before the war he read History at Peterhouse College, Cambridge, where he subsequently became a Fellow. He received his commission with the Yorkshire Regiment in late August 1914 and saw action with his battalion at the Second Battle of Ypres. He was killed during a German attack on his battalion's trenches. His MC, gazetted on 2 October 1915, was won as a second lieutenant and was awarded for conspicuous gallantry and resource on numerous occasions, securing the defence of his company's line, particularly on the night of 5 and 6 July 1915 near Wulverghem. Although exposed by the enemy's flares and under heavy rifle fire, and assisted by only one NCO, he carried eight 'knife rests' (entanglements) and placed them in position within forty yards of the enemy's line. Again, on the night of 6 and 7 August near Armentières, he was in charge of a wiring party in front of our fire trench. When a German machine gun was turned on the party, he successfully withdrew his men, but then returned with the same NCO and completed the work, showing an utter disregard for danger. Buried alongside him are two of his men, although they were killed almost a month earlier.

Captain John Earnscleugh BRYDON, Royal Army Medical Corps, was attached to the 4th Yorkshire Regiment. He died of wounds on 27 June 1917 and is buried in the next row (Plot I.C.17). Private Joseph Henry WILSON, 2/2nd Northumbrian Field Ambulance, is buried next to him and also died of wounds the same day, as did Private

Frank RIGG, 1/3rd Northumbrian Field Ambulance, though he happens to be buried just a few graves along from SPROXTON (Plot I.B.25). All three appear to have become casualties following a small operation carried out by the 5th Yorkshire Regiment and the 1/5th Durham Light Infantry on 26 June. Both battalions were part of the 50th (Northumbrian) Division.

Among the thirty casualties from the Northumberland Fusiliers are five officers. Captain John Middleton DOWNEND, 26th Battalion, was killed in action on 24 November 1917. Before the war he was the headmaster at the Boys' School in Hemsworth, West Yorkshire. *Officers Died in the Great War* shows the surname as 'Dowend' (Plot I.D.15).

Two others, Second Lieutenant David KINNAIRD and Second Lieutenant Geoffrey LAUGHTON, also 26th Northumberland Fusiliers (3rd Tyneside Irish), were both killed during a trench raid that took place on the night of the 5/6 December 1917 (Plots I.E.1 and 2). Although a small party under Second Lieutenant Jenkins got into the trenches and found them empty, the remaining three groups came under machine-gun fire, killing KINNAIRD and LAUGHTON, along with three other ranks, and wounding seven others. Two of the three killed are also buried here, though separated from the two officers. They are Serjeant John William SYMM and Private Edward GIBSON (Plots I.D.22 and 23). The third man killed that night is probably Private Lawrence JACKSON. Although shown in the CWGC register as serving with the 22nd Battalion, he was killed in action on 5 December 1917 and is buried next to SYMM and GIBSON in grave 21, Row D. The CWGC records show only seven Northumberland Fusiliers dying that day, two of whom can readily be ruled out as not having been involved in the raid. Taking the two officers into account, that only leaves Private JACKSON. Nearly all the Northumberland Fusiliers buried here are from the 34th Division and most of them are from the 21st or the 22nd (2nd and 3rd Tyneside Scottish) Battalions.

The CWGC records relating to Second Lieutenant Percy Reginald NEALE and Private Horace James SHEASBY show them as serving with the 101st Battalion (Buckinghamshire & Berkshire), Machine Gun Corps at the time of their deaths on 20 and 30 December 1917, respectively (Plots I.E.6 and 7). Their unit should read '101st Company, Machine Gun Corps', which was part of the 34th Division. The confusion probably arises because the Buckinghamshire and Berkshire Yeomanry merged in April 1918 and then went on to serve in the Machine Gun Corps.

The cemetery also contains twenty-eight identified burials from the Royal Field Artillery. Just over half are casualties from 1917 and are buried in Plot I. A second lieutenant, a corporal, and three gunners from 'A' Battery, 160 Brigade, Royal Field Artillery, killed in action on 6 February 1918, are buried amongst them. Two of the gunners had been awarded the MM (Plots I.E.21 to 25). The remaining casualties, all from 1918, died in the last few days of August and at the start of September. Among the 1917 casualties is a Major Forster Moore ARMSTRONG, 251st (Northumberland) Brigade, Royal Field Artillery, who was killed in action on 25 September 1917, aged 41 (Plot I.C.20). The 50th (Northumbrian) Division carried out several raids on enemy positions during September 1917, and consequently, artillery from both sides was frequently in action throughout the month. As well as causing many casualties among the infantry, artillery positions also came under heavy shell fire and with the same result.

The ten casualties from the Royal Garrison Artillery follow a similar pattern. The 1917 burials, from May and July, can be found in Plot I. They include Second Lieutenant Charles Arthur GREEN MC, 2/1st Lowland Heavy Battery (Plot I.C.24) and two other ranks from his unit who lie next to him. All three men were killed in action on 13 July 1917; one of them, Gunner Magnus SMITH from Shetland, was only 18 years old when he died. GREEN, who had been studying Classics at Worcester College, Oxford, when war broke out, had already shown an interest in military affairs by joining the OTC at the Royal Grammar School in Newcastle-upon-Tyne. In 1916 he joined the Royal Horse Guards OTC, and in August that year was gazetted as a second lieutenant. By the following January he was in France with the 2/1st Lowland Heavy Battery as a forward observation officer. During the April and May fighting he performed admirably and won his MC for gallantry and devotion to duty. The citation refers to one occasion in particular when he returned through a heavy barrage four times and brought back valuable information, including a vital message requesting reinforcements that saved a critical situation. His MC was gazetted on 26 July 1917. He and the two men buried next to him were killed by a shell that wounded several others. They were originally buried near to where they fell and it is therefore fitting that they were reburied together after the war.

The 1918 Royal Garrison Artillery casualties are from fighting at the end of August and the first two days of September.

Also in Plot I are four men of the 7/8th Royal Irish Fusiliers who were killed during operations to capture Tunnel Trench on 20 November 1917. One of them, Private Albert McCULLOUGH, originally from the Shankill area of Belfast, was just 16 years old when he was killed in action. All are buried side by side in Row D in graves 9, 10, 11 and 12. Rows B and C also start with two privates from the South Irish Horse (7th Royal Irish Regiment). Both were killed on 29 October 1917.

By comparison with many other regiments, very few battalions of the South Lancashire Regiment were ever involved in fighting around Arras, but there is a group of ten NCOs and privates buried here from the regiment's 2/4th Battalion, all of whom were killed in action on 28 August 1918. The battalion was part of the 57th (2nd West Lancashire) Division. They are to be found in Plot II, Rows A and B. The battalion's objective was the village of Hendecourt, whilst on its right the 9th King's (Liverpool) Regiment) was to capture Riencourt. The attack, which started at 12.30pm on the 28th, lasted several hours and was initially successful, though the 2/4th South Lancashire Regiment found its left flank exposed and had to withdraw from the village overnight. Both villages, however, were cleared the next day. The regimental history indicates that twenty other ranks were killed during the operation on the 28th and that a further five were missing in action. The CWGC records show a total of twenty-nine dead that day; seven are buried at HAC Cemetery, Écoust-Saint-Mein, one at Wancourt British Cemetery, one at Dury Crucifix Cemetery, and twelve others are commemorated on the memorial at Vis-en-Artois. It is therefore evident that a few of the 158 wounded died later that day.

Plot II contains seven officers and men of the 1st Royal Munster Fusiliers killed in action between 28 August and 2 September 1918, including two officers. Captain Colin Herbert CARRIGAN MC and Bar, was killed in action on 2 September, aged 23, serving with the 2nd Battalion. On 22 December 1914 the 2nd Battalion had attacked near Givenchy and had come under rifle and machine-gun fire from Givenchy Ridge. Lieutenant Colonel Bent and Major Thomson went forward and both were badly wounded. Thomson was killed soon after receiving his wound, but Bent was left on top of a dead German in a trench with a gaping wound to the side of his abdomen caused by a shell fragment that had left his intestine exposed. When darkness came, a search party went out, but it failed to find him and withdrew at around 1.30am the next morning. Half an hour later a small party went out, led by CARRIGAN, who brought his commanding officer back to the British lines after he had been lying exposed to the cold since 9.00am the previous day. Although Lieutenant Colonel Bent survived, he was unable to return to the front. He did continue serving at home in the UK and represented the regiment when the memorial to the battalion was unveiled at Étreux in the late 1920s.

CARRIGAN's MC was also won at Givenchy while serving as a second lieutenant with the 2nd Battalion. The citation states that on 25 January 1915 he handled his machine guns effectively and broke up a German advance. Then, showing gallantry and resource when forced to retire, he managed to extricate his machine guns under heavy fire before bringing them back into action 300 yards to the rear. The award was gazetted on 10 March that year. The regimental history also refers to his skilful judgement and leadership during the German March Offensive in 1918, especially on 27 March, though it does not comment on how he died other than to note that his death occurred during the attack on the Drocourt–Quéant Line. *Officers Died in the Great War* only shows the award of the MC, not the bar to it, and I can find no trace of any bar having been awarded or gazetted. Furthermore, the roll of honour in the regimental history only refers to him having been awarded the MC. He was, however, mentioned in despatches on 22 June 1915. He is buried next to three of his men who died with him on 2 September 1918. (Plot II.C.1)

Still in Plot II, in Row A, is Captain Gordon Thompson SHAW MC who was killed in action on 28 August 1918. SHAW's father, Sir Alexander William Shaw, was a successful businessman from Limerick who made his fortune in bacon curing by expanding the original business founded by his father. Although there is an entry in the *London Gazette* dated 7 June 1918 that shows the MC after his name, I can find no corresponding entry regarding the date on which it was gazetted. His obituary in a Limerick newspaper also refers to the award, as does the regimental history, which shows his MC gazetted on 1 January 1918 in the New Year's Honours List. He is shown in the regiment's roll of honour as serving with the 8th Battalion. That battalion amalgamated with the 9th Battalion in May 1916; later, in November that year, the composite formation was disbanded and its men transferred to the 1st Battalion. (Plot II.A.28)

Another officer in this cemetery with a gallantry award is Lieutenant Mark BRAWN DCM, 4th Bedfordshire Regiment. He was 38 years old when he was killed in action on 1 September 1918. His DCM was gazetted on 14 January 1916, and the citation on 11 March, while he was serving as a company serjeant major with the 9th Battalion, London Regiment (Queen Victoria's Rifles). It was awarded for conspicuous gallantry and devotion to duty, but not for any specific action. The citation only states that on each occasion he showed great bravery, skill, and a total disregard of personal risk. (Plot II.B.21)

He and three other ranks were killed that day during an air raid. The battalion was marching up from Boiry to Hénin when the incident occurred. Eleven others were wounded and twenty-six horses and mules were killed by the explosion. The three men killed with him are buried alongside him in graves 18, 19 and 20. Other men of the Bedfordshire Regiment are buried in this cemetery, but they all are casualties from the 2nd Battalion killed in action on 11 April 1917.

There are nine holders of the MM buried here. They are:

Gunner William Edward COMLEY MM, 'D' Battery, 82 Brigade, Royal Field Artillery, killed in action on 28 May 1917, aged 19. (Plot I.C.8)

Private Alfred BRADLEY MM, 54th Company, Machine Gun Corps, formerly Gordon Highlanders, killed in action on 6 June 1917, aged 26. (Plot I.C.13)

Lance Serjeant Thomas MARTIN MM, 1/5th Durham Light Infantry, died of wounds on 26 June 1917. *Soldiers Died in the Great War* makes no reference to his MM. (Plot I.C.15)

Corporal William RUSSELL MM, 'A' Battery, 160 Brigade, Royal Field Artillery, killed in action on 6 February 1918, aged 25. (Plot I.E.21)

Gunner David William JARDINE MM, 'A' Battery, 160 Brigade, Royal Field Artillery, killed in action on 6 February 1918. (Plot I.E.25)

Rifleman Robert MATTHEWS MM, 20th King's Royal Rifle Corps, killed in action on 27 February 1918. (Plot I.E.26)

Private Joseph BARLOW MM, 1st Royal Munster Fusiliers, formerly Manchester Regiment, killed in action on 28 August 1918. (Plot II.A.31)

Private Robin Carlyle MORLAND MM, 2/7th King's (Liverpool Regiment), killed in action on 1 September 1918. *Soldiers Died in the Great War* makes no reference to his MM. (Plot II.B.29)

Corporal Henry John VINCENT MM, 57th Battalion, Machine Gun Corps, formerly London Regiment, was killed in action on 30 August 1918 (Plot II.B.30). He is buried alongside three other men from the same unit, one of whom is Second Lieutenant Henry REED (Plot II.B.33). A fourth man from the same unit, Corporal Ernest Reginald MILLWARD, is buried separately, even though he was killed in action within the same twenty-four hour period as the others (Plot II.B.11).

Chapter Six

Dinner with Sassoon – A Middle Name of Murray – Last Confessions in a Barn

Summit Trench Cemetery, Croisilles

The cemetery is very isolated and is tucked on a bank adjacent to the A.1 Autoroute about a mile north-west of Croisilles. Just before the D.5 passes beneath the A.1, on the east side, nearest Croisilles, there is a track heading north that leads directly to the cemetery. The cemetery is signposted on the D.5 close to the track and is easy to find, whether coming from Croisilles or from the direction of Arras.

Summit Trench was captured with little difficulty and relatively few casualties on 24 August 1918 by 167 Brigade of the 56th (London) Division. The advance began at 7.00am and by 8.30am tanks and men from the brigade's three battalions had captured Summit Trench and were in the process of consolidating the position. The advance was part of a wider operation that involved the 52nd (Lowland) Division advancing to the north of the 56th (London) Division and the Guards Division pushing ahead to the south. The village of Croisilles lay slightly to the east of Summit Trench and reports had started to come in claiming that it had been abandoned, but patrols found that the village was, in fact, heavily defended, particularly by machine-gun detachments. After a bombardment failed to dislodge the garrison, the German artillery retaliated, firing gas shells into the British positions.

At 3.00am on 26 August 167 Brigade attacked again, but made no progress in the face of wire that still remained largely uncut and heavy fire from the many machine-gun positions now well established in and around the village. The following day 169 Brigade took over and continued the attack. The 2nd (City of London) Battalion, London Regiment (Royal Fusiliers), and the 5th Battalion, London Regiment (London Rifle Brigade), attempted to envelop the village from the north and made some progress, but the Guards Division attacking from the south was heavily counter-attacked, enabling the garrison in Croisilles to hold out, though its position was becoming ever more precarious.

Fortunately, further north, the 52nd (Lowland) Division and the Canadian 2nd Division had managed to enter the northern end of the Hindenburg Line and had begun to roll it up by working southwards. Croisilles was not captured until 28 August when the 1/8th Middlesex Regiment from 167 Brigade entered and occupied it after some initial fighting during the morning.

After the fighting the 56th (London) Division began collecting and burying its dead near to Summit Trench, a long trench that ran approximately north to south about 100 yards east of where today's cemetery is located. Today there are sixty-nine identified casualties here, all of whom belong to the 56th (London) Division, including two officers. Another five unidentified men lie with them.

Lieutenant Owen Henry GARRUD, 1/8th Battalion, London Regiment (Post Office Rifles), was killed in action on 24 August 1918, aged 24, during the initial attack when Summit Trench was captured. (Plot II.A.1)

Second Lieutenant George Houlden MERRIKIN, 1/2nd (City of London) Battalion, London Regiment (Royal Fusiliers), was killed in action on 27 August 1918, aged 40, while leading a party to recover wounded men from an earlier attack. Whilst doing so they came under fire and MERRIKIN lost his own life in the process of trying to save others. He and his party had already rescued eight men, but as they were going out for the ninth man in broad daylight he was shot dead. The CWGC register notes that he had been a clerk in Holy Orders before the war. He was the chaplain at Wellingborough School, a curate at Dulwich College, and precentor at Bristol Cathedral, but in October 1914 he decided to enlist as a stretcher-bearer with the Royal Army Medical Corps. However, in early January 1918 he accepted a commission and joined the 2nd Battalion at the end of April that year. (Plot I.B.1)

Lance Serjeant Victor James AYTON, 1/2nd (City of London) Battalion, London Regiment (Royal Fusiliers), was one of the men killed in an attack on Fooley Trench at 2.45am on 27 August 1918. He and his party from 'A' Company had managed to advance as far as the German wire protecting the trench, but they were killed there when they came under heavy machine-gun and rifle fire. The attack involved two platoons from each of 'A', 'C' and 'D' companies. It was the wounded survivors of this attack that MERIKIN had gone out to rescue. (Plot I.B.11)

It is also interesting to note the ages of many of the burials here; almost a third are twenty years of age or under. Battalions throughout the British army had been receiving drafts throughout the summer of 1918 to replace the losses incurred during the spring fighting. Battalion war diaries from May to early July often comment on the fact that many of the drafts sent to them contained a high proportion of inexperienced young men aged around nineteen.

Croisilles British Cemetery

The cemetery is located in the south-west corner of the village at the end of the Rue Eugène Hornez, which runs off the D.9 road to Saint-Léger. The earliest burials were made after the village was captured on 2 April 1917 by the 7th Division after an initial attempt had failed a few days earlier. The cemetery was then used until the German Offensive on 21 March the following year. These burials form Plots I and II. The village was recaptured by the 56th (London) Division on 28 August 1918 after a hard fight. Today, over half the burials are unidentified and there are fourteen special memorials commemorating men whose graves were destroyed by shell fire.

This is one of the very few cemeteries in and around Arras to contain significant numbers of casualties from Irish regiments, notably the Royal Dublin Fusiliers, which has fifty-one identified burials. An identical number of identified NCOs and men of the 2nd Coldstream Guards can also be found here. The four Leicestershire battalions that made up 110 Brigade of the 21st Division (6th, 7th, 8th and 9th Leicestershire Regiment) have almost as many, with fifty. In all, these three regiments make up almost a third of the 533 identified burials within this cemetery.

The 7th Division made two attempts to capture the village, the second of which was successful and took place on 2 April 1917. This is a recurring date on early head-stones, particularly in respect of the 2nd Queen's (Royal West Surrey Regiment), which has thirty-five burials from that date, thirty-one of which are identified, the majority in Plot I, Row A.

The 22nd Manchester Regiment, which was also part of the 7th Division, had made an earlier attempt to take the strongly held village on 28 March along with men from the 1st South Staffordshire Regiment. Their attack began at 5.15am, but met with little success. It was followed on 2 April by a much bigger effort involving the 4th Australian Division on the right, the 7th Division opposite Croisilles, and the 21st Division to its left, all backed by an artillery bombardment to cut the German wire that had halted the advance a few days earlier. This attack was successful and the villages of Croisilles and Écoust-Saint-Mein were captured and cleared that same day.

The majority of the 2nd Queen's (Royal West Surrey Regiment) who fell that day are to be found closest to the entrance to the cemetery in Plot I, Row A, though a few more are scattered elsewhere within the cemetery. One of the four officers from this battalion, Lieutenant Frank Cecil WOODS, was the son of Surgeon Major David Woods, Royal Army Medical Corps (Plot I.A.3). The other three are buried either side of him. One of them, Second Lieutenant Alfred Cyril FITCH (Plot I.A.2), lost his brother on 3 July 1916 on the Somme. Lieutenant Conrad William Fitch, 6th Queen's (Royal West Surrey Regiment), is buried in Aveluy Communal Cemetery Extension. The men of the 22nd Manchester Regiment are all NCOs or privates and the majority are to be found in Row C, straddling Plots II and IV; seven more are commemorated by Special Memorials 6 to 12.

Second Lieutenant Thomas LOWERY DCM, 15th Durham Light Infantry, was killed in action on 3 August 1917, aged 25. His DCM, gazetted on 24 June 1916, was won while he was serving as an acting corporal with the same battalion. The award was made in recognition of his conspicuous show of gallantry on four nights while carrying out wiring close to the enemy's position. Each night his little party was ham-pered by snipers. On the fourth night, after he had sent his party back, he advanced alone and bombed the snipers' post, enabling him to carry on working for another half hour. He subsequently went out with a corporal, again bombing the enemy, and com-pleted his work. (Plot I.B.23)

The highest-ranking casualty here is Major Valentine FOWLER, 10th Yorkshire Regiment. He was killed by shell fire on 2 June 1917, aged 40, and had seen action at Loos in 1915 and on the Somme the following year (Plot I.C.6). Next to him is Serjeant John DOWNING DCM, 10th Yorkshire Regiment, who was killed on the same day. DOWNING's DCM was gazetted on 13 February 1917 and was awarded for conspicuous gallantry in action after he and three other men had rushed an enemy machine gun, shooting its team and enabling the attack to be carried out successfully. (Plot I.C.7)

Captain Samuel POOL MC, Royal Army Medical Corps, was attached to the 8th Leicestershire Regiment when he was killed in action on 16 June 1917. His MC was gazetted on 25 November 1916 and was awarded for leading his stretcher-bearers with conspicuous gallantry and devotion to duty through heavy fire and collecting a number of wounded men lying out in the open. He worked continuously for forty-eight hours, displaying great courage and determination. (Plot I.D.12)

An officer who had won his gallantry award prior to his commission is Second Lieutenant Arthur Reginald DEAN DCM, 4th East Yorkshire Regiment. He was killed on 3 July 1917, aged 22, though *Officers Died in the Great War* shows his date of death as 4 July. His DCM was won as a private when serving with the 9th Duke of Wellington's Regiment. The award was gazetted on 21 June 1916 and was awarded for conspicuous gallantry during operations in which he worked his machine gun over the parapet under very heavy shell fire and accurate sniper fire in order to repulse an enemy counter-attack. (Plot I.G.9)

Second Lieutenant David Willis BINNIE, 9th (Glasgow Highlanders) Highland Light Infantry, is one of seventeen identified burials from that battalion and the Glasgow (Queen's Own Royal) Yeomanry. This latter unit has only ten casualties buried in France relating to the Great War, four of whom are to be found here. BINNIE attended Glasgow Academy and was originally commissioned in the 5th Battalion before joining the Glasgow Highlanders. His headstone has a family inscription taken from one of Rupert Brooke's war sonnets. He was killed in action on 27 May 1917, aged 21. During this period a number of small, often piecemeal, attacks were carried out along the new line in front of Arras, partly to improve local positions, but mainly to divert attention from the coming attack on Messines Ridge at the end of the first week of June. (Plot I.C.15)

Another notable family inscription can be found on the headstone of one of BINNIE's fellow officers, Second Lieutenant John Francis NEWLOVE (Plot I.G.15). He was killed in action on 25 June 1917, the day after the battalion had returned to the trenches around Croisilles. He was one of four men killed when a shell scored a direct hit on 'B' Company's HQ during a heavy bombardment, which also resulted in twelve other men being wounded. NEWLOVE had originally served in the Yorkshire Regiment before joining the Glasgow Highlanders and had been wounded at Loos in 1915. He was also at Fricourt on the Somme the following year. He had been married for only a month before he was killed and the inscription on his headstone reads: '*Who stands if freedom fall, who dies if England live*'. These are the last two lines of Rudyard Kipling's poem: 'For all we have and are'.

The date 20 November 1917 occurs on many of the headstones in this cemetery. This was the opening day of the Battle of Cambrai. However, none of these casualties fell in that particular battle. They fell during a simultaneous operation to capture Tunnel Trench and Tunnel Support Trench, which ran in front of the village of Fontaine-les-Croisilles, and which formed part of the Hindenburg Line. Tunnel Trench was a huge construction containing ample concrete shelters and many dug-outs about 30 feet below ground; furthermore, it was wired for demolition should its capture appear imminent. The tunnel itself was 7 feet high, 6 feet wide, and had entrances every 25 yards or so leading down to its many galleries. It also contained many recesses for the storage of food, ammunition and other supplies, as well as providing electric-lit sleeping accommodation for its garrison. It had originally been designed as a support trench for the Hindenburg Line, but since the Battle of Arras it had become part of the German front line in this sector.

Four reinforced concrete pill-boxes, named 'Jove', 'Mars', 'Vulcan' and 'Juno', provided extensive machine-gun cover and these were among the objectives for units of the 16th (Irish) Division on 20 November. A fifth pill-box, 'Pluto', lay in the path of the 3rd Division, along with Bovis Trench.

The operation had been well-rehearsed and was largely successful on the day. Within ten minutes Tunnel Trench and Tunnel Support Trench were occupied and the job of clearing the tunnel began immediately.

On the right of the 16th (Irish) Division's sector, the 6th Connaught Rangers saw heavy fighting. Here also, on the extreme left of the 3rd Division's attack, the 1st Northumberland Fusiliers ran into difficulties when its line was driven back in the afternoon by one of several counter-attacks that developed throughout the day. The 12th West Yorkshire Regiment on its right met little opposition. The gap between the 16th (Irish) Division and the 3rd Division had also been subjected to a dummy attack under a smoke barrage as an additional measure to assist both divisions to pinch out this part of the German defences west of Bullecourt.

Fighting eventually came to a conclusion on 23 November following an attack to recapture Jove strongpoint, which had been captured on the opening day but then lost during one of the enemy's counter-attacks. Combined casualties for both divisions came to just over 800.

Captain George Chaigneau COLVILL, 7th Royal Irish Regiment (South Irish Horse), was killed in action on 30 November 1917, ten days after the hard-won positions around Tunnel Trench had been consolidated (Plot II.A.11). He was one of four sons who served during the war and was educated at Winchester College and New College, Oxford. His brother, James, went on to command destroyers in the Second World War, whilst the other two, David and Robert, served in the Army, both attaining the rank of colonel. Robert Lowry Chaigneau Colvill, who had attended the Royal Military Academy, Woolwich, was wounded in the Great War, but finished his career as a colonel in the Royal Engineers. Like his brother George, David Chaigneau Colvill also attended Winchester College, but had then gone on to complete his education at Sandhurst. He served with the 2nd Oxfordshire & Buckinghamshire Light Infantry and won the MC in 1918, followed by the DSO in 1940 for gallant conduct in action against the enemy. He retired with the honorary rank of lieutenant colonel. Their father served as High Sheriff of County Dublin between 1910 and 1914.

The 16th (Irish) Division's burials are mainly from units that formed part of the centre and left sections of the attack on 20 November 1917. Out of the fifty-one casualties from the Royal Dublin Fusiliers who are buried here, fourteen were killed on 20 November 1917 and four more the following day. Corporal Christopher Joseph WALL DCM was one of those killed on the first day of the operation (Plot II.C.19). His DCM was gazetted posthumously on 6 February 1918 and was awarded for gallantry and devotion to duty during the attack on Tunnel Trench. He had gone forward to link up with the company on his right, but on his way there he found a party of men who were held up by fire from two machine guns. He at once took command of the situation and organized them into a bombing party, which he then led, capturing both guns and ten prisoners in a demonstration of great courage and initiative.

Amongst the eleven men from or attached to the 7/8th Royal Irish Fusiliers, who were killed on 20 November, are two officers: Second Lieutenant Leonard William BUTLER, aged 18, attached from the 4th Battalion, and Lieutenant William Frederick HUGHES, attached from the 10th Battalion (Plots II.C.13 and 14). Near to them, and also killed in action that day, is Company Serjeant Major Samuel CRAIG DCM, 7/8th Royal Irish Fusiliers Plot II.C.15). CRAIG was an acting company serjeant major when he won his DCM, which was gazetted on 13 February 1917. It was awarded for conspicuous gallantry in action. The citation states that he proved himself tirelessly, organizing men of different units in his vicinity, cheering them on and maintaining discipline under the most trying circumstances. Private Joseph NASH, 7/8th Royal Inniskilling Fusiliers, who is buried in the same row, held the MM. (Plot II.C.6)

There are also a few men from the 2nd, 6th and 7th Battalions, Royal Irish Regiment, the 7/8th Royal Inniskilling Fusiliers, and fewer still from the 1st Royal Munster Fusiliers, with just three identified burials. One of them, Serjeant Bertie Leopold PRINCE, 1st Royal Munster Fusiliers, who fell on 20 November 1917, had two brothers killed during the war (Plot II.C.11). Lance Serjeant Joseph Ernest Prince, 1st Dorsetshire Regiment, was killed in action on 30 September 1918 and is commemorated on the memorial at Vis-en-Artois. The other brother, Private Reginald Luke Prince DCM, was killed in action with the 1st Somerset Light Infantry on the Somme on 1 July 1916. He is buried at Serre Road Cemetery, No. 2. However, many more Royal Munster Fusiliers are buried at Croisilles Railway Cemetery, which is nearby.

Accompanying the infantry in the attack on Tunnel Trench were five parties from 174 Tunnelling Company, Royal Engineers. Their job was to clear the tunnels and underground chambers of demolition charges, a task which they achieved. Two men who were involved in that task are buried here and both were killed by shell fire. They are Serjeant Frank CLARK (Plot II.C.7) and Sapper William Frederick Patrick KIRWIN (Plot II.F.7).

Another member of the same tunnelling company, Sapper David EVANS, was killed three months earlier on 24 August 1917 (Plot I.D.22). Croisilles was subjected to heavy enemy shelling that day and two delayed action shells landed above one of the caves where Evans and others were working. The explosion caused fifty feet of the chamber to collapse. Of the six casualties, only EVANS died as a result of the incident, whilst the others were more fortunate, suffering shell shock, bruising and the effects of gas.

All the Royal Engineer casualties here date from the second half of 1917, including Sapper James BREMNER, 155th Field Company, who was also killed in action on 20 November. Others are from various units, including the 21st Signalling Company, 'J' Special Company, No. 3 Special Company, and a variety of other field companies.

The CWGC register shows a very early burial, but the year of death appears to be incorrect. *Soldiers Died in the Great War* shows that Private William Thirkell PRATT, 49th Company, Machine Gun Corps, was killed in action on 20 November 1917, not

1915 as shown in the CWGC register. In the context of this cemetery, this makes perfect sense and ties in with the operation against Tunnel Trench by the 16th (Irish) Division to which his unit was attached. (Plot II.C.22)

Company Serjeant Major John Alfred James FOX DCM is among the fifty-one men of the 2nd Coldstream Guards buried here. He began the war with the regiment's 3rd Battalion and won his DCM while he was serving with it. The action that led to the award occurred early on 25 August 1914 during the small, but brisk action at Landrecies.

The 4th Guards Brigade had bivouacked there for the night and had posted piquets around the approaches to the town. Aware that a French detachment might be passing through, a group was spotted coming down the road from the north-west beyond the railway line where the 3rd Coldstream had posted a small detachment of its men. Despite a ruse by the Germans, who replied in French when challenged, the Coldstream opened fire and throughout the night a fire-fight ensued. During that encounter the Germans brought up field guns in an attempt to force their way through the outpost line, across the railway and the River Sambre, and into the town. FOX showed great gallantry by helping to serve a machine gun throughout the night, at one point even repairing it under fire to ensure that it remained in action (Plot III.E.1). The 3rd Coldstream losses came to twelve men killed, 105 wounded, and a further seven were reported as missing. This gives some indication of the intensity of the fight and was one of many small actions that occurred during the days of the Retreat from Mons.

Three other men of the 2nd Coldstream Guards buried here hold the MM: Lance Serjeant John Holmes EDLINGTON MM (Plot III.A.17), Lance Corporal George William RONSON MM (Plot III.C.3) and Private Ernest George MANKTELOW MM (Plot IV.A.15). All three were killed in action on 27 August 1918.

The Guards Division as a whole is also very well represented here. In addition to the fifty-one men of the 2nd Coldstream Guards killed in action on 27 August 1918, there are burials from the 1st Grenadier Guards, 1st Welsh Guards, 2nd Scots Guards, and the Guards' Machine Gun Regiment, all of whom fell during the first phase of clearance around the village of Saint-Léger on 24 and 25 August. There are just two officers within this divisional group: Second Lieutenant Arnold Ashton Justice WARNER, 1st Grenadier Guards (Plot III.E.29) and Second Lieutenant George Edward BARBER, also 1st Grenadier Guards (Plot III.E.32). Both were killed in action on 24 August. The 2nd Coldstream did lose some of its officers, but the three that were killed on 27 August are buried in Mory Street Cemetery rather than here. Second Lieutenant BARBER was aged 19 when he was killed. He, like all but one of the men from his battalion, is buried in Plot III, Row E, along with the two privates from the 2nd Scots Guards.

Before its capture in November 1917 Tunnel Trench had been the objective of an earlier attack that took place on 27 May 1917 involving the 2nd Royal Welsh Fusiliers. One of its officers killed that day was Second Lieutenant Thomas Rathesay CONNING MC (Plot IV. B.3). He had been with the battalion for fifteen months and was wounded during a raid on 25 April 1916. An earlier raid on 8 April had not been successful after a Bangalore torpedo placed under the German wire had failed to explode. An effort had been made to recover it, but only the butt of it came away, leaving behind the front section, which remained lodged in the enemy's wire. The raid on the 25th was an attempt to remedy this.

He had also had a narrow escape during the early hours of 22 June 1916 while the battalion was holding trenches in the Givenchy sector. Feeling tired, he and Captain Blair decided not to go to the company's dug-out for a drink; a decision that inadvertently saved both their lives, as the Germans exploded a mine under it, which probably would have killed both of them. A raid then followed the explosion involving around 150 of the enemy and fierce fighting took place in which CONNING took part. The crater formed by the mine became known as Red Dragon Crater, a reference to the regimental badge. Later that year he also saw fighting with his battalion on the Somme around High Wood.

He was considered not only a very popular officer with the men, but also regarded as dependable, unflappable and a man of considerable experience, having served as bombing officer and with the Lewis gun section of his battalion. His MC was gazetted in the New Year's Honours List on 1 January 1917.

He is mentioned several times in *The War the Infantry Knew 1914–1919* by Captain J.C. Dunn DSO MC and Bar DCM, the battalion's Medical Officer. This work is surely one of the finest accounts of a battalion at war ever compiled. Shortly before moving up to Arras in the spring of 1917 CONNING had accompanied Siegfried Sassoon and several of his fellow officers to Amiens where they enjoyed dinner at the well-known restaurant, Godbert. Sassoon's only recollection of the event appears to have been the formidable cocktail of drinks they consumed.

It would appear that CONNING, normally a happy-go-lucky chap, had some kind of inkling that his time might finally be up. Before leading his company in the attack on Tunnel Trench on 27 May 1917 he took the trouble of '*arranging his affairs as if, for him, the end of everything had come*'. That afternoon he assisted some of his men out of their assembly trench, encouraging some and chaffing others who no doubt shared his own fears. He then led them under the barrage towards their objective. He was killed near the first line of German wire and the attack was an heroic failure in which the battalion lost ten officers and 155 men, approximately half of whom were killed.

As regards the Leicestershire Regiment, four of its battalions, the 6th, 7th, 8th and 9th, made up 110 Brigade of the 21st Division. The brigade was involved in the 3rd Battle of the Scarpe on 3 May 1917, when the 8th Battalion attacked south of Héninel towards the village of Chérisy and the 9th Battalion next to it attacked further south towards Fontaine-les-Croisilles.

North of the Héninel–Chérisy road, parts of Tunnel Trench were in British hands, but south of that location the Germans still held it strongly. In an effort to loosen the German grip on this section of Tunnel Trench even further, 64 Brigade, which was also part of the 21st Division, was ordered to attack on the left flank of the 8th Leicestershire Regiment and force its way down Tunnel Trench at right angles to the direction of attack by the two Leicestershire battalions. Overall, the attack was not a success, despite some of the Leicestershire men gaining a foothold along the Chérisy–Fontaine-lès-Croisilles road beyond Tunnel Trench. With assistance from the remaining two Leicestershire battalions, the remnants of this group had to withdraw during the evening from what had become a dangerous pocket that was very vulnerable to counter-attacks.

Just over a month later, on 15 June, 110 Brigade made a further attempt using the same plan. On this occasion the 58th (2/1st London) Division was to attack at right angles to the main assault on Tunnel Trench, which was carried out by the 12th and 13th Northumberland Fusiliers from the 21st Division's 62nd Brigade. This time, the Leicestershire Regiment's 8th and 9th Battalions were in support, the former going over at 2.30am. A combination of uncut wire, heavy counter-barrage and heavy machine-gun fire brought the attack to a halt, though again some men did manage to reach the German positions and fought it out in small, but fierce encounters with bomb and bayonet. In the prevailing circumstances, the 9th Leicestershire Regiment did not follow up the initial assault, since there was clearly no success to exploit and little chance of reaching their comrades to reinforce them.

Though the cemetery has no identified burials from the Leicestershire Regiment dating to 3 May, there are several from the subsequent attack and the days that followed throughout the months of June, July and into August. There are also men from the two battalions of Northumberland Fusiliers that took part in the attack on 16 June. One of the men killed on 15 June was Private John Henry HOLYOAK, 9th Leicestershire Regiment (Plot I.E.6). He and two of his cousins joined the 9th Battalion in September 1914. One of them was severely wounded at Ypres some months later and was invalided out of the army.

There are two Royal Flying Corps graves in this cemetery and three from the Royal Air Force who fell in 1918. Chronologically, the first is Second Lieutenant Harold BLYTHE, 32 Squadron, Royal Flying Corps (General List). He was reported missing on 2 February 1917, but is known to have died of wounds in German captivity on the 10th of the month. His squadron was engaged that day with nine enemy aircraft in what was described as a general encounter. (Plot III.E.9)

Next is Captain Charles Lindsay Murray SCOTT, 54 Squadron, Royal Flying Corps (Plot VI.C.19). He was reported missing on 15 February 1917 when flying a Sopwith Pup, but was later confirmed as having been killed in action that day. He was an only son and had initially served with the North Staffordshire Regiment, where his father had served as a lieutenant colonel. SCOTT was wounded during the heavy fighting at Hill 60 in Belgium in April 1915. After his recovery, he joined the Royal Flying Corps and spent five months as an observer before gaining his wings in July 1916. He also spent some time that year as an instructor on the Home Staff, but returned to the front in January 1917. He was killed just three days before his 25th birthday.

He was the nephew of General Sir Archibald Murray (hence his middle name) who served as chief of staff to Sir John French until January 1915 when he was replaced by Sir William Robertson. Robertson then succeeded him for a second time in December that year when he became Chief of the Imperial General Staff. Murray then went on to command the Egyptian Expeditionary Force until he was replaced by General Sir Edmund Allenby.

Lieutenant Leslie Nansen FRANKLIN, 56 Squadron, Royal Air Force, was killed in action, aged 20, on 14 July 1918 whilst flying a SE5 aircraft. (Plot I.C.1)

Lieutenants Arthur James VIVEASH and Thomas Alan JOHNSON, 13 Squadron, Royal Air Force, were killed in action on 28 August 1918 while flying an RE8 aircraft. (Plots III.F.2 and 3)

There are a number of other graves to note, including a number of gallantry award holders not already mentioned:

Serjeant Robert Batson CLARK MM, 1st East Yorkshire Regiment, attached 64th Trench Mortar Battery, killed in action on 1 July 1917. (Plot I.E.19)

Sapper William Henry COOK MM, 21st Signal Company, Royal Engineers, killed in action on 19 July 1917. (Plot I.F.3)

Corporal William PURVIS MM and Bar, 149th Company, Machine Gun Corps, killed in action on 26 June 1917, aged 27. *Soldiers Died in the Great War* shows only the award of the MM against his name. (Plot I.F.4)

Lance Corporal Robert RITCHIE MM, 5/6th Cameronians, killed in action on 22 June 1917. (Plot I.F.10)

Serjeant Victor Arthur PAGE MM, 20th Royal Fusiliers, killed in action on 20 June 1917. (Plot I.F.16)

Corporal William GILLESPIE MM, 'D' Company, 9th Northumberland Fusiliers (Northumberland Hussars Yeomanry), killed in action on 22 March 1918. (Plot III.C.15)

Serjeant Thomas ROSAM MM, 12th Northumberland Fusiliers, killed in action on 16 August 1917. The award of the MM is not recorded in *Soldiers Died in the Great War*. (Special Memorial 13)

Chronologically, the last burials are from the 129th Company, Chinese Labour Corps. Coolie Liu Hai CHENG died on 10 October 1919 and Ganger (Foreman) Sun Wen PIN died on 27 October that year. (Plots II.E.17 and 18)

A visit to this cemetery should be rounded off with a visit to Plot 7, which contains six members of 514 Squadron, Royal Air Force, who were killed when their Lancaster bomber came down on the night of 16 June 1944 while on a mission to bomb rail yards around Valenciennes. Flight Officer (Navigator) Arnold Hughes Morrison survived and managed to evade capture. He eventually returned to England on 9 September that year thanks to help from the Bordeaux-Loupiac Line after members of the local Resistance had initially sheltered him. He was awarded the DFC in December 1944.

The raid was one of two main operations carried out by the Royal Air Force on the night of 15/16 June. One operation targeted an ammunition dump at Fouillard and a fuel dump at Chatelhérault and all aircraft and crew on this mission returned safely. However, some of those who took part in the raids on Valenciennes and Lens were less fortunate; eleven Lancasters were lost out of a total of 224 aircraft involved.

Croisilles Railway Cemetery

Today's cemetery contains 181 burials, twenty-six of which are unidentified. It was begun by the 21st Manchester Regiment soon after it had helped to capture this area on 2 April 1917. From Croisilles British Cemetery it can be reached by retracing one's steps back along the Rue Eugène Hornez, turning right into the Rue du Tour des

Haies, then right into the Rue du Moulin. After about 200 yards the road eventually forks. The right fork is the road to take. After about half a mile and a couple of bends in the road there is a small track going off to the left. The cemetery lies at the end of this track and is best accessed on foot. There is very little space by the roadside for parking and in wet weather the ground can be muddy. It cannot be accessed from the D.5, the Rue du Pont, which runs between Croisilles and Écoust-Saint-Mein.

Tucked up against the railway embankment from which it derives its name, this cemetery is one to visit in conjunction with Croisilles British Cemetery. Indeed, the one may be considered an extension of the other. Many of the same dates recur, but the units involved are different. Whereas Croisilles British Cemetery contains burials from the 2nd Queen's (Royal West Surrey Regiment), which formed the left flank of the attack by the 7th Division's 91 Brigade on 2 April 1917, Croisilles Railway Cemetery contains casualties from the centre battalion in that attack, the 21st Manchester Regiment. On the brigade's right flank that day was the 1st South Staffordshire Regiment, but none of its casualties from that attack are interred here.

The 2nd Queen's (Royal West Surrey Regiment) attacked in a northerly direction back towards Croisilles from the point where the road meets the path to the cemetery. The 21st Manchester Regiment and the 1st South Staffordshire Regiment extended the line of advance, but angled back slightly across the fields between the road and the cemetery to a point roughly half way between Croisilles and Écoust-Saint-Mien. They attacked towards the railway embankment. From there the line was extended towards Écoust by the 9th Devonshire Regiment, the 8th Devonshire Regiment and 2nd Gordon Highlanders, all units from the 7th Division's 20th Brigade.

Thirteen of the twenty other ranks from the 21st Manchester Regiment recorded as killed on 2 April 1917 are buried in this cemetery, as well as one of the two officers, Second Lieutenant Ernest Harry RICHARDS (Plot I.A.12). They can be found in Plot I, Row A, together with a handful of men from the battalion who were killed in early summer that year while holding the line.

There are burials from the 1st South Staffordshire Regiment in this cemetery, but the eight identified casualties date between late April 1917 and July that year, and were incurred while holding the line.

The cemetery also contains casualties from the attack on Tunnel Trench on 20 November 1917 where the 1st Royal Munster Fusiliers and the 6th Connaught Rangers formed the right flank of the 16th (Irish) Division. Thirty-three identified NCOs and privates of the 6th Connaught Rangers killed that day are buried here along with one man who died the following day. Among the battalions of the 16th (Irish) Division, the one with the highest percentage of casualties that day was the 6th Connaught Rangers; thirty-four other ranks were killed and three officers and 109 other ranks were wounded.

A poignant footnote to this operation is offered by the battalion's commanding officer. In his excellent collection of letters, subsequently published under the title, *War Letters to a Wife*, Lieutenant Colonel Rowland Fielding writes:

> *We recovered all our dead and buried them in a little 'war' cemetery behind the embankment near what used to be Croisilles Railway Station, and not a single living man remained in the hands of the enemy.*

He also describes very movingly and with obvious affection how the men of the whole battalion queued up on the evening of 17 November to attend confession in an old patched-up barn in Ervillers. Canvas screens were erected to create makeshift confessional booths and the barn was dimly lit by one or two candles so that it resembled a church. The one battalion casualty who fell in this attack and who is not identified here with his comrades is Private Michael McHale. His grave was subsequently lost and he is therefore commemorated on the Arras Memorial. The thirty-three men can be found predominantly in Plot I, Rows C and D, directly behind the German graves on the right of the entrance, though three are buried very close to the Cross of Sacrifice.

There are also eleven identified officers and men from the 1st Royal Munster Fusiliers killed on 20 November 1917, including Second Lieutenant Charles Francis ENNIS (Plot I.C.5) and Lieutenant Francis George Vernon MacDANIEL (Plot I.C.4), who were attached from the regiment's 2nd Battalion. A further four men from the battalion are buried here, but they were killed in action prior to this attack. One of them, Private Michael RIDGE (Plot I.E.7), fell in action on 11 September 1917, not 1918 as shown in the CWGC records. All fifteen men are to be found in Plot I, Rows C and E.

The Irish character of this cemetery is further upheld by sixteen identified burials from the 6th Royal Irish Regiment, several of whom were killed in the attack on Tunnel Trench, though some fell in late August and early September that year, and some during the very last days of November when the new line was under consolidation. There is one officer among them: Lieutenant John Henry GRAYSON, who was killed in action on 20 November 1917, aged 20 (Plot I.D.7). The youngest soldier buried in this cemetery also served with the 6th Royal Irish Regiment, but he was killed prior to the Tunnel Trench operation; Private John SAMPSON was killed in action on 27 October 1917, aged 17 (Plot I.D.7). There are also twelve identified casualties from the 7th Leinster Regiment; and again, the dates on their headstones reflect the dates on those of the 6th Royal Irish Regiment.

Second Lieutenant William Travers SMITH is one of the five officers from the Royal Engineers who led one of the five parties of 174 Tunnelling Company that accompanied the 16th (Irish) Division in order to make safe German demolition charges on 20 November. He was killed in action by rifle fire, aged 28, and had been previously mentioned in despatches (Plot I.D.8). Another man from this company, Sapper Thomas Lewis BENNETT, who had formerly served with the Pembroke Yeomanry, is commemorated within the cemetery by way of a special memorial (Special Memorial 1). He was killed when a bomb exploded next to him. There are also two men from 156th Field Company, Royal Engineers: Sapper Walter William HUBBLE and Sapper James Charles QUANTRILL, both killed on 20 November 1917 (Plots I.D.6 and 22). Pioneer William FLYNN and Pioneer Thomas Norman EDWARDS, from 'J' Special Company, Royal Engineers, are buried next to each other. Both were killed on the last day of August 1917. They belonged to one of the specialist engineer companies that dealt with the discharge of gas (Plots I.A.9 and 10).

A small operation was carried out on 15 December 1917 and was described by IV Corps Commander, Lieutenant General Haldane, as a conclusion to the successful attack by the 3rd Division and 16th (Irish) Division three weeks earlier. Regimental sources for the 19th Royal Welsh Fusiliers show that four men were killed in the capture of Neptune Trench and a further sixteen were wounded. At least two of the wounded succumbed to their injuries, as six privates from that attack are now buried here. Privates George HEARN and Henry JONES, and Privates George FRATER and Samuel JOHNSON are buried in adjacent double graves (Plots I.E.17 and 18). Private Thomas CALLINAN and Private Henry PLANT lie next to them (Plots I.E.15 and 16). Corporal Harry AMOS, also 19th Royal Welsh Fusiliers, was killed exactly ten days later, on Christmas Day (Plot I.E.19). Two men serving with the 19th Royal Welsh Fusiliers, both named OWEN, but not related to each other, were killed on 23 and 24 December 1917 and are also buried next to each other. (Plots I.D.31 and 32)

Another group of headstones are those belonging to men from various battalions of the London Regiment killed throughout June 1917. All are buried in Plot II, Rows A or B, and most are from the 56th (London) Division. All but one of these eight men served with the 4th (City of London) Battalion, London Regiment (Royal Fusiliers), and were killed in action on 4 June 1917. Two other men buried here are shown in the CWGC register as serving with the 6th Battalion, London Regiment (City of London Rifles), which served with the 47th (London) Division. Both men were killed in action on dates in the middle of June when the 47th (London) Division was near Westoutre in Belgium following its involvement in the Battle of Messines. These two men had obviously been transferred or posted to the 56th (London) Division at some time prior to their death, though they are still shown serving with their former battalion as far as the CWGC records are concerned.

There are eleven gunners in the cemetery, ten of whom are from either the 105th or the 106th Battery, 22 Brigade, Royal Field Artillery. Nine of these ten were killed in action on the day prior to the opening of the Arras Offensive, 8 April 1917. All eleven are buried either in Plot I, Row B, or Plot II, Row A.

The cemetery consists almost exclusively of 1917 casualties; in fact, there are only three identified burials from the following year. Equally, there are very few gallantry awards buried here, just three. One of those is an officer from Anson Battalion, 63rd (Royal Naval) Division, killed on 5 September 1918. Lieutenant Richard DONALDSON MC, was from Glasgow and had studied there at the university between 1910 and 1914. His MC was gazetted on 1 January 1918, but the entry was corrected on 7 February that year in respect of his rank (Plot II.B.1). Two men from the 21st Manchester Regiment, Serjeant Charles HOPWOOD MM and Lance Corporal Joseph WHITTAKER MM, are the other gallantry award holders. HOP-WOOD was killed in action on 2 April 1917 and WHITTAKER was killed in action a couple of months later, on 24 June.

Écoust-St. Mein British Cemetery

This is a small cemetery that sits on the north-west edge of the village by the roadside on the D.5. Only eight burials are unidentified from a total of 151. The CWGC notes that two battalions, the 8th Battalion and the 9th Battalion, Devonshire Regiment, captured the village of Écoust on 2 April 1917 in blizzard conditions. However, there are no burials here before late August 1918, and the one casualty from the Devonshire Regiment, who is buried here, was actually attached to the Labour Corps. The CWGC register states that there was once a German extension to the communal cemetery, which is on the same side of the road about eighty yards away. This extension is now gone. Visible to the east of this location is Écoust Military Cemetery.

Nearly half of the cemetery is taken up by officers and men of the King's (Liverpool Regiment) who account for fifty-nine of the 143 identified casualties buried here. All but nine of the fifty-nine are from the regiment's 13th Battalion and all date from the end of August 1918 through to the middle of September. The 13th Battalion casualties were killed in action on 31 August and 1 September in a successful attack on Écoust by the 3rd Division.

The CWGC note attached to the entry for Serjeant John Pearson NEAL, 13th King's (Liverpool Regiment), shows that he had enlisted in the 1st City Battalion (Cotton Contingent) King's (Liverpool Regiment), which was then redesignated the 17th Battalion (1st Liverpool Pals). As regards the 'Cotton Contingent', this is a reference to the arrangements made at St George's Hall, Liverpool, on the opening day of recruitment when the tables were set out, one for each of the main areas of commerce in the city. One of these was for the Cotton Association; other tables were set out for the corn, sugar and timber trades. (Plot D.25)

Second Lieutenant Cyril HILLS MC, 2nd Suffolk Regiment, was killed in action on 30 August 1918, aged 32 (Plot A.47). His MC was gazetted on 2 December 1918 and was awarded for conspicuous gallantry during an attack when he went forward for 300 yards with an officer and three other men and rushed a machine-gun nest and its two guns, one of which he turned on the retreating enemy. Later he showed a grasp of the situation by filling up a gap in the defence, organizing the line with coolness, and behaving splendidly. He and thirty-seven men of his battalion, all killed in action on 30 August 1918, are buried here in Rows A and D.

The CWGC register shows that Private Alfred George RUMP died on 30 August 1916, but this is incorrect and the year of death should be 1918, the same as for the other men of the 2nd Suffolk Regiment (Plot D.40).

Private Ernest Frank ALBON, 2nd Suffolk Regiment was also killed in action on 30 August 1918 (Plot D.60). He lost a brother, Private Frederick John Albon, who served with the 7th Suffolk Regiment and was killed in action on 12 October 1916 on the Somme. He is commemorated on the Thiepval Memorial.

Captain William RAINE MC, 9th King's (Liverpool Regiment), and adjutant of the battalion, died of wounds on 8 September 1918, according to CWGC records. However, *Officers Died in the Great War* shows his death occurring the previous day, as does the regimental history. His MC was gazetted on 1 January 1917 in the New Year's Honours List. (Plot B.1)

Major Aylmer Louis Elliot FLEET MC, 'B' Battery, 56 Brigade, Royal Field Artillery, was killed in action on 10 September 1918, aged 29; he was the son of Vice

Admiral Henry Louis Fleet CBE. His MC was gazetted on 11 January 1919 and was awarded for conspicuous gallantry and devotion to duty, commanding his battery with energy and ability. On one occasion, he brought it up to close range and rendered valuable assistance to the infantry by his fire, contributing significantly to the success of the operations. The operations referred to were in Mesopotamia. (Plot B.7)

Lieutenant Robert DARLING MC, 9th King's (Liverpool Regiment), was killed in action on 16 September 1918, aged 27. He was commissioned as a corporal from the Northumberland (Hussars) Yeomanry in October 1915. His MC was gazetted on 25 August 1916 for his show of conspicuous gallantry during a raid on enemy trenches. At the conclusion of the raid he was one of the last to leave, and did so carrying a severely wounded man. Later on, he volunteered to go out to try to rescue a missing officer and, with the help of a private soldier, succeeded in bringing back his body, despite heavy shell and rifle fire. The raid took place on 28 June and is remembered because six battalions from the 55th (West Lancashire) Division took part in it. The missing officer was Second Lieutenant Herbert Angus Riley, aged 19, who is now buried at Wailly Orchard Cemetery. Private F. Winrow, the man who assisted Lieutenant DARLING, won the MM for his part in this act of gallantry. His award was gazetted on 24 August 1916 and it would appear that he survived the war. (Plot B.20)

Captain Malcolm Angus MATHESON MC, 6th Gordon Highlanders, died of wounds on 27 September 1918, aged 22. His MC was gazetted on 18 July 1917 and was awarded for conspicuous gallantry and devotion to duty after taking command of the company during an attack. The capture of all the objectives was largely due to his good leadership and personal bravery. The citation concludes that he set a splendid example throughout the operation. (Plot C.5)

In addition to the several holders of the MC, there are five holders of the MM here: Lance Corporal Ralph Theodore SMALL MM, 13th King's (Liverpool Regiment), killed in action on 1 September 1918, aged 32 (Plot A.44); Serjeant James Daniel Johnson MM, 9th King's (Liverpool Regiment), killed in action on 14 September 1918 (Plot B.19); Corporal Frederick Charles UPTON MM, 63rd (Royal Naval) Division Signal Company, Royal Engineers, died of wounds on 27 September 1918, aged 27 (Plot C.4); Serjeant John MYERS MM, 13th King's (Liverpool Regiment), killed in action on 31 August 1918, aged 21 (Plot D.16); and Lance Corporal Thomas CLARKE MM, 2nd Suffolk Regiment, killed in action on 30 August 1918, aged 21 (Plot D.57).

Another significant group of casualties are the fourteen men of the 1st Royal Scots Fusiliers. The group consists of one officer, Lieutenant John CHARLTON, and thirteen other ranks, who with the exception of one man, were killed in action on 2 September 1918. All of them can be found in Row A and Row D.

There are just six Commonwealth soldiers buried here, all of them Canadians. They are all September 1918 casualties and each man is from a different unit. One of the men, Private Rocky Karst JORDON, 47th Battalion, Canadian Infantry, was born in Naples, Italy. He died of wounds on 26 September 1918, aged 19, at the 3/2nd West

Lancashire Field Ambulance. His left arm and leg were badly injured when a shell burst near him while his battalion was assembling for the attack on the Marquion Line. In spite of immediate attention he died later that day. (Plot B.26)

One final grave of note is that of Private Thomas Robinson TETLOW, 12th Battalion, Tank Corps, who fell in action on 2 September 1918. He had previously served with the Royal Army Ordnance Corps. (Plot D.5)

Écoust Military Cemetery, Écoust-Saint-Mein

The cemetery can be seen from Écoust British Cemetery and sits just off the D.5E along a path on the north-east side of the village. It lies tucked up against the old railway embankment and its location had been part of the German defensive positions on 2 April 1917 when the village was first captured. Although the village of Écoust-Saint-Mein was captured by the 7th Division on 2 April 1917, there is not a single casualty buried here from that date. The 8th and 9th Battalions, Devonshire Regiment, captured the village, the latter attacking towards this cemetery from the fields just south of the communal cemetery, the former attacking further along close to where the D.956 and the D.10E4 enter the village.

The CWGC register tells us that there are seventy-eight identified burials here, which is exactly half the total, and that one special memorial commemorates another casualty known to be buried within this cemetery. What is unusual is that the cemetery contains almost as many unknown German soldiers as it does British. By far the majority of identified burials are from 1917 and these run from early April, when Écoust was captured, to the end of November. As such, the cemetery provides a ready snapshot of battalions that occupied this part of the line throughout that year. It is also a cemetery with few officers and no gallantry award holders.

All ten of the 1918 casualties, men of the 2/6th North Staffordshire Regiment, fell between 21 and 24 March, or during the early part of April. The CWGC register tells us that a number of graves, including almost all of those belonging to the North Staffordshire Regiment, were brought into the cemetery after the Armistice and buried in Plot II, Row B. The date of death for three of the North Staffordshire men, Privates Reginald MOSS, Thomas PERKIN and Sidney Watkiss ROSS, has never been precisely determined, but they almost certainly died of wounds in German captivity. *Soldiers Died in the Great War* shows all three deaths on 24 March. Their battalion belonged to the 59th (2nd North Midland) Division, which was completely overrun on 21 March 1918. It suffered the highest number of fatalities of any division that day and more than 2,000 of its men were taken prisoner, many of whom would probably have sustained wounds of some description. What is certain is that no battalion from this division was still fighting around Écoust-Saint-Mein by the evening of 21 March.

Lieutenant Colonel Thomas Bezley Houghton THORNE, 2/6th North Staffordshire Regiment, was one of those killed in action on the opening day of the German March Offensive. His is one of the graves referred to that was brought in after the war; he was 44 years old when he died. (Plot II.B.20)

Also buried in Plot II, Row A, are nine Australian artillerymen, eight of whom are buried consecutively. All nine have been identified and were killed in action in April

1917 serving with the 10th Brigade, Australian Field Artillery. Five of them fell on the opening day of the First Battle of Bullecourt, 11 April 1917. The 62nd (West Riding) Division, which also played an important part in the First Battle and Second Battle of Bullecourt, has twenty-five identified burials here. Not all of the sixteen men of the York & Lancaster Regiment buried here were killed during the fighting at Bullecourt in April and May 1917, but many of them were.

HAC Cemetery, Écoust-Saint-Mein

The cemetery lies on the D.956 just over half a mile from the centre of Écoust-Saint-Mein. The fields directly behind the north-west corner of the cemetery are those over which the 8th Devonshire Regiment made its attack on the village on 2 April 1917. The fields on the other side of the road opposite the entrance to the cemetery between the D.956 and the D.36E are where the 2nd Gordon Highlanders attacked that day.

Of the 824 identified casualties in this cemetery, 454 are from 1918 and 355 from 1917. A further nineteen are recorded as having fallen in 1916, though this figure now needs to be revised, since it can be confirmed that some are the result of simple error over the date of death.

Given its size, there are surprisingly few gallantry award holders buried here; just fifteen with the MM and three with the MC. There are also very few officers above the rank of lieutenant. One of the exceptions is Major Valentine Sandford LONGMAN, 19th Battery, Royal Field Artillery, who was killed in action on 1 September 1918, aged 32 (Plot VI.G.17). He is one of seventy from the Royal Field Artillery buried here, fifty-nine of whom are 1917 casualties. Four of the eleven 1918 casualties from this regiment were killed during the March fighting.

The cemetery was begun in April 1917 by the 2nd Battalion, Honourable Artillery Company, which formed part of the 7th Division. It therefore seems appropriate to start with the regiment from which the cemetery derives its name and which was the first to inter its men at this location. Many of the subsequent casualties were brought to this cemetery for reburial after the war, when a significant number of other cemeteries were decommissioned as battlefield clearances took place.

Fittingly, the most recent burials here included two men of the 2nd Battalion, Honourable Artillery Company who, together with the remains of seven other un-identified soldiers, are believed to have been killed at the Second Battle of Bullecourt. The bodies were discovered by a farmer in 2009 and the men were laid to rest on 23 April 2013. The two bodies that were identified are Lieutenant John Harold PRITCHARD and Private Christopher Douglas ELPHICK. Both men were killed on 15 May 1917 (Plots II.A.A.6 and 8). PRITCHARD, whose middle name is shown as 'Heriot' in the regimental history, served with the regiment from 1 March 1909 and went to France as a serjeant with the 1st Battalion in September 1914. He was wounded near Neuve Église in late November that year and again on 16 March the following year just south of Ypres. He was eventually commissioned and posted to the 2nd Battalion on 1st October 1916.

Today, the cemetery contains thirty-one officers and men of the 2nd Battalion, Honourable Artillery Company, including three officers buried together, all of them second lieutenants and all killed in action on 31 March or 1 April 1917 (Plots I.A.14

Funeral of Major Roderick Ogle Bell-Irving DSO MC, 16th Battalion, Canadian Infantry, near Agnicourt. He was killed in action on 1 October 1918 and is now buried in Éterpigny British Cemetery. (*IWM*)

The photograph was taken during the Battle of Arras near Hénin-sur-Cojeul. A small battlefield cemetery can be seen in the middle of the photograph with a shell bursting a little way beyond it near the road. (*IWM*)

A soldier's grave near Bullecourt. The grave is marked with a simple wooden cross and numerous shell cases. Possibly an artilleryman? The photograph was taken on 18 May 1917. (*IWM*)

This photograph was taken from the high ground south of Noreuil on 14 May 1917. The cemetery, with its wooden crosses, was begun soon after the village was captured six weeks earlier, on 2 April by 13 Brigade, Australian Infantry. The cemetery, Noreuil Australian Cemetery, still exists in a landscape that has hardly changed. The top of the sunken lane that runs alongside the cemetery is just traceable as a dark horizontal line across the middle ground. (*IWM*)

ter the war every effort was made to locate lost graves. Here a Graves Registration Unit is covering remains. (*CWGC*)

Another team begins the unpleasant, but necessary task of recovering the body of a fallen soldier after the war. (*CWGC*)

The photograph shows the bodies of soldiers arriving at a military cemetery for re-burial. (*IWM*)

carpenter making wooden crosses. (*Peter Taylor Collection*)

...indmill British Cemetery on the Arras–Cambrai Road with the remains of Monchy-le-Preux ...rely visible in the distance to the left of the Cross of Sacrifice. The vehicle belongs to the Imperial ...ar Graves Commission and carries the 'IWGC' initials on the side. A wreath appears to have been ...d at one of the graves. (*CWGC*)

The Faubourg d'Amiens Cemetery at Arras. The photograph was taken before the construction of the Arras Memorial. Note the variation in the types of wooden cross originally used to mark the graves of soldiers. (*Goodland Collection, CWGC*)

Floral tributes for a fallen soldier. The two women in the photograph appear to be the same ones from the previous photograph. (*Goodland Collection, CWGC*)

mason's yard containing some of the many headstones required to replace each wooden cross.
e enormity of the task can readily be appreciated. (*Goodland Collection, CWGC*)

day, headstones are cut by computer-programmed machines. Here, the inscription is being done
hand. (*Goodland Collection, CWGC*)

A vehicle used by a team from the Imperial War Graves Commission. (*Goodland Collection, CWGC*)

Bodies are still being discovered the battlefields. In 2009 a farmer found the remains of soldiers originally buried in May 1917 aft the Second Battle of Bullecourt. Two of the men were subsequen identified and all nine were re-buried with full military honours at HAC Cemetery, Écoust-Saint-Mein, on 23 April 2013. (*CWGC*)

HAC Cemetery, Écoust-Saint-Mein, on 23 April 2013. The funeral service takes place as the nine bodies are laid to rest. Members of the French *Souvenir Français* also pay their respects. (*CWGC*)

to 16). One of them, Second Lieutenant Ewart Stanley BRASS, had went France in February 1915 with 1st Battalion and had been wounded twice. He and Second Lieutenant Frederick Hodskinson GRAY, who had rejoined the regiment at the outbreak of war, were killed on 1 April. The third man, Second Lieutenant Arthur William JONES, was killed the following day.

Four NCOs from the battalion are buried adjacent to their officers; and a further twenty men who were killed in action on 31 March or 1 April 1917 can be found with them in Plot I, Row A. Just before dusk on 31 March, the Germans launched a raid on two posts held by the 2nd Battalion. One of these positions, an advanced post on the Mory–Bullecourt road, was captured. 'A' Company counter-attacked without success during the early hours of the following morning. A repeated attempt by 'C' Company a short time later also came to nothing. During these two actions heavy machine-gun fire caused the battalion around 200 casualties. A few days later, on 3 April, a party went out to recover the dead for burial, but it had to withdraw when it came under enemy shell fire and the officer in charge was wounded.

Among the other ranks of the Honourable Artillery Company, a few are worth further comment. The CWGC register records the death of Private Henry BEAUMONT, 2nd Battalion, Honourable Artillery Company, as 26 February 1917 (Plot I.A.27). This runs contrary to the regimental history, which records it as 31 March 1917. I am more inclined to go with this latter date, which not only coincides with the actions described above, but also because on 26 February the battalion was in support to the 1st Royal Welsh Fusiliers as they entered Serre. The regimental history also records that the following day, 27 February, the 2nd Battalion lost one of its NCOs, Serjeant Paul Marcus Bonner. He is buried in Queen's Cemetery, Bucquoy, not far from Serre. Had BEAUMONT died or been killed at the end of February, or even at the beginning of March, he would almost certainly have been buried much closer to where he died. For his body to be buried at Écoust in such circumstances would make no sense at all. Henry's brother, Freund Beaumont, also died in the war when his ship, HMS *Laurentic*, a requisitioned White Star vessel, struck a mine and sank off the coast of Donegal on 25 January 1917. When it went down 350 lives were lost, as well as a substantial quantity of gold, though this was later recovered. He is commemorated on the Plymouth Memorial.

Private John Leslie SWORDER, 2nd Battalion, Honourable Artillery Company, was another who had already lost a brother (Plot I.A.24). Charles Frederick Sworder went to France as a private with the 1st Battalion, Honourable Artillery Company, but the following year he received a commission and went on to serve as a second lieutenant in the 7th Suffolk Regiment. He was killed in action in Mash Valley on 3 July 1916 and is buried in Ovillers Military Cemetery on the Somme.

The CWGC register contains a note that Private Henry Charles TRINDER had joined the Honourable Artillery Company after leaving his position as Secretary to the President of the British Chamber of Commerce in Paris in 1915. He was killed in action on 31 March 1917; he was an only son. (Plot I.A.23)

Private Henry RIBSTEIN, 2nd Battalion, Honourable Artillery Company, is buried in a separate plot from the others, having been killed in action at a later date, 15 May

1917, at Bullecourt. A German counter-attack that day forced the left of the line held by the battalion to fall back. The line was subsequently restored by 'D' Company, assisted by remnants of 'B' Company, but it was another day of very heavy casualties for the battalion, which had five officers killed, three more wounded, and around 250 other ranks killed, wounded or missing. This left just four officers and ninety-four men to answer the roll call the following day. (Plot III.K.18)

Another man from the battalion, Private Walter Welford RAINER, who according to the CWGC register was born in British Guiana, is also buried in a different plot from the other casualties killed in action on 31 March 1917. The most likely explanation is that his body was not recovered until after the others. (Plot IV.D.27)

The 8th and 9th Battalions, Devonshire Regiment, which were also part of the 7th Division, now have a total of forty-six identified burials here. Their earliest casualties are from 27 March 1917, as the division edged forward towards the Hindenburg Line in the wake of the German retirement. Some days later, on 2 April, after four days of bombardment, both battalions were again involved in an attack that began at 5.15am. The 9th Battalion, which suffered heavily as it pressed through the gaps in the wire, still managed to advance and was able to clear machine-gun positions near the cemetery on the north-west edge of Écoust-Saint-Mein. The 8th Battalion encountered similar difficulties as it negotiated gaps in the wire, but the enemy's fire was partly subdued by supporting fire from Lewis guns, which enabled 'B' Company on the right to enter the village of Écoust-Saint-Mein. Here, each house had to be fought for and cleared in the face of determined resistance. 'D' Company eventually cleared its obstacles and linked up with 'B' Company along the railway embankment, leaving 'A' Company behind them to mop up. The subsequent counter-attacks were all met successfully and dealt with. Despite the day's success, some of the cost can still be counted here today where thirty-four identified casualties from both battalions have since been laid to rest. The casualty total for both the Devonshire battalions came to around 220.

Captain John Chantrey INCHBALD, 9th Devonshire Regiment, was among the casualties that day. He was 22 years old and had been a scholar at Winchester College and New College, Oxford. He landed in France with the battalion in July 1915 and had been mentioned in despatches. Like a number of officers and men of the 9th Devonshire Regiment, he was originally buried at one of the Mory–Écoust Road Cemeteries, but his grave was subsequently lost and he is now commemorated here by way of special memorial (Mory–Écoust Road Cemetery, Memorial 1). Next to him lie Captain David Humphrey BELLAMY, 10th Devonshire Regiment, attached 9th Battalion, Lieutenant Audley St John PERKINS, Second Lieutenant Richard Hamilton CARRICK and Second Lieutenant Edward McCartney READ, all 9th Devonshire Regiment. (Mory–Écoust Road Cemetery, Memorials 2, 3, 4 and 5)

Captain BELLAMY went overseas with the regiment's 10th Battalion in 1915 and had served with it in Salonika. He was one of a number of casualties that were caught by the machine-gun fire from the cemetery on the north-west side of Écoust-Saint-Mein. BELLAMY's father, Lieutenant Colonel Charles Vincent Bellamy DSO, was also commissioned in the Devonshire Regiment after leaving Plymouth College in

1886. He went on to serve throughout the Great War after periods with the Ceylon Light Infantry and the Southern Nigeria Volunteers. He was subsequently promoted to the rank of major and was in the Anzac sector in Gallipoli in 1915 with the Royal Engineers, followed by Egypt, before serving in France and Belgium between 1916 and 1918. During the war he was twice mentioned in despatches. His long and distinguished service was rewarded in the *London Gazette* dated 4 June 1917 when he was awarded the DSO in the King's Birthday Honours.

Lieutenant PERKINS met his death clearing trenches on the edge of the village.

Two officer casualties from the 8th Devonshire Regiment, buried rather than commemorated here, are Second Lieutenant Maurice Edward Edmonds FENWICK (Plot III.H.13) and Second Lieutenant Clement Daryl CALEB (Plot III.D.18). CALEB had been wounded on the Somme the previous year and was mortally wounded, aged 22, on the north side of Écoust-Saint-Mein, close to the station. He and FENWICK were among thirty men of the battalion killed or found to be missing after the day's actions on 2 April 1917. Nine of the casualties from the 8th Battalion are commemorated together (Mory–Écoust Road Cemetery, Memorials 9 to 17), as is another man (Special Memorial A.16).

After the capture of Écoust-Saint-Mein, the 8th and 9th Devonshire Regiment remained in the area, suffering further casualties, mainly from shelling. They also took part in operations in May around Bullecourt. Two officers buried in Plot IV were killed in action on 8 May 1917 during fighting to clear a small area in the southwest part of Bullecourt, known as the Red Patch. Resistance was fierce and bombing was the chief method employed by both sides to attack and defend small areas of trench and rubble. The 8th Devonshire Regiment took over from the 9th Battalion on the night of 8 May. By nightfall on 9 May, when it was relieved in turn by the 2nd Gordon Highlanders, the battalion had suffered eleven officer casualties and almost 250 other ranks killed, wounded or missing, all within the space of twenty-four hours. The two officers buried here are Second Lieutenants Charles John HOLDSWORTH (Plot IV.H.15) and Montague William Augustus SANDOE. (Plot IV.K.1)

Nineteen out of twenty-one NCOs and privates of the 2nd Gordon Highlanders now buried here fell during the fighting to capture Écoust-Saint-Mein during the final days of March or on 2 April 1917. The other two were killed a couple of months later, in June. During the latter days of August 1918 the 1st Gordon Highlanders were also involved in fighting in this area as part of the 3rd Division. Most of the 1st Battalion casualties are buried in Plot I, Row C, but others are scattered elsewhere, including some who had been transferred to the 1/14th Battalion, London Regiment (London Scottish). One of the 1st Gordon Highlanders, Private William BIRTLES, had been awarded the MM (Plot III.J.1). A further three men from the 1/6th and 1/7th Gordon Highlanders, killed in action during late March and early April 1918, are also buried here in Plot VIII.

Plot I, Rows B and C, contain a significant number of headstones belonging to men of the Royal Fusiliers: forty-four in total. They are from the 4th Battalion and most of them are dated 31 August 1918, though three men, who were killed or died of wounds a day either side, are buried elsewhere within the cemetery. Among the three is Lance Corporal Frank ROPER MM, one of two men from the battalion to have been decorated for gallantry. (Plot II.E.2).

The second gallantry award within this group of 4th Royal Fusiliers is Serjeant Stephen E. JETTEN MM. He was one of the casualties from the fighting on 31 August and was 28 years old when he fell (Plot I.C.9). Oddly, neither he, nor Lance Corporal Frank ROPER is shown as having been awarded the MM in *Soldiers Died in the Great War*. However, JETTEN's MM was gazetted on 10 October 1916 and was awarded for bravery in the field as a lance corporal, although the spelling of his surname is slightly different.

After taking up positions to the south-east of Écoust-Saint-Mein in preparation for the attack on 31 August, the 4th Royal Fusiliers advanced. However, many casualties had already occurred from shelling as they were forming up for the attack. Equally, the British artillery did not really deal effectively with strongpoints and other obstacles that lay in front of the Fusiliers, so that when the attack took place the battalions on either side made good progress, but the Royal Fusiliers ran into deadly machine-gun fire from a sunken road about 250 yards ahead of them and from another position on the southern outskirts of the village. Despite making several attempts to push on, the Fusiliers could make no headway and all but one of the officers became casualties. Two tanks that had gone forward in support of their attack were also soon put out of action and were unable to assist. The following day the battalion was able to advance, but only after the 1st Northumberland Fusiliers had cleared resistance from the sunken road around 8.00pm the night before with the aid of a creeping barrage.

Second Lieutenant William Francis PENWARDEN (Plot I.B.6) and Second Lieutenant Victor Albert AYRES (Plot I.C.7) both fell during these operations, as did a couple of veterans. Company Serjeant Major Thomas HAMBLETT, aged 39, had served in the South African War, while 36-years-old Private Frederick Thomas MARTIN had served for sixteen years prior to his death. By contrast, Private Cecil Frank RITCHLEY (Plot I.B.12), who was born in Nebraska, USA, and Private Robert George Henry CAMPLING (Plot I.B.21) were just 16 and 17 years old respectively when they were both killed in action on 31 August.

One final point with regard to the 4th Royal Fusiliers is that the CWGC register incorrectly shows Lance Corporal Percy TEE as having died on 31 August 1916. On that date the battalion was on the Somme. The correct date, in keeping with the battalion's movements, should be 31 August 1918, which is supported by the entry in *Soldiers Died in the Great War*.

The CWGC register should also show the date of death for Private John TOPHAM, 8th King's (Liverpool Regiment), as 30 August 1918 and not 1916 (Plot V.A.30). There are forty-three men from this regiment buried or commemorated here and all except one fell between 28 August and 2 September 1918. The 13th Battalion accounts for just under half of the total, many of whom fell on 31 August. The 13th King's (Liverpool Regiment) was part of the 3rd Division, the same division as the 4th Royal Fusiliers, and both were in action around Écoust-Saint-Mein at the end of August 1918.

TEE and TOPHAM are two of nineteen men shown in the CWGC register as having died in 1916. Another man whose year of death should read differently is Rifleman Andrew Beattie TURBYNE. His unit is shown merely as the King's Royal Rifle Corps, but he was killed on 29 August 1918, not 1916, serving with the 13th Battalion, London Regiment (The Kensingtons), which was affiliated to the King's Royal Rifle Corps. He had previously served with the Seaforth Highlanders and the Queen's (Royal West Surrey Regiment). (Plot IV.B.16)

There is quite a wide discrepancy regarding the death of Lance Corporal James DALGLEISH, 9th King's (Liverpool Regiment), who according to the CWGC register was killed on 7 April 1916, but who according to *Soldiers Died in the Great War* was killed on 16 May 1916. Like the few other genuine 1916 infantry casualties buried here, these men would have died of wounds in German captivity.

While the 7th Division was engaged in the capture of Croisilles and Écoust-Saint-Mein on 2 April 1917, the 4th Australian Division was busy capturing the village of Noreuil. The story of Noreuil that day is best told in connection with Noreuil Australian Cemetery. However, some of the casualties from that fight are buried here: eighteen men of the 51st Battalion, Australian Infantry, killed on 2 April in the advance around the northern edge of the village, the majority of whom probably fell soon after the advance began. There are two officers among the eighteen: Captain Louis Lionel SMITH (Plot II.E.3) and Second Lieutenant Joseph Henry MINCHIN (Plot II.E.4). Five other officers from this battalion were wounded and casualties amongst its other ranks ran to 198. Casualties amongst the 50th Battalion were even higher; five officers and ninety other ranks were killed out of a total of 360, though none happen to be buried in this cemetery.

In order to facilitate the cutting of wire in front of the Hindenburg Line near Bullecourt, three groups of Australian Field Artillery had been placed well forward in the shallow valleys that divided the villages of Écoust, Noreuil and Lagnicourt. However, their forward location made them vulnerable. In the action at Lagnicourt on 15 April 1917, when the Germans launched an attack along these valleys, the intention was not to capture or recover ground, but to inflict as much damage as possible on the artillery positions and destroy the guns in order to prevent, or at least disrupt, further offensive action against the Hindenburg Line.

When the Germans advanced down the valleys the gun batteries were easily overrun. Later that day, after the Australians had recovered the ground that had been temporarily overwhelmed, they found that only four 18-pounder guns and one howitzer had been spiked and that only one had been destroyed by shell fire. Many more had been prepared for destruction, but the charges had fortunately failed to detonate. The Germans claimed that twenty-two guns had been destroyed by demolition, which was clearly not the case, and all the undamaged guns were soon back in action once the sights and breech blocks had been refitted.

There are twelve identified Australian gunners buried here who were killed in this action on 15 April. All of them are from the 11th Brigade, Australian Field Artillery, and they can be found in Plot I, Row A. (Between I.A.1 and I.A.19)

There are also twenty-two identified Australian casualties from May 1917, notably fourteen men killed in the fighting at Bullecourt on 3 May, and a few more from the following two days. Like many groups within this cemetery, this collection of Australian artillerymen, infantry and pioneers is fairly scattered, in this case across four separate plots. However, all the infantry are from battalions belonging to the 5th and 6th Australian Brigades, which on 3 May 1917 attacked on the east side of the Bullecourt salient. Some of the artillery casualties are also from that date, whilst others fell on 12 and 27 May.

The 13th Battalion, London Regiment (The Kensingtons), and the 16th Battalion, London Regiment (Queen's Westminster Rifles), were in action between Croisilles and Bullecourt between 28 and 31 August 1918. They experienced heavy resistance and were even counter-attacked by a fresh German division early on the morning of the 30th, during which the 56th (London) Division was driven out of Bullecourt. A further consequence of that withdrawal was that the 3rd Division was forced to give up Écoust.

There are now thirty-two officers and men from the London Regiment buried here who fell between 28 and 30 August 1918, and while many are from the 13th Battalion, an almost equal number are from the 2/20th Battalion, London Regiment (Blackheath and Woolwich). This second-line Territorial battalion had been part of the 60th (2/2nd London) Division, but was detached in late June 1918 and on 9 August it became part of the 62nd (West Riding) Division. One headstone, that of Private Albert ACOURT, shows him to be from the 32nd Battalion, London Regiment, but he, like many others originally from that battalion, had been posted to the 16th Battalion (Queen's Westminster Rifles) to replace losses. It will also be noted that the CWGC register records Private Arthur Harry BEESLEY, 2/20th Battalion, London Regiment, as having died on 30 August 1916. He was, in fact, killed on 30 August 1918. (Plot IV.E.12)

One of the NCOs from the 13th Battalion, London Regiment, Serjeant Charles Henry William MAPLETHORPE, had been awarded the MM (Plot IV.B.8), but the family of another man from the same battalion, Private Arthur Frederick CORNWELL, killed in action on 29 August 1918 (Plot IV.A.19), is also of interest. His father, Private Eli Cornwell, died at home serving with the 57th Protection Company, Royal Defence Corps, on 25 October 1916, aged 64. However, Arthur's half-brother, Boy 1st Class John Travers Cornwell, was awarded the VC and also mentioned in despatches. He was only 16 years old when he was mortally wounded aboard HMS *Chester* on 31 May 1916 at the Battle of Jutland. After all of his gun's crew had been killed or wounded, and despite the extreme gravity of his injuries, he remained at his post awaiting orders until the end of the action. He died a few days later on 2 June in Grimsby. He is now commemorated on a memorial in Chester Cathedral dedicated to those on board who lost their lives, and some cottages in Hornchurch, Essex, were later named after him. He is buried in Manor Park Cemetery in East London, where both he and his father are commemorated together on the war memorial.

Another group of men from the London Regiment, mainly from the 7th Battalion (City of London) and the 10th Battalion (Hackney Rifles), were killed during the latter part of May and early June 1917. The majority of them are to be found in Plot III, Row F, including three officers: Lieutenant Alexander MANTLE, 7th Battalion (Plot III.F.30), Second Lieutenant Geoffrey Wilfred HILLS, 10th Battalion (Plot III.K.12) and Second Lieutenant Harold Benjamin SMITH, 7th Battalion. (Plot VI.B.1)

Casualties from the Royal Field Artillery have already had been referred to briefly, but not those of the Royal Garrison Artillery. There are just eleven identified burials from this heavy branch of the artillery and they date from early December 1917. The CWGC register shows three men buried next to each other from 'M' Anti-Aircraft Battery, killed in action on 22 January 1918 (Plots III.F.14 to 16). The register shows the man in the next grave, Private James Arthur BEAUMONT, aged 41, serving with the Army Service Corps, but he too was part of 'M' Anti-Aircraft Battery and was killed at the same time as the other three. There are also three men of 144th Siege Battery buried together, killed in action on 5 September 1918. (Plots VIII.C.29, C.30 and D.1)

In addition to the sixty-five Australian casualties, there are also seventeen identified Canadian soldiers here, including six drivers and a corporal from the 1st Canadian Division Ammunition Column who were killed the same day, 5 September 1918, and almost certainly as a result of the same incident. Fittingly, they are now buried together. (Plots VI.F.12 to 17)

From the other side of the Empire, there are just four men from the New Zealand Division buried in this cemetery. Three are artillerymen who were killed together on 27 September 1918 (Plots VII.D.8 to 10) and there is a lone infantryman from the 3rd Battalion, New Zealand Rifle Brigade, killed on the 10th of that month. (Plot VII.C.8)

A few other miscellaneous graves are worth mentioning in passing before leaving this cemetery. Private Arthur BATEY, 2/6th South Staffordshire Regiment, was killed in action on 21 March 1918, aged 20 (Plot VIII.B.31). His brother, Wilfred Batey, was killed in action with the 12th Durham Light Infantry on 7 June 1917 and is commemorated on the Menin Gate.

Captain Arthur Graeme WEST, 6th Oxfordshire & Buckinghamshire Light Infantry, was killed on 3 April 1917. Like a number of others during the Great War, he committed his thoughts to paper in the form of a diary, which was subsequently published under the title *Diary of a Dead Officer* (Plot VIII.C.14). There are only two other men from his regiment buried in this cemetery, both of them officers from WEST's battalion. Captain Athelstan Basil BAINES (Plot VIII.C.10) was 28 years old when he died. Before the war he lived with his wife at Saint-Cloud, Seine et Oise, in France. The other is Second Lieutenant James Arthur SELLAR, aged 23. He was the son of a clergyman and the CWGC register tells us that he had originally enlisted with the 19th Royal Fusiliers (2nd Public Schools Battalion) and had gone to France in 1915 before returning to England as an officer cadet and where he received his commission (Plot VIII.C.11). Both men were killed on the same day as WEST.

Rifleman John WOODHOUSE, 12th King's Royal Rifle Corps, died on 4 October 1917 when he was executed by firing squad. He went missing prior to his battalion's involvement in an attack near Langemarck in August and was found near Calais a fortnight later. His defence that he had become lost after returning from leave was easily dismissed. He was already under a suspended sentence of death and the division to which he belonged, the 20th (Light) Division, had already shot two men earlier that year, one as recently as September, the other in June. This last man was from the same battalion as WOODHOUSE, which may not have helped his case. (Plot VIII.C.23)

There are four identified casualties from the Royal Flying Corps killed in action in 1916. Taking them in chronological order, the first is Major Francis Fitzgerald WALDRON, 60 Squadron, Royal Flying Corps. He was wounded in aerial combat flying a Morane single-seat fighter on 3 July 1916 and, although his aircraft was seen by other members of his flight to come down under control, he died later that day in German captivity and his death was later confirmed. He had joined the cavalry in 1907, serving with the 19th (Queen Alexandra's Own Royal) Hussars, but went on to gain his flying certificate in 1912 at his own expense. He then joined the Royal Flying Corps in 1913 and was therefore one of the very early pioneers of military aviation. Later that year he had the honour of being the first to reach Montrose in the very first British military flight to Scotland. He also served as an instructor at the Central Flying School, but went to France in August 1914 as part of the first Royal Flying Corps contingent. He was mentioned in Sir John French's first despatch and in 1915 he was given command of a squadron. His father was Brigadier General Francis Waldron CB, Royal Horse and Royal Field Artillery, and his uncle was the Right Honourable Laurence Ambrose Waldron, MP for the St Stephens Green Division, Dublin. (Plot VIII.A.26)

Lieutenant William Powell BOWMAN, 11 Squadron, Royal Flying Corps, and Lieutenant George CLAYTON were killed together on 17 October 1916 whilst flying their FE2b. Both are buried in the same grave and both had previously served with the West Yorkshire Regiment before transferring to the Royal Flying Corps. BOWMAN had been a student at Leeds University when war broke out. He was considered a good flyer and on one occasion, when he was attacked by four enemy machines and his observer had been shot, he skilfully guided his machine down from 9,000 feet. In spite of extensive damage to the aircraft and an empty fuel tank, he managed to land it successfully behind his own lines. Their deaths occurred in aerial combat near Mory whilst on a reconnaissance mission for Third Army. (Plot VIII.C.7)

Captain Auberon Thomas HERBERT, 22 Squadron, Royal Flying Corps, was killed in action on 3 November 1916, aged 40, though his partner that day, Lieutenant Anderson, was taken prisoner. He was the son of the late Honourable Auberon Edward William Molyneux Herbert and was 8th Baron Lucas and the 11th Baron Dingwall. He was educated at Bedford Grammar School and went on to Balliol College, Oxford, and represented the university at rowing. After Oxford, he became a war correspondent for *The Times* in South Africa and during his time there he was wounded in the foot by a rifle bullet. The wound caused infection and he had to be evacuated back to England, by which time the only remedy was to remove the limb below the knee.

In 1905, he succeeded his uncle, Lord Cowper, in the baronies of Lucas and Dingwall. In 1907, he became Private Secretary to Lord Haldane at the War Office and then served as Under-Secretary for War the following year. Three years later he became Under-Secretary for the Colonies before moving to the Board of Agriculture as its Parliamentary Secretary. He became President of the Board in 1914 and took a seat in the Cabinet.

He joined the Royal Flying Corps in 1915, gaining his flying certificate and serving in Egypt before returning home as an instructor. He only arrived in France once the Somme battles were already under way. Though originally reported as missing, his death was confirmed a month later and his grave was eventually located in 1918 during the Advance to Victory. He was a personal friend of the writer John Buchan, who included an affectionate eulogy to him in his work *These for Remembrance*, which was privately printed in 1919, though it later gained wider readership. He was also a cousin of the poet, Captain the Honourable Julian Henry Francis Grenfell DSO, 1st Royal Dragoons, and his brother, Second Lieutenant the Honourable Gerald William Grenfell, 8th Rifle Brigade, both of whom fell in action during the war. Julian's best known work is *Into Battle*. (Plot VIII.C.17)

A further nine Royal Flying Corps casualties are buried here, all killed in 1917, as well as one flyer from the Royal Naval Air Service. They are all buried close to each other in Plot VIII.

Air Mechanic 2nd Class Hubert Victor GOSNAY was killed in action on 24 March 1917, aged 22 (Plot VIII.A.20). His pilot, Lieutenant James Russell Middleton, was injured and taken prisoner when their aircraft, an FE2b, came down behind enemy lines. Middleton survived for a while, but died from his wounds in Germany on 21 June that year and is buried at Cologne Southern Cemetery. Middleton was in Canada working as an engineer before the war and had initially enlisted in Lord Strathcona's Horse. He later transferred to the 7th Cameron Highlanders before joining the Royal Flying Corps.

The following day, Lieutenant John Stephen COOPER, 70 Squadron, Royal Flying Corps, and Second Lieutenant Alexander Norman McQUEEN, formerly 6th Gordon Highlanders, were killed in action in their Sopwith one-and-a-half Strutter aircraft. They died on 25 March 1917 and both men are buried next to each other. Their names appeared in the Royal Flying Corps Casualty List for April. (Plots VIII.C.15 and 16)

Flight Lieutenant Harry Redmond WAMBOLT, Royal Naval Air Service, was 24 years old when he was killed in action on 3 April 1917 in his Sopwith Pup. *Airmen Died in the Great War* shows his date of death as 4 March 1917. (Plot VIII.A.15)

Lieutenant Oswald Thomas WALTON, 18 Squadron, Royal Flying Corps, formerly 3rd South Lancashire Regiment, was killed in action flying an FE2b on 12 April 1917, as was the man with him that day, Air Mechanic John Campbell WALKER. Again, they are buried in adjacent graves. (Plots VIII.A.27 and 28)

Lieutenant David Rhys Cadwgan LLOYD, Royal Flying Corps, was killed in action on 16 June 1917, aged 20. He was described by his commanding officer as a *'fine and fearless flyer – almost the best in the squadron'* and *'an undeniable fighter'*. He joined the Essex Yeomanry on 16 September 1914 and was gazetted as a second lieutenant in the Loyal North Lancashire Regiment on 29 December that year. He served with the BEF from 30 November 1914 and was wounded on 1 July 1916. He transferred to the Royal Flying Corps on 28 September 1916 and was promoted to lieutenant on 1 March 1917. He returned to France on 19 April 1917, which was a critical time for the Royal Flying Corps. Pilots were urgently needed to replace heavy losses during a month that became known as 'Bloody April'. He was shot down and killed in aerial combat two months later when flying a Nieuport 23 aircraft over Marquion, near Cambrai. (Plot VIII.B.8)

Second Lieutenant Albert Alexander ALLEN, 46 Squadron, Royal Flying Corps, was killed in action on 11 October 1917 whilst flying a Sopwith Pup. (Plot VIII.A.42)

Second Lieutenant Sidney Walter RANDALL, 11 Squadron, Royal Flying Corps, and Lieutenant Walter de Courcey DODD, formerly 5th Royal Munster Fusiliers, died together on 31 October 1917 when their aircraft, a Bristol F2B, came down behind German lines. DODD was certainly alive when they crashed, but he died very soon after from his injuries. They are now buried next to each other (Plots VIII.A.45 and 46). DODD was one of three brothers who died during the war. Second Lieutenant Francis Joseph Dodd died at home on 31 October 1918 and is buried at Grantham Cemetery, Lincolnshire. He had originally enlisted in 1914 with the Royal Dublin Fusiliers before transferring to the Machine Gun Corps. Lieutenant John O'Connell Dodd, 6th Royal Munster Fusiliers, was killed in action just four days before the Armistice and is buried at Monceau-Saint-Waast Communal Cemetery.

Second Lieutenant Peter Francis KENT, 3 Squadron, Royal Flying Corps, was killed in action on 6 February 1918, aged 19, when flying a Sopwith Camel aircraft. (Plot VIII.D.13)

Reference has already been made to a number of 1916 casualties, particularly those where the year of death is incorrectly recorded. There is just one officer among this group: Second Lieutenant Charles Ferris BEVERLAND, 2nd Royal Inniskilling Fusiliers, died on 4 December 1916 (Pronville German Cemetery Memorial 34). He clearly died as a German prisoner and he is a genuine 1916 casualty. He was a member of the OTC at Queen's University, Belfast, between 1915 and 1916. The battalion history, which covers the period 1914–1916, makes no references to him and provides only a very general account of events during that period. However, in mid-November 1916 his battalion, which was part of the 32nd Division, was in the area of high ground just north of Beaumont Hamel in the vicinity of Munich Trench where the last phase of the Battle of the Somme was being played out. On 25 November the division handed over its trenches to the 7th Division. Presumably he was taken prisoner before that date although the circumstances of his capture remain very obscure.

There are three holders of the MC buried here:

Captain Alfred PARKINSON MC, 21st Manchester Regiment, was killed in action on 12 May 1917. His MC was gazetted on 19 April 1917, shortly before his death. It was awarded for conspicuous gallantry and devotion to duty in leading his platoon to its final objective and driving the enemy from their position. (Plot IV.K.2)

Captain Howard Kilbourne HARRIS MC, 3rd Essex Regiment, attached 11th Battalion, was killed in action on 22 February 1918. He was born in Ontario, Canada, and after attending University College (University of Toronto) he joined the Bankers' Bond Company. He enlisted in England and was commissioned in the 11th Essex Regiment. His MC was awarded for his part in leading an attack on enemy trenches in 1916 during which he assumed command and controlled operations with great coolness and skill. He had also been involved in the preparations for the attack. The award was gazetted on 30 May 1917. His death came while carrying out a reconnaissance on a German position. (Plot VIII.A.37)

Second Lieutenant Douglas Gordon KEMP MC, Royal Engineers, was killed in action on 21 March 1918. His MC was gazetted on 4 February 1918 and the citation appeared on 5 July that year. It was awarded for conspicuous gallantry and devotion to duty during an enemy attack when he had taken charge of a party and held his position with great courage and coolness until reinforcements arrived. He then took part in a counter-attack and assisted in capturing an important trench, which he held until relieved. His show of initiative and determination was described as 'splendid' at this critical time. (Quéant German Cemetery Memorial 27)

Holders of the MM, not already mentioned, are listed below:

Private Arthur SIMPSON MM, 13th King's (Liverpool Regiment), killed in action on 31 August 1918. (Plot I.C.10)

Private George Alfred REEVE MM, 8th King's Own (Royal Lancaster Regiment), killed in action on 28 August 1918. (Plot I.C.28)

Lance Corporal Herbert John MADELEY MM, 2/6th South Staffordshire Regiment, killed in action on 21 March 1918. (Plot II.C.3)

Driver William John EVANS MM, 'C' Battery, 91 Brigade, Royal Field Artillery, killed in action on 6 June 1917. (Plot II.E.5)

Serjeant J. HEATH MM, 'D' Battery, 281 Brigade, Royal Field Artillery, killed in action on 8 December 1917. (Plot III.G.27)

Serjeant James MERCER MM, 22nd Manchester Regiment, killed in action on 17 April 1917. (Plot III.K.15)

Rifleman Benjamin DRAYCOTT MM, 2/8th West Yorkshire Regiment, killed in action on 7 April 1917. (Plot IV.H.26)

Private Charles LOCK MM, 2nd (City of London) Battalion, London Regiment (Royal Fusiliers), killed in action on 15 June 1917. (Plot VI.D.14)

Serjeant Lester Louis DELMAS MM, 9th King's (Liverpool Regiment), killed in action on 28 August 1918. (Plot VI.F.6)

Private Percy Clifford GRAY MM, 27th Battalion, Australian Infantry, killed in action on 24 April 1917. (Plot VII.G.1)

Serjeant William KITCHEN MM, 21st Manchester Regiment, killed in action on 11 May 1917. (Special Memorial A.17)

Other battalions in action at the end of August 1918 were the 2/4th Loyal North Lancashire Regiment and the 2/5th King's Own (Royal Lancaster Regiment). Both of these formed part of the 57th (2nd West Lancashire) Division. Together, these two battalions have over thirty casualties buried here. Very little has been written about the 57th (2nd West Lancashire) Division, mainly because it came to the Western Front relatively late in the war in February 1917 and consisted of second line Territorial battalions. Its only battle honour that year was for the Second Battle of Passchendaele between 26 October and 7 November. However, it did play a greater part in the final advances the following year from late August through to October 1918.

Noreuil Australian Cemetery

This is one of my favourite cemeteries to visit and, like the Devonshire Cemetery on the Somme, it tells a particular story. The ground over which that story was written can easily be appreciated from the cemetery or from the crest of the spur that divides Noreuil from Lagnicourt. This cemetery has all the character associated with many of the so-called 'Pals' cemeteries on the Somme. It lies off the D.5 on the southern side of the village at the end of the Rue de la Chapelle. One of the sunken lanes used by the Germans to defend the village runs along the western edge of the cemetery. The left flank of the attack by the 50th Battalion, Australian Infantry, ran along the edge of this sunken lane, which was one of those barricaded. A machine-gun nest was also located nearby. It is a cemetery that deserves to be visited more frequently; it is not large and has just 219 identified casualties.

As they retreated to the Hindenburg Line in March 1917, the Germans temporarily held a line of villages in order to delay the British advance. Noreuil was one of those villages, along with Hénin, Croisilles, Écoust, Longatte, Doignies and Louverval. An unsuccessful attempt to capture this line had been made at the end of March, but on 2 April I Anzac Corps and the 7th Division made a renewed effort. 13 Brigade, Australian Infantry, was tasked with clearing Noreuil and then securing a line marked by the Lagnicourt–Bullecourt road. Overall, the day's fighting was successful, but the contest at Noreuil was prolonged, costly and lasted the entire day; 13 Brigade lost around 600 casualties, 360 of those borne by the 50th Battalion. Of that 360, five officers were killed that day, along with ninety other ranks.

The 51st Battalion, Australian Infantry, advanced along the spur on the north side of the village, but the 50th Battalion approached from the direction of Lagnicourt, which had recently been captured. This latter battalion was to advance downhill to the village and then wheel to the right up the valley that leads to the village of Quéant, leaving behind a detachment to deal with any garrison in the village itself. The spur of high ground to its right was to be secured by the 52nd Battalion, though this appeared only to involve the capture of a post.

The cemetery is quite unusual in that not only are all five officers from the 50th Battalion buried here, though four are shown as dying on 3 April 1917, but also the ninety other ranks from that battalion killed on 2 April are interred here with them. To find all the dead from a particular action in one place is indeed quite rare, especially on this scale, but the task was made easier in so far as the subsequent advance allowed an opportunity to collect the dead from the battlefield and to organize an ordered system of burial. Some of the graves were subsequently lost as a result of shell fire the following year during the German March Offensive, but it is certain that these men had been buried within the cemetery and it seems right and fitting that they are still be remembered here, even if only by way of special memorials.

One of the five officer casualties is Lieutenant William Paton HOGGARTH, 50th Battalion. According to C.E.W. Bean, who compiled the *Official History of the Australian Imperial Force during the Great War 1914–1918*, HOGGARTH held the distinction of being the first Australian to enter Mouquet Farm in August the previous year, despite being wounded during its capture. He was killed early in the attack on Noreuil when he and others were caught in enfilade from a German machine-gun nest positioned in the village cemetery. As he lay mortally wounded he urged his men on, declining offers of help. (Plot E.4)

The artillery barrage on the village had not been sufficient to subdue its garrison and fire came not only from its ruined buildings, but also from barricades in the sunken lanes leading to it.

Lieutenant Wilfred Vivian Hubert BIDSTRUP (Plot F.39) and Lieutenant Wilfrid Oswald JOSE (Plot F.31) were also mortally wounded in this initial phase of the fighting. BIDSTRUP was seen to empty his revolver at close range into the Germans before he fell. JOSE, who was a 10th Battalion officer, but attached to the 50th Battalion, was 21 years old and was born in China, the son of a clergyman. The CWGC register shows both as dying on the 3rd rather than 2 April.

Captain Harold Edwin Salisbury ARMITAGE (Plot C.21), 50th Battalion, is also shown as dying the day after the fight. He had taken his company into the village and had then gone on to link up with the 51st Battalion with a view to both groups pushing on to the objective, which was the road between Lagnicourt and Bullecourt. The detachments that were left behind in the village were not sufficient to overcome the garrison there and most were either killed or captured. When ARMITAGE and another company commander emerged from the village they were able to link up with the 51st Battalion away to the left on the higher ground, but not with Captain Todd, whose company had not entered the village, but had wheeled sharply to the right and made its way along the valley leading towards Quéant according to the plan. To complicate matters further, the Germans had dug a diagonal shallow trench about 250 yards in front of the Bullecourt–Quéant road. This had not shown up on any of the aerial reconnaissance photographs and it lay close to the point where the two battalions had intended to join up. This was now occupied and well-defended by the enemy.

The gap between Todd's force and the rest of the battalion was flagged up by ARMITAGE, whose message, conveyed by a runner, described the position on the right as 'precarious'. His message also pointed out that although casualties were increasing, his own position was being consolidated favourably. ARMITAGE was later shot through the head while trying to determine the enemy's strength opposite his position. He had previously been mentioned in despatches.

Sergeant William John JAMES (Special Memorial B.12) was sent by Todd to a location where two tracks meet on the crest of a small rise about 1,000 yards north-east of Noreuil and told to hold the position and defend the gap until reinforcements arrived.

However, this small detachment came under such heavy fire that it was forced to withdraw and JAMES was killed during this action.

The 52nd Battalion had dealt with the enemy post and had begun to dig in near the crest of the southern spur overlooking the valley where Todd and the remainder of his men were now pinned down and almost surrounded. The capture of the mopping up parties had allowed Germans from the village to attack Todd's men from the rear. As they did so, they placed captured Australian prisoners to the front, which made return fire impossible without endangering the lives of those captured.

By now, German opposition around the Lagnicourt–Bullecourt road, and down in the valley, had begun to stiffen after reinforcements had emerged from the direction of Quéant. A machine gun on the valley side of the spur was also sweeping the open ground east of the village. This was on the reverse slope to that occupied by the 52nd Battalion and the failure to capture and dominate this southern spur undoubtedly caused multiple casualties and prolonged the day's fighting.

In response to ARMITAGE's message, Lieutenant Esson Thomas James RULE took his platoon forward in an effort to locate and support Todd. This was the last platoon readily available to the 50th Battalion and RULE was mortally wounded in that attempt (Plot A.24). However, the remainder of this party was gathered together under Major Loutit, who had been sent up by the battalion's commander, Lieutenant Colonel Salisbury, and it eventually succeeded in eliminating a group of Germans that had been enfilading Todd's scattered positions. Loutit's force then occupied a crater, which allowed it to return fire on the German machine-gun position on the side of the valley and to command the gap between Todd and ARMITAGE's men.

By the early hours the next day the Germans had withdrawn, leaving the Australians to clear the battlefield of their dead. Further north, the other villages had been captured, but the fighting had also been heavy, particularly around Écoust-Saint-Mein. During the fighting for Noreuil the artillery of both sides had been quiet. Consequently, there were no casualties caused by shell fire, so that all the dead bodies on the battlefield remained intact.

In addition to the five officers, there are three sergeants, seven corporals, eight lance corporals and seventy-two privates from the 50th Battalion buried within the walls of this cemetery, including one whose rank is given as driver rather than private.

This cemetery is also the final resting place for two sets of brothers. Private Edward Charles CLAYTON was killed in action with the 52nd Battalion, Australian Infantry, on 12 April 1917, aged 29. His brother, Private William Alfred CLAYTON, aged 42, also served in the same battalion and was killed on the same day as Edward. Today, they rest side by side. (Plots E.5 and E.6)

Corporal Thomas BOSTON, aged 25 (Plot F.41) and Private Angus BOSTON, aged 28 (Special Memorial A.8), are also buried here, though not together. They were killed in action on 2 April 1917. Not only did they serve together in the 50th Battalion, Australian Infantry, but their army numbers are consecutive (3250 and 3249), indicating that they joined up together. Two other men, Privates Ernest Arthur NEWTON and Ernest Leslie NORMAN, both of whom served with the 50th Battalion, are commemorated next to each other and also have consecutive army numbers (1957 and 1958). (Special Memorials B.32 and B.33)

Australian burials continued in this cemetery after the capture of Noreuil. Ten casualties can be found dating to 15 April 1917, the date of a German attack on Lagnicourt; all except one of them are buried in Row F. The men in Row F all belonged to the 19th Battalion, the other soldier is from the 17th Battalion. A further twenty-two were killed in action between 16 April and 2 May 1917 and, like the men killed on 15 April, they are from battalions belonging to the 2nd Australian Division and all are NCOs and privates.

The remaining Australian burials from 1917 are confined to the first half of May. Most of the eighteen burials dating between 3 and 31 May 1917 are 5th Australian Division casualties, with just a handful of 1st and 2nd Australian Division men among them. On 3 May 1917, as part of a wider offensive known as the Third Battle of the Scarpe, the 2nd Australian Division attacked the eastern side of the salient around Bullecourt. This offensive, on a frontage of just over fourteen miles, involved eleven British divisions and two Canadian divisions, as well as the 2nd Australian Division. The attack by the 2nd Australian Division and the British 62nd (West Riding) Division at the southern end of this line became known as the Second Battle of Bullecourt.

Among the group of Australians killed during the May engagements is the highest ranking casualty to be found in this cemetery, Major George TOSTEVIN, 1st Company, Australian Machine Gun Corps. He was killed while carrying out a reconnaissance in preparation for a relief of the 1st and 5th Machine Gun Companies by the 3rd Machine Gun Company. (Plot F.7)

Captain Archibald Ramsay GARDNER, 55th Battalion, Australian Infantry, was killed by shell fire on 9 May 1917 (Plot H.12) and Second Lieutenant James KERR, also from the 55th Battalion, was killed in action nine days later on 18 May 1917 (Plot H.8). Near to him is Lieutenant William DENT-YOUNG, 11th Battalion, Australian Infantry, who was killed by shell fire on 5 May 1917. He was caught in an enemy barrage that caused casualties amongst a carrying party made up of men from the 10th Battalion. (Plot H.15)

With regard to Australian casualties, the final word rests with something of an enigma. Private William Ralph MARSHALL, 50th Battalion, Australian Infantry, is shown in the CWGC register as having died on 25 April 1918, Anzac Day. However, this makes no sense, as his battalion was nowhere near Noreuil that day. His battalion, part of 13 Brigade, was located south of Villers-Bretonneux, which is a very long way from here. He is commemorated by way of Special Memorial B.26, indicating that, although he is known to have been buried within this cemetery, his grave was subsequently lost by shell fire. It may be that the year of death should be 1917 rather than 1918. Even so, the 4th Australian Division was resting during this period, so the circumstances of his death, and particularly the date, appear to be something of a mystery.

Although Australian burials dominate this cemetery, there are burials from British units. Second Lieutenant William Lawrence BETTELEY MC, 7th Somerset Light Infantry, was killed in action on 25 June 1917, aged 46. The CWGC register notes that he had come from South America in order to serve. His MC was gazetted on 25 November 1916 and was awarded for conspicuous gallantry in action for his display of skill and courage while forming a defensive flank under heavy fire, in the course of which he was wounded, though he still remained at his post (Plot A.11). A short distance along the same row is Lance Corporal William Joseph SMITH MM, who was also killed in action with the 7th Somerset Light Infantry, but on 24 June 1917 (Plot A.23). The row contains a number of men from battalions of the 20th (Light) Division, including the 7th Duke of Cornwall's Light Infantry, the 10th, 11th and 12th Battalions, Rifle Brigade, the 7th Somerset Light Infantry and the 6th Oxfordshire & Buckinghamshire Light Infantry. Almost all were casualties of enemy shelling during the months of June and July as successive battalions carried out tours of duty in and around the front line in this sector.

Captain Henry Norman WALLER, 2/4th Duke of Wellington's Regiment, was killed in action on 3 July 1917, aged 27 (Plot H.4). A few other men from his battalion who died on or around the same date are also buried here, but not together, indicating that they were probably brought into the cemetery at different times after the Armistice from isolated graves nearby. At the start of the row is Second Lieutenant Norman Reid MITCHELL, 20th King's Royal Rifle Corps, who was killed in action near Bullecourt on 5 December 1917 (Plot H.1). He was born in Ceylon and went on to study at Glasgow University where he gained his Master's degree. He then became a church minister in Whitsome, Berwickshire, before enlisting in the Seaforth Highlanders. He continued to serve with that regiment at the front, and even obtained a temporary commission in it in October 1917. At the start of December, however, he transferred to the 20th King's Royal Rifle Corps, but was killed in the trenches during his first tour of duty with his new unit.

One particular grave here always strikes me as a little sad; sad because Lance Corporal George R. FRASER MM, 2nd Royal Scots, lies here alone when twenty-two of his comrades who fell on the same day happen to be buried close by at Vraucourt Copse Cemetery. The answer may be that his body was recovered at a different time to the others or because his body was recovered by a different burial party. Twenty-five NCOs and privates from that battalion lost their lives in the capture of Noreuil on 2 September 1918. FRASER, whose grave is Plot G.2, had formerly served with the Royal Scots Fusiliers and *Soldiers Died in the Great War* shows him as serving as a private at the time of his death.

Lagnicourt Hedge Cemetery

This small cemetery has sixty-two identified casualties and lies on the south-west side of the village of Lagnicourt-Marcel. From the direction of Noreuil on the D.5, the first turning on the right on entering the village is the D.36, which leads to Vaulx-Vraucourt. The turning on the right after that is the Rue des Boeufs. Take this turning and follow it around the western edge of the village. Take the next exit on the right, the Rue de Morchies, which is the D.18. About 150 yards down this road, turn right. This is the Rue de Beugny and the cemetery sits a short way down the road on the right.

The CWGC register also points out that Plot II was made by the Germans after they had overrun the village in March 1918 and refers to its former name, Lagnicourt No. 2 Cemetery. Two other cemeteries made in the commune by the Germans did not survive post-war concentrations. Plot I was added by the Guards Division after its 2nd Brigade retook the village in early September 1918.

The CWGC register notes that the cemetery was originally begun by the 7th Somerset Light Infantry in June 1917, although today the cemetery contains one private soldier (Plot I.C.9) from the 12th Battalion, Australian Infantry, killed in action two months previously on 15 April 1917, when the Germans launched a limited, but fierce attack against the 1st Australian Division and part of the 2nd Australian Division. Its aim was to destroy as many guns and artillery positions as possible, so as to delay any further attacks on the Hindenburg Line. The attack reached the villages of Noreuil, Boursies and Demicourt, and passed through and beyond Lagnicourt, all of which lay behind the Australian front line. The Germans withdrew later that day having destroyed some of the gun pits, though very few artillery pieces were damaged because the charges failed to detonate.

The 7th Somerset Light Infantry relieved the 12th King's (Liverpool Regiment) in the front line on 5 June 1917. This included an outpost situated about 500 yards east of the main front trench, just east of the village of Lagnicourt. On 7 June the battalion suffered its first casualties here. Four men were killed when the enemy shelled trenches occupied by 'C' Company. Apparently, some staff officers from the artillery had ventured down the line and were standing in the trench, obviously visible to the enemy. This prompted a brief, but very accurate bombardment. That day a further three men from the battalion were killed by sniper fire which came from the long grass that covered much of no man's land. These deaths clearly show the difficulties and hazards of taking over trenches, where often it took a while, occasionally with tragic consequences, to appreciate weak spots vulnerable to enemy observation. The seven casualties are buried together. (Plots I.A.7 to 13)

The 20th (Light) Division, to which the 7th Somerset Light Infantry belonged, did not take part in the Battle of Arras, but it did spend two periods on the extremities of that battlefield, once in the summer of 1917 in the Quéant sector, and again in 1918 in the Avion sector on the outskirts of Lens. Casualties from various battalions of this division can therefore be found within the cemeteries in both localities. The few casualties here from the 12th King's Royal Rifle Corps, the 12th Rifle Brigade and the 6th King's Shropshire Light Infantry are all from the 20th (Light) Division and are all random deaths rather than the result of specific operations; simply the result of holding the line. Likewise, a few 3rd Division casualties from the 1st Northumberland Fusiliers and 12th West Yorkshire Regiment can be found here, as well as a couple of identified casualties from the 2/8th West Yorkshire Regiment, which was part of the 62nd (West Riding) Division, and which date from the summer and early autumn of 1917.

Another interesting group of graves can be found in Plot I.B.16 to 21. They are a group of NCOs and privates from the 1/14th Battalion, London Regiment (London Scottish), who were killed in September 1917 during a two-month period in this sector. Until the third week of September trench routine had been very uneventful, but then the Germans began to put down a heavy bombardment on a post that formed part of the London Scottish line. On the 24th it was noticed that the enemy shelling was directed specifically at the wire around the post, indicating the likelihood of a raid. On the night of the 24th/25th the London Scottish put patrols out in no man's land and a wiring party went out to repair the gaps. All appeared quiet until 4.45am when the Germans suddenly put down a box barrage around the post which, despite the imminent risk, was still being held. The German raiding party did manage to get into the post and captured two sentries. The British artillery put down a bombardment on no man's land, mainly to catch the returning raiders, but also to break up any attempt to broaden the raid. Five of the six burials referred to above are casualties of this raid.

The sixth, who died of wounds two weeks later on 9 October, was Lance Corporal Francis James William DOWDEN (Plot I.B.20). On 8 October the London Scottish carried out a retaliatory raid on the German trenches opposite them. The raid by No. 11 Platoon, under Second Lieutenant Gibson, took out two bangalore torpedoes to blast a gap through the German wire. The first failed to detonate, but the second cut a gap sufficiently wide for the raiders to penetrate. However, another belt of wire lay between them and the German trench. As the group tried desperately to cut a gap by hand, they came under fire from short range and had to withdraw empty-handed. Four men were wounded and brought back, but one of them, Lance Corporal DOWDEN, succumbed to his wounds and died soon afterwards. All in all, the London Scottish has ten identified burials here in Plot I, but two of them from early September are to be found in Row A rather than Row B.

Elsewhere, reference has already been made to casualties from 20 November 1917 and the final few days of that month. These were from a secondary operation timed to coincide with the opening of the Battle of Cambrai. The objective of the operation was the capture of Tunnel Trench and its supporting trench system. Many casualties from this operation are buried in Croisilles British Cemetery and Croisilles Railway Cemetery. However, the four privates buried here, and who died between 20 and 29 November 1917, were not killed in the actual attack on Tunnel Trench. The 56th (London) Division was ordered to stage 'dummy' attacks on the day of the operation. A dozen 'dummy' tanks were placed out in no man's land and hundreds of 'dummy' figures were placed above the parapet along the divisional front to deceive the Germans opposite into believing that the British attack extended beyond its actual boundaries. A bombardment had also been put down around Quéant in the preceding weeks as part of that deception. The three casualties from the 3rd (City of London) Battalion, London Regiment (Royal Fusiliers), were almost certainly killed by retaliatory shell fire on 20 November, indicating that the Germans, at least for a short time, were taken in by the deception.

There are just six identified casualties from the period covering the German March Offensive when this part of the line was overrun. Most of these casualties can be found in Plot II, Row A, and are from the 9th Norfolk Regiment, the 1st Leicestershire Regiment, the 1st Wiltshire Regiment and the 2nd South Lancashire Regiment. They were killed between 24 and 26 March 1918. Just a few days earlier, on 21 March 1918, Second Lieutenant Eric Francis Seaforth HAYTER, 87th Battery, Royal Field Artillery, was killed in action aged 25. This was the day that the German Offensive began. Before the war he worked as an electrical engineer for the state railway in Victoria, Australia, but he came to England in order to enlist. He was hospitalized from the effects of gas early in 1917 and spent some time recovering in England before returning to the front. He was the only son of Colonel F.J. Hayter, who served at the Royal Military College in Australia. (Plot I.A.14A)

The remainder of the cemetery is taken up by casualties from operations in September 1918 as the Germans were forced back to the Hindenburg Line and the Canal du Nord. The Welsh Guards have nine identified casualties in Plot I, and there are six men from the 4th and 9th Field Ambulances, Royal Army Medical Corps, including two men with the MM: Private Frank BOTHWELL MM, 4th Field Ambulance, from Dublin (Plot I.C.4) and Corporal Joseph Peter GREEN MM (Plot I.C.1). Both were from the same unit and both were killed in action on 27 September, a day of heavy fighting. The Guards Division was heavily involved that day, but its casualties here precede that date.

Casualties in the Guards Division during the middle part of September 1918 were fairly few in number and generally occurred as part of the daily attrition between successive advances, usually the result of shelling. However, one incident of note was a raid carried out by the Germans on 17 September as No. 4 Company, 1st Welsh Guards, was being relieved by the 2nd Coldstream Guards east of Lagnicourt. Each side was holding opposite ends of a communication trench and the Germans made a bombing attack along it in an effort to dislodge their opponents. The raid was beaten back after a brief, but fierce, fight. Two of the casualties here from the Welsh Guards are from this date and could easily have been killed in this encounter.

Finally, the CWGC register provides the interesting comment with regard to Bombardier Albert James GODDEN, 26th Siege Battery, Royal Garrison Artillery, who was killed in action on 19 September 1918, aged 19 (Plot I.A.2). His parents are shown as residing at Rue de Kemmel, Wytschaete, Belgium, even though he is recorded as a native of Folkestone. Wytschaete was captured by the Germans on 1 November 1914, but its ruins were retaken on the opening day of the Battle of Messines by the 16th (Irish) Division. It was captured again by the Germans on 16 April 1918, but was retaken early on the morning of 28 September 1918 by the 34th Division, just nine days after Bombardier GODDEN's death.

Chapter Seven

A Mill and a Crucifix – From the Scarpe to the Piave – A Gallant Cheesemaker

Dury Crucifix Cemetery

In early April 1918 the new German front line ran just west of Orange Hill, with its support line just slightly west of Wancourt. Behind that another defensive line ran just west of the Bois du Vert and Chérisy; and yet another line, known as the Fresnes–Rouvroy Line, ran in front of Vis-en-Artois. The village of Vis-en-Artois was an integral part of this trench system and was, in effect, a large redoubt encircled by trenches, machine-gun positions and defensive positions on all sides.

Behind that was the Drocourt–Quéant Line, which was linked to the Fresnes–Rouvroy Line by a defensive trench known as the Vis-en-Artois Switch, which in turn ran diagonally south-east from the village to face Upton Wood and the village of Hendecourt-lès-Cagnicourt. The Drocourt–Quéant Support Line then ran behind the main line of that name and skirted the western edges of Dury and Mont Dury where it crossed the main D.939 and continued south.

Another diagonal switch line, the Buissy Switch, ran back from this system of defences, passing between the villages of Cagnicourt and Villers-lès-Cagncourt and then to the west of Buissy. This arrangement was not on the same scale as the Hindenburg Line, but it was a formidable set of obstacles and still provided the Germans with a very strong line of resistance. The task facing the Canadian Corps on 2 September 1918 was to break through this system beyond Dury. It did so, but at a cost of around 11,000 casualties, dead, wounded or missing.

Dury Crucifix Cemetery lies a few hundred yards south of the village of Dury. At the junction of the D.939 and the D.956, take the D.956 north towards the village. Continue for about half a mile along the D.956, to the point where the road forks. Take the right fork, which is the minor of the two roads. Follow this road to the cross-roads and turn right. The cemetery is a short distance down this road. The cemetery is clearly visible long before arrival, as it lies in open fields on the southern edge of the village.

Although this is a fairly large cemetery, containing 2,058 burials, only 292 are identified. The original graves belong mainly to men of the 46th Battalion, Canadian Infantry, and were made soon after the battalion had captured the village of Dury in conjunction with the 47th Battalion. These burials can now be found in Plot I, Rows A and B.

Of the 292 identified burials here, 122 come from Canadian units. They are mainly from the 4th Canadian Division, though some are also from the 3rd Canadian Division. With one exception, all of these men fell on 2 September 1918, or a day or so either side of it, as the Canadian Corps completed its assembly and then captured the Drocourt–Quéant Line. The one exception is Private John KUSKITCHU, 52nd Battalion, Canadian Infantry, whose date of death is shown in the CWGC register as 28 August 1916. However, records for the 52nd Battalion show his date of death as 28 August 1918, which in the context of this cemetery makes far more sense. (Plot I.E.48)

Although this part of the battlefield is mainly associated with the Canadian Corps and the fighting that took place here on and around 2 September 1918, the number of identified graves from British units outnumber those of Canadian units; there are now 170 British casualties buried here. Just over a third of them are from 1917, the majority being from April and May that year. No British or Canadian unit ever penetrated this far in 1917, but the CWGC notes are useful in this respect, informing us that the original battlefield cemetery was greatly enlarged after the Armistice and that it was used to bury men who had fallen to the west of this location during the various stages of the Battle of Arras in 1917. Nineteen men of the 2nd Essex Regiment and ten from the 2nd Seaforth Highlanders were also reburied here when Essex Cemetery in Éterpigny was closed. All of these men fell in September 1918. A number of Canadian dead from locations north of here were also brought to this cemetery for re-interment after the Armistice.

The youngest soldier buried here is Canadian. Private Frank Nathaniel YOUNG was killed in action on 2 September 1918, aged 17, serving with the 46th Battalion, Canadian Infantry. (Plot I.A.24)

Second Lieutenant Joseph Edward SMITH, 60 Squadron, Royal Air Force, was killed in action on 17 September 1918, aged 26, flying an SE5a. This was not a particularly heavy day in terms of casualties for the Royal Air Force, though enemy air activity was described as 'normal' and the weather was also reasonable. (Plot I.B.9)

Second Lieutenant Raymond Alfred CRUICKSHANK, 2nd Monmouthshire Regiment, was killed in action on 23 April 1917, aged 23. He was with his platoon when he was killed by a shell. He had been in France since December 1916 and was slightly wounded on 9 April 1917, a couple of weeks before his death. His unit was the pioneer battalion attached to the 29th Division (Plot I.F.51).

His son, also Raymond Alfred Cruickshank, served with 7 Squadron, Royal Air Force, during the Second World War and won the DFC and Bar. On 3 May 1941 he and his crew were returning from a sortie over Hamburg and had almost reached their air base in Cambridgeshire when their Sterling hit some trees. The aircraft crashed and flipped over killing all the crew members. His body was returned to the family home in Newport where he was buried in Newport (Christchurch) Cemetery. His DFC was awarded for gallantry during many raids and operations, but the citation singles out one particular occasion when he had bombed bridges over the River Meuse at one of the most heavily defended points within the target zone. Although his aircraft was damaged by heavy ground fire, he descended to low altitude and withheld his bombs until the right moment. The award was gazetted on 7 June 1940. The bar to his DFC was awarded for general gallantry during subsequent flying operations and was gazetted on 22 October 1940. Both awards were won with 7 Squadron, Royal Air Force.

Another interesting entry in the CWGC register is that relating to Private Theodore Ernest SUNBURY. He was another of those killed in action on 2 September 1918 and served with the Motor Machine Gun Mechanical Transport Company, Canadian Army Service Corps. The note in the CWGC register tells us that he was a Professor of Music; on his enlistment papers he gave his profession as musician. (Plot II.D.31)

Company Serjeant Major George Thomas MARCHANT, 2nd South Wales Borderers, was killed in action on 19 May 1917, aged 27, during an attack carried out by his battalion just east of Monchy-le-Preux in conjunction with the 1st Border Regiment and the 1st Royal Inniskilling Fusiliers. It was the same action in which Serjeant Albert White, 2nd South Wales Borderers, won his VC. MARCHANT had previously served with the Royal Welsh Fusiliers. (Plot II.E.34)

Captain Stuart Aloysius MOORE MC and Bar, 50th Battalion, Canadian Infantry, was killed in action on 2 September 1918. His MC was gazetted on 28 March 1917, but only under his first name. The entry was then corrected on 19 April. It was awarded for conspicuous gallantry and devotion to duty whilst leading a bombing party with great courage and initiative, bombing many dug-outs and inflicting many casualties on the enemy. During that operation he was wounded. The citation adds that he had also done fine work on previous occasions. The bar to it was gazetted on 2 December 1918 and was awarded for conspicuous gallantry and good leadership when he took his own and another company forward across 2,000 yards of ground in the face of determined resistance from machine-gun fire. The next day Captain MOORE and his men broke up a heavy counter-attack by the enemy and, although he was forced to give up some ground, the citation states that he disputed every inch of it and ensured that all the wounded were brought back with him. Throughout the two days he set a splendid example to those under his command. (Plot II.K.1)

Lieutenant Arthur Richard BATSON MC and Bar, 'C' Company, 50th Battalion, Canadian Infantry, was killed in action on 2 September 1918, aged 32. His death occurred shortly after he had secured his objectives. His men were consolidating their position under shell fire and he was in discussion with the company commander, Captain MOORE, on one of the flanks when they were killed by shell fire. His MC was gazetted on 17 September 1917 and was awarded for conspicuous gallantry and devotion to duty at a time when the situation was uncertain. He went forward alone and resolved the matter by carrying out a daring reconnaissance across open and fire-swept ground. The report that he sent back was of the greatest value. On previous occasions he had carried out similar reconnaissance work. The bar to his MC was gazetted on 7 March 1918 and again was awarded for conspicuous gallantry and devotion to duty. This time, after the main attack had failed, he collected and organized the stragglers and, by his example and courage, inspired them to fresh and successful efforts after two further attacks had also failed. (Plot II.K.2)

Second Corporal (Lance Corporal) Ernest CRADDOCK DCM, 1st Divisional Signal Company, Royal Engineers, was killed in action on 2 September 1918. His DCM was gazetted on 3 September 1918 and was awarded for conspicuous gallantry and devotion to duty while in charge of the brigade's forward exchange. After an enemy bombardment had cut the lines to the right-hand battalion, he went out at once, making his way through an intense bombardment and, at great personal risk, laid out two new lines. That same afternoon the buried cable route to the left hand battalion was also blown up. Again, and in full view of the enemy, he laid out overland lines under heavy shrapnel fire. He then maintained both of these lines the whole day and throughout the night. It was his courage and devotion to duty that enabled brigade HQ to keep in communication with the battalions on the left and right of the brigade front. (Plot II.K.39)

Private Reginald Arthur HARROP DCM, 50th Battalion, Canadian Infantry, was killed in action on 2 September 1918, aged 20. His DCM was awarded for conspicuous gallantry and devotion to duty during an attack in which he and two other men captured an enemy machine gun and its crew under heavy fire. The task was made more difficult owing to the position of the gun, which was firing from the apex of two belts of wire. Later, when his company was forced to fall back, he undertook to bring back his platoon officer who had been wounded, doing so at great personal risk. The citation concludes by stating that throughout these operations he behaved with marked courage and determination. The award was gazetted on 15 November 1918. HARROP was also posthumously awarded the *Médaille d'Honneur* (France) on 18 July 1919. (Plot II.K.46)

Second Lieutenant James Burgess MACDONALD, 6 Squadron, Royal Air Force, was killed in action on 30 August 1918, aged 19. His observer that day, Second Lieutenant F.C. Cook, was wounded. Their aircraft was an RE8 two-seater reconnaissance biplane that first came into service in late 1916. Activity by enemy aircraft that day was described as light and flying conditions were fine, but cloudy. (Plot II.K.54)

Lieutenant Norman Aubrey OUTERBRIDGE (Plot III.A.47) and Private Percy MERCER (Plot III.D.34) both fell while serving with the 1st Newfoundland Regiment. They were killed on 14 April 1917 defending Monchy-le-Preux. Lieutenant OUTERBRIDGE was the son of Sir Joseph and Lady Outerbridge of St John's, Newfoundland. Sir Joseph was a businessman, philanthropist and an enthusiastic supporter of the British Empire. He had chaired the Festival of Empire Committee in 1910–1911 and was one of the men responsible for the recruitment, administration, and provisioning of the hundreds of volunteers who flocked to the Newfoundland Regiment in 1914. Norman's brother, Captain Herbert Outerbridge, also served with the Newfoundland Regiment during the war and was awarded an OBE in the King's Birthday Honours List on 3 June 1919. MERCER was 18 years old when he died.

Second Lieutenant Clarence Wasson APPLEY, 8 Squadron, Royal Air Force, died of wounds on 2 September 1918. He was born in Brooklyn, New York, and his parents lived in New Jersey. He was 26 years old when he died (Plot III.D.5). The man with whom he was flying that day, Second Lieutenant Ralph Frederick Talbot, was also killed when their FK8 came down, but his body has never been identified and he is now commemorated on the Flying Services Memorial at Arras.

Second Lieutenant Frank Stanlie LAYARD MC, 1st Border Regiment, took part in an unsuccessful attack on the evening of 19 May 1917 just to the east of Monchy-le-Preux. During that attack he was in command of 'B' Company whose task it was to capture enemy positions near Cigar Copse and then establish two strongpoints, one east of the wood, the other on the south side of a trench known as Devil's Trench. However, his company came under heavy fire and the attack broke down. Once the attack had failed, many of the wounded were brought in under the cover of darkness, but LAYARD was among those who were still missing. His friend, Captain William Maurice (Pat) Armstrong MC, the brigade major attached to 86 Brigade, went out on successive nights in an effort to recover his body, but was killed by a German sniper on 23 May. He is now buried in Faubourg d'Amiens Cemetery in Arras. LAYARD, whose parents lived in Ceylon, was just 20 years old when he died. His MC was gazetted on 18 June 1917 and was awarded for conspicuous gallantry and devotion to duty while in command of a party of bombers carrying out a reconnaissance. Although his party came under heavy fire and incurred several casualties, he completed the task successfully and returned with valuable information. The success of the operation was attributed to his personal courage, determination, and leadership. (Plot III.E.11)

There are also four holders of the MM buried here, including one man, Sergeant William James CATTANACH MM, who was also awarded a bar. He was killed in action on 2 April 1918, aged 26, serving with the 21st Battalion, Canadian Infantry. The battalion war diary notes that his death was deeply felt by the men of his company and by all officers and men of long standing in the battalion. His battalion had experienced a quiet day in the trenches on 1 April, but around 9.30pm the Germans began a bombardment. The 18th Battalion, Canadian Infantry, was due to relieve the 21st Battalion that night, but the bombardment went on until 5.20am the next day and delayed the relief. It was during this period of shelling that Sergeant CATTANACH was killed. (Plot III.C.43)

Private Albert Victor WATERHOUSE, 46th Battalion, Canadian Infantry, had also won the MM. He was killed in action on 2 September 1918, aged 30. He was born in Lisburn, Northern Ireland, and had originally intended to join the Methodist Church. However, in May 1916 he decided to enlist and fought with distinction, winning his MM during the fighting east of Amiens in early August 1918. (Plot I.A.18)

The remaining two holders of the MM buried here are not from Canadian units, but from Scottish regiments. Private Hugh Harris GALBRAITH MM, 1st Royal Scots Fusiliers, died on 5 May 1917, almost certainly as a result of wounds (Plot III.B.31). Serjeant Daniel STEWART MM, 2nd Royal Scots, was killed in action on 3 May 1917. *Soldiers Died in the Great War* makes no reference to the award of his MM. (Plot III.G.39)

There are a few other graves worth noting, including eight members of the Tank Corps who were killed in action or who died of wounds on 2 and 3 September 1918. Six of the eight are from the 11th Battalion, including Second Lieutenant Hubert Graham Hamilton MARSHALL, whilst the remaining two are from the 9th Battalion. Five are buried in Plot III, Row C, two in Plot II, Row K, and the third in Plot II, Row D. Eighty-one tanks were deployed for the attacks on 2 September 1918, not just in this area, but as far south as the Bapaume–Cambrai road. The 9th, the 11th and the 14th Battalions of the Tank Corps were deployed to assist the Canadian effort against the Drocourt–Quéant Line. Their crews did very good work, particularly against machine-gun nests; casualties overall were fairly light, though the Germans did use anti-tank rifles to good effect near Villers-lès-Cagnicourt.

Dury Mill British Cemetery

The cemetery is another of those set in open countryside. At the junction of the D.939 Arras–Cambrai road, take the D.956 north towards Dury. Take the next right turn and continue straight on. The cemetery is easily visible from here and is reached via another small road that runs through the open fields. The cemetery is set back and reached via a small track.

Unlike Dury Crucifix Cemetery, where close to 85 per cent of the burials are un-identified, this one has only fourteen unknown soldiers out of a total of 333. The CWGC register states that the original mill that gave its name to the cemetery was largely destroyed when Dury and the German defensive positions to the west of this location were captured on 2 September 1918.

The cemetery is very much dominated by Canadian dead, nearly all of them from the Canadian 4th Division, which attacked north of the D.939, the Arras–Cambrai road, on 2 September 1918. Several of its battalions are well represented amongst the burials; there are sixty belonging to the 75th Battalion, fifty-four from the 87th Battalion, fifty-two from the 78th Battalion, forty-three from the 38th Battalion and twenty-nine from the 54th Battalion.

Sergeant Angus Roderick McNEIL DCM, 'D' Company, 85th Battalion, Canadian Infantry, won his award whilst carrying out duties as an acting sergeant. The citation states that during an attack and subsequent period of consolidation he handled his men with the utmost skill showing great courage and initiative in placing posts where they were required. During the night he secured valuable information by patrolling the ground to his front, and the following day he went out with a patrol in broad day-light under heavy machine-gun fire, even though he had been on duty continuously for thirty-six hours and had already taken part in two attacks. Throughout these operations he showed a very fine spirit of keenness and devotion to duty. The award was gazetted on 17 September 1917. Sergeant McNEIL was killed in action on 2 September 1918. Before the war, like many men from the Cape Breton area of Nova Scotia, he was a mariner by profession. (Plot I.A.23)

Private Clifford William BELL, aged 22, and his elder brother, Private Norval Delbert BELL, aged 25, were both killed in action with the 78th Battalion, Canadian Infantry, on 2 September 1918 during the fighting for Dury and Mont Dury. They are now buried close to each other, though perhaps an opportunity was lost to bury them side by side (Plots I.B.17 and 35). Sometimes individual battalions did have the chance to gather up their dead for burial after a battle, but this was not always practicable or even possible, depending on circumstances. I know of at least one occasion when a Canadian battalion chose to remain on the battlefield after it had been relieved until it had buried its own dead, a task it preferred to do rather than leave it to others.

Sergeant Frank SHRUBSHALL DCM, 38th Battalion, Canadian Infantry, won his DCM during the operations south of Lihons on 10 August 1918 when the advance by his platoon was held up by an enemy machine-gun post. He charged the position single-handed, and although the enemy got the gun away, he killed two of its crew. His brave action enabled his platoon to continue its advance. The citation concludes that during the entire operation his example and disregard for his own safety were an inspiration to the men of his platoon. The award was gazetted on 16 January 1919. He was killed in action on 2 September 1918, aged 38. (Plot I.C.27)

Lieutenant Archibald Cockburn BAIN MC, 75th Battalion, Canadian Infantry, was killed in action on 2 September 1918, aged 32. His MC was gazetted on 2 December 1918 and was awarded for conspicuous gallantry and devotion to duty during a night attack on a village in which he led his platoon straight through the main street with great dash, reaching a line of trenches some 250 yards beyond it. From there, he and his men engaged enemy machine-gun parties on both flanks. The speed at which he reached his final objective facilitated the occupation of the village and the capture of the trenches beyond it. (Plot II.A.25)

Lieutenant Matthew Maurice WALLACE MC, 54th Battalion, Canadian Infantry, was killed in action on 2 September 1918, aged 25. His MC was gazetted on 15 October 1918 and was awarded for his actions whilst leading a party of six on a reconnaissance of the enemy's wire. While his patrol was out it encountered an enemy patrol about thirty-strong, divided up into three parties. Lieutenant Wallace then deployed his men with great skill and waited until one of the enemy groups was within easy bombing distance. He and his party then attacked the enemy with bombs and revolvers, shouting in a manner that suggested he was in command of greater numbers. The enemy party was taken by surprise and fled in disarray, leaving behind a wounded man who was taken prisoner. During the encounter Wallace's party sustained no casualties. The citation concludes that this *'brilliant little exploit was largely due to the dash and initiative displayed by him'*. (Plot II.A.30)

Private John Smith SHAW MM and Bar, 102nd Battalion, Canadian Infantry, was either killed in action on 3 September 1918 or died from wounds sustained the previous day. His MM was gazetted on 23 February 1918 and the bar to it was gazetted posthumously on 24 January 1919. Back in Canada he was a farmer and had enlisted in April 1916. (Plot II.C.3)

There are several young soldiers buried in this cemetery who died when they were 18 years old, but there are also a couple of veterans of previous campaigns. One of these is Company Sergeant Major Joseph Moore COOPER, 87th Battalion, Canadian Infantry, who was killed in action on 2 September 1918, aged 42. He had previously served in the Sudan and in the South African campaign (Plot II.C.23). Private Albert Daniel Dyer MATTHEWS, 54th Battalion, Canadian Infantry, was another veteran of the South African campaign who fell during the fighting on 2 September. He was 40 years old when he was killed (Plot II.A.35).

There are just nine casualties from British units in this cemetery; three of them are airmen, three are members of the Tank Corps, and there are also three infantrymen. All of them are 1918 casualties. The three from the 9th Battalion, Tank Corps, are buried adjacent to each other and were killed in action on 2 September 1918. Second Lieutenant Frank Harold SMITH (Plot I.D.13) is buried between the other two men, Corporal Fred HARDMAN, formerly Lancashire Fusiliers (Plot I.D.14) and Private Herbert GARNER, formerly Northamptonshire Regiment (Plot I.D.12).

Lieutenant Hubert Wilton CLARKE, 40 Squadron, Royal Air Force, was killed in action on 2 September 1918, aged 19, while flying an SE5a machine. He had formerly served with the 28th Battalion, London Regiment (Artists' Rifles) and had been a pupil at Charterhouse School. He died during a period when the Royal Air Force was enjoying overall success against the enemy. Between 2 September and 8 September 1918 it brought down 101 enemy machines and drove another fifty-one down and out of control. Against this figure, sixty-six of its own aircraft were missing in action. Lieutenant WILTON, unfortunately, was part of that statistic. (Plot II.D.27)

Lieutenant Ewart Nutman UNDERWOOD and his observer, Second Lieutenant Cecil Muscroft COLEMAN, 11 Squadron, Royal Air Force, were killed in action on 6 September 1918 while flying a Bristol F2B aircraft. UNDERWOOD was 20 years old when he died and was an only son. (Plots II.E.2 and 3)

The three infantrymen, all privates, were also killed in action in September 1918. Two are from the 1st Loyal North Lancashire Regiment and are buried next to each other (Plots I.D.18 and 19). The other man is from the 5th Cheshire Regiment, the pioneer battalion of the 56th (London) Division. He is buried in Plot I and his grave is the first one in Row E.

There are nine holders of the MM buried in this cemetery, one of whom has already been referred to. The remaining eight are listed below.

Private Sidney HALE MM, 85th Battalion, Canadian Infantry, killed in action on 2 September 1918, aged 32. (Plot I.A.21)

Private Richard Henry HIGGINSON MM, 78th Battalion, Canadian Infantry, killed in action on 2 September 1918. (Plot I.B.7)

Private James Arthur ROBERTSON MM, 38th Battalion, Canadian Infantry, killed in action on 2 September 1918. He was a farmer from Braeside, Ontario, and his family had been one of the original families to settle and farm in that part of Ontario. He was also an officer of the Loyal Orange Lodge. He enlisted in August 1916. (Plot I.C.2)

Private Wilbert DRYNAN MM, 38th Battalion, Canadian Infantry, killed in action on 2 September 1918. (Plot I.C.22)

Private James GARROW, MM, 85th Battalion, Canadian Infantry, killed in action on 2 September 1918, aged 33. (Plot I.D.22)

Lieutenant Joseph Paget BAILEY MM, 38th Battalion, Canadian Infantry, killed in action on 2 September 1918, aged 22. (Plot I.D.27)

Lance Sergeant D'Arcy Oliver BORLAND MM, 75th Battalion, Canadian Infantry, killed in action on 2 September 1918. (Plot II.B.23)

Corporal John Leach MOWAT MM, 87th Battalion, Canadian Infantry, killed in action on 2 September 1918, aged 24. His Canadian army record shows the spelling of his surname as Mowatt. (Plot II.C.22)

Éterpigny British Cemetery

Éterpigny is situated a couple of miles north-west of Dury. To get there, take the Arras–Cambrai road, the D.939, passing through Vis-en-Artois and Haucourt. Continue along this road for a couple of miles as far as the junction with the D.956. Turn left and continue along this road as far as the next village, which is Dury. At the very northern end of Dury there is a small road running north-west towards Éterpigny. The cemetery is about a mile and a half down this road, on the eastern side of the village. The cemetery is small and was begun at the end of August 1918 by units of the British 1st and 4th Divisions. Of the sixty-six graves in this cemetery, fifty-six men have been identified. Twelve of these are Canadian, four of whom are holders of gallantry medals.

The four men from the 2nd Royal Sussex Regiment and the 1st Northamptonshire Regiment who were killed on 6 and 7 September 1918 are worth a brief mention. Both battalions formed part of the British 1st Division. Although this division spent the entire war on the Western Front, it spent very little of that time around Arras. One of the men, Lance Corporal George Frederick LESSONS, 1st Northamptonshire Regiment, came from Nottingham and was a professional footballer. (Plot A.1)

Sergeant Hugh Sylvester McLENNAN DCM, 16th Battalion, Canadian Infantry, was killed in action on 11 October 1918. His gallantry was posthumously acknowledged in the *London Gazette* just a few days after the Armistice on 15 November 1918. The citation records that he showed great ability in organizing the capture of machine guns and strongpoints, which at different times had impeded the advance, and not once did he fail to put any them out of action. He showed confidence in himself as well as resourcefulness, which kept all his men up to 'concert pitch' during the long advance. On 11 October his battalion was ordered to push out strong patrols in the direction of Sailly and the high ground that lay beyond the Drocourt–Quéant Switch. As it did so, it encountered heavy machine-gun fire from Férin. He was killed during this advance, leading his men as he had always done. (Plot C.16)

Private Eldon Elon ELSTON MM, 13th Battalion, Canadian Infantry, was killed on 10 October 1918, aged 28. He is one of three holders of the MM in this small cemetery. (Plot D.3)

Major Roderick Ogle BELL-IRVING DSO MC, 16th Battalion, Canadian Infantry, was killed in action on 1 October 1918. (Plot D.4). Though Roderick was born in Vancouver, his father, who had been born in Scotland, ensured that his boys were always aware of their Scottish heritage. The family lived a very comfortable life and Roderick's father, who was a prominent shipping agent, also had other business interests. Roderick was educated in Scotland, and on his return to Canada he became one of the original officers in the Highland Regiment, which in 1912 became the 72nd Battalion, Canadian Infantry, otherwise known as the Seaforth Highlanders of Vancouver.

Roderick followed his father into the shipping business where he initially worked as a clerk. On the outbreak of war he was transferred to the 16th Battalion, Canadian Infantry, serving as a lieutenant, though he only joined it at the front sometime after its arrival in France. However, he was with his battalion in time for the fighting at

Mount Sorrel in 1916 where he won his MC near Armagh Wood. The citation notes that when his company was held up by a machine-gun position, he managed to find an approach to the gun that was screened from view. He made his way alone towards it, rushed it, and bayoneted three of its crew. He was still fighting hand-to-hand with the fourth member of the team when help arrived. During the struggle he was forced to resort to the bayonet when his revolver became clogged with mud, making it completely useless. He then led his men forward and took command of another company on its way to the objective.

He was promoted to temporary major in June 1916 and on 1 July 1916 he became acting major. He was then promoted to the substantive rank in November after the fighting around Courcelette. In June 1917 he took temporary command of the 16th Battalion and was involved in the fighting at Hill 70 in August, and later on that year at Passchendaele.

On 30 September 1918 his battalion was ordered to capture the ground between Saucourt and Cuvillers, near Cambrai. At 5.00am on 1 October BELL-IRVING was following up behind his leading companies as they advanced towards the village of Cuvillers when the Germans counter-attacked. Throughout his military service he had never been far away from action, and on this occasion he was killed in the ensuing fight. His body was recovered, but not immediately, and he was buried on 17 October. His DSO was posthumously awarded in 1919.

His brother, Captain Allan Duncan Bell-Irving, served between 1915 and the end of the war with 7 Squadron, and later 60 Squadron, Royal Flying Corps, subsequently Royal Air Force. During his career Allan was shot down on three occasions, was wounded twice, and was awarded the MC and a bar. He had also commanded the School of Special Flying at Gosport and left the Royal Air Force in 1919. During the Second World War he served in the Royal Canadian Air Force, reaching the rank of Air Commodore, and was awarded the OBE. Two other brothers, Malcolm McBean Bell-Irving and Richard Bell-Irving, also flew during the war, another served in the Army, and two of his sisters served as nurses.

The fourth Canadian here with an award for gallantry is Lieutenant Stuart Robertson WIDMEYER MM, who also served with the 16th Battalion, Canadian Infantry. He enlisted in August 1915, arriving in France on 7 May 1916. Whilst still serving as a private, he was wounded on 9 April 1917 at Vimy Ridge. His MM was awarded to him sometime between that date and 4 November 1917, the date on which he was commissioned as a lieutenant. The battalion history makes no specific mention of his act of gallantry, though the date on which his MM was gazetted, 9 July 1917, tends to suggest that it was for actions on or around 9 April 1917. He was killed in action on 1 October 1918, the same date as BELL-IRVING. (Plot D.5)

The vast majority of British burials are from the 4th Division, which at midnight on the 26/27 August 1918 became attached to the Canadian Corps from Army Reserve in readiness for the operations to capture the Drocourt–Quéant Line.

On 30 August 1918 the 4th Division managed to capture the village of Éterpigny with little difficulty, though casualties amongst the 1st Somerset Light Infantry amounted to five officers and 190 other ranks. Most of these occurred from shelling shortly before zero hour, which was set for 4.00pm. The cemetery now contains twenty-four casualties from the last two days of August, all of whom were killed during the capture and consolidation of Éterpigny. Most of them belong to the 1st Somerset Light Infantry, but there are also some from the 1st Rifle Brigade, the 1st Hampshire Regiment and the 1st Royal Warwickshire Regiment, including Private George SMITH MM, 1st Royal Warwickshire, the only British gallantry award holder in this cemetery. (Plot C.9)

Next to him is Serjeant Percy George WEEKS, 1st Warwickshire Regiment, who was killed in action by a sniper on the same day as SMITH. When I last visited this cemetery there was a small note tucked into the CWGC register stating that WEEKS had previously been wounded by a bullet when it struck a wallet in one of his breast pockets. On that occasion it saved his life. If so, this is one of many accounts where articles frequently carried by soldiers, such as pocket bibles, notebooks and cigarette cases, were responsible for taking the impact of bullets and shrapnel balls, thereby saving the life of their owners. (Plot C.8)

Other burials from the 4th British Division include men from the 1st King's Own (Royal Lancaster Regiment) whose attack on 2 September 1918 was carried out in conjunction with the 2nd Essex Regiment, supported by the 2nd Lancashire Fusiliers. The plan had been to avoid a frontal infantry attack on the village of Étaing, which was to be left to the tanks once they had circumvented the marshy ground that lay in front of the village. As it happened, the tanks attacked Étaing Wood rather than the village of Étaing; consequently, some infantry casualties were caused by enfilade fire from the village, as well as from the area around Prospect Farm to the south.

Hamblain-Les-Prés Communal Cemetery
The village is about eight miles east of Arras and its communal cemetery is on the south-west side at the junction of the D.34 and the D.43 where the Rue de Boiry meets the Rue de Sailly.

There are just three burials here, from the Second World War, and all three are men of the 2nd Royal Inniskilling Fusiliers. They died during an encounter with the enemy on 23 May 1940 whilst out on patrol near the River Scarpe. One of the men, Second Lieutenant Hugh Richard KERRICH, was just 20 years old when he died. His father, Brigadier General Walter Allan Fitzgerald Kerrich DSO MC, had served with distinction in the Royal Engineers between 1914 and 1917 on the Western Front, then in Italy between 1917 and 1918. He was also awarded the *Croix de Guerre* (Belgium), which was gazetted on 19 August 1919. His DSO was won while commanding the Royal Engineers in Italy, attached to the 7th Division, during operations on the River Piave. Previous attempts to erect a bridge across the river had failed, but on the night of the 24/25 October 1918 Lieutenant Colonel Kerrich made a personal reconnaissance by wading into the river at various places until he found a suitable spot. Under enemy observation, he worked to throw a bridge across the river and to maintain it in spite of heavy shelling and bombing by enemy aircraft. None of his own men were skilled at bridging, especially across fast flowing waters, so he made use of Italian engineers to make up the skills deficit. His MC was gazetted on 14 January 1916. He continued to serve until his retirement in 1944.

Haucourt Communal Cemetery, Pas de Calais

Lying approximately eight miles south-east of Arras, Haucourt is a small village on the north side of the D.939 and its cemetery is situated in the north-east corner just off the D.9, which is the road to Éterpigny, opposite a small strip of woodland.

There are just three casualties from the Royal Air Force and, although they were buried here collectively, there is an individual headstone for each man. They are the crew of a Bristol Blenheim from 57 Squadron that had taken off from Hawkinge in Kent on a reconnaissance mission. On 22 May 1940 their aircraft crashed in a field just outside the village after it had been shot down, killing the entire crew. The men are Pilot Officer Roi Leonard SAUNDERS, Sergeant (Observer) Samuel Frank SIMMONS, and Aircraftman 1st Class (Wireless Operator) George Ross PIRIE.

Rumaucourt Communal Cemetery

Rumaucourt lies to the north of the D.939, which is the main Arras–Cambrai road. Once past the turning for Dury, heading south-east, continue for about two and a half miles to the junction with the D.19. Turn left here and continue along this road to the southern edge of the village. The communal cemetery lies opposite the large German Military Cemetery.

The CWGC register points out that the fifty-five German graves that used to be here have since been removed to the German Cemetery opposite. Although twenty-four of the thirty British graves here have been identified, eight of them are commemorated by special memorials. The identity of each of the eight men is known, but details regarding the exact location of their remains have been lost, though they are definitely buried here.

The earliest casualties are from the later part of 1916 and are not buried consecutively. They are: Lance Corporal George LONGHORN, 8th Border Regiment, who died of wounds on 29 October 1916 (Grave 7); Private G.B. LEA, 8th North Staffordshire Regiment, who presumably died of wounds on 26 November 1916, but who appears not to be shown in *Soldiers Died in the Great War* (Grave 19); and Private Frank ADAMS, 7th East Kent Regiment (Buffs), who died of wounds on 2 December 1916 and had formerly served with the Kent Cyclist Battalion (Grave 36).

There are two 1917 casualties, both from early April. Private Joseph Gilbert BARNEY, 2nd Honourable Artillery Company, is known to have died of wounds on 1 April 1917 whilst in German captivity. It is quite likely that he was wounded and captured as part of the garrison of a forward post. On the evening of 31 March 1917 a large party of Germans raided positions held by the battalion between Écoust-Saint-Mein and Mory, including a number of forward posts. The battalion suffered around 200 casualties when it made two attempts to recapture one of these posts during the early hours of the following day. The regimental history claims that Private BARNEY died as a prisoner in Germany in May 1917, but this seems highly improbable given that he is buried in this cemetery. (Grave 50)

The majority of the identified graves relate to 1918, the earliest of which are from the last week of March. Casualties from the 3rd Division and the 34th Division are interspersed with men from battalions of the 59th (2nd North Midland) Division and the 40th Division. The first three of these divisions were holding the section of front south of the River Cojeul when the German Offensive began on 21 March 1918. The 3rd Division lost ground, whilst the positions occupied by the 34th Division and the 59th (2nd North Midland) Division were overrun that day. The 40th Division was rushed forward from reserve to fill the gap created by the collapse of 59th (2nd North Midland) Division. A number of burials also relate to April and there is one from May. Several of these infantrymen are now commemorated by way of special memorials. Later casualties are from either the Royal Field Artillery or the Royal Flying Corps.

Captain Denys Charles WARE, 209 Squadron, Royal Air Force, obtained his flying certificate in October 1912 and was one of the original aviators who crossed to France with the British Expeditionary Force in 1914. He was with 5 Squadron, Royal Flying Corps at the time. He was wounded in 1916 and was killed in action on 20 September 1918, aged 26, whilst flying a Camel aircraft. According to *Airmen Died in the Great War* he had been awarded the MM, but this seems very unlikely and I can find no trace of this award in any of the Gazettes. (Grave 1)

Lieutenant Richard Hamilton O'REILLY and his observer occupy the next two graves. He and Second Lieutenant Leslie Edwin MITCHELL, 62 Squadron, Royal Air Force, fell on 29 September 1918. There is no clear answer as to how they were killed, but their BF2b aircraft was seen to break into pieces over Dury. Just before his death, MITCHELL had flown a number of times with Captain William Ernest 'Bull' Staton, who went on to score twenty-six victories. Captain Staton survived the war, but was captured at Singapore in 1942. He eventually retired as an Air Vice Marshal. Lieutenant O'REILLY is shown in the CWGC register as serving with the Canadian Engineers, but that was his former regiment. (Graves 2 and 3)

Finally, there is Lieutenant James Richardson MONTGOMERY, 3 Squadron, Royal Air Force. He was killed in action on 16 September 1918 (Grave 5). His brother, George Montgomery, was also killed during the war. He fell in October 1917 whilst serving as a second lieutenant with the 116th Battalion, Machine Gun Corps, aged 26. He is buried in Larch Wood (Railway Cutting) Cemetery, Belgium.

Vis-en-Artois British Cemetery, Haucourt

Despite its name, the cemetery is located on the D.939 at Haucourt rather than Vis-en-Artois. It is a large concentration cemetery containing 2,369 graves. Well over half of them are unidentified and there are several special memorials to soldiers known or believed to be buried here, as well as four men whose original graves have since been lost and who are now commemorated here. At least in appearance, the cemetery is now incorporated as part of the site that forms the Vis-en-Artois Memorial, though strictly speaking, the monument was added at the back of the original cemetery, which, of course, was very much enlarged after the Armistice.

Vis-en-Artois was captured by the Canadian 3rd Division on 27 August 1918 and the cemetery was begun soon after that when 430 burials were made; 297 of these were Canadian soldiers and 55 were men of the 2nd Battalion, Duke of Wellington's Regiment. This battalion was part of the British 4th Division, which in turn was attached to the Canadian Corps during these operations. These original burials can be found in Plots I and II. The cemetery continued to be used by Field Ambulances and some fighting units until October that year. After the Armistice a number of cemeteries were closed and concentrated into this one, whilst, at the same time, many isolated graves were brought in from the surrounding battlefields.

The cemetery was designed by J.R. Truelove, as was the memorial to the missing that forms the impressive backdrop.

Captain James STEEL MC, 10th Field Ambulance, Royal Army Medical Corps, was killed in action on 2 September 1918, aged 25. His MC was gazetted on 18 September 1918. The citation for it points out that he was one of the very few regimental medical officers who were with their unit throughout the whole period of the withdrawal, during which time he had tirelessly dressed the wounded, often under fire. Whenever his unit had to move, he personally assisted in evacuating the worst cases and, although he was wounded twice, he refused to leave his work, except to have his own wounds dressed. The withdrawal refers to the German offensive of March 1918. (Plot I.A.1)

Lieutenant Leslie COLEMAN and Second Lieutenant Charles Eric GARDENER, 5 Squadron, Royal Air Force, were killed flying together on 2 September 1918 in an RE8 aircraft. GARDENER was 19 years old when he died, as was COLEMAN. This was not a day of heavy losses for the Royal Air Force and its casualties for the entire Western Front that day amounted to just fifteen personnel, including those who died of wounds. GARDENER and COLEMAN were the only casualties from their squadron that day. (Plots I.A.42 and 43)

Major George Henry MUSGROVE DSO, 20th Battalion, Canadian Infantry, was killed in action on 28 August 1918, aged 36. He was killed by a bullet wound to the throat and died immediately. He was born in Walsall and had studied at Birmingham University. His military service dated back to his enlistment in the South Staffordshire Regiment in 1900 when he took part in the South African campaign. After that he served in the Canadian Militia until the outbreak of war when he volunteered to serve overseas, sailing for England with the first Canadian Contingent in October 1914. On 16 May 1915 he had his arm shattered during fighting around the location known as the Orchard near Festubert. His DSO was awarded for gallantry when, prior to a raid on enemy defences, he carried out detailed observation by reconnaissance. The raid was considered to be successful and some ground was gained as a result of it. The citation records that the success of the operation was mainly attributed to his thoroughness and skilled leadership. He had also personally supervised the forming up of the assaulting parties whilst under fire and ensured that battalion HQ was kept informed at each stage of the raid. His energy, keen sense of duty, and fearless conduct in the open, inspired all and contributed greatly to the success of operations carried out. (Plot I.B.19)

Serjeant William J. DE YOUNG MM and Bar, 20th Battalion, Canadian Infantry, was killed in action on 28 August 1918 (Plot I.B.23). His brother, Private Clifford Francis de Young, was killed in action on 14 June 1917 whilst serving with the 85th Battalion, Canadian Infantry, and had previously been wounded at Lens. He is buried at Cabaret Rouge British Cemetery.

Sergeant William Henry MURNEY MM and Bar, 'D' Company, 21st Battalion, Canadian Infantry, was killed in action by a sniper on 28 August 1918. He was one of the original members of his battalion and had served in France and Flanders since 1915. He was an experienced soldier who had fought at Courcelette on the Somme in 1916, at Vimy and at Passchendaele in 1917, and in August 1918 east of Amiens. His life before the war in Canada could not have been more different; he worked as a cheese maker. His MM was awarded for conspicuous gallantry and devotion to duty during a large enemy raid on our trenches. The raid took place under a heavy bombardment and the attacking force used flame-throwers. Despite this, MURNEY showed a complete disregard for his own safety and rallied those around him while all the time being under heavy bombardment and rifle fire. When his unit counter-attacked, he led his section forward with great courage. After the line had been re-established, he worked tirelessly to reorganize it whilst still under the enemy's bombardment. The award was gazetted on 25 April 1918. The bar to his medal, gazetted on 24 January 1919, was awarded for action at Marcelcave on 8 August 1918, where he again showed outstanding leadership. (Plot I.B.28)

Private Joseph Millard SEARS, 18th Battalion, Canadian Infantry, was killed in action on 28 August 1918, aged 36. Born in Nevada, he had previously served with the United States Coastal Artillery between 1906 and 1909, which was followed by service in the United States Marine Corps between 1910 and 1914. (Plot I.B.40)

Private David WHITEHEAD DCM, 3rd Battalion, Canadian Infantry, was killed in action on 30 August 1918. He had won his DCM as part of the leading wave during an advance in which he used his rifle with deadly effect. At a sunken road, where heavy machine-gun fire had checked the advance, he borrowed a Lewis gun and dashed forward, enfilading the road and 'absolutely annihilating' the garrison. Throughout the entire day and the following day, he carried out much work of a similar nature. The award was gazetted on 15 November 1918. (Plot I.B.51)

Sapper John BEVAN, 11th Battalion, Canadian Engineers, was killed in action on 2 September 1918, aged 51. He had previously served in the South African campaign and is one of several men buried in this cemetery to have done so. (Plot I.C.37)

Lieutenant John Labatt SCATCHERD MC and Bar, 11th Battery, 3rd Brigade, Canadian Field Artillery, was killed in action on 3 September 1918. His MC was gazetted on 4 December 1918. It was awarded for conspicuous gallantry and devotion to duty, going forward with the advancing infantry whilst in charge of a brigade patrol, keeping in constant touch with the situation and sending back information that enabled accurate and effective fire to be brought to bear by his gun batteries. Though constantly under fire, he was always on the spot to clarify any doubtful situation that arose. The bar, gazetted on 5 February 1919, was awarded for his role as reconnaissance officer during operations east of Arras. During this period he established a series of observation posts from which he was then able to maintain communication with his battery. He carried out these duties despite being under constant enemy machine-gun and shell fire. It was through his courage and untiring efforts that his battery was able to bring effective fire onto many enemy targets. The dates referred to in the citation are 31 September to 4 October, but these are clearly an error. (Plot I.C.44)

Captain Thomas Barker MERRICK MC, 4th Battalion, Machine Gun Corps, was killed in action on 2 September 1918, aged 25. His MC was gazetted on 20 July 1917 and was awarded for conspicuous gallantry whilst in charge of his machine guns. He was blown up by a shell and was buried on more than one occasion and, although his section had already suffered heavy casualties, he fought on with his gun with great bravery and skill, inflicting heavy casualties on the enemy. (Plot I.D.6)

The CWGC record for Gunner Harry HAWKINS, 116th Siege Battery, Royal Garrison artillery, is incorrect. He was killed in action on 11 September 1918, not 1916. (Plot I.D.21)

Lieutenant James Albert HOLLAND, 85th Battalion, Canadian Infantry, was killed in action during operations on 2 September 1918, aged 19. He had joined the battalion in mid August 1917 and was wounded on 25 October near Passchendaele. He did not rejoin his unit until 29 April 1918. (Plot I.E.1)

Lieutenant Eric Starmage Hamilton LANE, 85th Battalion, Canadian Infantry, was also killed on 2 September 1918, but had served rather longer than Lieutenant HOLLAND. According to the CWGC register, LANE enlisted in November 1915, but the battalion history shows him joining on 23 February 1915. He was serving with 'D' Company at the time of his death and was 22 years old. (Plot I.E.6)

Battery Sergeant Major Alexander Bartore SALMON DCM, 1st Battalion, Canadian Machine Gun Corps, was killed in action on 2 September 1918, aged 27. His DCM was awarded posthumously for conspicuous gallantry and devotion to duty at Cagnicourt on 2 September 1918, the day on which he was killed. When the officer in command of his section had become a casualty, he took charge of the men. He went forward and personally reconnoitred suitable commanding positions from which he was able to bring his guns into action, silencing those of the enemy. On three occasions he passed through heavy machine-gun fire in order to get ammunition forward to his guns. He was severely wounded during the day's fighting and died soon afterwards. (Plot II.A.49)

Serjeant Ernest James CLARK MM, Army Veterinary Corps, attached Royal Field Artillery, died of wounds on 3 September 1918, aged 27. Although not a fighting arm, men from the veterinary service were often well forward with the units to which they were attached, especially those attached to gun batteries and forward transport units, and therefore ran the same risks of injury and death. (Plot II.B.8)

Private James PETERS DCM, 54th Battalion, Canadian Infantry, was killed in action on 2 September 1918, aged 19. He won his DCM for his display of conspicuous gallantry and devotion to duty. The citation notes that he showed courage and judgement in two night raids on enemy trenches. On the first night he entered the trench with another man who was immediately wounded. Nevertheless, he continued his exploration and returned with intelligence regarding the enemy's defences. The next night he guided a raiding party to the same location. The raiders were successful in achieving their objectives and during the operation PETERS killed two of the enemy himself. The award was gazetted on 3 March 1918. In civilian life he had been a milkman. (Plot II.B.21)

Although some are listed as serving with the 10th Kite Balloon Section, seven men buried together in Plot II, Row C, were all attached to 37th Kite Balloon Section when they were killed in action on 5 September 1918. The men, in order of burial, are: Air Mechanic 2nd Class Harold Frederick LOVELL, aged 31; Corporal Alfred Charles BANKS; Private 2nd Class William Henry ADKIN, aged 44; Private 2nd Class Walter Joseph BRIDGE, aged 39; Private 2nd Class Henry James APPLETON, aged 44; Private 2nd Class George ELEY and Serjeant Charles Stanley MORRISON. *Airmen died in the Great War* does not throw any light on the manner of their deaths. (Plots II.C.22 to 28)

Captain Charles Eric ROBERTSON and Serjeant John Frazier CARR, 11 Squadron, Royal Flying Corps, were killed in action on 12 July 1917. ROBERTSON was commanding 11 Squadron at the time of his death and it is likely that he had chosen to fly that day. Both men are buried side by side. (Plots II.D.16 and 17)

Lieutenant Samuel JOHNSON MC, Royal Field Artillery, was killed in action on 24 September 1918, aged 38. His MC was gazetted on 13 January 1919 and was awarded for his consistent display of courage, energy, and determination whilst serving as liaison officer between his battery, the 303rd Siege Battery, Royal Garrison Artillery, and the infantry. He was often under heavy fire and often visited the front lines in search of information that frequently proved valuable. (Plot II.D.24)

Lieutenant Charles Franklin BUCHANAN MC, 7th Battalion, Canadian Infantry, was killed in action on 12 October 1918, aged 28. His MC was gazetted on 12 March 1919, but the citation only appeared on 8 October that year. It was awarded for conspicuous gallantry and initiative between 27 September and 1 October 1918 during fighting at Bourlon Wood. His company was held up by machine-gun fire, and though wounded, he collected up what men he could and continued to work his way forward, eventually capturing six machine guns and around fifty prisoners. He shot two of the enemy with his revolver, at which point the enemy's resistance broke down. The citation acknowledges that the position was captured thanks to his fearless leadership. (Plot II.E.18)

Private Thomas BLEZARD, 7th Battalion, Canadian Infantry, died on 12 October 1916, aged 26. The war diary states that the battalion had moved into trenches near Courcelette on the afternoon of 10 October. The following day it records that the whole area was subjected to shrapnel and high explosive shelling, which thankfully caused only slight casualties. On 12 October the 7th Battalion was relieved by the 2nd Battalion and moved back to Albert. It is therefore very surprising to find him buried here at Vis-en-Artois rather than behind our own lines somewhere on the Somme. Canadian military records also show 12 October 1916 as his date of death. The obvious explanation would be that he was captured and died in German captivity, but there is no specific mention in the battalion's war diary that any of its men were captured during that period. Whatever the circumstances of his death, his presence here is certainly unexpected. (Plot II.E.22)

Captain John Ross MACPHERSON DSO, Princess Patricia's Canadian Light Infantry, was killed in action on 26 August 1918, aged 28. He joined the battalion in the field in July 1915. His DSO, gazetted on 8 February 1918, was awarded for carrying out a personal reconnaissance after which he led his company forward under intense shell fire. Despite determined resistance, he and his company surrounded and captured an enemy strongpoint and its garrison. The citation concludes that his leadership, energy, and initiative were entirely responsible for the success of this operation, which straightened out the line in readiness for a further attack the following day. His three brothers also served, each as a lieutenant, and all three survived the war. He was also mentioned in despatches. (Plot IV.I.5)

Captain Stanley Donald SKENE MC, 15th Battalion, Canadian Infantry, was killed in action on 10 October 1918, aged 34. His MC was gazetted on 12 March 1919 and its citation appeared on 8 October that year. It was awarded for his actions during the crossing of the Canal du Nord on 27 September 1918. Fire from machine guns and snipers was hindering the work of engineers trying to throw bridges across the canal. Taking one of his men with him, he dislodged at least fifteen enemy posts and dealt effectively with any opposition. During the remainder of these operations he went forward under heavy fire and brought back valuable information. (Plot V.C.19)

Lieutenant Herbert Leigh Midelton DODSON 73 Squadron, Royal Air Force, formerly 46 Squadron, was killed in action, aged 23, on 25 August 1918 whilst flying a Camel aircraft. He was one of twelve members of the Royal Air Force who died that day on the Western Front. (Plot V.C.25)

Captain George Creasey KNEE, 4th East Yorkshire Regiment, attached 8th Battalion, was killed by shell fire in assembly trenches on 3 May 1917, although he is shown in the regimental history as a second lieutenant at the time of his death. The 8th East Yorkshire Regiment and the 7th King's Shropshire Light Infantry were in support that day behind the 1st Royal Scots Fusiliers and the 2nd Royal Scots for an attack on the Bois du Vert. The attack was brought to a halt soon after it began when it came under heavy machine-gun fire from Infantry Hill, causing heavy casualties. (Plot V.D.23)

Private John Duncan McRAE, 1st Canadian Mounted Rifles, was killed in action on 26 August 1918, aged 21. His brother, Private James George McRae, 10th Battalion, Canadian Infantry, had been wounded on 10 October 1916 at Courcelette on the Somme. He was evacuated as far as the medical facilities at Étaples, but he died there two days later on 12 October. The boys were born in Washington DC and it is believed that James was the first man from that Federal District to die in battle during the war. He was the first of the two brothers to volunteer, but was initially rejected on account of his height. John was wounded on 9 April 1917 at Vimy Ridge and spent nine months recuperating in England before returning to the front in June 1918. He died soon after receiving a mortal wound on the battlefield on 26 August 1918. (Plot V.E.16)

Major John Kenrick Lloyd FITZWILLIAMS MC, 25 Army Brigade, Royal Field Artillery, was killed in action on 30 August 1918. He had also been awarded the Russian Order of St Stanislaus, 2nd Class. His MC was gazetted on 16 November 1916 and was awarded for conspicuous gallantry in action. During an attack in which an enemy position was captured, he observed the fire of his battery from the infantry front line, often under heavy shell fire. Throughout the day he sent back reports that proved to be very accurate and most valuable, proving himself to be a gallant and capable battery commander. He was one of nine children. One of his seven brothers, Edward Crawford Lloyd Fitzwilliams, attained the rank of colonel; another, Duncan Campbell Lloyd Fitzwilliams, became a distinguished surgeon. Both men later received the CMG for services in their respective professions. (Plot V.G.1)

Lieutenant Dick INESON MC MM, 58th Battalion, Canadian Infantry, was killed in action on 27 August 1918, aged 27. His MC was gazetted on 13 January 1919 and was awarded for leading his platoon in an attack on a village. The fighting was said to have been sharp as he led his platoon against position after position, capturing thirty-one prisoners, including one officer. The citation concludes that the success of his company was largely due to his quick initiative, cool leadership, and daring example. (Plot V.G.2)

Captain Thomas St Pierre BUNBURY, 64 Squadron, Royal Air Force, was killed in action on 31 August 1918. His father was Major General William Edwin Bunbury CB, Indian Army, who served as quartermaster general in India between 1912 and 1916, and who commanded the Rawalpindi Division between 1916 and 1917. Thomas was his eldest son and the grandson of the Right Reverend Thomas Bunbury DD, Bishop of Limerick from 1899 until his death in 1907. (Plot V.G.4)

Private Frederick William KING, Princess Patricia's Canadian Light Infantry, was killed in action on 26 August 1918, aged 34. His father, Doctor William Frederick King, had been awarded a CMG in 1908 in recognition of his work in surveying and astronomy. (Plot VI.A.14)

Second Lieutenant Eric Thomas Somervell SALVESEN, 7th Royal Scots, attached 13th Battalion, was initially recorded as missing after the attack on 23 April 1917, but was actually killed in action that day, aged 19. The CWGC register shows only that his father was Mr J.T. Salvesen of 6, Rothsay Terrace, Edinburgh. His father, Johan Thomas Salvesen, was in fact the owner of a large shipping company and coal exportation business who, with his brother Frederick, had set up offices at Leith in Edinburgh and in South Georgia in the Falkland Islands.

Eric's elder brother, Lieutenant Christian Raymond Salvesen, 7th Royal Scots, was killed in Britain's worst rail disaster at Quintinshill near Gretna on 22 May 1915, aged 24. He was one of 230 who died, 218 of them servicemen, when the troop train he was travelling in collided with two other trains. A further 246 were injured. He is buried in Edinburgh (Rosebank) Cemetery.

Their cousin, Second Lieutenant Edward Maxwell Salvesen, was killed during the Second Battle of Ypres on 25 April 1915 whilst serving with the 2nd Royal Dublin Fusiliers. He is commemorated on the Menin Gate, Ypres. Edward's brother, Captain Frederick Malcolm Ross Salvesen, served during the war with the 82nd Punjabis, but died in December 1919, barely a year after the war had ended. Their father was the Rt Hon. Lord Salvesen. Grandfather to all four boys was the Norwegian shipping magnate, Christian Salvesen. In recent years the family business was bought out by another commercial transport company, 'Norbert Dentressangle'. Anyone visiting the battlefields of France and Belgium and using the motorways and Channel ports will be very familiar with red and white livery of the 'ND' freight trucks. (Plot VI.B.24)

Serjeant Robert Frederick CHANEY MM and Bar, 'A' Company 7th East Surrey Regiment, was killed in action on 8 July 1917. CHANEY won the bar to his medal during the opening phase of the 1917 Arras offensive. *Soldiers Died in the Great War* makes no reference to his winning the bar. (Plot VI.D.20)

Second Lieutenant William Francis MacDONALD MC, 3rd Seaforth Highlanders, attached 2nd Battalion, was killed in action on 31 August 1918, aged 21, near Rémy. His MC was gazetted on 29 November 1917, but I can find no citation to accompany it. (Plot VI.E.3)

Second Lieutenant Henry Charles FARNES, 48 Squadron, Royal Flying Corps, formerly King's Royal Rifle Corps, was killed in action on 6 July 1917 whilst flying an F2B aircraft. His observer that day, Corporal J.T. PARK, formerly 9th Black Watch, was killed with him. Their squadron was under the command of Major Keith Rodney Park MC and Bar, who went on to become Air Chief Marshal Sir Keith Park GCB KBE MC and Bar DFC DCL. The squadron claimed 317 victories during the war and thirty-two of its members became aces. The highest scoring ace was Major Park who was credited with twenty victories. (Plots VI.F.14 and 15)

Lieutenant Charles Conway SHAW MC, 39th Battalion, Machine Gun Corps, was killed in action on 31 August 1918. He joined the 6th King's (Liverpool Regiment) in November 1914. The CWGC register notes that his parents lived in the Gironde region of France, but does not show his place of residence before or during the war. His MC was gazetted on 18 September 1918 and was awarded for conspicuous gallantry and devotion to duty, directing the fire of his machine guns using great judgement and precision whilst under heavy shell fire, successively engaging enemy troops, transport and a field gun battery with great effect. Later on, he successfully covered the retirement of other troops. Throughout these operations he set a great example of courage and cheerfulness that inspired his men with great fighting spirit. (Plot VI.G.2)

Sergeant Leonard HARDING DCM, 4th Battalion, Canadian Mounted Rifles, was killed in action on 28 August 1918. He had previously served in the Canadian Cavalry before transferring to the Canadian Mounted Rifles which, in spite of its title, fought as an infantry unit. His DCM was gazetted on 28 March 1918 and was awarded for conspicuous gallantry and devotion to duty in an attack. After his officer was killed early on in the action, he took charge of his platoon and led it to its objective in spite of heavy resistance. When his flank became exposed he was forced to withdraw, an operation which he skilfully carried out. He then established a defensive line in touch with the unit on his flank. He later assisted in breaking up an enemy counter-attack, after which he immediately led a patrol into no man's land and captured two prisoners. Throughout these operations he set a splendid example of courage and devotion to duty. (Plot VI.G.21)

Almost three in every five burials within this cemetery belong to Canadian units and all of them are 1918 casualties. There are also three men from the Newfoundland Regiment who were killed in action near Monchy-le-Preux on 14 April 1917. One of them, Private Alfred E. CAKE, was just 16 years old when he fell (Plot VIII.F.18). Private Herbert LEDREW is buried in the same plot, a few rows further back (Plot VIII.A.3). He was just 20 years old when he was killed. Canadian army records show quite a number of men with the same surname serving either with the Newfoundland Regiment, or with family connections to Newfoundland, which suggests that some, at least, were probably related. Private Jabez STEAD, the third Newfoundland man here, is buried not too far away. He was 19 years old when he was killed. (Plot VII.F.20)

Second Lieutenant David Rankin CROMB, 3rd Royal Scots, attached 13th Battalion, was killed in action 23 April 1917, aged 20. Before the war he was a medical student at Edinburgh University and held a Master's degree. (Plot VII.A.24)

Lance Corporal Wilfrid James STAINES, 9th Royal Fusiliers, was killed in action on 23 June 1917, aged 26 (Plot VII.B.4). His brothers, Archie and Sydney Charles, also died whilst serving. Sydney died at home on 16 April 1916 as a private in the 5th Cold-stream Guards. He is buried at Hadleigh (St James the Less) Cemetery, Essex. The other brother, Bombardier Archie Staines, 96th Siege Battery, Royal Garrison Artillery, was killed in action on 15 August 1917, the day of the Canadian attack at Hill 70 near Loos. He is commemorated by way of a special memorial at Loos British Cemetery (Cité Calonne Military Cemetery, Memorial 9).

According to the CWGC records, Private Leon Andrew DELAUNEY, 116th Battalion, Canadian Infantry, was killed in action on 27 August 1918, aged 17. However, his service records appear to be at odds in so far as they show his age as 20 when he enlisted on 17 December 1917. His parents lived in Mexico City and according to Canadian records, he spent two years serving in Mexico, although the notes do not elaborate further. Born in the United States, it seems likely that those two years were spent serving with the United States Army. What is certain is that he was killed in action during the fighting around Infantry Hill and the village of Boiry-Notre-Dame. (Plot VIII.C.5)

Captain Edmond William Claude Gerard de Vere PERY, 32 Squadron, Royal Air Force, was killed in action on 18 May 1918, aged 24. He was killed when he and fellow pilot, Lieutenant Hooper, engaged two enemy machines above Étaing near the River Scarpe. His aircraft was seen to spiral out of control as pieces of it began to break off. Nevertheless, he somehow managed to regain control of it and landed it in no man's land, but in doing so he probably sustained some injuries. Having just survived an extremely hazardous descent, he was then very unfortunate in that the Germans began shelling the location where he had just landed. He is believed to have died soon afterwards, though the precise circumstances of his death are not known. He was an Old Etonian who held the honorary title of Viscount Glentworth. His father, William Henry de Vere Sheaffe Pery, was 4th Earl of Limerick and lived at Dromore Castle, County Limerick. Edmond was succeeded by his uncle, Edmund Colquhoun Pery GBE CH KCB DSO, who also served during the war. His DSO was won in March 1918 after rallying and reorganizing troops whilst under fire near Ervillers and at Ayette during the retreat. (Plot IX.A.26)

Serjeant Frederick KIRTON DCM, 'A' Company, 7th South Staffordshire Regiment, was killed in action on 1 September 1918, aged 29. His DCM was gazetted on 6 March 1918 and was awarded for conspicuous gallantry and devotion to duty after several casualties had been caused by enemy snipers. He went out alone, located them, and then led his section against them with great skill and judgement, killing one and capturing three others. (Plot X.A.120)

Second Lieutenant Brian Edward GLOVER DCM, 8 Squadron, Royal Flying Corps, was killed in action on 13 March 1916. Lieutenant Gilbert Dennis James GRUNE, who was flying with him that day, was also killed when their BE2c was shot down over enemy lines by the German ace, Max Immelmann. GRUNE had joined the Royal Field Artillery in November 1914, but in 1915 he transferred to the Royal Flying Corps. He was 22 years old when he died. Second Lieutenant GLOVER's DCM was gazetted on 17 November 1915 whilst serving as a corporal with the 47th Divisional Signal Company, Royal Engineers. It was awarded for conspicuous gallantry between 21 September and 1 October 1915 during operations carried out between Les Brebis and Loos, where he had constantly carried despatches and operational orders under very heavy shell fire, never once failing to deliver his messages. Both men are now buried next to each other. He was also awarded the *Médaille Militaire*. (France) (Plots XI.A.1 and 2)

Second Lieutenant Percy Rogers PALMER MC, Royal Flying Corps, who had formerly served with the Royal Welsh Fusiliers and the Leicestershire Regiment, was killed in action on 25 May 1917. His MC was gazetted on 17 April 1917, but his name was wrongly transcribed and the citation was originally shown under the name of Percy Reginald Palmer. This was corrected in the *London Gazette* dated 18 June 1917. The citation notes that he had shown conspicuous gallantry and devotion to duty firing a Bangalore torpedo under most difficult conditions, showing great courage and determination. In addition to this, he had gone out into no man's land and rescued two wounded men. His award was won while he was serving with the Leicestershire Regiment. (Plot XI.B.13)

Lieutenant Dudley Joseph de Angulo BIRD, 29 Squadron, Royal Flying Corps, was killed whilst flying his Nieuport 23 on 27 June 1917, aged 23. He had previously served in the Royal Field Artillery. *Royal Flying Corps Communiqué No. 94* notes that aircraft from 29 Squadron had set off on a patrol during the evening of 27 June. During that sortie they came across six Albatros scouts and became involved in a fight with them. The squadron destroyed two of the six enemy machines and drove down another out of control. However, there is no mention of any losses on the part of 29 Squadron, and certainly no mention of Lieutenant BIRD. His family lived at Bradfield Hall, Norwich. (Plot XI.B.14)

Flying their RE8 machine, Lieutenant W.H. BUCKERIDGE and Second Lieutenant Allan Gilbert MALCOLM, 52 Squadron, Royal Air Force, were both killed in action on 2 October 1918. The CWGC register shows Second Lieutenant MALCOLM's parents living in Buenos Aires. Both men are now buried next to each other. (Plots XI.C.7 and 8)

Second Lieutenant Arthur Webb EDWARDS, 41 Squadron, Royal Flying Corps, was killed in action on 10 October 1917 in his DH5 aircraft. This was a day on which there was very little flying owing to wind and rain. Some aerial activity had been possible during the early morning and again during the evening. (Plot XI.D.9)

Lance Corporal Jasper HOULISON, 1st Gordon Highlanders, and Private Harold THOMAS, 10th Royal Welsh Fusiliers, formerly Montgomeryshire Yeomanry, died of wounds in German captivity a few days after the attack at Serre on 13 November 1916 during the Battle of the Ancre. Both men would have been buried by the Germans and then reburied here after the war. They died on 19 and 18 November respectively. (Plots XI.F.6 and 8)

Second Lieutenant Arthur Allister BLYTON, 'A' Battery, 70 Brigade, Royal Field Artillery, was killed in action on 5 September 1918, aged 26. The CWGC register points out that he was the nephew of the Honourable Mrs Alister Campbell of Colchester. His father, Edmund Van Houtte Blyton, played football for Lincoln City. (Special Memorial 7)

There are five Australian casualties buried here who fell between 12 and 15 April 1917 when the Australians were involved in fighting around Bullecourt. There are also two South African soldiers buried in the cemetery, both belonging to the 75th Battery, South African Heavy Artillery, but they are buried separately from each other. Both men were killed in September 1918, though a week apart.

There are forty-three holders of the MM buried here. In most cases, I have only referred to those awarded a bar to the original medal. Thirty of them are from Canadian units. One of them, Sergeant George Arthur BAILEY MM, 52nd Battalion, Canadian Infantry, who was killed in action on 28 August 1918, had also been awarded the *Croix de Guerre* (France). The CWGC register incorrectly notes his regiment as the Royal Canadian Regiment. (Plot V.J.23)

Vis-en-Artois Communal Cemetery
This cemetery is located on the north side of the village. Heading back towards Arras from Vis-en-Artois British Cemetery, the road to take is the D9E, which is the road out towards Boiry-Notre-Dame. Turn right here. After about 250 yards the road divides. Take the left fork and the cemetery sits a little further ahead on the right-hand side.

There is just one identified grave here. According to the CWGC register, Second Lieutenant Rowland Murray WILSON-BROWNE, 12 Squadron, Royal Flying Corps, died as a prisoner of war on 21 July 1917, aged 19, even though his headstone shows his date of death as 31 July 1916. His is a special memorial on the east side of the cemetery. Although the exact location of his grave is unknown, he is known to be buried in this cemetery.

Chapter Eight

'A Gallant English Officer' – Sewing Machines and a Portuguese Count – A Mysterious Death in the Woods

Cagnicourt British Cemetery

The cemetery is easy to find and is located by the roadside on the D.13 on the eastern edge of the village of Cagnicourt. The village itself is about twelve miles south-east of Arras and lies south of the D.939, which is the main Arras–Cambrai road. It was the scene of heavy fighting on 2 September 1918 when the Canadian Corps captured the Drocourt–Quéant Line and the 1st Canadian Division captured Cagnicourt itself. The CWGC register informs us that there used to be a German cemetery adjacent to where the current cemetery now stands, but it was removed after the war. The British cemetery was used briefly for about a month after the fighting and was then added to after the Armistice. There are a few casualties commemorated here from the Second World War and over half of the graves relating to the Great War are unidentified. Out of almost 300 burials, only 103 casualties have been identified.

One man whose grave has been identified is Captain Sidney Edward COWAN MC and two Bars. What is truly remarkable about this British airman is that he was only 19 years old at the time of his death, which occurred on 17 November 1916. Cowan had been an original member of 24 Squadron, Royal Flying Corps, back in September 1915. In spite of his age, he rapidly set about building a reputation for tactical skill as a single-seat fighter ace. Although he only ever achieved seven victories in total, his attitude when confronting enemy aircraft was extremely aggressive. His second victory on 4 May 1916 saw him drive down a German machine which hit a wire fence as it landed causing it to break up. For many pilots this would have been enough, but COWAN dived again and emptied his remaining drum of ammunition at the fleeing pilot and his observer, both of whom had managed to climb out of the wreckage and were running across a field. He hit one of them and the other took refuge in a nearby shed. His own luck then appeared to have run out as his engine failed. He made a bumpy landing on the enemy side of the line, but miraculously, the jolt appears to have released the jammed mechanism and his engine sprang back into life, enabling COWAN to take off without coming to a halt. He then came under heavy fire from the ground, but managed to get back to his aerodrome safely.

Later that year he took part in several aerial combats above the Somme battlefield and in the skies above Bapaume. On 3 August he and his squadron were engaged in combat for forty-five minutes between Flers and Sailly-Saillisel, during which COWAN claimed his fourth victory. Six days later, he sustained slight wounds, but was back in action on 16 September above Sailly-Saillisel, where he brought his sixth victim down in flames. By November 1916 he had moved from 24 Squadron to 29 Squadron where he took command of 'C' Flight, but on 17 November luck finally turned against him. As he and another pilot from his unit dived on one of three German machines, COWAN collided with his colleague and both planes plunged behind enemy lines.

The other pilot involved in the fatal collision was Second Lieutenant William Spencer Fitzrobert Saundby, who is now commemorated on the Flying Services Memorial at Arras. However, COWAN's body was subsequently recovered by the Germans, who then buried him in the small cemetery at Ablainzevelle. We know this from a letter written to his family by a British officer who came across his grave sometime later and recognized COWAN as a former pupil from his school, Marlborough College. The Germans had placed a cross on the grave bearing the inscription: '*In memory of a gallant English officer*'. After the war, for some unknown reason, COWAN's body was reburied miles away in Cagnicourt British Cemetery.

COWAN's MC was awarded in May 1916, his first bar was added in October and the second bar was awarded on 14 November just three days before his death. His was truly an amazing fighting record.

His brother, Captain Philip Chalmers Cowan, 56 Squadron, Royal Flying Corps, formerly 8th Manchester Regiment, was killed in action on 8 November 1917, aged 22. He has no known grave and is therefore commemorated on the Flying Services Memorial at Arras. Captain Sidney Edward COWAN's grave is right by the entrance to the cemetery in front of the Cross of Sacrifice, which somehow seems very appropriate. (Plot II.B.13)

Despite his youth, COWAN is not the youngest man buried in this cemetery, as there are two privates from the 1/8th Middlesex Regiment, both aged 18, who were killed in action on 12 and 13 October 1918. They are Private Charles William WELLARD and Private William Edward WOOD. (Plots I.D.12 and 18)

Second Lieutenant Norman Rausch de POMEROY, 11 Squadron, Royal Flying Corps, was killed in action on 20 October 1916 while flying an FE2b. His observer, Lieutenant William Black, was taken prisoner and survived the war. They were shot down over Douai by Erwin Böhme. Black had tried to climb out of his seat and into his pilot's when their machine went out of control, but he was unable to do so. He must have believed that he was going to die, but miraculously he survived the crash, though with injuries. Their aircraft came down somewhere to the north-west of Monchy-le-Preux and de POMEROY was buried by the Germans. They were the fourth of Böhme's twenty-four victories. (Plot I.A.17)

Second Lieutenant William STEVENSON MC, 147th Heavy Battery, Royal Garrison Artillery, was killed in action on 18 September 1918, aged 39. His MC was gazetted on 30 July 1919 and was awarded for his actions on 29 August 1918 after he had brought half of his battery up to an advanced position between Chérisy and Hendecourt while continuously under an enemy barrage. He showed great coolness and courage the whole time as he endeavoured to complete this work so that the guns could be brought into action by daybreak. The citation also refers to his work a few days later, on 2 September, when one of the guns suffered a premature explosion causing casualties. He was conspicuous in evacuating the wounded and helped to extinguish the subsequent fire whilst under constant heavy shell fire. The citation concludes that his conduct had been consistently gallant throughout all of these operations and that he had shown marked energy and enterprise on all occasions. The CWGC register notes that he was the headmaster at the Church of England School at Haydock in Lancashire. (Plot I.B.1)

Another fine account of battalion life in the trenches is *The Journal of Private Fraser*, edited by Reginald H. Roy and published in 1985. It recounts the experiences of Private Donald Fraser, 31st Battalion, Canadian Infantry, who later transferred to the Canadian Machine Gun Corps. One of the many individuals mentioned in his account is Private Dennis (Red) DRISCOLL. He describes how both of them had a narrow escape one night on 29 December 1916 when their unit was in trenches near Souchez. One of the constant hazards of trench life was sniping, and this was particularly prevalent in that sector. Fraser describes how they were emptying sandbags when a bullet came whistling past DRISCOLL's head and struck some corrugated iron, causing sparks to fly up a few inches from Fraser's own feet. DRISCOLL was eventually killed in action on 27 September 1918, aged 27, serving with the 2nd Battalion, Canadian Machine Gun Corps. (Plot I.B.9)

The Reverend William Henry TOMKINS, Chaplain 4th Class, attached 7th South Staffordshire Regiment, died on active service on 28 September 1918. He had followed his father into the ministry and had served in Salonika and Palestine before moving to the Western Front. (Plot I.C.7)

Air Mechanic 1st Class Andrew MORRISON, 11th Reserve Lorry Park, Royal Air Force, was killed in action on 4 October 1918. (Plot I.C.11)

Second Lieutenant Frank Alexander BAKER MM, 14th Battalion, London Regiment (London Scottish), was killed in action on 1 October 1918 (Plot I.C.12). He is one of four holders of the MM buried in this cemetery.

Second Lieutenant George Deans LUGTON, 8th Cameronians, was killed in action on 30 November 1917, aged 22. He was born in Chicago, but at some point his parents came to live in Glasgow where he worked for the *Scotsman* newspaper. LUGTON was not serving with the 8th Battalion at the time of his death, as it was in Egypt between January 1916 and April 1918. Without reference to his file at the National Archives it is impossible to speculate as to which regiment or battalion he was attached. (Plot III.D.25)

The remaining three holders of the MM buried here are: Private Charles Henry MADDEN MM, 13th Battalion, London Regiment (Kensingtons), killed in action on 3 October 1918 (Plot I.C.21); Serjeant George COWELL MM, 18th Army Field Brigade, Royal Engineers, killed in action on 30 September 1918 (Plot I.C.22); and Captain Leonard WATTS MM, 3rd (City of London) Battalion, London Regiment (Royal Fusiliers), killed in action on 9 October 1918, aged 21 (Plot I.D.7).

Cagnicourt Communal Cemetery

There is just one burial here. Sergeant (Flight Engineer) Eric WHITE, 426 Squadron, Royal Canadian Air Force, was killed in action on 13 June 1944. His aircraft, a Halifax MK III, caught fire and came down near Villers-lès-Cagnicourt whilst taking part in a raid over Cambrai. He and Squadron Leader Ian Mackenzie McRobie were killed and two of the crew were taken prisoner. Three of the crew, however, managed to evade capture. McRobie's body was never found, but WHITE was buried here by local villagers. The other crew members were able to jump from the aircraft before it crashed. It is believed that they were shot down by a German night fighter. Squadron Leader McRobie is now commemorated on the Runnymede Memorial.

Dominion Cemetery, Hendecourt-lès-Cagnicourt

The cemetery is located about one and a half miles north-east of Hendecourt-lès-Cagnicourt. It lies in open fields, slightly west of where the Drocourt–Quéant Line cut across the battlefield on 2 September 1918. It can be reached via the small road that links Hendecourt-lès-Cagnicourt with Cagnicourt. After leaving the first of these two villages heading east, there is a track running north at right angles. Take this track for about 300 yards to where it joins a similar track, again at right angles. Turn right and the cemetery is easily visible in the open landscape. Looking west from the cemetery there is an irregular shaped wood about a quarter of a mile north of Hendecourt-lès-Cagnicourt. This was known to the troops as the Crow's Nest and during the fighting here it was home to a number of German machine-gun detachments that put up strong resistance in front of the main defensive position. As a battlefield cemetery, this is a very fine example, all the better for its remoteness and beautiful sense of isolation among quiet fields.

Although the cemetery was begun by the Canadians after the capture of the Drocourt–Quéant Line and its defences, the village of Hendecourt-lès-Cagnicourt was actually secured by troops from the 57th (2nd West Lancashire) Division and the 52nd (Lowland) Division during their overnight advance on 1 September, which lasted into the early hours of the following morning.

For such a small cemetery, with only 226 identified casualties, it contains a real wealth of gallantry awards, including a VC and no fewer than thirteen holders of the MM, two of whom were also awarded a bar. There are also four recipients of the MC, five with the DCM, one DFC and one MSM. It is a cemetery that is well worth visiting, particularly with regard to understanding the Arras battlefield in the early autumn of 1918.

The majority of casualties are from the Canadian 1st Division's attack on the Drocourt–Quéant Line, which took place on 2 September 1918 south of the Arras–Cambrai road. Today, there are 111 Canadians buried here who fell that day. One of them is Lieutenant Alex CAMPBELL-JOHNSTON, 16th Battalion, Canadian Infantry. He was 16 years old, and thus under age, when he joined up as a private in 1915. He then served with the battalion in France from 1916 until his death at the age of 18. (Plot I.C.25). Private Ronald Alfred CAMPBELL-JOHNSTON, 7th Battalion, Canadian Infantry, Alex's elder brother, was killed the following day, 3 September 1918, aged 29, while taking part in the same operations. Although he is not buried next to Alex, he is buried in this cemetery just a few rows away (Plot I.G.13). Their brother, Alexander Campbell-Johnston, also served with the Canadian Expeditionary Force but survived the war.

This cemetery has a very high proportion of casualties from the Quebec Regiment, particularly the 13th and 14th Battalions, both of which came from the Montreal area. Among the regiment's fifty burials is Lieutenant Archibald Liddell McLEAN MC DCM, 14th Battalion, Canadian Infantry. His DCM was awarded whilst serving as a lance corporal and deployed as a runner. It was gazetted on 17 January 1916 and the citation for it appeared two months later on 14 March. It was awarded for conspicuous gallantry whilst carrying despatches under heavy shrapnel and rifle fire and for bravery and resource in carrying messages from the advanced line to the battalion HQ under trying conditions. While doing so, he was under shrapnel fire the whole time. His MC, gazetted on 22 October 1917, was awarded for conspicuous gallantry and devotion to duty whilst conducting the defence of an important strongpoint. Although rendered unconscious by an exploding shell, he recovered and remained in charge continuously for thirty hours, during which his personal gallantry proved a key factor in repelling several enemy counter-attacks. He was killed in action on 2 September 1918. (Plot I.A.24)

Next to him is Lieutenant Francis Joseph HURLEY DCM MM, 14th Battalion, Canadian Infantry, who was killed in action on 1 September 1918 (Plot I.A.25). HURLEY's DCM was gazetted on 26 July 1917 when he was a company sergeant major. It was awarded for conspicuous gallantry and devotion to duty after he had charged an enemy machine gun single-handed, capturing the gun and killing three of its crew. Later on that day he was wounded twice, but still carried on to the objective where he assisted others in its consolidation. Unfortunately, there is no reference to his MM in the published work *The Distinguished Conduct Medal: Awards to Members of the Canadian Expeditionary Force 1914–1920*, nor in the list of awards to men of the 14th Battalion in the *Canadian Great War Project*. The MM is also not shown against his name in *Officers of the Canadian Expeditionary Force who Died Overseas 1914–1919* and I can find no trace of it in any of the Gazettes.

The 14th Battalion, Canadian Infantry, has another four recipients of the MM buried here. All of them were killed or died of wounds on 1 and 2 September 1918. They are Sergeant William Cassells McARTHUR MM, who came from Coatbridge in Scotland (Plot I.C.7); Private Jack McGARRY MM (Plot I.D.6); Private Alexander PETRIE MM (Plot I.D.22) and Lance Corporal George Clifton McKENZIE MM (Plot I.F.11).

Captain Morten Joseph MASON MC, 16th Battalion, Canadian Infantry, was killed in action on 2 September 1918, aged 34. Following enlistment on 22 September 1914, he initially served with the 14th Battalion and went to France as a private on 9th February 1915. He was then promoted to lieutenant on 7 March 1916 and was wounded later that year on 4 September. His MC was gazetted on 26 July 1917, two months after his promotion to acting captain. It was awarded for conspicuous gallantry and devotion to duty after he had led his men to their final objective under heavy fire. Even though he was wounded twice during the advance, he set a fine personal example to his men. He had also been awarded the *Croix de Guerre* (Belgium). (Plot I.B.1)

Sergeant James STEPHEN DCM, 16th Battalion, Canadian Infantry, was killed during the attack on the Drocourt–Quéant Line on 2 September 1918. His DCM was awarded posthumously and was gazetted on 15 November the same year. It was awarded after the officer in charge of his platoon was wounded when it was still a mile from its objective. Sergeant STEPHEN then took charge and led the platoon forward. It had to wheel to the left in order to capture some guns, which it did successfully in spite of heavy machine-gun fire. The citation notes that the attack was successful thanks to his grasp of what was required and his determination to see the task through. Unfortunately, he was killed later that day. Thirty-one of the thirty-four burials here from the 16th Battalion were killed on 2 September. The other three died the previous day. (Plot I.B.7)

Lieutenant Otto Bertel KRENCHEL MC DCM, 13th Battalion, Canadian Infantry, was killed on 2 September 1918, aged 35. According to the CWGC register, his parents came from Copenhagen, Denmark, where his father worked as an apothecary. He won his DCM serving as a corporal with the 17th Battalion and it was gazetted on 14 March 1916, the same day as Lieutenant McLEAN's. The citation records that KRENCHEL had shown conspicuous gallantry in saving a machine gun, and later, when his section was in a very exposed position, he held the ground with great bravery for forty-eight hours after the rest his battalion had been relieved, remaining there until the relieving battalion was able to replace him. His MC was gazetted posthumously on 13 January 1919 and was awarded for gallantry during an attack on a village, leading his platoon with great determination on one of the flanks. Thanks to good tactical handling on his part, his platoon overcame several strongpoints, thereby enabling the rest of his company to advance. At one point, he charged a machine gun with three other men and, although the others were wounded, he rushed the post, capturing two prisoners and killing the remainder of the crew. Later that day, he carried out a very daring reconnaissance and brought back valuable information. (Plot I.C.24)

Easily lost amongst the many Canadian dead is a British infantryman, Private Stephen CLEARY, 1st Royal Munster Fusiliers, who was killed in action on 2 September 1918 (Plot I.E.23). The 1st Royal Munster Fusiliers by this stage of the war had become part of the 57th (2nd West Lancashire) Division, a second-line Territorial division that had no existence before the war. It had remained in the south-east of England until February 1917 when it crossed to France, serving there and also in Belgium until the end of the war. In addition to Private CLEARY there are two officers and twelve other ranks buried here from British artillery units, all of whom are September 1918 casualties. Otherwise, this is very much a Canadian cemetery.

One of the main reasons why this cemetery is visited is on account of the VC holder buried here. Sergeant Arthur George KNIGHT VC, 10th Battalion, Canadian Infantry, died on 3 September 1918 as a result of wounds received the previous day. His VC was awarded posthumously and was gazetted on 15 November, a few days after the Armistice. It was won near Villers-lès-Cagnicourt for actions on the day prior to his death during his battalion's attack on the Drocourt–Quéant Line. The actions leading to the award began when his bombing section became held up. He went forward alone, bayoneting several machine gunners and trench mortar crews and forcing the remainder to retire. He then brought forward a Lewis gun and directed its fire at the enemy as they were retreating. As he and his platoon were pursuing the enemy, he saw about thirty of them go into a tunnel running off one of the trenches. He again went forward alone, killing one of the officers and two NCOs and capturing twenty prisoners. Later on, he again routed another enemy party single-handed, but on this occasion he was wounded. Despite medical attention he died the next day, aged 32. He originally came from Haywards Heath in Sussex, but had lived and worked in Regina, Saskatchewan, before the war. He had also been awarded the *Croix de Guerre* (France) in November 1917. (Plot I.F.15)

Private George David HAYS DCM, 7th Battalion, Canadian Infantry, was killed on 3 September 1918. Canadian army records show the spelling of his surname as 'Hayes'. His DCM was awarded posthumously and was gazetted on 30 October 1918. It was awarded for conspicuous gallantry and devotion to duty when his platoon was suddenly held up by machine-gun fire. He rushed forward and threw a grenade into the gun's emplacement, and in company with another man, who was immediately wounded, he charged the enemy with the bayonet, killing three and taking three others prisoner. During the whole time that he was carrying out this daring exploit he was under enfilade fire from another enemy machine gun. The citation goes on to conclude that his conspicuous gallantry and dash were worthy of very high praise. (Plot I.G.14)

Second Lieutenant Leonard Thomas WHITE MC, 133rd Heavy Battery, Royal Garrison Artillery, was killed in action on 21 September 1918. His MC was gazetted on 26 July 1918 and was awarded for conspicuous gallantry and devotion to duty in maintaining communication and observation posts whilst under shell, gas, and machine-gun fire. He frequently sent back valuable information and his personal example encouraged his signallers to maintain the lines. Buried next to him is Major Arthur Bracebridge CHALLIS, who was killed in action on the same day, aged 46, commanding the 133rd Heavy Battery. CHALLIS had been awarded the Territorial Decoration for long service. This medal was instituted in 1908 and the qualifying period for it was twenty years, with war service counting as double and service in the ranks counting as half. (Plots II.C.2 and 3)

Lieutenant Victor Henry McELROY DFC, Canadian Engineers, attached 3 Squadron, Royal Air Force, was killed in action on 2 September 1918. His DFC was gazetted on 3 December 1918 and was awarded for conspicuous courage and determination in attacking enemy troops, transport, huts and other facilities. In all of these operations he achieved marked success at low altitudes, inflicting heavy casualties on the enemy even though his machine was frequently riddled by heavy hostile fire. (Plot II.D.3)

Some of the holders of the MM have already been referred to, but the remaining ones are listed below. Included in this list is the one holder of the MSM, who was also a Canadian soldier.

Private Le Roy Maitland BUCK MM, 2nd Battalion, Canadian Infantry, killed in action on 2 September 1918. (Plot I.A.1)

Private Harry SEIVWRIGHT MM, 13th Battalion, Canadian Infantry, killed in action on 2 September 1918. (Plot I.A.21)

Corporal Lois Milton MORTON MM, 16th Battalion, Canadian Infantry, killed in action on 1 September 1918. He was mortally wounded when a shell burst near to him and another man as they were going to get a stretcher to assist with the wounded. He died very soon afterwards on the battlefield. His brother, Lawrence, also served with the Canadian Infantry and survived the war. (Plot I.B.8)

Lance Corporal Alfred Howard HASTINGS MM and Bar, 16th Battalion, Canadian Infantry, killed in action on 2 September 1918. (Plot I.B.9)

Corporal Robert CURRIE MM, 16th Battalion, Canadian Infantry, killed in action by machine-gun fire on 2 September 1918. He had been promoted to corporal two weeks before his death. His MM was awarded for gallantry in connection with a raid that took place in the early hours of 13 February 1918. CURRIE, who was a lance corporal at the time, was in command of one of the leading sections. When his section came across three belts of uncut wire he showed great bravery and pluck in getting his men through the obstacles and into the German trenches. He then led his men with bombs against the garrison, driving the enemy back into their dug-outs and clearing the way for the rest of the raiders. He then continued to lead his men down the German trenches, bombing many of the dug-outs and inflicting many casualties. Finally, he gathered his men and withdrew, bringing back the wounded and a prisoner. (Plot I.B.19)

Sergeant Francis Everett HEALD MM, 15th Battalion, Canadian Infantry, killed in action on 1 September 1918. (Plot I.B.23)

Lieutenant John MORRICE MM and Bar, 1st Battalion, Canadian Infantry, killed in action on 2 September 1918. His MM was gazetted on 19 December 1916 and the bar to it on 20 June 1917. His brother, Private James Ritchie Morrice, was killed in action serving in the same battalion on 5 June 1916 near Sanctuary Wood. He is buried in Ypres Reservoir Cemetery. His other brother, Private Adam Morrice, was also killed in action. He fell on 4 October 1917, aged 20, serving with the 2nd Gordon Highlanders. He is commemorated on the Tyne Cot Memorial. (Plot I.D.2)

Private William John BROOKS MM, 15th Battalion, Canadian Infantry, killed in action on 1 September 1918. (Plot I.D.23)

Staff Sergeant David HUTCHINSON MSM, 2nd Tramway Company, Canadian Engineers, killed in action on 9 September 1918. (Plot II.A.8)

Gunner Norman GIBBINS MM, 163rd Siege Battery, Royal Garrison Artillery, died of wounds on 17 September 1918. Unfortunately, there is no reference to his MM in *Soldiers Died in the Great War*. (Plot II.B.8)

Lance Bombardier John C. SHANKS MM, 163rd Siege Battery, Royal Garrison Artillery, killed in action on 20 September 1918. (Plot II.B.16)

Sergeant Alfred Henry BEADLE MM, 163rd Siege Battery, Royal Garrison Artillery, killed in action on 27 September 1918, aged 42. (Plot II.C.17)

Quéant Communal Cemetery, British Extension
The cemetery lies on the north-west side of the village, which in turn is about sixteen miles south-east of Arras. It is just on the edge of the village on the D.38 leading to Riencourt-lès-Cagnicourt. It has almost 300 burials, 270 of which have been

identified. There were once around 600 German graves on the north side of the communal cemetery, but these have long since been removed.

The village lies at the southern end of what was the Drocourt–Quéant Line, which linked the Hindenburg Line with the Lens defences. The position was captured on 2 September 1918, mainly by the Canadian Corps, but the 112 Canadian soldiers buried here are all casualties of the fighting that took place around the Canal du Nord and Cambrai in late September and the first part of October that year. During that period Quéant was home to the 4th Canadian Divisional Advanced Dressing Station. According to the war diary of the 12th Field Ambulance, Canadian Army Medical Corps, around 10,000 casualties passed through its hands here between 27 and 30 September 1918.

One of those casualties was Captain Andrew ROSS MC, a senior member of the 12th Canadian Field Ambulance, who died of wounds on 29 September 1918, aged 42 (Plot C.35). I can find no trace of his MC in the *London Gazette*. Canadian army records do not show the award of the MC next to his name and there is also no mention of any award of the MC against his name in *Officers of the Canadian Expeditionary Force Who Died Overseas*.

Private William FAITHFUL DCM, 46th Battalion, Canadian Infantry, was killed in action on 27 September 1918. His DCM was awarded for actions that day near Cambrai, during which he showed conspicuous gallantry and devotion to duty after all his officers and NCOs had become casualties. Of his own initiative, he took charge of his platoon and led it to its objective. He successfully dealt with two machine guns and their crews, thus allowing all the assaulting waves to proceed during the attack. Though wounded, he continued to command the platoon until the objective was reached. The citation concludes that he showed great courage and initiative throughout the operation. His award was gazetted on 2 December 1919 (Plot B.31). Buried just along from him is Private Raymond P. LAWTON MM, also from the 46th Battalion, Canadian Infantry. He too was killed in action on 27 September 1918. (Plot B.33)

Private Thomas LECHOW DCM, 7th Battalion, Canadian Infantry, was killed in action on 29 September 1918. His DCM was awarded for conspicuous gallantry and devotion to duty during the advance east of Arras between 2 and 4 September 1918. When he noticed two of the enemy mounting a machine gun on the parapet of a truck, he rushed forward, passing through our own artillery barrage, and captured both men and the gun. His prompt initiative undoubtedly saved his platoon many casualties. The award was gazetted on 16 January 1919. (Plot B.65)

Lieutenant Thomas John MOULDS MC and Bar, 3rd Battalion, Canadian Infantry, died on 27 September 1918 from wounds received the same day. The battalion's war diary refers to him only in a long list of casualties at the end of September. His MC was gazetted on 1 January 1918 in the New Year's Honours List and the bar to it on 8 March 1919. The bar was awarded for conspicuous gallantry and leadership during operations at Bourlon Wood on 27 September. When his company was held up by heavy enemy machine-gun and artillery fire he pushed his platoon forward by sections, outflanking a battery of 77mm field guns, capturing them with the remainder of their crews. He rushed the next position in a similar manner, killing the gun crews and capturing both guns. In doing so, he secured his company's objectives and, though wounded, he remained with his men while the position was consolidated. (Plot C.11)

Lieutenant Samuel Lewis HONEY VC DCM MM, 78th Battalion, Canadian Infantry, died of wounds on 30 September 1918. His VC was awarded posthumously for several acts of bravery between 27 and 29 September 1918 whilst taking part in operations at Bourlon Wood. When all the other officers in his company had become casualties, not only did he take command, he also carried out the necessary re-organization and led the men forward, gaining his company's objective. However, when casualties continued to occur amongst the men as a result of enfilade fire, Lieutenant HONEY went out, located the machine-gun nest responsible, rushed it, and captured the guns and ten prisoners single-handed.

Later, under his leadership, his company repelled four enemy counter-attacks. Yet again, he went out alone, located an enemy post, and then led a party against it, capturing the post and three machine guns. On 29 September he led his company against another strong enemy position, but was eventually wounded and died later the same day. This was also the final day of operations around Bourlon Wood.

His DCM was awarded for conspicuous gallantry and devotion to duty. When his platoon commander was wounded, he assumed command and led his men forward in the face of terrific fire until he was compelled to dig-in owing to heavy casualties. He held the position for three days, encouraging his men by his splendid example. The award was gazetted on 16 August 1917 and his MM was gazetted on 26 April 1917, though some records show the date as 10 January 1917. His MM was won in con-nection with a raid on German trenches in late February 1917 when he performed excellent work, clearing a communication trench and establishing a block in spite of strong opposition. When the raiding party withdrew, he personally covered the retirement of his own section and that of another while under heavy fire from grenades. (Plot C.36)

Major General Louis James LIPSETT CB CMG, General Staff, commanding the British 4th Division, is one of the highest-ranking casualties buried on the Western Front. He was born in County Donegal, but was educated in England, firstly at Bedford School, then at Sandhurst. He was commissioned in 1894 and took part in campaigns on the North-West Frontier of India and in the South African War. He was serving with the Royal Irish Regiment in 1914, but happened to be attached to the Militia in Winnipeg at the time. When the Canadian Expeditionary Force was being assembled, he was appointed lieutenant colonel of the former militia unit, the 90th Rifles, which subsequently became the 8th Battalion, Canadian Infantry. He then took the battalion to Belgium, where it played an heroic part in the Second Battle of Ypres in April 1915. After that, he rose to command the Canadian 2 Brigade, which included his beloved 8th Battalion. When Major General Mercer was killed in action at Mount Sorrel in June 1916, he was a natural choice to take over command of the Canadian 3rd Division.

He retained that position throughout the rest of the war until September 1918 when he took command of the British 4th Division. On 14 October, while venturing forward, perhaps further than an officer of his rank ought to have done, he was hit in the jaw by a sniper's bullet. Although badly wounded, he was tended to by his brigadier who encouraged him to make a dash to a nearby wood. LIPSETT was able to make the short journey, but once within the relative safety of the wood he collapsed and died soon afterwards.

His body was taken back to Quéant where his funeral took place. The service was attended by HRH the Prince of Wales, General Horne, Commander of the First Army, and Lieutenant General Currie, Commander of the Canadian Corps. He was 44 years old when he died and was buried with full military honours, the firing party coming from his old unit, the 8th Battalion. He was the last British and Dominion general to be killed in the Great War. He was also awarded the *Croix de Guerre* (France). (Plot F.1)

The cemetery also contains men from units belonging to the 57th (2nd West Lancashire) Division. There are small numbers of men from the 1st Royal Munster Fusiliers and the 2/4th and 1/5th Loyal North Lancashire Regiment, but greater numbers from the King's (Liverpool Regiment). The division's 171 Brigade was composed entirely of battalions of the King's (Liverpool Regiment), as was a third of 172 Brigade. The division, like all second-line Territorial units, did not exist prior to the outbreak of the Great War. When it went to France in February 1917 it became part of II Anzac Corps. Although it played an heroic part in the Second Battle of Passchendaele during the latter part of October and the first week of November 1917, it saw far more action during the final advances through northern France in the autumn of 1918, notably around Arras, the Canal du Nord, and Cambrai.

Amongst the men of the King's (Liverpool Regiment) are two officer casualties from the 2/7th Battalion: Lieutenant Percy Whittle PITTOCK (Plot C.7) and Second Lieutenant Stanley HIGGINS (Plot C.6). Both men were killed in action on 27 September 1918 during operations near Bourlon Wood.

A further twenty-one identified casualties of the King's (Liverpool Regiment) are now buried here. All twenty-three men fell between 8 and 29 September 1918, including eight on 11 September and nine on 27 September. Fourteen are from the 2/7th Battalion, whilst the others come from the 2/6th, the 2/8th and the 2/9th Battalions. Lieutenant Anthony STEEL, who fell on 11 September 1918, is shown in the CWGC register as serving with the Labour Corps, but he was attached to the 2/8th King's (Liverpool Regiment) at the time of his death (Plot A.17).

Another officer, also attached to the King's (Liverpool Regiment), was Lieutenant Sidney Edward Bush SAGE. He was attached to the 2/6th Battalion from the 6th Gloucestershire Regiment and died of wounds on 13 September 1918 at the 3/2nd (West Lancashire) Field Ambulance, which at that time was located at Quéant. (Plot A.12)

There are two more officers buried here belonging to units of the 57th (2nd West Lancashire) Division. They are Lieutenant Edgar Cyril COMLEY MC, 4th Royal Munster Fusiliers, attached 1st Battalion, who was killed in action on 27 September 1918 (Plot B.42) and Second Lieutenant James Lawton HARROP, 4th Loyal North Lancashire Regiment, who died of wounds on 13 September 1918 (Plot A.22).

COMLEY's MC was gazetted on 17 September 1917 and was awarded for conspicuous gallantry and leadership whilst in charge of his platoon. The citation notes that he showed great coolness and utter disregard for his own safety whilst under an enemy barrage, moving about amongst the men and encouraging them by his own personal example. It goes on to add that he led a successful attack on an enemy strongpoint, showing the utmost gallantry, after which he did much to plot out defensive trenches around the position whilst under heavy shell fire.

There is also a small Scottish element to the cemetery, thanks to the inclusion of eleven officers and men of the 6/7th Gordon Highlanders in Rows D and E. Among them is Captain Percy Melville MACKENZIE, 2nd Gordon Highlanders, the son of Peter Mackenzie, Count de Serre Largo (Portugal), of Tarlogie House, Tain, which lies just north of Inverness. The Portuguese title came via Captain MACKENZIE's mother, whose family was of Portuguese descent. His father, Peter, was the nephew of George Ross Mackenzie who rose from being a machine engineer with the Singer Sewing Machine Company to become its fourth president. Under his presidency, he sent his five sons and Peter, his nephew, to various parts of the world to manage and promote the company's business, and it was while he was travelling in this capacity that Peter met his Portuguese wife. Captain MACKENZIE's wife, Helen, came from a prominent family in the Scottish Borders that claimed ancestry back to the Earls of Douglas (Plot D.4). MACKENZIE was killed in action on 6 October 1918.

A week later, another officer of the battalion, Captain Alexander REID MC, died from his wounds. I can find no trace of his MC in any of the Gazettes, nor is there any reference to it in *Officers Died in the Great War*. (Plot E.5)

There are also eight officers and men from battalions belonging to the Highland Light Infantry that made up part of the 52nd (Lowland) Division, namely the 5th, 6th and 7th Battalions. Lieutenant Peter Alexander Earle McCRACKEN is shown in the CWGC register as serving with the 9th Battalion, but must have been attached to one of the above units, as the 9th Battalion (Glasgow Highlanders) was on the old Somme battlefields on the day he was killed in action, which was 16 September 1918 (Plot A.37). A few graves along the row is Lieutenant James Robert Grant MUIR, 1/7th Highland Light Infantry, who died of wounds the following day, aged 21 (Plot A.41), as did the man next to him, Captain Kenneth McAlpine ROSS, Royal Army Medical Corps, who was attached to the 1/5th Highland Light Infantry. (Plot A.42)

The Cameronians has six of its officers and men buried here. Captain William Scott Branks WILSON, 6th Cameronians, was killed in action on 19 September 1918, aged 39. He was educated at Hamilton Academy and then read Law at Glasgow University. On graduation he went into practice as a solicitor in Motherwell. At the outbreak of war he readily volunteered, believing that it was his duty to participate. Whilst overseas, serving in Palestine and France, he wrote many letters home to his wife, and these were published privately after his death under the title, *On Active Service*. It was said that he had a keen, dry sense of humour and that he was well liked within his battalion. On 19 September 1918 he was standing outside the entrance of his dug-out, not far from Moeuvres, when a shell exploded near him. He was hit by several fragments from it and died instantly. (Plot A.57)

Buried next to Captain WILSON is Private Alexander BULLOCH, 7th Battalion, Cameronians. He lost two brothers during the war. Walter served as a corporal with the 5/6th Cameronians and was killed on 21 May 1917, aged 24. His other brother, William, was a sapper with the Royal Engineers and was killed on Hogmanay, 31 December 1917, aged 33. Walter, who has no known grave, is commemorated on the Arras Memorial and William is buried at Trois Arbres Cemetery, Steenwerck, close to the Belgian border. (Plot A.56)

Buried in the next row is Second Lieutenant Alexander McGLASHAN, 7th Cameronians, who fell on 27 September 1918, aged 24. (Plot B.41)

Lieutenant Colonel Edward Stephen GIBBONS DSO, Middlesex Regiment, was killed in action on 19 September 1918, aged 35. He began his military career in December 1902. His DSO, gazetted on 1 December 1914, was awarded for his coolness and zeal as a captain whilst serving with the 1st Middlesex Regiment at Le Maisnil on 21 October in what the citation refers to only as 'a serious emergency'. The serious emergency occurred after the 1st Middlesex Regiment had been sent up to support the 2nd Argyll & Sutherland Highlanders at Maisnil. After subjecting their position to a heavy bombardment, the Germans attacked in the afternoon and fighting then continued throughout the rest of the day and well into the evening. However, when a detachment of French cyclists on the left flank gave way, the position had to be abandoned. Many wounded had to be left behind in the subsequent withdrawal as a new defensive position was hastily organized to the rear. Lieutenant Colonel GIBBONS was the son of Sir William Gibbons, KCB. (Plot A.58)

A significant number of artillerymen of various ranks can be found scattered throughout the cemetery. There are twenty-nine from the Royal Field Artillery and eighteen from the Royal Garrison Artillery. The highest ranking amongst them is Major Harry Burton EMERTON MC, 'B' Battery, 178 Brigade, Royal Field Artillery who, like many of those buried here, was killed on 27 September 1917. He was 26 years old when he died. His MC was gazetted on 2 December 1918 and was awarded for his work in going forward constantly ahead of his unit in order to select battery positions during an advance, thereby enabling it to provide effective support to the infantry. The citation also refers to an incident when he rushed over to an ammunition dump that had been set on fire next to his battery and, at great personal risk, managed to get the flames under control. (Plot B.54)

Two more artillery officers are buried in Row E, one of whom is Lieutenant Leslie Willoughby FRANKLIN, 10th Battery, 147 Brigade, Royal Field Artillery. Although he was educated at Dulwich College, London, the CWGC register notes that he was born at Kobe in Japan. He is also one of many men listed on the Great War Memorial in Yokohama. He died of wounds on 16 October 1918 (Plot E.15). Of the two officers from the Royal Garrison Artillery, Second Lieutenant Cecil Harry MORETON, 22nd Heavy Battery, was killed in action on 17 October 1918, aged just 19. He had been a pupil at Blundell's School in Tiverton, Devon. (Plot A.39)

Listed below are several NCOs and other ranks, not already mentioned, who were awarded the MM, a number of whom served with the Canadian Expeditionary Force.

Private Angus Charles McCALLUM MM, 102nd Battalion, Canadian Infantry, killed in action on 27 September 1918, aged 29. (Plot B.32)

Corporal Henry Augustus Morris BILSTON MM, 27th Siege Battery, Royal Garrison Artillery, killed in action on 27 September 1918. (Plot B.45)

Serjeant Clifford SCARGILL, 2/7th King's (Liverpool Regiment), killed in action on 27 September 1918, aged 22. (Plot C.4)

Bombardier Frank GOLD MM, 5 Brigade, Canadian Field Artillery, killed in action on 29 September 1918. (Plot C.28)

Private C. STEWART MM, 6/7th Gordon Highlanders, killed in action on 6 October 1918. (Plot D.7)

Corporal Olly WALPOLE MM, Canadian Corps Cyclist Battalion, killed on 11 October 1918, aged 23. (Plot D.30)

Sergeant Eric Mackay SULLIVAN MM, 21st Battalion, Canadian Infantry, died of wounds on 12 October 1918, aged 39. He was born in Wagga Wagga, New South Wales, where his father worked for the local newspaper. When he enlisted with the Canadian Expeditionary Force he stated that he had worked as a printer and that he had previously served in the South African War with the Imperial Bushmen as a squadron sergeant major. His MM was won during his battalion's advance near Marcelcave on 8 August 1918. On or around 12 October he was wounded in the hip by shrapnel and was taken to No. 9 Canadian Field Ambulance where he was treated, but subsequently died. (Plot D.32)

All in all, this is a very worthwhile cemetery to visit. In addition to the above entries, the following may also be of interest.

Major George William MARTIN, 17th Northumberland Fusiliers, was killed in action on 17 September 1918, aged 47 (Plot A.38). The 17th Battalion was a pioneer battalion and from 31 May 1918 it had been attached to the 52nd (Lowland) Division. The regimental history describes 17 September as a bad day for the battalion. Major MARTIN and Lieutenant McKay had been making their way towards Pronville and had reached the crossroads there when a shell exploded close to them. McKay was badly wounded, but '*poor old MARTIN*' was killed. He had been one of the original members of the battalion when it had embarked for the front on 20 November 1915. He had already completed his time and was already described as '*an old soldier*' when the war began. However, he insisted on doing his bit and left his '*snug post*' at York in order to serve abroad. He served initially as a serjeant major, then as quartermaster, and went on to serve as adjutant of the battalion. He was well respected and many of the battalion's officers and men attended his funeral, which took place in a field cemetery between Quéant and Bullecourt.

Armament Staff Serjeant Walter Henry STUBBS, Army Ordnance Corps, was killed in action on 19 September 1918. He is one of twenty men of such rank who were killed or who died during the Great War. Nineteen of them fell while serving overseas. The role of the Army Ordnance Corps revolved mainly around the supply and storage of armaments, particularly shells. Much of its work took place around railheads, but teams also worked closer to the front line at times, particularly in the case of repairs and salvage. (Plot A.53)

Sergeant Tom Hobart SCOTT, Canadian Corps Gas Services, died here on 22 September 1918, aged 37. He is one of only two men from this particular unit killed in the Great War. The other man was also a sergeant and is buried at Étaples. (Plot B.7)

There are no men from the Australian Imperial Force buried in this extended part of the communal cemetery, but there are three gunners from the New Zealand Field Artillery, one of whom had been awarded the MSM (Plot B.11). Farrier Serjeant Reginald John HANCOCK MSM, died on 22nd September 1918, a few days before the other two men who were from the 9th Battery. All three men are buried in Row B.

Air Mechanic 2nd Class William (Bib) NEWBURY, 46th Kite Balloon Section, Royal Air Force, died on 4 October 1918. He is the only member of the Air Services buried in this cemetery. I am unaware of any account of his death. (Plot C.47)

Private Frederick Horace PARKER, 7th Canadian Area Employment Company, Canadian Labour Corps, died on 3 October 1918, aged 55. He is the oldest man buried in this cemetery. (Plot C.49)

Private John Jeffrey NICHOLLS, 5th Field Ambulance, Canadian Army Medical Corps, had also been awarded the MSM and died of wounds on 12 October 1918. He was born in Kingsbridge, South Devon, though he enlisted in Toronto on 21 November 1914. He died at No. 10 Canadian Field Ambulance where he was taken after being wounded by shrapnel from an enemy shell when it exploded. He and a colleague were guiding two motor ambulances to the regimental aid post of the 24th Battalion, Canadian Infantry, near Iwuy, when the shell landed on the road between the two vehicles. He was wounded in the thigh and lower abdomen and his right femur was also badly broken. Despite prompt medical attention he died later. (Plot D.58)

Three casualties are buried together in collective grave E.15A. The men are not from the same unit, but they did die on the same day, 16 October 1918. One is a driver from the Royal Field Artillery, but the other two are infantrymen from the 1/4th Duke of Wellington's Regiment and the 1/6th Argyll & Sutherland Highlanders. I can only presume that the men were originally buried together on the battlefield, but were unable to be identified individually when exhumed and brought here after the war.

Finally, there is just one grave from 1919, a Chinese labourer attached to the 58th Company, Chinese Labour Corps, who died on 3 April that year. (Plot E.19)

Quéant Road Cemetery, Buissy

The cemetery is situated approximately half way between the villages of Quéant and Buissy on the D.14. On the 1918 battlefield, the site occupied a central position in open fields between Quéant and Cagnicourt, about a mile or so in front of the Buissy Switch. The Bois de Bouche lies just to the north of the cemetery, and beyond that is the Bois de Loison. This area was captured by the 14th and 15th Battalions, Canadian Infantry on 2 September 1918.

Today, this is a reasonably large cemetery, though it started out quite modestly with just seventy-one original graves in what is now Plot I, Rows A and B. The site was close to No. 2 and No. 57 Casualty Clearing Stations and was conveniently placed to take burials from both of these medical facilities. However, it was greatly enlarged after the Armistice when over 2,000 graves were brought in from the surrounding battlefield and eight other cemeteries were decommissioned. Although the majority of graves are unidentified, the cemetery does contain fifty-six special memorials commemorating men known or believed to be buried here, in addition to special memorials to twenty-six others who were originally buried in German cemeteries, but whose graves were subsequently lost or destroyed.

Only 35 per cent of the graves are identified and 378 of these are from 1917. Of the 533 burials from 1918, 394 are from the last few months of the war during the final advance.

The earliest casualty is Private Samuel PODMORE, 2nd Gordon Highlanders, who may have died as a German prisoner of war, though *Soldiers Died in the Great War* records that he was killed in action. His date of death in the CWGC register is recorded as 25 September 1915, the opening day of the Battle of Loos, when his battalion attacked with its right flank on the Vermelles–Hulluch Road, which incidentally formed the boundary between I Corps and IV Corps. His battalion managed to reach the junction with the Lens–La Bassée road where it dug in just short of Hulluch. The plot where he is now buried gives a fairly clear indication that he was a later addition, quite possibly from one of the cemeteries that was closed after the war. (Plot VI.A.13)

As regards Canadian casualties, there are two officers and eighty other ranks buried here. They come from a number of battalions, but all of them were killed or died of wounds towards the end of September or during the early part of October, in other words from the fighting around the Canal du Nord and Cambrai. Some are buried in Plots I and III, but many more are buried in Plots VII and VIII.

Lieutenant Reginald Gordon SPEAR MC, 46th Battalion, Canadian Infantry, who died of wounds on 23 October 1918, is one of those buried in Plot I. The battalion war diary provides a very detailed account of the difficult fighting that took place the previous day in the Faubourg de Paris district of Cambrai when Lieutenant SPEAR was wounded. SPEAR's MC was gazetted on 30 July 1919 in recognition of his actions near Cambrai on 27 September 1918 when he rendered valuable assistance by withdrawing men of his company from forward posts to the assembly positions under heavy shelling. During the attack on the 27th he handled his platoon with great tactical skill and, although wounded, he gallantly led it to its objective in the face of very heavy shelling and machine-gun fire. Later on, when his company was held up by direct machine-gun fire, he established a line of defence with his platoon in a very forward position and maintained communication with other units in his battalion, making several journeys across fire-swept areas in order to accomplish this. (Plot I.A.16)

Lieutenant Lucian Albert YOUNG, 1st Somerset Light Infantry, was one of three officers who died of wounds received during the attack across the Écaillon River on 24 October 1918. He died two days later, aged 28. In spite of the fact that they were facing inevitable defeat, the Germans still offered stiff resistance where defensive opportunities existed, and especially near rivers and canals. Casualties amongst the 1st Somerset Light Infantry amounted to eight officers and 149 other ranks as a result of operations on 24 October. The river, which in reality was little more than a stream about eight feet wide and five feet deep, was wired on both banks and wire had also been immersed within the river itself. It was crossed by means of four portable bridges, three of which had to be held in place by men wading into the water to secure them. This caused delays as well as casualties, though covering fire helped to subdue enemy machine-gun and trench mortar fire coming from the opposite bank. (Plot I.A.30)

Lieutenant Edward Cuthbert HOCKING, 151 Squadron, Royal Air Force, formerly Loyal North Lancashire Regiment and Royal Field Artillery, was killed in action on 28 October 1918, aged 22, whilst flying a Camel aircraft. He is one of eleven Royal Air Force burials in this cemetery, seven of whom can be found in Plot I. Row B. (Plot I.B.9)

Lieutenant Charles Edward HUTCHESON, 27 Squadron, Royal Air Force, was killed in action on 30 October 1918, aged 19 (Plot I.B.15). Second Lieutenant Ernest Andrew HOOPER, who was his observer that day, was killed with him, also aged 19. (Plot I.B.12)

Serjeant Sydney Frank BRIGGS DFM, 21 Squadron, Royal Air Force, died on 7 November 1918, aged 28, from influenza. The DFM, or Distinguished Flying Medal, was a relatively recent award and had only been introduced on 3 June 1918. His DFM was gazetted on 21 September 1918 and was awarded for distinguished service in an attack on an enemy seaport when he sunk an enemy destroyer by a direct hit from a bomb. He was serving as a private (aerial gunlayer) when he won the award. (Plot I.B.27)

There is some discrepancy regarding the date of death for Air Mechanic 1st Class, Sidney Arthur BAKER, 27 Squadron, Royal Air Force. *Airmen Died in the Great War* shows his death as occurring on 9 October 1918, whereas the CWGC register shows his date of death as 9 November 1918. Neither source makes any comment on how he died. (Plot I.B.32)

Air Mechanic 1st Class Herbert KNOWLES, 49 Squadron, Royal Air Force, died of wounds on 9 November 1918. His observer, Serjeant Horace Lewis DODSON, also died that day and is buried next to him. Given that the Armistice was just forty-eight hours away, there was a surprising amount of air activity that day. Although contact with enemy aircraft was described as light, the Royal Air Force made several attacks on aerodromes and carried out a bombing raid on the railway station at Enghien. (Plots I.B.34 and 35)

The Royal Field Artillery is represented by twenty-nine identified burials. Amongst them is Gunner Thomas LESLIE, 'D' Battery, 91 Brigade, Royal Field Artillery, who died on 11 November 1918 (Plot I.B.30). There is another casualty buried next to him who died the same day: Private Walter CORNES, 1st Somerset Light Infantry, died of wounds on Armistice Day. (Plot I.B.31)

One of the interesting characters buried in this cemetery is Major Benjamin Bennett LEANE, 48th Battalion, Australian Infantry. He fell on 10 April 1917, aged 24, and was one of several men killed in an enemy barrage as the Australian troops began to withdraw from no man's land just as it was becoming light following the decision to postpone the attack on Bullecourt until the following day (Plot I.C.1). Another brother, Lieutenant Colonel Allan William Leane, 28th Battalion, Australian Infantry, was killed in action on 4 January 1917, aged 44. He is buried at Dernancourt Communal Cemetery just behind Albert. The brothers were part of a famous military family, three of whom were associated with the 28th Battalion, which was nicknamed 'The Joan of Arc Battalion', because it was 'made of all Leanes'.

Second Lieutenant Allan Edwin Leane, a cousin of theirs, and son of Colonel Edwin Thomas Leane, was killed in action on 2 May 1917, aged 23, serving with the 48th Battalion, Australian Infantry. The CWGC register shows his rank as captain and he is commemorated on the Australian National Memorial at Villers-Bretonneux.

Company Serjeant Major Ernest William JAMIESON DCM, 14th Battalion, London Regiment (London Scottish), was killed in action on 29 August 1918, aged 36. His DCM, gazetted on 20 July 1917, was awarded for conspicuous gallantry and devotion to duty in extinguishing a burning lorry under heavy shell fire, saving the vehicle and enabling the wounded to be rescued. (Plot I.D.1)

Second Lieutenant Mark NETTLESHIP, 1st King's Own Scottish Borderers, attached 1/4th Battalion, was killed in action on 1 September 1918, aged 25 (Plot II.C.26). His brother, Second Lieutenant Thomas Nettleship, was killed in action on 22 March 1918, aged 32, whilst serving with the 1/5th Northumberland Fusiliers. He has no known grave and is commemorated on the Pozières Memorial on the Somme.

Lieutenant Ewen Colquhoun Richardson HAMILTON-JOHNSTON, 2nd King's Own Scottish Borderers, attached 1/4th Battalion, was killed in action on 1 September 1918, aged 22 (Plot II.C.29). His brother, Captain Douglas Charles Hamilton-Johnston, 2nd Black Watch, was killed in action in Mesopotamia, at Hanna, leading an attack on Turkish positions on 21 January 1916. Douglas had been wounded earlier in the war, first by a shell at Festubert on 10 December 1914 and again on 3 March 1915 in trenches near Neuve Chapelle.

Major John Crosby WARREN MC, 7th Sherwood Foresters, is one of thirty-four officers and men from that regiment buried in this cemetery. Twenty-four of them, including Major WARREN, died on 21 March 1918 when the German Offensive began, and all apart from one of the thirty-four were killed or died between 17 and 28 March. Major WARREN was educated at Sedbergh School and Trinity College, Oxford. His MC was gazetted on 18 November 1915 and the accompanying citation is unusually specific as to the location, date, and circumstances in which it was won. It was awarded for conspicuous gallantry at the Hohenzollern Redoubt on 13 October 1915 when, with a party of just four men, he held back the enemy in the trench system known as Little Willie for three hours. Once the enemy had occupied the trench behind him, he withdrew across the open to the western face of the redoubt where he built and occupied a barrier. He then personally helped to defeat a strong attack using bombs and held the trench for fourteen hours. The citation also notes that he had previously come to notice for similar gallant conduct. He had also been mentioned in despatches. (Plot II.F.18)

The Sherwood Foresters here are from various battalions, including the 2nd, the 2/5th, the 2/6th and the 2/7th Battalions, but are scattered throughout different parts of the cemetery. Captain Marmaduke Marshall SHAW MC, 3rd Sherwood Foresters, attached 2nd Battalion, was killed in action on 21 March 1918, aged 21. His MC was gazetted on 17 September 1917 and was awarded for his actions while in command of reinforcements for our front line. He sent back men who had already been engaged in severe fighting and who presumably were exhausted, and then held on with his detachment until ordered by divisional HQ to withdraw. During this time he had had little or no sleep for three days and two nights. While holding his trench he showed splendid fearlessness, as well as great skill and energy in consolidating the position (Plot VI.H.29). Lieutenant Albert CATTERALL, 7th Battalion, was also killed on 21 March 1918, aged 24. (Plot III.D.23)

Lieutenant William Fleming Oliphant MORRISON, 8th Royal Scots, attached 2nd Battalion, was killed in action on 2 September 1918, aged 26. After 'C' Company had forced its way into Noreuil, capturing the garrison there, he took a small party of men over the slight ridge that separates Noreuil from Lagnicourt in order to secure the village against the threat of counter-attack from the south-east. German resistance, however, was already beginning to stiffen and his group met opposition from a party of the enemy defending Lagnicourt Trench. Lieutenant MORRISON was killed in the ensuing fight which lasted for two hours. The remnants of his party were eventually forced back to the outskirts of Noreuil, which by now had come under heavy fire. (Plot III.A.2)

As well as MORRISON, the 2nd Royal Scots also lost Lieutenant Alexander Stuart Robertson MC, that day. Like MORRISON, he too was an 8th Battalion man attached to the 2nd Battalion. He is buried at Vraucourt Copse Cemetery, Vaulx-Vraucourt, where twenty-two of the battalion's twenty-five other ranks killed that day are now buried, including Private Hugh McIver VC MM and Bar. Another 8th Battalion officer, Lieutenant James Graham MYLNE, 8th Royal Scots, attached 4th Royal Scots, was killed in action on 2 September 1918. He is buried here with Lieutenant MORRISON in the same plot a couple of rows away. (Plot III.C.7)

Another casualty from the fighting on 2 September 1918 is Serjeant David Brown POLLOCK DCM, 7th Cameronians. His DCM was gazetted on 1 May 1918. It was awarded for his prompt action as he and others were approaching their final objective. Noticing an enemy machine gun still in action on the flank, he rushed it without hesitation, bayoneting two of the team and driving off the remaining five. He then remained with the captured gun until his section arrived. His own men and the rest of the platoon would no doubt have sustained many casualties had it not been for his prompt actions (Plot I.D.2). Of the fourteen NCOs and men of the 7th Cameronians buried in this cemetery, ten of them were killed in action on 2 September 1918, the same day as Serjeant POLLOCK, though he is the only one not buried in Plot IV.

Second Lieutenant James ATKINSON MC, 1st Royal Scots Fusiliers, was also killed in action on 2 September 1918. His MC was gazetted on 26 September 1918. It was awarded for conspicuous gallantry, going out alone in broad daylight and discovering an enemy post. The next day he took two men with the intention of capturing it.

As they were trying to capture the sentry, about twenty of the enemy emerged from nearby shelters. One of ATKINSON's men threw a bomb at them, badly wounding one of the party, who was then hurriedly dragged back to our lines as a prisoner. In order to cover their withdrawal, Second Lieutenant ATKINSON kept the enemy back by hurling further bombs. The citation concludes by stating that throughout this entire operation he displayed great courage and coolness and obtained an important identification. (Plot IV.A.22)

There are 299 men buried here from the Australian Imperial Force and all of them were killed within a short space of time. The first casualties are from the final ten days of March 1917 as advanced parties edged their way towards the Hindenburg Line, and in doing so had to deal with rearguard units defending positions and villages in front of it.

According to the CWGC register, Captain Percy Herbert CHERRY VC MC, 26th Battalion, Australian Infantry, was killed in action on 27 March 1917, aged 21. However, a number of accounts show it as 26 March, including the *Australian Dictionary of Biography*. His VC citation also seems to imply that he died on 26 March, and another man, reported to have been killed by the same shell as CHERRY, is shown in the CWGC register as dying on the 26th.

CHERRY had already demonstrated great courage and character in 1916 during the fighting around Pozières. During an enemy counter-attack a German officer approached CHERRY's position, whereupon both men fired at each other from close quarters. A shot from the German officer struck CHERRY's steel helmet, but CHERRY returned fire and mortally wounded his opponent. After the enemy's attack had been defeated, the dying German officer asked CHERRY to post some letters for him, which he agreed to do. CHERRY was also wounded that day during the fighting.

The day before CHERRY was killed in action he took a party of men through the village of Lagnicourt, where they encountered stiff opposition, especially from a large crater blown in the centre of the village. He sent three messages back, the first requesting that Stokes mortars be brought forward in order to bring suppressing fire on the defenders before he and his party rushed the crater.

After waiting half an hour he sent back another message: '*Can't wait for Stokes, having a "go" at it, will report result later.*' CHERRY and his men then rushed the crater, bayoneting all the occupants. After carrying out this assault he sent another message back confirming that the obstacle had been cleared. After more fighting around some German dug-outs, CHERRY's men eventually met up with other units that had been sent around the flanks of the village. Then, in spite of orders for his own unit to return to reserve, he used his initiative and kept his party in advanced posts near the road leading to Doignies in order to deal with any counter-attack. His VC was awarded for his exploits around Lagnicourt during the period described.

His MC was won in November 1916 at Malt Trench, near Warlencourt, on the Somme, where he was wounded as he rushed two machine guns, one of which he subsequently turned on the enemy. As with his VC, the MC was not gazetted until after his death. Unfortunately, he was killed when a shell burst near to where he was standing in one of the many sunken lanes around Lagnicourt. Before going to France he had served in Egypt and also at Gallipoli where he was wounded on 1 December

1915, just as the evacuation of the peninsula was beginning to get under way. (Plot VIII.C.10)

Second Lieutenant Arthur JERRY MM, 28th Battalion, Australian Infantry, was mortally wounded by the same shell that killed CHERRY. Both men were in a sunken lane east of Lagnicourt when the shell exploded. Earlier that day the Germans had launched a counter-attack, pinning the Australians against the extremities of the village. In order to minimise their own losses, the Germans then broke off their infantry attacks, which allowed their artillery to put down a bombardment on the Australian positions, inflicting further casualties and delaying any further advance. Earlier that day, Second Lieutenant JERRY had been responsible for capturing some machine guns whose crews had been sheltering in an area of dead ground. He had then set up his own gunners on the south-east side of the village in order to deal with the counter-attack. (Plot VIII.B.12)

Lieutenant Fred Williams CORNER, 26th Battalion, Australian Infantry, also shared the day's exploits with CHERRY. As the group entered Lagnicourt, it was fired on from a farmhouse built around a courtyard on the edge of the village. The occupants were able to fire from windows and doors, temporarily forcing the Australians to take cover until bombers were able to rush the entrance to the courtyard. At the same time as the bombers assaulted the courtyard and its buildings, one of the Lewis gunners accompanying them offered support by firing from the hip. Resistance was soon overcome and no prisoners were taken. Lieutenant CORNER then pushed on ahead of the main group towards the centre of the village, but was killed near the rim of the crater that was later rushed by CHERRY and his men. (Plot VII.H.1)

Lieutenant William Ernest S. COOK, 28th Battalion, Australian Infantry, was another of the officers killed on 26 March 1917 during the fighting for Lagnicourt. (Special Memorial D.1)

Of the 119 casualties from April 1917, fifty-four were killed on 11 April during the fighting that became known as the First Battle of Bullecourt. Another twenty-one are from the German counter-attack on 15 April 1917, the intention of which was to destroy as many Australian gun batteries as possible in order to hinder or prevent further attacks on the Hindenburg Line in the Bullecourt sector. A further 150 burials relate to the following month, eighty of which are from 3 May 1917, the start of the Second Battle of Bullecourt. Many of these casualties were brought here after the Armistice from various nearby locations and therefore tend to be spread across different parts of the cemetery.

Amongst those killed on 11 April are Second Lieutenant Herbert James HAMMOND, 48th Battalion, Australian Infantry, aged 39 (Plot I.E.22) and Corporal A. COOPER MM, 47th Battalion. (Plot IV.F.29)

Two more holders of gallantry awards are among those killed during the large German raid on 15 April 1917. Sergeant George KIRKPATRICK MM, 17th Battalion, Australian Infantry, had also been previously mentioned in despatches. (Plot III.F.11). The other man, Private John Ernest JOHNS MM, 12th Battalion, is buried elsewhere in the cemetery. (Plot VI.G.34)

The earliest of the British 1917 casualties is Second Lieutenant James Herbert SAYER, 15 Squadron, Royal Flying Corps. He was originally reported missing in action, but his death was later confirmed as having occurred on 3 April 1917. He was only 19 years old when he died, but had already been mentioned on several occasions in the *Royal Flying Corps Communiqués* in January 1917 in connection with his flying skills, particularly at low altitude whilst carrying out contact patrols. (Plot VIII.G.25)

Buried near to SAYER, in Plot VIII, Row G, is Second Lieutenant George Beaumont BATE, 18 Squadron, Royal Flying Corps, who was mortally wounded on 29 April 1917 when he and his pilot, Second Lieutenant Dinsmore, attacked three enemy aircraft whilst on escort duty. They sent one down in flames and damaged another sufficiently to put it out of action. However, the third one managed to return fire as they were pursuing it, one of the bullets hitting Second Lieutenant BATE. Their FE2b aircraft was also seriously damaged and Dinsmore only just managed to land it behind British lines. (Plot VIII.G.11)

There are twenty-nine British burials dating to May 1917 and similar numbers for the months of June and July, though there are just a handful from the remaining months of the year. Among these are two British airmen from 15 Squadron, Royal Flying Corps, who were killed in action in their RE8 on 10 December 1917. They are Second Lieutenant Leonard Hubert THIERRY (Plot VII.B.31) and his observer, Air Mechanic Richard Thomas LEE. (Plot VII.A.32)

One of the casualties from May 1917 is Reverend, the Honourable Maurice Berkeley PEEL MC and Bar, Chaplain 4th Class, who was 44 years old when he was killed on 14 May 1917. He was the fifth son of 1st Viscount Peel and the grandson of Sir Robert Peel who twice served as British Prime Minister. His MC was gazetted on 18 February 1915 and the bar to it on 17 April 1917. His MC was awarded for services in connection with operations in the field. The bar was awarded for his conspicuous gallantry and devotion to duty after he went out to a line of advanced patrols with two stretcher-bearers and succeeded in bringing in several wounded men, subsequently working for thirty-six hours in front of the captured position where he rescued many more wounded men under very heavy fire. (Plot V.A.31)

His son, Major David Arthur George Peel, 2nd Irish Guards, died of wounds on 12 September 1944, aged 33, two days after winning the MC during the advance towards the Escaut Canal. He had been ordered to capture the bridge at De Groote Barrier, which was being prepared for demolition and was defended by a large garrison of Germans supported by three 88mm guns. After the first tank to approach the position was met with anti-tank rounds, Peel made a personal reconnaissance of the position before formulating a plan to use part of his unit to give covering fire whilst he led another party across the bridge on foot. He and his men charged the German defences around the bridge and secured it intact. He is buried at Leopoldsburg War Cemetery in Belgium.

Second Lieutenant James AMOS, aged 18, and his pilot, Second Lieutenant John James BORROWMAN, both members of 22 Squadron, Royal Air Force, were killed in action in their Bristol F2B on 29 August 1918 and are now buried next to each other. BORROWMAN had been wounded a few weeks earlier on 10 August. (Plots V.E.3 and 4)

Captain Henry Beresford SPENCER, West Somerset Yeomanry, was killed in action on 2 September 1918, aged 37. His father had also served as a captain, but in the 5th Gloucestershire Regiment. His maternal grandfather was General Marcus Beresford who served as Commandant of Bangalore; whilst on his father's side of the family his grandfather was Reverend the Honourable Charles Frederic Octavius Spencer and his great-great-grandfather was George Spencer, 4th Duke of Marlborough. His was a very familiar middle class upbringing that rested firmly on the values and traditions of Church and Army, but whose recent ancestry was also rooted in the landed gentry of England. At the time of his death he was serving with the Tank Corps. (Plot VI.E.15)

Lieutenant Cecil Arthur Henry HUDSON DCM MM and Bar, 8th Battalion, Canadian Infantry, died, aged 25, in somewhat unusual circumstances. The 8th Battalion's war diary for 26 September 1918 opens by recording the discovery of Lieutenant HUDSON's body lying over a log in an area of woodland just outside a camp near Hendecourt. His rifle was found beneath his body. A court of enquiry was convened the same day and it was concluded that he died of accidental injuries. His funeral took place that same afternoon.

He had won his DCM for conspicuous gallantry and devotion to duty as a signalling sergeant, following up the attacking companies and laying a line under heavy fire as they moved forwards. When the line was destroyed by shelling he established a lamp signalling station near the front line. He also located a party of enemy snipers and killed three of them, returning with a most valuable reconnaissance report. Though wounded, he remained on duty with the greatest courage and determination until he was incapacitated by another wound. The award was gazetted on 28 March 1918. His MM was gazetted on 21 December 1916 and the bar to it on 18 July 1917. (Plot VI.F.15)

Captain Archibald Douglas Hewitt CLARK-KENNEDY, 5th Royal Scots Fusiliers, was killed in action on 18 September 1918, aged 30. He was the son of the late Captain and the Honourable Mrs. Clark-Kennedy of Knockgray, Carsphairn, Galloway in Scotland and had previously been mentioned in despatches. His brother, Captain Alexander Kenelm Clark-Kennedy, 1/5th King's Own Scottish Borderers, was killed in action on 19 April 1917, aged 33, and is buried in Gaza War Cemetery.

The Clark-Kennedy family owned considerable land in the Dumfries and Galloway area of Scotland and one of its ancestors, Lieutenant General Clark-Kennedy, had fought in the Peninsular War and at Waterloo where he commanded the centre squadron of the 1st (Royal) Dragoons, capturing the Eagle and Colours of the French 105th Regiment.

On a hill above Carsphairn on the family estate there is a very fine cairn memorial where the two brothers are commemorated along with other men from the parish who fell during the Great War. The memorial was unveiled in 1923 by another celebrated member of the family, Lieutenant Colonel William Hew Clark-Kennedy VC CMG

DSO and Bar. He won his VC on 27 and 28 August 1918 whilst commanding the 24th Battalion, Canadian Infantry, near Wancourt, leading his men against a series of machine-gun positions that were holding up the advance. He was also awarded the *Croix de Guerre* (France). He returned to Scotland from his home in Canada in order to unveil the memorial. The memorial has since been inscribed with the names of men from the parish who fell in the Second World War. (Plot VII.D.20)

There are casualties here from the early days of September 1918 belonging to battalions of the Royal Naval Volunteer Reserve that made up much of the 63rd (Royal Naval) Division. Of the twenty-two officers and other ranks buried here, seventeen of them fell between 1 and 4 September 1918. One of the officers, Sub Lieutenant Edward George Cummings UNWIN, had served in the ranks with the division at Galipoli in 1915 and only received his commission as an officer in early October 1917. He was killed in action on 3 September 1918, aged 22. He is shown in the CWGC register as serving with the Hood Battalion, though the authorized history of the 63rd (Royal Naval) Division shows him as one of six officers killed in action in the first week of September 1918 with the Hawke Battalion rather than Hood. (Plot VII.E.31)

A further twenty-two officers and men from the 1st Battalion, Royal Marine Light Infantry, can also be found here in Plots V, VI and VII. Most of these men fell between 2 and 5 September 1918, with just two whose dates of death are shown occurring towards the end of the month. Amongst them is Private Joseph William BRINDLEY DCM, 1st Royal Marine Light Infantry, who was just 20 years old when he was killed in action on 5 September 1918. His DCM was gazetted on 16 January 1919 and was awarded for operations on 25 August 1918 near Grévillers. When his detachment was held up by fire from a machine gun during the early stages of an attack, he went forward single-handed and captured the gun and its entire crew. The citation concludes that his gallantry and determination were an inspiration to all ranks (Special Memorial A.1). Another man from his battalion is Private Edwin FERRIDAY, Royal Marine Medical Unit, Royal Naval Division. He was killed on 27 September 1918. (Plot VII.F.27)

The youngest casualty here is Rifleman Thomas King SPEER of the Rifle Brigade. At the time of his death he was serving with the 28th Battalion, London Regiment (Artists' Rifles). This was one of several battalions of the London Regiment to receive men from disbanded battalions of the Rifle Brigade in 1918. His parents lived in Texas, USA and, although he is now commemorated by a special memorial, he is known to have been buried close to that part of the cemetery. He was 17 years old when he died of wounds on 27 September 1918. (Plot VII.F.32)

Lieutenant Alfred Henry HISCOX, 208 Squadron, Royal Air Force, died of wounds on 28 September 1918. His wounds were incurred three weeks earlier on 6 September whilst flying a Camel aircraft. The fact that he is buried here suggests that he may have died as a German prisoner of war. Had he landed behind our own lines, he would surely have been buried further to the west of this location, perhaps even at one of the hospitals near the coast, particularly given the gap between the date he was wounded and the date of his death. (Plot VII.G.13)

There is just one casualty from 1919. Sapper J. CARBERRY, 4th Light Railway Company, Royal Engineers, died on 18 April 1919. I can find no trace of him in *Soldiers Died in the Great War*. (Plot VII.H.28)

Lieutenant Harvey Gerald Burns DRUMMOND, MC, 1st Scots Guards, was killed in action on 3 September 1918, aged 20. He was the son of the late Major A.S. Drummond, Scots Guards. His MC, gazetted on 2 December 1918, was awarded for conspicuous gallantry after his company commander was wounded in an attack. He took charge of the company and, in spite of a heavy mist, succeeded in reaching the final objective where he was untiring in his efforts to reorganize and consolidate the position while under heavy shell fire. The citation also records that not only did he set a fine example, he was also largely instrumental in the capture of two machine guns and their teams. (Plot VIII.E.20)

An early 1918 casualty was Company Serjeant Major Robert McKay MITCHELL DCM, 6th Black Watch, who was killed in action on 20 January 1918. His DCM was gazetted posthumously on 17 April 1918 and, although it refers to conspicuous gallantry and devotion to duty, the citation makes it clear that it was not connected to any specific incident or act of gallantry, but to a course of conduct over a period of time, commenting that his courage, cheerfulness, and powers of leadership, often under the most trying conditions, had always set a splendid example to all ranks. (Plot VIII.F.33)

Second Lieutenant Milton George CRUISE, 213 Squadron, Royal Air Force, was killed in action on 20 September 1918, aged 23, flying a Sopwith Camel. He was a Canadian by birth and enlisted in December 1915. (Plot VIII.G.22)

As well as the one casualty from 1915, there are also six casualties from 1916. One of them, Second Lieutenant Joseph Eric RUSSELL, 7th Queen's (Royal West Surrey Regiment) is shown in *Officers died in the Great War* as having been killed in action on 23 November 1916, aged 23 (Plot VIII.D.5). Next to him is a private from the 7th Queen's Own (Royal West Kent Regiment) who died the previous day. The battalion war diary points out that Second Lieutenant RUSSELL was one of three officers missing in action during operations on 18 and 19 November to capture Desire Trench. The casualty figures show just ten other ranks killed in action over the two days, with a further seventy-five wounded, but a staggering 172 men missing. Second Lieutenant RUSSELL and Private Ernest Michael BARNES would probably have died as prisoners, presumably as a result of wounds received during that period.

The remaining four men are to be found in Plot VIII, Rows D and F. One is a lance corporal from the 2nd Suffolk Regiment and the other three are privates from the 2nd King's Own Yorkshire Light Infantry, the 10th Royal Welsh Fusiliers, and the 10th Cheshire Regiment. They would also have died in German captivity, almost certainly as a result of wounds.

Finally, the cemetery contains thirty-eight men who held the MM. This is too great a number to list here and reference has already been made to a few of them. However, there are still a few worth noting, including three not already mentioned who also won a bar.

Private Archibald LAW, MM and Bar, 102nd Battalion, Canadian Infantry, was killed in action on 25th October 1918. (Plot I.A.23)

Sergeant Albert Pole MM and Bar, 4th Royal Scots, was killed in action on 21 September 1918, aged just 20. *Soldiers Died in the Great War* shows his surname as 'Poole'. (Plot VII.C.40)

Corporal Albert BURLEY MM and Bar, 1st King's Royal Rifle Corps, was killed in action on 10 September 1918. *Soldiers Died in the Great War* only shows the award of the MM against his name. (Plot VIII.D.18)

Private Thomas HAXTON MM, 7th Battalion, Canadian Infantry, is one of several men who were killed outright on 6 October 1918 when a German high explosive shell scored a direct hit on a hut near Écluse where they were billeted (VII.G.34). Eight other men killed in that incident are buried here with him in Plot VII, Rows G and H. They are Privates SWAIN, FRAZER, McLEOD, HANLON, COWARD and HOWE in Row G, whilst the remaining two, Corporal ENDACOTT and Private MATHESON, are in Row H (Plots VII.H.32 and 34). Private HAXTON is one of six Canadians here with the MM. There are also seven Australian soldiers buried here with the MM.

Quebec Cemetery, Chérisy

The cemetery lies roughly half a mile down a farm track that runs south from the D.9 approximately half way between Chérisy and Vis-en-Artois. The track is suitable for vehicles, especially in dry weather. The cemetery has 195 burials, twelve of which are unidentified. The CWGC register points out that Chérisy was captured by the 18th (Eastern) Division on 3 May 1917, but was lost later that night. The village then remained in German hands until it was captured the following year by the Canadian 2nd Division on 27 August. The line reached by the Canadian 2nd Division on 27 August ran more or less where the cemetery now stands. The earliest burials are from 26 August 1918, though there are only two of them.

As the name suggests, this is another cemetery that is overwhelmingly Canadian in character. It takes its name from the Province of Quebec on account of the fact that almost half of the 189 Canadians buried here come from just two battalions of the Quebec Regiment: the 22nd Battalion, Canadian Infantry (French Canadians) and the 24th Battalion, Canadian Infantry (Montreal). Both battalions were part of the Canadian 2nd Division, which on 27 and 28 August 1918 attacked south of the Arras–Cambrai road. Some progress was made towards the Fresnes–Rouvroy Line, but a combination of uncut wire and heavy machine-gun fire from the direction of Upton Wood caused the advance to falter towards the end of the first day. The Canadians then dug in overnight between Sun Quarry and Vis-en-Artois.

The following day the same units renewed their attack, whilst the Canadian 3rd Division did likewise north of the Arras–Cambrai road. However, the attack soon came to a halt, this time mainly on account of depleted numbers, though uncut wire and determined heavy fire from the German defences were still an important factor. The heavy casualties on both days are reflected within the walls of this cemetery.

There is just one officer amongst the sixty-one men of the 22nd Battalion who now lie here. Lieutenant Louis Stanislas VIEN, the son of a prominent Canadian lawyer and politician, was killed in action on 27 August (Plot C.6). Another officer from the

22nd Battalion, Lieutenant Louis Rodolphe Lemieux MC, was wounded that day, but he died two days later and is buried at Ligny-St Flochel British Cemetery. He too was the son of a Canadian politician, the Honourable Rodolphe Lemieux MP. Lieutenant Lemieux had also been awarded the *Légion d'Honneur* (France). The 22nd Battalion's war diary records that forty-three other ranks were killed in action over the two days, but also adds that a further thirty-five were missing in action with many more wounded. Buried here amongst the battalion's dead are seven men who were recipients of the MM. Two of them also gained a bar to the original medal. Private Emery LAMBERT MM and Bar, was born in Maine, USA. He was killed in action on 27 August 1918, aged 20 (Plot B.26). Private Hormidas HAYENS MM and Bar, was killed in action the following day, aged 45. (Plot C.15)

The 24th Battalion casualties include one holder of the MM, Private François PELLETIER (Plot D.18), and three officers, two of whom won the MC. Captain Philip Ilderton WALKER MC, 24th Battalion, Canadian Infantry, was killed in action on 28 August 1918 and came originally from Newcastle-on-Tyne, though he was educated in Montreal. His MC was gazetted on 16th September 1918, soon after his death. It was awarded in recognition of his quick thinking and organizational abilities when a trench held by his company was obliterated by shell fire. He skilfully repositioned his men so as to reduce casualties, but still retain control of his front. When the enemy did attack his position, he personally directed the firing of a Lewis gun and the rifle fire of his company with such devastating effect that the attack was completely broken up and very heavy casualties were inflicted on the enemy. The citation refers to his conspicuous gallantry and coolness. (Plot B.29)

The other two officers of the battalion are Lieutenant John Cecil SHIPWAY (Plot C.11) and Lieutenant Percival George TUCKER MC (Plot C.25). TUCKER's MC was gazetted on 11 January 1919 and was awarded for conspicuous gallantry and devotion to duty in an attack. In spite of heavy fire, he pressed forward with his platoon and reached his objective well ahead of his battalion. Still under fire, he immediately consolidated his position and established communication with the units on his flanks.

Private John Bryan RYALS, 24th Battalion, Canadian Infantry, was killed in action on 28 August 1918, aged 24. The CWGC register gives quite a detailed account of the educational establishments that he attended, including the Gordon Institute in Barnesville which was founded by John Brown Gordon, one of Lee's generals during the American Civil War. In 1890 the institute set up a department of military studies. When he left there, Private RYALS went on to study at Vanderbilt University in Nashville, Tennessee, and then Columbia University in New York. He began his military service in March 1917 and was killed in action between Chérisy and Upton Wood. (Plot B.23)

There are smaller numbers from other battalions of the Canadian 2nd Division, particularly the four that made up the Canadian 4th Brigade, namely, the 18th, 19th, 20th and 21st Battalions, including two officers. Lieutenant John Clamson SPENCE, 18th Battalion, Canadian Infantry, was killed by a sniper, aged 31, somewhere between Guémappe and Chérisy (Plot A.47). Lieutenant Sydney Baker COOPER

MM, 19th Battalion, Canadian Infantry, won his MM serving in the ranks of the battalion (Plot A.14). Both men were killed in action on 27 August 1918.

During the fighting on 27 and 28 August both sides relied heavily on the firepower of their machine guns. The Canadian machine gunners were heavily involved on both days when thirty-seven of them were killed outright. The majority of those killed were from the 2nd and 4th Battalions, Canadian Machine Gun Corps. Thirteen officers and men belonging to these two battalions are buried in this cemetery.

Captain Frank Llewellyn MUCH MC, 'C' Battery, 2nd Battalion, Canadian Machine Gun Corps, had enlisted in Montreal in September 1915, though he was born in Brecon, South Wales. He had taken part in fighting at Passchendaele in 1917 and also at Amiens on 8 and 9 August 1918. On 26 August 1918 the German defence relied heavily on its machine gunners. Consequently, Captain MUCH and his men were extremely busy that day taking on machine-gun nests that were holding up, or likely to hold up, the infantry attacks.

On one such occasion Captain MUCH carried out a personal reconnaissance of some ground that had been made impassable for the infantry owing to the siting of a group of German machine-gun positions. Having taken stock of the situation, he skilfully moved two of his own guns to more favourable positions and got them into action. The unexpected fire, not only from the front, but also on both flanks, threw the German gunners into confusion and several of the crews attempted to make a run for it, but were cut down by the Canadians' fire. Sadly, two days later, and after much fine work of a similar nature, Captain MUCH was wounded and died that same day, 28 August.

His MC was awarded for his gallantry and dedicated work during the fighting on and around 8 August near Amiens, but particularly for his skill and courage on 26 August. When heavy casualties had occurred amongst the infantry during an enemy counter-attack, he personally brought up four of his guns to fill a gap in the line under heavy fire. The enemy's fire was so intense that all his NCOs and two of his gun crews were soon killed or wounded, and he was also severely wounded. However, the enemy's advance was checked, thanks to his valuable contribution, gallantry and disregard of danger. The citation concludes that throughout the entire operations that month he had set a splendid example to his men. The award was gazetted posthumously on 5 October 1918 and the citation for it appeared on 11 January 1919. He was 38 years old when he died and left behind a widow and two children. The CWGC record incorrectly shows his initials as 'F.E.' but notes that his father had attained the rank of lieutenant colonel. (Plot D.19)

On the same day that Captain MUCH was killed, two other officers from his battalion also lost their lives. Lieutenant Clifford Weldon TRAVIS, 2nd Battalion, Canadian Machine Gun Corps (Plot D.14) and Lieutenant James Gordon BOLE (Plot D.25) were killed in action on 28 August 1918. Lieutenant BOLE was born in Moose Jaw, Saskatchewan, but enlisted in Toronto in November 1914 where he was then living and studying Law. Prior to that he had been an active member of the local militia, the Queen's Own Rifles. On 28 August 1918 the village of Cagnicourt was heavily defended, and so each Canadian machine-gun battery sent four of its eight guns forward with the infantry attack to offer close support. The attack started well enough, but was soon held up by German machine-gun positions around Upton Wood and a location next to it known as Sable Pit. The ensuing battle between the machine gunners of both sides was extremely fierce and the 2nd Battalion, Canadian Machine Gun Corps, sustained eight officer casualties that day in addition to further losses amongst the other ranks, several of whom are buried within this cemetery.

The latest burials here are from 9 and 10 of September 1918 and consist of one officer and four men of the 49th Battalion, Canadian Infantry, who are all buried next to each other (Plots E.1 to 5). There is also a group of three officers from the 87th Battalion, Canadian Infantry, buried next to each other who were killed in action on 2 and 3 September 1918 during the attacks on and around the Drocourt–Quéant Line.

Lieutenant Albert LLOYD MC, 87th Battalion, Canadian Infantry, died on 3 September, aged 24. His MC was gazetted on 7 March 1918 and was awarded for his coolness and organizational ability. The day prior to an attack he had rendered valuable service in organizing supplies and arranging dumps. On the day of the actual attack he went forward to make a reconnaissance. On seeing a section of men about to be cut off by the enemy, he organized a party to provide covering fire, enabling the men to get back to our line safely. The citation also notes that during the attack, when all the officers in his vicinity had become casualties, he took command of the situation and held the line against several enemy counter-attacks.

Early on 3 September, Royal Air Force patrols reported that the Germans appeared to be evacuating Saudemont and Écourt-Saint-Quentin. The 87th Battalion, Canadian Infantry, sent out patrols which were able to confirm this, and then advanced to take up the ground vacated by the enemy. However, the German withdrawal allowed its artillery to put down a heavy bombardment on both villages and it was during this barrage that Lieutenant LLOYD was killed by a shell near Saudemont (Plot A.37). On either side of him are Lieutenant Gerald Saunders FOGARTY and Lieutenant Leonard Francis TASKER, both of whom were killed in action on 2 September. (Plots A.36 and A.38)

Another son of a Canadian politician is also buried in this cemetery. Lieutenant Roger Morrow PORTER, 2nd Battalion, Canadian Infantry, was killed in action on 30 August 1918, aged 20. His father was Edward Guss Porter KC MP. (Plot B.49)

Several of the holders of the MM buried here have already been mentioned; those that have not are as listed below:

Sergeant Harold Baker AULT MM, 3rd Battalion, Canadian Infantry, killed in action on 27 August 1918, aged 20. (Plot A.23)

Private Georges BOUCHARD MM, 22nd Battalion, Canadian Infantry, killed in action on 27 August 1918, aged 23. (Plot C.21)

Corporal Hormisdas MORISSETTE MM, 22nd Battalion, Canadian infantry, killed in action on 28 August 1918, aged 21. (Plot C.34)

Lance Corporal Joseph LABRIE MM, 22nd Battalion, Canadian Infantry, killed in action on 27 August 1918, aged 20. (Plot C.44)

Lance Corporal Charles DUAL MM, 22nd Battalion, Canadian Infantry, killed in action on 28 August 1918, aged 24. (Plot D.4)

Private Wilfrid GRIMARD MM, 22nd Battalion, Canadian Infantry, killed in action on 27 August 1918. (Plot D.44)

The cemetery contains just four British soldiers. They are all NCOs or privates who fell on dates between the end of August and early September 1918. This small contingent consists of one artilleryman and three infantrymen belonging to the 52nd (Lowland) Division and the 57th (2nd West Lancashire) Division.

Riencourt-lès-Cagnicourt Communal Cemetery

Riencourt-lès-Cagnicourt is situated about ten miles south-east of Arras on the D.13 where it meets the D.38. The cemetery can be found on the north-east side of the village on the D.13 as it heads towards Cagnicourt.

There is just one burial here: Pilot Officer Frederick William RATFORD, 253 Squadron, Royal Air Force. His Hurricane Mark 1 was shot down by a ME 109 on 19 May 1940 just south of Arras.

Sun Quarry Cemetery, Chérisy

The cemetery is located on the D.38 about a mile south-east of the village of Chérisy. The CWGC register points out that the name of the cemetery is derived from a flint quarry that was known to the troops as Sun Quarry. It has 191 burials, only seven of which are unidentified. It was made after the September fighting here by Canadian units.

The majority of burials are from infantry battalions belonging to the Canadian 2nd Division, notably the 22nd Battalion and the 24th Battalion, both from Quebec; the 26th Battalion from New Brunswick; the 29th Battalion from British Columbia and the 31st Battalion from Alberta. The majority of them were killed in action during the final days of August 1918 attacking a series of trenches in front of Upton Wood and the village of Hendecourt-lès-Cagnicourt, though in the case of the 29th Battalion, its men were killed in early September attacking the Drocourt–Quéant Line.

For a relatively small cemetery there is a wealth of variety contained within its walls, including a wide diversity of non-infantry arms. In addition to Canadian infantry there are thirteen men from the Canadian Machine Gun Corps, mainly from the 2nd Battalion attached to the Canadian 2nd Division. There are also burials from the Canadian Field and Garrison Artillery, Canadian Engineers, Works and Signalling Companies, and a private from the 2nd Canadian Field Ambulance. Further diversity can be found among the small contingent of British soldiers here.

Lance Sergeant Robert Henry JACKSON DCM, 3rd Battalion, Canadian Infantry, was killed in action on 30 August 1918. He was hit and killed instantly by machine-gun fire whilst advancing east of Chérisy. He was a native of County Monaghan in Ireland, though he was living and working in Toronto when he enlisted. His DCM was gazetted on 15 November 1918 and was won after his platoon officer and sergeant had both been killed attacking a machine-gun nest. He then took command and re-organized the men, cleverly manoeuvring them and capturing the position, which consisted of two guns and eighteen men. He then led his platoon to its final objective, saving casualties by his skilful handling of the situation. The citation concludes that he set a splendid example to his men. (Plot A.24)

Private John Samuel NICHOLSON MM, 26th Battalion, Canadian Infantry, was killed in action on 28 August 1918. His MM was won in connection with operations a few weeks earlier on 8 August, when his company was held up under heavy fire. NICHOLSON rushed his Lewis gun up to one of the flanks and put down fire onto the strongpoint that was responsible, causing it to cease firing. He then rushed the post, capturing the gun and dispersing its crew. By this action and throughout the advance that day, he proved to be of great assistance to his platoon commander. Canadian army records show that he was 19 years old when he was killed and that he enlisted at the age of 16. His profession is recorded as school teacher, which seems at odds with his age. He may have been an assistant teacher which was not unusual in rural areas at that time. (Plot B.10)

Sergeant Edward Albert V. PALMER MM, 26th Battalion, Canadian Infantry, was killed in action on 28 August 1918. He was born in Bermondsey, London, and was 25 years old when he died. He was also one of four men from the 26th Battalion who were awarded a *Croix de Guerre* (Belgium) on 10 December 1917 in connection with fighting during the latter stages of the Third Battle of Ypres. (Plot C.24)

Private Harold PAYNE, 2nd Battalion, Canadian Infantry, is also an interesting case, but not unique. Back in Canada he became an Anglican minister after graduating from Huron College in 1916 with High Honours in Divinity and Arts. However, soon after that he decided that his calling was to fight rather than to serve as an army chaplain or in some other non-combatant role. He was killed in action on 30 August 1918. (Plot D.2)

Lance Corporal Garth Leland MILLER MM, 26th Battalion, Canadian Infantry, was killed in action on 28 August 1918. His MM was also won on the opening day of the advance on 8 August 1918 near Amiens. When both his platoon commander and sergeant became casualties, he led the men forward to their objective under intense rifle and machine-gun fire. He was 21 years of age when he died. (Plot D.10)

Other Canadian recipients of the MM are: Private Edward JONES MM, 15th Battalion, Canadian Infantry, killed in action on 30 August 1918 (Plot A.5); Corporal Frederic C. MANSFIELD, MM, 3rd Battalion, Canadian Infantry, killed in action on 30 August 1918 (Plot B.2); and Private Daniel Vincent McDONALD MM, 26th Battalion, Canadian Infantry, killed in action on 28 August 1918 (Plot C.23).

One or two other graves that may be of interest are also buried in Row C. Captain James Lloyd EVANS, 5th Battalion, Canadian Infantry, had previously served during the South African campaign. He was killed in action on 1 September 1918, aged 39, by a machine-gun bullet at the start of an attack near Hendecourt-lès-Cagnicourt (Plot C.1). Captain George Allan McGIFFIN, 24th Battalion, Canadian Infantry, who was killed in action on 27 August 1918, had previously been wounded on the Somme at Courcelette in 1916. (Plot C.15)

There are some British burials here too, thirty-one in all. Amongst them are six officers belonging to, or attached to the 57th Battalion, Machine Gun Corps, 57th (2nd West

Lancashire) Division, who were killed on 6 September 1918. (Plots E.15-E.20) There is also a solitary officer from the Royal Air Force, Lieutenant John Jack MOLLISON, 208 Squadron, Royal Air Force, killed in action whilst flying on 27 August 1918, aged 20 (Plot C.11), and Private John LECKIE, 14th Battalion, Tank Corps, killed in action on 2 September 1918. These casualties serve to further illustrate the 'all arms' nature of this battlefield cemetery. In fact, of the thirty-one British soldiers buried here, only two are infantrymen, though according to the CWGC register there are four. However, Lieutenant Frederick John STANDRING, 8th Royal Scots, and Lieutenant Andrew Abercromby GARDNER, 6th Argyll & Sutherland Highlanders, were both attached to the 57th Battalion, Machine Gun Corps, when they were killed in action on 6 September 1918 (Plots E.17 and E.18). The majority of the British burials are gunners.

Lieutenant MOLLISON's brother, Lieutenant William Allan Mollison, was also killed during the war. He had originally enlisted in the 9th (Glasgow Highlanders) Highland Light Infantry, but went on to serve with the 2/6th Duke of Wellington's Regiment. He was invalided back home on two occasions after contracting rheumatic fever. He did, however, return to the front and was attached to the 52nd Company, Machine Gun Corps when he died. His unit was about to be relieved from the front line on 13 September 1918 when a shell burst and William was injured in several places by fragments. He was hospitalized and appeared to be making a recovery when septicaemia set in and he died on 1 October 1918. He is now buried at Terlincthun British Cemetery. The machine gun unit to which he was attached may have been the 52nd Battalion rather than the 52nd Company as shown in the CWGC records. (Plot C.11)

Captain George Charles TAYLOR, Royal Army Veterinary Corps, attached 26 Brigade, Royal Field Artillery, died of wounds on 6 September 1918, aged 24. He had graduated in London in early July 1916. He is one of thirty-three members of the Royal Veterinary College recorded as having been killed or having died of wounds during the Great War, though many more died during the conflict as a result of illness, disease or natural causes. He is one of only two officers from the Royal Army Veterinary Corps buried in the Arras area. He died of gunshot wounds to the back. (Plot F.2)

Captain Cyril Warner WEEKES MC, Royal Field Artillery, was killed in action on 16 August 1918, shortly after his MC was gazetted on 3 June 1918 in the King's Birthday Honours List. It was awarded for distinguished service in connection with military operations in France and Flanders rather than any particular act of gallantry. He had been a member of the University of London's OTC. WEEKES is one of several officers and men buried here from the Royal Field Artillery and the Royal Garrison Artillery who were killed or who died of wounds in September 1918. (Plot G.6)

Upton Wood Cemetery, Hendecourt-lès-Cagnicourt

The cemetery contains 226 casualties, most of whom are Canadian infantrymen; 218 of them are identified and there is one special memorial to a man known to be buried in the cemetery. It derives its name from the wood next to it, though it is known locally as Bois d'Hendecourt. The nearest village is Hendecourt-lès-Cagnicourt, which is about ten miles south-east of Arras and about one mile south of the wood and its cemetery. Heading north-east from the village along the D.956, the cemetery is clearly visible in the fields over to the left with the wood behind it. The village fell to the 57th (2nd West Lancashire) Division and the 52nd (Lowland) Division on the night of 1/2 September 1918, just hours prior to the attack on the Drocourt–Quéant Line.

Upton Wood was situated 1,500 yards west of the Drocourt–Quéant Line and was a key part its forward defences. The capture of the wood and the ground just to the east of it was vital to the Canadian Corps in order to secure suitable jumping off positions closer to the main German lines, which were the last significant defences west of the Canal du Nord in front of Cambrai. For their part, the Germans defended the approaches to the Drocourt–Quéant Line with energy and determination, even counter-attacking through Upton Wood on 31 August and 1 September, only to be driven out again.

The Germans had used wooded areas extremely well in the past, particularly on the Somme in 1916. South of Upton Wood they also occupied the small copse known as the 'Crow's Nest'. As long as the Germans held these two locations the Canadian 1st Division would be denied access to good jumping off positions for the main attack on 2 September. At 4.40am on 30 August 1918 the 1st, 2nd and 3rd Battalions, Canadian Infantry, attacked the enemy's trenches and positions around Upton Wood, which were heavily defended by German machine gunners. The following day the 8th Battalion, Canadian Infantry, made further small gains in the face of heavy counter-attacks.

The cemetery here contains fifty-one dead belonging to the 1st Battalion, Canadian Infantry. These men were killed on 30th August 1918 as they attacked from the direction of Sun Quarry towards Upton Wood and the village of Hendecourt-lès-Cagnicourt. The 2nd Battalion also has fifteen of its men buried here from 30 and 31 August. By contrast, the 3rd Battalion has very few burials, but it did remove thirty-one of its men from the battlefield for burial at Valley Cemetery not far from here.

Private Lazarus CONSTANT, 2nd Battalion, Canadian Infantry, was killed in action on 30 September 1918, aged 22. He came from the Pas Agency, which was part of the Cree Nation, although his surname disguises the fact that he was of Native American descent. (Plot A.6)

There are two Canadian officers with gallantry awards buried here. The first of them is Lieutenant David MILNE MC, 10th Battalion, Canadian Infantry, who died of wounds on 2 September 1918, aged 30. The actions for which he received the award occurred near Villers-lès-Cagnicourt on the same day that he was killed. His MC was awarded for his marked display of courage and devotion to duty and for leading his men with great skill. Throughout the day he made several daring reconnaissance patrols under very heavy fire, returning on each occasion with valuable information. He also led his men skilfully and with dash, beating down all opposition before them. It was during the final assault on the sunken road to the east of Villers-lès-Cagnicourt that he received the wounds from which he later died. Although the sunken road was an enemy strongpoint, it was captured under his dash and leadership. His MC was gazetted on 18 February 1919, but the citation did not appear until 1 August that year. (Plot A.29)

Private Herbert Pollexfen ROBINSON, 7th Battalion, Canadian Infantry, is buried next to Lieutenant MILNE and was killed in action on the same day, aged 41. The CWGC register notes that his widow lived in Los Angeles, California. His attestation papers show his occupation as rancher and that he was 41 years old when he enlisted. The papers also indicate that he had previously served with the Manchester Regiment and the Royal Irish Fusiliers between 1884 and 1902 and that he was born in Burma. The CWGC register points out that his late father was Colonel Barnes Slyfield Robinson, whose first reference in the *London Gazette* was as an ensign without purchase in the 89th Regiment of Foot in December 1852. That regiment merged with the 87th Regiment of Foot in 1881 to become the Royal Irish Fusiliers. On 21 May 1884 Lieutenant Colonel Robinson, Royal Irish Fusiliers, was made a Commander of the Order of the Bath (CB). (Plot A.30)

Corporal Allan Brander ANGUS DCM, 5th Battalion, Canadian Infantry, was killed in action on 1 September 1918. His DCM was won as a battalion stretcher-bearer. The citation notes that he had remained in no man's land for a period of three days attending to the wounded at great personal risk to himself. After thirty-six hours on duty, when he learned that there was still a wounded man in no man's land, he took a stretcher party through heavy fire and brought the man in. He is one of forty-eight men buried here from the 5th Battalion, Canadian Infantry, who were killed or were mortally wounded on 1 September 1918. (Plot A.36)

The commanding officer of 'D' Company, 1st Battalion, Canadian Infantry, Captain Adam Miller WILLIAMSON, is buried here. Early on the morning of 30 August 1918 he had led his company forward near Upton Wood, but by late morning he found himself in command of his battalion's entire front line position. As he was reorganizing his men the Germans counter-attacked, whereupon he and the rest of his battalion also counter-attacked and fierce fighting took place. Later that day Captain WILLIAMSON was killed by a shell as he was making his way back to Battalion HQ. His runner had been taken to make up a Lewis gun team and he had set out alone, which is possibly why his body was not discovered until the following day. (Plot B.15)

Private James Wellington JOHNSON, 1st Battalion, Canadian Infantry, was killed in action on 30 August 1918, aged 23. The CWGC register notes that he was a native of the Six Nations Reserve, Ontario. As the name suggests, this was a Native American Reserve, though Canadian records do not identify him as a Native American (Plot B.27). Another member of the Six Nations Reserve is also buried here. Private Jacob ISAAC, who served with the 1st Battalion, was killed in action on 30 August, though in his case Canadian records confirm that he was a Native American soldier. (Plot A.2)

Private Tokutoro IWAMOTO MM, 10th Battalion, Canadian Infantry, was killed in action on 2 September, aged 38. He was an only son whose father still lived in Kobe, Japan. He was one of a number of Japanese, or soldiers of Japanese parentage, who served with the Canadian Expeditionary Force during the Great War. His MM was won at Hill 70 near Loos on 15 and 16 August 1917 where he displayed great keenness and fearlessness, accounting for many of the enemy. On 16 August he mopped up several dug-outs in the Chalk Pit single-handedly, capturing around twenty prisoners. (Plot D.24)

Lieutenant George Percival St John BELFORD, 1st Battalion, Canadian Infantry, was killed in action on 30 August 1918, aged 21. The CWGC register shows his father as Major James Franklin Beatty Belford, but makes no reference to his war service. Major Belford was an Anglican minister who enlisted in August 1917 and served as a Canadian Army Chaplain. At some stage he returned to Canada where he raised a forestry battalion before returning with it to France. George's two brothers, Lieutenant Franklin Robert William Beatty Belford and Lieutenant James Henry Belford, served with the 87th Battalion, Canadian Infantry, and survived the war, though both were seriously wounded. Although Franklin survived the war, he died at the relatively young age of 43. (Plot D.33)

Captain Charles Bryan ROBINSON MC, 7th Battalion, Canadian Infantry, was killed in action on 2 September 1918. His MC was gazetted on 22 October 1917, but the accompanying citation did not appear until 11 March the following year. It was awarded for conspicuous gallantry and devotion to duty as a lieutenant after he had taken command of his company at a critical time when all the other officers had become casualties. Casualties amongst the NCOs and other ranks were also high, but his personal courage and ability enabled those remaining with him to hold on to a difficult position throughout the day until relieved later that night, in spite of heavy artillery and machine-gun fire. (Plot E.40)

Private Louis WHITE, 5th Battalion, Canadian Infantry, was killed in action close to this cemetery on 1 September 1918. Although the surname under which he served gives nothing away, he was a Native American from the Sweetgrass Reserve where his tribal name was Louis White Cloud. (Plot F.8)

Lance Sergeant David HAMPTON MM, 10th Battalion, Canadian Infantry, was killed in action on 2nd September 1918. His MM was won at Hill 70 on 15 August 1917 whilst in charge of a Lewis gun team. When another Lewis gun team lost its NCO and ran out of ammunition, he arranged for ammunition to be brought up to it and then got the gun back into action. He also carried out a very daring reconnaissance of ground in front of his battalion's most forward position and later led two platoons up to it after dark. (Plot F.12)

A number of other men buried here who also held the MM are listed below.

Private Edward WILMOT MM, 5th Battalion, Canadian Infantry, killed in action on 1 September 1918, aged 25. (Plot A.9)

Private Frank SWAN MM, 11th Battalion, Canadian Infantry, killed in action on 1 September 1918, aged 21. (Plot A.12)

Private Ernest George ALLWOOD MM, 7th Battalion, Canadian Infantry, killed in action on 2 September 1918, aged 34. (Plot A.23)

Sergeant Herbert Laughlin GOUGEON MM, was reported to have been killed instantly by a bullet near Upton Wood on 30 August 1918. His MM was gazetted on 13 March 1918. (Plot B.14)

Lance Sergeant John BRIGHT MM, 1st Battalion, Canadian Infantry, killed in action on 30 August 1918. (Plot D.7)

Sergeant Thomas Melville KILPATRICK MM, 4th Battalion, Canadian Infantry, killed in action on 31 August 1918, aged 24. (Plot E.1)

Lance Corporal Robert SMITH MM, 10th Battalion, Canadian Infantry, killed in action on 2 September 1918. (Plot E.14)

Sergeant Frederick William BARNES MM, 'C' Company, 8th Battalion, Canadian Infantry, killed in action on 31 August 1918, aged 22. (Plot E.31)

Private William Leslie WRIGHT MM, 10th Battalion, Canadian Infantry, killed in action on 2 September 1918. (Plot F.11)

There are very few burials from British units. They consist of just one man from the Royal Field Artillery, killed on 19 September 1918 (Plot F.30); four privates from the Royal Munster Fusiliers, all of whom were killed in action on 2 September 1918; three men from the Army Service Corps who fell on 28 September 1918 (Plot F.32 and 34); and a private from the 2/4th South Lancashire Regiment, killed on 2 September 1918 (Plot E.22). Two of the Royal Munster Fusiliers are buried next to this last casualty (Plot E.23 and 24), the other two in the next row (Plot F.21 and 22).

Valley Cemetery, Vis-En-Artois

The isolation of this small battlefield cemetery, with its single tree and surrounded by fields, gives it an air of tranquillity surpassed by few cemeteries on the Western Front. It lies south of the D.9 approximately half way between the villages of Chérisy and Vis-en-Artois. It is reached via a small track that runs south from the D.9 and which crosses a brook, otherwise known as the River Sensée. Looking north-east from the cemetery, the top of the Vis-en-Artois Memorial is just about visible on the horizon above the buildings and trees in the village of Haucourt.

Exhausted after its efforts during the previous two days, the Canadian 2nd Division was relieved by the Canadian 1st Division on the night of the 28/29 August 1918. The 1st Division's objective was the Fresnes–Rouvroy Line and the Vis-en-Artois Switch. Little happened on the 29th, but at 4.00am on the 30th the division began its attack. The 1st and 2nd Battalions went forward from their positions near Sun Quarry towards the German trenches and strongpoints around Hendecourt-lès-Cagnicourt. The 1st Battalion, Canadian Infantry, captured Upton Wood, whilst the 3rd Battalion made its assault just south of the village of Haucourt, where the Fresnes–Rouvroy Line joined the Vis-en-Artois Switch. Here it was able to link up with the 2nd Battalion. The Germans put up fierce resistance and made several attempts to retake lost positions by counter-attacking, though each attack was eventually driven back by the Canadians. However, in the face of stiff opposition that day, the 3rd Battalion was unable to capture all its objectives. A number of enemy trenches managed to hold out, including Opera Trench and a strongpoint to the south-east of Vis-en-Artois, known as the 'Ocean Work', but these fell the following day, 31 August.

The cemetery was begun by the 3rd Battalion, Canadian Infantry, in early September 1918 following the fighting around Upton Wood, and in particular the capture of Orix Trench on 31 August 1918. Orix Trench was part of the Vis-en-Artois Switch, a defensive line that ran about 1,200 yards east of this cemetery and about the same distance from the eastern edge of Upton Wood and parallel to it. The CWGC register notes that the battalion brought back thirty-one of its officers and men to this location. All thirty-one share the same grave reference (Plot A.10), indicating that they were buried in one large grave, along with another Canadian soldier belonging to the 19th Battalion. Another six Canadian soldiers are buried here whose graves were brought in from the surrounding battlefield in September 1918. They too are buried in Row A.

There are a number of gallantry awards and a few British and Australian burials from 1916. There are also four men of the Royal Field Artillery killed in action on 1 and 2 September 1918. The CWGC register gives an insight into the work that was being carried out between 1924 and 1925, referring specifically to the closure of Thilloy German Cemetery south of Bapaume. Four Australian and three British soldiers were taken from that cemetery and reburied here at around the same time as a number of isolated graves were also brought in. These additional graves now form Rows B and C. It was around this period that many of the cemetery concentrations took place. The cemetery now has sixty-nine burials in total, nineteen of which are unidentified.

Captain Norman Victor CLIFF MC and Bar, is one of the 3rd Battalion casualties killed in action on 30 August and is the highest ranking officer buried here (Plot A.10). His MC was gazetted in the King's Birthday Honours List on 3 June 1918 and was awarded for services in the field. However, the bar to it, gazetted on 2 December 1918, was awarded for conspicuous gallantry and leadership after he had led his company in an attack to its final objective. He then took it forward a further 1,000 yards in order to secure some high ground that overlooked the position. The following day he established a line of outposts and pushed out patrols, capturing a machine gun and eighteen prisoners.

The CWGC register notes that he had enlisted in August 1914 and had served on the Western Front since February 1915. It also notes that he was wounded in 1917, though, if that were the case, it is not mentioned in the battalion's war diary. However, he was wounded by shrapnel in May 1915 at the Orchard, near Festubert, whilst serving as a private with a machine-gun detachment. The wound to his hip was sufficiently serious to cause him to be discharged from military service and he returned to Canada, albeit temporarily. Back in Toronto he was understandably welcomed as a war hero. He had also taken part in fighting during the Second Battle of Ypres, and while he was at home recuperating he gave an account of his experiences to the local newspaper.

After making a good recovery, he re-enlisted in September 1916 and was offered a commission, which he accepted. He went on to take part in operations at Passchendaele in early November 1917 and at Amiens on 8 August 1918, and is referred to on several occasions in the battalion's war diary. His brother, Lieutenant Harold Cliff, also served during the war with the artillery.

Lieutenant Edward SLATTERY DCM MM and 2 Bars, 3rd Battalion, Canadian Infantry, was also killed in action the same day (Plot A.10). His DCM was won as a sergeant for actions at Fresnoy where, according to the citation, he showed great dash and gallantry in leading his platoon to its objective. Through his personal supervision and gallantry, he and his platoon then repulsed several hostile counter-attacks. The citation concludes that his determination and devotion to duty set a splendid example to his men. The award was gazetted on 26 June 1917. His MM was gazetted on 9 December 1916 following fighting on the Somme in September and October. The bar to it was gazetted on 9 July 1917 and relates to the fighting in April at Vimy Ridge. The second bar was won in connection with the fighting at Passchendaele and was gazetted on 23 February 1918. He came from Newfoundland rather than Canada and was 23 years old when he was killed. Slattery's younger brother, Private Michael Slattery, who also held the MM, was killed in action on 14 August 1917. He is buried at Villers Station Cemetery and served with the 87th Battalion, Canadian Infantry.

Another man buried here who apparently lost a brother during the war is Private Arthur Christopher FISHER. Arthur lies here with his comrades from the 3rd Battalion after he was killed in action or died of wounds on 31 August 1918 (Plot A.10). Canadian army records do not specify the manner of his death. According to the CWGC register, his brother, Albert William Fisher, also died during the war, but there appears to be no trace of him in the CWGC records. I have also been unable to trace Albert in Canadian records.

Corporal Frederick MARSH DCM, 3rd Battalion, Canadian Infantry, won his DCM as a private. It was awarded for conspicuous gallantry and devotion to duty after an attack had become held up by heavy machine-gun fire from a strongpoint. He led his section around one of its flanks and bombed it before the occupants were even aware of his presence, killing everyone in it and capturing the gun. The citation concludes that his great courage and quick initiative were undoubtedly responsible for resolving a critical situation and that his behaviour on this occasion was in keeping with his gallant conduct throughout operations. The award was gazetted on 28 March 1918. (Plot A.10)

Two other members of the 3rd Battalion, Canadian Infantry, buried here in Plot A.10, also hold gallantry awards. They are: Company Sergeant Major George RODGER MM and Bar, 3rd Battalion, Canadian Infantry, killed in action on 30 August 1918, aged 26. He came from Cupar in Fife and had enlisted in 1915; and Private Charles DAVIS MM, 3rd Battalion, Canadian Infantry, killed in action on 31 August 1918, aged 29.

Sergeant Samuel NEWELL MM and Bar, 19th Battalion, Canadian Infantry, was another Newfoundlander who served with the Canadian Expeditionary Force. He fell on 27 August 1918, aged 25, whilst fighting with the Canadian 2nd Division. He was buried here with the men from the 3rd Battalion, Canadian Infantry, probably at or around the same time.

Though there are few British burials, there is one gallantry holder among them. Sergeant Alfred Aaron LANGFORD MM, 'C' Battery, 174 Brigade, Royal Field

Artillery, was killed in action on 1 September 1918, aged 26 (Plot A.5). Three other men of the Royal Field Artillery are buried in adjacent graves, all killed in action on 1 or 2 September 1918.

Private Arthur James MILSOM, 8th Royal Warwickshire Regiment, who died on 29 August 1916, is one of four British infantrymen buried here (Plot C.15). His brother, Private Henry John Milsom, was killed in action on 15 June 1917 whilst serving with the 10th Field Ambulance, Royal Army Medical Corps. He is buried at Level Crossing Cemetery, Fampoux. All four men would have died of wounds as prisoners of war. Their battalions: the 10th Cheshire Regiment, the 2nd Wiltshire Regiment, the 8th Royal Warwickshire Regiment and the 2nd Royal Berkshire Regiment, were all engaged on the Somme at the time of their deaths. They are the casualties who were brought here from Thilloy German Cemetery and are referred to in the CWGC register, though Private George Hugo DURANT's remains were never located when the bodies were exhumed. He is commemorated here by way of special memorial. Similarly, the four infantrymen from the Australian Imperial Force, who died on various dates during the latter half of 1916, would have died in German hands, almost certainly from wounds or injuries.

Villers-lès-Cagnicourt Communal Cemetery

The village of Villers-lès-Cagnicourt lies about twelve miles south-east of Arras and is situated just south of the D.939 Arras–Cambrai road. The cemetery is on the north side of the D.13, which runs through the village.

In late August 1918 it lay behind the Drocourt–Quéant Support Line and the Buissy Switch close to where these two defensive positions converged just south of the main road. On 2 September 1918 the Canadian 1st Division managed to penetrate as far as the Buissy Switch, where it dug in. The following day patrols were sent forward, but the Germans had already vacated the last part of their defensive positions around the Drocourt–Quéant Line and were withdrawing back to their next line of resistance, which was the Canal du Nord and the heights of Bourlon Wood.

There are just two British soldiers buried here: Warrant Officer Class II, Staff Sergeant Major Horace William Gilbert PARKER, 2nd Armoured Reconnaissance Brigade, Royal Armoured Corps, who died on 24 May 1940, aged 35, and Private George Joseph ALLEN, 2nd Battalion, Wiltshire Regiment, who also fell the same day.

Chapter Nine

Two Deaths in a Dublin Park –
The Mammoth of Morchies –
A Swiss Imbroglio

Beugnâtre Communal Cemetery

The communal cemetery is really part of the churchyard and, as with so many villages in this part of France, the church spire is an easy landmark to pick out. Beugnâtre lies very close to the A.1 Autoroute, about two miles north-east of Bapaume. From Arras the easiest way to reach it is to follow the D.917 south and take the small turning off to Favreuil, which is sign-posted. Pass through Favreuil to the junction with the D.956 and turn left. The churchyard and cemetery are on the very east side of the village, just off the Rue de Frémicourt. For anyone familiar with north London, the village is twinned with the former London Borough of Finsbury.

There are ten burials here, two of whom are officers from 4 Squadron, Royal Flying Corps, who are buried next to each other. Second Lieutenant Eustace Bertram LOW was just 18 years old when he and his observer, Second Lieutenant Albert Fisher GIBSON, were killed in a flying accident on 24 March 1917. GIBSON, who had previously served with the 4th Leinster Regiment, had the misfortune to be killed on his 21st birthday. Second Lieutenant LOW had only been at the front since early January that year and had little operational flying experience. He had received his commission in August 1916, soon after leaving Haileybury College. The aircraft he was flying that day was a BE2c. (Graves 7 and 8)

Of the remaining eight casualties, three are men from the 2/10th Battalion, London Regiment (Hackney Rifles), who were killed in action on 11 May 1917 and five are Australian soldiers killed in March and May 1917. The three Australians who died in March are infantrymen, whereas the two from May are artillerymen.

Boyelles Communal Cemetery Extension

The village of Boyelles lies just off the D.917 about 8 miles south of Arras. The cemetery is situated about 300 yards to the north of the village in open fields and is quite detached from the village itself. The Rue Principale is the main turning off the D.917 and leads into the centre of the village. Once in the centre of the village the road to take is the Rue d'Hénin, which is the road that leads north and away from the village and back on to the D.917.

The CWGC register notes that the village was captured on 19 March 1917 by the 7th Division and remained in British hands until it was overrun in March the following year during the German Offensive. It was then retaken on 23 August 1918 by the 56th (London) Division. The register also notes that the 21st, 33rd and 56th Divisions made particular use of the cemetery during the two periods when the village was under British occupation. It now has 142 burials, five of which are unidentified, and four German graves still remain.

Just over a quarter of the identified burials here are from artillery units covering both 1917 and 1918. The main group of 1917 casualties are the eight men killed on 11 May 1917, one of whom was Wheeler Quartermaster Serjeant Robert EDWARDS DCM, 'A' Battery, 150 Brigade, Royal Field Artillery, who was killed in action, aged 41. His DCM was gazetted on 17 December 1914 and was awarded for conspicuous bravery whilst serving with 6th Battery, Royal Field Artillery, at Le Cateau on 26 August 1914. In the midst of the battle he had repaired equipment under heavy fire and had frequently helped to run up single guns to the infantry's firing line (Plot I.D.8). Like all the 1917 graves in this cemetery, these men are all buried in Plot I. The 1918 burials are in Plot II.

There are also two 1917 burials from the Royal Garrison Artillery. Second Lieutenant Frank Jefferson FARNHAM, 239th Siege Battery, Royal Garrison Artillery, was killed in action on 15 April 1917. The CWGC register notes that he was a keen college sportsman and had served with the infantry between September 1914 and February 1916 (Plot I.C.1). The other man was also from the same siege battery, but was killed ten days later on 25 April and is buried a few graves along (Plot I.C.4).

The main group of artillerymen from 1918 cover just a few days of fighting at the end of August. Most of them fell on the 27th August and were from the 1/2nd London, Heavy Battery. Four of the men are buried together (Plots II.D.1 to 4), whilst the other four from that unit are buried two rows away, but similarly as a group of four. (Plots II.F.9 to 12)

Three days later two men of 123rd Siege Battery, Royal Garrison Artillery, were killed in action. One of them is Second Lieutenant Ronald Henry SAMPSON, whose father, Charles Henry Sampson, was a Fellow of Brasenose College, Oxford, and had been a tutor there since 1882. His son, Ronald, was educated at Lancing College, Shoreham, in Sussex and was 20 years old when he died (Plot II.G.3). Before the war, Ronald had intended taking Holy Orders, but the outbreak of war changed all that and he became a private in the Royal Field Artillery. He was then selected for a commission and was sent for training with the Royal Garrison Artillery. He was eventually commissioned in December 1917 and went to France the following month. His brother, Christopher Bolckow Sampson, did enter the clergy and went on to become a chaplain to Her Majesty Queen Elizabeth II in 1958. The other man from that unit, Lance Bombardier Thomas Bennett WHITE, is buried next to him. According to *Soldiers Died in the Great War* he was a Territorial soldier from Chiswell in Dorset who served with the Dorset Battery and who died of wounds on 30 August 1918. (Plot II.G.4)

The majority of the 1917 infantry burials are from various units of the 21st Division, including twelve Northumberland Fusiliers from the 12th and 13th Battalions, as well as the division's pioneer battalion, the 14th Northumberland Fusiliers. All died during the period between the end of March 1917 and the middle of July that year.

The CWGC register shows two officers, Captain Cyril Arthur Mecrate BUTCHER and Second Lieutenant Ernest Stanley STEPHENS, each serving with a different infantry unit. BUTCHER is shown serving with the 10th Yorkshire Regiment and STEPHENS with the 1st Lincolnshire Regiment. However, when they were killed in action on 6 July 1917 they were both attached to the 62nd Trench Mortar Battery. (Plots I.F.1 and 2)

Second Lieutenant Harold Edward JOBLING, 7th Leinster Regiment, was 19 years old when he died of wounds on 9 September 1917. The previous day the British had fired off 1,000 gas projectiles using trench mortars from a position just behind the sector covered by his battalion. Tragically, some of these fell short, one of which severely wounded him and also accounted for two other lives. He was the son of Major Alfred Jobling who served with the York & Lancaster Regiment. (Plot I.F.9)

Two more officers killed in 1917 can be found in nearby graves, one behind the other in Rows C and D. Captain John Morris OWEN, 2nd Royal Welsh Fusiliers, was killed in action on 23 April 1917, aged 30 (Plot I.C.3). He had been previously wounded in January 1916 in an attack on some craters near Auchy, south of the Bethune–La Bassée Road. Lieutenant Robert Ward Shepherd ROBERTSON, 4th Queen's (Royal West Surrey Regiment) attached 19th Company, Machine Gun Corps, was killed on 27 May 1917 (Plot I.D.3). He had enlisted in the Royal Montreal Regiment in August 1914 and had then served as a private for almost a year on the Western Front before receiving a commission in January 1916. Buried behind them is Serjeant William Frederick CAMP-JERMYN, 'A' Company, 1/4th Suffolk Regiment, who was killed in action on 27 June 1917, aged 19. He held the Medal for Military Valour (Italy), which was awarded to him in March 1916 (Plot I.E.3). He is buried next to an officer and two privates from his battalion.

Finally, with regard to 1917 burials, there is Second Lieutenant Thomas John OWEN, 29 Squadron, Royal Flying Corps, who was killed in action on 8 April 1917 while flying a Nieuport 23 single-seater aircraft. This was the day before the opening of the Battle of Arras and the strain on pilots and observers was considerable as they sought to carry out a variety of tasks on behalf of other units and formations, especially the artillery. He is one of two airmen buried here. (Plot I.A.7)

As far as 1918 casualties are concerned, there are quite a number of 3rd Division burials here dating to the early part of the year prior to the German Offensive in March. Most notable within this group are casualties from the 2nd Royal Scots, the 1st Royal Scots Fusiliers, and the 7th King's Shropshire Light Infantry. They are buried in Plot II, Rows A and B. Corporal William MANFORD MM, is the only gallantry award among them (Plot II.B.1). There are also a number of burials from the 4th (City of London) Battalion, London Regiment (Royal Fusiliers) in Plot II, Rows C and E, including one of its officers, Captain Cyril William ROWLAND MC, who was killed in action on 23 August 1918, aged 23, when his battalion captured the village of Boyelles with the assistance of four tanks. He is referred to in the battalion history as ROWLANDS. His MC was gazetted on 4 February 1918 and was awarded for his part in the recapture of a section of the Hindenburg Support Trench on 24 November 1917. After capturing the trench, he and his men held it for two days.

He and several others were singled out for their fortitude and vigilance throughout the operation. (Plot II.C.4)

Second Lieutenant Herbert SCOTT, 8 Squadron, Royal Air Force, was killed in action on 23 August 1918, aged 29, while observing for his pilot, Lieutenant John Ross Robert Gordon McCallum. Both men died when their AWFK8 aircraft, a twoseater reconnaissance/bomber, came down. Although SCOTT is buried here (Plot II.F.2), McCallum, who was a Canadian flyer, is buried at Douchy-les-Ayette British Cemetery.

L'Homme Mort British Cemetery, Écoust-Saint-Mein

The cemetery lies between the villages of Écoust-Saint-Mein and Mory on the D.10E4 and is on the Mory side of the A.1 Autoroute. It is not particularly difficult to find, but it is isolated. Passengers on the TGV service from Lille to Paris will get a good, but very brief view of the cemetery by looking right, provided they do not blink.

The cemetery is a combination of original burials and others that were brought here after the Armistice. The original ones are to be found in Plot I, Row A, on the right, closest to the side wall. This part of the cemetery was begun by the Grenadier Guards in August 1918. A further 152 graves were then brought here after the Armistice, including a number of soldiers of the New Zealand Division, who are now buried in Plot II to the left of the entrance. Today there are sixty-four identified casualties out of a total of 166. As a cemetery, it feels somewhat dislocated owing to its isolation, and by virtue of its proximity to modern transport infrastructure, which now carves its way through this part of the battlefield.

Captain Pulteney MALCOLM, King's Company, 1st Grenadier Guards, was reported missing in action on 25 August 1918 after a failed attack around L'Homme Mort and Bank's Trench (Plot I.A.1). He was buried by the Germans near to where he fell along with several of his men. He had been wounded on two occasions, first with the 4th Grenadier Guards at Loos on 27 September 1915, and again on 16 April 1917, while serving with the Household Battalion at Arras. He only returned to active service in 1918. At the time, he happened to be away from the fighting, but he was called back to command the King's Company, 1st Grenadier Guards, for its attack on 25 August after his battalion had been reduced to just seven officers and 212 other ranks owing to heavy casualties from the previous two days of fighting. He had to ride and then walk a considerable distance overnight on the 24/25 in order to take up that command, arriving just in time for the attack at 4.30am.

There was a heavy ground mist when the attack took place, causing the eight tanks assigned to the attack to lose direction. No. 3 Company, which started alongside the King's Company, was ordered to return to its jumping off position, a trench known as Mory Switch, after the tank supporting it broke down near Bank's Trench. The company's commanding officer, Lieutenant Hawkesworth, had also been wounded. As the fog lifted, MALCOLM's company numbered only around forty men and No. 4 Company was sent up to support it. The tank allotted to the company was also hit causing damage to its engine and water cooling jacket. By chance another tank was located nearby and was redirected to support the attack by the King's Company.

There was even a bizarre moment of confusion as a party of around 150 Germans in Bank's Trench became clearly visible as the mist cleared. None of them seemed to be prepared to fight, but equally none of them seemed to be about to surrender. When the disabled tank was hit yet again and the other was also put out of action, the attack broke down completely and the survivors returned to Mory Switch, which by now had come under heavy fire. The only success that day on this part of the front was at Hally Copse, and the 1st Grenadier Guards, now exhausted and badly depleted, was relieved by the 2nd Battalion on the night of the 25th.

Captain MALCOLM came from a family with an impressive military and naval pedigree. His father, Lieutenant Colonel Pulteney Malcolm, had previously served in India and won the Albert Medal for attempting to save life on land. He was later awarded a DSO for services in the Mashud-Wasiri operations. On his return to England he served as Chief Constable of Kingston-on-Hull between 1904 and 1910, then as Chief Constable of Cheshire Constabulary in 1910. In 1913 he was made a member of the Royal Victorian Order. During the Great War he served as Assistant Adjutant and Quartermaster-General on the Divisional Staff of the New Armies, a role for which he was mentioned in despatches. He was also given the temporary rank of lieutenant colonel on 29 May 1917. Sadly, Pulteney, was his only surviving son.

Captain MALCOLM's grandfather was General Sir George Malcolm GCB, who had commanded the Bombay Army. Sir George, who was the nephew of Admiral Sir Pulteney Malcolm (1768–1838), was one of three sons. Another of Sir George's uncles was Admiral Sir Thomas Pasley (1734–1808) who served in the Seven Years' War, the American Revolutionary War, and the French Revolutionary Wars. It was during the latter campaign, at the ripe old age of 60, that Sir Thomas lost a leg at the Glorious First of June in 1794 when the British, under Lord Howe, engaged the French Atlantic Fleet as it was escorting a grain convoy to France from America. The British sank seven French ships that day resulting in 4,000 French casualties whilst the British losses came to 1,200. Another 3,000 Frenchmen were captured.

Admiral Sir Pulteney Malcolm had fought under Nelson and also with Wellington, whilst his brother, Sir James Malcolm, fought in the American Revolutionary War, the Napoleonic War, and the American Wars of 1812. A third brother, Sir John Malcolm, joined the East India Company as a cadet and went on to become a distinguished soldier and diplomat in India and Persia.

Several of the graves following on from Captain MALCOLM are men of the 1st Grenadier Guards who were killed in action with him, including Private Alexander WILSON MM, whose gallantry award does not appear next to his name in *Soldiers Died in the Great War* (Plot I.A.6). Private Albert Henry PASCOE, 1st Grenadier Guards (Plot I.A.7), is recorded as having died on 20 August 1918, whereas he was actually killed on 25 August, along with the rest of his comrades who fell that day and who are now buried here with him. Serjeant William Henry CUSHEN, 2nd Grenadier Guards, is shown as having been killed on 25 August 1918, though *Soldiers Died in the Great War* records his date of death as 27 August. (Plot I.A.13)

The largest group of casualties belongs to the 1st Battalion, Otago Regiment, New Zealand Division. The majority were killed on 25 August 1918, though a few were killed or died of wounds the following day. Their attack took place just north of Bapaume towards the main road linking it with Arras. The morning attack had encountered heavy machine-gun fire from enemy positions near to the road and from Monument Wood. The attack had also run up against several strongpoints whose presence had caused the various units to separate. To make matters worse, the tanks designated for the attack were delayed by fog, and when they did finally appear they began firing on the New Zealanders in the belief that they were Germans. As soon as the fog began to lift, the tanks were all disabled by German anti-tank rounds, four of them near Monument Wood.

The tanks did, however, manage to cause such a distraction that the infantry was able to push on and deal with the strongpoints, and by 9.00am the Otago Regiment had reached the Bapaume–Arras road, though by then it had lost the barrage. Any further efforts to continue the advance were postponed until 6.30pm when the attack was renewed. Monument Wood was eventually taken, machine-gun fire from near the cemetery was overcome, and our artillery fire was successful in breaking up a counter-attack. A second attempt by the enemy to retake the positions along the road and around the cemetery was also repulsed. The 1st Canterbury Regiment, whose attack took place closer to Bapaume, sustained fewer casualties, though machine-gun fire from the north-west edge of the town had been heavy. Casualties for the 1st Otago Regiment came to seven officers and 211 other ranks.

There were further New Zealand casualties amongst the 3rd (NZ) Rifle Brigade, which entered Bapaume on 29 August. Opposition here was fairly light, but rear-guards offered just enough resistance to allow the majority of Germans in and around the town to withdraw over the Bancourt Ridge and back to the Hindenburg Line. Although, strictly speaking, these events belong to the Battle of Albert, the narrative should help the visitor to understand the presence of so many New Zealanders in this cemetery.

The cemetery contains two members of the 1st Otago Regiment with gallantry awards: Sergeant Walter Anderson McMILLAN MM and Sergeant William SULLI-VAN MM were both killed in action on 25 August 1918. (Plots II.C.4 and 14)

Private Robert BORTHWICK, 2nd Highland Light Infantry, is buried here separated from the rest of his fallen comrades. He is one of around 150 other ranks who became casualties when the battalion attacked Béhagnies on 23 August 1918. Private BORTHWICK's company, which was on the right of the battalion's attack, came under heavy machine-gun fire once it had cleared Gomiécourt. Béhagnies was found to be strongly defended and the battalion's commanding officer, Lieutenant Colonel Walter Lorrain Brodie VC MC, was killed in the attack just after midday. Heavy resistance continued throughout the following day until the village eventually fell to the battalion on the 25th with assistance from the 24th Royal Fusiliers. Most of Private BORTHWICK's comrades killed during this fighting can be found either at Gomiécourt South Cemetery, Bienvillers Military Cemetery, or commemorated on the Vis-en-Artois Memorial. Lieutenant Colonel Brodie VC MC, is buried at Bien-villers Military Cemetery. Sadly, Private BORTHWICK is buried here alone. His was almost certainly one of the graves brought here after the Armistice. (Plot I.B.4)

Easily lost amongst the August 1918 casualties are two men who died earlier that year during the time of the German Offensive in March. Private Frederick Cecil HARRINGTON, 2/5th Lancashire Fusiliers, fell on 25 March 1918, aged 19. His battalion was part of the 55th (West Lancashire) Division. According to *Soldiers Died in the Great War*, he was killed in action, but the really puzzling thing is that he is buried here at all. In mid-February 1918 his battalion moved to the area just south of the La Bassée Canal and by mid-March it had moved again, this time to the Givenchy sector just north of the canal. He is now buried a long way from either of those locations. Even allowing for post-war concentration of isolated graves from other battlefields, his presence here is somewhat unusual and certainly unexpected.

Private James WHEELHOUSE, 10th Queen's (Royal West Surrey Regiment), was killed on 21 March 1918. His unit was part of the 41st Division, which on the opening day of the German Offensive was in Third Army Reserve. The division began to move towards the fighting at the end of the first day after detraining at Achiet-le-Grand and Albert. It seems reasonable to assume that Private WHEELHOUSE was killed somewhere between Achiet-le-Grand and the village of Favreuil where the battalion spent the night. The men are buried next to each other. The battalion war diary makes no reference to any casualties that day. (Plot I.C.1 and 2)

Among the 1917 casualties are three men of the 4th Yorkshire Regiment who fell during the attack around the Wancourt Tower on 23 April 1917 (Plots II. Row A.13, 14 and 16). Another casualty from the same brigade is Second Lieutenant Frederick William HEAP, 5th Durham Light Infantry, whose battalion had been in action that day in support of the initial attack by the 4th Yorkshire Regiment and the 4th East Yorkshire Regiment. (Plot II.A.8)

There are also four casualties from the fighting that took place south of Arras in May 1917. Three are from the 8th and 10th Rifle Brigade, whilst the fourth is Company Sergeant Major James Edward Lewis HINTON MM, 5th Oxfordshire & Buckinghamshire Light Infantry, who was killed in action on 3 May 1917, aged 25. All of the men are buried in Plot I, Rows D and E. The 10th Rifle Brigade was part of the 20th (Light) Division, whereas the other two battalions belonged to the 14th (Light) Division.

Of the many tanks put out of action on the 25th August, one crew member, Private Clarence NEWELL, 7th Battalion, Tank Corps, happens to be buried here. Although he is the only one from that battalion buried in this cemetery, four other men from his unit killed in action that day are now buried at Achiet-le-Grand Communal Cemetery Extension. All in all, just over forty tanks attached to III and IV Corps went into action on 25 August 1918, resulting in sixteen deaths. (Plot II.B.10)

Morchies Military Cemetery

The village of Morchies is situated close to the right angle formed by the D.917, the Arras–Bapaume road, and the D.930, the Bapaume–Cambrai road. However, from Arras, I prefer to take the D.5, which runs in a south-easterly direction from Beaurains on the edge of the southern suburbs of Arras and passes through the villages of Neuville-Vitasse, Hénin-sur-Cojeul, Croisilles, Écoust-Saint-Mein, Noreuil and

Lagnicourt-Marcel. Morchies lies approximately a mile west of this last village and the D.18 connects the two. Morchies Military Cemetery is just outside the village on the right-hand side and is easily seen from the D.18 a short distance from the road. The CWGC register points out that Morchies was adopted after the war by the London Borough of Barking.

The reason I prefer to take this route is because it provides an opportunity to take in a number of other cemeteries; more importantly it cuts right through the line of outpost villages in front of the Hindenburg Line that were briefly, but stubbornly defended by the Germans between the end of March 1917 and 2 April when they were captured.

The capture of the villages from Croisilles to Noreuil on 2 April, together with those of Louverval and Doignies, was vitally important with regard to the Battle of Arras which was now just a week away. Although the intention was to capture Vimy Ridge and advance on either side of the River Scarpe, the hope was also to breach the northern end of the Hindenburg Line, thus widening the offensive along the key axis of the Arras–Cambrai road. This would have caused the Germans a great deal of pressure and anxiety ahead of the French attacks a week later. However, for this to happen it was crucial that British and Australian troops were close enough to the Hindenburg defences and that the artillery was satisfactorily dug in to allow it to support the infantry attacks.

Only seventy-four of the 163 burials here are identified, though there are eight special memorials to soldiers known to be buried within its boundaries and a further ten soldiers originally buried by the Germans whose graves were lost through subsequent shell fire (Morchies Memorials 1 to 10). Thirteen German graves still remain. The Germans were responsible for burying a total of seventy-six British soldiers here after they captured the village on 21 March 1918 and the CWGC register points out that these now lie in Rows B, C and D.

Captain John Sydney BOAST MC, 2nd South Lancashire Regiment, is one of those commemorated here (Morchies Memorial 2). He had originally enlisted in the South Lancashire Regiment as a drummer boy in 1894 and later served with the 1st Battalion in the South African War, as did his brother, Sydney Thomas Boast, who was awarded the DCM during the campaign. Their father had also been a soldier and had served in the Crimean War and the Indian Mutiny. In 1914, John went to France as a sergeant with the 2nd Battalion and was wounded twice before the year was out. Both brothers were mentioned in despatches on 8 October 1914, and Sydney was mentioned for a second time a few weeks later in Sir John French's despatch on 20 November.

John then received his commission for gallant conduct in the field and by the end of 1915 he had attained the rank of captain. He was awarded the MC on 3 June 1916 in the King's Birthday Honours List. He temporarily took command of the battalion on 3 September 1916 after both its commanding officer and second in command became casualties during an attack at the Leipzig Salient, near Thiepval on the Somme. He was killed in action, shot though the head, on 22 March 1918 near Morchies.

Sydney, who had reached the rank of major, was also awarded the MC. Whether by coincidence or not, it was gazetted on 3 June 1916 in the same Birthday Honour's List as John's award. Sydney's son, Frederick, also served in the same battalion of the regiment as his father and uncle. He survived the war, but was killed in the early hours of 28 December 1919 in Phoenix Park, Dublin, aged 20. He went to investigate the sound of gun fire with four other soldiers of the guard at Vice-Regal Lodge, the official residence of the Lord Lieutenant of Ireland. They came across a man, Laurence Kennedy, and when Frederick challenged him a struggle ensued in which Boast and Kennedy were both shot dead.

Another member of the family, Lieutenant S.W. Boast MC, also served with the 2nd South Lancashire Regiment during the war and survived. His MC was awarded on 3 June 1918 in the King's Birthday Honours List.

Serjeant Thomas Alphonsus O'HARA DCM, 11th Lancashire Fusiliers, was killed in action on 19 January 1918. His DCM was gazetted on 22 January 1916 and was awarded for gallantry during a raid on German trenches south of the Le Touquet–Warneton railway line on the night of 28 December 1915. With the assaulting party, he penetrated the German trenches for some fifty yards and successfully bombed the enemy while he himself was under heavy rifle fire and bombs. He was second-in-command of his party for the operation in which he and his men hurled around eighty bombs at the enemy before retiring. (Plot C.1)

Fifty-two of the identified graves are from 1917, seventeen of which belong to men of the Australian Imperial Force, including one officer, Second Lieutenant Frederick John SANDERSON, 6th Battalion, Australian Infantry, who died on 4 May 1917 (Plot A.8). Like SANDERSON, most of these Australian casualties are from the 1st Australian Division and were killed or died of wounds between the end of March and the beginning of May 1917.

There are also men of the 56th (London) Division among the 1917 casualties; seven from the 1/14th Battalion, London Regiment (London Scottish) and an equal number from the 12th Battalion (The Rangers). The three men shown as belonging to the 11th Battalion, London Regiment (Finsbury Rifles), must have been posted to one of the battalions within the 56th Division, since the 11th Battalion did not serve on the Western Front. Three men from the 13th Battalion, London Regiment (Kensingtons) and one from the 9th Battalion, London Regiment (Queen Victoria's Rifles) are also buried here.

The 1918 burials are mainly 25th Division or 6th Division casualties from the German March Offensive or from the months leading up to it. The men belong to the 11th Lancashire Fusiliers, the 3rd Worcestershire Regiment, the 1st West Yorkshire Regiment and the 1st Leicestershire Regiment. However, there are also a handful of casualties from September 1918 when the village was recaptured.

Lieutenant Arthur William MACNAMARA DFC, 12 Squadron, Royal Air Force, was killed in action on 3 September 1918, aged 19 (A.3). His DFC was awarded for courage and skill in successfully carrying out several photographic reconnaissance missions in spite of attempts by enemy fighters to hinder his efforts. The impressive citation notes that on one occasion, when he was about six miles behind enemy lines, he was attacked by superior numbers of the enemy, but by a series of skilful manoeuvres he drove them off and was able to carry on with his work in spite of extensive damage to his own machine. During that flight he managed to take 126 photographs. MACNAMARA and his observer, Lieutenant Hallgrimur Jonnson MC, were killed when they were shot down over Beugnâtre, near Bapaume. Jonsson has no known grave and is therefore commemorated on the Flying Services Memorial at Arras. His MC was awarded in connection with his supervision of a working party while serving with the Canadian Infantry.

There is one other gallantry award buried here: Corporal Edward Thornton FERGUSON MM, 2nd Trench Mortar Battery, Royal Garrison Artillery, who was killed in action on 22 September 1918. (Plot D.13)

One final anecdote perhaps should be mentioned here, though it concerns an exhumation rather than a burial. On 30 July 1917 a French scientist, described as a geologist, arrived in Morchies to examine some excavations made by No. 2 Section, 174 Tunnelling Company, Royal Engineers. Whilst digging they came across the skeletal remains of a mammoth and, in the interests of science and no doubt curiosity as well, they had informed the authorities. This unusual and bizarre moment of archaeological discovery is recorded in the company's war diary.

Morchies Australian Cemetery

This CWGC cemetery lies on the opposite side of the village to the previous one, in other words on the south side. From Morchies Military Cemetery it is easy to find. Continue through the village on the D.18 and the cemetery is immediately apparent on the left hand side.

This cemetery was begun in March 1917 and was used by units of the Australian Imperial Force through until April. There are twenty Australian soldiers here in total, ten of whom are from the 11th Battalion, Australian Infantry, and were killed or died of wounds on 6 and 9 April 1917. There is one officer amongst them: Second Lieutenant John Terence McMAHON, 3rd Field Company, Australian Engineers, who was killed on 9 April 1917. (Plot B.11)

The other burials are 1918 casualties, four of whom were buried by the Germans in March when the village fell on the first day of their offensive. All four men are from the 11th Queen's (Royal West Surrey Regiment) and were killed in action or died of wounds on 23 March. Only one of the sixty-one burials here is unidentified.

Despite the name of the cemetery, two thirds of the burials are British soldiers. Apart from the four who died in March 1918, thirty of them are from battalions of the 3rd Division and died in the fighting a few miles east of here near Havrincourt and the Canal du Nord, on 27 September 1918. Within this group are twelve men of the 7th King's Shropshire Light Infantry, all of them buried in sequence, eleven of whom were killed on 27 September, including Second Lieutenant Harold AMEY (Plot E.1)

Similarly, there are sixteen officers and men of the 2nd Royal Scots buried in Rows C and D, all of whom are September 1918 casualties. The two officers, Captain Richard Douglas CROSSMAN MC and Second Lieutenant Francis James MITCHELL, are shown as serving with the 3rd and 4th Battalions, but were attached to the 2nd Battalion when they died. (Plots D.8 and D.9)

The battalion's objective on 27 September was a section of strongly held trenches north of Flesquières. These positions were captured with little difficulty and with relatively few losses, and most of the casualties occurred after the battalion had taken all its objectives. The problem was a familiar one; failure to mop up had left large numbers of Germans in the rear and, rather than surrender, they decided or were persuaded to resist.

Captain CROSSMAN was hit in the arm, almost certainly by a sniper. As he was waiting to have his wound dressed he was hit again, this time in the head, killing him instantly. The 2nd Royal Scots had no option but to deal with the situation and began bombing back down the trenches. It was during this phase of the operation that Second Lieutenant MITCHELL was killed as he stood on the parapet, identifying pockets of enemy activity and directing his men towards them. He was almost certainly targeted and killed by a sniper. Fortunately, the Royal Scots were assisted in their task when other elements of 76 Brigade began to arrive. The Germans found themselves surrounded, at which point seven officers and 260 men surrendered. These numbers demonstrate very clearly the extent to which the mopping up had been overlooked. This was an organizational failure and could probably have been avoided.

CROSSMAN's MC had been gazetted on 26 July 1918. It was awarded for conspicuous gallantry and devotion to duty during an attack in which his right flank became exposed. Realizing this, he formed a defensive flank with his company and then held the position for two days. The citation states that during this period he sent back valuable information and inspired confidence amongst all those around him.

The most senior casualty is Major Thomas Francis Pennefather BREEN, 142nd Field Ambulance, Royal Army Medical Corps, who was killed in action on 18 September 1918, aged 28. His Field Ambulance was also part of the 3rd Division. (Plot C.10)

Finally, there are three holders of the MM buried here. They are: Private R.R. GENNOE MM, 11th Battalion Australian Infantry, killed in action on 6 April 1917 (Plot B.5); Bombardier Frederick William DELLOW MM, 49th Battery, Royal Field Artillery, killed in action on 16 September 1918, aged 23 (Plot C.4); and Private Alexander WAUGH MM, 2nd Royal Scots, killed in action on 27 September 1918, aged 30 (Plot D.11).

Morchies Communal Cemetery

The communal cemetery is adjacent to Morchies Military Cemetery, although strictly speaking, it is the other way round. There are eight men buried here, five of whom are identified and fell in September and October 1916. One of them, Serjeant William FRASER MM, 1/5th Duke of Wellington's Regiment, died of wounds on 8 September (Grave 2). Two of the men are from Canadian Infantry units. The five men, if not all eight, would have died as prisoners of war, almost certainly as a result of wounds.

Mory Abbey Military Cemetery, Mory

The cemetery is about a quarter of a mile north of the village of Mory, opposite l'Abbaye Farm, on the road out to Écoust-Saint-Mein and just west of the junction of the D.10E4 and the D.36. It is set well above the level of the road and contains 514 identified casualties. Mory fell into British hands in March 1917 as the Germans pulled back to the Hindenburg Line, but it was retaken by them the following March after a stubborn defence by the 34th Division and the 40th Division. There are still 230 German graves on the west side of the cemetery. As the CWGC register points out, some of these date between March and August 1918 and were made by the Germans themselves, whilst those who fell during September 1918 were buried by the British. The village was captured at the end of August 1918 by the Guards Division and the 62nd (West Riding) Division. After the war three other nearby cemeteries were closed and their graves were brought here.

The 2nd Battalion, Honourable Artillery Company, has two officers and twenty identified other ranks buried here, split between Plots I and II, though all are 1917 burials. One of the two officers, Second Lieutenant George Frederick FARMILOE, was a very good cricketer and had joined the battalion in France as recently as 7 June 1917. He was killed just three weeks later, on 26 June, the day after his battalion had taken over trenches by the railway embankment, near Bullecourt. Private Egerton Browning LEIGH was killed with him that day and both men are now buried next to each other. (Plots I.I.8 and 9)

Second Lieutenant Robert James FLORY MC, 2nd Honourable Artillery Company, was killed two days later on 28 June 1917 when a shell landed on a dug-out that was being used by 'D' Company as its HQ. He had won his MC six weeks earlier during an attack in which he spent the whole day moving about the line supervising and encouraging his men in spite of sniper and machine-gun fire. The award was gazetted on 18 July 1917. Company Serjeant Major George Shirley Maxwell ROBINSON and Serjeant John Clifford DRINKWATER were also killed by the same shell. All three men are now buried side by side (Plots I.J.1–3). Private Charles Howard TRUBSHAWE was killed the same day, but not in the same incident as the other three. (Plot I.J.4)

The battalion with the largest representation is the 2nd Grenadier Guards, which has fifty-nine identified burials here. A further fourteen other ranks from the regiment's 1st Battalion can also be found with them. With just one exception, all of these men were killed or died of wounds between 23 and 27 August 1918 during fighting around the villages of Mory and Saint-Léger. The majority fell on 27 August attacking the German positions at L'Homme Mort and Bank's Trench. The one exception is a private from the 1st Battalion, killed on 14 September further towards Cambrai and the Canal du Nord.

Although the regimental history of the Grenadier Guards is not especially helpful in terms of references to individuals, particularly with regard to other ranks, it does provide some biographical detail with regard to its officers.

Second Lieutenant Francis Jasper LANGLEY, 2nd Grenadier Guards, joined the battalion in December 1917 and was wounded the following March whilst fighting to recover a post after it had been captured and its occupants put out of action by shell fire. He rejoined the battalion a few months later, on 23 June. His death came on 27 August 1918 whilst leading his platoon against a machine-gun nest at L'Homme Mort, near Bank's Trench. Though he was mortally wounded in the attack, the position was eventually taken after a hard fight in which the remainder of the garrison, numbering around twenty men, was captured. (Plot IV.C.17)

Second Lieutenant Hugh Adair FINCH, 2nd Grenadier Guards, is shown as having died on 27 August 1918, but the precise circumstances and date of his death cannot be confirmed. What is certain is that he was sent out with a small party of eight men on the night of 25/26th with instructions to locate enemy positions in front of his battalion's own position. The area, which covered a wide frontage, was relatively ill-defined in terms of fixed posts and positions. Nothing more was heard from his patrol and nothing could be ascertained regarding its fate or whereabouts until the advance on the 27th when Finch's body was found about 1,000 yards in front of the line that had been established two days earlier. It seems likely that his patrol had made contact with an enemy patrol and was cut off or killed in a fight. (Plot IV.C.19)

Lieutenant Cyril GWYER, 2nd Grenadier Guards, had only been with the battalion since April 1918. His death on 27 August came when he and his men from No. 2 Company emerged from Hally Copse and were met by a hail of machine-gun fire before they could move out into artillery formation. He was killed almost immediately and two of his fellow officers were wounded, one of whom was the company's commanding officer, Captain Smith. Having suffered around 50 per cent casualties, Smith ordered the men to go to ground. Throughout the day the survivors did manage to work their way forward in support of No. 3 Company, as originally intended, though they remained pinned down by intense machine-gun fire from positions 200 yards ahead of them where slightly higher ground provided ideal conditions for the defending garrison. Lieutenant GWYER, who was educated at Winchester School and Christ College, Oxford, joined the Duke of Lancaster's Own Yeomanry Regiment in 1914. In 1915 he married Constance Frances Monckton, a descendant of John Monckton, 1st Viscount Galway. Her family owned several estates in Staffordshire, including Stretton Hall. (Plot IV.C.20)

Second Lieutenant Howard William STEWART, Guards' Machine Gun Regiment, attached 4th Grenadier Guards, was killed on 27 August 1918. He had been wounded twice, once on 11 October 1917, and again on 27 March 1918. (Plot V.C.6)

Second Lieutenant Roderick Magrath OLIVER, 2nd Grenadier Guards, was educated at Winchester School and New College, Oxford, before working in London as a solicitor. He was killed in action on 27 August 1918. He was also a member of the MCC. (Plot V.C.16)

There is only one gallantry award amongst this group of officers and men of the Grenadier Guards. Serjeant Walter William BELCHER DCM, 1st Grenadier Guards, won his award for conspicuous gallantry and devotion to duty after the enemy had made a determined attack in great strength and had penetrated a small section of the front line. He immediately organized bombing parties and led them with splendid courage and determination, driving back the enemy. The rapidity with which the enemy was ejected and with heavy losses was largely due to his excellent leadership and the example he set to his men. Sadly, he was killed in action on 25 August 1918, aged 24. (Plot V.C.27)

Although the CWGC register shows the rank of Arthur Horace GRACE, 2nd Grenadier Guards, as gunner, this is merely a typographical error, as his headstone shows it correctly as 'guardsman', as do other records. He had also served in the South African War and was 36 years old when he was killed in action. (Plot V.D.10)

Men from the other four regiments of Foot Guards can be found in this cemetery, though in far smaller numbers. All, apart from one man, fell during the latter days of August 1918 and there are two winners of the MM amongst them. Corporal Edmund Charles MATTHEWS MM, 1st Irish Guards, was killed in action on 27 August (Plot IV.D.24) and Serjeant Henry Mountain DAY MM, 2nd Scots Guards, was killed in action three days earlier on 24 August. (Plot IV.E.12)

Among the eight men of the Royal Flying Corps now buried here, Captain Henry Arthur TAYLOR MC, 27 Squadron, was the first one to lose his life. He was just 18 years old when he and another man, Second Lieutenant Stephen Dendrino, were reported missing on 27 September 1916, a day that was described as cloudy with rain and not very favourable for flying.

TAYLOR was educated at Charterhouse School followed by the Royal Military College, Sandhurst. He had gone to France towards the end of April 1916, but soon after that he joined the Royal Flying Corps. He quickly established himself as a very promising flyer and the major part of the *Royal Flying Corps Communiqué* for 13 July 1916 is devoted to an attack made by TAYLOR and three other pilots of 27 Squadron who, in their Martinsyde single-seat fighter bombers, had been developing a technique to navigate to their target whilst flying above the cloud.

The targets on 13 July were the Douai–Cambrai and Denain–Cambrai railway lines. The four Martinsydes flew all the way above the clouds before dropping down onto their targets. TAYLOR dropped one of his bombs from a height of 800 feet onto a train as it was travelling north, but the bomb failed to explode. He then dropped a second bomb from 500 feet onto another train as it was pulling up at a junction just west of Aubigny-au-Bac. The bomb landed about ten yards from the railway line near the front of the train where it exploded, derailing the tender and two trucks and also causing a squadron of cavalry nearby to scatter. The damage and chaos were enough to disrupt a transport convoy three and a half miles in length as it was passing along the Fressies–Cambrai road. TAYLOR's attack was the only one during that sortie to cause physical damage, despite many of the bombs falling extremely close to trains on both lines. His exploits that day were recognized the following month by the award of the MC, which was gazetted on 19 August 1916.

A couple of weeks earlier, on 1 July, TAYLOR had also attacked and brought down an opponent whilst escorting a Morane biplane on a reconnaissance mission over Cambrai, Busigny and Etreux. He and the rest of the escort were harassed and attacked throughout the flight, but the operation was carried out successfully.

Two days before his death, TAYLOR was promoted within his squadron to flight commander with the rank of temporary captain. During an operation that day he drove down another enemy plane out of control north-east of Péronne. Sadly, he was shot down on 27 September 1916 whilst leading a patrol when his flight was attacked by a much larger enemy formation (Plot III.E.5). Second Lieutenant Stephen Dendrino, who died with him, is commemorated at London Cemetery, Neuville-Vitasse.

Although TAYLOR's rank as captain was a temporary one, it is nevertheless represents an extraordinary achievement given his age. I cannot recall coming across any

British flyer of that rank younger than him in over thirty years of research on the Western Front.

Captain Alan John MacDonald PEMBERTON MC, 22 Squadron, Royal Flying Corps, had previously served with the Leinster Regiment after receiving his commission in 1911. He was the son of Major General W.W. PEMBERTON and was 24 years old when he died of wounds in German hands on 3 November 1916. This was described as a difficult day for flying on account of high winds and a day on which 22 Squadron had to report six of its members missing in action. PEMBERTON had initially gone to France with the Leinster Regiment in December 1914 and had taken part in fighting the following year at Ypres and the nearby village of Saint-Éloi. He had also been mentioned in despatches. He joined the Royal Flying Corps in January 1916 and had only been flying operationally for about a month before his death (Plot IV.A.23). His observer, Second Lieutenant L.C.L. Cook, was taken prisoner.

Second Lieutenant Herbert Marshall HEADLEY, Royal Flying Corps, was reported missing on 11 March 1917, aged 19, and was an only son. His death was later confirmed by the Germans as having occurred that day. He had originally enlisted as a trooper in a cavalry regiment, aged 17, but in May 1915 he obtained a commission in the Royal Field Artillery and went to the front in January 1916. In May 1916 he transferred to a trench mortar battery, serving with it until his transfer to the Royal Flying Corps in December 1916. It is known that on 11 March 1917 his machine was hit whilst flying at a height of around 8,000 feet. Despite having been wounded, he continued to fire at his attackers as his machine lost height over enemy lines. His body was subsequently recovered from the wreckage of his aircraft and he was buried by the Germans (Plot V.B.9). His pilot that day, Serjeant Henry Philip Burgess, also died in the crash and is commemorated on the Flying Services Memorial at Arras.

Second Lieutenant John THWAYTES, 4 Squadron, Royal Flying Corps, had previously served with the Border Regiment before transferring to the Royal Flying Corps. He and his observer that day, Second Lieutenant Hugh Temple BOURNE, aged 23, were killed in action flying a BE2c on 18 March 1917. (Plot IV.C.6 and 7)

Second Lieutenant Eric ELGEY, 59 Squadron, Royal Flying Corps, was killed in action on 19 March 1917 after he was set upon by six enemy aircraft and shot down near Croisilles while observing the German retreat south of Arras. He had previously been a member of the OTC at the University of London. Second Lieutenant ELGEY died that day along with his pilot, Captain Eldred Wolferstan BOWYER-BOWER, who had previously served with the East Surrey Regiment. BOWYER-BOWER was the only son of a serving officer in the Royal Engineers, Captain Thomas Bowyer-Bower. A couple of weeks later, after the capture of Croisilles on 2 April, his father was made aware of a grave marked by a cross made from pieces of a wrecked plane upon which there was a small inscription written in pencil: '*Two unknown Captains of the Flying Corps*'. Believing that one of them could be his son, the father was given permission to exhume the bodies. When the grave was uncovered, one of the bodies was indeed that of his son, the other was his observer, Second Lieutenant ELGEY. Both bodies were removed and brought back for reburial in a nearby village, which although not stated, would seem to have been Mory. (Plots I.D.7 and 8)

Another former member of London University's OTC was Lieutenant Elias TREM-LETT DSO, 9th Devonshire Regiment, attached 208th Company, Machine Gun Corps. His DSO was awarded for conspicuous gallantry and devotion to duty at Bullecourt on 3 May 1917 when he organized and led a bombing party that succeeded in working its way along a stretch of trench for 500 yards. During this operation he displayed admirable coolness and resource, which proved a great encouragement to those with him. His award was gazetted on 26 July 1917. He died of wounds on 23 May 1917, aged 27. (Plot I.G.4)

Second Lieutenant Claude Peregrine BERTIE, 59 Squadron, Royal Flying Corps, formerly 6th (London) Brigade, Royal Field Artillery, was also killed in action on 19 March 1917. He was 26 years old and was the only son of Lieutenant Colonel the Honourable George Bertie who lived in Ecclestone Square in London's Belgravia. He had served in the Territorial Army since 1909, but when war broke out he immediately volunteered to serve abroad, as did many Territorials. He served at the front from February 1915 until September that year when he was invalided home suffering from an attack of diphtheria. A year later, in September 1916, he joined the Royal Flying Corps and went to France with his squadron in February 1917. On the day that he was reported missing he had gone up to reconnoitre the Hindenburg Line and its defences. His death was later confirmed, though the man flying with him that day, Second Lieutenant F.H. Wilson, was taken prisoner. (Plot I.C.8)

There is quite a wide diversity of men and units in this cemetery. Even amongst the fourteen men of the Royal Engineers, the variety of roles is very marked. They include those involved in road construction, light railways, gas warfare, cable and communications, signaling, tunneling, as well as men from routine field companies. Most are buried in Plot I, though a few are spread across Plots II and III, along with a handful of casualties from the Royal Army Medical Corps.

Lieutenant Colonel James Houghton Henry CHADWICK DSO, 24th Manchester Regiment (Oldham Pals), was killed in action on 4 May 1917, aged 36. Before the war he was an Inspector of Schools. When war broke out he enlisted as a private, but was granted a commission in November 1914, after which he served with his battalion until his death. He was posthumously mentioned in despatches on 25 May 1917 and his DSO was also gazetted posthumously on 4 June that year as part of the King's Birthday Honours List. His battalion, a pioneer unit, was ordered up towards Bullecourt to dig a trench connecting with the front line, which at that point ran parallel and just north of the railway embankment. There was some confusion over where the actual lines ran, and so CHADWICK and his batman, Lance Corporal Robert ARCHER MM, went forward to clarify and, if necessary, rectify the situation. As they were making their way there, a German shell exploded near them, mortally wounding both men. They were taken to a dressing station where they died, in spite of efforts to save them.

ARCHER, who came from Belfast, had been awarded the MM in September 1916 for dedicated service throughout the Battle of the Somme rather than for any specific act of gallantry. ARCHER and CHADWICK were buried together (Plots I.C.9 and 10). Three other men belonging to the original Oldham Pals can also be found in this cemetery. All three were killed by shell fire. They are Serjeant Isaac HOUGHTON (Plot I.I.7), Serjeant Frank STOTT (Plot I.T.8) and Private Tom Cockcroft BENNETT (Plot II.J.8).

Towards the end of 1917 this sector was occupied by the 3rd Division, but even after the subsidiary operations on and around 20 November had come to an end, the sector still remained active in places and sections of trench were frequently targeted for bombing raids. On 11 December the 4th Royal Fusiliers took over trenches from the 8th East Yorkshire Regiment in the Noreuil right sub-sector. The following day a German raid captured Pudsey Trench, which the 4th Royal Fusiliers was then ordered to retake, along with another trench, London Support Trench. A heavy German bombardment prevented the immediate recapture of these positions, but they were eventually retaken and held. However, on 15 December our own artillery put down a barrage with tragic consequences when it fell short of the now revised front line. Second Lieutenant Frederick Sidney GODDARD, 4th Royal Fusiliers, was killed by one of the shells, but the bombardment was also responsible for causing another sixty-five casualties amongst men of the battalion. Second Lieutenant GODDARD and nine of those sixty-five men can now be found in Plot II at the start of Row F.

The co-ordination of artillery bombardments with infantry activity was always crucial and relied not only on communication, but also on both sides keeping to an agreed plan. On the night of the 22/23 July 1917 'D' Company, 1st Royal Welsh Fusiliers, carried out a raid on the far side of Bullecourt, entering the German posts near the crucifix on the Hendecourt road. They were assisted by men of the 2nd Honourable Artillery Company whose role it was to distract German attention over on the right of the main raid. Finding the posts empty, the Royal Welsh Fusiliers pushed ahead to Bovis Trench, which formed part of the German main line. This was not part of the agreed plan. The raid was also intended to be carried out by stealth, with no preliminary or supporting bombardment either before or during the operation.

At Bovis Trench, where the German wire was found to be strong and intact, a message was sent back requesting that Bangalore torpedoes be brought forward to blow gaps in it. This inevitably led to a delay during which time the platoon lying out by the German wire was discovered and came under heavy machine-gun fire. The object of the raid had been limited to the initial line of posts, and although in the circumstances the decision to push on further in search of prisoners might have appeared worth the risk, this was not part of the plan that was agreed with the artillery. The agreement had been for the artillery to open fire on Bovis Trench at the conclusion of the raid. When the time came for the bombardment to commence, it fell on the platoon that was now pinned down close to the German wire and still waiting for the arrival of the Bangalore torpedoes. The party was therefore forced to retire to the original line of German posts through a hail of shells. In the event, although the posts had been abandoned by the enemy, they were also found to be unsuitable for retention, and so the original plan to dig a communication trench linking them up to our own front line was also abandoned. Several men of the 1st Royal Welsh Fusiliers who lost their lives when they were caught in the bombardment of Bovis Trench can be found in Plot II, Row I.

Lieutenant Colonel Richard Annesley WEST VC DSO and Bar MC, North Irish Horse, commanding the 6th Battalion, Tank Corps, was killed in action on 2 September 1918, aged 40. WEST's DSO was gazetted in the New Year's Honours List in 1918, whereas all the other awards were for gallantry rather than service in the field. What is remarkable is that they were all won during a very short period of time between 8 August 1918 and his death less than a month later. The bar to his DSO, gazetted on 7 November 1918, was awarded for actions on 21 August during the attack on Courcelles. When the infantry had lost its bearings in dense fog, WEST, who was on horseback, gathered up a group of them and led them through the village in the face of heavy machine-gun fire, despite having two horses shot from under him. The citation concludes that it was his courage and leadership that ensured the village was captured.

On 2 September his own battalion of light Whippet tanks had been designated to follow up the infantry and some heavier tanks with a view to exploiting any opportunities that presented themselves during the advance. WEST rode up close behind the infantry in order to be able to judge the right moment to deploy his tanks. At one point the enemy began to put in a counter-attack against the depleted line of advancing infantry whose flanks were now exposed. Realizing the potential setback to the infantry's prospects of advancing further that day, WEST rode out in front of them under very heavy machine-gun fire and rallied them. After taking charge of the situation and detailing NCOs to replace the officer casualties, he rode up and down in front of the men urging them to fight on until he fell riddled with machine-gun bullets. To his enormous credit the counter-attack was repulsed. For this outstanding show of bravery and leadership he was awarded the VC. (Plot III.G.4)

A further fourteen identified casualties belonging to the Tank Corps can be found in this cemetery, all of whom are from the 12th Battalion. Twelve were killed on 2 September, whilst the remaining two were killed just prior to that date. The Drocourt–Quéant Line, which was a switch line linking the Hindenburg defences in the south with the defences around Lens, was attacked on 2 September. The 12th Battalion, Tank Corps, was deployed that day in support of the 3rd Division and the 62nd (West Riding) Division when they attacked at 5.30am towards the high ground near Lagnicourt in front of the Hindenburg Line. With just eighteen hours to go before the actual attack, there had only been sufficient time to address the infantry's officers with regard to tactics and co-operation with the tanks. The time constraints also meant that there had been no opportunity for any prior reconnaissance of the ground by either infantry or tank officers, not least because the starting line for the attack had been in enemy hands the previous day. The area around Lagnicourt and Noreuil had many sunken lanes with high banks and the clay-like nature of the ground made conditions less than ideal. As the attack got under way, many of the tanks were knocked out, whilst some ditched and mechanical failure put others out of action. The infantry's verdict on the tanks that day varied considerably; some claimed that they were of little use, whilst others praised them for providing valuable assistance until such time as they were knocked out or were otherwise disabled. Ten of the men are buried in Plot III at the start of Row F, with the remainder in Plot IV, Rows C and E, or Plot V, Row D.

Serjeant David John MORGAN DCM, 119th Heavy Battery, Royal Garrison Artillery, was killed in action on 17 September 1918, aged 38. He was a veteran of the South African campaign and had won his DCM as a corporal, though the award was gazetted on 21 October 1918, after his death. The citation pays tribute to him by stating that he had always kept his gun detachment at a high state of efficiency and had shown great coolness while under heavy fire, noting that on one occasion he had brought in wounded men across ground that was under heavy shell fire. (Plot III.G.5)

Second Lieutenant George Barton SPENCER, 13th Rifle Brigade, was killed in action on 25 August 1918, aged 28, during the Second Battle of Bapaume. He was one of four officers and forty-six other ranks from the battalion who were killed during this phase of fighting between 21 and 26 August. A further seven officers and 252 men from his battalion were also wounded during the same period. Around 400 German prisoners were captured in these operations, including some bearing the Gibraltar battle honour borne by the 73rd Hanoverian Regiment. A German officer who served with the 73rd Regiment was Ernst Jünger. He was wounded at Favreuil, near Bapaume, but managed to evade capture and survived the war. He went on later to write two classic books on the war, *Storm of Steel* and *Copse 125*. (Plot IV.A.3)

The CWGC register shows Rifleman Harry George Albert DOWNEY serving with the 104th Battalion, King's Royal Rifle Corps, at the time of his death on 25 August 1918, but he was actually killed serving with the 13th Battalion. The CWGC note regarding his battalion is quite possibly a reference to the 109th Battalion rather than the 104th Battalion and could simply be a typing error. From 1 September 1916 the 19th King's Royal Rifle Corps became a Training Reserve Battalion and was redesignated as the 109th Training Reserve Battalion. Its purpose was to act as a reserve for the regiment's 16th and 17th battalions. Similarly, the 28th Royal Fusiliers was redesignated as the 104th Training Battalion and acted as a reserve to feed the 18th and 19th Royal Fusiliers. At some stage DOWNEY was posted to the 13th King's Royal Rifle Corps, but probably via the 109th Training Battalion rather than the 104th Training Battalion. *Soldiers Died in the Great War* records his surname as Douney and shows him serving with the 13th Battalion at the time of his death. It also confirms that he had formerly served with what it refers to as the '19th Training Reserve'. (Plot IV.A.11)

Private Albert LEE DCM MM, 2nd Leinster Regiment, was killed in action on 25 August 1918, aged 29. His DCM, gazetted on 14 November 1916, was awarded for conspicuous gallantry in action. After the battalion bombers had dealt with all the dug-outs within their objective, Lance Corporal LEE, with great bravery and showing a total disregard for his own personal safety, pushed on through our own barrage and assisted in clearing a village of the enemy, thus greatly facilitating the second phase of the advance. (Plot IV.A.18)

Captain John Francis BENNETT, 9th Hampshire Regiment, attached 2/4th Battalion, was killed in action on 26 August 1918 along with nine other ranks when they came under heavy machine-gun fire from the Beugnâtre–Mory road and the high ground in front of their first objective (Plot V.A.13). Another five identified men from the 2/4th Hampshire Regiment are buried here in Plot V. Row A, including two winners of the MM: Private Henry Charles MOY MM, and Private Harry HEWITT MM (Plots V.A.16 and 18). All five men died between 26 and 30 August 1918. Captain BENNETT's headstone bears the unusual regimental badge of the Hampshire Cyclist Battalion.

Among the wide variety of units represented in this cemetery are a handful of cavalry-men. Three of them, Private Albert Henry Herbert ADAMS, Private Donald PEARCE and Private Henry RICHARDS, 17th Lancers (Duke of Cambridge's Own), were all killed in action on 28 March 1917 whilst following up the German withdrawal to the Hindenburg Line and are now buried together (Plots V.B.16 to 18). Another cavalryman, Lance Corporal John BROWNLIE, (Queen's Own Royal) Glasgow Yeomanry, fell in action on 12 May 1917. (Plot I.E.4)

Second Lieutenant Charles Maxwell PULLAN, 2nd West Riding Brigade, Royal Field Artillery, was killed in action, aged 20. He was directing the fire from his battery when a shell burst in the observation post he was occupying, mortally wounding him on 21 March 1917. He died the following day. (Plot V.D.26)

When the 59th (2nd North Midland) Division was overwhelmed on 21 March 1918, the 40th Division was committed to battle in support of the right flank of the 34th Division, which was adjacent to the 59th (2nd North Midland) Division's posi-tion. The 40th Division was one of four held in GHQ Reserve prior to the start of the battle. However, virtually all the casualties buried here from the 59th and 40th Divisions pre-date this fighting and come mainly from the period between December 1917 and the middle of March 1918. By the standards of the Western Front this was a quiet period. Casualties from the 2/6th South Staffordshire Regiment, together with a smaller number of men of the 2/5th and 2/6th North Staffordshire Regiment, the 2/5th Lincolnshire Regiment, and the 2/5th and 2/6th Sherwood Foresters, can be found predominantly in Plot III. All of these battalions were part of the 59th (2nd North Midland) Division.

The men of the 40th Division are mainly from the 13th Yorkshire Regiment, the 20th and 21st Middlesex Regiment and the 12th Suffolk Regiment. On 21 March 1918 the HQ of 178 Brigade of the 59th (2nd North Midland) Division was located in the sunken lane that runs south-west from Mory towards Béhagnies. It was joined there later that day by the HQs of 120 and 121 Brigades of the 40th Division. The 40th Division is often referred to as a bantam division, though not all of its men were below regulation height.

The gallantry award holders in this cemetery, to which reference has not already been made, are listed below:

Corporal John CAMPBELL MM, 252 Tunnelling Company, Royal Engineers, died of wounds on 18 April 1917. (Plot I.C.2)

Serjeant George BRADLEY MM, 'D' Battalion, Machine Gun Corps (Heavy Branch), died of wounds on 3 May 1917. (Plot I.D.1)

Lance Corporal Albert John MOORE MM, 19th Royal Welsh Fusiliers, killed in action on 31 January 1918. (Plot III.A.1)

Serjeant William Austin HAYES MM, 2/5th North Staffordshire Regiment, killed in action on 21 March 1918. (Plot III.D.5)

Private Alfred CRABTREE MM, 1st Royal Berkshire Regiment, killed in action on 24 August 1918. (Plot III.E.1)

Private John SPARROW MM, 2nd Suffolk Regiment, killed in action on 30 August 1918. (Plot IV.D.9)

Private John LUMSDALE MM, 5th Duke of Wellington's Regiment, killed in action on 27 August 1918. (Plot V.A.7)

Serjeant Harry WELLS MM, 1st Royal Berkshire Regiment, killed in action on 24 August 1918. (Plot V.B.20)

Serjeant Rowland LIMBERT MM, 1st Royal Berkshire Regiment, killed in action on 24 August 1918. (Plot V.B.21)

Mory Street Military Cemetery, Saint-Léger

The cemetery is located on the D.36E on the south side of the village, about two miles north of Mory. The location is set above a very good example of a sunken road. From inside the cemetery and looking south, west and then north it is possible to appreciate the possibilities that this location, and locations like it, offered the German machine gunners in late August 1918. It is a small cemetery with just sixty-six burials, five of which are unidentified. Like the nearby village of Mory, Saint-Léger was occupied by the 7th Division in March 1917, lost after a stubborn defence by the 34th Division and the 40th Division a year later, then retaken by the 62nd (West Riding) Division and the Guards Division in late August 1918.

This cemetery consists mainly of officers and men from the Guards Division who were killed in action between 24 and 27 August 1918. The majority of them are from the 2nd Coldstream Guards, though many more casualties from this battalion can be found not too far away at Croisilles British Cemetery. However, all the officers from the battalion who were killed in action on 27 August, or who died of wounds that day, are buried here. By the end of the day's fighting the 2nd Coldstream Guards had lost 111 other ranks killed and 189 wounded, leaving the battalion strength at only 140.

Lieutenant Gerard Charles BRASSEY, 2nd Coldstream Guards, was the second son of Major Leonard Campbell Brassey, MP for the Peterborough Division of Northamptonshire, who went on to become 1st Baron Brassey of Apethorpe in 1938. Gerard was educated at Eton where, in 1917, he became captain of the Oppidans, a term used to refer to the majority of boys at Eton who are common entrants, as opposed to the much smaller group of King's Scholars. His uncle, Lieutenant Colonel Edwin Brassey, commanded the 2nd Coldstream Guards from March 1918 to May 1919, and was therefore Gerard's commanding officer at the time of his death. Gerard was just 19 years old when he fell on 27 August 1918 near Saint-Léger and had only been at the front with his uncle's battalion since March of that year. (Plot A.4)

BRASSEY's mother, Lady Violet Mary Brassey, was the daughter of Charles Henry Gordon-Lennox, 7th Duke of Richmond. Gerard's cousin, Lord Bernard Gordon-Lennox, a major with the 2nd Grenadier Guards, was killed in action at the First Battle of Ypres and is buried in Zillebeke Churchyard, near Ypres. Between 1915 and 1918 the Brassey family's London residence, 40 Upper Grosvenor Street in Mayfair, was turned into an auxiliary hospital for officers and was affiliated to Queen Alexandra's Military Hospital. Lady Brassey was also distantly related to the Egerton family of Tatton Hall in Cheshire, a family that also suffered loss during the war.

Lieutenant Guy Frederick Beckham HANDLEY MC and Bar, who had also been mentioned twice in despatches (Plot A.3), and Captain Edward Jeffery WATSON-SMYTH, who had been with the regiment since February 1915 (Plot A.8), were also killed in action on the same day as Lieutenant BRASSY. HANDLEY had only been with the battalion since early December 1917, though he was an experienced soldier. He was 35 years old when he died and had won his MC serving with the York & Lancaster Regiment. It was gazetted on 25 November 1916 and was awarded for conspicuous gallantry in action after leading his men with great courage and determination. Although wounded, he remained at his post and consolidated the position. Later that day, he and his men repulsed an enemy counter-attack on the position. The bar to his MC was gazetted on 20 August 1917 and was awarded for conspicuous gallantry and devotion to duty during an attack. Prior to the assault he showed a splendid example, steadying the men under a heavy enemy barrage as he visited the entire battalion front, reorganizing where necessary. After the attack he remained in command of the captured position for three days in succession. The citation adds that his personal example and utter disregard of danger inspired all ranks to fresh efforts and enabled the position to be consolidated. Captain WATSON-SMYTH was 21 years old when he died and was already an experienced officer and soldier.

Two other men here belonging to the 2nd Coldstream Guards also hold gallantry awards. They are Serjeant Austin Edward HOOPER MM (Plot B.5) and Lance Corporal Thomas Edwin CLIFFORD MM (Plot B.9). Both men were killed in action on 27 August 1918.

Although the thirty-five identified casualties of the Coldstream Guards dominate this small cemetery, it also contains six NCOs and men of the 2nd Scots Guards who were killed in action a few days earlier, as well as two privates from the 1st Irish Guards killed on 27 and 28 August. Amongst this group is Serjeant Adolphus Harry WADE DCM, 2nd Scots Guards, who won his gallantry award in May 1915 at Festubert whilst serving as a private. He and another man were bringing up a trench mortar across ground that was swept by machine-gun fire when his comrade was killed in front of him. In spite of the continuing danger to himself, WADE proceeded with the task and brought the trench mortar forward to where it could be brought into action. He was 24 years old when he was killed on 24 August 1918. (Plot C.3)

On the night of 28 August, which was cold and showery, the 8th King's Own (Royal Lancaster Regiment) began its move towards Écoust in the wake of the previous days' fighting. The following day it pushed out patrols in order to maintain pressure on the German rearguard units. Between here and the Hindenburg Line the ground was ideally suited to this type of defence and gave the German machine-gun teams several opportunities to make their presence felt. Second Lieutenant William Leonard SMART, attached to the 8th Battalion from the Lancashire Fusiliers, was killed in action, along with twenty other ranks, whilst dealing with some of these rearguard units. A further twenty men were also wounded. He and another man from the battalion, Private Harry RUSHWORTH, are buried next to each other. (Plots A.7 and A.6)

Serjeant Thomas LOCKE MM, 'B' Battery, 74 Brigade, a Londoner born in Hackney, is one of seven identified casualties here from the Royal Field Artillery. His brigade was in support to the Guards Division throughout the advances in late August and he died of wounds on 30 August 1918. The remaining six were all killed a week later, on 6th September, and were from different artillery brigades.

Although there are a number of 1917 casualties commemorated here, their headstones are special memorials. Unfortunately, their graves were destroyed, either during the German March Offensive, or the Allied advance in late August 1918. The four men of the 21st Manchester Regiment were part of the 7th Division and were killed in action during the pursuit of the Germans as they fell back towards the Hindenburg Line shortly before the Battle of Arras began (Special Memorials 3, 4, 5 and 6). Private Joseph William CUTTELL, 6th Northamptonshire Regiment, was killed in similar circumstances on 20 March 1917. (Special Memorial 1)

St Léger British Cemetery

The village of Saint-Léger lies about eight miles south of Arras. It was captured in March 1917, but lost in March the following year during the German Offensive in spite of a gallant attempt to hold it by the 34th Division, supported by the 40th Division, which had been sent forward from reserve. In 1918 part of the third system of British trenches ran about 500 yards east of Saint-Léger, but about half a mile north of the village these defences connected to the rest of the third system, which then ran from a point about half a mile north-east of Judas Farm, then on towards Hénin. Saint-Léger was abandoned on 22 March 1918 after a temporary line had been taken up a couple of hundred yards east of Judas Farm. The following day the 31st Division linked up with the remnants of the 34th Division at this location, relieving it after two heavy days of fighting in which the 34th Division lost close to 4,000 casualties, nearly half of whom were reported as missing in action.

Saint-Léger was then re-captured by the Guards Division and the 62nd (West Riding) Division in late August 1918. On the night of 24 August 1918 the Guards Division's line ran though Judas Farm and joined that of the 56th (London) Division, about half a mile further north.

This cemetery is very well tucked away next to an old railway embankment, now disused and densely wooded. If coming from the direction of Hamelincourt along the D.12, continue for about a mile east of the junction with the D.917. The road then forks by the side of a large farm. This is Judas Farm. Bear right here and continue for just over a mile. The cemetery will be clearly visible in the fields over to the left. If arriving from any other direction, it is best to make for the centre of the village where the D.9 meets the D.12. Take the D.9 on the west side of the junction and almost immediately there is a small road branching off. Take this small road and the cemetery is over on the right. Either way, the cemetery is accessed via a track. It contains 191 casualties, only seven of whom are unidentified.

The cemetery contains fourteen identified casualties from the 1st South Staffordshire Regiment. This was one of two battalions given the task of capturing the village of Croisilles on 28 March 1917. It began its advance from a position to the north-east of Saint-Léger Wood, but initial success was soon dashed after one of its companies was heavily counter-attacked once it had reached the German wire on the south-west side of Croisilles. The other company reached its objective, which was a sunken lane, but came under heavy fire and was then counter-attacked. It was soon cut off and isolated from the rest of the attack and was then virtually annihilated. Another company from the battalion tried to reach those who were desperately hanging on, but was unable to reach them. All the South Staffordshire men buried here are either NCOs or privates and are to be found mainly in Row C.

Apart from the 1st South Staffordshire Regiment, casualties from other battalions of the 7th Division can be found here, although in far fewer numbers. One of them, Captain Thomas Trelawny BEATY-POWNALL, 3rd Border Regiment, attached 2nd Battalion, was killed in action on 24 March 1917, aged 35 (Plot A.4). His brother, Major George Ernest Beaty-Pownall DSO, also served with the same battalion, although he was later killed commanding the 1st King's Own Scottish Borderers on 10 October 1918, aged 41. He had previously fought in the South African War and had also been wounded there. He is buried at Lijssenthoek Military Cemetery in Belgium. Their father, Lieutenant Colonel George Albert Beaty-Pownall, had served with the Royal Artillery.

Another brother, William Charles Beaty-Pownall, had died of bullet wounds at Laing's Laager, Matabeleland in 1896. Yet another member of the family, Charles Pipon Beaty-Pownall, went on to become a Rear Admiral and an aide-de-camp to King George V. He served with distinction in the Royal Navy, particularly in 1914 when he played a significant part in landing the expeditionary force under Brigadier General Dobell at Tiko at the start of the campaign in the Cameroons. He was subsequently awarded a CMG for his services.

Private Richard Benjamin HOTCHKISS, 1st Royal Welsh Fusiliers, was killed in action on 3 April 1917, aged 20 (Grave B.3). His brother, Private Frederick Hotchkiss, also fell and is buried at Beersheba War Cemetery. Frederick died on 6 November 1917 whilst serving with the 1st Herefordshire Regiment.

The 110 Brigade, belonging to the 21st Division, consisted of four battalions of the Leicestershire Regiment, namely, the 6th, 7th, 8th and 9th Battalions. There are twenty-eight men from these battalions now buried here, including two officers. They were killed on various dates between April and July 1917 and are therefore widely dispersed throughout the cemetery between Rows C to F. Second Lieutenant Charles Ronald SAYERS, 9th Leicestershire Regiment, was killed in action on 13 April 1917 (Plot C.21). His brother, Lieutenant Keith Raymond Sayers, 23 Squadron, Royal Flying Corps, formerly Queen's Own (Royal West Kent Regiment), was also killed in action later that year, on 9 September 1917, aged 21. He has no known grave and is commemorated on the Flying Services Memorial at Arras.

A number of the burials relate to an operation carried out to coincide with the opening of the Battle of Cambrai. This was the attack on part of the Hindenburg Line known as Tunnel Trench. Captain Gerald J. FITZGIBBON, 10th Royal Dublin Fusiliers, was killed in action during this attack on 20 November 1917 (Plot G.4). He is one of a small group of men from three different battalions of Royal Dublin Fusiliers to be found in Rows G and H who were killed or who died of wounds during that attack, or in the ten days that followed it, just prior to the 16th (Irish) Division leaving this area at the start of December. Amongst them is Serjeant James

MERRINS MM and Bar, 2nd Royal Dublin Fusiliers, who died of wounds, very likely here at Saint-Léger where a number of field ambulances were located. *Soldiers Died in the Great War* records the same man as James Merrin and only shows the award of the MM next to his name, not the bar. However, the identical army number shows that this is the same individual who is buried here. The *London Gazette* shows that both awards were conferred posthumously; the first gazetted on 4 February 1918, the bar two months later on 2 April 1918. (Plot H.5)

Serjeant William DELANEY MM, 2nd Royal Irish Regiment, is another 16th (Irish) Division casualty who died from wounds sustained in the attack on Tunnel Trench on 20 November 1917 (Plot G.3). Corporal Horace Louis MORROW MM, 11th Hampshire Regiment, is one of five identified casualties in this cemetery from the 16th (Irish) Division's pioneer battalion. He and his comrades were killed or died of wounds either in the run up to operations on 20 November 1917 or the following day when the battalion's main task was to consolidate the captured positions. This was a vital part of the operation. (Plot G.7)

Attempts to capture Tunnel Trench earlier in the year had involved several minor operations during May and June. A good account of these operations, and the reasons for their failure, can be found in *The War the Infantry Knew 1914–1919* by Captain J.C. Dunn. The war diary of the 1st Queen's (Royal West Surrey Regiment) also has a good account of a small operation, carried out nearby on the morning of 29 June 1917, aimed at seizing several posts in and around Kitten Trench and then establishing a block there. The attack was carried out at company strength, but met strong resistance and was soon called off, thankfully with few casualties. Four men who died during this operation are buried together. (Plots F.18 to 21)

There are also thirteen NCOs and privates of the 2nd Worcestershire Regiment who, like the 1st Queen's (Royal West Surrey Regiment), belonged to the 33rd Division. Most of them were killed in action on or around 23 April 1917 when the Battle of Arras moved into its second main phase, often referred to as the Second Battle of the Scarpe. Two of these men, Corporal John MUDGE (Plot C.31) and Serjeant Solomon NASH (Plot C.32), have army numbers that suggest that they may have been with the battalion when it was involved in the heroic counter-attack at Gheluvelt on 31 October 1914, though I have been unable to confirm this. A number of men from the 101st Field Ambulance, attached to the 33rd Division, are also buried here in Row E, many of whom were killed around the same time as the Worcestershire men.

A small group of seven officers and men from the 1st East Lancashire Regiment are scattered between Rows D, E, and G. All of them were killed or died of wounds on 12 and 13 March 1918 during their first tour of front line duty as part of the 34th Division. The 1st East Lancashire Regiment had previously served with the 4th Division, but under the reorganization in February 1918 that reduced the number of battalions in a brigade from four to three, the 1st East Lancashire Regiment found itself in trenches near Boisleux-Saint-Marc and Saint-Léger, detached from its old division. Although the beginning of March was a quiet period, the first twelve days spent in the line was longer than the battalion had been used to. When it was eventually relieved, it found that its billets and other facilities were very poor and complained bitterly that the out-going battalion appeared to have done absolutely nothing to make life more bearable. The battalion clearly felt a little homesick. Morale, *esprit de corps*, and leadership would be critical factors in the days ahead.

There are several more gallantry awards buried in this cemetery. They are: Second Lieutenant Frederick George COLES MC, 16th Trench Mortar Battery, Royal Field Artillery, killed in action on 25 September 1917, aged 33. His MC was gazetted in the King's Birthday Honours List on 4 June 1917 (Plot B.5); Private William Graham HOPKINS MM, 9th Devonshire Regiment, killed in action on 22 April 1917 (Plot D.18); and Corporal James Sidney SATTLER MM, 104th Battery, 22 Brigade, Royal Field Artillery, killed in action on 27 April 1917, aged 23. His artillery unit was part of the 7th Division and had been in action at Mametz in 1916 during the fighting on the Somme (Plot E.8).

There is just one burial from the 9th April 1917, the opening day of the Battle of Arras, and that is Sowar Allah Yar KHAN, 36th Jacob's Horse, an Indian cavalry regiment that was part of the 1st Indian Cavalry Division. The division had also been part of operations to follow the German withdrawal back to the Hindenburg Line. He was the only man from his regiment to lose his life on 9 April. (Plot A.7)

Vaulx Australian Field Ambulance Cemetery

Vaulx-Vraucourt is situated twelve miles south-south-east of Arras. As with Noreuil Australian Cemetery and Lagnicourt Hedge Cemetery, I would always suggest using the D.5 from Arras, rather than the D.917 Arras-Bapaume road, in order to take in the string of villages that formed the last line of resistance before the Germans began the final stage of their withdrawal behind the Hindenburg Line in late March 1917.

The cemetery lies just over half a mile south of the village on the D.10E4. On exiting the village in the direction of Beugnâtre, the cemetery is clearly visible in the fields. The CWGC register notes that it was begun in April 1917, soon after the village was captured, and that it remained in use until February 1918. When the Germans retook Vaulx-Vraucourt in March the following year, they added to it with a number of burials of their own. A peculiarity of this cemetery is that it now contains more German than Commonwealth graves.

This is a small cemetery, where fifty-one of the fifty-two casualties are identified, the first of whom fell on 9 April 1917. Other burials followed throughout the month, including Major Alastair Cosmo Burton GEDDES MC, 17th Kite Balloon Company, Royal Flying Corps, who was killed in action on 19 April 1917, aged 25. After completing his studies in 1914 at Edinburgh University where he gained a Bachelor of Science degree, he joined the Royal Naval Air Service and went to France in August 1915. He then joined the Kite Balloon Section of the Royal Flying Corps and was awarded the MC in January 1917 in the New Year's Honours List. In April that year he was made a Chevalier of the Légion of Honour. His father, Professor Patrick Geddes, was Professor of Botany at Dundee University. He is the only casualty here from April 1917 who is not a member of the Australian Imperial Force. (Plot B.14)

The Second Battle of Bullecourt, which began on 3 May 1917, gave rise to further burials, including a number of men attached to the 3rd, 7th and 14th Australian Field

Ambulances. Among the Australian dead are two officers who were killed in action on 6 May. One of them is Lieutenant Norman DOUGALL MC, 10th Battalion, Australian Infantry. His MC was gazetted on 18 June 1917 and was awarded for leading a counter-attack that drove back the enemy, saving the situation at a critical time. The citation gives no further details regarding the circumstances of the award (Plot B.18). The other officer, Lieutenant Kenneth Koeppen WENDT, was just 18 years old when he was killed (Plot B.21). Both men had been in action a few weeks earlier at Lagnicourt. In fact, the citation for DOUGALL's MC bears close resemblance to an action at Lagnicourt described by C.E.W. BEAN, author of the *Official History of the AIF in the War of 1914–1918*.

As May unfolded, Australian burials ceased; in fact, no further burials took place until July that year when units of the 62nd (West Riding) Division began burying their dead here adjacent to the medical facilities. After playing a key part in the First and Second Battles of Bullecourt, the division remained in this sector where it held the line until the end of September. Again, there was a gap of several months before burials resumed in December 1917, though in relatively small numbers. These late 1917 casualties are either from the Royal Garrison Artillery or the 4th South Staffordshire Regiment.

Amongst the May casualties are two gallantry award holders; Private Jean Louis Michel GALLANTY MM, 7th Field Ambulance, Australian Army Medical Corps, who died of wounds on 5 May 1917 (Plot C.13) and Private John UNCLE MM, 6th Battalion, Australian Infantry, who died on 8 May (Plot C.15). Both awards were gazetted on 27 October 1916 and both men were mortally wounded during a week of heavy losses when around a third of the stretcher-bearers belonging to the 2nd, 5th, 6th 7th and 14th Australian Field Ambulances became casualties.

There are just a few casualties who fell in January and February 1918, some of whom are men of the 4th South Staffordshire Regiment. The last burial here is an officer of Drake Battalion, Royal Naval Volunteer Reserve. Sub Lieutenant George HUNTER was killed in action near the Achiet-le-Grand–Arras railway line on 21 August 1918 and was one of four sub lieutenants from that battalion who lost their lives during the final week of August. (Plot A.5)

Vaulx Hill Cemetery, Vaulx-Vraucourt

Vaulx Hill Cemetery is located about 500 yards north-east of the village on the D.36. Of the 856 graves here, almost 600 are identified. There are twenty-nine special memorials to men known or believed to be buried here, as well as four soldiers now commemorated on this site who were originally buried in other cemeteries, but whose graves were lost by shell fire. The vast majority of burials are 1918 casualties, but there are still 128 relating to the previous year.

Heavy fighting took place here during the German Offensive in March 1918 when Vaulx Vraucourt was defended by men of the 6th Division. Three of its battalions are well represented here: the 2nd Durham Light Infantry, the 1st West Yorkshire Regiment and the 11th Essex Regiment. There are also some casualties from the 25th Division, and even the 41st Division, both of which were in reserve on the 21st March, but soon became involved in fighting to the north of Bapaume.

Although Vaulx Vraucourt was captured and occupied by British and Dominion troops in March 1917, no cemetery existed on this site until September 1918 when seventeen graves were made in what is now Plot I, Rows A and B. The cemetery was very much enlarged after the Armistice as graves were brought in from the battle-field and from the closure of other cemeteries. Nevertheless, there are four casualties here from 1916, three of which can be found in Plot I, Row C, the other in Plot III, Row F.

Captain George Edward COCKERILL, 16th Battalion, London Regiment (Queen's Westminster Rifles), died of wounds in German captivity on 3 July 1916 fol-lowing the attack by the 56th (London) Division at Gommecourt on 1 July 1916. He is known to have fallen that day, along with two other officers from that battalion, but little is known about the exact circumstances of his death. (Plot I.C.15)

Private George William WRIGHT, 1/5th Sherwood Foresters, died the same day as Captain COCKERILL, 3 July 1916. *Soldiers Died in the Great War* makes the distinc-tion between soldiers who died of wounds and soldiers who died whilst on military service; WRIGHT is shown as having died, but there is no reference to wounds. However, his battalion did attack on 1 July 1916 north of Gommecourt Wood. His burial here suggests that he may well have suffered the same fate as COCKERILL. (Plot I.C.10)

Second Lieutenant John Mortimer McBAIN, 231 Brigade, Royal Field Artillery, is recorded as having died from his wounds on 9 July 1916, aged 20. It would be highly unusual for gunners to be captured during a time of offensive action by their own side, since by virtue of their role they would almost always be behind the front line. Forward observation officers, however, were an exception to the rule and would often be located in front line trenches, sometimes going out into no man's land to inspect damage to the enemy's wire. This may well explain how he was wounded, and possibly captured. (Plot I.C.11)

Plot I also contains fifty-eight New Zealanders. All apart from one man are from one of the four battalions of the 3rd New Zealand (Rifle) Brigade and were killed or died of wounds between 26 and 31 August 1918 during the fighting around Bapaume. These men can be found in Rows A, B, C and E. According to the CWGC register, twenty-two of them were brought here after the Armistice from New Zealand Cemetery No. 17, which was at Favreuil.

Second Lieutenant John DENSEM DCM, 4th Battalion, 3rd New Zealand (Rifle) Brigade, was killed in action on 26 August 1918. His surname in the CWGC register is recorded as 'Densen', but his DCM is gazetted under the above spelling. It was gazetted on 1 January 1918 and was awarded while he was serving as a lance sergeant. The citation, which was gazetted on 17 April that year, states that he worked day and night in a heavily shelled area supervising working parties and guiding parties forward under heavy fire. By his initiative and using his energy, he carried out his task of establishing a forward dump with great success. (Plot I.A.27)

Lieutenant Cecil Harold SEWELL VC, 1st Queen's Own (Royal West Kent Regi-ment), was killed in action serving with the 3rd Battalion, Tank Corps, whilst supporting an attack by the New Zealand Rifle Brigade on 29 August 1918, aged 23

(Plot I.D.3). He was killed going to the aid of another tank after it had ditched in a shell hole. Its crew were trapped inside the machine, which had caught fire. SEWELL got out of his own tank under heavy fire and managed to dig away sufficient earth to enable the crew to escape, though they had by then managed to put out the fire. It was while he was returning to his own machine that he was hit several times and killed next to his gunner, Private William KNOX, who is now buried in the next grave. (Plot I.D.2)

Private Thomas PATERSON, 2nd King's Own Scottish Borderers, was killed in action on 26 August 1918, aged 19 (Plot I.D.12). His brother, Private William Paterson, was killed serving with the 5th Cameron Highlanders on 26 September 1918 and is buried in Gwalia Cemetery in Belgium.

Lieutenant John William DARLOW MC, 1st Queen's Own (Royal West Kent Regiment), was attached to the 16th Royal Warwickshire Regiment when he was killed in action on 29 August 1918, aged 24. His MC was gazetted on 2 December 1918 and was awarded for his inspiring leadership and courage whilst commanding a support company during an advance. Seeing that gaps had occurred in the attacking line, he skilfully pushed forward platoons to fill those gaps. The following day he led a patrol forward and cleared a gully, capturing nine prisoners and a machine gun that otherwise would have held up the advance. (Plot I.E.23)

Company Quartermaster Serjeant Frank BOOTH DCM, 2nd Battalion, Machine Gun Corps, was killed in action on 10 September 1918, aged 27. His DCM was won while he was serving as a private in the Oxfordshire & Buckinghamshire Light Infantry. It was awarded for conspicuous gallantry in action after he had set up his machine gun in the open in order to break up an enemy counter-attack. When all his gun crew had become casualties and his gun had been put out of action, he continued the fight by sniping at the enemy, causing them heavy casualties. The citation concludes that his coolness and bravery under fire had been most marked. The award was gazetted on 14 November 1916. (Plot I.J.22)

Serjeant Joseph HAVENHAND DCM, 5th King's Own Yorkshire Light Infantry, was killed in action on 2 September 1918. His DCM was gazetted on 22 October 1917 and was awarded for conspicuous gallantry and devotion to duty at a critical moment in an attack when his company was held up by heavy machine-gun fire from a concrete strongpoint. Taking a few men with him, he succeeded in getting close enough to the post to bomb it. This act of gallantry enabled his company to advance and capture its first objective. The citation appeared on 26 January 1918. *Soldiers Died in the Great War* shows him serving with the 2/4th Battalion of his regiment at the time of his death. (Plot I.K.1)

Private James McPHEE, 2nd Highland Light Infantry, is shown in the CWGC register as having died on 19 December 1918, after the Armistice (Plot II.A.10). His army number is identical to that of Private James McPHIE, 2nd Highland Light Infantry, who is recorded in *Soldiers Died in the Great War* as having been killed in action on 12 September 1918. Also buried with him in this cemetery are three other men from his battalion who were killed in action on 12 September or who died of wounds that day, as are several of his other comrades who fell around that date. I am therefore inclined to believe that the September date is the more likely of the two, particularly as one of the three casualties who died on 12 September, Private Andrew JOHNSTONE, is buried a few graves away from him (Plot II.A.15). The discrepancy is almost certainly a simple clerical error whereby the day and month of death have become almost inverted and consequently confused.

The highest-ranking casualty buried in this cemetery is Lieutenant Colonel Bertram Alexander Gordon WATTS DSO, 4th Australian Field Artillery, who was killed in action when his dug-out was hit by a shell on 10th April 1917. His DSO, gazetted on 3 June 1916 in the King's Birthday Honours List, was awarded for distinguished service in the field. He was 37 years old when he died (Plot II.B.3). Killed with him were members of his staff, including Captain Brian Hamilton MACK, 7th Field Ambulance, Australian Army Medical Corps, aged 24 (Plot II.B.4) and Lieutenants Herbert George HARDING, aged 34, and Guy Kennedy DAVENPORT MC, who was eight years his junior. DAVENPORT's MC was gazetted on 1 January 1917 in the New Years Honours List. HARDING and DAVENPORT are buried together in the same grave. (Plot II.B.6)

Captain Guy Brooke BAILEY, 52nd Battalion, Australian Infantry, was killed in action on 28 March 1917, aged 33 (Plot II.F.19). He and HARDING had both been previously mentioned in despatches.

Second Lieutenant Reginald William COOK MC, 3rd Devonshire Regiment, attached 1st Battalion, was killed in action on 1 September 1918, aged 26. His MC was awarded for his gallantry, skill and endurance after his company commander had become a casualty. He took command of his company and showed great ability protecting the entire divisional flank. He remained on duty throughout the operation and only had his wounds dressed once the situation had become stable. His award was posthumously gazetted on 5 November 1918. (Plot II.B.26)

In the days prior to the first attack on Bullecourt on 11 April 1917, the Australian Field Artillery positions in the shallow valleys around Noreuil and Lagnicourt came under shell fire from German batteries, which inevitably caused casualties amongst the Australian gunners. Some of those casualties are buried here amongst the nineteen men from 4, 5, 6 and 12 Brigades, Australian Field Artillery, who were killed or who died of wounds in April and May 1917. Also buried with them are a handful of men from the 5th, 7th and 13th Field Ambulances, Australian Army Medical Corps, two of whom held the MM. They are Private Alfred Edgar RICHARDS MM, 13th Field Ambulance, Australian Army Medical Corps, who was killed in action on 27 March 1917 (Plot II.F.22) and Lance Corporal A. BAILEY MM, 5th Field Ambulance, Australian Army Medical Corps, killed in action on 24 April 1918 (Plot II.G.14).

On 20 March 1917 an advance force under the command of Brigadier General John Gellibrand, later to become Major General, carried out a bold attempt to pinch out the village of Noreuil, which lay just in front of the Hindenburg Line. The village turned out to be more heavily defended than had first been thought and casualties from the operation came to thirteen officers and 318 other ranks, thirty-eight of whom were recorded as killed. Of the fifty that were reported missing, some were actually captured after they failed to receive the order to withdraw.

The units involved were the 21st Battalion and the 23rd Battalion, Australian Infantry. The CWGC records now show that twenty men from the 23rd Battalion were killed or died of wounds on 20 March 1917 and forty-four from the 21st Battalion; rather more than were originally reported. Inevitably, some of the wounded would have died after the original casualty return had been filed, as would some of those initially reported missing in action. Most have no known grave and are commemorated on the Australian Memorial at Villers Bretonneux.

However, one officer, Lieutenant David Stanley EVANS, 23rd Battalion, Australian Infantry, is buried in this cemetery (Plot III.B.15) along with three of his men killed in that operation, two of whom are buried near him (Plot III.B.17 and 19). The other is buried elsewhere in the cemetery (Plot I.G.1). EVANS had been acting adjutant of the battalion and was shot whilst trying to make his way to a group of men led by a fellow officer.

Another interesting casualty from 1917 is Second Lieutenant Charles Gustave Rochefort MACKINTOSH, 18 Squadron, Royal Flying Corps, who was killed in action on 5 April 1917, aged 38. He was educated at the City of London School and had also spent some time living in Germany before the war. In 1913, as a German and French speaker, he went to Switzerland where he worked as a journalist for the *Daily Mail*, and also as a winter sports representative for the Royal Automobile Club. It was here that he was accused of spying, along with a number of other journalists, and spent several weeks in prison before being tried by court-martial, though fortunately he was acquitted.

When the war broke out he volunteered for the Royal Flying Corps and initially flew as an observer. On 5 April 1917 he was wounded three times whilst in action. His pilot that day, Lieutenant Harry Atheling Russell Boustead, managed to land their FE2b aircraft behind British lines, though MACKINTOSH was already dead. Unfortunately, Lieutenant Boustead died from his wounds a few hours after landing. He is now buried at Pozières British Cemetery on the Somme. (Plot II.B.10)

Serjeant Charles McGREGOR DCM, 1st Cheshire Regiment, was killed in action on 2 September 1918, aged 31. His DCM was awarded for courage and determination after the advance of his battalion was held up. Single-handedly, he killed the enemy detachment responsible for the hold up, capturing its machine gun, thereby saving the battalion many casualties. His behaviour throughout the day was described as a splendid example of conspicuous gallantry and devotion to duty. (Plot II.C.1)

Lieutenant George Henry ADNEY MC, 7th Battalion, Tank Corps, was killed in action on 2 September1918, aged 21. His MC was gazetted on 15 February 1918 and was awarded for his part in three attacks carried out in a single day. On two occasions he led parties of infantry forward in the attack. He also gave valuable assistance to the infantry in two other attacks, showing great skill and courage. The citation, which was not gazetted until 16 July 1918, actually refers to four attacks, not three. (Plot II.C.16)

Although shown in the CWGC register as serving with the Herefordshire Regiment, Private James WILTON was one of a number of men from the regiment's

1/1st Battalion who were posted to the 7th King's Shropshire Light Infantry. Others were transferred to other battalions of the King's Shropshire Light Infantry and also served overseas. (Plot II.F.2)

Second Lieutenant James MIDDLETON MC, 7th King's Shropshire Light Infantry, was killed in action on 2 September 1918 near Lagnicourt, aged 29. His battalion advanced around 4,000 yards that day capturing three 77mm guns, thirty-two machine guns, eight trench mortars, three anti-tank rifles and 235 prisoners. He had previously served with the Lancashire Fusiliers as a private, then as a lance corporal, before transferring to the Border Regiment as an NCO. He was then gazetted as a second lieutenant in the South Wales Borderers. His MC is acknowledged in the regimental history of the King's Shropshire Light Infantry and in *Officers Died in the Great War*, but I can find no trace of it in any of the Gazettes. (Plot II.F.3)

Captain Roland Maddison VAISEY, 36 Brigade, Royal Field Artillery, was killed in action on 7 September 1918 (Plot II.H.1). Prior to serving during the war he worked as a partner in his father's law firm. His son, Sergeant John Roland Maddison Vaisey, was killed on 30 September 1941, aged 25, serving with 58 Squadron, Royal Air Force. He and fellow crew members took off from their airbase at Linton-on-Ouse in their Whitley aircraft in the late afternoon of 29 September on a bombing mission over Stettin as part of a combined force of Whitley, Stirling, Wellington, and Halifax bombers. Their aircraft was one of eight that failed to return and all five crew members were reported missing, presumed killed. He and his crew are commemorated on the Runnymede Memorial.

Lieutenant Alfred Maxwell WILLIAMSON-NAPIER, 75 Brigade, Royal Field Artillery, was killed in action on 12 September 1918. He had been awarded the *Croix de Guerre* (France). (Plot III.A.2)

Captain Ernest Bowen SHELLEY, 1st Grenadier Guards, died on 12 September 1918 near Havrincourt when a shell burst, killing him and wounding two of his fellow officers. He was wounded on the Somme near Arrow Head Copse in September 1916. His brother, Major George Edward Shelley, served with the 4th Grenadier Guards and was wounded at Loos in September 1915, but survived the war. (Plot III.A.13)

Second Lieutenant Colin Winder WARWICK MC, 5th Border Regiment, attached 8th Battalion, was killed in action on 22 March 1918 near Vaulx Wood, aged 26. Despite being surrounded on three sides that day, several detachments from his battalion held out for four hours before retiring. He was killed sometime during that engagement, though the exact circumstances of his death remain obscure. His MC was gazetted on 25 August 1917 and was awarded for conspicuous gallantry and devotion to duty after he had led his platoon against a strong enemy position, capturing forty prisoners and killing many others. Through his skilful handling of the attack, his platoon suffered only one casualty. Later that day, he also outflanked and captured another enemy strongpoint, capturing its machine gun and killing its crew. He then went on to attack a field gun position, killing the crew and capturing the gun. The citation concludes by stating that throughout the operations he displayed the greatest gallantry. (Plot III.C.15)

Lieutenant Gavin Ferguson YOUNG, 3 Squadron, Royal Air Force, was killed in action on 2 September 1918 whilst flying a Sopwith Camel. I have yet to come across any account of how he died. He was one of sixteen members of the Royal Air Force who died on the Western Front that day and the only one from 3 Squadron. (Plot III.E.6)

Second Lieutenant Herbert Edward ARNOLD, 5 Squadron, Royal Flying Corps, is another man shown in *Officers Died in the Great War* as simply having died whilst on military service. However, *Royal Flying Corps Communiqué No. 68* shows him as missing in action on Boxing Day 1916 along with his observer, Lieutenant Insoll. This is corroborated by the entry in *Airmen Died in the Great War*, which shows ARNOLD as having been killed in action on Boxing Day. They had, in fact, taken off at 9.15am on 26 December to carry out a bombing raid on Vaulx-Vraucourt, one of several locations behind German lines that were targeted that day. They managed to reach their target, but were shot down close to the village. ARNOLD clearly died from his injuries, but Insoll was taken prisoner. Just prior to the Christmas period, ARNOLD's squadron had been deployed on observation duties for the artillery. ARNOLD had originally served with the Royal Fusiliers, but joined the Royal Flying Corps in 1916. (Plot III.F.20)

Private Joseph Wright HARRISON DCM, 5th King's Own Yorkshire Light Infantry, was killed in action on 2 September 1918. *Soldiers Died in the Great War* shows the year of his death as 1915, which is incorrect. He had formerly served with the Manchester Regiment and the Northumberland Fusiliers. HARRISON, who came from Standish, near Wigan, was serving with the 23rd Northumberland Fusiliers when he won his DCM, which was gazetted on 3 September 1918. It was awarded for conspicuous gallantry and devotion to duty whilst in charge of a Lewis gun team. Under heavy fire, he repeatedly rushed his gun forward to within a hundred yards of the advancing enemy. In doing so, he held up parties as they were trying to advance and inflicted heavy casualties on them. (Plot III.J.12)

Two men in Plot III at the start of Row K were killed on Christmas Eve 1917. Private Ellis Eaves HOLMES and Private William HUMPHREYS, 2nd South Lancashire Regiment, were in a dug-out with their comrades when it collapsed. A rescue attempt was undertaken and after several hours those inside were brought out, though both men were found to be dead (Plots III.K.1 and 2). The two men next to them also served with the same regiment, but belonged to the 8th Battalion, not the 2nd Battalion, and died a month later.

Major Bertram Chambré PARR, Oxfordshire & Buckinghamshire Light Infantry, attached 2nd South Staffordshire Regiment, was killed in action on 3 September 1918. Although the CWGC register gives no biographical details, his mother was the Honourable Constance Lavinia Harriet Plunkett, daughter of Admiral Edward Plunkett, 15th Lord Dunsany. (Plot III.K.17)

The remaining gallantry awards in this cemetery are all holders of the MM and are listed below:

Sergeant Robert ELLMERS MM, 2nd Battalion, 3rd New Zealand (Rifle) Brigade, killed in action on 26 August 1918, aged 20. (Plot I.B.22)

Private Sampson Edwin JASPERS MM, 1st Duke of Cornwall's Light Infantry, killed in action on 30 August 1918. (Plot I.E.4)

Private Ambler WOODHEAD MM, 2/4th Duke of Wellington's Regiment, killed in action on 30 August 1918, aged 21. *Soldiers Died in the Great War* makes no reference to his MM. (Plot I.H.8)

Serjeant John E. STURGESS MM, 2nd Highland Light Infantry, killed in action on 11 September 1918, aged 19. *Soldiers Died in the Great War* makes no reference to his MM. (Plot I.J.7)

Serjeant Frederick Hyde BROWN MM, 276th Siege Battery, Royal Garrison Artillery, killed in action on 13 September 1918, aged 24. (Plot I.J.26)

Private Ernest SMITH MM, 5th King's Own Yorkshire Light Infantry, killed in action on 2 September 1918. (Plot I.K.12)

Rifleman George LUMLEY MM, 8th West Yorkshire Regiment, killed in action on 2 September 1918, aged 22. (Plot I.K.19)

Corporal George Thomas WORTH MM, 'A' Battery, 155 Brigade, Royal Field Artillery, killed in action on 10 September 1918. (Plot II.A.14)

Serjeant John William RYAN MM, Royal Engineers, killed in action on 17 December 1917. (Plot II.A.28)

Lance Serjeant John Samuel BASS MM, 1st Bedfordshire Regiment, killed in action on 2 September 1918, aged 34. (Plot II.C.3)

Private Joel TOOTH MM, 5th King's Own Yorkshire Light Infantry, killed in action on 2 September 1918. *Soldiers Died in the Great War* shows him as killed in action on 20 July 1918 and makes no reference to the award of his MM. However, it does note that he came from Staffordshire and had previously served with the Northumberland Fusiliers. An entry in the *London Gazette* dated 7 October 1918 confirms the award of the MM to a Private J. Tooth, Northumberland Fusiliers, who came from Staffordshire, with an army number identical to the one shown in *Soldiers Died in the Great War*. (Plot II.E.2)

Serjeant P. FOX MM, 5th King's Own Scottish Borderers, killed in action on 2 September 1918, aged 32. There appears to be no trace of this soldier in the relevant volume of *Soldiers Died in the Great War*, but his MM was gazetted on 11 February 1919. He came from Pontefract. (Plot II.F.28)

Private Thomas William HOWE MM, 2/4th York & Lancaster Regiment, killed in action on 2 September 1918, aged 27. (Plot III.J.26)

Private William POTTS MM, 2/4th King's Own Yorkshire Light Infantry, killed in action on 2 September 1918, aged 19. His MM was gazetted on 11 February 1919. Like Private Joel TOOTH, he had previously served with the Northumberland Fusiliers, and his entry in *Soldiers Died in the Great War* also makes no reference to the award of the MM. (Plot III.K.18)

Corporal Charles LEWIS MM, 8th West Yorkshire Regiment, killed in action on 1 September 1918, aged 19. (Plot III.K.25)

Vraucourt Copse Cemetery, Vaulx-Vraucourt

The cemetery lies about 1,000 yards north-north-east of the village of Vaulx-Vraucourt, just off the D.36E, which is the road that runs north from the village towards Écoust Saint-Mein. The cemetery can be seen from the road, but is reached via a farm track that runs off to the right.

The cemetery, which was begun in April 1917, originally contained fewer than half the number of graves we see today. Most of these were the consequence of fighting by the 3rd Division on 2 and 3 September 1918. However, in 1928, a nearby cemetery, Vraucourt ADS Cemetery, was closed owing to its location. The ground there, which often became waterlogged, made the site difficult to maintain, and so the bodies were exhumed and brought here. Today, 98 of the 104 burials are identified.

A significant number of those 3rd Division casualties are from the 2nd Royal Scots. All twenty-three men were killed in action on 2 September 1918, including Lieutenant Alexander Stuart ROBERTSON MC, 8th Royal Scots, attached 2nd Battalion. They now lie buried here in Plot I, Rows A and B. ROBERTSON's MC was posthumously gazetted on 2 December 1918 and was won whilst commanding his company during an attack on Noreuil in which he was killed. The citation points out that by spotting and clearing out a number of machine-gun posts that had been passed over by the attacking lines of infantry he undoubtedly saved many casualties. He also personally ensured that his flanks were in touch with other units during the attack, demonstrating not only gallantry, but also great organizational skills.

The 2nd Battalion lost two officers and twenty-five other ranks that day and a further four officers and 132 other men were shown as wounded or missing. Most of the men who fell are buried here. As for the others, Lance Corporal George R. Fraser MM, 2nd Royal Scots, is buried in Noreuil Australian Cemetery and Privates Swanston and Howitt are buried in Vaulx Hill Cemetery. The other officer, Lieutenant William Fleming Oliphant Morrison, also shown in the CWGC records as 8th Battalion, Royal Scots, but who was actually attached to the 2nd Battalion, is buried at Quéant Road Cemetery, Buissy. Once Noreuil had been captured, Morrison was ordered to push on with two platoons to clear the ridge south-east of the village, but his group was forced to withdraw after two hours of fighting and heavy losses. He was amongst those killed in the encounter.

One grave of particular note is that of Private Hugh McIVER VC MM and Bar, 2nd Royal Scots (Plot I.A.19). His VC was won on 23 August 1918 just east of Gomiécourt. It was there that he had braved heavy artillery and machine-gun fire, showing a total disregard for his own safety whilst carrying messages back and forth as a runner. At one point, single-handedly, he pursued an enemy scout who was making his way back to a machine-gun post. Attacking the post, he killed six of the occupants and captured twenty others along with two machine guns. By eliminating the threat posed by the position he enabled his company to advance without further hindrance. Later, he placed himself in considerable danger when he stopped a tank from mistakenly firing on our own troops, thereby saving many lives.

His MM was gazetted on 19 September 1916, and the bar two years later, on 21 October 1918. He had originally enlisted in August 1914 and so was a very experienced soldier. On 23 August 2008, the 90th anniversary of his winning the VC, a memorial to him was unveiled in the village of Courcelles-le-Comte. Several of his relatives attended the ceremony, complete with pipes and drums. Although the circumstances surrounding his VC are well documented, I have yet to find any account of the actions that led to the award of the MM or the bar to it.

Around a third of the current graves belong to Australian soldiers who were killed or who died of wounds in April and May 1917. A fair number of them hold gallantry awards and all are buried in Plots II and III. These are graves that were removed from Vraucourt ADS Cemetery and brought here in 1928. All fell during the fighting at the First and Second Battles of Bullecourt or during the German raid at Lagnicourt on 15 April, or in the days immediately following these actions.

Captain Norman Craig SHIERLAW MC, 13th Battalion, Australian Infantry, was killed on 11 April 1917. He enlisted in June 1915 and was a Fellow of the Royal College of Surgeons in Edinburgh before the war. The citation for his MC states that for two days he had continually attended to the wounded under heavy fire, noting that he had also done fine work on many other occasions. The award was gazetted on 26 March 1917 (Plot I.B.13). Nearby is Private William George WALTERS MM, 4th Battalion, Australian Infantry, who was killed in action on the last day of April 1917. (Plot II.B.8)

Buried next to WALTERS is Second Lieutenant Richmond Gordon HOWELL-PRICE MC, 1st Battalion, Australian Infantry, who was killed on 4 May 1917, aged 20. His was another one of those families that really distinguished itself during the war. He was the youngest of six sons who gave service to the Empire. Richmond originally enlisted as a trooper in the Australian Light Horse in December 1915 and served briefly in the Middle East before gaining a commission with the 1st Battalion, Australian Infantry. He was wounded on 3 May 1917 during the Second Battle of Bullecourt and died the next day. Three days after his death he was awarded the MC. (Plot II.B.7)

The eldest son, David, who was born in 1881, had previously served in the South African War and worked as a staff officer with the Australian Imperial Force during the Great War. John, who was born in 1886, went on to win the DSO for his actions as a lieutenant on board the submarine HMS *C3* during the raid on Zeebrugge on 23 April 1918. He survived the war and died in 1937. Another brother, Frederick, was also awarded the DSO in the King's Birthday Honours in June 1919 after serving as a major in Palestine.

Another brother, Lieutenant Colonel Owen Glendower Howell-Price DSO MC, commissioned in August 1914, commanded the 3rd Battalion, Australian Infantry. He won his MC at Lone Pine in the Gallipoli campaign in 1915 where he was also mentioned in despatches. He then fought at Pozières on the Somme in 1916 and was again mentioned in despatches. On 3 November 1916, whilst supervising work on a machine-gun emplacement prior to an attack near Gueudecourt, he was shot through the head and died of his wound the next day at the casualty clearing station, aged 26. He is buried at Heilly Station Cemetery, Méricourt-L'Abbé. His DSO was gazetted on 1 January 1917 in the New Year's Honours List.

Following Richmond's death, Lieutenant General Birdwood is said to have moved Phillip Llewelyn Howell-Price DSO MC, to a position on the staff at I Anzac Corps, but Phillip, who had enlisted in the 1st Battalion, Australian Infantry, as a private in

September 1914, soon had a decision to make. On learning that his old battalion was about to go into battle at Broodseinde during the Third Battle of Ypres, he insisted on joining it. Sadly, he was killed on 4 October 1917, aged 23, when he was caught in the artillery barrage. He, like his brother Owen, had landed at Gallipoli and was severely wounded at Lone Pine, where he was also mentioned in despatches. His DSO was awarded for his part in leading a raiding party on enemy positions near Armentières on 27 June 1916. He also fought on the Somme in July 1916 near Pozières, and again in November that year at Gueudecourt. He was also wounded the following year at Bullecourt and his MC was won in June at the Battle of Messines.

Although Phillip was an experienced officer, perhaps General Birdwood thought that he had fought long and hard already, hence the decision to retain him on the staff. However, Phillip's sense of duty towards his old battalion proved the greater attraction for him. He has no known grave and is commemorated on the Menin Gate.

Two other captains from the Australian Imperial Force are also buried here. Captain James Gordon TYSON MC, 3rd Battalion, Australian Infantry, was killed on 3 May 1917, aged 22 (Plot II.B.11); Captain Norman Gilbert PELTON, 58th Battalion, Australian Infantry, was killed by shell fire on 12 May 1917, aged 36 (Plot II.A.11). TYSON's MC was gazetted on 18 June 1917 and was awarded for gallantry after leading half of his company forward during the initial stages of an attack and capturing an enemy strongpoint that had been holding up the advance.

There are two other gallantry award holders buried here. Private Charles NICHOL-SON MM, 7th Shropshire Light Infantry, was killed in action on 2 September 1918 and is one of ten men from that battalion buried here and who fell the same day (Plot I.B.21). Corporal Albert YATES MM, 12th Rifle Brigade, died of wounds on 2 June 1917 (Plot II.A.3).

Chapter Ten

An Unusual Revelation on Good Friday – Early Days with Fabian Ware – Two Trees, a Sunken Road and a Railway Cutting

Bellacourt Military Cemetery, Rivière

Coming from Arras, the most direct way to this cemetery is via the Arras–Doullens road, the N.25. Continue along this road to Beaumetz-lès-Loges and then take the D.7 south towards Bellacourt. After about 400 yards the road divides, but bear right and stay on the D.7. About 800 yards further on the cemetery should become apparent. It sits just off to the left at a small crossroads on the north side of the village in fields. Bellacourt is part of the commune of Rivière and is about six miles south-west of Arras.

This cemetery was begun by the French in October 1914 and still retains just over a hundred French graves. The cemetery also used to contain a number of American graves from July and August 1918, but these have since been removed. The 46th (North Midland) Division used it from mid-July 1916 and thirty-four of the seventy-five 1916 casualties buried here are from the division's 139 Brigade, which was made up of four battalions of the Sherwood Foresters: the 1/5th, 1/6th, 1/7th and 1/8th Battalions. Most were killed by shell fire, including Lieutenant Charles Edward Victor CREE, 6th Sherwood Foresters, who was killed on 20 July 1916 by a shell that wounded fifteen other men and killed the three men buried next to him. (Plot I.G.5 to 8)

Second Lieutenant Thomas George INGLESANT, 7th Sherwood Foresters, was killed in action on 28 August 1916 (Plot I.B.3), just a few weeks before his brother, Serjeant John Herbert Inglesant, 1/4th Leicestershire Regiment, who fell on 22 September. He is buried at Bailleul Communal Cemetery Extension.

Second Lieutenant John Hugh BONE, 6th East Surrey Regiment, was killed in action on 22 July 1916, aged 24. The 6th Battalion was deployed on garrison duty in India during the war and it is difficult to determine the battalion with which he was serving at the time of his death. He is shown in *Officers Died in the Great War* as serving with the 6th Battalion. The regimental history makes no reference to his death, nor do any of the relevant battalion war diaries, including the battalions of the London Regiment affiliated to the East Surrey Regiment, the 21st Battalion (First Surrey Rifles) and the 23rd Battalion (County of London). He could well have been attached to a trench mortar battery. (Plot I.B.5)

The 55th (West Lancashire) Division also made use of the cemetery between March 1916 and the end of the year. Small numbers of casualties from the 1/5th South

Lancashire Regiment, the 1/5th Loyal North Lancashire Regiment, the 1/5th, 1/6th and 1/10th King's (Liverpool Regiment) can be found here, along with a handful from the 16th, 17th and 18th Battalions of the Manchester Regiment, which belonged to the 30th Division.

Lieutenant Arthur Reginald Bewes CHAPMAN, 1/5th Loyal North Lancashire Regiment, was killed in action on 6 June 1916, aged 20. He had been gazetted back in August 1914 after cutting short his studies at St John's College, Cambridge, in order to serve. (Plot I.F.8)

Captain Edward Meredydd LLOYD-EVANS, 1/5th King's Own (Royal Lancaster Regiment) is the only casualty here from that battalion, which was also part of the 55th (West Lancashire) Division. He was an only son and was killed in action on 14 March 1916 during what the war diary describes as a quiet period. He had been wounded previously during the Second Battle of Ypres. (Plot I.F.10)

The cemetery remained relatively unused throughout 1917. Twenty-seven of the thirty-one burials that year are casualties from February, March and April. Bellacourt was not used as a location for casualty clearing stations during the Battle of Arras, though it was used for billeting. One of the casualties from the spring of 1917 is Lance Corporal Frederick Howard BOUGH, Mounted Military Police, who was killed in action on 19 March 1917. He had previously served with the Duke of Lancaster's Own Yeomanry. (Plot I.M.8)

The CWGC register refers to the 58th (2/1st London) Division's use of the cemetery during the spring of 1917. The 2/3rd, 2/4th, 2/6th, 2/10th, 2/11th and 2/12th Battalions all have casualties here in Plot I, Rows K, L and M.

Corporal Thomas STOCKHAM, 503rd (Wessex) Field Company, Royal Engineers, who died of wounds on 10 March 1917, was one of six brothers who served, though he appears to be the only one to have lost his life during the war. (Plot I.L.3)

The majority of the casualties in this cemetery are from 1918; in fact, 327 of the 432 identified casualties here are from that final year of the war. There is only one unidentified burial in the entire cemetery.

Between March and July 1918 the Canadian 2nd Division spent a good deal of time in trenches between Neuville-Vitasse and Tilloy-lès-Mofflaines. The 173 Canadians buried here come mainly from infantry battalions belonging to that division. A number of gallantry awards can be found amongst them. They are as follows:

Company Sergeant-Major William McAULIFFE MM, 19th Battalion, Canadian Infantry, killed in action on 2 April 1918. (Plot II.B.1)

Lance Corporal Thomas Percival MASON MM, 18th Battalion, Canadian Infantry, killed or died of wounds on 3 April 1918. (Plot II.B.12)

Sergeant Charles Frederick FRANKLIN MM, 24th Battalion, Canadian Infantry, killed in action on 10 April 1918. (Plot II.C.3)

Lance Corporal Alexander Claud HARDING MM, 28th Battalion, Canadian Infantry, killed in action on 12 May 1918, aged 25. (Plot II.J.1)

Private Hamilton Trelford MITCHELL MM, 28th Battalion, Canadian Infantry, killed in action on 12 May 1918 (Plot II.J.2). The CWGC register states that his brother, Private Hugh Brown Mitchell, also fell during the Great War, but the

CWGC records offer no exact match. Canadian army records, however, show Hugh as serving with the 28th Battalion, Canadian Infantry. He was killed in action on 6 November 1917 near Passchendaele, but has no known grave and is commemorated on the Menin Gate.

Lance Corporal William Francis MOORE MM, 21st Battalion, Canadian Infantry, killed in action on 16 June 1918. (Plot II.O.11)

Sergeant Joseph Alfred BIDDISCOMBE MM, 26th Battalion, Canadian Infantry, killed in action on 23 June 1918. (Plot II.P.11)

The CWGC entry for Private Emmerson Ross CAMPBELL, 26th Battalion, Canadian Infantry, who was killed in action on 7 May 1918, aged 19 (Plot II.H.2), refers to his brother Douglas, who also fell during the war, though the CWGC records show no exact match. Canadian army records also fail to positively identify him.

The most senior Canadian officer buried here is Captain Benjamin Ethelbert NICHOLLS MC and Bar, 20th Battalion, Canadian Infantry. He was killed in action on 8 May 1918. Unusually, his MC and the bar to it were gazetted on the same day, 18 October 1917 (Plot II.H.6). A few days after his death, Lieutenant Theodore James GEERNAERT, 23rd Battery, 5 Brigade, Canadian Field Artillery, was killed in action on 12 May 1918. The CWGC register tells us that prior to moving to Canada he had served as a quartermaster serjeant in the Royal Field Artillery. (Plot II.H.11)

Private Leopold DELISLE, 22nd Battalion, Canadian Infantry, was executed on 21 May 1918. The offence which sealed his fate took place on 29 March 1918 when he went missing. He was discovered and arrested just over a week later. However, he also had a very poor history of disobedience, including drunkenness, absence from parades, insubordination, and even refusal to parade. On one occasion he had struck an officer and had served a prison sentence for that offence. On release, he returned to his battalion. No further offences were recorded against him until he went absent, but with such a poor record prior to going missing, there was little chance of leniency and he was sentenced to death and shot. (Plot II.J.6)

According to the CWGC register, Private Walter Oswald LARSEN, 27th Battalion, Canadian Infantry, who was killed in action on 25 June 1918, had a brother who was killed in the war serving with the American Expeditionary Force. His brother was George Larsen and he served with the 18th Battalion, 1st American Division. The boys came from Sacred Heart, Minnesota. A number of Americans chose to enlist north of the border in Canada during the early years of the war, including Walter. (Plot II.P.12)

With just one exception, British casualties from the final year of the war date from 28 March onwards and, like the Canadian dead, they run through to July. There are several interesting graves among this group.

Private Wilfred John MARTIN, 2nd South Staffordshire Regiment, who was killed in action on 10 May 1918, aged 19, had two brothers who fell in the Great War (Plot II.H.10). The first to die, on 26 May 1915, was Lance Corporal Herbert William Martin, 1/23rd Battalion, London Regiment, and he is commemorated on the Le Touret Memorial. The other brother, Second Corporal Alan Stewart Martin,

29th Divisional Signal Company, Royal Engineers, died of wounds on 11 May 1918, aged 22, just a day after Wilfred.

Lieutenant Oswald Nelson MASH MC, 'D' Battery, 174 Brigade, Royal Field Artillery, was killed in action on 1 June 1918. Gazetted on 5 March 1918, his MC was awarded for his actions during a bombardment when a dump of howitzer charges adjacent to his battery was set on fire by a shell. There were also gas shells amongst the burning charges. MASH showed great coolness and courage in rushing over to the fire and extinguishing it. In doing so, he prevented an explosion that would otherwise have had serious consequences for his battery's position and those working with it. (Plot II.M.7)

Second Lieutenant Bruce Lorence CAPELL MC, 2/1st (North Midland) Brigade, Royal Field Artillery, died on 7 June 1918, aged 21. CAPELL won his MC after heavy casualties had occurred amongst his men as a result of enemy shell fire. His coolness and his splendid example rallied the rest of the men and kept them in action. When not doing that he superintended the dressing and removal of wounded men. His award was gazetted on 15 March 1918. (Plot II.O.3)

Major Bertie Christopher Butler TOWER MC and Bar, 4th Royal Fusiliers, died of wounds on 22 August 1918, aged 30, while leading the battalion after its commanding officer had been badly wounded. His MC was gazetted on 14 January 1916. The bar to it was gazetted on 18 September 1918 and was awarded after he had made several reconnaissance patrols under heavy machine-gun and artillery fire. On each occasion he brought back valuable information and showed great energy and determination (Plot III.F.1).

Another of his brothers, Major Kingslake Fritz Butler Tower, also served with the Royal Fusiliers during the war. He had narrowly escaped death in 1914 when the 4th Royal Fusiliers briefly defended the canal at Mons; bullets knocked his hat off, another struck his rifle and two more passed through his puttees. He was eventually wounded a couple of weeks later on 9 September. Another two brothers had followed in their father's footsteps by choosing to serve in the Royal Navy. One of those brothers, Ion Beauchamp Butler Tower DSC, entered the Royal Navy in 1904 and went on to reach the rank of rear admiral. He was unfortunately killed in Regent Street, London, during an air raid on 14 October 1940. He is buried in Kensal Green (All Souls) Cemetery, north London, and was 51 years old when he died. At the time he was serving as liaison officer to the Commander-in-Chief, Home Forces, General Sir Alan Brooke. The other brother, Sir Francis Thomas Butler Tower KCB CB OBE, became a vice admiral in the Royal Navy.

Major Bernard Charles TENNENT MC, 7th Field Ambulance, Royal Army Medical Corps, was killed in action on 22 August 1918. Next to him is another officer from the same Field Ambulance unit, Captain Raymond BREWITT-TAYLOR MC, who died of wounds the same day. Serjeant Robert CARRUTHERS MM, also died of wounds, but not until the following day (Plots III.F.3 to 5). BREWITT-TAYLOR, who was educated at University College School and St Bartholomew's Hospital in London, was made a Chevalier of the Order of Leopold II, a Belgian honorary award. The CWGC register also notes that he was born in China where his father had been

Commissioner of Customs. TENNENT's MC was gazetted on 24 August 1917 and was awarded for conspicuous gallantry and devotion to duty. The citation records that he had continually exposed himself to danger whilst under heavy shell fire in order to visit his posts in the front trenches, and that he had done so with the utmost fearlessness. He also dressed many men out in the open, again regardless of personal danger, and when some of his stretcher-bearers became casualties he took their place, and even assisted by carrying the wounded himself. BREWITT-TAYLOR's MC was gazetted on 27 July 1918 and was awarded for conspicuous gallantry and devotion to duty after he had searched for a missing stretcher-bearer for two hours under heavy shell fire. He eventually found the man lying wounded in a shell hole and brought him back to our own lines. Throughout nine days of fighting he constantly went out for wounded men under fire and brought them back in similar circumstances.

Regimental Serjeant-Major William BURT DCM, 1/7th Middlesex Regiment, was killed in action on 23 August 1918, aged 36. His DCM was gazetted on 26 November 1917 while he was serving as a company quartermaster serjeant with the East Kent Regiment (The Buffs). It was awarded for conspicuous gallantry and devotion to duty while bringing rations to the battalion in the front line. He had gone forward, making a personal reconnaissance of the route before taking all his pack animals to the forward dump through heavy shelling during which several animals became stuck in the mud. He then remained at the dump under shell fire until the carrying parties had left. The citation ends by stating that his remarkable coolness and cheerfulness under difficult conditions had an excellent effect on the men. The citation appeared on 6 February 1918. (Plot III.F.7)

Lieutenant Gilbert Edgar ADAMSON MC, 1/7th Middlesex Regiment, was killed in action on 24 August 1918, aged 23. He was a pupil at the City of London School between 1906 and 1914 and began studying at Merton College, Oxford, but left in 1915 in order to serve. He won his MC for conspicuous gallantry and devotion to duty during a night raid on enemy trenches. On the night of the raid he was responsible for taping out the line of the advance from our front line position. In doing so, he enabled the exact point of entry to be reached after crossing 600 yards of no man's land. He personally led his party with great courage and gallantry and gained that part of the objective allocated to it, despite strong enemy resistance, which had been expected. The citation goes on to add that his fine example and leadership contributed greatly to the success of the raid. His award was gazetted on 13 September 1918. (Plot III.G.2)

There are thirteen men buried here with the MM. Those not already referred to are listed below:

Serjeant Patrick John LYONS MM, 'Z' 30th Trench Mortar Battery, Royal Garrison Artillery, killed in action on 7 December 1916. (Plot I.J.9)

Driver Charles STALLWOOD MM, 'A' Battery, 174 Brigade, Royal Field Artillery, killed in action on 29 May 1918. (Plot II.L.13)

Lance Bombardier William DEAKINS MM, 'A' Battery, 76 Brigade, Royal Field Artillery, killed in action on 20 June 1918. (Plot II.O.13)

Serjeant Harry George PEIRCE MM, 25th Battalion, Machine Gun Corps, killed in action on 26 August 1918. He had previously served with the Middlesex Regiment. (Plot III.C.5)

Gunner William Cyril SEED MM, 12th Siege Battery, Royal Garrison Artillery, killed in action on 28 March 1918. (Plot III.E.6)

Blairville Churchyard

The churchyard is in the centre of the village in the Rue de l'Église. The village is south of the D.34 between Ransart and Ficheux and is about six miles south-west of Arras.

There are just two casualties buried here. Both are 1918 casualties and their graves can be found in the south-east corner of the cemetery. They are Private William HARRISON, killed in action on 21 March 1918 whilst serving with the 6th Battalion, Tank Corps, but who had formerly served in the Machine Gun Corps, and Private James NELSON, 6th Royal Scots Fusiliers, who died on the 23rd February that year.

Boisleux-Au-Mont Communal Cemetery

The cemetery lies outside the village of Boisleux-au-Mont on its north-west side. From Arras, take the D.917 south towards Bapaume as far as Boiry-Becquerelle. Turn right here along the D.35 and continue as far as Boisleux-au-Mont. In the centre of the village turn right again, taking the D.36, which is the road to Ficheux. The cemetery lies about half a mile further on down this road on the left hand side. The two graves from the Second World War lie closest to the road and are in a separate plot from the others. The village is about five miles south-west of Arras.

There are only eight burials here and two of them are from the Second World War. They are: Private George WHITELEY, 10th Durham Light Infantry, aged 21, who was killed between 19 and 21 May 1940. He was from Pudsey in Yorkshire. The other is Private John Ball WATSON, 1st Tyneside Scottish (Black Watch), whose date of death is known to have occurred on 21 May 1940.

The remaining six graves are from 1918. Three of them are connected to fighting around the eastern outskirts of Boisleux-Saint-Marc during the March Retreat. In chronological order they are:

Private Cyril Arthur HOLMES, 1st Grenadier Guards, aged 22, killed in action on the 28th March 1918. (Grave 1)

The Reverend Edward Reginald GIBBS, Chaplain 4th Class, Army Chaplain's Department, attached 1st Grenadier Guards, died on 29 March 1918, aged 32. His father was a Minister at East Budleigh in Devon. The battalion war diary notes only that he was killed by a random shell on what was otherwise a quiet day, although it also mentions that three officers and seven other ranks were wounded that day, which happened to be Good Friday. It appears that he had been conducting the funeral of a soldier shortly before he was killed. GIBBS studied at Haileybury College and Keble College, Oxford, and before the outbreak of war served as personal chaplain to the Archbishop of York, who subsequently commissioned a wooden tryptich in GIBBS's memory in St Andrew's Church, Bishopthorpe. The tryptich, essentially an altar piece, remains open throughout the year, but on Good Friday its doors are closed for the entire day to reveal a brass memorial plaque dedicated to the memory of GIBBS. One of his brothers, Lieutenant Colonel William Beresford Gibbs, 3rd Worcestershire Regiment, was mortally wounded by shell fire on 3 September 1916, aged 35, near Thiepval. He is buried on the Somme in Blighty Valley Cemetery, Authuille Wood. Another three brothers also served. (Grave 2)

Second Lieutenant Cecil Clarence MAYS, 1st Grenadier Guards, was killed on 30 March 1918, aged 23. He had joined the battalion while it was serving in the Ypres Salient in September 1917 and was mortally wounded by a machine-gun bullet. (Grave 4)

Captain Lionel de Jersey HARVARD, 1st Grenadier Guards, was killed in action on 30 March 1918. It was an ancestor of his, John Harvard, who in 1663 founded Harvard University in Massachusetts, one of the Ivy League institutions. Lionel was born in Lewisham and went on to spend four years at Harvard where he took an Arts degree. He then joined the Inns of Court OTC and subsequently gained a commission in the Grenadier Guards. He was involved in the fighting at Ypres in 1917 and had been wounded on the Somme at Lesboeufs in September 1916. He left behind a widow and a young son. His brother, Lieutenant Kenneth O'Gorman Harvard, was killed in action with the 2nd Grenadier Guards on 1 August 1918, aged 20, and is buried at Artillery Wood Cemetery in Belgium. Lionel is buried in Grave 5.

Lieutenant the Honourable Harold Fox Pitt LUBBOCK, 2nd Grenadier Guards, was killed in action on 4 April 1918, aged 29 (Grave 3). He was the son of the late John Lubbock, 1st Baron Avebury, whose family home was Kingsgate Castle in Kent. Harold had already served in Gallipoli and Palestine as a captain with the West Kent Yeomanry before becoming a lieutenant with the Grenadier Guards. His brother, Captain the Honourable Eric Fox Pitt Lubbock, was killed in action on 17 March 1918 while serving with 45 Squadron, Royal Flying Corps, and had been awarded the MC. He is buried at Lijssenthoek Military Cemetery in Belgium. Harold died on the 4th April 1918 when a shell pitched into the trench where he was standing during a period of heavy artillery fire. Lance Corporal Thomas Teagle MM was mortally wounded by the same shell that killed Lieutenant LUBBOCK and died the same day, aged 23. Six other men were also wounded in the explosion. Teagle is buried in Bucquoy Road Cemetery, Ficheux, about eight miles south-south-west of here on the D.919. It is well worth a visit, but lies outside the area of this book. It is the cemetery where Private Joe Standing BUFFALO is buried; he was killed in action on 29 September 1918 whilst serving with the 78th Battalion, Canadian Infantry. He was the grandson of Chief Sitting Bull of Little Big Horn fame and lived at Fort Qu'Appelle, Saskatchewan.

Private Richard AYRES, 1st Grenadier Guards, was killed in action on 16 August 1918. (Grave 6)

Ervillers Military Cemetery

This is a small cemetery situated on the south-west side of the village. It is in the Rue de l'Église, not far from the village church. The layout of the cemetery is fairly irregular and is really a succession of individual plots.

The present site was originally a German cemetery until they withdrew behind the Hindenburg Line in March 1917. The Germans had used it to bury a number of prisoners who had died of wounds. After the German withdrawal, the cemetery was used by a number of British units that just happened to be in the area at the time. After the war, a few other graves that had been made in the Mayor's garden were transferred to this cemetery and more than a hundred German graves were removed at the same time. The original burials made by the Germans are the fifteen unidentified graves.

For such a small cemetery the casualties come from a wide variety of units, including the infantry, the Royal Engineers, the Machine Gun Corps, the Royal Field Artillery, the Royal Army Medical Corps and the Royal Flying Corps. There is just one Australian soldier buried here, Private Athol Powys FOWLER, who died on 26 March 1917 when serving with the 25th Battalion, Australian Infantry. His family, who lived in New South Wales, clearly wished to keep the link with Wales through their son's name. His battalion had been involved in operations near Noreuil around the time of his death. (Plot E.8)

There is just one officer among the fifty-two identified casualties now buried here. Second Lieutenant Robert Thomas DAVIES, 21st Manchester Regiment, died of wounds during the fighting at Écoust and Croisilles on 2 April 1917 when the 7th Division captured both villages. Both locations formed part of a last temporary defensive line for the German rearguards before the final withdrawal behind the Hindenburg Line took place. Second Lieutenant DAVIES was 24 years old when he died. (Plot A.2)

The infantry casualties, or at least those that are identified, are mainly from battalions of the 7th Division, though there are a few from the 62nd (West Riding) Division, which was involved in the fighting around Bullecourt in April and May 1917.

Captain Herbert SPANNER, 27 Squadron, Royal Flying Corps, was killed in action on 28 December 1916, aged 23, while flying a Martinsyde G102, which was a single-seat fighter/bomber aircraft. He was a Canadian airman who came from Toronto. He was initially reported as missing in action that day, but his death was later confirmed. (Plot D.4)

Air Mechanic 2nd Class James BOON, 4 Squadron, Royal Flying Corps, was killed while acting as an observer on 24 March 1917. The aircraft was a BE2c flown by Second Lieutenant D.K. Sworder who was injured in the crash. (Plot E.6)

The earliest of the identified casualties are eight NCOs and men from the 2nd Royal Warwickshire Regiment who were killed in action on 21 March 1917 after the Germans had left Ervillers. By 18 March the outpost line of the 7th Division ran along the eastern edge of the village. Between 19 and 21 March the outpost line was edged forward to just east of Boyelles and Saint-Léger. All eight men are buried in their own plot at the far end of the cemetery from the entrance. (Plot F.1)

Gomiécourt South Cemetery

The D.9 runs along the northern edge of the village of Gomiécourt where there is a junction. Turning off the D.9 into the village, continue through it and exit on the south side. About a hundred yards down the road is a 'T' junction. Turn left here and the cemetery lies in open fields on the south-east side of the village. This is not a large cemetery and most of the 206 graves relate to identified casualties. With regard to those buried here, there are a few casualties of interest buried in Plot IV.

The CWGC register shows two men who fell in August 1916, both of them privates. The date of death given for Privates Herbert THOMPSON, 13th King's Royal Rifle Corps, and Albert James WHITE, 5th Duke of Wellington's Regiment, is 25 August. However, THOMPSON's battalion had already moved to the Béthune area on 20 August 1916 and did not return south until the last week in October. The 1/5th Duke of Wellington's Regiment, which happened to be on the Somme in August 1916, was well behind the lines at the time that WHITE is supposed to have died. The 2/5th Battalion was still at home in England. Both these battalions of the Duke of Wellington's Regiment amalgamated at the end of January 1918 to form the 5th Battalion. Taking into account these battalion movements, it is far more likely that both men were not killed in action on 25 August 1916, but on the same day two years later in 1918. Therefore, I believe there are no 1916 casualties in this cemetery.

Other than three casualties who fell in March 1918, the cemetery consists almost entirely of men who died during the advances in August 1918, with just a few casualties from the following month. The village of Gomiécourt was successfully captured soon after 4.00am on 23 August by the 3rd Division, with very few casualties. As a consequence, very few men from this division are buried here.

Most of the men buried here who fell in August 1918 are from three divisions of the British Army. The first is the 62nd (West Riding) Division. It has twenty-four NCOs and privates of the 2/4th York & Lancaster Regiment buried here, twenty-two from the 2/4th and the 5th King's Own Yorkshire Light Infantry, seventeen from the 2/4th and 5th Duke of Wellington's Regiment, and ten from the 2/20th Battalion, London Regiment (Blackheath and Woolwich). This last battalion had been attached to the division as recently as 9 August. Most of these casualties occurred during operations between the villages of Mory and Vaulx-Vraucourt.

From the 2nd Division there are eighteen NCOs and privates from the 2nd Highland Light Infantry, sixteen NCOs and privates from the 24th Royal Fusiliers, with smaller numbers from the 2nd Oxfordshire & Buckinghamshire Light Infantry, the 2nd Royal Scots and the 1st Royal Berkshire Regiment.

On 23 August 1918 the 2nd Highland Light Infantry advanced in a south-easterly direction towards Béhagnies from positions north of Gomiécourt. At the same time, the 24th Royal Fusiliers pushed out towards the village of Sapignies, with the 2nd Oxfordshire & Buckinghamshire Regiment in reserve. Some of the Whippet tanks accompanying the attack were put out of action and others became dispersed and drifted towards the 37th Division's sector. The Highlanders came under machine-gun fire from locations north of their position and were also held up in front of Béhagnies by field guns firing at point blank range, as well as machine-gun fire from the village. The battalion's commanding officer was killed during the attack.

The 24th Royal Fusiliers came under heavy fire too, but succeeded in capturing a position north-west of Béhagnies, as well as two field guns. Without support from the tanks, and in the face of heavy machine-gun fire, neither Béhagnies nor Sapignies were taken on 23 August. However, both units were successful two days later when the 2nd Highland Light Infantry and the 24th Royal Fusiliers captured Béhagnies and the 2nd Oxfordshire & Buckinghamshire Light Infantry took Sapignies.

The other division with significant casualties here is the 37th Division. Its men are from the 10th Royal Fusiliers, the 13th Rifle Brigade and the 13th King's Royal Rifle Corps. On 23 August this division was operating directly south of the 2nd Division. The 13th Rifle Brigade and the 13th King's Royal Rifle Corps captured Achiet-le-Grand and the 10th Royal Fusiliers took Bihucourt. On 25 August the 13th Rifle Brigade sustained casualties from machine-gun fire protecting the western side of Favreuil, but eventually managed to link up in the village with New Zealanders from the 1st Battalion, Otago Regiment, later that day. The 10th Royal Fusiliers and the 13th King's Royal Rifle Corps also made progress on 25 August in spite of difficulties experienced by the 62nd (West Riding) Division on their left flank.

Regimental Serjeant Major William Francis DOUGLAS, 2/4th Oxfordshire & Buckinghamshire Light Infantry, was 44 years old when he was killed in action on 21 March 1918. His battalion was part of the 61st (2nd South Midland) Division. He was a veteran of the South African campaign and went to France with the 2/4th Battalion in May 1916 as a regimental serjeant major. His had been a steady hand during those two years on the Western Front, where his previous military experience had proved extremely valuable. He was mentioned in despatches in recognition of his fine work with the battalion. (Plot IV.F.14)

Another veteran of the South African campaign was Company Serjeant Major Frederick William WATSON MC DCM and Bar, 5th King's Own Yorkshire Light Infantry, who was killed in action on 27 August 1918, aged 38. He had been a soldier since the age of 18 and had joined the King's Own Yorkshire Light Infantry in 1897. Between 1908 and 1909 he served in the Mediterranean and also spent a year of his service seconded to the Northern Nigeria Regiment. By the outbreak of war he was already an experienced soldier and was promoted to company serjeant major with the 2nd Battalion. His previous military experience was almost certainly a factor in the decision to leave him behind as an instructor when the battalion embarked for the front and it was only in January 1917 that he went to France with the regiment's 2/5th Battalion.

His DCM was awarded for his fine work on 8 March 1917 during a daylight raid when he established and maintained an important post under difficult circumstances, thereby allowing a party from the 10th Essex Regiment next to him to carry out a bombing attack on a section of enemy trench. As always, doing the right thing at the right time was critical to success, and his courage and determination during this operation were rightly recognized by the award of the DCM.

However, his career was somewhat chequered. Within the first four years of his service he had earned two badges for good conduct, but later on there were several lapses in discipline that led to sanctions. The most serious of these was in August 1917 when he was found drunk on duty and was reduced in rank to sergeant. After his fall from grace he was posted as a training instructor, though still within the 62nd (West Riding) Division and, although the disciplinary hearing had reduced him in rank, it did take into consideration his previous good work and experience, and probably the fact that the previous month he had been wounded on two consecutive days. His posting as an instructor, which would have allowed him a few months away from the stresses of the front line, seems to have done the trick, and he regained his rank as a company serjeant major soon after his return to the battalion.

His MC was gazetted on 7 November 1918 and was awarded for conspicuous gallantry and good leadership. When the officers from two of his company's platoons had become casualties, it was his leadership that kept the men going forward under fire. On one occasion, when cut off, he skilfully led his party out of immediate danger to a more sustainable position, fighting all the time as he and his men withdrew. On another occasion, after his battalion had overrun some enemy dug-outs during its advance, he captured seven German officers and over a hundred other ranks with the assistance of just an officer and one other man. Sadly, on 27 August 1918 a machine-gun bullet struck him in the back of the neck and he died within minutes. It was men like WATSON who were so often the cohesive force that held many a battalion together, particularly in 1918, a time when most battalions contained a high proportion of inexperienced young soldiers. His immense presence and influence would have been deeply missed.

Citations of the Distinguished Conduct Medal in the Great War 1914–1920 contains no record of any bar awarded to his DCM, nor is there any reference to it in any of the gazettes. However, *Soldiers Died in the Great War* does show the award of the bar against his name, as does his headstone. (Plot IV.E.3)

Captain John RODGERS MC, 2/4th York & Lancaster Regiment, was killed in action on the 2nd September 1918, aged 22. He was awarded the MC for his actions at Mory on 25 August 1918, just a week before his death. When all the other company commanders had become casualties, he reorganized the men, going from position to position under heavy artillery and machine-gun fire, inspiring them to beat off an enemy counter-attack. This enabled his battalion to take up an advanced line, which was later consolidated under his fine leadership. The award was gazetted on 1 February 1919. His battalion was part of the 62nd (West Riding) Division. His regiment was very much associated with South Yorkshire and the city of Sheffield, where his family had been involved for a number of years in the manufacture of very high quality cutlery. Sheffield, of course, was famous throughout the world for its stainless steel, particularly its fine cutlery. (Plot IV.E.2)

Though a relatively small cemetery, there are quite a few holders of the MM.

Private David WILSON MM, 2nd Highland Light Infantry, killed in action on 23 August 1918, aged 24. (Plot I.A.3)

Serjeant Percival PEMBERTON MM, 5th Duke of Wellington's Regiment, killed in action on 26 August 1918, aged 26. (Plot I.C.3)

Corporal William SCOTT MM, 13th Rifle Brigade, killed in action on 25 August 1918, aged 23. (Plot I.E.8)

Serjeant Albert Charles MOORE DCM MM, 1st King's Royal Rifle Corps, was killed in action on 24 August 1918, aged 23. His MM was gazetted on 10 April 1918 and his DCM on 15 November the same year. The DCM was awarded for conspicuous gallantry and devotion to duty while part of a battle patrol during which he led an attack on an enemy machine-gun post, capturing the gun and killing two of its crew. He then assisted his officer in working the captured gun against an enemy reinforcement party and subsequently did invaluable work repelling enemy bombing attacks. He personally accounted for at least five of the enemy and showed fine courage and leadership throughout the operation. (Plot II.A.5)

Serjeant Thomas JACKSON MM, 1st King's Royal Rifle Corps, killed in action on 24 August 1918, aged 29. (Plot III.A.7)

Private Richard James BUNKER MM, 2/4th York & Lancaster Regiment, killed in action on 26 August 1918, aged 34. (Plot III.E.7)

Serjeant Arthur Dean BLACKBURN MM, 2/5th Duke of Wellington's Regiment, killed in action on 30 August 1918, aged 18. (Plot IV.A.2)

Private Rudolph Buckley LISTER MM, 2nd Suffolk Regiment, was killed in action on 23 August 1918, aged 24. He was an only son and had won his MM for bravery as a runner on 14 October 1916 at the Schwaben Redoubt whilst serving with the Cambridgeshire Regiment (Plot IV.F.2). Buried in the next grave to LISTER is Lance Corporal George Gordon EDWARDS, 1st King's Royal Rifle Corps, who died of wounds on 23 August 1918, aged 53. (Plot IV.F.3)

Finally, there is one casualty from the Tank Corps: Private Reginald Normand GRIFFITHS, 6th Battalion, Tank Corps, who was killed in action on 23 August 1918. (Plot II.D.8)

Le Fermont Military Cemetery, Rivière

Rivière, where this cemetery is located, is made up of several small settlements that seem to have fused together over time to create one village. From Arras, the best approach to the cemetery is to take the D.3 that runs through Wailly. Approximately 500 yards after leaving Wailly, there is a small road off to the right. Take this road and continue to the 'T' junction, then turn left. The cemetery is situated about 200 yards down this road, which runs parallel to the D.3 and to the north of it. The CWGC sign is well placed and does indicate where to come off the D.3. The cemetery contains eighty burials and the CWGC information relating to it points out that the cemetery register is held at the Mairie, which is only open on certain days and between certain times.

The cemetery was begun by the 55th (West Lancashire) Division in 1916, but was not actively used after March 1917 when, effectively, it was closed. The CWGC information incorrectly states that there is just one burial dating to 1918, as there are two members of the Chinese Labour Corps who died on 7 October that year, as well as Driver Frederick Richard PRIOR, Royal Field Artillery, who died at the time of the German March Offensive and is the casualty referred to in the CWGC notes.

There are sixty burials from 1916 compared with just eighteen from the first three months of 1917. However, all seventy-eight men died or were killed in action whilst holding the line, or just prior to following up the German withdrawal to the Hindenburg Line.

Half of the 55th (West Lancashire) Division was made up of six battalions of the King's (Liverpool Regiment). The cemetery contains eighteen NCOs and men from five of those six battalions, as well as one man from the regiment's 11th Battalion, which was the pioneer unit attached to the 14th (Light) Division. That division also has burials here dating between the end of 1916 and the start of January the following year. These casualties are from the 7th, 8th and 9th Rifle Brigade and the 7th and

8th King's Royal Rifle Corps. Other battalions of the 55th (West Lancashire) Division that used this cemetery are the 2/5th Lancashire Fusiliers, the 1/4th Loyal North Lancashire Regiment, and the 1/4th King's Own (Royal Lancaster Regiment), but their casualties are not here in significant numbers.

A handful of men belonging to the 12th (Eastern) Division can also be found here, including Second Lieutenant Denis George DESLANDES, 7th East Surrey Regiment, who was killed in action on 27 November 1916 when his battalion's trenches were subjected to heavy trench mortar fire. He is one of four officers in this cemetery. (Plot II.D.5)

There does not appear to be any clear reason why three corporals of the 4th Battalion, Special Brigade, Royal Engineers, should be buried together (Plots II.A.4 to 6), when another member of that unit is buried separately (Plot II.B.2). All four men were killed on the same day, 28 June 1916. It strikes me as odd that they were not buried consecutively, even if they were killed at different times of the day. The only other casualty buried here who was killed that day is in Plot II, Row C. The man buried in Plot II, Row B, Pioneer Henry George DENNE, is of lower rank, but that would not normally account for his separation from the others.

Finally, there are three NCOs with the MM in this cemetery. They are: Sergeant John Richard ASPDEN MM, 8th Rifle Brigade, killed in action on 3 October 1916 (Plot I.D.8); Sergeant Archie James BARRETT MM, 6th East Kent Regiment (The Buffs), killed on 13 September 1916 (Plot II.A.7); and Lance Corporal William H. WILLIAMS MM, 1/7th Duke of Wellington's Regiment, killed on 28 February 1917 (Plot II.E.7). Neither WILLIAMS nor ASPDEN is shown as having been awarded the MM in the respective volumes of *Soldiers Died in the Great War*.

Moyenneville (Two Tree) Cemetery

This is a delightful cemetery set in splendid isolation at the end of a long track, but it is not the easiest to locate. The track leading to it is not suitable for vehicles and is best tackled on foot. Moyenneville sits on a rise on the D.32. Towards the southern end of the village the road bends almost at right angles and a small road runs off it in a south-westerly direction. Take this side road and park up. A couple of hundred yards further along is where the road divides again. Ignore the track off to the right, which leads to the village cemetery. Take the grassy, and sometimes very muddy, farm track instead and walk about 500 yards to the cemetery.

The first occasion that I visited this cemetery I could not find it, but it was early March and there was a heavy early morning fog with visibility down to about fifty yards. I returned in the afternoon and found it bathed in spring sunshine. There are thirty-three identified casualties buried here and around half as many again whose identity remains unknown.

The cemetery gets its name from a couple of tree stumps that remained once the area around Moyenneville and Saint-Léger had been cleared. The really puzzling thing is why the cemetery was made here at all, especially when the communal cemetery is on the very edge of the village next to open fields. The graves are from two distinct, but very brief periods of fighting. The CWGC register tells us that the cemetery was made sometime after the capture of Moyenneville on 21 August 1918, but it does not tell us whether the August casualties were collected from the battlefield and buried at the same time as those who fell in March that year, or whether the March casualties were subsequently gathered up and brought here to lie with those who died in August. Would it not have been easier to reconstruct the cemetery elsewhere, perhaps closer to the village? On reflection, this tiny cemetery must surely have been a very good candidate for closure after the Armistice. The fact that it still remains never ceases to amaze me. We, as visitors to the battlefields, owe a huge debt of thanks to landowners and to the CWGC for preserving and maintaining original burial sites, such as this one. This alone makes a visit to this cemetery worthwhile.

All the burials are from 1918 and all of them are either privates or NCOs. Just over half relate to the German March Offensive. These eighteen graves are mainly men of the 15/17th West Yorkshire Regiment. In the first week of December 1917 the 15th West Yorkshire Regiment, the original 'Leeds Pals', received just over 250 men from another Leeds (Bantam) battalion, the 17th West Yorkshire Regiment. In February 1918, further reorganization took place within the British army, as a result of which 4 (Guards) Brigade joined the 31st Division and was slotted in beside the division's other two brigades, which consisted entirely of units belonging to regiments from the north of England. The changes saw brigades within the British army reduced from four battalions to just three. The 15/17th West Yorkshire Regiment, 13th York and Lancaster Regiment, and 18th Durham Light Infantry made up 93 Brigade.

It should also be pointed out that none of the thirteen Guardsmen buried in this cemetery belong to the 4th (Guards) Brigade. The casualties here were part of the Guards Division that captured the village on 21 August 1918, ahead of fighting around Saint-Léger a few days later.

As the CWGC register rightly points out, the 15/17th West Yorkshire Regiment made a determined stand on the high ground around the village against repeated German attacks in late March 1918. The 31st Division took over this part of the shifting line on 23 March from the battered 34th Division. The 15/17th Battalion initially occupied a position close to the village of Boyelles and Judas Farm, which in rebuilt form still stands today. The 13th York & Lancaster Regiment took up a position alongside, whilst the 18th Durham Light Infantry remained in support. The following day the 31st Division fended off two German attacks, one in the morning, the other in the afternoon. Unfortunately, the 40th Division was forced to give up ground to the south, and so the 31st Division began an orderly retirement westwards. On 25 March it took up a line between the villages of Moyenneville and Ablainzevelle, completing the move in the early hours of the 26th. When a further retirement was ordered later that day, the 15/17th West Yorkshire Regiment lost touch with the brigade's other two battalions, both of which had already moved west of Moyenneville, leaving the Leeds men with both flanks in the air.

When the Germans attacked on the 26th, they took the village and the ridge of high ground to the south-west. Any continued resistance was wholly dependent on holding this key defensive position. Realizing the importance of retaking the ridge, the men of the 15/17th West Yorkshire Regiment counter-attacked and drove the Germans off the high ground whilst one of its platoons counter-attacked through the village, restoring the position for the time being. That same afternoon the Germans fought their way back into the village, forcing the Leeds men to retire towards its western edges where they managed to hold on. By now the men were so exhausted that an intended counter-attack was cancelled on the grounds that it was unlikely to succeed.

By 27 March the only viable option was to abandon Moyenneville and retire further west. In order to cover the withdrawal, Serjeant Albert Mountain selected ten men to accompany him, taking as much ammunition as they could muster, with a view to holding the ridge for as long as possible, after which they themselves would attempt to break off and retire. They were successful in buying time throughout the morning, but by mid-afternoon the Germans had managed to work around both flanks. Having left it to the last moment, the small party then tried to retire. Serjeant Mountain did manage to escape and was subsequently awarded the VC for his bravery, but some of his party were killed whilst others, probably wounded, were captured.

As the CWGC register makes very clear, this minor action delayed the German advance on this part of the battlefield for thirty-six hours. The men of the 15/17th West Yorkshire Regiment really did put up an outstanding performance and their headstones here are all the more poignant when their story is told. Although much attention has been given to the heroic stands made at many of the redoubts on 21 March, locations such as this have been neglected. Three men of the 18th Durham Light Infantry are also buried beside them.

At 4.35am on 21 August 1918, the 2nd (Guards) Brigade captured Moyenneville in an attack that began in heavy mist. The smoke from the artillery barrage combined with the mist to reduce visibility, which proved to be something of a mixed blessing. Although it masked the presence of the advancing troops, it was also a hindrance in that it made contact between platoons more difficult. The objectives were Moyenneville and the Arras–Albert railway line that ran just east of the village. The attack itself was successful and by 11.30am all objectives had been secured. The 1st Scots Guards and the 1st Coldstream Guards made the initial advance before the 3rd Grenadier Guards passed through them to capture the railway line. Once the Germans realized that the village had been lost, they bombarded it, causing an uncomfortable day for the Coldstream Guards, who had halted there in order to reorganize. Patrols were pushed out that night east of the railway line, but no further advance was attempted.

All of this was a preliminary to a much larger push that was to take place on 23 August. On the 22nd a German counter-attack was broken up without too much difficulty, after which the Germans reverted to bombarding the village and the area surrounding it, causing more casualties amongst the Coldstream Guards. The following day the 3rd Grenadier Guards continued their advance from the railway line and the 1st Scots Guards advanced towards the village of Hamelincourt.

On 23 August the Guards Division faced far stiffer opposition. After the capture of Moyenneville, 2 (Guards) Brigade was relieved by the 1st Grenadier Guards, the 2nd Scots Guards and 1st Welsh Guards of 3 (Guards) Brigade. The next few days involved some very difficult fighting in the vicinity of Saint-Léger where the countryside, with its small copses, sunken lanes and hedgerows, was ideally suited to defence. Private Sidney COOLING, 1st Grenadier Guards, and Private James Edward FRIDAY, 1st Welsh Guards, both of whom are buried here, were killed near Saint-Léger rather than Moyenneville. COOLING's name is shown in *Soldiers Died in the*

Great War as 'Couling'. He was killed in action on 26 August (Plot A.8). Private FRIDAY died of wounds on 24 August. (Plot B.4)

There are just two gallantry awards in this cemetery. Lance Corporal John W. LANGLEY MM, 1st King's (Liverpool Regiment), was killed in action on 11 August 1918 (Plot A.21). Serjeant Angus CONNOR MM, 1st Scots Guards, was killed in action on 21 August 1918 (Plot B.2). There is no reference to LANGLEY's MM in *Soldiers Died in the Great War.*

To complete this cemetery, there are two men from the Royal Field Artillery, both of whom were killed during the advance in August 1918, very likely as a result of German shelling. They are from different brigades. The 74th Brigade was attached to the Guards Division, whereas 155 Brigade was part of an Army Brigade rather than any particular division.

Railway Cutting Cemetery, Courcelles-le-Comte

The village of Courcelles-le-Comte is about sixteen miles south of Arras. The cemetery lies well outside the village and to the south, on the west side of the railway line. From Arras, the best route to take is the N.17 towards Bapaume. Continue as far as Ervillers and in the centre of the village turn right on to the D.9. On the edge of the village, the D.9 splits, but bear left and continue towards Gomiécourt. About 400 yards west of the village there are two tracks, one running north, which leads to Warry Copse Cemetery, and another running more or less straight ahead. Take this latter track and continue over the railway line, taking care when crossing. Railway Cutting Cemetery lies along a footpath running parallel to the railway line. There are ninety-two identified burials, one of which is commemorated by a special memorial.

Like nearby Warry Copse Cemetery, this one tells the story of the attack by the 3rd Division on 21 August 1918. However, here at Railway Cutting Cemetery, we find many more casualties from the 1st Northumberland Fusiliers. The battalion faced heavier resistance that foggy morning than some of the others, and today, twenty-three of its men are buried here, all of whom were killed in action or died of wounds on 21 or 23 August 1918. Those killed on 21 August came up against German positions on the high ground south of Courcelles-le-Comte. Those who died two days later either fell during enemy counter-attacks the following day or from an attack later that evening when the 1st Northumberland Fusiliers recaptured the positions lost earlier in the day.

Corporal John SCOTT MM, 1st Northumberland Fusiliers, is one of those who died of wounds on 23 August. His entry in *Soldiers Died in the Great War* does not refer to his MM (Plot A.56). The date of death shown in the CWGC register for Private Frederick John SHURROCK, 1st Northumberland Fusiliers, is incorrect. It should be recorded as 23 August 1918 rather than 3 August 1918. (Plot A.44)

On 21 August the 4th Royal Fusiliers was in support to the 1st Northumberland Fusiliers. Eleven of its casualties can be found here, including two officers. All were killed or died of wounds on 21 or 22 August 1918. One of the officers, Lieutenant Lawrence Picton EVANS, 6th Royal Fusiliers, attached 4th Battalion, was 42 years old when he was killed on 21 August (Plot A.53). Next to him is Captain Barrie Dow

ROBERTSON, 4th Royal Fusiliers, who was killed in action the following day. (Plot A.54)

These eleven casualties make up just over half the total of twenty Royal Fusiliers in this cemetery; four are from the 23rd Battalion, three are from the 10th Battalion, and the remaining two are from the 24th Battalion. The 10th Royal Fusiliers, which formed part of the 37th Division, was successful in clearing the village of Ablainzevelle on 21 August, capturing it with little opposition, except for the north-west corner. That part of the village had not been touched by the artillery barrage on account of its proximity to the jumping off positions and therefore took longer to deal with.

That same day, the 23rd Royal Fusiliers, belonging to the 2nd Division, reported a number of casualties on its part of the battlefield as a result of earlier gas shelling. The fields of long grass through which the advance took place had become contaminated with mustard gas residue.

Two days later, on 23 August, the 24th Royal Fusiliers advanced directly through the position now occupied by this cemetery and beyond the railway line, towards the village of Béhagnies, whilst further south the 23rd Royal Fusiliers advanced on Sapignies.

As at Warry Copse Cemetery, we also have men from the King's (Liverpool Regiment). Captain James Alexander Campbell JOHNSON, 8th King's (Liverpool Regiment), attached 13th Battalion, is one of ten casualties from his battalion buried here (Plot A.57). There is also a gallantry award among this group. Corporal William BURNS MM, 13th King's (Liverpool Regiment), formerly Royal Irish Fusiliers, was killed in action on 21 August along with the others (Plot A.45). Private Jesse Willie HALL, 13th King's (Liverpool Regiment), is recorded in the CWGC register as having been killed in action on 1 August 1918. Again, the entry for his death is incorrect and should be recorded as 21 August 1918. (Plot A.18)

Other 3rd Division units with burials here are the 1st Royal Scots Fusiliers with four men, including Captain Robert Lindsay McMUTRIE, all killed on 21 August 1918. The 2nd Suffolk Regiment has ten of its men here who were killed or died of wounds on 21 or 23 August 1918. Private Arthur John BIDWELL MM, 2nd Suffolk Regiment, is one of those who died on 21 August (Plot A.58). His brother, Lance Corporal John Bidwell, 8th Battalion, London Regiment (Post Office Rifles), also served, but died at home on 19 March 1918. He is buried in Highgate Cemetery, London. The 1st Gordon Highlanders has one officer, Second Lieutenant Donald Hamilton McGREGOR (Plot A.7), and four other ranks buried here.

There are also a handful of casualties from the 63rd (Royal Naval) Division and two men from the Tank Corps. Private Harry Edward EVENDEN is shown as serving with the 6th Battalion, Tank Corps, and was killed in action on 23 August 1918 (Plot A.47). Serjeant James MURRAY's battalion is not shown, but he also died serving with the Tank Corps. (Plot B.14)

There is one final gallantry award holder buried here: Corporal Andrew EATOUGH MM, 2nd Division, Ammunition Column, Royal Garrison Artillery. He was killed in action on 28 August 1918. (Plot C.11)

Sunken Road Cemetery, Boisleux-Saint-Marc

This is one of those cemeteries that seems to have few visitors. I only visited it for the first time in February 2011, almost thirty years after my first visit to the battlefields of France and Flanders. Like many of the cemeteries that sit between the Somme battlefield and Arras it has plenty to offer, even to the casual visitor, and is well worth a visit.

The cemetery is situated in an isolated location in open farmland to the north-east of Boisleux-au-Mont. From the D.917 take the D.35 at Boiry-Becquerelle and head west towards Boisleux-au-Mont. Approximately half way between the two villages the D.35 makes a double bend. At the point of the second bend there is a small road or track running north. About 600 yards up this road is the cemetery. This road eventually links up with the D.34 and the village of Mercatel to the north.

A number of regiments are well represented within this cemetery; the King's (Liverpool Regiment), the Highland Light Infantry and the Royal Fusiliers, as are several divisions: the 57th (2nd West Lancashire) Division, the 63rd (Royal Naval) Division and the Guards Division. Another feature of this cemetery is the high proportion of gallantry awards. Of the 416 identified casualties here, no fewer than twenty-six have gallantry awards, which equates to one in every sixteen headstones. Only two graves are unidentified and there are still four German graves to the right of the entrance in Plot I.

Just under a fifth of the casualties are from 1917 and there are also some burials from the German Offensive in March 1918. However, the vast majority of burials are from battles fought during the latter part of 1918, particularly around the Canal du Nord between 27 September and 1 October and the Second Battle of Cambrai on 8 and 9 October.

All this fighting took place a good distance to the east of this cemetery, but it was here that six casualty clearing stations were located at various times between 9 September and 27 November 1918, and so most of the men buried here died of wounds rather than on the battlefield. Casualty clearing stations are large facilities and cannot be moved easily or quickly, so that it was often difficult for them to keep pace with the advances that were being made by the troops at this stage of the war. At one point, between 28 September and 12 October 1918, there were four casualty clearing stations operating in this area at the same time. These were No. 38, No. 19, No. 1 and No. 30. During that period the distance between the battlefields and these facilities was between twelve and eighteen miles.

Captain Percival Elliot COX, 4th Northumberland Fusiliers, died of wounds on 23 May 1917, aged 26. The 149th Brigade was in reserve on 20 May pending an attack by the 33rd Division. As the attack went reasonably well and no counter-attacks developed, 149 Brigade was not used. However, on the night of the 22nd it took over from 19 Brigade and 100 Brigade in the Hindenburg Line. It is quite likely that he was wounded during that relief, or shortly after it. His battalion was part of the 50th (Northumbrian) Division. (Plot I.A.3)

Lieutenant Ernest Edward PARSON MC, 124 Brigade, Royal Field Artillery, died of wounds on 1 June 1917. His MC was gazetted on 30 July 1917 and awarded for conspicuous gallantry and devotion to duty whilst acting as forward observation officer.

When the infantry was held up by bombers and machine-gun fire from an enemy strongpoint, he organized an attack on it, capturing seventeen prisoners and a machine gun. (Plot I.E.12)

Captain Henry Edward STEWART, 8th Royal Sussex Regiment, was killed in action on 1 June 1917 near Hénin-sur-Cojeul. His battalion was attached to the 18th (Eastern) Division as pioneers. He was the only son of Sir Edward and Lady Philippa Stewart. His mother was one of eleven children born to Henry Granville Fitzalan-Howard, 14th Duke of Norfolk. One of Henry's uncles was the 15th Duke of Norfolk who also died in 1917. Henry's father received his knighthood that same year for services during the war. In 1914 he had worked closely with Fabian Ware as part of a contingent from the British Red Cross Society that had initially crossed to France as a medical unit. However, both men soon began to take an interest in the marking and recording of soldiers' graves and the subsequent care of them. That interest became the War Graves Registration Commission, which became the Imperial War Graves Commission, which in turn became the Commonwealth War Graves Commission. Captain Henry Edward Stewart was educated at the Oratory School and New College, Oxford, where he graduated. He had accompanied his battalion to France in July 1915 and was mentioned in despatches. (Plot I.F.14)

Corporal Walter SHEARSMITH MM and Bar, 2/5th Duke of Wellington's Regiment, was 25 years old when he died of wounds on 13 September 1918. His MM was gazetted on 18 October 1917. I can find no trace of the bar being gazetted, though it is acknowledged in *Soldiers Died in the Great War*. (Plot II.A.1) Another man, Private Sydney Shearsmith, is commemorated on the Arras Memorial. He was killed in action on 3 May 1917 whilst serving with the same battalion. Both men came from Worlaby in Lincolnshire and enlisted at Barton in Lincolnshire; their army numbers are almost consecutive. It seems highly likely that they were related, and were probably brothers, though the CWGC records do not confirm this. Curiously, neither man is listed on the war memorials at Worlaby or at Barton-on-Humber.

Private Thomas FLETT, 5th Duke of Wellington's Regiment, died of wounds on 12 September 1918, aged 19. He was one of many who had lied about his age on enlistment and was just 15 years old when he joined the army, though he only served for a short time on the Western Front before his death. His family operated a shipping business in Sunderland. (Plot II.A.9)

One headstone stands out as the only Indian soldier buried here. Havildar Major Kirpa SINGH was serving with the 2nd Division Ammunition Column when he died on 12 September 1918, leaving his widow, Punna, in Peshawar. It is unusual to find any reference to female next-of-kin for Indian soldiers, though the state where they resided is often mentioned in the CWGC register. (Plot II.A.11)

Another interesting and unusual headstone is that of Second Lieutenant George James Paul HOLTON, Middlesex Hussars, attached 1st Reserve Battalion, London Regiment (Royal Fusiliers). He died on 16 September 1918, aged 24, and came from Mill Hill, London. The regimental badge is that of his yeomanry regiment. (Plot II.B.21)

Gunner Eric Parkes GREENHOUGH, New Zealand Field Artillery, was killed in action on 26 September 1918. The CWGC register make no reference to an award that he received for bravery in New Zealand when he was just 12 years old. The award was made for rescuing a man who was drowning off the beach close to where he lived. (Plot II.F.26)

Three of the Guards Division casualties are from the German Offensive in March 1918 and are buried next to each other (Plots I.G.2 to 4). On 21 March 1918 the Guards Division was near Warlus, just south of Arras, but it was soon called into action and fought strongly as it fell back through Boyelles and Boiry-Becquerelle between 23 and 30 March 1918. By the end of the month it eventually held a line along the eastern outskirts of Boisluex-Saint-Marc and just to the east of Boiry-Saint-Martin. However, the majority of the Guards Division casualties buried here are from the last two weeks in September and the first week of October 1918. This may seem surprising, particularly as the division passed through the area just south of Boisleux-Saint-Marc in late August 1918 when it attacked the village of Saint-Léger. In mid-September the division was further east around Moeuvres, and later that month it was involved in fighting south of the Bapaume–Cambrai road in the Hindenburg Support Line.

Serjeant Albert Henry EVANS DCM, 1st Welsh Guards, died of wounds on 17 September 1918. His DCM was not conferred for any single act of gallantry, but for continuous gallantry and devotion to duty. The citation notes that for a period of eighteen months he performed his duty in a most exemplary and praiseworthy manner and showed an absolute disregard for danger and the greatest devotion to duty. He worked alongside Lieutenant A.H. Picton-Phillips, a popular and very able doctor attached to the battalion, whose place was then taken by the charismatic Captain Lionel Matthew 'Mick' Rowlette DSO MC, an Irishman with a wicked sense of humour. EVANS soon became Rowlette's right-hand man, and both men did splendid work together, most notably at Gouzeaucourt in 1917 during the Battle of Cambrai. Unfortunately, EVANS was mortally wounded on 16 September 1918 during a period of heavy shell fire and died the following day. He was described as a quiet, smiling, smart man; of medium height with clear blue eyes, square jaw, and a cheery word for every stricken man; never weary and never flustered. (Plot II.C.12)

Rowlette survived the war, but was wounded twice during his military service. On one occasion, at Ypres in July 1916 during a heavy bombardment, he crawled a considerable distance over open ground to attend to two wounded men. In spite of his own wounds, he later went out again in order to attend to seven more wounded cases until he was eventually removed from the battlefield to have his own wounds dressed. His actions that day earned him the DSO. He was also a larger than life character. He and a fellow medical officer, attached to the Grenadier Guards, once performed a race along the rafters of their billet during the officers' Christmas dinner in 1916. He often shared a joke with the men, and once took great delight when he was cursed by nearly every man in the battalion as he inoculated them against typhoid.

Lieutenant John Marshall SMITH, 9th (Glasgow Highlanders) Highland Light Infantry, was killed in action on 27 September 1918, aged 24. At the time of his death he would have been attached to some other unit. The 9th Highland Light Infantry was much further south, near Épehy, when he died. The more likely explanation is that he was attached to one of the regiment's other battalions, such as the 1/5th, the 1/6th or the 1/7th, which were all part of the 52nd (Lowland) Division. (Plot II.E.3)

Sometime before the war, Lieutenant William Archibald MACKENZIE had gone to Canada, where he worked for the Canadian Bank of Commerce, though he was originally from Uig on the Isle of Skye, where he grew up. In September 1914 he enlisted as a private in the 4th Cameron Highlanders, transferring to the King's Own (Royal Lancaster Regiment) when he received his commission in March 1918. He had seen a good deal of action during his service, including operations at Neuve Chapelle and Loos in 1915. He had also taken part in fighting on the Somme in 1916 and at Vimy Ridge, Givenchy and Cambrai the following year. He was badly wounded leading his company near Cambrai on 29 September 1918 and died the same day, aged 28, serving with the 2/5th King's Own (Royal Lancaster Regiment). (Plot II.E.29)

Lieutenant George Harvey ROCHESTER MC, 54th Battalion, Canadian Infantry, died on 28 September 1918, aged 24, from wounds incurred the previous day near Bourlon Wood. Although his battalion gained its objectives, casualties were described in the war diary as 'fairly heavy' and were largely caused by machine-gun fire. His MC was gazetted on 2 December 1918 and was awarded for conspicuous gallantry and resource in leading his platoon, which was on the extreme right of the Corps attack. In the face of very heavy fire, he worked his men forward section by section for several hundred yards, personally seeing that every advantage of cover was taken. He then led the final rush on his objective where he captured three machine guns. The manner in which he handled the advance saved many casualties, even though he had shown a total disregard for his own safety. (Plot III.A.24)

Second Lieutenant Frederick HODGKISS MC, 3rd Loyal North Lancashire Regiment, attached 2/4th Battalion, died of wounds on 8 October 1918, aged 32. His MC was gazetted on 11 January 1919 and was awarded for conspicuous gallantry and devotion to duty during three days of fighting near the village of Moeuvres between 7 and 9 September 1918. In one attack on a village, he collected and organized a number of men belonging to another company and led them forward with his own platoon. Later, he dashed up to an enemy machine gun and, with the enemy's own stick grenades, he personally wounded all the crew, throwing some forty grenades and accounting for seven of the enemy, setting a fine example to all those around him. He joined the Loyal North Lancashire Regiment in 1914 as a private and was in France in time to take part in the Battle of Loos. He had also served as a sniper and as a Lewis gunner, and had fought in the Battle of the Somme where he was wounded. He received his commission at the start of 1918 and managed to remain with his preferred regiment. (Plot III.C.24)

The highest ranking officer here is Lieutenant Colonel Robert Romney Godred KANE DSO and Bar. The bar, which is not shown on the headstone or in the CWGC register at the time of writing this book, was gazetted on 1 January 1919 after his death, which occurred on 1 October 1918 whilst commanding the 1st Royal Munster Fusiliers. He was educated at the Oratory School in Edgbaston, followed by the Royal

Military College, Sandhurst. The son of a Dublin judge, he began his association with the Royal Munster Fusiliers in March 1910, serving in India and Burma until war broke out. He served on the Staff at Gallipoli from the time of the initial landings until July 1915, followed by further service as a staff officer in France. He was wounded twice during the war and was awarded the *Légion d'Honneur* (France). He was also mentioned in despatches. His DSO was awarded for distinguished service at Gallipoli. I have notified the CWGC with regard to the bar so that its records can be amended. (Plot III.E.20)

The day after Lieutenant Colonel KANE died of wounds, Serjeant Frederick Arthur GODFREY DCM and Bar MM, 1st Royal Munster Fusiliers, also died from his. He was one of ten men from his battalion who were presented with the MM on 20 December 1916 at Derry Camp, near Spanbroekmolen in Belgium. His DCM was gazetted on 22 October 1916 and was awarded while he was serving as a corporal in recognition of his marked gallantry and devotion during an attack in which he was wounded. In spite of his wound, he continued regardless, saying: '*It is nothing*', before leading and cheering on two further attacks. The citation points out that when these attacks finally broke down owing to heavy machine-gun fire, it was with some difficulty that he was restrained from going on himself. The bar to his DCM was won during the attack on Pronville, south of Cambrai, on 30 September 1918, where he was again wounded as his company was crossing the canal bridge. He refused to go back to have his wounds dressed, but instead went back to help some of his comrades who had also been wounded, even saving some from drowning. He then got men from his company across the canal and, as all the officers had been wounded, he took charge of the survivors and led them in the attack. He was wounded three times before he was eventually parted from his men. The citation closes by stating that he behaved splendidly throughout the entire operation, which strikes me as something of an understatement. He was evacuated from the line for medical treatment, but sadly died of his wounds a few days later on 2 October 1918. He was 28 years old when he died; the bar to his DCM was gazetted posthumously on 2 December 1918. (Plot III.F.23)

There are two more Irish gallantry awards buried here: Serjeant Albert SOMERS MM and Bar and Serjeant George S. GATES MM. Both served with the 2nd Royal Irish Regiment and both died of wounds. GATES died on 1 October 1918 (Plot III.B.16), SOMERS the following day. (Plot III.F.10)

The 63rd (Royal Naval) Division also brought many of its wounded here during the period of fighting around Moeuvres, Inchy, and the Canal du Nord, a phase known as the Second Battle of Cambrai, which took place in late September and the first week of October 1918. By early October there were five casualty clearing stations based in this area, a distance of twelve miles from the actual fighting. By the end of September the Germans had still not been cleared from the western banks of the canal and the division's first task was to secure a footing on the eastern bank opposite Moeuvres before advancing to take the higher ground beyond it, the spur that runs south-west from Bourlon Wood. After accomplishing this, the division continued its advance by working its way down the Hindenburg Support Line in a southerly direction. Three of the division's battalions, the 7th Royal Fusiliers, the 4th Bedfordshire Regiment and the 28th Battalion, London Regiment (Artists' Rifles), were involved in these operations, along with men from the Royal Naval Volunteer Reserve and Royal Marine Light Infantry. Some of their dead are now buried here.

Major John FORSTER MC, 7th Royal Fusiliers, died of wounds on 2 October 1918. He had won his MC during the later stages of the Battle of the Somme. On 13 November 1916 at the Battle of the Ancre, FORSTER had rallied his men and remnants of other units after the initial attack by 'C' and 'D' companies had broken down. With what was left of his own company, which was 'C' Company, he reached the German front line where he held on all day. He was involved in the March Retreat in 1918, and on the opening day he was buried twice as shells exploded around him on his way to Battalion HQ. By 23 March, being the most senior officer remaining, he assumed command of his battalion and led it through the difficult days of retreat. (Plot III.E.12)

Private Frederick MILLUCCI, 1st Battalion, Royal Marine Light Infantry, was 18 years old when he was killed in action on 4 October 1918 (Plot III.E.27). The CWGC register notes that his brother also fell, but a search of its records reveals no trace of any other soldier of the same surname. He and Private Frederick John WAR, 1st Coldstream Guards, are the youngest casualties buried in this cemetery. (Plot II.C.9)

Captain Wilfred READMAN, 9th Loyal North Lancashire Regiment, died of wounds on 30 September 1918, aged 24. Although the CWGC register shows him serving with the 9th Battalion when he died, that unit was disbanded in France on 12 August 1918, having been reduced to a composite battalion with the 8th Border Regiment in late June and temporarily transferred to the 50th (Northumbrian) Division. He was transferred to the 2/4th Battalion, which was part of the 57th (2nd West Lancashire) Division, and was fatally wounded during operations around the Canal du Nord. (Plot III.F.4)

Reference has already been made to a number of men with gallantry awards, including some of the twenty-three recipients of the MM buried here. Serjeant Henry TRUSLER MM and Bar, 1st Battalion, Royal Marine Light Infantry, who died of wounds on 30 September 1918, aged 22, is another of those men. His MM was gazetted on 6 August 1918, but the bar to it was added posthumously on 11 February 1919 (Plot III.B.11). The other MM holders buried here are listed below:

Gunner William HAZEL MM, 36th Siege Battery, Royal Garrison Artillery, died of wounds on 22 May 1917. (Plot I.A.17)

Corporal Thomas Owen SANDERS MM, 1st King's (Liverpool Regiment), died of wounds on 18 September 1918, aged 23. (Plot I.C.10)

Serjeant William James YEOWELL MM, 9th King's Royal Rifle Corps, died of wounds on 28 May 1917, aged 26. (Plot I.D.10)

Corporal Reginald Joseph DIGWEED MM, 2/4th Hampshire Regiment, died of wounds on 14 September 1918, aged 21. (Plot II.A.18)

Private George SKILBECK MM, 1/9th Durham Light Infantry, died of wounds on 14 September 1918, aged 20. (Plot II.A.25)

Private Charles NOBES MM, 9th Durham Light Infantry, died of wounds on 14 September 1918, aged 38. (Plot II.B.12)

Gunner Percy William JACKSON MM, 127th Heavy Battery, Royal Garrison Artillery, died on 17 September 1918, aged 26. (Plot II.C.3)

Private George Rippon HARDY MM, 1st Northumberland Fusiliers, died of wounds on 21 September 1918, aged 20. (Plot II.D.23)

Serjeant Alexander COLVILLE MM, 1/5th Royal Scots Fusiliers, died of wounds on 21 September 1918, aged 23. (Plot II.D.24)

Private George PALMER MM, 'Z' Company, 1st Northumberland Fusiliers, died of wounds on 21 September 1918, aged 21. (Plot II.D.30)

Serjeant Frederick Edward William DAVIS MM, 93 Brigade, Royal Field Artillery, died of wounds on 26 September 1918, aged 30. (Plot II.F.24)

Private Edward G. ORMSBY MM, 1/6th Highland Light Infantry, died of wounds on 29 September 1918, aged 21. *Soldiers Died in the Great War* makes no reference to his MM. (Plot III.A.25)

Staff-Serjeant Arthur Robert VISICK MM, 111th Heavy Battery, Royal Garrison Artillery, died of wounds on 5 October 1918. (Plot III.C.13)

Private Charles MOSLEY MM, 9th King's (Liverpool Regiment), died of wounds on 7 October 1918. (Plot III.C.14)

Private James Bell HARVEY MM, 1/2nd Lowland Field Ambulance, Royal Army Medical Corps, died of wounds on 9 October 1918, aged 21. (Plot III.C.28)

Lance Corporal Thomas Edward JONES MM, 9th King's (Liverpool Regiment), died of wounds on 3 October 1918, aged 26. (Plot III.E.13)

Leading Seaman George R.F. REES MM, Anson Battalion, Royal Naval Volunteer Reserve, died of wounds on 1 October 1918, aged 21. (Plot III.F.19)

Lance Corporal Edward Francis DUERDEN MM, 2/7th King's (Liverpool Regiment), died of wounds on 1 October 1918, aged 26. (Plot III.F.21)

Finally, there are a few men who had previously served elsewhere than on the Western Front. Corporal Albert BUTLER, 'A' Company, 1/4th Royal Scots, had previously served in Gallipoli, Egypt and Palestine and had enlisted in August 1914 (Plot III.E.3). Private William Robert LARNER, 1st Battalion, Royal Marine Light Infantry, had also enlisted in 1914 and had previously served in Gallipoli (Plot III.A.10). Similarly, Gunner Alfred George Frederick MASTERS, 28th Battery, 4 (Wessex) Brigade, Royal Field Artillery, enlisted in August 1914, but then went to India in December that year before subsequently serving in France. (Plot III.B.2)

Warry Copse Cemetery, Courcelles-le-Comte

This small cemetery was made after the village of Courcelles-le-Comte had been captured by the 3rd Division on 21 August 1918. Out of a total of forty burials only two are unidentified. The cemetery is on the south-east side of the village, just east of the Achiet-le-Grand–Arras railway line. It can be reached from the village along the D.9E. Immediately east of the railway line there is a track running south-east towards Gomiécourt. The cemetery sits a couple of hundred yards off this track tucked up against the railway embankment. If approaching from the direction of Gomiécourt, the cemetery is easily visible from the same track running north-west towards Courcelles-le-Comte.

The largest group of men buried here belongs to the King's (Liverpool Regiment). There are sixteen in all, including two officers, Second Lieutenant Harry WASH-BROOK, 5th King's (Liverpool Regiment), who was killed in action on 22 August 1918 (Plot A.12) and Lieutenant Reginald James BARRETT, 6th King's (Liverpool Regiment), who was killed on 21 August 1918 (Plot A.21). However, both officers happened to be attached to the 13th Battalion when they were killed. One of the remaining fourteen NCOs and men was twice decorated. Lance Serjeant Charles Napier MITCHELL MM and Bar, 13th King's (Liverpool Regiment), was killed in action on 21 August 1918. Both awards were gazetted posthumously, the MM on 29 August, a week or so after his death, and the bar soon afterwards on 7 October. Regrettably, neither award is shown against his name in *Soldiers Died in the Great War*. (Plot A.27)

The attack on 21 August took place at 4.55am in thick fog, which proved to be something of a mixed blessing; on the one hand it offered some cover from view, whilst on the other it made visibility and communication more difficult. By 8.45am the men of the 13th King's (Liverpool Regiment) had managed to link up along the railway line with their comrades from the 7th King's Shropshire Light Infantry and the 1st Royal Scots Fusiliers. The right of the 3rd Division's attack turned out to be more of a challenge when the 1st Northumberland Fusiliers came up against stronger opposition, as did the left flank of the 63rd (Royal Naval) Division. Despite gallant efforts by the 4th Royal Fusiliers to support the Northumberland men, enemy machine-gun fire higher up the slope was sufficiently heavy to prevent them joining the division's other units on the railway line.

The fog also resulted in many of the tanks losing their way, so that they were unable to support the initial advance. Later on, thirteen of them did manage to reach the second objective. Private Arthur SEAMAN, 15th Battalion, Tank Corps, was a member of one of those crews and was killed in action on 21 August. He had previously served with the Cameronians. (Plot A.24)

Casualties from all three brigades of the 3rd Division can be found here, including eight NCOs and privates of the 1st Gordon Highlanders who are buried consecutively. All of them were killed on 23 August 1918, two days after the capture of Courcelles-le-Comte (Plots A.33 to A.40). Another NCO and five privates from the 1st Royal Scots Fusiliers, killed on 22 and 23 August 1918, are also buried consecutively (Plots A.1 to A.6). Other headstones relating to the 3rd Division belong to men from the 2nd Suffolk Regiment, the 8th King's Own (Royal Lancaster Regiment) and the 2nd Royal Scots.

Mercatel Communal Cemetery

The village of Mercatel is situated about four miles south of Arras on the main Arras to Bapaume road. The cemetery is located on the south side of the village about 400 yards or so south of the church. There are just seven identified casualties here out of a total of twenty. The graves are located east of the entrance. All seven are men of the 1st Black Watch (Tyneside Scottish) who were killed in action on 20 May 1940 during the fighting that took place just south of Arras.

Two of the seven, Private Albert Edward McLUCKIE, aged 24, (Grave 2) and Private Ernest NIXON, aged 23, (Grave 18) have consecutive army numbers. Private John McCORMICK (Grave 1) was 40 years old when he died. Six of the seven hailed from County Durham.

The battalion went to France as part of the British Expeditionary Force and was employed in airfield construction. On 20 May 1940 it found itself caught between Mercatel and Ficheux, virtually encircled and engaged in a battle that lasted several hours against German infantry and tanks converging from the north, west and east. A few survivors were able to withdraw from the position, which had clearly become untenable, but many more were taken prisoner.

Chapter Eleven

A Mystery off the Cornish Coast – Coffee and Small Comforts – Orchids and Orchards

Agnez-lès-Duisans Communal Cemetery

There are just three Second World War casualties buried here, one of whom is unidentified. Both identified men served with the 4th Royal Northumberland Fusiliers and died on the same day, 20 May 1940. In Grave 1 is Fusilier Richard William Davidson PATTISON, aged 25; next to him in Grave 2 is Fusilier Robert SCOTT, aged 27.

Barly French Military Cemetery

The cemetery is easy to find. It lies about 500 yards south of the village of Barly on the D.8. The French began the cemetery in September 1915 and it still retains a number of French graves. The CWGC register notes that it was also used by British Field Ambulance units between March 1916 and May 1918. There are now twenty-eight identified casualties buried here from Britain and the Dominions in what is still very much a French military cemetery.

The cemetery was used in 1916 by the 55th (West Lancashire) Division to bury its dead and it remained in use until 1918. Although there are a few burials dating to 1917, over half the British and Commonwealth plot consists of 1918 burials, including six men from units of the Indian Labour Corps buried alongside three of their fellow countrymen who died in 1917. One of these men, Labourer DAIDAN, 49th North-West Frontier Province, Indian Labour Corps, died on Christmas Day 1917. According to the CWGC register, all nine Indian graves were brought in from various locations after the Armistice.

The first two graves to note are in Plot II, Row A. Private Joseph BRENNAN, 1/8th King's (Liverpool Regiment), was shot for desertion on 16 July 1916, the same day that Private J. SLOAN was also shot for his act of desertion. BRENNAN's battalion was also known as the Liverpool Irish. SLOAN's battalion was the 1/4th King's Own (Royal Lancaster Regiment) which, like the 1/8th King's (Liverpool Regiment), was part of the 55th (West Lancashire) Division. SLOAN had gone absent while on a bombing course and a witness at his trial claimed that he had seen him remove his equipment before making off. He was arrested in Rouen six days later. The trial of both men took place on consecutive days. The fact that both men came from the same brigade was almost certainly a factor in deciding their fate. The Battle of the Somme was also in full swing and, although the division was not directly involved in the fighting at that stage, both men were undoubtedly executed as an example to others within the division at what was clearly a critical time for the British army. Whatever the reason for the omission, *Soldiers Died in the Great War* does not include SLOAN's name in the roll call. (Plots II.A.11 and 13)

Private John Thomas BOOTH, 1/5th York & Lancaster Regiment, died on Christmas Day 1916. He is not shown in *Soldiers Died in the Great War* as having died from wounds or having been killed in action, and so presumably he died of sudden illness or some other natural cause. (Plot II.A.17)

Captain Egerton Lowndes WRIGHT MC, 1st Buckingham Battalion, Oxfordshire & Buckinghamshire Light Infantry, was killed in action on 11 May 1918, aged 32. A member of the MCC, he had also captained the Oxford University XI. His death came whilst serving as brigade major with 6 Infantry Brigade, but he had joined his parent battalion back in September 1914. His MC was gazetted in the New Year's Honours List on 1 January 1918. His brother, Captain Philip Lowndes Wright DSO MC, who also served with the Oxfordshire & Buckinghamshire Light Infantry, wrote a history of the 1st Buckinghamshire Battalion after the war. Both his decorations were for service during the war rather than specific acts of gallantry. The MC was awarded in the New Year's Honours List on 1 January 1917 and the DSO in the King's Birthday Honours List of 3 June 1919.

Beaumetz-lès-Loges Communal Cemetery

This is another easy cemetery to find. It lies just outside the village of Beaumetz-lès-Loges to the north of the village on the D.7, which is the Arras–Doullens road.

There are just twenty-nine casualties in a small plot set aside at the far end of the civilian cemetery. The majority are from 1916, beginning in May that year and continuing through to December. Burials ceased after May 1918. The 55th (West Lancashire) Division began burying its dead here and its battalions are very evident, especially those of the King's (Liverpool Regiment).

Lieutenant William James JONES, 6th King's (Liverpool Regiment), and three others from that battalion were killed on 28 June 1916 during a raid carried out by six battalions of the 55th (West Lancashire) Division. JONES and his men are buried together. (Plots A.6, A.7, A.8 and A.9) According to the regimental history, these were the only four men from that battalion killed in the operation. A few days later, on 1 July, as the Battle of the Somme opened, Lance Serjeant Ernest BEESTON MM and two others from the 6th King's (Liverpool Regiment) were killed in action, though the 55th (West Lancashire) Division did not take part in the opening day of the battle. BEESTON's MM was awarded for his part in the raid of 28 June, although it was gazetted much later on 19 February 1917. (Plots B.7, B.8, B.9)

Of the seven men buried here who died in 1917, Regimental Serjeant Major Charles Thomas LAYLAND MSM, 5th Royal Scots, attached 12th Battalion, is worth a brief pause. He was killed in action on 4 January 1917, aged 40. On 2 January the 12th Royal Scots had carried out a raid on the enemy's trenches, but had found them unoccupied. Although the raid caused no losses or damage to the Germans, they retaliated with trench mortar fire over the next few days, no doubt in the hope of deterring any future incursions. It is highly likely that LAYLAND was killed during one of these bombardments. By tragic coincidence, his MSM was gazetted on 1 January 1917 in the New Year's Honours List, a few days before his death.

Berneville Communal Cemetery

Berneville is about five miles south-west of Arras and lies just to the north of the N.25. The D.67 runs north from the N.25 into the village of Berneville and is known as the Rue d'Arras. As the D.67 enters the village on the east side, it bends to the left, but there is also a small side road to the right. The cemetery sits just along this side road, more or less at the junction

There are six burials here, evenly split between the First and Second World Wars. The three First World War casualties are from March 1917. Drummer Frederick ROSE, 2nd West Yorkshire Regiment, and Private Ellis HOLT, 19th Manchester Regiment, were executed for the crime of desertion on 4 March 1917. ROSE was a regular soldier, but he went missing on 18 December 1914 as his battalion was making its way to trenches near Fleurbaix in preparation for an attack. The attack never took place that day, but ROSE had already made his way back behind the lines. Remarkably, he evaded detection for two years, apparently residing with a woman in the town of Hazebrouck. The circumstances of his arrest are not entirely clear, but it appears that a neighbour reported his presence and he was subsequently taken into custody.

Private HOLT was one of the many who had answered the call to serve when war broke out. As a Salford man, he joined the Manchester Regiment and became a member of the 19th Manchester Regiment, otherwise known as the 4th Manchester Pals. He had already deserted once and had been sentenced to two years penal servitude with hard labour, but the sentence had been suspended. His second offence offered no such opportunity for redemption.

Buried between these two men is Rifleman John KING, 7th King's Royal Rifle Corps, who died on 16 March 1917. Contrary to at least one source, he was not executed, though he does not appear to have died in action.

From the Second World War there are two privates from the 8th Durham Light Infantry who were killed in action or died of wounds on 21 and 22 May 1940. The final grave is that of Flying Officer (Pilot) Gilbert Francis Moncreiff WRIGHT, 605 Squadron, Royal Air Force, who was killed in action on 22 May 1940, aged 36, when his Hurricane was shot down near Arras.

Fosseux Communal Cemetery

The village of Fosseux is about ten miles south-west of Arras. The cemetery is on the east side of the village and just to the north of the D.66. It can also be reached via the D.59. There is just one British casualty buried here. Private William THOMSON, 11th Durham Light Infantry, was killed in action on 21 May 1940, aged 22. He is buried not far from the main calvary in the cemetery.

Gouy-en-Artois Communal Cemetery Extension

Gouy-en-Artois is situated about nine miles south-west of Arras and the cemetery is on the south side of the village on the road leading to Bavincourt, opposite a heavily wooded area. It is a tiny cemetery with just forty-four CWGC graves and four

German burials. The majority of burials here relate to the Battle of Arras 1917 and almost all of them are April casualties.

Probably the most visited grave in this cemetery is that of Brigadier General Charles Bulkeley BULKELEY-JOHNSON CB, ADC General Staff, commanding the 8th Cavalry Brigade. He was wounded on 11 April 1917 and died almost immediately after being hit by a bullet to the head. He was presumed to have been shot by a sniper while making his way forward to try to ascertain the situation following the cavalry's efforts to support the infantry at Monchy-le-Preux.

His military career began in 1887 when he was commissioned in the 2nd Dragoons (Royal Scots Greys). However, he spent the duration of the South African War in Egypt, where he remained until 1903. In November 1899, for his services in connection with these operations, he was mentioned in despatches. In 1911 he was given command of his regiment, and in August 1914 he embarked with for France as part of the 5th Cavalry Brigade. His promotion to brigadier general in command of the 8th Cavalry Brigade occurred in November that year. (Plot A.30)

Buried next to him is Second Lieutenant, the Honourable George Seymour DAWSON-DARMER, 10th (Prince of Wales's Own Royal) Hussars, who died of wounds on 13 April 1917. He was the son of the 5th Earl of Portarlington in Ireland and had previously served as a captain in the Dorset Yeomanry at Gallipoli (Plot A.31).

His nephew, the son of the 6th Earl, was Air Commodore George Lionel Seymour Dawson-Damer, who was killed during the Second World War in mysterious circumstances. He was on board a Vickers Warwick aircraft that took off from RAF Lyneham on 17 April 1944 in order to attend a meeting with the Yugoslav Partisan leader, Tito. Not long into the flight, during the early hours of the morning, the aircraft exploded in mid-air just off Newquay on the Cornish coast. All sixteen people on board were killed, including the pilot. One version of the story maintains that the aircraft was carrying a quantity of gold to fund clandestine operations in Europe run by British agents, some of whom were believed to be among the passengers.

The cemetery was used by a number of divisions during the Battle of Arras and most of the casualties buried here would have died of wounds. The divisions that used the cemetery in April 1917 were the 14th, the 56th, the 30th and the 21st Divisions, all of which were in action on the opening day of the Battle of Arras on the section of front stretching from the southern suburbs of Arras to the village of Croisilles under VII Corps. There are also a handful of subsequent burials from the 33rd Division and the 50th (Northumbrian) Division.

There is just one gallantry award buried here: Lance Corporal George Robert RAYNER MM, 9th King's Royal Rifle Corps, who died on 10 April 1917. His award was gazetted on 11 November 1916, though the entry in *Soldiers Died in the Great War* makes no mention of the award, nor can I find any trace of him, or his award, in the *King's Royal Rifle Corps Chronicle* for 1916. (Plot A.8)

There are just five identified casualties from 1918, four of whom are from the 2nd Royal Scots, which on 28 March 1918, along with other units from the 3rd Division, was involved trying to stem the spread of the German advance south-east of Arras (Plots A.44 to 47). With them is a driver from the 40th Division Ammunition

Column who died in April 1918. The 40th Division was also involved in the fighting immediately south of Arras during the last week of March 1918.

The CWGC register also shows one man, Private Edgar BRYAN, as being from the 70th Battalion, Yorkshire Regiment. This should be interpreted as the 7th Battalion.

Habarcq Communal Cemetery Extension

Habarcq is about seven miles to the west of Arras. The communal cemetery is on the north side of the village on the D.61, the road leading to Haute-Avesnes, and the extension is alongside it. There are 179 burials relating to the Great War and fifteen from the Second World War, eleven of which are unidentified.

The village was used by a number of field ambulances from March 1916 when British troops began to arrive in the area to take over from the French. However, burials ceased towards the end of March the following year once the Germans had withdrawn to the Hindenburg Line and the British Third Army advanced to take up the ground that had been vacated. Only two burials took place after that date and they are buried in Plot V, Rows G and H, in each case the second grave in the row. Some 378 French graves still remain from the early part of the war before the British took over; there are no holders of gallantry awards buried in this cemetery.

Sapper Francis Lynch HENDERSON, 1/2nd (Durham) Field Company, Royal Engineers, died on 6 June 1916 from wounds received during an enemy air raid, aged 22. He rejoined the army from the Reserve list on 5 August 1914, the day after Britain had gone to war. (Plot I.J.5)

Second Lieutenant Victor MacDonald BOWLING, 12 Squadron, Royal Flying Corps, died from his injuries on 4 March 1917 after accidentally crashing. He was 18 years old when he died and joined the Royal Flying Corps directly from school in August 1916, arriving in France in January 1917 (Plot V.J.1). His father, Alfred BOWLING, was master of the SS *Enosis*, which was carrying coal to Malta from Barry in South Wales when the ship was sunk by a German submarine on 18 November 1915. He is commemorated on the Tower Hill Memorial in London.

Second Lieutenant Percival Fossy Thackaberry BURNS was serving with the 13th King's (Liverpool Regiment) when he died of wounds on 21 March 1917, aged 22. He had been an undergraduate at Trinity College, Dublin. He had also been mentioned previously in despatches. (Plot V.K.6)

Second Lieutenant James Walker THORBURN, 6th Cameron Highlanders, died of wounds on 12 March 1917, aged 27. His brother, Lance Corporal William George Thorburn, 23rd Royal Fusiliers (1st Sportsman's Battalion), was killed in action on 17 February 1917, aged 19, and is buried in Regina Trench Cemetery, Grandcourt. (Plot V.L.2)

Second Lieutenant William Stanley JOHNSON, 7th East Surrey Regiment, died of wounds on 17 March 1917, aged 20. His battalion relieved the 6th Queen's (Royal West Surrey Regiment) late on the afternoon of the 15th in trenches near Arras. For the following two days his battalion also supplied working parties and it was on the second day that a shell caused devastation to JOHNSON's platoon, killing six men outright and wounding another fourteen. Despite being moved to Habarcq and its medical facilities, Second Lieutenant JOHNSON's life could not be saved (Plot V.L.7). The six men who were killed instantly by the shell were buried together at Faubourg d'Amiens Cemetery in Plot II, Row H. The battalion suffered a further four casualties from shelling that day.

Second Lieutenant William Adam Mackie NIVEN, 29 Squadron, Royal Flying Corps, was killed whilst flying a DH2 aircraft on 28 October 1916. The weather was not particularly conducive to air operations that day. He had also served in German South-West Africa in 1914–1915 with the Transvaal Scottish under General Botha. He came to England early in 1916 where he obtained his commission in the Royal Flying Corps. (Plot VIII.A.5)

Second Lieutenant Edgar Percy GAY, 6th Duke of Cornwall's Light Infantry, was killed in action on 6 January 1917 (Plot VIII.C.8). His name is incorrectly referred to in the CWGC register; his surname was actually GRAY. The regimental history makes a brief comment on his death. On 1 January his battalion took over trenches from the 10th Durham Light Infantry in the H.2 sub-sector near Arras. On 6 January the 10th Durham Light Infantry returned to carry out a raid. The raid went ahead and the raiders came and went, leaving the 6th Duke of Cornwall's Light Infantry to bear the consequences, which came in the form of heavy shelling. Second Lieutenant GRAY was badly wounded by one of the shells and died the next day. Raids of this nature were always unpopular with those who were left holding the trenches when, as the regimental history puts it, '*the other lot cleared off*'.

On 17 April 1916 Private Thomas SANDERS, 14th Royal Warwickshire Regiment, was with a working party carrying out wiring when he was hit in the thigh by a sniper's bullet, which then made its exit via his stomach. Captain Ehrhardt rushed to his aid, but he too received a bullet wound to his thigh as soon as he reached SANDERS, presumably from the same sniper. An old school friend of theirs, Lieutenant Emile Jacot, went to the assistance of both men accompanied by Serjeant Weatherhead, and at great personal risk to themselves they managed to bring both men back to safety. Ehrhardt eventually made a recovery, but was discharged from military service. When operated on it was found that the bullet had fragmented. Pieces of it were removed from Ehrhardt's stomach, but those in his back were presumably too close to the spine and they were left inside him. Unfortunately, and despite making it back to the brigade's Field Ambulance at HABARCQ, Private SANDERS died from his wounds on 20 April after contracting gangrene. (Plot VIII.D.1)

Captain Edward Brassey EGERTON, 'D' Squadron, 17th Lancers, died of wounds on 1 September 1916, aged 27. He was the son of Lady Mabelle Egerton and was married to the daughter of the 4th Marquess of Ormonde. He was educated at Eton and Christ Church College, Oxford, before joining the 17th Lancers in 1909 and serving in India as a lieutenant. He went to France in November 1914 and married in August 1915 (Plot VIII.E.3).

Shortly after the outbreak of war, his mother, Lady Mabelle Egerton, drove across to France with her father in the family's Sunbeam carrying parcels for the Red Cross and St John's Ambulance. At Rouen she was asked if she could boil up some water so that troops carrying dry rations, such as Oxo cubes and tea, could have a hot drink. And so, from such humble beginnings in a side shed, the 'Rouen Station Coffee Shop' was born. At its height, it provided around 6,000 cups of tea per day to troops entering or leaving France via Rouen and became one of the largest canteens in France, selling items such as soap, sandwiches, cakes, tea, coffee and other small comforts. It carried on providing this facility throughout the war. Lady Egerton was also involved in the provision of small comforts to soldiers invalided home on ambulance trains from Rouen; in 1918 she was awarded a CBE in recognition of her work. Two of Edward's brothers served in the Royal Navy. Henry Jack Egerton CB, became a vice admiral, whilst Commander Hugh Sydney Egerton won the DSC. The Egerton family is the same one that had a long association with Tatton Hall in Cheshire, now run by the National Trust. (Plot VIII.E.3)

Serjeant David Brown WALKER, 11 Squadron, Royal Flying Corps, died on 16 September 1916 from wounds received the previous day, aged 19. His squadron had been busy that day flying as escort to 12 Squadron, which dropped thirty-eight bombs on Bapaume railway station from heights of between 200 and 800 feet. The bombing was very accurate and caused significant damage to the railway line and station infrastructure, including several trucks and a train that were badly damaged after repeated hits. While the raid was in progress, 11 Squadron became heavily engaged with several enemy machines as they worked hard to protect the bombers. Four enemy aircraft were brought crashing to the ground, one of which was shot down by Second Lieutenant William Powell Bowman with WALKER as his observer. Two more enemy aircraft were also driven down out of control during the encounter.

Aircraft from 11 Squadron returned to Bapaume later that day, attacking the town and the village of Achiet-le-Petit before they were intercepted by ten enemy machines near Vélu, whereupon a severe fight took place. This is likely to have been the fight in which WALKER was badly wounded (Plot VIII.E.4). Bowman survived the encounter, but was reported missing in action a month later on 17 October following aerial combat over Mory while on a reconnaissance operation for Third Army. Bowman's death was only confirmed in March the following year and he is now buried at HAC Cemetery, Écoust-Saint-Mein.

Captain Vincent Charles CLARKE, 10th Durham Light Infantry, died from accidental injuries on 12 October 1916, aged 22. He had been out on a patrol and was returning to the trench when he was fired on mistakenly by one of the sentries, mortally wounding him. This was one of the great potential hazards of patrolling no man's land at night. (Plot VIII.F.5)

Lieutenant Norman HARGREAVES, 29 Squadron, Royal Flying Corps, had previously served with the 4th East Lancashire Regiment and was killed in action on 23 November 1916 while flying a DH2 aircraft single-seater aircraft. (Plot VIII.F.7)

Private Hugh FLYNN, 18th Highland Light Infantry, died by firing squad here at Habarcq on 15 November 1916. His case would not have been helped by the fact that the same sentence had been confirmed and carried out nine days earlier in relation to another man from his battalion and for the same crime of desertion. That man is also buried in this cemetery. Private FLYNN did not have any previous history as regards disciplinary matters, but it was clearly felt that a further example had to be made in order to deter others. (Plot VIII.G.7)

Second Lieutenant George Allan EXLEY, 5th King's Own Yorkshire Light Infantry, attached Royal Flying Corps, was killed while flying on 14 January 1917. When war broke out, he initially enlisted in the Royal Engineers and trained as a despatch rider at York. He was later commissioned and transferred to the King's Own Yorkshire Light Infantry before joining the Royal Flying Corps early in 1916. Unfortunately, his operational flying career was extremely brief, as he had only been at the front for a fortnight before he was killed. On the date of his death, and for several days after, the weather had been particularly poor and very little flying had taken place. (Plot VIII.H.9)

Captain Reginald William MACLUCKIE, 3rd Argyll & Sutherland Highlanders, attached 9th West Yorkshire Regiment, had spent time in South Africa as a civil engineer after graduating from Edinburgh University with a Bachelor of Science degree. When war broke out he came home and enlisted in the 3rd Argyll & Sutherland Highlanders, but went to France with another of the regiment's battalions after gaining his commission in March 1915. He served as a brigade bombing officer and later commanded a trench mortar battery. He died of wounds on 11 August 1918. (Plot VIII.J.3)

Private John McQUADE, 18th Highland Light Infantry, was executed on 6 November 1916 for the offence of desertion. His record as a soldier had been poor and he was already under sentence of a year's imprisonment for disobedience, though this had been suspended. He was shot in Habarcq and was buried here. (Plot VIII.J.7)

Second Lieutenant Francis Carey CLEMENTS, Cable Section, attached 'F' Corps Signals, Royal Engineers, died from wounds on 11 January 1917, aged 24. Before the war he had been training to be an electrical engineer. (Plot VIII.J.9)

Private John Robert DAVIES, 14th Field Ambulance, Royal Army Medical Corps, died of wounds on 7th March 1916, aged 33. He was a veteran of the South African campaign where he served with the 2nd Battalion, King's (Liverpool Regiment) as a mounted infantryman. (Plot VIII.K.1)

Lieutenant Frederick William Robertson TURNER, 2nd (Glamorgan) Company, Royal Engineers, was killed in action on 5 August 1916, aged 25. His unit was part of the Territorial Army. Much credit and attention has been given to men of Kitchener's New Army, and rightly so, but it should be remembered that many men had offered themselves for military service long before the war as part of the Territorial system. Their contribution and commitment, not least the decision of many of them to serve overseas from the outset, deserves equal credit and recognition. (Plot VIII.K.3)

Of the four identified casualties from the Second World War, three are men of the 8th Durham Light Infantry, killed in action on 21 May 1940, and the fourth is a private from the Army Catering Corps, who died on 1 September 1944, aged 41. All can be found in Plot 5, Rows F and G.

Haute-Avesnes British Cemetery

The cemetery is on the south-west side of the village on the road to Habarcq, not the north side as noted in the CWGC records. It lies outside the village itself, but is located by the roadside in fields and is easy to find. If arriving from the D.939, the main Arras–Saint-Pol road, just continue through the village of Haute-Avesnes following the signs for Habarcq and the cemetery will become apparent on exiting the village. It contains 142 CWGC burials and eight German graves. All of the casualties here are identified.

Throughout the war the village of Haute-Avesnes was always in French or British hands and it was much used for billeting purposes. It also sits just off the main Arras–Saint-Pol road, about halfway between the important villages of Étrun and Aubigny-en-Artois, where a number of casualty clearing stations were located. Most of those buried here would have died of wounds, though it is possible that some may have been brought back for burial by their battalions, or may even have died unexpectedly from illness, accident, or natural causes. It was also within shelling range, and as a billeting area, it would also have been a legitimate target for aerial bombing.

According to the CWGC notes for this cemetery, it was begun by the 51st (Highland) Division in July 1916. Despite this, there are no casualties from that division buried here for that year. The division spent the first two weeks of July instructing the 60th (2/2nd London) Division in trenches around Neuville-Saint-Vaast and Roclincourt before moving to Doullens, Lucheux and Baudricourt on 14 July. There are, however, a handful of men from the 60th (2/2nd London) Division buried among the 1916 casualties.

All the casualties from 1916 are buried in Row A.1 to A.16, though for some reason there is one March 1917 casualty occupying grave A.15. There is just one officer among this group of men in Row A: Captain J.W.J. CRAIG, Royal Horse Artillery, 1/1st (Berkshire) Brigade, attached to 'B' Battery, 300 Brigade, Royal Field Artillery, whose death occurred on 26 July 1916. The Stock Exchange roll of honour correctly identifies him as John William Archibald CRAIG. (Plot A.8)

The 51st (Highland) Division did use the cemetery after its return to the Arras front in February 1917, when it took over familiar trenches in its old sector near Roclincourt and relieved the 9th (Scottish) Division. Both divisions then made use of the cemetery during April 1917. Some 75 per cent of the total burials here are from 1917 and most of them, not surprisingly, are casualties who fell between April and July that year. As well as men from the two Scottish divisions, including seven South Africans, there are also casualties from the 4th Division, the 34th Division and the 37th Division.

Among the 1917 casualties are two cavalrymen. Private William Francis ALLEN, 5th (Princess Charlotte of Wales) Dragoon Guards, died of wounds on 11 April 1917, the day on which the cavalry were involved in the capture of Monchy-le-Preux. Acting as the advanced guard of the 1st Cavalry Brigade, the 5th Dragoon Guards had gone forward on 10 April, but after conferring with the commanding officers of the 1st King's Own (Royal Lancaster Regiment) and the 2nd Duke of Wellington's Regiment, they withdrew to the village of Athies. Both battalion commanders took the view that mounted action was not a realistic possibility, certainly not north of the River Scarpe, and that deployment in a dismounted capacity was likely to prove no more effective than their own infantry. The 5th Dragoon Guards did sustain casualties that day from shell fire, even though the regiment did not go into action, and Private ALLEN died the following day from his injuries. (Plot C.3)

Buried a few graves along from him is Private Harry Edward STIRLING, 2nd Dragoon Guards (Queen's Bays), who died of wounds on 13 April 1917, aged 25 (Plot C.8). His regiment also sustained a handful of casualties whilst at Athies on 11 April 1917, two of whom are now buried at Point du Jour Military Cemetery and another at Athies Communal Cemetery Extension.

Second Lieutenant Henry George BRUNSDON, 9th Royal Scots, is recorded in the regimental history as having been killed in action on 23 April 1917 near Roeux. On the night of 23/24 April, after a heavy day's fighting, the battalion withdrew to the support line and was then relieved the following night when it moved back to Arras. In *Officers Died in the Great War* he is shown as dying of wounds on the 24th April. In the circumstances, this seems the more likely date of death and it agrees with records held by the CWGC. The majority of officers and men of his battalion who were killed in action on 23 April are buried far closer to where they fell than he is. It is extremely unlikely that his dead body would have been brought back here for burial a couple of days later. He is likely to have been on his way to one of the nearby casualty clearing stations when he died, either very late on 23 April or the following day. (Plot C.9)

Another interesting grave is that of Second Lieutenant Frank Reginald SEELY, 1st Hampshire Regiment, who died of wounds on 13 April 1917, aged 20 (Plot C.14). He was the eldest son of Major General, the Right Honourable, John (Jack) Edward Bernard Seely CB CMG DSO who was Secretary of State for War between 1911 and 1914 and who, with Sir John French, had been forced to resign as a result of The Curragh Incident. 'Jack' Seely went on to serve as a brigadier general during the war and commanded the Canadian Cavalry Brigade in what was the last true, great cavalry charge of the war at Moreuil Wood on 30 March 1918. He was also a great friend of Sir Winston Churchill and played an enormous part in public life after the war. The family had several homes, but is most associated with its estate on the Isle of Wight, which was managed by Frank's great-uncle, Colonel Harry Gore Browne, a VC winner in the Indian Mutiny.

Several of Frank's cousins were killed serving their country. Captain Charles Grant Seely, 8th Hampshire Regiment, was killed in action in Palestine on 19 April 1917. He is buried in Gaza War Cemetery. His brother, Squadron Leader Nigel Richard William Seely, was killed in action on 10 May 1943 serving in the Royal Air Force. He is buried in Brook (St Mary's) Churchyard, Brighstone, on the Isle of Wight. The third cousin to fall was Lieutenant Colonel William Evelyn Seely, South Nottinghamshire Hussars, who was killed on 6 June 1942 and who is commemorated on the Alamein Memorial.

There are also three gallantry award holders buried here. Second Lieutenant Reginald Arthur BROWNING MC, 20th Northumberland Fusiliers (1st Tyneside Scottish) died of wounds on 10 April 1917 (Plot B.21), as did Lance Corporal Harry Mansfield LOWE MM, 11th Royal Scots (Plot B.28). Second Lieutenant BROWNING's MC was gazetted on 13 February 1917 and was awarded for leading a successful raid on the enemy's trenches, which he did with great courage and skill, setting a splendid example to those around him.

Lance Corporal Cecil Thomas LAWSON MM, 10th Royal Fusiliers, died on 23 April 1917 from wounds received when his own battalion and others from the 37th Division's 111 Brigade fought their way to just beyond the Roeux–Gavrelle road in what was otherwise a disappointing day. (Plot C.37)

Buried close by is Lieutenant Gerard Thomas MANBY-COLGRAVE, Army Service Corps, attached 221st Siege Battery, Royal Garrison Artillery, who died of wounds on 21 April 1917, aged 31. He was an only son whose military service encompassed several branches of the army, including the 2/1st Kent Cyclist Battalion and the Royal Army Medical Corps. His family had purchased the ancient manor house at Cann Hall (Canon's Hall) in Essex in 1671 and the estate remained in the family, at least partly, until 1900. Gerard was also Lord of the Manor of Little Ellingham in Norfolk. (Plot C.23)

The most senior officer buried here is Major Percy WILTSHIRE, 1st (East Anglian) Brigade, Royal Field Artillery, commanding the 251st Siege Battery, Royal Garrison Artillery, who died of wounds on 25 April 1917, aged 45. (Plot D.7)

There are just nine graves relating to 1918, three of which are from the Chinese Labour Corps and who are buried at the far end of the cemetery near the Cross of Sacrifice. Several other Chinese Labourers who died between January and June 1919 can also be found here. Five other graves belong to men of the 1st Somerset Light Infantry (Plots E.1 to E.5) who were killed in action or who died of wounds between 28 March and 5 April 1918, including Captain Alfred Cyril PARSONS, who fell on 29 March. The remaining casualty in this group is a lance corporal of the 2nd Seaforth Highlanders. The 2nd Seaforth Highlanders and the 1st Somerset Light Infantry were both part of the 4th Division, which had been heavily involved in the fighting at Arras in 1917. Even after that, the division had a long-standing association with the area just north of the River Scarpe and defended that location during the latter part of March and early April, when the Germans widened their offensive to include the sector near Arras.

Izel-lès-Hameau Communal Cemetery

The village of Izel-lès-Hameau lies to the west of Habarcq on the D.54, which runs off the D.939 Arras–Saint-Pol road near Duisans, passing through Hermaville on the way. The cemetery itself can be found on the north-west side of the village next to open countryside near the junction with the D.75E1.

There are six identified casualties in this cemetery, five of whom are men of the Royal Flying Corps. The solitary infantryman is Serjeant William WATSON, 13th King's Royal Rifle Corps, who died of wounds on 6 April 1917. (Grave 6)

Taking the Royal Flying Corps casualties in chronological order, Second Lieutenant Eric ARMITAGE, 45 Squadron, Royal Flying Corps, was killed in a flying accident in his Sopwith Pup on 4 October 1917. The official communiqué for that day states only that the weather was '*very bad indeed*'. This was probably a contributory factor in the incident that led to his death. He was 19 years old when he died and an only son. At the outbreak of war he enlisted in the Royal Garrison Artillery and obtained his commission in the Royal Field Artillery before joining the Royal Flying Corps. (Grave 3)

Second Lieutenant Allan James BALLANTYNE, 46 Squadron, Royal Flying Corps, died from his wounds on 10 November 1917. He too was 19 years of age and was also flying a Sopwith Pup when he was wounded. He joined the Royal Flying Corps in February 1917 and served with several squadrons before joining 46 Squadron. (Grave 4)

Second Lieutenant Herbert WALSH, also from 46 Squadron, Royal Flying Corps, was killed in action on 30 December 1917 whilst flying a Sopwith Camel. The *Royal Flying Corps Communiqué* for that day merely states that no service flying was possible owing to the weather. (Grave 2)

Lieutenant Robert Leighton Moore FERRIE MC, 46 Squadron, Royal Flying Corps, was reported missing in action in his Sopwith Camel on 3 January 1918, aged 19 (Grave 5). He joined the Royal Flying Corps in late 1916 and flew with 46 Squadron from the middle of June 1917 until his death. He soon became a very proficient flyer and began to come to notice during the latter part of 1917.

His MC was gazetted posthumously on 4 February 1918 and was awarded in connection with a busy and hazardous seven-day period that began on 20 November, the opening day of the Battle of Cambrai. Despite very poor flying conditions that day, he led his flight to Caudry aerodrome where it dropped bombs from around 400 feet, destroying one shed and badly damaging another. Having successfully completed the mission, he led his flight safely home landing in heavy mist. On 23 November he again flew at very low altitude, this time over Bourlon, dropping bombs on the village and attacking enemy infantry. During the attacks he fired off 500 rounds of ammunition and on his return he was able to report back regarding the position of British troops. On 26 November he flew another mission at low altitude, bombing Inchy and scattering enemy troops with his machine gun. The citation also points out that he had already scored two victories and had contributed to several more.

The hazardous nature of the low level operations carried out during those seven days can be gauged by the fact that his flight commander, Captain Arthur Stanley Gould Lee, was shot down by ground fire on three occasions near Cambrai on 22, 23 and 26 November. Nevertheless, he was luckier than FERRIE and went on to score seven victories in fifty-six aerial combats. He survived the war and became a marshal in the Royal Air Force. He retired in 1946 and wrote a number of books, including, *No Parachute, Open Cockpit* and *Flypast*.

Serjeant Frederick INGHAM, 102 Squadron, Royal Air Force, died on 7 April 1918, aged 21. *Airmen Died in the Great War* gives no indication as to the manner of his death, nor does it mention any type of aircraft. (Grave 1)

Noyellette Communal Cemetery

The cemetery is situated just east of the village of Noyellette, which in turn lies about eight miles west of Arras and about half a mile west of Habarcq. The D.339 is the easiest route to take from Arras. This road runs off the main Arras–Saint-Pol road, the D.939. The road between Habarcq and Noyellette splits approximately half way between the two villages. Bear left here and the cemetery is about 400 yards along the road on the right.

There are just four airmen buried here, casualties from an operation undertaken by 98 Squadron, Royal Air Force, on 21 September 1943. Flying Officer Arthur George Gordon ATKINS, aged 20, is buried in Grave 1. The other three are buried in Collective Grave 2 and 3. They are Flying Officer (Navigator) Samuel Arthur Raymond TANNER, Flight Sergeant Allan Rothery BREAKSPEAR and Sergeant (Air Gunner) Kenneth Stanley Henry LAWSON. The men died when their Mitchell II aircraft was shot down by an enemy fighter near Hesdin. TANNER's brother, Melville, also served with the Royal Air Force as an observer and died on 3 September 1940. His Blenheim IV aircraft crashed about seven miles north-east of Huntingdon soon after taking off from Upwood Airfield on a training flight. He is one of ten servicemen buried in the churchyard of St John the Baptist at Clydach-on-Tawe, Glamorganshire.

Wanquetin Communal Cemetery

Wanquetin is situated about seven miles west of Arras on the D.59, approximately two and a half miles west of the village of Warlus. The communal cemetery is on the east side of the village with the extension behind it backing on to open fields. It is adjacent to the main road running east-west through the village and is easy to locate.

There are just eight burials in the communal cemetery. All are 1916 casualties, two from March 1916 and the remainder from late November. The March casualties are from the Royal Field Artillery and Royal Engineers, whilst the later ones are from battalions of the 12th (Eastern) Division and the 35th (Bantam) Division.

Wanquetin Communal Cemetery Extension

The arrival of the 41st Casualty Clearing Station at Wanquetin in October 1916 gave rise to the extension to the communal cemetery, which until then had been the only cemetery here. The current extension was designed by Sir Reginald Blomfield and contains 222 identified casualties from the Great War, several of whom are of interest, and nine from the Second World War.

According to the CWGC register, the earliest casualty buried here is Private Arthur WORDEN, 17th Lancashire Fusiliers, who died of wounds on 15 December 1915. In fact, Private WORDEN died a year later on 15 December 1916. (Plot I.A.14)

Private WORDEN is one of twenty identified casualties from the middle year of the war, many of whom are from either the 35th (Bantam) Division or the 12th (Eastern) Division. All are buried consecutively in chronological order of death. There is one gallantry award amongst them: Private William Whyndom PALMER MM, 11th Middlesex Regiment, who died on 18 December 1916 (Plot I.A.15). Further along the row is the headstone of Private Owen Rohan WATERS, 7th Norfolk Regiment, who died of wounds on Christmas Day 1916. The battalion's war diary makes no reference to casualties that day and records only that Christmas was spent out of the line at Gouy-en-Ternois. On 17 December, the day before the battalion was relieved, the diary notes that one man was killed and four more were wounded by enemy trench mortar bombs. Presumably, Private WATERS was one of the four men injured in that incident. (Plot I.A.18)

The cemetery continued to be used throughout the first part of 1917 up to and including May. Burials then ceased until 1918. Most of the 1917 casualties are from battalions belonging to the 14th (Light) Division, which relieved the 12th (Eastern) Division the week before Christmas 1916.

One of the 1917 casualties is Captain William Strain SMITH MC, 1st Royal Scots Fusiliers, who died of wounds on 23 March 1917, aged 29. His unit was part of the 3rd Division and there are several other men from that battalion buried here with him who died between March and April that year. His MC was gazetted on 23 October 1916 while he was serving as a temporary second lieutenant. It was awarded for his part in a bombing raid in which he led his men along an enemy trench. The raid resulted in the capture of around 300 prisoners. (Plot I.B.22)

Another officer casualty is Captain Alexander Armstrong REES, Royal Army Medical Corps, whose death occurred on 4 February 1917. He was an only son and was attached to the 7th Royal Sussex Regiment. The battalion history covering the Great War, published in 1934, gives very few details about him. It notes that he was the referee for an inter-battalion soccer match in January on a 'very muddy field' and it also records that his death occurred at a casualty clearing station, presumably as a result of wounds or injury. He had only been with the battalion since November the previous year. (Plot I.B.15)

Private Joseph FERGUSON, 1st Royal Scots Fusiliers, was executed on 20 April 1917 after being convicted of desertion for the third time. He was already under a suspended sentence of death when he went missing whilst attached to a tunnelling company of the Royal Engineers. His absence of three months was compounded by the fact that he was arrested wearing another man's tunic bearing the DCM ribbon and that of a French decoration. The court would no doubt have been reminded of an earlier deception on his part after he had been invalided home in 1915 to recuperate from wounds. Whilst recovering he re-enlisted, but under a different name. Why he should have done this is not clear, though it is perhaps more likely to have occurred in order to evade some liability or difficulty at home rather than anything to do with army life. He was a regular soldier who had chosen to join the army in 1913, though prior to 1914 he had very little experience of army life and its discipline. (Plot I.C.13)

There are also two curious entries in the CWGC register regarding two men of the Queen's (Royal West Surrey Regiment) whose unit is shown only as '15th Company'. Privates Ernest DONNE and Charles Osborne HARVEY were killed in action on 16 May 1917 whilst serving with the 123rd Company, Labour Corps. The reference to '15th Company' is presumably a reference to a company within the Labour Corps in which they had previously served rather than a reference to their former regiment. Although both men share the same grave number, they have separate headstones. Also, the spacing of the headstones suggests two separate graves rather than a single grave for both. (Plot I.C.14)

Also sharing the same grave reference as Privates DONNE and HARVEY are two men from the Army Ordnance Corps. At first glance this appears odd because the CWGC register shows that they died on different dates. Second Lieutenant Archibald MULLIN was killed on 5 April 1917, but Corporal Frederick E. WATERS died nearly six weeks later on 16 May, the same day as DONNE and HARVEY, and perhaps even as a result of the same incident. Their burial alongside Second Lieutenant MULLIN therefore seems to be completely incongruous. However, *Officers Died in the Great War* shows the date of death for MULLIN as 16 May 1917. The balance of probability therefore suggests that the entry for MULLIN in the CWGC register is incorrect and that his date of death should be the same as the others. Although this goes some way towards explaining the sequence of these four burials, it does nothing to explain why all four men have individual headstones with regular spacing between them and yet share the same grave reference.

The majority of burials in this cemetery are from 1918. The first of these casualties are officers and men of the 15th (Scottish) Division who fell during the uncertain days between 28 and 31 March when the British lines in front of and to the south of Arras came under pressure as the Germans attempted to broaden the scope of their main offensive, which had begun a week earlier. The critical day of fighting around Arras was 28 March. Eleven of the twenty casualties here, who fell between that date and the end of the month, did so on 28 March and can be found in three small groups (Plots I.C.16 and I.C.17, Plots I.D.1 to I.D.3, and Plots I.E.1 to I.E.6). Amongst them are several officers, three of whom are from the 10th Cameronians.

Captain Gavin McCALL MC DCM MM, 10th Cameronians, was killed in action on 28 March 1918, aged 32. His DCM was won as a serjeant for conspicuous gallantry in action when he assumed command of his company and led it with great courage and determination, capturing his objective and consolidating the position. The award was gazetted on 21 December 1916. His MC was gazetted on 27 September 1918 and was won as a second lieutenant after he had displayed courage and great leadership at a critical moment when our lines had been pushed back by an enemy counter-attack, thereby exposing his right flank. At this point, McCALL took charge of two companies whose officers had become casualties and opened fire, holding his position until it was almost surrounded (Plot I.D.1). Buried next to him are two fellow officers: Second Lieutenant John William KERR, 10th Cameronians, who was also killed in action on 28 March 1918, aged 23, and Lieutenant George William JAMIESON, 5th Cameronians, attached 10th Battalion, who was killed in action the same day, aged 24. (Plots I.D.2 and 3)

Buried nearby is Serjeant Todd EAGLESHAM MM, 10th Cameronians, who was also killed in action on 28th March 1918, and who, like Lieutenant JAMIESON, came from Glasgow. His MM was gazetted on 9 December 1916 and was awarded in connection with the fighting on 15 and 16 September when the 15th (Scottish) Division captured the village of Martinpuich. EAGLESHAM had served with the battalion from the very outset and had been a constant source of support to his officers and men alike. His brother, John, also served. (Plot I.E.2)

Another officer casualty from the 15th (Scottish) Division is Second Lieutenant George James ROSS, 6/7th Royal Scots Fusiliers, who was killed on 30 March 1918, aged 25. According to the information in the CWGC register, he lived in Malaya before the war, working as a rubber planter. *Officers Died in the Great War* shows his date of death as 30 January 1918, which is clearly incorrect. (Plot I.C.15)

Of the 162 burials here from 1918, well over half of them fell during the months of April, May, June and July, months which, relatively speaking, were very quiet. Casualties from this period are the result of normal attrition associated with holding the line and occurred through shelling and the everyday routine of trench warfare, including patrols and raids.

It was during this period that the Canadian 1st Division held the line just south of the River Scarpe. The Canadian 2nd Division extended that line south to a point more or less opposite Croisilles. The Canadian casualties here come from both these two divisions, though the majority are from the latter of the two.

One Canadian of interest is Lieutenant John A. GORDON, 4th Battalion, Canadian Infantry, who was killed in action on 4 April 1918, aged 26. He was a friend of Lieutenant J.H. Pedley, author of the memoir, *Only This*. Pedley knew him from school days and recalled the moment of his death just after both men had finished breakfast. Pedley had decided to accompany him down to a sap at the end of one of the trenches, but when Lieutenant GORDON's batman reminded them that neither was carrying any bombs, GORDON had asked him to go and bring a couple. As GORDON was holding up some strands of wire so that Pedley could pass beneath, two shots rang out and GORDON fell mortally wounded. Pedley knelt down and cradled his head, describing how his eyes were still open, but glazed. Despite calling his name, GORDON was unable to make any verbal response and gradually the colour faded from his cheeks.

Pedley recalls the blunt, but pragmatic words of advice from Sergeant Mackay, who had just arrived on scene: '*Get him back out of there for God's sake, and get yourself into shelter or there'll be two of you to be carried out.*' Pedley then describes how he untangled Lieutenant GORDON's hands from the barbed wire while Sergeant Mackay grabbed his feet as they laid him out on the floor of the trench. As Pedley was placing GORDON's arms across his chest he noticed the fatal wounds, one in the neck and one in the stomach. He then removed GORDON's watch and a silver identity disk and gave them to his batman. Pedley goes on to describe the depression he felt at witnessing his friend's death. His memoir is well worth seeking out. (Plot I.E.10)

Corporal Joseph KAEBLE VC MM, 22nd Battalion, Canadian Infantry, was mortally wounded during a strong attack carried out by the enemy near Neuville-Vitasse on 8/9 June 1918. All but one of his Lewis gun team had become casualties from the German barrage that preceded the attack. When it lifted, KAEBLE immediately jumped over the parapet with his Lewis gun and fired directly into the advancing Germans. He was wounded several times, but still carried on at his gun and kept the enemy from advancing further until he fell. Even as he lay dying, he kept firing his gun at the enemy, who by then had begun to retire. His actions won him the VC, which was gazetted posthumously on 13 September 1918. His MM, obviously earned prior to his winning the VC, was actually gazetted after it on 7 October 1918 (Plot II.A.8).

Next to him is Private Peter Paul DESJARDINS, who was killed in action on the same day and was from the same battalion as KAEBLE. It would be interesting to know his part in the events that day and whether he was that last member of the Lewis gun crew with KAEBLE when he made his heroic stand, though it is unlikely that we shall ever know. The battalion war diary provides an additional report on the episode, but makes no specific mention of others who were part of KAEBLE's team. (Plot II.A.7)

Around midnight on 18/19 July 1918 an enemy aircraft dropped a single bomb onto the transport lines near Wanquetin where members of the 28th Battalion, Canadian Infantry, were sleeping. Thirteen men were killed outright and a further fifteen were wounded, one of whom later died. The thirteen dead were buried here on 19 July and now lie in Plot II, Row B.

On the night of 28 July 1918, the 16th Battalion, Canadian Infantry, carried out a raid known as the Llandovery Castle Raid. The Canadian Hospital Ship, *Llandovery Castle*, was returning to England after conveying sick and wounded men back to Halifax, Nova Scotia, when it was sunk on 27 June 1918 by a German submarine off the south-west coast of Ireland. All fourteen Canadian nurses perished and only twenty-four of the 258 persons on board survived. As a consequence, feelings had been running especially high amongst men of the Canadian Corps and, although the operational order for the raid refrains from using such words as 'retaliation' or 'revenge', it does set out three objectives: to obtain identifications, to destroy enemy positions, and to '*raise Hell, generally*'. The number of men involved in the raid was not particularly great, just nine officers and 150 other ranks. When the raiding parties entered the German trenches astride the Arras–Cambrai road, they found that the enemy had already vacated them, at least temporarily. The Canadian casualties, which amounted to one officer and five men killed and twenty wounded, were caused by our own barrage. Three NCOs and one private from the raid are buried here. (Plots II.B.23 and 24, and Plot II.C.1. and 2)

Four Royal Air Force casualties can be found in Plot II, all of whom belonged to 27 Squadron, Royal Air Force. Second Lieutenant Arthur Frederick MILLAR and Second Lieutenant John Varley LEE were killed in a collision with Second Lieutenant John Hetherington DICKSON and Serjeant Stephen Bernard PERCIVAL, who also died. PERCIVAL had been awarded the *Croix de Guerre* (France). Both crews were flying DH9 aircraft when the accident happened on 14 August 1918. All four men are now buried next to each other. (Plots II.C.8 to 11)

Amongst the fifty-nine British burials between April and July 1918, twenty-eight are Seaforth Highlanders, twenty-five of whom are from the 8th Battalion, which formed part of the 15th (Scottish) Division. Some are buried in Plot I, Rows E and F, the remainder in Plot II, Rows A and B. There is one gallantry award: Sergeant John MITTEN MM, 8th Seaforth Highlanders, formerly of the Cameron Highlanders, who was killed in action on 2 April 1918 (Plot I.F.5), as were the two officers from the battalion, Second Lieutenant John MACKINNON (Plot I.E.19) and Second Lieutenant William Hutton DIXON (Plot I.F.4). MITTEN's MM was won serving as a private with the Seaforth Highlanders rather than his former regiment and was gazetted on 11 July 1917. The 56th (London) Division also used the cemetery to bury its dead during the spring and early summer of 1918, particularly the 1/7th Battalion, Middlesex Regiment, whose men can be found in the same part of the cemetery as the Seaforth Highlanders.

An interesting, though cryptic entry can be found in the CWGC register relating to Gunner George Ellerker Walter STEPHENS, 38th (Welsh) Heavy Battery, Royal Garrison Artillery. With regard to his death it reads: *'When undertaking a hazardous task for which he volunteered'*. He was 20 years old when he was killed in action on 9 June 1918. Unfortunately, there are no further clues as to how he died or the nature of the task in which he was involved. (Plot II.A.9)

There are two more holders of gallantry awards buried here: Sergeant Henry ANDERSON MM, 1st Company, 3rd Battalion, Canadian Machine Gun Corps, and Private Norman BLACKBURN MM, also 3rd Battalion, Canadian Machine Gun Corps. Both men were killed in action on 24 September 1918 or died of wounds the same day (Plots II.E.6 and II.E.23). They and twenty other men from the battalion died during a daylight bombing raid on Warlus. Private Oscar POWELL, who was one of those wounded in the incident, died the following day. (Plot II.E.4). The remaining twenty men are buried sequentially either side of him, indicating that they were all laid to rest on or immediately after 25 September. (Plots II.E.2 to E.24)

Nine burials from the Second World War can also be found here. All are NCOs or privates, and all except one fell in action on or around 21 May 1940. Private Robert Dixon Turner McPARLIN, 11th Durham Light Infantry, is shown as having died on 15 April 1940. Six of the men are from the 8th Durham Light Infantry and two are from the 4th Royal Northumberland Fusiliers. (Plots 2. F.1 to 9)

Warlincourt Halte British Cemetery, Saulty

The cemetery is situated on the north side of the N.25 Arras–Doullens road and is well signposted. It lies beyond the intersection with the D.26, the road that runs north through Gombremetz to Saulty, just a couple of hundred yards east of the intersection with the D.23.

It was used by No. 20 and No. 43 Casualty Clearing Stations between June 1916 and May 1917. The 1/1st South Midland Casualty Clearing Station was also based here in February 1917, as was No. 32 Casualty Clearing Station between April and June the same year. The cemetery's relevance to the Battle of Arras, and the reason for its inclusion in this book, is that Plots VII, VIII, IX, and X consist entirely of casualties from the fighting there in April and May 1917. Besides, it is just thirteen miles from Arras.

After June 1917, as the CWGC register points out, the cemetery was fairly dormant until May and June the following year, when it was used by a number of Field Ambulances. After the war it was enlarged to accommodate some nearby cemetery closures. Today it contains 1,266 graves, only eight of which are unidentified. There are still a number of German graves here, along with two French burials. For anyone interested in the northern end of the British attack on the Somme on 1 July 1916 this is a very useful cemetery to visit.

Second Lieutenant John GIBSON, 8 Squadron, Royal Flying Corps, was killed whilst flying on 19 June 1916, aged 28 (Plot I.D.16). His observer that day, Lieutenant Thomas Stanley Roadley, was injured in the crash, but survived until the following year when he was killed in action on 17 August. He is buried at Harlebeke New British Cemetery, in Belgium.

Lieutenant William Aubrey BOWERS, 1/5th North Staffordshire Regiment, is one of a number of officers and men from battalions of the 46th (North Midland) Division who died of wounds at Warlincourt following the attack at Gommecourt on 1 July 1916. BOWERS died from shrapnel wounds on 2 July, aged 29. He and his family lived in very comfortable circumstances at Caverswall Castle near Stoke-on-Trent, Staffordshire, where the family had mining interests. The Wedgwood family owned the castle before them. He was educated at Winchester School and at New College, Oxford, where he became a member of the University's OTC and gained his Master's degree. He was a good sportsman who enjoyed playing cricket and football. He was also a member of the North Staffordshire Hunt. (Plot I.E.1)

Second Lieutenant Otto Hans Herman LORENZEN, 7th Middlesex Regiment, attached 1/5th Lincolnshire Regiment, died at No. 20 Casualty Clearing Station on 2 July 1916 from wounds incurred the previous day near Gommecourt. He was mortally wounded close to the enemy's front line trench where the wire was uncut. As he and others tried to force their way through it, they came under ferocious rifle and machine-gun fire. Having enlisted in September 1914, he initially served with the 3/9th Battalion, London Regiment (Queen Victoria's Rifles), and was promoted to corporal before he received his commission at the end of September 1915. Before the war he and his wife lived in East Finchley, not far from his parents' address in the Bishop's Avenue, which is on the edge of Hampstead Heath. (Plot I.E.2)

Second Lieutenant Charles Thomas Hinton VAISEY, 8 Squadron, Royal Flying Corps, died of wounds on 1 July 1916 (Plot I.E.8). He had been wounded two days earlier while flying with his observer, Lieutenant Charles Edward Murray Pickthorne, who was unhurt in the incident. Pickthorne wrote to VAISEY's father informing him in some detail of his son's death. When three hostile machines attacked them, VAISEY was badly wounded in the back by an initial burst of fire from one of his opponents. At first he believed that VAISEY was dead, but in spite of the gravity of his wounds, and evidently in great pain, VAISEY somehow managed to fly back to the aerodrome where he made an almost perfect landing, undoubtedly saving the life of his observer. However, in his letter, Pickthorne very much understated his own involvement in the whole affair.

With only four days' operational flying experience behind him, Pickthorne had actually climbed out of his seat in mid-air and had briefly taken control of the machine. In doing so, he inadvertently roused VAISEY, who until then had been unconscious. Lieutenant Pickthorne also had the presence of mind to use his wireless set to let those on the ground know that a doctor would be required should they make it back to the aerodrome.

VAISEY, whose two brothers also served at the front, had been farming sheep in Australia when the war broke out, but like many, he returned to England to enlist. VAISEY's determination and ability are all the more remarkable, as he and his observer were over enemy lines when he was wounded. Pickthorne survived the war and his later claim to fame was that on 11 March 1917 he drove down an enemy Albatros Scout, forcing it to land close to our own front line. When the pilot tried to make his way back across no man's land to his own front line, he was shot and wounded by Australian troops, who then captured him. The pilot turned out to be

Crown Prince Friedrich of Prussia. Pickthorne was awarded the MC soon after that. (Plot I.D.16)

Lieutenant Colonel William BURNETT DSO, 1/5th North Staffordshire Regiment, died on 3 July 1916 from wounds received near Gommecourt two days earlier on the opening day of the Battle of the Somme. He was 36 years old when he died at No. 20 Casualty Clearing Station. He was mortally wounded after leaving his battalion HQ to try to clarify the situation with regard to his battalion's attack, which had broken down. Having been urged to press on with the attack by brigade HQ, he was reluctant to do so until he was fully aware of the situation and obviously felt that he needed to make a personal reconnaissance before trying to reorganize his men. He was later found slumped in a communication trench with a bullet wound to the abdomen.

Three other battalion commanders from the 46th (North Midland) Division were killed in action on 1 July 1916. His battalion had been in support that day, but was caught in a heavy German barrage that prevented it moving forward to assist its sister battalion, the 1/6th North Staffordshire Regiment.

In civilian life BURNETT had been a colliery manager and was very active within the local football and cricketing circles in Hednesford where he lived. On the outbreak of war, he commanded the Hednesford Company of the South Staffordshire Regiment (Territorials) and later went to France with the regiment's 1/5th Battalion before transferring to the 1/5th North Staffordshire Regiment. (Plot I.F.5)

Lieutenant Ronald Duncan WHEATCROFT, 1/6th Sherwood Foresters, died on 2 July 1916 from wounds received the previous day near Gommecourt. He was educated at Rugby School and New College, Oxford, and was 26 years old when he died. He was hit by a bullet and shell fragments whilst trying to cut a gap in our wire during the attack (Plot I.F.14). His body was brought back by Serjeant Wagg, who also went out that day and rescued several other men, including Serjeant Thomas GREEN MM, who died from his wounds on 3 July (Plot I.F.3). WHEATCROFT's brother, Second Lieutenant George Hanson Wheatcroft, who was also a pupil at Rugby School before going on to Trinity College, Cambridge, was killed in action on 11 August 1915 whilst serving with the Royal Garrison Artillery. He is buried at Mailly-Maillet Communal Cemetery Extension.

Captain Francis Bradbury ROBINSON, 1/6th Sherwood Foresters, also died of wounds on 3 July 1916. He was an only son and had joined the Territorials when he was 19 years old. He had been a captain since October 1915 and was serving as the brigade's machine gun officer when he was fatally wounded (Plot I.F.6). ROBINSON had been hit in the stomach and had then fallen into a wire entanglement. He is the officer referred to in the VC citation for Captain John Leslie Green, Royal Army Medical Corps, who was attached to the 1/5th Sherwood Foresters. Green went out and removed Captain ROBINSON from the wire under heavy fire rifle and grenades, dragging him into a shell hole where he dressed his wounds. He had almost managed to bring him back to safety when he himself was fatally hit. Green, whose body was only recovered in March 1917, is buried at Foncquevillers Military Cemetery.

Corporal Herbert Edward BROWN, 1/5th South Staffordshire Regiment, died of wounds on 5 July 1916. His widow is shown as residing in Remagen in the Rhineland,

Germany, though *Soldiers Died in the Great War* shows his place of residence as Wandsworth, London. Corporal BROWN may have been wounded during the attack on Gommecourt on 1 July, but could also have received his wounds a short while after that, before the battalion was relieved and before it moved to Ransart early the following day. He was 25 years old when he died. (Plot I.G.7)

Second Lieutenant Charles Fifield HOLTOM, 1/5th North Staffordshire Regiment, died of wounds on 4 August 1916. He was a pupil at Stonyhurst, the renowned Catholic school in the north of England. In July 1914, after leaving school, he went to work with his father, who was a solicitor. A month later his life changed dramatically when he enlisted as a private in the North Staffordshire Regiment. He was gazetted as a second lieutenant in February 1915 and a few months later he was serving on the Western Front. He was wounded in action on 13 October 1915 at the Hohenzollern Redoubt, as the Battle of Loos was reaching its final stages, and spent some months recovering from his injuries. When he was passed fit he did not return to his battalion immediately. However, when he did return to it on 3 July 1916 it was a very different battalion to the one he had left behind. (Plot I.J.6)

Private Albert BAGULEY, 1/6th Sherwood Foresters, was killed in action on 24 September 1916. His brother, Ernest, was killed in action in Belgium, serving as a private with the 2nd Sherwood Foresters on 9 August 1915. Ernest Baguley is commemorated on the Menin Gate at Ypres. (Plot II.G.10)

Second Lieutenant Frank Collett Reeve BEECHEY, 13th East Yorkshire Regiment, died of wounds on 14 November 1916, aged 30 (Plot II.J.8). Three of his brothers also served and fell during the war. Serjeant Bernard Charles Reeve Beechey was killed in action on 25 September 1915 at Loos whilst serving with the 2nd Lincolnshire Regiment, aged 38. He is commemorated on the Ploegsteert Memorial. Private Charles Reeve Beechey, 25th Royal Fusiliers, died of wounds on 20 October 1917 in East Africa and is buried in Dar Es Salaam War Cemetery. Lance Corporal Harold Reeve Beechey, 48th Battalion, Australian Infantry, was killed in action on 10 April 1917. He has no known grave and is commemorated on the Australian National Memorial at Villers-Bretonneux.

The 1/1st Monmouthshire Regiment was the pioneer battalion attached to the 46th (North Midland) Division for most of the war, and it too was in action on 1 July 1916. The following day the division was withdrawn from the front and went into billets around Berles-au-Bois about ten miles behind the line. This was the last the division would see of the fighting on the Somme, but for the pioneers it was a different matter. Over the next few months the 1/1st Monmouthshire Regiment would make regular trips to the front line to carry out maintenance work, dig and improve communication trenches, bring up stores and provide working parties for whichever of the division's units happened to be holding the line near Gommecourt and, on occasions, for adjacent divisions too. Casualties within the battalion were never heavy, but they did occur fairly frequently. There are ten men from the 1/1st Monmouthshire Regiment buried here, but they are scattered between the different plots, according to when they died.

Amongst this group is Second Lieutenant Stanley Earl RICHARDS, who died of wounds on 29 August 1916. He was educated at Cardiff High School and before the war had worked at the head office of the National and Provincial Bank in Cardiff. He was also a keen sportsman and excelled at hockey, which he played at club level for Abergavenny and Newport, and also represented Wales at international level. He joined the army in July 1915 and served for a while with the Inns of Courts OTC before being gazetted to the Monmouthshire Regiment in September that year. He went to France in early 1916, where he was soon wounded in the foot, but after a few months' convalescence he returned to the front in July. Here he would have regularly supervised the working parties and various tasks carried out by his men in the Gommecourt sector. He was wounded on 26 August and was taken to No. 20 Casualty Clearing Station at Boisleux-au-Mont where he died three days later. He was buried here at Warlincourt Halte rather than the communal cemetery at Boisleux-au-Mont. (Plot III.A.7)

Captain William Herbert HEDGES MC, 1st (North Midland) Field Company, Royal Engineers, is shown in *Officers Died in the Great War* as having died on 22 August 1916, aged 23, as opposed to being killed in action or dying of wounds. His MC was gazetted in the King's Birthday Honours List on 5 June 1916 (Plot III.A.12). His father, William Ross Hedges of Birmingham, was the chemist who invented and patented Hedges Mentholated Snuff, which is still available today.

Corporal Tom Ernest WEBB MM, 1st Monmouthshire Regiment, died of wounds on 14 October 1916. He came from a large family near Chepstow, which included eight brothers. He had joined the Monmouthshire Territorials in March 1913 whilst serving his apprenticeship in a shipyard and was one of the many part-time soldiers who immediately volunteered to serve overseas on the outbreak of war. He went to the front in February 1915 where he saw a good deal of action; firstly, at the Second Battle of Ypres, where the 1/1st Monmouthshire Regiment served as the pioneer battalion of the 28th Division, then at Loos and the Somme where it was attached to the 46th (North Midland) Division in the same role. We know from a letter written to his family by his commanding officer that he died on 14 October 1916 when a shell exploded near him in the village where he was billeted during a bombardment by the Germans. His experience, cheerfulness, and coolness made him a reliable man to have around and he frequently acted as a runner for his battalion commander, though he was also a good sniper. His MM was gazetted on 27 October 1915 for bravery in the field, but he also received a mention in despatches on 1 January 1916 for gallant and distinguished service in the field. (Plot III.B.13)

Lieutenant John Henry Tandy LIDDELL, 6th King's Royal Rifle Corps, attached 1st Battalion, died of wounds on 17 November 1916. He was educated at Winchester School and Pembroke College, Oxford, and was a member of the Inner Temple. Within a few days of the outbreak of war he was commissioned in the Special Reserve, King's Royal Rifle Corps, and went to France a month later with the 2nd Battalion, where he saw action on the Marne, the Aisne, and at Ypres, where he was wounded on 31 October 1914. He returned to France in August 1916, but was wounded again later that year, on 13 November, during the attack on Serre by the 2nd Division. He died from his wounds four days later. (Plot III.E.1)

Lieutenant Geoffrey Bache SMITH, 19th Lancashire Fusiliers, was serving as adjutant of the battalion when he died on 3 December 1916, aged 22, having being wounded by shrapnel four days earlier on 29 November. SMITH was a pupil at King Edward's School, Birmingham, which J.R.R. Tolkien had also attended. Both men went on to Oxford, though SMITH studied at Corpus Christi College, Tolkien at Exeter College, and it was here that they became good friends. A volume of SMITH's poetry was published in 1918 under the title, *A Spring Harvest*. The preface to it was penned by Tolkien. (Plot III.G.2)

Lieutenant Colonel Percy Arnold LLOYD-JONES DSO, Royal Army Medical Corps, died of wounds on 22 December 1916, aged 40. He was also awarded the Order of the Crown of Italy and had been mentioned in despatches. As well as gaining a Bachelor of Arts degree, he was also a Bachelor of Medicine and a Member of the Royal College of Surgeons, but he had previous military experience too, having served in the South African campaign. In the intervening years he worked with the Red Cross and was awarded the Italian Red Cross Medal for his work during the Messina earthquake, which occurred on 28 December 1908 killing tens of thousands. He then went on to serve with the British Red Cross during the Balkan War in 1912–1913. His DSO was gazetted on 23 June 1915 for distinguished service in the field. (Plot III.H.3)

Second Lieutenant Francis William HUBBACK, 2/6th Battalion, London Regiment (City of London Rifles), died of wounds on 12 February 1917, aged 32. In 1911 he married Eva Marian Hubback (née Spielman), an English feminist and women's champion on issues such as birth control, eugenics, and women's suffrage. At the time of her husband's death she was teaching Economics at Newnham College, Cambridge. He had also studied at Cambridge, where the couple met, and had attended Trinity College. (Plot IV.J.8)

Second Lieutenant Edwin Albert POPE, 8 Squadron, Royal Flying Corps, was killed in action flying a BE2c on 27 February 1917. His observer, Second Lieutenant Hubert Alfred JOHNSON, was also killed with him that day. They were shot down in flames over Blairville by the German ace, Werner Voss, and were his tenth victory in a career that spanned forty-four victories. (Plots V.B.3 and 4)

Private Samuel Irving PREECE, 1/8th Sherwood Foresters, died of wounds on 5 March 1917, aged 24. The CWGC record states that he had also served as a Brother of the Sacred Mission at Kelham Theological College. The Anglican religious order, founded in 1893, carried out its work in South Africa, Japan and Australia, as well as in England. The college, near Newark, was built by Sir George Gilbert Scott, the man who designed St Pancras Station. (Plot V.C.14)

Captain George WENDEN, 35 Squadron, Royal Flying Corps, was killed whilst flying on 16 March 1917. His observer, Lieutenant G. McKerrow, was unhurt. WENDEN had also served with the Border Regiment after receiving his commission in November 1914. (Plot V.E.1)

Second Lieutenant John MUIRHEAD, 59 Squadron, Royal Flying Corps, was also killed in action on 16 March 1917, aged 25, flying an RE8 aircraft. He would appear to be his squadron's only fatality between 15 and 17 March. The squadron's note-book/diary refers to Lieutenant MUIRHEAD's death on 16 March, but offers no explanation as to the circumstances in which it occurred. However, we do know that his squadron was mainly involved in reconnaissance work at around this time. (Plot V.E.2)

Major John Henry NUNN, 149 Brigade, Royal Field Artillery, died of wounds on 1 April 1917, aged 32. His unit was part of the 30th Division, which around the time of his death would have been in the Mercatel area opposite Neuville-Vitasse and Saint-Martin-sur-Cojeul. Although he lived in west London before the war, his parents lived in Wexford, Ireland. *Wisden*, the cricketing almanack, refers to him as a '*good Irish bat*' and notes that he played for the Phoenix Cricket Club, the oldest cricket club in Ireland. (Plot V.G.4)

Second Lieutenant Arthur Cyril YOUNG, 8 Squadron, Royal Flying Corps, was just 19 years old when he and his observer, Second Lieutenant Robert Campbell CAMERON, were brought down on 2 April 1917. YOUNG died from his wounds. When he joined the Royal Flying Corps in August 1916 he achieved his boyhood ambition, which was to become a pilot. He went to France at the end of the first week in March 1917 where his dreams survived the harsh reality of operational flying for barely a few weeks. Second Lieutenant CAMERON also died of his wounds. (Plots V.G.6 and 7)

Lieutenant Albert EMMERSON, 12 Squadron, Royal Flying Corps, formerly 5th Leicestershire Regiment, was killed in action on 4 April 1917, aged 25, whilst fly-ing as an observer (Plot V.H.6). His pilot, Second Lieutenant Karl Christian Horner, who was 20 years old, also died that day, though he is not buried here with him. Horner is buried a few miles north of here at Avesnes-le-Comte Communal Cemetery Extension.

Second Lieutenant Geoffrey Chasemore BURNAND, 48 Squadron, Royal Flying Corps, was killed in action on 7 April 1917. The CWGC register shows that he left Argentina, where he had been working as a railway engineer, in order to enlist. When he resigned from his job in November 1915 and came home it was with a view to joining the Royal Flying Corps. He achieved that ambition, despite the fact that he had been badly injured in a railway accident, which had left him crippled. He even-tually went to France in January 1917. (Plot V.J.5)

Serjeant Reginald James MOODY, 8 Squadron, Royal Flying Corps, was killed in action with his observer, Second Lieutenant Edmund Eric HORN, on 4 March 1917 when their BE2d aircraft was shot down in flames near Berneville by German ace, Werner Voss. They were his twelfth victory. HORN had volunteered for the Royal Army Medical Corps on his 17th birthday and went to the front three months later where he was gassed. He was then commissioned in the Middlesex Regiment and saw action throughout much of 1916 before transferring to the Royal Flying Corps in December that year. (Plots VI.B.10 and 11)

Second Lieutenant Harold William TAGENT, 8 Squadron, Royal Flying Corps, had formerly served with one of the Public Schools Battalions (Royal Fusiliers) and the 4th Royal Irish Fusiliers. He was killed in action on 24 March 1917 whilst flying a BE2e aircraft. His observer that day, Second Lieutenant Geoffrey Thomas GRAY, was also killed with him. TAGENT was an only son and was commissioned in the Royal Irish Fusiliers in May 1915. He and GRAY were on a photographic mission when they were attacked and shot down, eventually falling on our side of the line. (Plots VI.E.3 and 4)

Lieutenant Hugh NORTON, 8 Squadron, Royal Flying Corps, was killed in action on 24 March 1917, aged 24, flying a BE2d aircraft (Plot VI.E.7), His observer, Second Lieutenant Reginald Alfred William TILLETT, formerly Royal Gloucestershire Hussars, also died with him (Plot V.F.15). The CWGC register notes that NORTON had enlisted on the outbreak of war. He was educated at Wellington College, where he had been a member of its OTC, before going on to King's College in London where he studied Chinese. He was about to go to the Far East to take up a position when war broke out. He immediately joined the Inns of Court OTC and from there he obtained a commission in the King's Own (Royal Lancaster Regiment). He served in France and in the Balkans as a signaling officer before going to Egypt, after which time he transferred to the Royal Flying Corps. He was considered a promising pilot, but was killed within a few weeks of his return to France. He and Second Lieutenant TLLETT were shot down above Boisleux-Saint-Marc by the German ace, Werner Voss, who marked them up as his twenty-second victory.

Major Henry Harley FOWNES, Royal Garrison Artillery, was killed in action on 17 March 1917, aged 30. He grew up in comfortable circumstances at Goldspink Hall in the Jesmond district of Newcastle-on-Tyne. (Plot VI.D.9)

Lieutenant Colonel Andrew Reginald BERRY, CB, 2/9th Battalion, London Regiment (Queen Victoria's Rifles), died of pneumonia on 24 March 1917, aged 48. The CWGC register notes that he had been a captain in the Rifle Brigade's Reserve of Officers. He had also served as a major in the 19th Middlesex Volunteer Rifle Corps (St Giles and St George's, Bloomsbury) which had been part of the Militia prior to 1908. This unit, which was affiliated to the Rifle Brigade, later merged with the 1st Middlesex Volunteer Rifle Corps to become the 9th Battalion, London Regiment (Queen Victoria's Rifles). (Plot VI.E.9)

Captain Claude Holdsworth HUNT, XVIII Corps HQ, Royal Field Artillery, died of wounds on 2 April 1917, aged 31 (Plot VI.G.1). His wife remarried in 1926. Her new husband, Lieutenant Colonel Aubrey Vere Spencer DSO, had served with the 2nd Oxfordshire & Buckinghamshire Light Infantry during the war and went to France with the British Expeditionary Force in August 1914. His DSO was awarded in connection with the intense fighting during the First Battle of Ypres, particularly between 21 and 23 October.

Lieutenant Harold George COLLINS, 48 Squadron, Royal Flying Corps, was killed in aerial combat on 9 April 1917, aged 22 (Plot VI.J.14). At the start of the war he enlisted in the Queen's Own (Royal West Kent Regiment) but then accepted a commission in the Army Service Corps. It was in early 1916 that he transferred to the Royal Flying Corps, where he was well regarded as a flyer. Commenting on his death, his commanding officer pointed out that, although he had been badly wounded in the right hand during the early part of the engagement, COLLINS had continued fighting and had fired his machine gun in an heroic manner until he was again wounded, this time fatally. He was dead by the time he and his colleague returned to their base. His pilot that day, Lieutenant John Herbert Towne Letts, was unhurt and landed their Bristol F2A aircraft safely after their aerial combat with Richthofen's Jasta 11 near Arras. Letts, who had only just taken over as flight commander from Captain William Leefe-Robinson VC, went on to become a very experienced flyer, but was accidentally killed soon after taking off on 11 October 1918. He is buried at Bac-du-Sud British Cemetery, Bailleulval.

Captain Thomas Edward BURKE, 1st King's Shropshire Light Infantry, attached 5th Battalion, died on 11 April 1917, aged 28, after being wounded near Telegraph Hill. He had previously served with the Royal Irish Constabulary in Enniskillen. (Plot VII.C.6)

Second Lieutenant Robert Harry GROVES MC, 'C' Company, 3rd (City of London) Battalion, London Regiment (Royal Fusiliers), died of wounds on 12 April 1917, aged 21. His MC was gazetted on 20 June 1917 and was awarded for conspicuous gallantry and devotion to duty. Whilst digging in, his company came under heavy machine-gun fire. By his gallantry and example he succeeded in getting his men dug in, despite being consistently exposed to fire. (Plot VII.D.1)

Company Serjeant Major Harry BEESTON DCM, 5th King's Shropshire Light Infantry, died of wounds on 10 April 1917. His DCM was won during operations in which all his officers had been either killed or wounded. He then took charge, organizing and leading the men of his company throughout the day. During that time he displayed the greatest bravery, moving about freely in order to keep his men together in the advance, exposed to hostile fire of all kinds. The award was gazetted on 14 November 1916. (Plot VII.E.15)

Lieutenant Geoffrey Charles Martyn LEECH, 9th King's Royal Rifle Corps, died on 9 April 1917, aged 26. He was wounded in action near the Harp on the opening day of the Battle of Arras, almost certainly as a result of the machine-gun fire that met the leading companies as they left their assembly trenches. (Plot VIII.A.9)

Captain Charles Edward STEWART MC, 10th Durham Light Infantry, died of wounds on 10 April 1917, aged 29. In civilian life he had been a Writer to the Signet in Edinburgh. His MC was gazetted on 4 June 1917 in the King's Birthday Honours List. (Plot VIII.B.1)

Captain Walter Herbert Leonard WADDAMS MC, 1/1st (City of London) Battalion, London Regiment (Royal Fusiliers), died of wounds at No. 43 Casualty Clearing Station on 12 April 1917, aged 25. His MC was gazetted on 16 November 1916 and was awarded for conspicuous gallantry in action after he had established a post with great courage and determination under very heavy fire, setting a fine example to his men. (Plot VIII.D.7)

Serjeant Herbert HUGHES, 4th (City of London) Battalion, London Regiment (Royal Fusiliers), died of wounds on 15 April 1917, aged 19. The CWGC register states that he was the youngest son and that he was one of six brothers who served during the war. (Plot VIII.H.1)

Lieutenant Henry COWARD, 1st Border Regiment, died of wounds on 20 April 1917, aged 37. His father, Sir Henry Coward, was a British conductor who died in 1944 and who toured the world presenting music with the Sheffield Choir. He also lectured on music at the University of Sheffield. (Plot VIII. J.12)

Captain Eric William COULSON-MAYNE, 'D' Company, 5th Durham Light Infantry, died of wounds on 25 April 1917, aged 20. The CWGC register points out that he was an only son and had passed the entrance exam for the Royal Military College, Sandhurst, but instead chose to accept an immediate commission in the Bedfordshire Regiment in order to go overseas sooner. He joined his battalion in Belgium in May 1915. The record also notes that he was wounded in 1915 whilst serving with the 1st Bedfordshire Regiment. During his convalescence he refused to remain idle and served as a recruiting officer. In 1916 he served as intelligence officer with the Bedfordshire Regiment before subsequently transferring to the Durham Light Infantry. (Plot IX.A.15)

Private Thomas BRIGHAM, 1/10th Manchester Regiment, had been a member of the Territorial Army prior to the war. Like many of them, he volunteered for overseas service and served in Egypt and Gallipoli before going to the Western Front. He had been absent on two previous occasions and was already under a suspended sentence of death when he went missing again. In such circumstances there was very little room for leniency and he was found guilty and shot by firing squad on 3 June 1918, aged 22. (Plot IX.C.15)

According to the CWGC register, Private Abraham COLLINS, 43rd Mobile Veterinary Section, Royal Army Veterinary Corps, died of wounds on 27 April 1917, aged 35. However, *Soldiers Died in the Great War* gives his date of death as 24 July 1917, quite a wide discrepancy. (Plot IX.D.3)

Lieutenant Hugh Cecil PATTERSON and his observer, Corporal Robert EDWARDS, 48 Squadron, Royal Flying Corps, were killed in a collision as they were returning from a patrol in their Bristol F2B on 30 April 1917. PATTERSON, an only son, was educated at Marlborough School. He went to France in November 1915, but then returned home, obtaining a commission in the Bedfordshire Regiment later the following year. He was attached to the Royal Flying Corps in November 1916, but remained in England until 18 April 1917 when he returned to France as a pilot. Sadly, he was killed twelve days later. (Plots IX.F.15 and 16)

Second Lieutenant George Neil HUNSTONE, 11 Squadron, Royal Flying Corps, was killed in action on 28 June 1917, aged 19, whilst flying a Bristol F2A (Plot IX.H.14). His observer, Second Lieutenant H.D. Duncan, was wounded, but survived the incident. HUNSTONE was educated at Marlborough College and had joined the Artists' Rifles in 1915. He was commissioned in February 1917 and gazetted as a flying officer in May that year. Unfortunately, he was killed the day after joining his squadron.

Air Mechanic 2nd Class Kenneth OLIVER, an observer with 55 Squadron, Royal Flying Corps, was killed in action in a DH4 aircraft on 23 April 1917. His pilot, Lieutenant A.M.N De Levison, was wounded, but survived. (Plot X.C.1)

Second Lieutenant Douglas Archibald RIGBY DCM, 5th Cameronians, died of wounds on 24 April 1917, aged 37. His DCM was won as a serjeant major whilst serving with the same battalion and was gazetted on 30 June 1915. It was awarded for conspicuous ability and devotion to duty over a period of time and concludes by stating that Serjeant Major Rigby had performed excellent work. (Plot X.C.3)

Second Lieutenant Eyre Percival MORRIS, 8 Squadron, Royal Flying Corps, was killed in action on 1 May 1917, as was his observer that day, Lieutenant Valentine Ralph PFRIMMER, when their BE2e came down. PFRIMMER is shown serving with the Canadian Field Artillery rather than the Royal Flying Corps. Any soldier belonging to the Canadian Expeditionary Force, who then went on to serve with the Royal Flying Corps or the Royal Air Force, is always shown in CWGC records under their Canadian unit. (Plots X.G.3 and 4)

Second Lieutenant Albert James LUCAS, 66 Squadron, Royal Flying Corps, died of wounds on 16 May 1917, aged 22. He had been wounded two weeks earlier on 3 May and it can only be presumed that his injuries were so severe that he was unable to be moved back to one of the many military hospitals or that he died suddenly after initially showing signs of recovery. (Plot XI.A.4)

Second Lieutenant Frank James FOSTER, 11 Squadron, Royal Flying Corps, was killed in action on 23 August 1917, aged 27. His observer, Lieutenant David Grant DAVIDSON, who had formerly served with the 2nd Divisional Signaling Company, Canadian Engineers, also died that day. Although both men were Canadians, FOSTER had joined the Royal Flying Corps without ever having served with the Canadian Expeditionary Force, whereas the opposite was true in the case of his colleague. For this reason, the CWGC records show them under different units. (Plots XI.A.13 and 14)

Second Lieutenant Charles Cowley DENNIS, 11 Squadron, Royal Flying Corps, and his pilot, Lieutenant George Eric MIALL-SMITH MC, aged 22, were killed in action on 25 September 1917 when their Bristol F2B came down. MIALL-SMITH had won his MC as a temporary second lieutenant with the 8th Norfolk Regiment. It was gazetted on 23 October 1917 and was awarded for conspicuous gallantry in action. After he had worked his way around an enemy strongpoint that was holding up the advance, he attacked the position with a group of men from several regiments, capturing it and taking around 160 prisoners. Second Lieutenant DENNIS joined the 18th Battalion, London Regiment (London Irish) in spring 1915. He was later commissioned in the 19th Battalion, London Regiment (St Pancras Rifles), but was then wounded. It was while he was recovering from his wounds that he transferred to the Royal Flying Corps. (Plots XI.B.6 and 7)

Lieutenant Mortimer Sackville WEST, 11 Squadron, Royal Flying Corps, was killed on 11 November 1917 whilst flying a Bristol F2B. His observer that day, Captain John Albert REVILL, a Canadian, was also killed and is buried next to him. WEST achieved five victories before his death, the last one over the village of Cagnicourt on 11 September, exactly two months before he was killed (Plots XI.B.8 and 9). WEST's brother also served during the war. Second Lieutenant John Preston Sackville West, 'D' Battery, 189 Brigade, Royal Field Artillery, was killed in action on 14 June 1917, aged 28. He is buried at Railway Dugouts Burial Ground (Transport Farm) outside Ypres. There appears to be no obvious or direct connection to the well-known Sackville-West family, though some distant link is a possibility.

Second Lieutenant George Henry WHYTE, 49 Squadron, Royal Flying Corps, was killed in action on 4 December 1917 whilst flying with his observer, Second Lieutenant Charles Ernest CODDINGTON, formerly 10th King's (Liverpool Regiment). Both men are buried side by side. WHYTE, according to the CWGC register, was a native of Argentina where both his parents lived. (Plots XI.B.11 and 12)

Pilot Serjeant George PICKARD and his observer, Flight Serjeant Harry MILLS, 11 Squadron, Royal Flying Corps, were killed in action in their F2B aircraft on 25 January 1918. (Plots XI.B.13 and 14)

Lieutenant John Herbert MORRIS, 49 Squadron, Royal Flying Corps, was killed whilst flying a DH4 aircraft on 6 March 1918, aged 19. His observer, Air Mechanic 1st Class W.G. Hasler, was injured, but survived the incident. It would appear that the men were not involved in any active operations that day, but were either testing the aircraft or training in it when their engine suddenly failed. Their machine burst into flames on impact with the ground and Hasler was lucky to survive. (Plot XI.B.15)

Captain Edward Dugdale D'Oyley ASTLEY, 3rd Royal Berkshire Regiment, attached 1st Battalion, was killed on 1 June 1918, aged 21, when a shell burst close to his tent whilst his battalion was out of the line. His funeral took place the following day at Warlincourt Halte. Captain ASTLEY was educated at Charterhouse School and had joined the Royal Berkshire Regiment at the outbreak of the war. He was also mentioned in despatches for his part in an attack on Munich Trench on 14 November 1916 after the other officer with him had become a casualty, leaving him in command of the operation (Plot XI.C.19). The battalion war diary notes that the same shell that killed ASTLEY also killed two other ranks and wounded a further eight, one of whom died later that day. All three men were buried alongside ASTLEY the next day. (Plots XI.C.16, 17 and 18)

A few days later three more officers belonging to the 1st Royal Berkshire Regiment were killed. Second Lieutenant Spencer Charles BERESFORD, aged 35, Second Lieutenant Henry Morris AVERY, aged 24, and Second Lieutenant Arthur Leslie ROW MM, had set out on 5 June to make a reconnaissance of the forward area to be taken over by the battalion, but became caught up in an enemy bombardment. All three men were killed by shelling. Second Lieutenant ROW is one of fourteen holders of the MM buried in this cemetery. (Plots XI.C.12, 13 and 14)

Second Lieutenant Thomas Peacock JOHNSTON, 18 Squadron, Royal Flying Corps, was killed in action on 20 May 1917, aged 27, flying an FE2b aircraft. Shortly after his death, 18 Squadron was equipped with DH4 aircraft and became a bomber unit. Prior to that the squadron had operated as a fighter and reconnaissance unit and had often carried out observation work on behalf of the artillery. (Plot XII.A.5)

According to the CWGC records, Second Lieutenant Edward Sharp AMBLER, 2nd Scots Guards, was killed in action on 8 May 1918. However, regimental records show his death occurring three days later on 11 May. The regimental account states that he became disorientated whilst out on patrol and lost his way. When he eventually returned to our lines he was mistaken for part of an enemy patrol and was killed by rifle fire from one of the battalion's sentries. (Plot XII.B.5)

Second Lieutenant William Alexander FLEET and Second Lieutenant George Edward Archibald FitzGeorge HAMILTON, 1st Grenadier Guards, were both killed in action by a shell on 18 May 1918 while the battalion was out of the line. FLEET had joined the battalion the previous year while it was at Ypres and was gassed during his first tour of the trenches. He returned to the front in March the following year. In connection with his death, the regimental history points out that during this period casualties out of the line were often higher than in the front line, as the enemy's artillery tended to bombard the rear areas on a daily basis, particularly with gas shells.

The CWGC record makes no reference to HAMILTON's background, but he was the son of Sir Charles Edward Archibald Watkin Hamilton, 5th Baronet. His mother was the daughter of Rear Admiral Sir Adolphus FitzGeorge, second son of Prince George, Duke of Cambridge. HAMILTON's godparents were none other than Queen Mary and King George V. He was also a direct descendant of Lord Hamilton, who married the daughter of King James II of Scotland. HAMILTON's parents took the rather unusual step of choosing to convert to Islam. (Plots XII.B.6 and 7)

Second Lieutenant Rupert Maurice CHAMBERLAIN, 2nd Scots Guards, died of wounds on 20 May 1918, aged 20. He had set out with one of two parties on a listening patrol trying to detect whether the Germans were building up to an attack on that part of the front. However, the night of 19 May was one of bright moonlight and when both parties were discovered they came under machine-gun fire. CHAMBERLAIN was hit in the head even before he had got beyond our wire and he died on the way to the dressing station (Plot XII.B.9). His brother, Second Lieutenant Eric Dunstan Chamberlain, was killed in action during the German counter-offensive at Cambrai on 30 November 1917 while serving with the 1/5th Loyal North Lancashire Regiment and is commemorated on the Cambrai Memorial at Louverval.

Buried next to Second Lieutenant CHAMBERLAIN is Private William EARL, 1/7th Lancashire Fusiliers, who was shot by firing squad on the morning of 27 May 1918, aged 22. A conscripted soldier, EARL had gone missing a month earlier. Given the short period of time between his desertion and execution, he cannot have been at large for very long before his arrest and subsequent trial. (Plot XII.B.10)

Private Herbert BURMAN, VI Corps, Troops Mechanical Transport Company, Army Service Corps, was killed in action on 27 May 1918, aged 27. The CWGC register shows that he enlisted on 4 August 1914, the day that hostilities were declared between Britain and Germany. (Plot XII.B.14)

The case of Lance Corporal Frederick HAWTHORNE, 1/5th South Staffordshire Regiment, is an interesting one. Towards the end of July 1916 his battalion was ordered to carry out a night raid on some German trenches and HAWTHORNE had been placed in charge of a section of the raiding party. On the evening of the raid he made strong representations to one of his officers about the wisdom of carrying out such an operation in bright moonlight. His concerns were overruled, and when the raiders began to move forward, HAWTHORNE and his men failed to follow and remained in their trench. He was placed under arrest for cowardice and tried in the usual manner. The fact that he had set a bad example to his men was no doubt an aggravating factor at his trial. After he had complained to the officer, some of his men had even spoken out in support of him, but their subsequent willingness to remain with him had only made matters seem worse. His battalion also belonged to the 46th (North Midland) Division, whose performance on 1 July had come in for some very close scrutiny. The perceived failure of the division was attributed, at least in part, to poor leadership and resolve. Some senior officers had already faced severe criticism, discipline within the division was being questioned and reputations were clearly at stake. Although the facts were very clear in HAWTHORNE's case, the real motives behind his execution remain far more opaque. (Plot XII.C.8)

The remaining twelve holders of the MM, not already referred to, are listed below:

Serjeant Thomas GREEN MM, 1/6th South Staffordshire Regiment, died of wounds on 3 July 1916, aged 28. He was almost certainly wounded on 1 July 1916 just north of Gommecourt. (Plot I.F.3)

Serjeant Harold William YOUNG MM, 1/4th Leicestershire Regiment, died of wounds on 13 August 1916, aged 25. *Soldiers Died in the Great War* makes no mention of his MM. (Plot II.F.8)

Serjeant Joseph HENLEY MM, 1/8th Sherwood Foresters, died of wounds on 5 March 1917. (Plot V.C.15)

Serjeant George FLEMING MM, 1/5th South Staffordshire Regiment, died of wounds on 22 March 1917, aged 21. (Plot V.E.14)

Lance Serjeant James Schofield SHEARD MM, 1/4th Duke of Wellington's Regiment, died of wounds on 18 February 1917, aged 21. (Plot VI.A.6)

Serjeant Arthur KEEN MM, 35th Siege Battery, Royal Garrison Artillery, died of wounds on 31 March 1917. (Plot VI.F.4)

Rifleman George CALLEN MM, 8th King's Royal Rifle Corps, died of wounds on 13 April 1917. *Soldiers Died in the Great War* makes no reference to his MM. (Plot VII.D.9)

Gunner Sidney Frank SAUNDERS MM, 1st Siege Battery, Royal Garrison Artillery, died of wounds on 18 April 1917. (Plot VII.J.6)

Lance Corporal Clifford John Allan HOARD MM, 5th King's Shropshire Light Infantry, died of wounds on 27 April 1917. (Plot IX.E.13)

Private Albert Herbert WHYATT MM, 7th Queen's Own (Royal West Kent Regiment), died of wounds on 6 May 1917. (Plot IX.H.3)

Private John Willie HOWELL MM, 6th King's Own Yorkshire Light Infantry, died of wounds on 20 May 1917. (Plot XII.A.2)

Corporal John Reginald CHURCH MM, 1st Queen's (Royal West Surrey Regiment), died of wounds on 22 May 1917, aged 19. (Plot XII.A.11)

Finally, there are a handful of cavalrymen who fell during March and April 1917. In chronological order of death they are: Private John BROWNE, South Irish Horse, died on 29 March 1917 (Plot VI.F.3); Private Peter McGUIRE, 5th (Royal Irish) Lancers, died of wounds on 10 April 1917 (Plot VII.A.12); Private James McKINLAY, 6th Dragoon Guards (Carabiniers), died of wounds 8 April 1917 (Plot V.J.15); and Private John Henry WARD, 16th (The Queen's) Lancers, died of wounds on 17 April 1917 (Plot VIII.J.7).

Warlus Churchyard

The village of Warlus is about five miles west-south-west of Arras. The churchyard site is situated west of the D.18 in the middle of the village on the Rue de Boel, which runs off the Rue du Maréchal Leclerc, otherwise known at this point as the D.18.

There are two men from the 1st Scots Guards buried here. After heavy fighting on the Somme in September 1916 the 1st Scots Guards moved to Warlus. Here there were some welcome opportunities for rest and recreation as well as training. Lance Corporal William DORANS was killed accidentally on the 26th October 1916 during one such training session involving the use of Lewis guns. Private Henry ASPINALL died three weeks later on 10 November 1916, which was the battalion's last day at Warlus before returning to the front line. Three other men who died earlier that year are commemorated by a special memorial panel. All three are Indian Army men, two belonging to the Army Hospital Corps, the other a Sikh member of the 16th Indian Cavalry, Sanitary Section, attached to King Edward's Own Cavalry.

Warlus Communal Cemetery

The cemetery lies approximately 600 yards north of the village of Warlus on the D.62 in open fields in the direction of Agnez-lès-Duisans.

It contains two groups of French graves. In the south-east corner, amongst the French burials, is a solitary CWGC headstone to Rifleman Albert Edward PARKER, 7th King's Royal Rifle Corps. He died alone on 15 May 1916, aged 35, when he was executed by firing squad somewhere in Warlus. He was found guilty of desertion and offered the mitigation of drunkenness at his trial. (Plot A.1)

Private Richard COWE, 8th Durham Light Infantry, is buried nearby. He fell on 21 May 1940. The cemetery register does not show a grave number.

Wailly Communal Cemetery

The main part of the village lies on the north side of the D.3, which runs from the south-western suburbs of Arras towards Rivière and then on to the village of Foncquevillers at the northern end of what was the old British front line on 1 July 1916. The cemetery lies outside the village to the north-west at the end of Rue de Verdun. On leaving Wailly Orchard Cemetery, continue along Rue des Alliés to the small cross roads and turn right. This is the Rue de Verdun and the cemetery lies about 700 yards further on in open fields.

There are two members of 7th Battalion, Royal Tank Regiment, buried here. Both were killed during the brief, but fierce action on 21 May 1940. The encounter with three German divisions by just under sixty tanks of 4th and 7th Battalions, Royal Tank Regiment, south-east of Arras, was costly, but disrupted the German armoured push across Artois, albeit for just a very short period of time. The dead are Sergeant REPPEN and Trooper Arthur ALEXANDER. There is a further burial here, but the soldier is unidentified.

Wailly Orchard Cemetery

The cemetery lies on the north side of the village. The D.3 from Arras divides shortly after entering Wailly. The left fork is the continuation of the D.3, but ignore this and take the right fork, which passes through the heart of the village and becomes the Rue de l'Église. After a hundred yards, take the next right, the Rue de Dainville, then the next left, which is the Rue des Alliés. The cemetery is about 200 yards on the left. There are 351 identified burials. The CWGC register points out that although the cemetery stands above the village, it was screened from enemy observation by a high wall.

In the week prior to the opening of the Battle of the Somme, no fewer than seventy raids took place at various locations between Gommecourt and Ypres. On 28 June 1916, during daylight hours, the 55th (West Lancashire) Division sent six raiding parties into the German lines, and would have sent out a further party had it not been for a change in wind direction following the discharge of gas and smoke. Four battalions of the King's (Liverpool Regiment), the 1/5th, 1/6th, 1/7th and 1/9th, took part in the raid that day along with men from the 1/4th Loyal North Lancashire Regiment and the 2/5th Lancashire Fusiliers. All of these battalions belonged to the 55th (West Lancashire) Division.

Second Lieutenant Herbert Angus RILEY, 1/9th King's (Liverpool Regiment), was one of the men killed on 28 June. His battalion went over at around 5.35pm and met with opposition once inside the enemy's trenches. This resistance was dealt with, but RILEY was found to be missing when the battalion withdrew. Second Lieutenant Darling and Private Winrow returned to the sap where the party had initially entered the German lines and recovered Second Lieutenant RILEY's body. He was just 19 years old. (Plot I.D.2)

After the raid on 28 June 1916 there were no significant events, or incidents of any note, on this part of the front between Wailly and Bretencourt. The history of the 55th (West Lancashire) Division simply states: '*Nothing of further importance took place during our tenure of this front.*' The history of the King's (Liverpool Regiment) also makes little comment, though there was still the day to day business of holding the front and patrolling also took place regularly.

Forty-seven of the 351 identified casualties in this cemetery are from the King's (Liverpool Regiment). Twenty-one of these are from 2 July 1916, including Second Lieutenant Eric JONES, 1/9th King's (Liverpool Regiment). (Plot I.E.3)

Company Serjeant Major Charles Harold Augustus YOUNG MM, 'C' Company, 6th Queen's Own (Royal West Kent Regiment), was killed in action on 2 December

1916, aged 28. His death occurred a few days before an intended raid on the enemy's trenches. He is one of ten men from the 6th Battalion buried here, seven of whom fell during the first week of December. (Plot I.A.13)

Second Lieutenant Richard Wake TWINING, 1st Devonshire Regiment, was killed in action on 1 July 1916, aged 21. He enlisted in August 1914 and was gazetted in the 1st Dragoon Guards in November that year. He transferred to the Devonshire Regiment in August 1915. At the start of the war his father was working for the Admiralty as a surgeon. (Plot I.C.7)

Gunner William STEWART, 55th (West Lancashire) Division Ammunition Column, Royal Field Artillery, was killed in action on 2 July 1916, aged 21. The CWGC register notes that he was an only son and shows his parents' home address in Preston, Lancashire, as 'Wailly Orchid'. It may be that the family mistook the name of the cemetery, or that the notification forwarded to them showed the cemetery as 'Orchid' instead of 'Orchard'. Equally, the name might be a deliberate play on words, perhaps conjuring up a favourite flower or some other poignant reminder of their son. Who knows? (Plot I.D.4)

Second Lieutenant John Scarlett PYM DCM, 6th Queen's (Royal West Surrey Regiment), was killed in action near Wailly on 5 December 1916, aged 25 (Plot I.H.11). According to the battalion war diary, he was killed at around 9.00pm when two heavy trench mortar shells exploded close to him. He was in charge of the left section of a raiding party when the incident occurred, though the raid itself had already been cancelled fifteen minutes earlier. The prospects for the raid had initially looked good; the enemy's wire was adequately cut and the evening was cloudy, but when the cloud cleared the officer in charge of the operation decided against going ahead with it.

The explosion that killed Second Lieutenant PYM also killed three other men and wounded twelve others, one of whom died very soon afterwards before he could be evacuated. All five men are now buried consecutively. Lance Corporal Frank DEDMAN, Lance Corporal John Richard Thomas BUCKLAND, and Private Albert DEVEREUX were killed outright, and Private Arthur James COE died from his injuries. (Plots I.H.7 to 11)

Second Lieutenant PYM won his DCM whilst serving as a corporal with the Royal Canadian Dragoons. It was gazetted on 21 September 1915 and was awarded for conspicuous gallantry and devotion to duty at Festubert on 26 May 1915. The citation records that between 6.00am and 7.00am he had crawled out into no man's land for about a hundred yards to reach a wounded man. Unable to recover him alone, he called for assistance. A sergeant came to his aid, but he too was shot and wounded in the thigh. PYM then returned to his trench, but at around 5.00pm he and two other men made another attempt to remove the wounded man; this time their efforts were successful. The citation ends by pointing out that PYM and the others were under continuous shrapnel and rifle fire during the rescue.

The cemetery was hardly used in 1917. There were just two burials from the 8th Rifle Brigade in January 1917 and one from the King's (Liverpool Regiment) in early July that year. These are to be found in Plot I, Rows H and J.

Private John William Brooks RICHARDS, 2nd Suffolk Regiment, formerly Royal Army Service Corps, was killed in action on 24 March 1918. He was the eldest of three brothers who served in the Great War, two of whom fell (Plot II.A.9.) Private William Lee Brookes RICHARDS, 115th Company, Machine Gun Corps, was killed in action the day after his brother, on 25 March 1918, aged 19. He is commemorated on the Tyne Cot Memorial.

Two officers from the 8th King's Own (Royal Lancaster Regiment), Second Lieutenant Arthur HEWETSON and Second Lieutenant Arnold BAILEY, were killed in action whilst directing defensive fire on 24 March 1918. On 22 March the battalion withdrew behind Wancourt and completed its move during the early hours of the following day. On the 23rd it was heavily involved in holding back successive German attempts to break through, and at one location a trench block was disputed for twelve hours. The battalion was then withdrawn into brigade reserve the following day. (Plots II.A.13 and 14)

Private James Harold BACON, 2nd Battalion, Canadian Machine Gun Corps, died of wounds on 16 May 1918. He is possibly one of several casualties caused that day when a large working party came under shell fire after it was spotted walking along the railway line north of Wailly at around 8.30am. (Plot II.E.23)

Second Lieutenant Walter Francis WOOLF, 7th King's Shropshire Light Infantry, was killed in action on 27 March 1918, aged 20. He had been wounded at the Battle of the Ancre in November 1916 during the 3rd Division's attack on Serre. He returned to his battalion in 1917, but was killed, along with Second Lieutenant David Leonard PRICE, near Hénin when the battalion's trenches were all but obliterated by the German bombardment that preceded the infantry attacks the following day. WOOLF's father served in the army as a major.

Second Lieutenant David Leonard PRICE was 24 years old when he was killed by shell fire. He was one of several officers who had joined the battalion earlier that month from the recently disbanded 5th Battalion. Also killed with them that day was Private Albert Victor MABBUTT MM, 7th King's Shropshire Light Infantry. The CWGC register notes that he had also been awarded the *Médaille Militaire* (Belgium). His MM was gazetted on 2 November 1917 and was awarded for bravery in the field; the Belgian decoration was gazetted posthumously on 15 April 1918. (Plots II.B.4 to 6)

Lieutenant John Alexander MAIN MC, 278th Railway Company, Royal Engineers, was also killed in action on 27 March 1918, aged 36. His MC was gazetted on 26 July 1918. It was awarded for conspicuous gallantry and devotion to duty whilst acting as liaison officer with railway-mounted guns of the Royal Garrison Artillery. By his untiring energy he ensured that the railway lines, upon which the guns depended, were continually maintained, despite considerable damage from shell fire. This enabled the guns to remain in action until the last moment when they were successfully withdrawn along with all the ammunition. (Plot II.B.11)

Lieutenant Edgar Smith SPURR MC, 25th Battalion, Canadian Infantry, was 32 years old when he was killed in action on 14 June 1918. His MC was gazetted on 18 October 1917, the citation appearing on 7 March 1918. It was awarded for conspicuous gallantry and devotion to duty whilst serving as intelligence officer with his battalion. Although constantly exposed to the most intense artillery fire, he ensured that his HQ was updated continuously with regard to the situation when all other means of communication had failed. When a strong enemy counter-attack was developing on one of his battalion's flanks, he made his way up the line through a heavy barrage, reorganized the advance, and established posts against strong enemy opposition. He accomplished this at a time when all the company's officers had become casualties. (Plot II.D.2)

Lieutenant Pierre Eugene GUAY MC, 22nd Battalion, Canadian Infantry, was killed in action on 1 May 1918, aged 24. His MC was gazetted on 18 October 1918 and the citation for it appeared the following year on 7 March. It was awarded for conspicuous gallantry and devotion to duty in organizing his platoon for an attack and leading it with splendid initiative and determination, capturing an enemy machine gun single-handed and putting its crew out of action. Later on, when another battalion in the front line was under counter-attack, he showed great coolness and courage, leading his platoon through an intense barrage in order to bring ammunition up to it. (Plot II.E.3)

Air Mechanic 2nd Class Frank Richard CROFT, 12 Squadron, Royal Air Force, was just 18 years old when he was killed in action on 29 May 1918. *Airmen Died in the Great War* makes no reference to the type of aircraft that he was flying that day, but it does show that he was flying alone. He was one of only two Royal Air Force casualties that day on the entire Western Front; the other was killed in Belgium whilst making a parachute descent from a balloon. (Plot II.G.14)

Private Allan McINTYRE MM and Bar, 25th Battalion, Canadian Infantry, was killed in action on 5 June 1918, aged 25. Fellow gallantry award holder, Lieutenant George E. ROCHE MM, who also served with the 25th Battalion, Canadian Infantry, was killed in action a few days later on 8 June 1918, aged 27, though at the time of his death he was attached to the 5th Canadian Light Trench Mortar Battery. (Plot II.H.3 and 4)

In total, 189 Canadians are buried here and all are 1918 casualties, including sixty from the 22nd Battalion, Canadian Infantry (Quebec Regiment). Four of the sixty are holders of the MM and are buried in Plot II. They are: Sergeant Adelard BEDARD MM, killed in action on 11 April 1918 (Plot II.B.3); Company Sergeant Major Armand MAGGIO MM, killed in action on 28 May 1918 (Plot II.G.1); Private Omer BLANCHET MM, killed in action on 30 March 1918 (Plot II.C.7); and Private Francois LANGLOIS MM, killed in action on 8 June 1918 (Plot II.H.8).

Private George GIROUARD, 22nd Battalion, Canadian Infantry, was killed in action on 18 June 1918, aged 34. He had been wounded on three previous occasions and, although he had been discharged from the military, he subsequently decided to re-enlist. (Plot II.H.10)

Another officer from the 25th Battalion, Canadian Infantry, is buried a little further along the same row. Lieutenant Edward Charles Cameron BING, was killed in action on 11 June 1918. (Plot II.H.13)

There is a total of 101 identified burials from 1916 shown in the CWGC register. However, one of them, Private Henry Edwin MOORE, 31st Battalion, Canadian Infantry, was killed in action two years later than the date shown in the register. He is the only attributed 1916 casualty not buried in Plot I. He is to be found buried in sequence elsewhere in the cemetery with three other men from the 31st Battalion, all of whom were killed in action on 25 June 1918. (Plot III.F.1 to 4)

Three officers from the 31st Battalion, Canadian Infantry, killed the same day, are also buried here. Next to them is another man who was possibly a company runner or a member of the company's HQ staff. They are Lieutenant John Norman MEE (Plot III.B.2), Lieutenant Chester Hamilton IRVINE (Plot III.B.3) and Private Francis Cornelius LOCK (Plot III.B.4). The other officer is Captain Herbert NORRIS DSO, 31st Battalion, Canadian Infantry (Plot III.B.1). All four men were killed in action on 25 June 1918. They were killed during a raid on enemy trenches at Neuville-Vitasse in which thirteen other ranks also lost their lives.

Captain NORRIS had served in the South African campaign with the 2nd Queen's (Royal West Surrey Regiment) between 1901 and 1902. He enlisted with the 31st Battalion, Canadian Infantry, in mid-November 1914 and was wounded at Saint-Éloi in April 1916. His DSO was awarded for gallantry at Courcelette on 15 September 1916 and was gazetted on 14 November that year. The citation states that after all the officers of his battalion had become casualties he had taken command of the entire unit, organizing and consolidating the position under very heavy fire, displaying high qualities of initiative and leadership.

The battalion had rehearsed its raid at Wailly, which explains why the burials were made here. The battalion war diary notes that the objectives of the raid were achieved, namely the destruction of several trench mortars and other emplacements, including a number of dug-outs. Twenty-one prisoners were also brought back, though other members of the garrison were killed. The diary also notes that the raiders had carried a Union Jack into the enemy's lines and had left it flying from a pole over Neuville-Vitasse. Attached to the pole was a letter addressed to the Commandant of the 10th Company, 65th Infantry Regiment, containing a copy of a wireless message referring to the Allied success on the Italian front.

Private Earl Avalon FISSETTE, 29th Battalion, Canadian Infantry, was killed in action on 29 June 1918, aged 24 (Plot III.E.3). The CWGC register notes that he had originally enlisted in Brock's Rangers at Haldimand. This particular unit, which was raised in Haldimand County and the Six Nations' Indian Reserve, consisted of men of Native American origin, including its officers, and was later redesignated as the 114th Battalion. However, the battalion was broken up soon after it arrived in England and was used to provide drafts for other Canadian battalions already on the Western Front. The Canadian government had considered the idea of an all-Native American unit, but this had been rejected, mainly for practical reasons. As the recruitment pool was relatively small, the formation of a battalion would have been difficult, maintaining it would have been impossible, and, of course, tribal differences existed. Another reason was that many Native Americans had useful skills, making them ideal for work such as sniping and scouting; it made far more sense to distribute those skills amongst existing battalions. However, the Canadian government also believed that the integration of Native Americans within existing battalions would greatly assist the process of social integration back home, particularly after the war.

Lieutenant Daniel LIVINGSTON MM, 25th Battalion, Canadian Infantry, was badly wounded in the leg during a night patrol. He was brought back to Wailly, but subsequently died on 7 April 1918. He had won his MM as a private at Courcelette in 1916 where he had served as a runner and had carried messages back and forth under heavy fire. His brother, Harrison, who was serving in the same battalion, was able to attend his funeral (Plot III.H.1). Another three of his brothers served in the Great War. Alexander served in the United States Navy and was awarded the *Croix de Guerre* (Belgium) for assisting the crew of a Belgian ship after it had been damaged by enemy action. Stanley, who was wounded on three occasions fighting with the United States Infantry, won a Citation Star for Valour, the *Croix de Guerre* (France), as well as the Purple Heart. William, who had won the MC at Vimy Ridge on the opening day of the Battle of Arras, was subsequently awarded a bar.

Other Canadian gallantry award holders buried here are: Corporal John Harvey APPS MM, 6th Battalion, Canadian Light Trench Mortar Battery, killed in action on 20 April 1918. He had enlisted in November 1914 (Plot II.E.1); Driver William Stewart STANLEY MM, 5 Brigade, Canadian Field Artillery, killed in action on 13 May 1918 (Plot II.E.17); and Sergeant Walter GREENWAY MM, 28th Battalion, Canadian Infantry, killed in action on 21 May 1918, aged 31 (Plot II.F.7).

Bibliography

In addition to the works referred to below, I have made extensive use of battalion war diaries held at the National Archives, Kew, and elsewhere. Similarly, I have referred to numerous Rolls of Honour, mainly those relating to schools, colleges, and universities but also those held by professional and commercial bodies, as well as other organizations throughout Britain and various parts of the world. Another key source of reference was the collection of battalion war diaries that forms part of the Canadian Great War Project.

It will also become evident to the reader that I have consulted just about every divisional and regimental history relevant to this work, whether from my own collection, through the British Library or the reference section of the Imperial War Museum, London. The works listed below do not include those specifically mentioned within the text. The following titles are merely the works to which frequent reference was made; it is by no means exhaustive.

Military Operations in France & Belgium 1914 (2 Volumes); 1915 (2 Volumes); 1916 (2 Volumes); 1917 (3 Volumes); 1918 (5 Volumes) (All Appendices and Maps). Brig. General Sir James E. Edmonds, CB, CMG. IWM & Battery Press, 1995.

Military Operations: Gallipoli (2 Volumes). Brig. General Aspinall-Oglander CB CMG DSO. IWM & Battery Press.

Military Operations: Italy 1915–1919. Brigadier General Sir James Edmonds CB CMG D. Litt and Major General H.R. Davies, CB. IWM & Battery Press.

Military Operations Macedonia (2 Volumes). Captain Cyril Falls. IWM & Battery Press.

Military Operations Mesopotamia (4 Volumes). Brigadier General F.J. Moberly CB CSI DSO. IWM & Battery Press.

Military Operations Egypt & Palestine (3 Volumes). Lieutenant General Sir George Macmunn KCB KCSI DSO & Captain Cyril Falls. IWM & Battery Press.

Military Operations Togoland and the Cameroons. Brigadier General F.J. Moberly CB CSI DSO. IWM & Battery Press.

Military Operations East Africa. Lieutenant Colonel Charles Hordern. IWM & Battery Press.

The Register of the Victoria Cross. Compiled by Nora Buzzell. This England Books, 1988.

VCs of the First World War: Arras & Messines 1917. Gerald Gliddon. Sutton, Stroud, 1998.

VCs of the First World War: The Spring Offensive 1918. Gerald Gliddon. Stroud History, 2013.

VCs of the First World War: The Final Days 1918. Gerald Gliddon. Sutton, Stroud, 2000.

The Distinguished Service Order 1886–1923, Parts I & II. Sir O'Moore Creagh VC GCB GCSI and E.M. Humphris. J.B. Hayward & Son, 1978.

Citations of the Distinguished Conduct Medal in the Great War 1914–1920, Section One; Section Two (Part One); Section Two (Part Two); Section Three; Section Four. Naval & Military Press, 2007.

Recipients of the Distinguished Conduct Medal 1914–1920. R.W. Walker. Military Medals, Birmingham, 1981.

Recipients of the Distinguished Conduct Medal 1855–1909. P.E. Abbott. J.B. Hayward & Son, 1975.

The Distinguished Conduct Medal to the Canadian Expeditionary Force 1914–1920. David K. Riddle and Donald G. Mitchell. Kirkby Marlton Press, 1991.

Recipients of Bars to the Military Cross 1916–1920: To which is added MCs to Warrant Officers 1915–1919. J.V. Webb, 1988.

The Distinguished Flying Cross and how it was won 1918–1995. Nick Carter. Savannah, London, 1998.

The Distinguished Flying Medal: A Record of Courage 1918–1982. I.T.Tavender. J.B. Hayward, 1990.

For Gallantry in the Performance of Military Duty: An Account of the Use of the Army Meritorious Service Medal to Recognize Non-Combatant Gallantry 1916–1928. J.D. Sainsbury. Samson Books, London, 1980.

Soldiers Died in the Great War 1914–1919: Parts 1 to 80. J.B. Hayward & Sons, 1989.

Officers Died in the Great War 1914–1919: Parts I & II (3rd Edition). HMSO. Samson Books Ltd, 1979.

The House of Commons Book of Remembrance 1914–1918. Edward Whitaker Moss Blundell. Elkin Mathews & Marrot, London, 1931.

Officers of the Canadian Expeditionary Force who died Overseas 1914–1919. N.M. Christie. Eugene G. Ursual, 1989 (Canada).

Airmen Died in the Great War 1914–1918: The Roll of Honour of the British and Commonwealth Air Services of the First World War. Chris Hobson. Hayward, 1995.

Royal Flying Corps (Military Wing) Casualties and Honours during the War of 1914–1917. Captain G.L. Campbell RFA and R.H. Blinkhorn. Picton Publishing, 1987.

British Regiments 1914–1918. Brigadier E.A. James OBE TD. Samson Books Ltd, London, 1978.

The Bond of Sacrifice Volumes I & II. Naval & Military Press Ltd, 1992.

De Ruvigny's Roll of Honour: A Biographical Record of Members of His Majesty's Naval and Military Forces Who Fell in the Great War 1914–1918. Marquis de Ruvigny – London Stamp Exchange, 1987.

British Battalions in France & Belgium 1914. Ray Westlake. Leo Cooper, London, 1997.

British Battalions on the Western Front: January to June 1915. Ray Westlake. Leo Cooper, London, 2001.

British Battalions on the Somme. Ray Westlake. Leo Cooper, London, 1994.

British Regiments at Gallipoli. Ray Westlake. Leo Cooper, London, 1996.

Above the Lines. Norman L.R. Franks, Frank W. Bailey and Russell Guest. Grub Street, London, 1993.

Above the War Fronts. Norman L.R. Franks, Russell Guest and Gregory Alegi. Grub Street, 1997.

Royal Flying Corps Communiqués 1915–1916. Edited by Christopher Cole. Tom Donovan, London, 1990.

Royal Flying Corps Communiqués 1917–1918. Edited by Chaz Bowyer. Grub Street, London, 1998.

Royal Air Force Communiqués 1918. Edited by Christopher Cole. Tom Donovan, London, 1990.

Under the Guns of the Red Baron. Norman Franks, Hal Giblin and Nigel McCrery. Grub Street, London, 1995.

The Royal Flying Corps in France: From Mons to the Somme. Ralph Barker. Constable & Co. Ltd, London, 1994.

The Royal Flying Corps in France: From Bloody April 1917 to Final Victory. Ralph Barker. Constable & Co. Ltd, London, 1995.

The Underground War – Vimy Ridge to Arras. Phillip Robinson and Nigel Cave. Pen & Sword Military, Barnsley, 2011.

The Student Soldiers. John McConachie. Moravian Press, Elgin, 1995.

The Sword of the North: Highland Memories of the Great War. Dugald Macechern. R. Carruthers & Sons, Inverness, 1993.

A Medico's Luck in the Great War: Royal Army Medical Corps Work with the 51st (Highland) Division. David Rorie. Milne & Hutchinson, 1929.

Warriors of the King: Prairie Indians in World War I. Lloyd James Dempsey. Association of Canadian Archivists, 1999.

Native Soldiers – Foreign Battlefields. Janice Summerby. Veterans Affairs Canada, Communications Division, 1993.

With the Royal Army Medical Corps at the Front. Evelyn Charles Vivian, 1914.

A Stretcher Bearer's Diary: Three Years in France with the 21st Division. J.H. Newton. A.H. Stockwell, London, 1932.

A Lack of Offensive Spirit? – The 46th (North Midland) Division at Gommecourt, 1st July 1916. Alan MacDonald. Iona Books, 2008.

Orange, Green & Khaki: The Story of Irish Regiments in the Great War 1914–1918. Tom Johnstone. Gill & Macmillan & Co., Dublin, 1992.

'Come On, Highlanders': Glasgow Territorials in the Great War. Alec Weir. Sutton Publishing Limited, Stroud, 2005.

The Letters of Agar Adamson. Edited N.M. Christie. CEF Books (Canada), 1997.

In Good Company: The First World War Letters & Diaries of the Hon. William Fraser, Gordon Highlanders. Edited by David Fraser. Michael Russell (Publishing) Ltd, Salisbury, 1990.

Shot at Dawn. Julian Putkowski & Julian Sykes. Wharncliffe Publishing Ltd, Barnsley, 1989.

With Rifle & Pick. Janet Dixon and John Dixon. Cwm Publications, Cardiff, 1991.

Prelude to Victory. Brigadier General E.L. Spears CB CBE MC. Jonathan Cape, London, 1939.

Surrender Be Damned: A History of the 1/1st Battalion, The Monmouthshire Regiment, 1914–1918. Les Hughes & John Dixon. Cwm Press, Caerphilly, 1995.

Brigadier General R.B. Bradford VC MC and his Brothers. Privately Printed, Eden Fisher & Co. Ltd, London. Copy signed & dated 1928.

Campaign in South-West Africa 1914–1915. Brigadier General J.J. Collyer. Pretoria, Government Print, 1937.

University of London OTC: Roll of Honour 1914–1919. Military Education Committee, University of London, 1921.

Etonians Who Fought in the Great War 1914–1919. (No Author or Publisher Shown)

Record of Service of Solicitors & Articled Clerks in HM Forces 1914–1918. Spottiswoode, Ballantyne & Co. Ltd, 1920.

Tanks in the Great War. J.F.C. Fuller DSO. John Murray, London, 1920.

The New Zealand Division 1916–1919 – Colonel H. Stewart CMG DSO MC. Whitcombe & Tombs Ltd, 1921.

The South African Forces in France. John Buchan. IWM & Battery Press, 1992.

The A.I.F. in France Volumes III, IV, V, VI. C.E.W. Bean. University of Queensland Press, 1982–1983.

Tyneside Scottish: (20th, 21st, 22nd & 23rd (Service) Battalions, Northumberland Fusiliers). Graham Stewart and John Sheen. Leo Cooper, London, 1999.

Tyneside Irish: (24th, 25th, 26th & 27th (Service) Battalions, Northumberland Fusiliers). John Sheen. Pen & Sword, Barnsley, 1998.

The First Birmingham Battalion in the Great War 1914–1919: Being a History of the 14th (Service) Battalion of the Royal Warwickshire Regiment. J.E.B. Fairclough. Cornish Brothers Ltd, Birmingham, 1933.

Birmingham Pals: (The 14th, 15th & 16th (Service) Battalions, Royal Warwickshire Regiment). Terry Carter. Pen & Sword, Barnsley, 1997.

Liverpool Pals: (The 17th, 18th, 19th & 20th (Service) Battalions, King's Liverpool Regiment). Graham Maddocks. Leo Cooper, London, 1991.

Bradford Pals: (The 16th (Service) Battalion, West Yorkshire Regiment). Ralph N. Hudson. Bradford Libraries, 2000.

Leeds Pals: (The 15th (Service) Battalion, West Yorkshire Regiment). Laurie Milner. Pen & Sword Books, Barnsley, 1998.

Hull Pals: (The 10th, 11th 12th & 13th (Service) Battalions, East Yorkshire Regiment). David Bilton. Leo Cooper, Barnsley, 2002.

The Tigers: (The 6th, 7th, 8th & 9th (Service) Battalions, Leicestershire Regiment). Matthew Richardson. Leo Cooper, London, 2000.

Salford Pals: (The 15th, 16th, 19th & 20th (Service) Battalions, Lancashire Fusiliers). Michael Stedman. Leo Cooper, London, 1993.

Accrington Pals: 11th (Service) Battalion, East Lancashire Regiment. William Turner. Leo Cooper, London, 1998.

The Blast of War: A History of Nottingham's Bantams: The 15th (Service) Battalion, Sherwood Foresters, 1915–1919. Maurice Bacon and David E. Langley. Sherwood Press, Nottingham, 1986.

Kitchener's Pioneers: The 5th (Service) Battalion, Northamptonshire Regiment. Geoffrey Moore, 1978.

On the Somme: The Kitchener Battalions of the Royal Berkshire Regiment 1916. Colin Fox & Others. University of Reading, 1996.

Arras To Cambrai: The Kitchener Battalions of the Royal Berkshire Regiment 1917. Colin Fox & Others. University of Reading, 1997.

Their Duty Done: The Kitchener Battalions of the Royal Berkshire Regiment. Colin Fox & Others. University of Reading, 1998.

Manchester Pals: The 16th, 17th, 18th, 19th, 20th, 21st, 22nd & 23rd (Service) Battalions, Manchester Regiment). Michael Stedman. Leo Cooper, Barnsley, 2004.

Cotton Town Comrades: The Story of the Oldham Pals Battalion. K.W. Mitchinson and I. McInnes. Bayonet Publications, 1993.

Sheffield City Battalion: (The 12th York & Lancaster Regiment). Ralph Gibson and Paul Oldfield. Barnsley Chronicle, 1988.

Barnsley Pals: (The 13th & 14th York & Lancaster Regiment). Jon Cooksey. Leo Cooper, London, 1996.

Campaign Reminiscences: The 6th Seaforth Highlanders. R.T. Peel and Captain A.H. Macdonald. W.R. Walker, Elgin, 1923.

List of Officers and Other Ranks of the Rifle Brigade Awarded Decorations, or Mentioned in Despatches for Services during the Great War (Published as Appendix to Above Work). Lieutenant Colonel T.R. Eastwood and Major H.G. Parkyn. The Rifle Brigade Club.

List of Officers and Other Ranks of the Rifle Brigade Awarded Decorations, or Mentioned in Despatches for Services during the Great War (Published as Appendix to Above Work). Lieutenant Colonel T.R. Eastwood and Major H.G. Parkyn. The Rifle Brigade Club.

The Bomber Command Diaries 1939–1945. Martin Middlebrook and Chris Everitt. Viking, Harmondsworth, 1985.

The History of the Northamptonshire Regiment 1934–1948. Brigadier General W.J. Jervois. Printed for the Regimental History Committee, 1953.

Index of Cemeteries